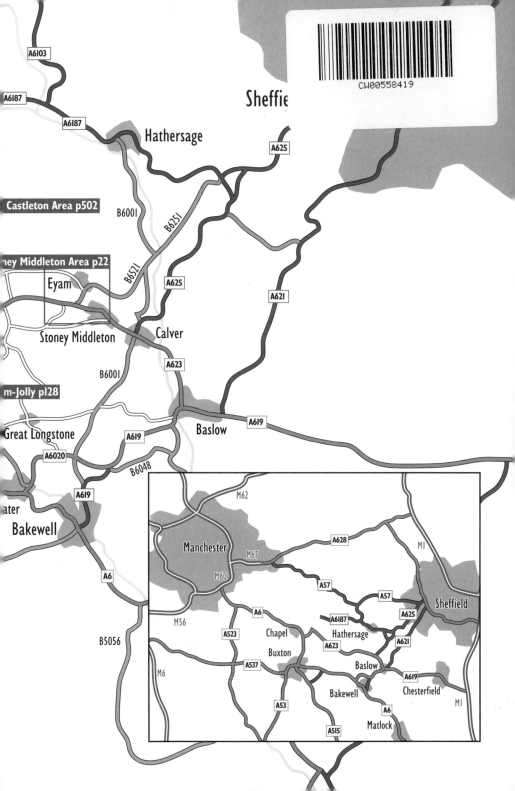

Peak Limestone
North

By Gary Gibson and Ian Carr
Series Editor: Niall Grimes
Researched and compiled by
a team of guidebook volunteers

British Mountaineering Council

177–179 Burton Road, Manchester M20 2BB

Peak Limestone North

By Gary Gibson and Ian Carr and a team of volunteers. Designed and typeset by BMC/Niall Grimes

First printed 2015
ISBN 978-0-903908-38-2

Cover photo: Mina Leslie-Wujastyk on Mecca Extension, F8c, Raven Tor (page 224). **Photo:** Niall Grimes.
Cover design: Allen Williams.

⛰ BMC CRAG CODE
www.thebmc.co.uk

Access	Check the Regional Access Database (RAD) on www.thebmc.co.uk for the latest access information
Parking	Park carefully – avoid gateways and driveways
Footpaths	Keep to established paths – leave gates as you find them
Risk	Climbing can be dangerous – accept the risks and be aware of other people around you
Respect	Groups and individuals – respect the rock, local climbing ethics and other people
Wildlife	Do not disturb livestock, wildlife or cliff vegetation; respect seasonal bird nesting restrictions
Dogs	Keep dogs under control at all times; don't let your dog chase sheep or disturb wildlife
Litter	'Leave no trace' – take all litter home with you
Toilets	Don't make a mess – bury your waste
Economy	Do everything you can to support the rural economy – shop locally

BMC Participation Statement — Climbing, hill walking and mountaineering are activities with a danger of personal injury or death. Participants in these activities should be aware of and accept these risks and be responsible for their own actions and involvement.

Table of Contents

Introduction	5
Acknowledgements	6
Climbing Notes	8
Access and Conservation	12
Visitor's Information	14
Crag Beta Pages	18

1 Stoney Middleton Area **22**

Stoney Middleton	24
Goddard's Quarry	78
Stoney West	79
Cucklet Delf	88
Golden Wall	89
Horseshoe Quarry	90
Tom's (Roadside) Cave	126

2 Water-cum-Jolly **128**

The Upper Circle	134
Vision Buttress	134
Stormflight Area	135
Jackdaw Point	136
Inch Test Buttress	139
Ping Pong Area	142
Psyche's Buttress	144
The Keep	145
Strip Search Wall	145
Lammergeyer Buttress	150
Ivy Buttress	151
Rubicon Wall	152
Waterfall Crag	164
Black Buttress	164
Moat Buttress Area	165
Swamp Wall	174
The Cornice	175
Two Tier Buttress	181
Witchcraft Wall	181
Church Buttress	182
Central Buttress	184
Mill Buttress	196
Mill Race Buttress	197
Ravensdale	198
Crag X	212
Monsal Viaduct Buttress	213

3 Raven Tor Area **214**

Raven Tor	218
Tideswell Dale	248
Ergonomic Buttress	251
Raven's Foot Buttress	251
Slip and Slime Buttress	251
Squirrel's Buttress	252

Blackwell Dale	254
Beginner's Wall	256
Sean's Roof	258
Zippy's Roof	260
Roadside Wall	260
Griff's Buttress Area	262
The Ravine	264

4 Chee Dale **266**

Blatant and Blackwell	272
The Sidings	278
The Embankment	284
Max Buttress	290
The Nook	296
The Cornice	304
Rhubarb Buttress	320
Chee Tor East	323
Chee Tor	324
Dog's Dinner Buttress	348
Nettle Buttress	352
Two Tier Buttress	358
Long Wall	374
Runyon's Corner / Moving Buttress	380
Railway Buttress	391
The Obelisk	391
The Lifts	392
Plum Buttress	398
The Cuttings	404
Topley Buttress	404

4 The Buxton Area **406**

Conies Dale	410
Smalldale	412
Devonshire (Beerhouse) Buttress	422
Deep Dale	424
Craig-y-Biceps	434
Staden Quarry	436
Lovers' Leap	452
Harpur Hill	454
Aldery Cliff	492

5 The Castleton Area **502**

Winnats Pass	504
The Arch	505
Odin's Cave	506
Peak Cavern	506
Cave Dale	507
Bradwell Dale	509
Eldon Hole	509
Graded Lists	510
Index	515

Ian Carr on Brachiation Dance, F7b+, at Water-cum-Jolly's Cornice (page 109). Photo: Richie Brooks.

Introduction

Spring, 1933. Three young men cower on the end of a ledge, perched high above the village of Stoney Middleton. They are about to complete an historic ascent. Above them towers 65 feet of vertical limestone. One of them, twenty-three year old Frank Elliott, steps out onto the rock and starts making his way up what is known locally as the Great Ridge. He climbs tentatively up a groove near the arête: "It was pretty rotten. There was tons of loose rock. We were chucking it down all the time," Elliott recalls. His companions, Gilbert Ellis and Harry Dover, look on but are unable to offer much help: despite the rope running to the leader, there is little to stop a fall. Elliott is essentially soloing. Climbing on-sight, placing no pegs, he continues with his tour-de-force eventually arriving at the flat grass above.

At the time, gritstone was the climbers' rock. Limestone was too steep and unstable to embark on, given the equipment and fitness of the day. But with this ascent, following a relentless, steep, loose, unprotected and exposed ridge, Elliott, Dover, and Ellis had just made history and given birth to Peak Limestone Climbing.

Climbing on limestone steadily gained popularity from the 1950s, initially as a training ground for hard aid-climbing then, later through the 1970s and 1980s, as a forcing ground for hard free-climbing. Today, in 2015, traditional climbing on limestone is on the decline. Popular routes have become polished, in-situ gear has deteriorated and many of the routes have returned to nature. Safer, middle-grade sport routes have become the choice of many climbers visiting the limestone cliffs and quarries.

Yet, once you get the taste, these white walls hold some of the most challenging and adventurous routes in the Peak. The dales, ridges, caves and quarries of the White Peak have a great spectrum of climbing styles and levels of difficulty. Airy trad leads high above the valley at Stoney Middleton; technical, vertical sport climbing on Horseshoe Quarry's classic walls; savage lakeside bouldering on Rubicon; out-of-the-way grade sevens on Water-cum-Jolly's Moat Buttress and Cornice; history-heavy pumpfests battling up Raven Tor's mighty walls; getting groovy on Chee Tor's ferny-but-flawless Extremes; going for one more redpoint in the evening light on Two Tier Buttress; power-draining undercutting in the shady cool intensity of Chee Dale's Cornice; bridging big space as the ravens circle close on a Ravensdale VS; rattling off a dozen leads in three hours at Harpur Hill; drenched in the late sun of an August evening on Smalldale's fantastic Main Wall.

Hopefully this new book will lead you to these experiences, and many more besides. Since 2012, a team led by Gary Gibson and Ian Carr has been working towards producing a new limestone guide. Plans for a single guide covering the whole of the Peak District were quickly discounted as the size of the task became clear. Consequently, this guide is the first of two volumes: Peak Limestone North and Peak Limestone South.

Recent development in the region has concentrated primarily on sport climbing. This guide documents that development, from some of the hardest routes in the country to the many middle-grade climbs that have appeared on previously unclimbed crags and long-forgotten venues. A large number of these routes have never appeared in print before.

Gary and Ian have had long standing relationships with the Peak. Both started their climbing careers in the late-70s, and have been closely involved in new routing, making early repeats of new climbs and in maintaining the quality of climbing in the area. Gary's intimate knowledge, especially in Chee Dale and the bolted quarries, make him an ideal candidate for the job.

One big aspiration for this guide is that, by shining a light on the great trad crags in the area, by leading efforts to clean up and regear routes, and by ensuring that lines and descriptions are accurate at the time of publication, climbers will once again turn their desires to the tremendous traditional challenges on Peak limestone. Stoney Middleton, Chee Tor, Central Buttress, Staden Quarry and Ravensdale, to name but a few, will give experiences that will live long in the memories of the adventurous. And, as hopefully the crag shots will show, they are not the overgrown Babylons that you may have been led to believe.

A final hope is that as you read this guidebook you are aware of the unparalleled knowledge and mammoth efforts of the contributors that have gone into producing this guidebook. The BMC stands proud in producing definitive guides and in maintaining the historical records for the Peak. We look forwards to this book's Southern counterpart.

Ian Carr
March 2015

Acknowledgements

The Northern Limestone climbing area has been a development ground in the Peak for many years. We therefore owe a debt of gratitude to all those who have pioneered before us. This includes the new routers, the equippers, the clubs, and their members. We would also like to acknowledge the on-going support of the BMC and the previous authors, editors and members of the BMC's Guidebook Committee.

For this book, the starting points for the scripts were initially the previous versions of the BMC's Limestone guidebooks; for which the current writers are eternally grateful. These were however up to 30 years old and needed a great deal of updating, editing and modernising. The geography had remained the same, but many routes had changed unrecognisably, either lost to vegetation or rationalised by the development of sport climbs.

Gary Gibson and Ian Carr undertook this challenging task. Gary's knowledge, commitment and downright dogged approach to this job provided the basis of this book, especially in the dales and quarries, where he has recently undertaken large amounts of re-gearing. In addition, both Gary and Ian spent many hours at a desk or walking the dales to verify the developing material for this guide.

Many others contributed written sections, opinions, photographs, support, knowledge and all the other input that goes into creating the book and Gary and Ian would like to thank and acknowledge these contributors.

Written sections were provided by: Rupert Davies, Jon Fullwood, Paul Harrison, Graham Hoey, Martin Kocsis, Simon Lee, Mark 'Zippy' Pretty, Lynn Robinson, Roger Whetton.

A strong team of local devotees and activists helped in developing and checking scripts. Particularly thanks go to: Kristian Clemmow, Rupert Davies, Graham Hoey, Steve McClure and Mark 'Zippy' Pretty.

Various other contributions were also made by: the ever supportive Hazel Gibson together with John Atkinson, Malc Baxter, Phil Burke, Steve Clarke, Steve Clegg, Simon Cundy, Bob Dearman, Al Evans, Neil Foster, Rick Gibbon, Seb Grieve, Colin Hughes, Mike Hunt, Phil Kelly, Dominic Lee, Bill McKee, Paul Mitchell, Keith Myhill, Keith Sharples, Nick Taylor, Roger Treglown, Dave Williams.

The final proofs were diligently checked and commented upon by Graham Hoey and Geoff Radcliffe. Graham & Geoff maintaining their 30 year plus contribution to the BMC's set of definitive guides to the Peak District.

The following photographers contributed the images that make this book shine; Eric Andrew, Dan Arkle, John Atkinson, Paul Bennett, Geoff Birtles, Andy Birtwistle, Richie Brooks, Ian Carr, Jon Clark, Rob Clifton, John Coefield, Liam Dobson, Alex Ekins, Paul Evans, Neil Foster, Jon Fullwood, Gary Gibson, Tim Glasby, Niall Grimes, Mike Hutton, Chris Jackson, Bob Keates, John Kirk, Dan Lane, Jon Leighton, Steve Lewis, Stuart Littlefair, Chris Lockyer, Adam Long, Alex Messenger, Andy Newton, Ian Parnell, Mark Rankine, Mark Scott, Keith Sharples, David Simmonite, Nick Smith, Michael Watson. A special thanks goes to Phil Kelly for his help in historical photo research.

A big thanks goes to the people behind the website peakbouldering.info for help in compiling bouldering sections.

Design and crag photography by Niall Grimes.

A very special thanks must go to those involved in securing access to these crags, including: Catherine Flitcroft, Rob Dyer, Henry Folkard, Jon Fullwood.

BMC Guidebook Committee
Les Ainsworth, Nick Bond, Ian Carr, Neil Foster, Niall Grimes, Dave Turnbull, Richard Wheeldon.

Previous editions of this book

Rock Climbs on the Mountain Limestone of Derbyshire: Graham West (Ed.) 1962

The Northern Limestone Area: Rock Climbs in the Peak, Volume 5 – Paul Nunn (Ed.) 1969

Northern Limestone: Rock Climbs in the Peak, Volume 4 Chris Jackson & Dave Gregory (Ed.) 1980

Peal Limestone Stoney: Peak District Climbs, Volume 3 Geoff Milburn (Ed.) 1987

Peak Limestone Chee Dale: Peak District Climbs, Volume 4 Geoff Milburn (Ed.) 1987

Peak Limestone Wye Valley: Peak Rock Climbing - Sixth Series, Volume 2. Chris Wright, Graham Hoey & Geoff Milburn (Ed.) 1999

From Horseshoe to Harpur Hill
Gary Gibson (Ed.) 20014

Gary Gibson on Poison Flowers, F6a+, on Golden Wall (page 89). Photo: Andy Birtwistle.

Climbing Notes

First Ascent Details

In order to give as much space to actual route information as possible, it was decided not to include detailed first ascent information, but to make the information available as a download from the BMC website. Consequently, alongside preparing the text of the guidebook, we have also brought the historical record up-to-date. The guidebook team, together those acknowledged above, specifically Graham Hoey, have been a great assistance in pulling all this information together.

First ascent information can be downloaded from the BMC website. Search for Peak Limestone North Web Support where you will find links to all first ascents.

Online Crag Info

Several crags and buttresses that have been climbed on over the years have now become lost and overgrown. While they are no longer relevant in a printed guide, this information is still part of the definitive record. For this reason we have placed the details of these routes and crags on the BMC website. Search the BMC website for Peak Limestone North Web Support where you will find links to all these crags.

Fixed Equipment

A lot of the routes in the guidebook rely upon fixed gear. The quality and age of which varies from route to route. With modern glue-in type, or larger diameter stainless steel bolts, it is quite easy to recognise that a route has been recently re-equipped. However, there still remain some older bolts and or pegs that date back to the first ascent. It can not always be assumed that what looks good, is good. Therefore, as always, it is the individual's judgement when relying upon fixed protection and belays.

Bolt Replacement

During the production of this guide, many routes have been re-equipped, either individually or in an organised way, supported by local bolt funds and the BMC.

Special thanks must go to the equippers and re-equippers of modern and some not-so-modern sport climbs. These climbers give their time, effort and sometimes their own money in maintaining the equipment, belays and general crag environments. The enjoyment of these routes is maintained and enhanced by a very small number of dedicated local climbers.

Sportsclimbs.co.uk – Gary Gibson's bolt work is supported by the BMC's Better Bolt Fund but also by individual contributions from the climbing community. Gary has re-equipped a significant proportion of the routes in this guidebook.

Kristian Clemmow and Mark Pretty have made a great contribution, not only by their efforts in re-equipping a great number of dilapidated routes but also for sharing their knowledge of the climbs, not to mention their own high-grade new route additions in the process.

The Peak Bolt Fund (**http://thepeakboltfund.blogspot.co.uk/**) is also partially funded and supported by the BMC's Better Bolt Fund, as well as individual contributors. This has also been instrumental in kick-starting the modernisation of crags like Raven Tor.

The BMC's Technical Committe, and Technical Officer Dan Middleton, have been instrumental in improving and modernising the overall standards by providing best-practice advice, materials and training in the placing of modern bolts. Here, special thanks is given to Jim Titt of Bolt Products (www.bolt-products.com) for the supply of his quality-engineered products.

Thanks are also due to those unnamed individual contributors, who under their own steam replace threads, pegs and bolts as and when required, usually out of their own pocket.

Any bolting done on any of the crags in this book must be done so with thought and sensitivity in order to preserve the historical integrity of routes and not endanger access to crags. The BMC Peak Area Committee has produced a set of guidelines that are worth considering if you are thinking of placing a bolt.

If you would like to get involved in the crucial work of rebolting sport climbs then search the BMC website for Peak Limestone North Web Support where you will find links to these groups.

Sarah Clough on Gabriel, VS 4c (page 46). Photo: Nick Smith.

Grades

This is a guide to traditional routes, sport routes, some aid routes and boulder problems. To differentiate, traditional routes are identified with a blue number, sport climbs with a green number and boulder problems in red.

1 Traditional Route

2 Sport Route

3 Boulder Problem

Traditional route grades

The system of grading for routes is the traditional British system, a combination of adjectival and technical grades, and assumes the leader has a normal rack, including standard camming devices, nuts, slings, quickdraws etc. The adjectival grade gives a sense of the overall difficulty of a climb. This will be influenced by many aspects, including seriousness, sustainedness, technical difficulty, exposure, strenuousness or rock quality. It is an open-ended system, and currently runs from Easy to Extremely Severe. Along the way, and in ascending order, are Moderate (M), Difficult (D), Hard Difficult (HD), Very Difficult (VD), Hard Very Difficult (HVD), Severe (S), Hard Severe (HS), Very Severe (VS), Hard Very Severe (HVS) and Extremely Severe (E), the last category being split into E1, E2, E3 etc.

The second part of the grade, the technical grade, is there to give an indication of the hardest move to be found on the route. They come onto the scale somewhere around 4a and currently run in order of ascending difficulty: 4a, 4b, 4c, 5a, 5b, 5c, 6a, 6b, 6c, 7a, 7b.

Bouldering grades

The Fontainebleau (Font) system is used in this guide. To avoid any confusion with the technical aspect of traditional British route grades or with sport grades, bouldering grades will always have the word 'Font' in front.

Sport grades

The French system is used, with a 'F' in front: F5, F6a, F6a+, F6b etc.

Aid climbs

This book still contains a small number of aid climbs (graded A1, A2, A3 etc).

Stars, daggers and black spots

Stars (none, one, two or three) have been used in this guide to indicate quality. An un-starred route is by no means a bad route.

Certain routes will have a dagger † symbol by them. This indicates a route where the guidebook team may have doubt about some aspect of the route, such as being unsure of the line, or having an unconfirmed grade due to insufficient repeats, or perhaps the nature of the climbing or protection have altered since a previous ascent. It is not meant to cast doubt on a first ascent.

Also, the dreaded black spot (●) means a route is known to be in a particularly dirty or dangerous condition.

New routes, first ascents etc.

Details of first ascents, including name, grade, individuals involved, date and style of ascent, or any improvements, amendments or corrections to FA lists, should be sent to: guides@thebmc.co.uk.

UK adj.	UK tech	French sport	US	Aust.	UIAA
M	3a		5.2	10	I
D	3b	F1	5.3	11	II
VD	3c	F2	5.4	12	III
S	4a	F3	5.5	13	IV
HS	4b	F4	5.6	14	IV+
VS	4c	F4+ / F5	5.7	15	V-
HVS	5a	F5+	5.8	16	V
		F6a	5.9	17	V+
E1	5b	F6a+	5.10	18	VI-
		F6b	5.10+	19	VI-
E2	5c	F6b+	5.11a	20	VI
E3		F6c	5.11b	21	VI+
		F6c+	5.11c	22	VII-
E4	6a	F7a	5.11d	23	VII
		F7a+	5.12a	24	VII+
E5	6b	F7b	5.12b	25	VIII-
E6		F7b+	5.12c	26	VIII
		F7c	5.12d	27	VIII+
E7	6c	F7c+	5.13a	28	IX-
		F8a	5.13a	29	IX
E8	7a	F8a+	5.13b	30	IX+
E9		F8b	5.13a	31	X-
		F8b+	5.14a	32	X
E10	7b	F8c	5.14b	33	X+
		F8c+	5.14d	34	XI-
E11		F9a	5.14a	35	XI

Font	UK tech	V grade
Font 1	3a	
Font 2	3b	
Font 3	3c	V0-
Font 4	4a	
Font 4+	4b	V0
	4c	
Font 5	5a	V0+
Font 5+	5b	V1
Font 6A	5c	
Font 6A+		V2
Font 6B	6a	V3
Font 6B+		V4
Font 6C	6b	
Font 6C+		V5
Font 7A		V6
Font 7A+		V7
Font 7B	6c	V8
Font 7B+		V9
Font 7C		
Font 7C+	7a	V10
Font 8A		V11
Font 8A+		V12
Font 8B		V13
Font 8B+	7b	V14
Font 8C		V15

Further Bouldering Info

A lot of details of eliminates is beyond the scope of this book. For more information, see this book and website.

peakbouldering.info This is a resource for creating a database of new problems, votes on grades etc, videos and photos. Go and check it out.

Peak District Bouldering This is the classic guide to all Peak bouldering, by Vertebrate Graphics.

Chris Sharma on Mutation, F9a, Raven Tor (page 162). Photo: Adam Long.

Access and Conservation

The inclusion of a crag in this guide does not imply the right to climb there.

The landscape of the Peak District is owned and managed by a variety of different groups with a variety of interests. These include farmers, conservation groups, quarrying companies and private landowners. Despite this, climbers enjoy access to the vast majority of the crags that lie within this landscape.

As climbers, we must behave in a reasonable and responsible way if we are to maintain access to these sensitive areas.

Please read the access notes at the start of each section to find information parking, approaches and any seasonal restrictions.

Always approach crags by the route described in the text. From time to time the BMC will agree temporary restrictions on some crags. This will usually be to allow birds to nest. If this is the case there will be signs in place on the approach.

Always park considerately and be polite to local residents and other users.

If you are considering any bolting activities then be aware of any ethical or environmental concerns. See the note to this effect in the Climbing Notes section.

Try not to leave unsightly quick-draws in place overnight.

The most up-to-date information for all access issues is to be found on the BMC's Regional Access Database. This is the definitive source of access info on the web. From bird restrictions and parking advice to sensitive approaches and advice on local ethics. This is the place to go to find out whether you can climb on a crag and just how to approach it. Find it online at **www.thebmc.co.uk/rad** or download the RAD App onto your mobile device.

If you encounter any problems or have any questions about access issues in the area, your first call should be your BMC Local Access Reps. Search the BMC website for contact details, email office@thebmc.co.uk or phone 0161 4454500.

Right: Toe-tingling access to Two Tier Buttress, Chee Dale. Photo: Ian Parnell.

Local Amenities

Pubs

The Moon, Stoney Middleton, S32 4TL
Phone: 01433 630203
Three Stags Heads, Between Stoney Middleton and Tideswell on the A623, SK17 8RW; Phone: 01298 872268
Red Lion, Litton, SK17 8QU
Phone: 01298 871458
Anglers Rest, Millers Dale, SK17 8SN
Phone: 01298 871323
Monsal Head Hotel, Monsal Head, DE45 1NL
Phone: 01629 640250
Miners Arms, Eyam, Hope, S32 5RG
Phone: 01433 630853
The Quiet Woman, Earl Sterndale, SK17 0BU
Phone: 01298 83211
The Bulls Head, Ashford-In-The-Water, DE45 1QB
Phone: 01629 812931

Cafés

Cintra's Tearoom, Hathersage, S32 1BB
Phone: 01433 651825
Yonderman, A623, Wardlow, SK17 8RW
Phone: 01298 873056
The Scarlett Rose Coffee Shop, adjacent to Hitch n Hike, S33 0AL;
Phone: 01433 651250
Outside Cafe, Hathersage, S32 1BB
Phone: 01433 651936
Hobb's Cafe, Monsal Head, DE45 1NL
Phone: 01629 640346
Palmers Cafe, Calver Crossroads (A623/B6001), S32 3XU
Phone: 01433 639458
Bookstore Brierlow Bar, A515 Brierlow Bar, SK17 9PY
Phone: 01298 71017
The Eating House, Calver
Phone: 01433 631583
The Green Pavilion, Buxton, SK17 6DR (down the hill from Jo Royle's Shop)
Phone: 01298 77309

Climbing shops

Outside, Main Road, Hathersage, Derbyshire, S32 1BB
Phone: 01433 651936
Jo Royle Outdoor, 6 Market Place, Buxton, SK17 6EB
Phone: 01298 25824
Hitch n Hike, Hope Road, Hope Valley, S33 0AH
Phone: 01433 651013

Things to do with the family

Peak District Online, Derbyshire. Peak District
www.peakdistrictonline.co.uk
Peak District National Park: Home
www.peakdistrict.gov.uk/
Things to see & do - Visit Peak District
www.visitpeakdistrict.com/see-and-do/
Hathersage Swimming Pool; S32 1DU
Phone: 01433 650843

Show Caves in Castleton and Buxton

Peak Cavern: The UK's largest cave entrance for guided tours of cave network with unusual rock formations. Castleton, S33 8WS; Phone: 01433 620285
Blue John Cavern: An illuminated limestone caves with marine fossils, bones, mineral mines plus a craft shop. Castleton, S33 8WA; Phone: 01433 620638
Speedwell Cavern: This consists of a horizontal lead miners' adit leading to the cavern itself, a limestone cave. Boat tours of 18th-century lead-mining caverns 450m below ground and a huge subterranean lake. Castleton, S33 8WA, Phone: 01433 620512
Treak Cliff Cavern: Part of the Castleton Site of Special Scientific Interest and one of only two sites where the ornamental mineral Blue John is still excavated. Network of caverns with rare Blue John stone and stalactites, for guided tours and visitor centre. Castleton, S33 8WP; Phone: 01433 621487

Monsal Trail

This linear route along Midland Railway's former London to Manchester line begins near the historic market town of Bakewell then, via tunnels, cuttings and dramatic viaducts, heads through the dramatic limestone scenery of the Wye Valley past old quarries and nature reserves. Mostly level, well surfaced and entirely traffic-free. Car parks and toilets at Bakewell, Hassop, Monsal Head and Miller's Dale.

Start/Finish: End of Coombs Road, Bakewell/Topley Pike, east of Buxton; Length: 8.5 miles / 13.7km;

Cycle hire: Cycle hire at Bakewell, Hassop Station and Thornbridge Outdoors (eastern end) and Blackwell Mill (western end). **peakdistrictcycleways.co.uk**

Geoff Birtles on The Flakes Direct, E2 5c, at Stoney Middleton, (page 63). Photo: Bob Keates.

The BMC

The British Mountaineering Council (BMC) is the representative body for climbers, hillwalkers and mountaineers in England and Wales. It exists to promote their interests and to protect their freedom. Since its formation in 1944 it has worked, negotiated and acted in the many different aspects of outdoor life to ensure that the rights and freedoms that we share can continue in a responsible and sustainable way.

It has many core programmes that cover a broad spectrum of activities, which include: negotiating and securing access to hillwalking and climbing areas; promoting cliff and mountain conservation for the benefit of users and the environment alike; representing the interests of climbers, hillwalkers and mountaineers in the broader political world; promoting and advising on good practice in the worlds of training, equipment and facilities; promoting British climbing and British climbers throughout the world through international meets and the support of everything from bouldering competitions to Himalayan expeditions; supporting specialist programmes and events centred around youth, safety and excellence; organising and promoting events in the world of competitions; providing expert advice on all aspects of climbing wall use, design and management; support and advice to climbing, hillwalking and mountaineering clubs; providing the definitive record of climbs through its guidebook programme; giving up-to-date information on all aspects of work programmes; providing top class insurance cover for all members.

If you are not a member, and would like to support the work that the BMC does on your behalf, then contact us on the addresses below. If you would like to volunteer to help in one of the many projects the BMC are active in please visit the website and see what the BMC is involved in at the moment, then get in touch. For these, or any other inquiries, contact us at:

EMAIL: office@thebmc.co.uk **WEB:** www.thebmc.co.uk
TELEPHONE: 0161 4456111

The BMC Peak Area

The BMC Peak Area is pleased to support the BMC Guidebook Committee as it presses forward with its successful programme of high quality guidebooks to rock climbing in the Peak. Our team of regional access volunteers continue to do sterling work throughout the area. Without them, Peak District guidebook volumes might be considerably slimmer.

The Peak Area is one of nine BMC areas in England and Wales, and is right at the heart of the British climbing community. We are lucky to have a very active local area. Turnout at the area meetings is consistently high and the standard of discussion and debate reflects the passion members feel about their area. By getting involved with your local area, you can influence local and national issues and support the work of the BMC.

The Peak Area meets five times a year; meetings are spread throughout the region giving as many people as possible the opportunity to attend at least one. Attendance is usually around 40-50, and the debate is always lively, but friendly. Every meeting sees new faces, which is essential if we are to keep evolving and meeting the needs of what is one of the biggest concentrations of climbers anywhere in the world. Meeting information is hosted on the BMC Local Areas site – http://community.thebmc.co.uk/peak In addition to the meetings we organise litter picks, crag clean-up sessions, and the odd social. If you've got an interest in climbing in your local area, we encourage you to come along to a meeting and find your level of involvement.

To keep members informed about what's happening in the area, we publish a newsletter a few days before each meeting, and the area has its own Facebook page – **www. facebook.com/bmcpeakarea**

The BMC and Guidebooks

The BMC first became involved in publishing Peak District guidebooks in 1972 and has had a continued involvement ever since. Over those years, and even before, there have been trials and tribulations, dramas and controversies, much hair pulled out and much of it gone grey. However, what cannot be denied is that there has now been over 40 years of tremendous definitive guidebooks to one of the world's best climbing areas. The roll call of volunteers who are responsible for this series of guides is too long to list, but they are heroes one and all.

Today, under the auspices of the current guidebook committee chaired by Ian Carr, this work carries on. The BMC guides being produced in 2015 continue to build upon the standard of what has gone before. Times may change, but quality, inspiration, innovation and dedication remain the same. Thanks to this the current series of BMC guides to the Peak and Pennine, with further guides for further afield planned, provide everything a climber could want from a guide, with definitive information to all routes and bouldering presented in a clear and enjoyable way.

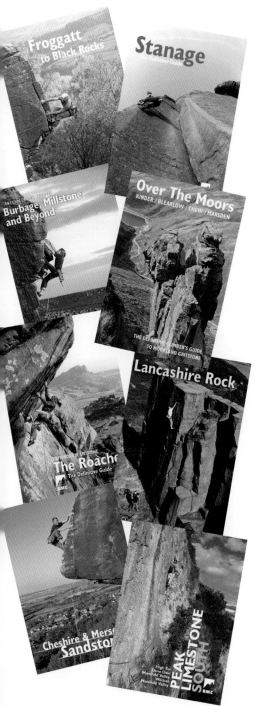

BMC Definitive Guides

Froggatt to Black Rocks
A definitive guide to the southern reaches of the eastern edges. This book takes all the great features of a BMC guide to give a truly bumper, breathtaking book. Featuring some of the best climbing photography yet seen in a guide.

Stanage
A definitive guide to The Queen of Grit. Detailing all the routes and all the bouldering along the three miles of this magnificent crag, it is the essential guide for anyone climbing on the crag. The guide features, for the first time in a British guide, bouldering circuits, set out in grade ranges along the crag. Also features a personal selection of five favourite routes from over 40 climbers.

Burbage, Millstone and Beyond
A definitive guide to the gritstone edges near the city of Sheffield. An award-winning guide that combines exhaustive research and detailed information with inspiration and entertainment, as well as great historical information.

Over The Moors
The upland gritstone crags that ring the mighty moorlands of Kinder, Bleaklow and the Chew Valley are some of the most noble outcrops in the land. Where jagged adventures, breathtaking scenery and sublime routes meet to give the wildest climbing on gritstone.

The Roaches
The tremendous crags of the Western Edges get the BMC treatment in this well-loved guidebook. Fun, inspiration and information are all dealt out in equal measure.

Lancashire Rock
A definitive guide to all rock climbs in the Lancashire area, from the quarries and edges of the gritstone area in the south, to the limestone escarpments in the north.

Cheshire and Merseyside Sandstone
The crags, quarries and bluffs of Cheshire and Merseyside sandstone have a charm and beautiful variety all their own. From the heights of Helsby to the pits of Pex, from Frogsmouth sport to Frodsham solos, it's all here. Here is a book that lays the delights of sandstone open for all to see.

Peak Limestone South; Available 2016
The companion to the North guide will be the last in the curent series of BMC definitive guides to the Peak District, focusing on the Matlock, Dovedale and Manifold-Valley limestone crags.

Visit the BMC Shop for all these titles

CRAG BETA PAGES

Crag	page	Crag quality	Aspect	Sun	Approach time	Dries after rain	Rains proof routes	Quantity and grade range	Season (J F M A M J J A S O N D)
Stoney Middleton	24	★★★★★	S	from noon	5-15 minutes	yes	some	Many eliminates Font 4 to Font 8A+	
Goddard's Quarry	78	★	S	not much	5-15 minutes	yes	some		
Stoney West	79	★★★	S	from noon	15 minutes	yes	no		
Cucklet Delf	88	★	E	AM	8 minutes	no	yes	9 problems Font 6C to Font 7C+	
Horseshoe Quarry	90	★★★	SW	from noon	5 minutes	yes	no		
Roadside Cave	126	★	S	none	roadside	no	yes		
Vision Buttress	134	★	S	from 2pm	20 minutes	yes	no		
Jackdaw Point	136	★★	S	from noon	20 minutes	yes	none		
Inch Test	139	★★	SW	PM	20 minutes	yes	none		
Ping Pong	142	★★★	W	from 2pm	20 minutes	yes	none		
The Keep	145	★	SW	from 3pm	15 minutes	yes	none		
Lamergeyer Buttress	150	★	SE	not much	15 minutes	yes	none		
Rubicon Wall	152	★★★★	S	from noon	10 minutes	yes	lots	33 problems Font 5 to Font 8B	
Black Buttress	164	★	NW	from 4pm	15 minutes	yes	no		
Moat Buttress	165	★★★	NW	from 3pm	15 minutes	yes	some		
Swamp Wall	174	★	NW	not much	20 minutes	no	none		
The Cornice	175	★★★	E	till noon	20 minutes	no	lots		
Two Tier Buttress	181	★	E	till noon	20 minutes	no	none		
Church Buttress	182	★	N	from 5pm	20 minutes	no	none		
Central Buttress	184	★★★★	NW	Sun	15 minutes	yes	none		
Mill Buttress	196	★	N	none	20 minutes	no	none		
Ravensdale	198	★★★	W	from noon	15 minutes	yes	none		
Crag X	212	★★	NE	not much	10 minutes	yes	none		
Monsal Buttress	213	★	SW	from 2pm	15 minutes	yes	none		

Season key: unlikely / possible / likely

CRAG BETA PAGES

Trad climbing					Sport climbing					Crag beta
VD to HS	VS to HVS	E1 to E3	E4 and above	total	F1 to F4+	F5 to F6a+	F6b to F6c+	F7a and above	total	General rundown of the best features of the crag and a note on the conditions.
14	51	112	78	255		3	13	17	33	Year-round classic trad, VS to E5. Recent sport, F6c to F8a+, historic bouldering, Font 6A to Font 8A+. Very dry, sunny, not much seepage, clean, polished, scruffy, noisy.
					2	3	2		7	A rently-developed wall with a few vertical clip-ups.
1	7	7	3	18		9	21	2	32	Bolted wall climbs in the F6s. Sheltered, popular, seepage free, can be hot, leafy.
										A small, steep wall of crimpy limestone. Obscure, leafy and shady.
1	6	16	2	25	17	127	114	11	269	Lots of vertical sport climbs in the F6s. Very popular. Very dry, sunny, not much seepage, sheltered, polished, sometimes loose. Mainly south-west facing but other aspects also.
										Hardcore. Good for a bit of dirty power. Shady, seeps in winter, ugly.
			2	2				3	3	An out-of-the-way wall with a couple of classy F7c/ F7c+ redpoints. Access issues.
	6	8	3	17						A nice wall of vertical trad climbing where the best routes are actually pretty good. Very sunny and sheltered. A bit nettle-ridden in summer. Climbing possible in winter.
	2	10	4	16				4	4	A few untravelled trad routes and four heavyweight sport routes, F7c to F8b. Sunny, sheltered and pleasant.
	2	6	5	13				1	1	A good, quiet little crag, well worth a visit for a handful of great trad leads from E1 to E5.
1	1	2	2	6				1	1	Pretty obscure. A few unstarred climbs that will please seekers of solitude.
			7	7				5	5	A long shady, unvisted cobweb-covered bulge. Its day has gone. Perhaps it will return.
		3	17	20			3	23	26	Brilliant bouldering, sport and trad. Everything is hard and classic. Polished and popular. Quite rainproof. Seeps in winter and hot in the sun. Good on a wet day.
		3	1	4				1	1	A little wall with a nice view.
		4	5	9			11	30	41	A rejuvenated buttress that now provides great sport climbing, F6a to F8b. A nice lakeside setting with lots of shade.
							1	2	3	A dark wall.
							3	25	28	Roof heaven. An wave of pump and power. Great for sport routes from the mid-F7s to the mid-F8s. Slow to dry. Secluded, shady and impressive.
							4		4	A wall of nice limestone.
	3	6	2	11						A few secluded trad routes with an esoteric vibe. Shady, exposed and clean.
	8	19	21	48			10	11	21	Big and brilliant. Classic trad, E3 to E6, recent sport, F6c to F7c. Quick drying, lots of shade, big, quiet and full of character.
1	16	8	2	27						Shady and in need of a bit of love.
7	36	18	4	65						Classic trad, VS - E1. Lofty, quick drying, sunny, impressive, quiet, a bit loose and polished.
						3	10	9	22	Short, punchy sport climbs, F6c to F7b. Shady, some rain shelter, cold in winter, close to a busy road.
							1	2	3	A blocky wall with a nice approach.

Crag	page	Crag quality	Aspect	Sun	Approach time	Dries after rain	Rains proof routes	Quantity and grade range	J F M A M J J A S O N D
Raven Tor	218	★★★★★	SW	from noon	roadside	yes	yes	70 Font 6A to Font 8B+	
Tideswell Dale	248	★	all	all day	1-15 minutes	yes	none	10 Font 5 to Font 7C+	
Squirrel's Buttress	252	★★	S	not much	10 minutes	yes	no	10 Font 5 to Font 7C+	
Blackwell Dale	254	★★★	all	all day	1-5 minutes	yes	some	65 problems Font 5 to Font 8A+	
Blackwell / Blatant	272	★★	S	from noon	10 minutes	yes	none		
The Sidings	278	★	S	from noon	15 minutes	yes	none		
The Embankment	284	★★★	S	from noon	20 minutes	yes	some		
Max Buttress	290	★★★	S	till 2pm	20 minutes	yes	none		
The Nook	296	★★	S	not much	25 minutes	no	none		
The Cornice	304	★★★★★	NE	not much	20 minutes	no	yes		
Chee Tor	324	★★★★★	W	from 1pm	25 minutes	no	none		
Dog's Dinner	348	★★	SW	from noon	15 minutes	yes	some		
Nettle Buttress	352	★★	N	from 4pm	20 minutes	yes	none		
Two Tier Buttress	358	★★★★★	NW	from 3pm	20 minutes	yes	some		
Long Wall	374	★★★	NW	from 3pm	25 minutes	no	none		
Runyon's / Moving	380	★★	N	from 5pm	20 minutes	yes	none		
The Lifts	392	★★	N	from 4pm	15 minutes	yes	none		
Plum Buttress	398	★★★★	NW	from 4pm	15 minutes	yes	none		
Conies Dale	410	★★	NW	from 3pm	20 minutes	no	none	12 problems Font 6B to Font 7C+	
Smalldale	412	★★★	N	from 5pm	7 minutes	yes	none		
Devonshire Buttress	422	★★	S	from 11am	6 minutes	yes	none		
Deep Dale	424	★★	all	all day	6-20 minutes	yes	some	8 problems Font 6B+ to Font 8B+	
Craig-y-Biceps	434	★★	N	from 5pm	3 minutes	no	no		
Staden Quarry	436	★★★	N	not much	8 minutes	yes	none		
Harpur Hill	454	★★★	E, W, N	all day	10 minutes	yes	none		
Aldery Cliff	492	★★★	SE	till 3pm	roadside	no	none		

Areas: RAVEN TOR AREA, CHEE DALE, BUXTON AREA

VD to HS	VS to HVS	E1 to E3	E4 and above	total	F1 to F4+	F5 to F6a+	F6b to F6c+	F7a and above	total	Crag beta — General rundown of the best features of the crag and a note on the conditions.
		1	3	4				88	88	Powerful and polished redpoints of the highest order. Ultra classic power-problems in the Font 7 and 8s. Sheltered, mostly rainproof, hot in the sun, winter seepage, polished, popular.
	2	2	1	5				13	13	Lots of small buttresses with short, steep and fingery bouldering in the high Font 6s and 7s, some pretty classic. Some harder sport routes. Shady, sheltered and slow drying.
										A bouldering venue for strong connoisseurs. Great rock. Leafy and sheltered.
	1			1				13	13	Lots of vertical sport climbs in the F6s. Very popular. Very dry, sunny, not much seepage, sheltered, polished, sometimes loose. Mainly south-west facing but other aspects also.
					11	26	4		41	A couple of nice, solid vertical walls delivering lots of sport climbs in the F6s. Sunny, open, quick drying, clean, midgy.
	7	11	5	22			2	2	4	Esoteric, fingery trad. Sunny, fresh, clean, seepage-free, quiet. Winter warmth.
		3	3	6			6	23	29	Cranky sport climbs, F7a to F7c. Sheltered, sunny, some seepage, open, an early-drying crag.
		2	3	5			5	15	18	Pumpy sport, F6c to F7b. Sheltered, fairly quick drying, popular.
		3		3				12	12	Powerful roof climbing. Quite seepy and dirty in early season. Slow to dry. Shady.
		4	10	14			7	72	79	Powerful, top-class sport climbs, F7a to F8b+. Shady and cool, tree-covered, sometimes humid, slow drying, rainproof.
	11	39	36	86			1	12	13	Classiy trad, VS to E5. Technical sport climbing F7c+ to F8a. Quite shady and cool, dirty in early season, can be leafy and humid in summer.
		3	5	8			3	7	10	Fingery sport and a monster boulder traverse. Dry, clean, leafy, sheltered.
		2	7	9		2	8	7	17	Classy sport climbs in the F7s or a cool E5. Slow-drying, dirty in early season, shady, quiet, good rock.
	1	7	13	21	1		12	60	73	Top-quality sport, F7a to F8b. Quick drying, clean, classic, solid, popular.
	3	7	5	15			4	31	35	Quality summer sport, F7a to F8a. Slow-drying, shady, sheltered, sometimes dirty.
2	21	11	11	45		1	12	21	34	A fun trad day VS to E1, with the odd sport hit. Runyon's is a sunless and sometimes dank corner. Moving Buttress is open and exposed but with some vegetation.
2	6	10	2	20		1	9	11	21	A random Chee Dale adventure. Exposed and quick-drying.
	2	8	1	11			6	12	18	Brilliant mid-grade trad and fresh sport, F6c to F8a. Clean, exposed, quick drying, little seepage.
										Fun, low-to-mid Font 7s in a nice spot. Secluded, sheltered, summery, fresh, seepy.
		6	6	12	15	30	15		60	Great, tall vertical sport climbs, F6b to F7a+. Generally shady, seepage free, cold in winter, unique location.
						1	10	10	20	A quick sport hit, F6b to F7b. Sunny, clean, dry, open, fresh.
19	22	36	5	79		1	5	12	18	Hard bouldering. Forgotten low and mid-grade trad and sport climbs in a beautiful place. A quiet, wooded valley, wet in winter.
			1	1		2	8	17	27	Quick, steep summer sport in the F7s. Shady, seeps in winter and after rain, nettly and planty in summer.
2	21	44	11	78				1	1	Classic summer trad, HVS to E2. Shady, mostly clean, can be a bit planty, quiet.
1	25	27	1	54	11	137	108	31	287	Great for doing lots of F5s and F6s. Exposed, quick-drying, industrial, not always solid, quiet.
8	21	16		45						Mid-grade slabs on cool days and summer evenings. Sheltered, friendly, some polish, vegetation and loose rock in sections.

THE STONEY AREA

STONEY MIDDLETON / STONEY WEST / HORSESHOE QUARRY +++

Steve McClure on Windhover, E2 5c (page 63). Photo: Ian Parnell.

Stoney Middleton

Trad: 255 (VD to E6) **Sport:** 33 (F5 to F8a+)
Bouldering: Many eliminates (Font 3 to Font 8A+)
Aspect: South **Sunshine:** From late morning **Season:** All year
Conditions: Very dry, sunny, not much seepage, clean, polished, scruffy, noisy
Best for: Year-round classic trad, VS to E4. Recent sport, F6c to F8a+,
historic bouldering, Font 6A to Font 7C+ **Approach:** 5 - 15 minutes

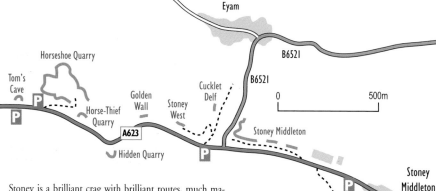

Stoney is a brilliant crag with brilliant routes, much maligned by those who judge books by their scruffy, dusty, polished covers. Fantastic testpieces through the mid and upper grades, combined with one of the most reliable climates in the area, make this a must-visit crag for most. Don't be put off by the shoddy reputation, thundering road or dusty environment; once you step off the ground you are in for some of the best routes around with steep, pumpy, technical and generally well-protected climbing all the way. The polish is no myth, all the same, so learn to love it.

Trad Climbing: Stoney contains a plethora of famous trad routes. Some may say that they are past their best, but others will argue that Stoney remains up there with the best trad crags on Peak limestone. Whatever you think, working through the grades at Stoney will give you one of the best apprenticeships going. The rock quality varies a great deal from section to section, ranging from perfect (and polished) to downright lethal (usually not polished).

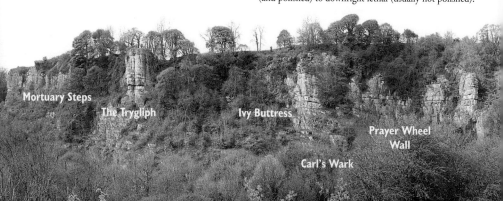

B6521

The Quarry

Slurper Wall

Mortuary Steps

The Triglyph

Ivy Buttress

Prayer Wheel Wall

Minus Ten

Wee Doris

Bitter Fingers

Tower of Babel

Windy Buttress

Garage Buttress

A623

Carl's Wark

P

Sport Climbing: There is an increasing number of sport routes, mainly on Garage Buttress. Early desperates such as *Little Plum* (F8a) have been complemented with a score of recent routes such as *Ming the Merciless* (F8a+) and *The Big Apple* (F8a). Of interest to the masses will be a recent clutch of longer, high-quality sport pitches with a parade of recent routes from the fives to the low sevens.

Bouldering: Stoney is one of the original homes of Peak bouldering and for lovers of polished eliminates of the highest historical pedigree the crag will provide endless return visits. Surprisingly brilliant, once you get into it, and often in condition in all seasons.

Conditions and Aspect: Stoney is a sheltered all-year-round venue. The rock dries very quickly after showers, but can seep after prolonged periods of rain. The whole area generally faces south and gets all the sun going. Summer shade can be found in the angles of the many bays, overlooked by trees. Likewise, warmth can be found from the weakest mid-winter sun. Windy Buttress stands proud high above the dale floor giving a welcome breeze in the summer when the higher dale can be humid. However, the front face can also be baltic if the winter wind is blowing across the crag.

Parking and Approach: Good off-road parking is available in a large lay-by just west of the village of Stoney Middleton on the left of the main A623. See the approach map for access to each buttress. Parking adjacent to the substation on the Eyam road is discouraged due to the need for 24/7 emergency access. Approaches take from 5 to 15 minutes.

Access Issues: Stoney is a SSSI, although there are no access issues. The designation is primarily for geological reasons but also covers the limestone flora. There are currently no access issues here though ownership of the various venues is by six different landowners. The crag's main landowner, Adrian Heath, is a great supporter of climbing on Stoney Middleton and recognises the significance of the crag and encourages responsible climbers to continue their activities.

Minus Ten   Wee Doris   Bitter Fingers   Tower of Babel   Windy Buttress

The Quarry

A perfect venue for pump lovers who don't give a damn about pretty landscapes. Two big vertical walls deliver tough action in the Extremes: be prepared for some forceful climbing and the odd urgent moment. Some of the routes here are brilliant and, especially around the E4 grade, are some of the best of their type in the Peak. The action is accompanied by an electric hum from the substation and after a day here climbers have been known to glow in the dark.

The walls face south and west and get afternoon and evening sun. Very sheltered. They don't suffer too badly from seepage but can get very hot on warm sunny days. Traditionally climbers have parked in a lay-by next to the walls on the B6521 Eyam road. However access problems now mean it's better to walk in from the main approach in the village, along the base of the crag or along the road. This takes about 15 minutes.

Forty five metres left of the main bay is a bay, now overgrown, that contained **Orang Utang**, HS (1970s).

Descent: Follow a series of ledges down the left side of the crag.

Immediately to the left of the descent is a clean wall: **The Dead Girls**, E4 6b (1987), climbs the smooth wall and desperate strip overhang by a huge reach to a marginally easier headwall; **Fortune**, E1 5b (2012), is the short corner and thin crack; **Disappointment**, E2 5c (2012), is the technical wall right again.

I Roraima HVS 5b 1970s
21m Gain the arête by pulling in from the left then climbing it on its left-hand side.

2 Holy Schmitt E3 5c ★ 2012
21m A surprising and worthwhile find. Exit the groove in the arête directly and make a long move to the break. Continue up the right-hand side of the sharp arête above, moving rightwards onto the wall at the top to finish.

3 Helmut Schmitt E6 6b ★★ 1980
21m An impressive test of finger-strength and stamina with just sufficient protection. Climb the slim groove in the arête and swing right along the break to gain the wall: direct is 6c. Zigzag first left and then right past a good jug to gain a break (peg). Move slightly left and back right (reachy) or direct (desperate) to pass the small overlap and gain the final roof by a fingery sequence. A final draining pull rightwards through this gains the respite of good finishing holds.

4 Cabbage Crack E4 6a ★★ pre-1960/1979
21m This classic product of the Seventies gives pushy and well-protected action. Follow the steep wall and groove 4m to the right of the arête. Climb the overlap using thin cracks to gain larger holds in a break below a thin crack. Either climb this (ouch) or bypass it on the right to the overhang (peg). Continue via a short crack before finishing slightly rightwards. **Photo on page 29.**

5 Jasper E3 5c ★★ 1963/1975
21m Marginally easier but no less strenuous. From below the overlap on *Cabbage Crack* (pegs) swing right and up with difficulty into a widening groove. Undercut this leftwards to better holds and an easier finish on the headwall (as for *Cabbage Crack*). A more direct start is possible via a shallow groove and a hole at 6a.

6 The Heat E6 6b 1980
22m Something of an enigma, but good climbing despite the lack of protection. Climb the shallow groove in the wall 5m to the right of *Jasper*, passing a break, to gain the crux of *Jasper*. Pull up and out rightwards into a right-facing groove. Finish direct up the headwall.

7 Oliver E4 6a ★★★ 1979
24m The best route on these walls, a true limestone classic. Climb the yellowy groove to reach a break. Swing left, then climb boldly up quartz holds and a layaway, to gain the next break. Swing right to good wires and cam placements. A tough rockover-cum-lurch gains improving holds leading up to another break and the brilliant headwall.

8 The Millionaire Touch E4 6b ★★★ 1976/1980
27m Tough and fingery at the crux and well-endowed with sound protection. Climb the thin, bulging crack with hard moves leftwards to get established on the upper wall above the bulge (peg). Move up to the main break before stepping left and climbing the upper wall rightwards through a bulge to the top. Superb!

9 X Calibre E5 6b 2001
27m Something of an eliminate. Climb the initial crack of the previous route before swinging right and up the wall above the break to a thin flake (two pegs). Hard moves gain the upper wall which provides steep climbing past the 'X'.

10 Brown Corner HVS 5a ★ 1961
26m The huge corner has the feel of a route very much from a bygone era. Begin up the crack in its right-hand wall. Superb when clean and dry, which is rare.

II One 'ard Move E6 6b ★ 1988
28m The impressive wall to the right of *Brown Corner* has a particularly hard central section and a loose finish. Several pegs help protect the crux.

12 Damocles E3 5b ★ 1963/1970s
30m The impressive hanging crack gives an intimidating pitch that is nowhere desperate but gives a very atmospheric climb. Sadly neglected of late, but worthy of star(s) when clean.

13 Golden Boy E5 6a ★ 1995
35m A long and lonely pitch up the centre of the wall. Climb a thin crack (peg) to a break (peg). Pull through the overlap with difficulty onto a short left-facing flake. Fingery and sustained moves up the wall above, slowly easing, gain better holds and an overlap, leading to the sanctuary of a ledge above. Finish via the thin crack in the wall to the right, as for *Emotional Rescue*.

14 Emotional Rescue E5 6a ★★ 1980
35m An impressive pitch with a big feel. Start up *John Peel* then transfer into a thinner crack on the left. Follow this, bold and fingery (poor peg) until more amenable climbing gains the prominent break. Follow a series of small corners leftwards to a ledge and finish up the thin cracks in the headwall to the right.

15 John Peel E2 5b ★   1965
30m The prominent old-style crack gives a pitch requiring respect, even today. Once above the tricky overhang, move left to climb a series of hollow flakes with care and a short left-facing corner to the top.

16 The Creeping Flesh E4 6a   2001
20m A short and fingery lower wall. Climb a series of thin cracks past a peg with an insecure sequence to gain better holds below an overlap. Pull through this (peg) on good holds before proceeding carefully to a bolt belay.

17 Icarus E1 4a, 5b, 5a   1964
The girdle. Climb the crack (HS 4a in its own right) to a belay. Move left along easy rock and then traverse a break to belay in *Brown Corner*. Continue along the break in a fine position to finish up *Jasper*.

18 Vicky E1 5b   1993
15m Climb the arête and continue past the left-hand side of the overhang to gain a ledge with a bolt belay. The wall to the right was once bolted to give **Victoria Barcelona**, F6c (2012).

Airlie Anderson on Cabbage Crack, E4 6a (page 27). Photo: David Simmonite.

Slurper Wall

The clean, steep corner 35m to the right is *Acrophobia*. The wall left of this provides a clutch of newly-cleaned routes, the first beginning at a shallow groove on the edge of the slope above *Gollyberry*.

24 Is Ya Ready? E2 5b — 2012
20m Climb the shallow groove and nose to reach ledges leading to an blanker section. A steep pull up and a swing right leads to an exit up a triangular niche.

25 Whasupwithi? E2 5b — 2012
20m Climb the groove, continuing directly to the breaks beneath the upper bulge (peg). Overcome this on good, hidden holds into the recess above.

26 Is Ya Alright? E3 5c — 2012
20m Climb the faint right-hand rib of the groove to reach a vague break below the capping bulge. A series of long, bold moves through this lead to a small tree at the exit.

27 How it Be? E2 5c ★ — 2012
20m Climb the shallow groove to reach a ledge. Continue via a second groove to a steepening (peg). Fine, airy moves rightwards gain gratifying jugs at the exit.

28 Get Six into the Mix E3 5c ★ — 2008
20m A good route with a bold finish. Climb the corner and continue up the wall to the upper break. Extending moves through an overlap lead to a short exciting finale.

19 Daedalus E3 6a ★ — 1993
15m Climb the thin crack in the left wall of the corner with strenuous pulls and a long stretch to pass the final overhang to the ledge above.

20 Psychopath E1 5b — 1960s
24m The corner is increasingly vegetated.

21 Lard Wall E5 6a — 1987
24m The vague thin crack gives fingery climbing (peg), to a large break. Swing right and finish up *Gollyberry*.

22 Gollyberry E3 6a ★ — 1964/1970s
24m The prominent crack system leads to a problematic overhang. Once above this, either scramble off or abseil from whatever may be available.

23 Chuck Berry E3 6a — 2012
15m A problematic start gains good holds (peg). A faint crack (peg) leads to a ledge. Continue more easily into a groove and bolt belay.

29 Will Ya be Ready? E2 5c ★ — 2012
20m A fine pitch. Use the arête to reach a ledge and continue to another ledge. Stand on the beak of rock to the right, and continue up to a niche below the overlaps. Long moves slightly leftwards through this lead to good holds and a tree belay off to the right.

30 Acrophobia HVS 5a ★ — 1963
30m Good climbing with a fine line and sufficient protection. Climb the corner with a problematic lower bulge. At the top, either abseil off or climb the groove on the left to finish. **Prolapse**, VS (1963), avoided the crux start by starting up *Get Six into the Mix*.

31 Fallout HVS 5b — 1970s
30m The bulge above the long groove has had a recent rockfall. Dangerous and loose.

32 J. Arthur E1 5b — 1963
30m Slightly better, but still a bit rank. Climb the slim corner and crack before making a long rising traverse across the wall to finish up a crack with broken rock

above. A lower traverse across the break and yellow wall to join *Easy Action* is also 5b.

33 Arachnid E3 6a ★ 2001
25m Pull up the wall and swing along the first break into the centre of the wall. Climb this (peg), difficult at first, until improving holds and protection gain the overlap. Pull through this (peg) and climb the wall to a bolt belay.

34 Easy Action E1 5b ★ 1976
30m Climb *Arachnid* to reach a thin crack slightly to the right. Follow this with an awkward exit left onto a ledge. Finish up the upper section of *The Slurper*.

35 The Slurper E1 5c ★ 1965/1970
30m Good climbing up the thin crack system, which proves most difficult in its lower reaches, to a good ledge and possible belay. Step left and follow the fine continuation crack to the top.

36 The Disillusioned Brew Machine E3 5c 1985
35m The shallow scoop directly above the possible belay of *The Slurper* leads to a bulge. Pull rightwards through the bulge into a dirty finishing groove.

37 Drink and Be Merry E4 6b 2012
35m Good clean climbing with a hard start and airy climbing above half-height. Hard moves gain a thin crack and arête leading to ledges. From the top of these, swing up and right and climb the intimidating wall (peg) to better holds and a flake crack. At the bulges above (peg) pull through on good holds to easier ground.

Mortuary Steps Buttress

A fine airy buttress giving a bunch of pushy pitches high above the deck. An easy descent is to the right of the buttress.

38 Co-Conspirator E2 5b, 5b   2011
1. 18m Climb the left wall of the corner via a series of bold moves to reach a grassy ledge. Continue up a thin crack to a larger grassy area and continue leftwards to a belay on a small ledge below a white corner.
2. 12m Move up into the corner and climb it (peg) to a small capping overhang. Pull right and continue up a rib to the right to the top.

39 Flared Beginnings VS 4c   2011
12m From the belay on *Co-Conspirator*, pull through the bulge on the right to a hand-jamming crack and climb this.

40 Drainpipe Groove VS 4b, 4c   1960s
1. 18m Climb the corner to a belay at the break.
2. 12m Pull through some hollow rock to reach a cracked groove leading to the top.

41 Straight Leg E2 5b   2011
12m From the belay on *Drainpipe*, climb the wall above, somewhat boldly at first past a peg. Good climbing. **a** The overgrown groove is **Dome's Groove**, VS 4c (1963).

42 The Profusionist E3 5c   2001
12m From the belay on *Drainpipe Groove*, move right and climb the wall to the right of the crack, passing a thread on the lower wall. Steep climbing on positive holds and with a difficult bulge at half-height.

The next routes all start up the first pitch of Mortuary Steps. Belays are taken in the mid-height break.

43 Death is Part of the Process E4 6b   1987
30m From a thread belay in the break 5m to the right of *The Profusionist*, climb the steep bulging wall past a bolt and two pegs, to finish up a thin crack.

44 Speed Kills E4 6a ★ ★   1977/1979
30m A technical and fingery pitch with difficult but well-protected climbing. Hard moves into the groove/scoop (peg on the left), gain improving holds in the groove itself. Follow this to the top.

45 In Formalin E5 6b ★   2001
30m A desperate little affair straight up the centre of the bulging wall (peg). High in the grade.

46 The Morgue E4 5c ★ 1971/1981

30m Make worrying moves around the bulge to gain a prominent short flake. Move up this (peg) before stepping right into its continuation crack. This leads to a good flake on the left and a finish at the yew tree.

47 Grave Snatcher E5 6b 2012

30m Clip the thread on the right then make extending moves up the bulging arête (peg) to reach a good flake. Use the crack on the left to continue to a finish up a short groove.

48 Mortuary Steps HVS 4a, 5b ★★ 1961

A fine route, hard for the grade, and with a big atmosphere.
1. 18m Follow slabby rock and a groove on the left of the buttress and take a belay below the groove on the arête.
2. 12m Pull through the bulge (thread) into the groove and follow it (peg) to the top.

49 Cardiac Arrest E4 6a ★ 1979

30m Impressive and difficult climbing on the edge of the buttress. Appropriately named. From the belay on *Mortuary Steps*, step right and make difficult moves through the bulge into the groove in the arête. Follow this leftwards to a break from where an intimidating swing right gains a thin crack in a fitting position to finish. **b Hart Attack**, E5 6b (1985), climbs straight through the final bulges past two pegs.

50 Beta Blocker E5 6b ★ 2001

30m A direct assault on the front face of the buttress, with reasonable protection. From the belay on *Mortuary Steps*, step right and make technical moves through the initial bulges 2m to the right of *Cardiac Arrest*. Gain a good hold, from where a sequence of intricate pulls gains the final crack of *Cardiac Arrest*.

55 Golden Lips E2 5b — 2012
12m The wall and groove to a more difficult finish.

56 Carbon Neutral E4 6a ★ — 2012
12m The wall gives fine climbing with limited protection (peg in the break), to a superb finish on the headwall.

57 Diamonds and Rust E2 5c ★ — 1987
11m The crack runs out and gives taxing final moves.

58 Blood Diamond E4 6a — 2012
11m The wall gives tough moves from the thin break (peg) and a scary move or two on the headwall.

The Triglyph

The cool tower 40m along the path.

59 Who the Hell E1 5c — 1971
26m Climb the overhanging wall before moving right after 5m to tackle a loose bulge.

60 To Hell and Back E3 5b — 1985
25m A poor route climbing the arête to the right.

61 How the Hell VS 4c ★ ★ — 1950
26m A fine climb up the left-hand crack. At the top, a variety of finishes are possible.

62 Hell Hath No Fury E2 5b — 1997
24m The blunt arête gives a worrying little pitch.

63 What the Hell VS 4b ★ ★ — 1957
26m The best route on the buttress following the main, central crack.

64 Morning Crack S ★ — 1950
20m The right-hand crack gives a good introduction to crack climbing.

51 Little Capucin HVS 5b ★ — pre-1960/1975
30m Climb the centre of the front face of the buttress (limited protection) to the break (belay). Continue up the thin crack in the centre of the wall by some fine moves.

52 Midi HVS 5a, 5a — 1970s
30m Do the first pitch of *Little Capucin* to the belay. Follow the short corner on the right, trending leftwards to finish close to the top of *Little Capucin*.

53 Dead on Arrival E4 5c ★ — 1985
30m A high-level girdle. From the bush on the second pitch of *Dome's Groove*, move up and traverse the break into *Mortuary Steps*. Step down and swing right on a good hold into *Cardiac Arrest*. Follow this to finish via *Little Capucin*.

A smaller buttress up and to the right of a vague descent path gives a handful of short pitches.

54 Silver Tongues E1 5b — 2012
12m A wall leads to an arête and short finishing crack.

Ivy Buttress

65 Naze VD 1957
20m The wall leads to a short corner which in turn leads to the second corner on the left.

66 Marasmus E3 5c 1970s
20m The wall left of the arête gives a bold route on good rock.

67 Childline E2 5b ★ 2012
20m Climb the lower front face of the arête (peg) onto its left-hand side. Fine climbing up this, with minimal protection but excellent rock, leads to the top.

68 Child's Arête HVS 5a 1960s
20m Follow *Childline* and continue up the right-hand side of the arête with some caution at the exit.

69 Emanon HS 1960s
20m Tackle the bulge and continue via a shallow corner.

70 No Rantzen E2 5c 2012
20m Climb the face (thread) and continue past an overlap up the fine pillar of rock above. Exit with care.

Tiger Wall Area: The bays left of Carl's Wark, and below the path leading to the substation, contain some esoteric routes. The first of these is about 200m left of Carl's Wark on a wall with a thin crack up the centre. **Just What the Doctor Ordered**, E1 5b (1986), is the wall left of the crack finishing left of the tree (needs uncovering). **Costa Brava**, HVS 5b ★ (1980), gives good climbing up the thin crack past an old peg. Twenty five metres right is a wall at a higher level. **Holly**, HVS 5c (2013), is the crack on the left to a big hole. **Willow**, HVS 5c (2013), is the next crack finishing pleasantly on good holds. **Liquid Dream**, HVS 5a (1986), is at the right-hand end.

Tiger Wall: Fifty metres right is a wall with the remnants of a stone shelter at its right-hand end. **Tiger Crack**, E2 6a (2013), is the thin crack in the centre of a wall to a jug then past two ledges. Right of a tree at the base of the wall is a pillar between mossy ledges: **Tiger Direct**, VS 4c (2013), climbs the pillar and finishes directly up the groove; **Tiger Traverse**, HVS 5a (2013), goes from the top of the pillar then follows the leftward-rising traverse and finishes up the ledges of *Tiger Crack*. Right again is a ledge at 4m: **Tiger Groove**, HS (2013), climbs up onto the ledge and follows the groove above finishing slightly left. Two metres right is **Has She Been?**, S (2013), following the broken groove to a step right to finish after the break; **Mompesson Rich Pickings**, MVS 4c (2013), is the girdle of Tiger Wall. Climb *Has She Been?* to the break and follow it left to finish up the ledges of *Tiger Crack*.

Carl's Wark

Beneath Prayer Wheel Wall is a quarried wall at road level. This can be approached from the road or by descending a path at the end of the track. It can remain damp after rain.

71 Little Crack VS 5a 1970s
6m The thin crack at the far left-hand side of the face.

72 More Air Than Chocolate Font 6A
The pockets, moving into the groove to finish.

73 Carl's Wark Traverse Font 7B
Jerry Moffatt's fierce and fingery traverse. Move right to finish up *Bubbles Wall Start*.

74 Flake and Pillar E1 5b 1970s
14m Climb the prominent crack; tricky at half-height.

75 Squeak E5 6a 1991
13m From the break on *Flake and Pillar*, move right and climb the wall directly. Bolder since the demise of a peg.

76 Au Revoir Monodoigt Font 7B
A hard highball, very testing on your vertical savvy.

77 Bubbles Wall Direct Font 6C
The direct start to the classic route is fingery and bold thanks mainly to the hole below.

78 Bubbles Wall E3 5c ★ ★ ★ 1975
15m A classic and strenuous pitch. Climb *Flake and Pillar* to the break and traverse right to a niche. Pull up and step left to a series of hollows which lead to the break. Finish rightwards. Doing the direct start makes the route E4 6b.

79 Black Kabul E5 6a ★ 1981
15m The upper wall to the right gives a bold exercise. Step left from the start of *Carl's Wark Crack* and climb the wall to a large hole (Friend 4). A big stretch and a bold pull off a finger edge gain the next break. Finish directly, more easily.

80 Carl's Wark Crack E2 5c ★ ★ 1968/1970s
14m Pumpy action.The superb crack gives a fine strenuous battle, the start of which is polished. It can be very muddy after rain or pleasantly air-conditioned in summer.

81 Scarab E6 6b ★ ★ 1976/1979
15m A classic 'scare-fest' from the Eighties with fine climbing and limited, but sound, protection. Climb the thin crack. Move left to a niche and commit to the wall above via a short, thin crack and plenty of small holds. Finish direct up the thin crack.

82 All Systems Go E6 6c ★ 1985
15m *Scarab's* fiercer neighbour. From the break, move up to a thread and launch up the wall above via a faint line of weakness, tiny holds and no more protection before the break is reached. Finish via the thin crack of *Scarab*.

83 Green Crack VS 4c ★ 1970s

15m The corner gives a good pitch but only in dry conditions. It can be finished via the crack on the left at 5b.

84 Soapsuds Traverse Font 6B+

Go rightwards across the lower break, move up, then back left along the higher one.

85 Soapsuds E3 6a ★ 1979

12m Fittingly named. Climb the wall and crack past the break before a series of tasty moves on small holds gains a further break. Finish more easily. **Shaky Crack**, VD (1960s), is a poor route taking the flake to the right.

86 Aerospace HVS 4c ★ 1979

24m Traverse the upper break from left to right.

Jake Oughton on Bubbles Wall, E3 5c (opposite page).
Photo: Dan Lane.

Stoney Middleton History

The grey cliffs that tower over the A623, as it winds out the tight Peak District village of Stoney Middleton, sit relatively quietly today. The dust has settled on their long and shining history. As you walk around its quiet bays today you would never guess how great a past these walls have. Yet it was here that history was made. Where the boldest limestone route of its day was climbed in 1933. Where the hardest routes around were forced in the days of big boots and sling runners. Where, not for the first time, a carpenter would say "Our Father" and the books would be written. Where a route would be climbed as possibly "the hardest route in the world" in 1981 by a climber who would call himself the best in the world. Where international visitors would come to see the state of the art and where, under a Thatcherite government, weekend and full-time migrants would come to the grey cliffs to climb, to doss and to sometimes live. Today, loved and mocked in equal measure, these limestone walls hold claim to be the most historic and important cliffs in the history of Peak District limestone climbing.

Climbers first began to explore what had been left for them soon after the local quarrymen had ceased activity. J.W. Puttrell and Henry Bishop climbed *Mineshaft* (1910) and *The Flue (Fingal's Flue)* in 1918. It wasn't until 1933 that Frank Elliott, Gilbert Ellis and Harry Dover climbed *The Great Ridge*, now known as *Aurora*. This was quite a feat, virtually protectionless. Around this same time, Eric Byne and Clifford Moyer went on to record *Fingal's Cave* and *The White Knight*. Nothing else is recorded until the 1950s when the Valkyrie Club comprising Joe Brown, Ron Moseley, Slim Sorrell, Nat Allen and Don Chapman, arrived on the scene. Well-versed in crack climbing, they climbed a host of new routes, including *Morning Crack* and *How the Hell*. Full-on aid-climbing also arrived when Brown and Moseley pegged their way up *Brown's Overhang* (later known as *Kink*), the first route above Windy Ledge. With the Valkyrie's transformation into the Rock and Ice came Don Whillans, who added *Thrutch* and *Frisco Bay*. With this, Stoney Middleton gained and maintained an intimidating reputation.

The Cioch Club gathered outside the Lovers' Leap cafe in the 1960s. Behind: John Atkinson, Dave Nowill, Jack Street partially covered, Jim Ballard, Brian Starkey, Colin Crookes and Brian Moore. Front: Sheila and Bryan (Tanky) Stokes and Geoff Birtles. Photo: Chris Jackson.

Jack Street on Dead Banana Crack, (page 55). Photo by Bob Keates.

Tom Proctor, Stoney's greatest climber.
Photo: Geoff Birtles.

and Geoff Birtles. They took an early interest in new routing with Bob Dearman and Graham Hawker making the first route on Garage Buttress with *Helicon*, then an aid climb. John Atkinson climbed *Padme* free on which Webb had used 2 pegs for aid. Significantly, Street and Birtles climbed *Jasper*. Although they used some aid, it was a bold venture, and a sign of things to come. Chris Jackson also made an impact with an almost-free version of Dearman's aid climb *The Flakes*. Moore was an active aid climber and he climbed *Pendulum* with Pete Fieldsend on aid which would in due course become a classic free climb. The same freeing would happen many years later to the aided *Little Plum* by Jackson and Birtles which took five days to ascend. Most of the new climbs and developments at Stoney for the five years from 1962 were the work of the Cioch Club.

It was with these events, together with the increased popularity of the Stoney Cafe and Moon Inn amongst climbers, that 'the Stoney Scene' arrived. Climbers of the day based themselves at Stoney for the weekend, dossing and camping up the dale. A tradition, that would last for the next 20 years.

The next decade of development was dominated by Tom Proctor, a quiet and powerfully-built carpenter. Knowing the place like the backs of his large hands he peppered the cliff with a host of high-class routes that were as hard as anything else in the country. Proctor, often with, and cajoled by, Geoff Birtles, added five high-class routes; *Pickpocket, Our Father, Dies Irae, Scoop Wall* and *Wee Doris*. These routes pushed the boundaries of the existing grading system and still remain highly respected today.

But challenge was on the way. Gabe Regan's *Bitter Fingers* and *Scarab* stand as testament to this period of activity. In the mid- to late-70s attention turned to the quarried sections. Birtles increased his tally with the addition of *The Millionaire Touch* and *Oliver*. Proctor excelled with a free ascent of *Circe* and left his final calling card, *Four Minute Tiler*, in 1980.

Stoney was perhaps at its summit of popularity between the mid-70s and mid-80s. Huge unemployment created a dole culture and young and old alike had endless time on their hands, only punctuated by once-a-fortnight visits to sign on. These time-rich-money-poor climbers often centred themselves at Stoney where they would doss in one renowned hovel or other – the Woodshed, Land of the Midnight Sun, or on Windy Ledge itself. They would subsist on the minimum of food and spend cold mornings cuddling one cup of tea in the cafe, cold evenings huddled round a half pint of orange juice in The Moon. By day they devoured the routes on Stoney or struck out on foot or hitched to other local crags.

It wasn't until the Sheffield University Mountaineering Club showed interest did things move on again. Dave Johnson, Dave Mellor and Jack Soper led the assaults. The SUMC teams initially climbed up the dale with ascents of *Gabriel, Pearly Gates* and *Minus Ten* but then turned their attention to the near pristine Windy Buttress. The team established the classic *Windhover* largely free and the hard aid climb, *Kingdom Come*. The routes from this period provided years of aid-elimination opportunities for future generations.

In 1961 a new stage of development took place when Barry Webb produced some classics that include, *Padme, Mortuary Steps* and *Brown Corner*. Likewise, the imposing crack of *Medusa* was climbed by Len Millson. Jack Street added some of the hardest routes of the era. *Jasper, John Peel, Boat Pusher's Wall* and *Dead Banana Crack* were all big deals at the time.

In 1962 another team arrived, the Cioch Club, including Jack Street, Chris Jackson, John Atkinson, Brian Moore

Tom Proctor attempting to free climb pitch 2 of Menopause (page 64). Photo: John Kirk.

These up-and-coming youngsters snapped away at the Proctor classics. Chris Hamper freed *Menopause*, originally attempted by Proctor, and repeated *Circe*. New blood, including Jerry Moffatt, Dougie Hall, Simon Nadin and Paul Mitchell, swung into action, with many stylish repeats. John Kirk freed one of the last major lines, *Kingdom Come*.

The big news story in the early-80s was the freeing of *Little Plum* by Jerry Moffatt. This desperate route was probably as hard as any route in the world at the time. *Easy Skanking* by Andy Pollitt broke the modern trend by attacking similar rock but with as much boldness as technical difficulty. Simon Nadin, on top form, proved a point by soloing *Menopause*, on-sight, an incomprehensible feat.

The millennium started slowly but soon gathered speed with the development of Garage Buttress as a sport crag. In 2002, Mark Pretty started the task with *Lover's Leap* and later *The King of Ming*. Pretty continued the development in 2007 with the addition of *Ming the Merciless* his hardest addition, at F8a+. Not to be outdone, Kristian Clemmow added another fine F8a, *The Big Apple*.

In 2012, Gary Gibson and Nick Taylor began scouring the area for unclimbed rock. During this period they added a large number of new trad routes, the best of which are the direct finish to *Dead Banana Crack*, *Top Banana*, *Adios Tango* and *Sign My Name*. In the following few years Gibson continued the development of the Garage Buttress area where he added a number of low grade, instantly popular sport climbs. The best of these are *Dreamcatcher*, *I Hate You* and the momentous *Four Thousand*, Gary's four thousandth new route.

2014 continued with the addition of more hard sport climbs by Clemmow and Pretty, *Dig Deeper* F8a and *Just Glue 'em Back*, F7b. Finally, and to top it all off, Clemmow added the hardest of them all, *Tollbar*, F8a+, bringing development to a near conclusion.

At the time of writing, you will often see climbers on the Garage Buttress sport climbs, but if you wander up the dale then you will find quiet and solitude. The classic trad routes remain as good and as testing as they have always been. So take a short walk and test your mettle.

A fuller climbing, and area, history can be found on the Stoney Middleton Heritage website. Search for it.

Ian Carr

Windy Ledge dossing scene, 1975. Photo: Mark Scott.

Kristian Clemmow on the first ascent of Tollbar, F8a+ (page 75). Photo: Keith Sharples.

Prayer Wheel Wall

A fine wall, good for rattling off a load of lower and middle-grade climbs. There are good tree belays on the ledge and the best descent is to walk off leftwards rather than abseil.

1   Omelette E3 6a   1976
9m   Climb the wall above the pothole. The size of the route is doubled by the depth of the hole.

2   Om E1 5b   pre-1960/1963
9m   The innocuous crack is a popular testpiece.

3   Shit Wall E2 5b   1979
12m   The dirty-looking wall via a faint crack is better than it appears. Censorship removed!

4   Nowt Said E2 5c   2014
15m   The wall to the finish of *Shit Wall*.

5   Mani E2 5b ★   pre-1960
15m   Excellent face-climbing requiring some care. Climb the wall directly above a shallow hole to the break. A tricky rock-up gains the next break. Step left and continue directly to the top via a thin crack.

6   Blinkers E2 5c ★   1982
15m   Climb the shallow depression. From a ledge at 5m, step left and climb up left of a thin streak. Move slightly right towards the top and exit slightly leftwards.

7   Padme HVS 5a, 4c ★ ★   1961/1963
Very much a classic but suffering due to its popularity.
1. 16m   Climb the shallow depression, trending rightwards to a series of good holds (peg) leading leftwards to a ledge and tree belay. Walk off or persevere.
2. 12m   Move right and climb a corner and overhang to finish up a groove on the right.

8   Sign My Name E3 5c ★   2012
25m   A surprising find, low in the grade. Boldly climb the wall and pass a peg to a pair of pegs at the final thin break. Tricky moves slightly rightwards and up lead to a sloping ledge (peg). Climb the thin crack above to a junction with *Padme* and pull through the overhang before moving right for the final slim corner.

9 Asparagus VS 4b ★   **pre-1960**
21m The angle gives pleasant climbing. From a small ledge, move right and finish up a short wall to a tree belay. **a Looking Through Gary Gibson's Eyes**, HVS 5a (1979), leaves *Asparagus* before climbing the wall to the left.

10 Brassiere Strap S   **1963**
45m From the belay on *Padme*, traverse right to *Rosehip Wine*. Weave on rightwards into *Aux Bicyclettes*. Continue along a ledge and across the top of *Gabriel* to finish.

11 Robin E2 5b   **1963/1986**
21m A bit of an eliminate, up the wall and vague rib.

12 Cock-a-Leekie Wall E2 6a ★   **1960s**
21m A classic little technical testpiece. Climb the centre of the bold wall to reach a ledge. Pull up to a thin break and step right before delicate moves lead up the short blank wall to a ledge. Finish to the trees more easily. **b** It is possible to climb a shallow groove just to the left at E4 6a.

13 Vinegar Fly VS 5a   **1979**
18m Climb the short tricky wall moving right onto the arête. Finish via the corner above.

14 Minestrone HVS 5a   **1957**
27m Climb the groove to an overhang and step left to ledges leading left to *Asparagus*. Finish up the corner that *Asparagus* avoids.

15 Rosehip Wine HS 4b ★   **1961**
18m Climb up to the base of the corner and follow it to a ledge. Step left and finish up a second corner.

The slim pillar on the right is **Whine, Whine, Whine**, E1 5b (2012). **The Thorn**, VS 4c (1960s), climbs the shallow groove and left-hand wall to the right. **Jungle Arête**, VD (1963), is the loose arête to the right.

16 Pollyanna E1 5b   **1960s**
12m The overhanging crack gives nice jamming.

17 Lesley Ann E3 6a   **2012**
12m From 5m up *Pollyanna*, swing right along the break and extricate a sequence of difficult moves up the wall (peg) to a ledge. Use the tree for descent.

18 Horizon VD   **1957**
21m The right wall of the corner. **a** The corner is S.

26 Fingal's Flue VS 4c ★   pre-1900
29m A classic of its genre, very entertaining. Climb the
back of the cave to enter a black hole, emerging back into
daylight a little higher. Continue up the easy chimney.

27 Fingal's Cave HVS 5a   1933
29m Bridge up the inside of the cave close to its entrance
to gain a hole in the roof. Finish up the chimney of *Fingal's
Flue*. Feels alarmingly bold until gear is eventually found.

28 The Groper VS 4c   1963
30m Pass the overhang and continue up the tower above.

29 No Statesman E3 6b   1988
15m The thin crack starting over a bulge.

30 Scurvy Knave HVS 5b   1984
10m Climb the easy broken wall and continue straight
up the wall just to the left of a hanging bush.

31 The White Knight VD   1933
30m Climb to a ledge then left up the face to the gully.

Pearly Gates Buttress

The large towering buttress provides an impressive profile
and a number of good routes.

32 Ben E2 5c   1976
30m The centre of the wall and the arête above are
climbed to reach a white band. Move left for 3m before
climbing the centre of the wall above to the top.

33 Gabriel VS 4c ★ ★   1957
20m A good climb that can be made great by continuing
up *The Pearly Gates*. Climb the corner to a ledge (peg), and
traverse rightwards and finish up the wall. **Photo on page 9.**

34 The Pearly Gates VS 4c ★ ★   1959
18m Fine exposure. Climb the wall above the belay. Traverse left and climb the groove. The groove can also be
reached by going left at a low level to another ledge and
approaching it from the left. The wall right of the final
groove may also be climbed at 4c.

35 Solitaire E1 5b ★   1966
18m The centre of the wall gives a pleasant pitch with
minimal protection.

36 Haven't Got a Cluedo E2 5c ★   2011
18m Climb directly from the initial crack of *Solitaire*.

37 St Peter E1 5b   1960s
14m The sharp arête has a baffling overlap complete with
plenty of polish and veneer.

19 Canine of Brine E2 5b   2012
22m The arête is bold with a tricky move below half-
height. Continue straight, pulling through the top bulge
directly above the corner where *Juggernaut* moves right.

20 Juggernaut HVS 5a   1965
30m Climb easy rock to reach a corner. Up this with a
difficult section past a peg. Continue directly to the bulge
and move right beneath this to finish up a groove.

21 Scanner E1 5b   2011
22m Climb up the centre of the wall, bold. From good
ledges, trend left and finish directly via a bulge.

22 Master of Tides VS 4c   2012
22m Climbs the arête finishing up easier ground.

23 Lost Horizon VD   1957
24m Climb the wall past a ledge moving left into a corner. Up this then trend left to finish at the top of *Horizon*.

24 Aux Bicyclettes VD   pre-1960
24m Climb the arête to a ledge. Finish up the crack.

25 The Crux HVS 5c   1986
24m The thin crack in the left wall of the cave.

38 St Paul E3 5c 1982

14m The bold wall to the right of the arête proves surprisingly tough but rewarding. Take a Friend 1½.

39 Parachute VS 4b pre-1960

14m The highly-polished corner.

40 Parr Kor E5 6a 2011

14m The centre of the wall without recourse to the arête. Just sufficient protection and good, albeit bold, climbing.

41 Roman Candle VS 4c 1961

14m Gain the arête and climb it on its left.

42 Au Gratin HS 4a pre-1960

14m Climb the arête with a mantel at 4m and with the help of a groove higher up.

43 Honeysuckle Lane E1 5b 2011

15m The shallow groove 2m right of the arête gives a good, bold pitch. **Suckle the Honey**, HVS 5a (2011), climbs the groove to the right and from a small tree moves left to join its parent route.

44 Moss Side E2 5b 2011

10m The fine fossil-encrusted wall to the right.

Minus Ten Wall

A great big wall with a fistful of testing pitches from VS to E5. It is clean and often stays quite dry in the rain. The assortment of polished, chalked holds at its base is the world-famous Minus Ten Bouldering Wall. Evening shade.

45 Minus Wall HVS 5b   1960s
14m The wall via a thin crack and loose finish.

46 Minus Ten VS 4c ★   1959
15m An excellent test of your jamming skills; underestimate it at your peril. **a Great Escape**, HVS 5b (1976), traverses the break rightwards to finish up *Cointreau*.

47 Jam Sandwich E5 6b ★   1985
18m Just that; squeezed-in but with much to recommend it. Climb the narrow wall by highly technical moves, (two pegs) to a big move and a swing left on a pocket at the top.

48 Traffic Jam E5 6b ★★   1979
19m The route of the wall, but gone are the days of queuing for this one. Climb to a ramp leading up to a thin break. Swing left and make an almighty move to gain

the next break. Finish more easily. **b** A reachy and equally classic direct version goes up from the thin break at E5 6b – fewer moves but fewer holds!

49 Double Scotch E2 5c ★★   1960s
18m Pumpy, chunky fun. The steep crack has a hard start. From the niche, move leftwards onto the headwall.

50 Cointreau VS 4c   pre-1960
20m The wider crack leads to a ledge. Finish via the corner past some ledges to the top.

51 The Flashing Fisher E3 5c   1984
20m The upper wall immediately to the right via a series of pockets and moving leftwards past a peg. Worthwhile.

52 Pygmies Walk Tall E1 5b ★   1967/1970s
24m From a ledge part way up *Thrutch*, move leftwards to an overlap. Pull through this and the overlaps above to reach a break. Move right to finish via a groove.

53 Thrutch HVS 5a   1952
20m The main corner past a ledge until an awkward mantelshelf rightwards onto a second ledge. Finish easily.

Dave Johnson on Double Scotch, E2 5c (opposite page). Photo: Jon Leighton.

Monosod, E2 5c (2013), starts up *Thrutch* and after 4m takes a gently-rising line up and left, passing the thin break on *Traffic Jam*, to finish up *Minus Ten*.

Minus Ten Bouldering

The shiny wall at the base of the crag is one of the original homes of Peak District bouldering. Since the 1970s, the technically minded have plied their craft on the slopers and crimps, producing such classics as the *Kirton Dyno*, the *JABP*, *Young Americans*, *Quent's Dyno*, *Zippy's Sidepull*, *Sean's Problem*, *One Arm Bandit* and, the ultimate in 1990's power-eliminates, *Pinch II*.

Detailing problems is beyond the scope of this book as they're essentially all eliminates and all have lists of rules detailing which holds you use, and more importantly, which ones you can't. For details, check out Peak District Bouldering (Vertebrate Publishing) or peakbouldering.info.

It is long past the heyday of its popularity where, in the years before climbing walls, the best climbers in the area would gather and work out fiendish exercises.

Today it is still a great place to work out on fingery, friction-dependent, body-position-critical, dynamic problems. It benefits from staying dry in the rain and remains seepage-free in the winter.

George's Wall, 20m right of the corner of Thrutch, offers a couple of problems.

54 George's Wall Dyno Font 7B
An enormous break-to-break dyno from the low jug about a metre and a half left of the arête.

55 George's Groove Font 6A+
The groove just right, a metre left of the arête.

Wee Doris Bay

This is one of Stoney's most impressive sections. Its main wall is seamed with cracks and delicate features which give a group of classic pitches. **Hammer**, VS 4b (1970s), is the wall 5m right of the left-hand arête of the wall and **Whet**, E2 5b (1985), is the bold wall just right again.

56 Sickle E1 5a   1965
12m   Climb the wall to reach a ramp (thread). Move awkwardly leftwards up this and finish directly.

57 Syntax Error E2 5c   1974
42m   Traverse the horizontal break with difficult moves to gain *Pickpocket*. Finish up the corner of *Frisco Bay*.

58 Boat Pusher's Wall E3 5c ★ 1966

18m A renowned frightener from the mid-Sixties. Climb the bold wall to a small ledge. Continue, still very bold, to reach a second, smaller ledge from where awkward moves gain a short and better-protected finishing groove.

59 Big Boris E6 6b ★ 1988

18m A very worthwhile pitch aiming for the bald-looking headwall. Make bold fingery moves to a small ledge and continue slightly leftwards to gain the overlap. Difficult moves through this (where once there was a bolt) lead onto the headwall and a thin break (peg). Finish easily.

60 Wee Doris E4 5c ★★★ 1968

18m The classic Stoney thrill ride. A sustained and pumpy pitch that is perfectly safe although it's likely to feel exciting to hard-pressed leaders. Boulder the shiny initial wall (small wires). Take a deep breath and attack the steep crack above, passing good protection, until draining moves allow an ungainly exit.

The most notable ascent to date was a streak where the climber attached himself by a rope tied round his testicles, a practice that the BMC does not recommend.

61 Medusa HVS 5a ★★ 1961

24m The compelling central crack gives a big butch pitch full of merit. Another essential tick and an eye-opener for the wall-trained (who may well dispute the grade!)

62 Gesemini E3 6a ★ 1964/1977

25m *Medusa's* twin. Cautious and precarious moves up the wall gain a thin crack leading with difficulty to the break and the wide crack above. Described here with the direct start; the original line stepped right from *Medusa* at the break into the upper crack at HVS 5a ★.

63 Pickpocket E4 6a, 4c ★★ 1968/1976

30m Yet another ever-dry classic, very much in the Stoney mould. Climb the polished wall aiming for a short crack. Pull up leftwards onto a thin ramp (crux) and stretch for a pocket to its left. Climb delicately upwards to a break and thin cracks above. Another hard stretch gains a wider break. Pull up the wall above to gain the ledges of *Golden Gate*; follow these easily leftwards to finish with care up the front of a slight pillar. Fagin brilliant!

a The Artful Dodger, E5 6b (2015), climbs the wall (pegs) and huge pockets to the right. Romp excitedly up these to the break.

64 Balthazaaaaah E5 6a ★   2012

30m An alternative to *Pickpocket* with a fine upper section. From the thread on *Pickpocket*, step up and out left and make a hard pull to better holds (peg). Continue directly to a wide break (thread), where a very long move gains good holds. Move up with urgency until holds on the arête gain a ledge. Finish easily via a crack on the right.

65 Frisco Bay VS 4c ★★   1952

30m Climb the wall just right of the large corner to reach a tree and then step left into the main corner. Follow this to a thrutchy exit onto the ledge. Finish direct via the open corner which is easier by starting it slightly to the right.

66 County Marin E4 6a   2012

28m From the tree on *Frisco Bay*, climb the wall just right of the corner via a flake and a tricky move to reach a thin crack leading to the ledge. Continue up the wall right of the corner to a break (peg), and make hard moves up a slim nose to big holds and an exit requiring a little care.

67 Bay of Pigs E1 5b, 5a   1976

1. 18m From the tree on *Frisco Bay*, climb the striking thin crack system with a tricky exit onto the ledge (peg and nut belay).
2. 12m Continue up the wider crack above to an awkward exit.

68 The B.A.R.T. Extension E5 6b, 5b 2012

1. 18m Climb the left arête of the prominent gash (*Golden Gate*) to the right to a ledge. Continue by technical moves to reach the next break and then by an almighty undercut manoeuvre to reach the top and a hard mantelshelf exit. Only those with a mega-reach should apply.
2. 12m Continue up the excellent but bold wall above to a thread. Move right and exit with care through the ivy.

69 Golden Gate HVS 5a, 4b ★★★ 1950

A fine big classic despite the sheen. Learn to love it.
1. 18m Climb the deep chimney crack and follow it before making awkward moves up and right to a tree belay.
2. 18m Traverse left along the ledge to the corner and continue leftwards in a fine position onto a slight pillar. Finish up the exposed arête to the left.

70 Hinges E1 5b, 5a ★ 1976/2012

A good two-pitcher now cleaned up and straightened out.
1. 18m Climb the left-hand side of the wall to a tree and pass a smaller tree onto the slabbier face above. Tiptoe delicately up the right-hand side of this (small wire protection) to the mid-height ledge.
2. 15m Step up left and climb the fine clean wall above to a cleaned finish rightwards. The original finish lies up the poorer crack to the right (4c).

71 Bingo Wall E2 5b, 5a ★★ 1966

A super little route climbing the left-hand side of the wall.
1. 15m Climb the crack just right of the chimney to an overlap and avoid it by rocking through its left-hand side. Step back right above and climb the wall to a tree belay.
2. 15m Climb the wall behind the tree, pulling leftwards over a small overhang. Finish up the superb knobbly wall.

72 Mindblind E5 6b 1984

15m Contrived but tough. Climb the very faint groove in the centre of the wall and exit through the overhang onto the easier headwall. Uses a side-runner in *Kelly's Eye* at this grade. E6 without.

73 Kelly's Eye E4 6a ★ 1979

15m Another fine testpiece. Climb the wall to the right to gain the flake or 'eye'. Swing left and through the slight overlap to reach a break. Finish via the fine thin crack.

74 The Brighton Line E1 5b, 5b ★ 2012

A surprising find with two excellent pitches.
1. 15m Climb the tight groove to reach a ledge. The sharp arête gives good holds (peg), and a final pull onto the ledge.
2. 15m The thin crack directly behind the belay to a rightwards exit.

75 End of the Line E1 5b 2012

15m From the ledge climb the right side of the wall.

Dead Banana Bay

This is the third of the big bays in the centre of the crag. The fantastic right wall is featured with forceful cracks and grooves and several classics. It is bounded on the right by a prominent arête with a large chimney to its right, itself quite often used as a means of descent. **a** The faint groove in the left arête of the slim left-hand wall leads to a hideously vegetated corner: **Bluefinger**, VS 4c (1968).

76 Flavour of the Month E6 6b † 1986

10m The pocketed wall provides difficult moves. Poorly protected since the removal of a bolt.

77 My Personal Pleasure E6 6c † 1986

19m Climb the faint crack to gain a break (pegs). Move up and right to a good hold and pull straight up above this to reach a faint break. Step left onto the arête and finish up this. Not climbed since the removal of two bolts.

78 Belinda E4 6a ★ 1974

18m A bold offering with excellent, though somewhat insecure, climbing. Step left from *Froth* to gain and follow a thin crack. This gains the break and shallow groove above. Climb this to a second break. E3 with side-runners. **b The Rainbow Woman**, E3 6a (1984), traverses the break crossing the left wall of the corner.

79 Froth VS 4b, 4c ★★ 1959

A classic; a fine first pitch and a superb and airy second.
1. 18m Climb the main corner to a ledge just below the
break. **c Wallop**, VS 4b (1959), escapes left from the ledge.
2. 15m Traverse right along the break using a chert frieze
into a niche. Pull onto the wall above to reach a tree, or continue along the break to a ledge and belay. Abseil descent.

80 Born Again E2 5c 1989

18m A direct line up the wall and vague pillar of *Froth*.

81 Mottled Wall E4 5c 1976

18m A super problem when clean; it often isn't. Gain the
thin break and make precarious moves up the wall to gain
an easier groove leading leftwards to the belay on *Froth*.

82 Mingtled Wall E2 6a ★ 1976

18m Start up *Dead Banana Crack* then branch left into
Mottled Wall. Take the thin crack branching right from
the groove to the break and escape left. Much better is to
join and continue up *Top Banana*; E3 6a ★★.

88 Sag Line E4 6b   2013
18m Climb the wall just right of *Fe Fi Fo Fum* to join it at the crack. Step up and follow the wall between it and *Okra*.

89 Beanstalk E3 5c   1969/1971
18m The reasonably-protected arête, climbed on its left-hand side.

90 The Blood of an Englishman E3 5c ★   2012
21m The arête purely on its right, with an unprotected start and a bold upper section. Excellent rock and climbing.

91 Augean VS 4c ★   1964
21m The crack onto the arête. Finish via the crack above.

92 Hercules E5 5c ★   1971
17m A bold experience up the wall to the right. Gain a ledge at 4m by an insecure move. Pull boldly up the wall above via a series of pockets moving leftwards to an ivy-choked crack. Follow this to a difficult exit.

93 Sisyphean E4 6a ★   2012
15m Climb the crack left of the corner and pull up leftwards to the break (peg). Step left and pull up to a hollow then up the bold wall to the right (peg), to a ledge and bolt belay.

94 Ivy Grotto Direct HVS 5a   pre-1960
20m The steep vegetated corner.

95 From Here to There E1 5b   1975
36m Traverse the walls from right-to-left starting up *Ivy Grotto Direct* and finishing up *Wallop*.

96 Slab and Arête HVS 5a   1970s
19m Climb the slab to reach a ledge. Move up a scoop on the left and traverse right onto the top of the protruding arête. Finish easily above.

97 Nowt About E2 5c   2012
18m Climb the short arête onto a ledge and attack the block overhang above via good holds onto the short sharp arête. Finish more easily above.

98 Anything Corner VS 4b   traditional
18m The clean cut-corner gives a worthwhile pitch.

99 Nip, Zip, Diddly E2 5c   2012
18m A pleasant pitch taking the sharp arête and the overlap above. Once established, wander up the left arête.

100 The Mineshaft D   pre-1900
24m The massive polished chimney is more often used as a descent.

83 Dead Banana Crack E1 6a ★ ★ ★   1965/1968
24m A fine route that got its name from the state of the leader's fingers after the first ascent. Gain the thin crack from the right. Make a particularly frustrating move to reach easier but sustained climbing leading to the break. Traverse right to finish, or better, pull rightwards through the steep blocky wall above. **Photo on page 39.**

d A fine alternative steps left and climbs the headwall past a peg on the left: **Top Banana**, E3 6a ★ ★ (2012).

84 The Great Leveller E6 6b   1988
22m An extremely tough and technical wall. Start up *Bitter Fingers*. Protection is low for the crux, which involves a huge reach from a painful mono undercut!

85 Bitter Fingers E4 6a ★ ★ ★   1976
22m A classic product of the Seventies, it has since become a much-coveted pitch. Climb the wall to reach an undercut flake. Move up and right into the thin crack and peg. Gain the break via a hard move then swing left to a good jug just above. Increasingly difficult moves up the crack lead to the headwall where easier moves gain the ledge. **Photo on page 57.**

86 Okra E5 6a ★   1980s
22m Leave *Fe Fi Fo Fum* and move left and up to the break on *Bitter Fingers*. Move right and boldly climb the wall.

87 Fe Fi Fo Fum HVS 5a ★ ★   1964
18m The fine flake crack gives a classic pitch full of good jams and jugs.

101 A.N.Other El 5c

1970s

12m The groove to the right of *Mineshaft* climbed direct.

102 Shellfish Shuffle S

pre-1960

24m The slabby wall further to the right trending leftwards at the top to finish at 'the winding room'.

To the right is a cave at 12m.

103 Tantalus HS 4b

1960s

1. 15m Climb up to the cave and traverse right to a groove which leads to a ledge and tree belay.

2. 20m Traverse right to a clean groove and climb this finishing via a short chimney. It is also possible to finish directly above the tree.

Tom's Roof Bouldering

Tom's Roof is the other classic venue for slippery polished eliminates, which complements Minus Ten's technical verticality with its brutal roof-swinging.

It was first developed by the King of Stoney, Tom Proctor, who worked out the original classic crossing the overhang using the matching-flake in the centre of the roof. The cave was the place where Jerry Moffatt famously developed horrendous power-stamina circuits before his all-crushing tour of the United States in the 1980s.

The original problem, from big undercuts, to the edge, then to the lip, is Font 7A. Other famous, harder problems - *The Womb, Punker Bunker, Pete's Power Pull, Power Allowance, Quintessence*, and *Jerryatricks* - generally use the central roof hold in various ways. Check out Peak District Bouldering (Vertebrate Publishing) or peakbouldering. info for rules and regulations.

It is approached up *The Mineshaft*, the gully 10m right of *Fi, Fi, Fo, Fum*. It seeps in winter and stays dry in the rain.

Mark Rankine on Punker Bunker, Font 7A+, one of the many variations at Tom's Roof. Photo: Alex Rankine.

The classic Stoney E4 testpiece, Bitter Fingers (page 55). Photo: Dan Lane.

The Tower Of Babel

Sixty metres to the left of Windy Buttress is this distinguished and imposing detached pinnacle. The best descent from this area is to go leftwards to *The Mineshaft*. The first six routes are gained by scrambling up a polished chimney on the left to reach a belay.

1 Babylon By-Pass HVS 4b   pre-1960
17m The chimney line. Poor.

2 Babelicious E1 5b   2012
28m Climb straight up the wall to a small undercut ledge. Pull over the bulge and finish up a shallow groove.

3 Glory Road VS 4b ★★   1951
21m Fine climbing following the left-hand groove, but polished as Sin!

4 The Glory Trail E2 5c   2001
21m Climb into the right-hand groove. Move left onto the arête and climb this with an airy section through a bulge.

5 Sin VS 4c ★★★   1952
23m A fine climb and no pushover. Move into the right-hand groove and follow it by bridging and jamming.

6 Lucy Simmons E2 5b ★★   1968
23m The front face of the tower gives a scary pitch with a complete sense of isolation. Follow *Sin* to the horizontal break at half-height. Swing right onto the exposed front face and climb it to the top in a heightened state. **Photo this page.**

7 Lucy Simmons Variation E2 5b ★   2012
28m A fine direct start on good rock. Climb the lower wall 5m right of the chimney up a thin crack to reach the groove of *Sin*. Step up and right onto the front face and follow this to meet and finish up the original.

8 The Tower of Babel E1 5b   1957/1963
33m Start down and to the right of *Glory Road*. Climb the front face of the tower via a thin crack for 7m and move right to gain an obvious groove leading to the top.

9 Towerfull E5 6a   2012
33m A very bold pitch. From a lower level around to the right, climb the lower wall via a short corner by bold moves to gain a ledge. With a good nut runner up and left, climb the face on the right via a flake to a good jug up and left (peg). Pull up and right and climb the fine face by a tricky starting move to gain ledge above. Easier climbing gains a ledge.

John Crook on Lucy Simmons, E2 5b (this page). Photo: Dan Lane.

Around to the right is a short blackened corner marking the foot of the right-hand side of the tower.

10 Revulva E1 5b   1963/1976

21m Make a tricky start up the corner and pull through the overhang on the left. Finish up the easier corner.

11 Revolva E1 5a   2012

12m The worthwhile cleaned face to the right via good moves on compact rock.

Last Stand, HVS 5a, climbs poor rock to the right via a thin crack and **Truffle**, VS 4c (1965), climbs the groove in the loose vegetated arête to the right passing a small overhang.

Windy Buttress

The large imposing buttress is without doubt the most impressive at Stoney. Its elevated position gives the place a very open feel, with a sense of exposure belying its height. This area dries very quickly but can be cold in the winter winds.

It is reached by following a track up the left-hand side of the lower buttress and contouring back to the right. Those with a sense of exploration may be interested to know that you can make a groping through trip via Keyhole Cave and emerge next to the *Aurora* descent gully, even without a torch!

Descent: There are abseil points above *Inquisitor* and *Scoop Wall* and a descent gully on the right, around from *Aurora*.

Starting from the left-hand side of the ledge and just right of the cave is:

1 Chantrelle E1 5a   1970s
18m   The wall and bulge to gain a left-facing groove leading to the top.

2 Do Nothing E3 5c   1980
18m   Climb the thin crack just right and pull left through the large bulge into a slim finishing groove. Some poor rock.

3 Inquisitor E2 5c ★   1963/1967/1976

21m From the top of the initial groove, pull right through the bulge (two pegs) to gain a more prominent groove. Follow this escaping left at the top. Slightly rattly in places.

4 Black Teddy E3 5c   1979

30m From the roof of *Inquisitor*, step right and use undercut holds to reach the traverse line of *Alcasan*. Traverse to a flake on the right and climb this to where it fades. Step left and finish via a hairline crack. Worthwhile.

5 Tuba Mirum E5 6b ★★   2013

24m A superb little find with generally good protection. Start 2m left of *Dies Irae*. Climb the shattered wall (peg) via a small left-facing corner (peg) to the breaks. Use the large undercut flake on the left (on *Black Teddy*), step right and pull through the bulge (peg) onto the excellent wall – this is right of *Black Teddy*. Climb straight up the wall with bold moves to gain and finish up *Dies Irae*.

6 Dies Irae E2 5c ★★   1964/1968

24m An essential Stoney tick and a good introduction to the E-grades on the buttress. Climb a thin crack (peg) and bulge to a small niche. Stretch up left and pull onto the wall above. Step up to a thin break and tiptoe 2m left on small chert footholds past an old peg. Pull up rightwards onto a flake; move left at its top to pull up the final wall. Traverse off left to avoid the tottering cornice.

7 Stuff the Turkey E4 6b ★   1987

24m A tight line but with good climbing. Tackle the short steep wall and bulge, thread and peg. Continue in a direct line through the bulges (bolt) onto the headwall (peg). Finish direct via a hairline crack.

8 Circe E5 6b ★★★   1963/1977

20m A classic encounter with overhanging territory: a tough crux with sustained climbing thereafter. Follow the left-hand of two shallow grooves, passing a bolt rightwards with difficulty. Follow undercut holds out rightwards (peg), until a big pull establishes you on the upper wall. Saunter up this to the top. **Photo below.**

9 Swine Vesicular E5 6b   1984

18m Very strange. The right-hand groove to its top then make difficult moves to gain *Circe* just after its crux.

10 Gaspera E5 6b ★   1988

15m Climb the steep wall just to the left of the chimney-crack (peg) to reach the overlap (peg). Long moves through this on flat holds (bolt) lead to an easing in angle and difficulty.

11 Kink E5 6c ★★   1951/1977

15m An impressive, well-protected and powerful pitch taking the roof crack which stops most climbers dead in their tracks.

Dominic Lee on the powerful undercutting section just above the 6b crux of Circe, E5 (above). Photo: Keith Sharples.

12 **Kinky** F7c ★   **2007**
12m The short bulging wall and large strip roof provide a stern test of physique and ability.

13 **Kellogg** E5 6b ★ ★   **1969/1974/1976/7**
21m A technical and fingery testpiece which spits off many a suitor. Boldly boulder the start to good holds next to a big peg. Move up to the overlap (old pegs). Pull leftwards into the tight groove (usually after trying all possible options) and follow it, easing, to the top.

14 **Nice in Nice** E5 6b ★   **1987**
20m Follow the faint groove (peg), step right (thread), and climb through the bulges (three bolts and a peg), to arrive at a convenient lower-off.

15 **Kingdom Come** E5 6b   **1959/1978**
26m To the right lies a small hanging groove 5m above the ledge. Gain the groove boldly and with difficulty (pegs), then climb it to a ledge. Pre-clipping the pegs (E4) would seem sensible, given the state of the rock on the crux. Move through the bulge above to enter a black groove and follow it to a clean corner leading to the top. An enjoyable finish is to follow *The Flakes Direct*.

16 Special K E4 6a ★ 1971

26m A bold, hard start gives access to easier but well-positioned climbing above. Begin by making sure your second is lashed securely to the crag, 4m left of the *Windhover* arête. Climb the bulge with commitment (crux, Friend 0.5) to reach a good flake. Continue up the wall to an overhang which can be crossed on huge holds to reach the headwall. Take a fairly direct line above following the twin cracks with difficulty.

The next group of routes share a common start that has got harder over the years. The 5c section of these routes is essentially this bouldery start.

17 The Flakes E2 5c, 4c ★ ★ ★ 1964/1970s

36m A super outing with everything that is good about Windy Buttress. Atmosphere, exposure and great climbing and good protection where it matters. Careful ropework eliminates the need to belay below the final corner. Start up *Windhover*. Difficult moves lead to the big undercut flake. Follow the line under the large overhangs. A short section at their end where the footholds disappear gives a couple of insecure moves to reach a hanging belay. **Photo on back cover.** Finish easily up the corner or, better is:

18 The Flakes Direct E2 5c ★ ★ ★ 1964

30m Brilliant; follow *The Flakes* and climb the bulge above with difficulty (peg on the lip - not a foothold), to finish via the fine flake and crack above. Careful ropework recommended. **Photo on page 15.**

19 Armageddon E2 5c ★ ★ ★ 1964

27m Perhaps the best of the bunch? Wonderful climbing and positions. Start up *Windhover* and follow it to below its final crack. Traverse left to a short corner and move up (two pegs) before traversing left to the finishing crack.

20 Windhover E2 5c ★ ★ 1958/1960

24m The original and classic encounter on this section of the crag. A mean start leads to a narrow ledge on the crest of the buttress. Step left and up for 5m then move right to the arête and climb up either side of this to a ledge. Finish via the steep, awkward crack (jams!) above or, easier, **a** the groove just right of the arête. **Photo on page 22.**

Misha Nepogodiev and Ed Shaw high above the road on Alcasan, E2 5c (page 64). Photo: Neil Foster.

21 Transmaiacon MC E5 6a † 1988
22m A bold and intimidating pitch up the bald-looking wall just to the right of the arête. Cross the bulge rightwards to finish up *Choss*. Some dreadful rock.

22 Choss E1 5b 1964
23m A poor pitch. Climb the groove 6m right of the arête and at the bulge (peg) traverse left before climbing the wall to finish via the upper groove of *Windhover*.

23 Dross E5 6b 2001
23m A very tough bulge. From the top of the corner on *Choss*, step right and climb the overlap by extending moves leftwards to reach a short crack. A long pull here gains better holds leading onto the wall. Finish straight up to a tree taking care with the finishing holds.

24 Scoop Wall E3 5c ★ ★ ★ 1955/1968
23m One of the great Stoney pitches. Heave up the initial bulges into a sentry box and hence to the main bulge. Make long moves on good holds (old peg), rightwards through this to where a steep crack (thread) leads to a rest below the upper bulge. Crux pulls (peg) gain a short crack on the left and the top. **Photo on page 67.**

25 In Corpus E5 6a 2001
18m A strange concoction. From 5m up *Scoop Wall*, step right, thread, and climb up to the bulge, thread. Step right and pull through it into a shallow scoop (peg) and climb this exiting right and up to the *Our Father* belay.

26 Our Father E4 6b, 5a ★ ★ ★ 1968
One of the iconic pitches of Stoney Middleton made famous by the antics of its Sixties and Seventies hero, Tom Proctor. Well-protected after the bouldery start but not to be underestimated.
1. 14m Athletic manoeuvres onto the lip of the roof (Font 6C) gain the hanging flake (small wires before a good peg). At its top, step right along the break (peg and threaded wire) and make an undercut stretch (long thread) to jams in the overlap above – the crux for shorties. Pull leftwards through this with conviction and up to the cave.
2. 10m Step right to finish up a pleasant groove.

27 Menopause E5 6a, 6b ★ ★ 1960s/1971/1980
A fantastic top pitch, much the stuff of legend until tamed by Chris Hamper. Incredibly, it has been soloed on-sight by Simon Nadin. Start at the right-hand side of the overhangs.
1. 15m Make difficult moves through the right-hand side of the bulges and follow a thin crack to join *Our Father* below the overlap. Continue as for this to the cave belay.
2. 9m Step left and make a series of difficult moves up the bulging wall to enter the slim hanging groove. Climb this to a bolt belay. **Photo on page 41.**

28 Hysterectomy E5 6c 1981
9m Desperate. Pull out of the right-hand side of the cave and make hard moves past a peg runner into a thin crack and groove-line leading to the top.

29 Adios Tango E4 6a ★ ★ traditional/2012
21m A surprising discovery giving excellent, open, wall climbing. From the far end of the ledge, pull through the initial bulge (peg), to good holds leading to another bulge (two pegs). Long moves through this gives better holds at a break (peg on left). Continue boldly up the wall (thread on left) to reach another break where a step right gains a small ledge. Climb the thin crack in the headwall, onto a small ledge on the left (thread) from where a final difficult section gains good holds leading to the top.

30 Tiger Trot VD pre-1960
9m A short pleasant traverse linking the end of Windy Ledge to a large ledge on the arête.

31 Alcasan E2 4c, 5b, 5a, 5c, 5c, 5b ★ ★ ★ 1964/1970s
A monumental traverse of the buttress gives a very atmospheric climb.
1. 45m Follow the first and second pitches of *Aurora* (Route 38) or *Aurora Arête* (Route 39) as far as *The Altar*.
2. 20m From *The Altar*, traverse left to a peg and move down and make some tricky moves left into the *Our Father* cave.
3. 14m Traverse left into a corner and descend awkwardly for 2m. Continue traversing left to a belay around the arête on *Windhover*.
4. 15m Traverse left as for *Armageddon* and then swing round under the roofs to follow *The Flakes* to its belay.
5. 11m Traverse left with difficulty (peg), then make a difficult sequence of moves down into the groove of *Kellogg* past two pegs. Traverse across the wall into *Kink*.
6. 35m Move left into the groove of *Circe* and move up this for 3m. Move left around the arête and continue across the wall in a superb position to the finishing groove of *Inquisitor*. **Photo on page 63.**

steep gully descent

abseil point

The Lower Corner

The next group of routes are found at road level 20m to the left of the chimney and descent route dividing Windy and Garage Buttresses.

32 You Are Only Mortal E4 6b   1984
33m The centre of the wall. Amble up the grass above.

33 Immortal Combat F6b+   2012
11m The problematic wall.

34 Breathing Underwater E4 5c   1980
30m Climb the shallow groove finishing past a poor peg runner to the grass. Amble up this to Windy Ledge.

35 Memnon E2 5b, 5c ★   1950s/1963
1. 30m Some good climbing but care is needed. Climb the large corner (poor peg) escaping left onto the grass. Climb up (poor rock and no more gear) to Windy Ledge.
2. 21m At the end of Windy Ledge is a groove. Climb this to an overhang and pull through this with difficulty (peg). Once above, move right and finish via a series of grooves. Some dubious rock but sound gear can be placed.

A better alternative is to go slightly left above the bulges to finish direct via a crack as for *Adios Tango* (**Membrane** E3 5c ★).

36 Black Power E5 6b   1987
27m Take a direct line up the wall with powerful moves on black rock (peg).

37 Racial Harmony E4 5c   1978
27m The ivy-threatened wall leads to the second of two pegs. Pull slightly to the left and make bold moves back right through an overhang to finish up a cracked upper wall.

38 Aurora VS 4c, 4c ★ ★ ★   1933
Another wonderful classic full of poise and charm.
1. 30m Climb the steep wall leading onto the right-hand side of the arête. Follow this past a good ledge where a step left leads onto the arête proper. Climb this, moving slightly right onto a wall leading to a ledge below a groove.
2. 21m Bridge and jam the delightful groove until just below the top. Move out left onto a ledge on the arête - *The Altar* - and finish in a fine position.

39 Aurora Arête HVS 4c, 5a ★ ★   1963
1. 30m As for *Aurora*.
2. 21m Move out left onto the face and climb the groove (pegs) to an overhang which can be passed to the right. Continue directly passing *The Altar* en-route to the top.

40 Melting Pot E3 5c   1978
21m A poor, loose route taking the cracks right of *Aurora Pitch 2* then moving right (peg) to pull through overlaps. Climb the groove moving right and back left to finish.

41 King Kong HVS 5b   1960s
21m Start just left of the entrance of the cave to the right and about halfway up the gully. Climb a corner and crack through a bulge. Traverse left into a finishing corner.

Naomi Buys on Scoop Wall, E3 5c (page 64). Photo: Mike Hutton.

Garage Buttress

Recent developments have seen Garage Buttress going from an obscure traditional venue with an odd bolted showpiece to becoming the crag's main sport climbing area. Thanks to the efforts of Mark Pretty, Kristian Clemmow and Gary Gibson, these walls are now adorned with good clip-ups from F5 to F8a+. A super-quick approach, sunny aspect and lack of seepage make them a great choice, especially useful in winter. The trad climbs are still as good as ever.

On the far left of the buttress, right of the gully that leads down from the top of Windy Buttress, is a poor wall. **The Fluff Pirate**, HVS 5a (1985), begins part way up the gully and climbs a groove: **Fluffy Roo Meets the Woodentops**, F6b (2013), is a direct line up the wall to the right; **Scrubber**, HVS 5a (1978), climbs an arch. Right again is a now-overgrown buttress. Right again is a tower protruding through the vegetation. **Pineapple**, HVS 5a (1960s), climbs a groove, overhang and crack; **Blue Banana**, HVS 5a (1964), is just right; **Leprosy**, VS 4c (1968), is right again.

Compositae Area: The next routes lie on the white tower. A Severe scramble gains a tree belay below a groove.

1   Ticket to the Underworld E4 5c   1979
17m   Climb the wall left of the groove to a small ledge on the right. Make a powerful move through the overhang (peg), followed by bold moves up the large hanging flakes, scary. After a tricky exit right, continue more easily to a tree belay and an abseil descent.

2   Compositae Groove HVS 5a ★   1961
18m   A fine little route that deserves more attention. Follow the groove past two pegs to a small overhang. Swing left onto the arête and continue up to a tree belay.

3   In Composite E2 5b   2012
15m   Climb the bold wall to the right of the groove (peg) to a ledge (peg on left). Pull over a slight bulge and continue more easily to a small ledge and bolt belay.

Reloaded Area: The next section contains a good number of newer mid-grade sport climbs and the odd older trad route. They are best approached by scrambling up below *Rippemoff* and following a fixed rope leading leftwards then traversing using the trees into the bay.

Ernie, E1 (1970s), climbs the left-hand corner of the bay.

4   Trigger F7a+   2012
11m   Climb the wall to the overlap. Desperate moves lead to good holds leading rightwards to a belay.

Right: Kristian Clemmow on Virgin King, F7b (page 76).
Photo: Keith Sharples.

Mark Pretty on The Lover's Leap, F7b+ (page 75).
Photo: Keith Sharples.

5 Two Ton Ted from Teddington F6b+   2012
11m The wall and overlap. Littered with good flake holds, but pretty loose.

6 Grotty Totty E1 5b   1970s
19m Climb the wall left of the tree to an overhang. Pull over on flakes to an arête which is followed past a tree.

7 Knockin' on the Bread Man's Door F6c ★ 2012
18m A fine pitch starting from a bolt belay by a small tree. Climb to the break then over the bulges to a good ledge. Easier climbing leads past a final bulge to a tree.

8 Happy Wanderer E1 5b   1970s
17m Climb the wall to the break. Continue up left-facing flakes and pull over a small overhang onto the upper wall. Move up and trend rightwards to a bolt belay.

9 Bohemian F6b+ ★   2012
15m An excellent open wall pitch with only a short hard section. From a bolt belay to the right, or the tree below, climb the wall just right of a flake to reach the break. A difficult pull gains better holds leading leftwards across the wall to a small ledge and the belay just above.

10 Empty Cartridge F6b+ ★   2012
18m From a bolt belay down and to the right of the yew tree, climb the easy wall and then the wall just to the left to gain the main break. A problematic move above this leads to good jugs and the belay.

11 Unloaded F6c   2012
15m From the belay of *Empty Cartridge*, climb the easy wall and continue up the more problematic wall to reach the break. Extending moves from an undercut gain better holds above. Pull out onto a ledge and easier ground leading to the belay.

12 Reloaded F6b+ ★   2012
18m Another good find. Climb the shallow groove to reach the break. Pull onto the wall above on good holds to reach easier ground leading to a ledge. Finish up the fine headwall.

13 Matrix E3 4a, 5b 1970s

21m From the belay of *Reloaded*, move up to a ledge and climb the shallow groove on the right to the main break. Move up to an overhang and undercut right before pulling over on good holds into a short groove. Traverse back left into another short groove (bolts) and climb this finishing up the headwall (peg on the right). It is also possible to finish directly from the short groove.

14 Matricide E4 6a ★ 2013

19m A good and involving route, high in the grade. From a hanging belay to the left of *I Hate You*, climb the technical wall (3 bolts) to the break (thread) and junction with *Matix*. Make extending moves directly through the roof (bolt) to arrive at the right-facing groove of *Matrix*, old bolt cluster. Continue straight up (wires needed) to a bolt belay just below the top.

15 I Hate You F7a ★ 2012

18m Great climbing, but requiring a blinkered approach. Climb the easy faint groove onto a slab. Overcome the tricky bulge to gain a good hold and the break just above. Extending moves through the right edge of an overlap gain a good rail, from where technical and fingery moves lead to a rounded break. One final pull gains good holds and the belay.

16 Four Minute Tiler E5 6b ★★ 1980

25m An impressive route, Tom Proctor's final calling card. Start from a ledge 5m left of a low peg belay. Move left for 2m and climb a shallow groove and flake to the break. Step right and pull desperately through the bulges above to gain a thin break. Swing right for 3m and pull up to some good flakes. Continue directly up the headwall, (two pegs) to a lower-off. **a Alex, it was Really Nothing**, E5 6b (1987), continues up the headwall past a peg.

17 Colonel Bogey E4 6a ★★ 1979

24m A great route, low in the grade, with some exciting climbing. From just right of a low peg belay, climb the bold wall to a flake. From the narrow ledge above step right (two pegs) and up into a shallow scoop, which is gained with difficulty and followed to the break. Make a hard pull up to gain the left-hand of two grooves. Climb this to its end. Follow the blunt rib (peg) just to the left to the top, or more easily, move right to finish. **b** Alternatively, start 2m to the right and reach blindly up right to good holds then go boldly up and left to the pegs, 6a.

18 La Belle et la Bete E5 6b ★ 1986

28m Follow the previous route to the two pegs. Move up and leftwards to gain the break. Step right and pull through the bulge (bolt) to reach a short hanging groove. Pull into this with difficulty (bolt) and then swing left into *Four Minute Tiler* to finish at a bolt belay.

19 Helicon E2 5c ★★ 1963/1970

22m A great direct line – quite high in the grade, some would say E3. Climb the groove to the capping overhang. Reach left then make a difficult pull (peg) up to the break. Gain the right-hand of the two slim grooves above and follow it to a tricky exit (peg) up the wall above.

20 Rippemoff E2 5c, 5a ★★ 1965/1971

A fine route with a distinctive crux.

1. 17m As for *Helicon* to the break. Traverse right for 6m to a comfortable stance complete with pegs.

2. 17m Move back left for 2m and climb over the bulge onto the headwall. Follow a thin crack in this to finish via a groove on the right.

21 Pullemdown E5 6a † 1983

24m A big scary outing that has had few, if any, repeats. The headwall involves intricate climbing on very good rock, but with little protection. Start up *Helicon* then swing right to climb a creaking flake to meet the traverse of *Gerremdown*. Pull directly through the bulge above to reach the main break of *Rippemoff*. Continue directly onto the steep headwall above, following a line just left of a thin crack. Where the crack ends, step left to a thin flake (crux) and finish direct.

22 Snatchemoff E4 5c ★ 2013

17m An excellent find, just worth the grade for an on-sight. From the belay of *Rippemoff*, pull straight over the bulge (hidden good wire placement) onto the excellent white wall. Climb straight up the centre of this on good, small holds but tricky gear placements, until a slightly rightwards exit leads to the top.

23 Chewemoff E3 5c, 6a ★ 1968/1979

1. 17m As for *Rippemoff*.

2. 12m From just left of the arête to the right, move up and then right with difficulty (peg) to finish via an easier groove and wall.

24 Gerremdown E3 4c, 5c † 1969

1. 12m Climb the groove as for *Rippemoff* but traverse right at the overhang to a belay on a large flake below a groove.

2. 15m Climb the main groove, or the trickier one just right, to the break. Step right, pass a thread, and attack the imposing roof on distant but big holds. Cut loose and pull over to an easier finishing groove (lower-off on the right).

The next route starts at ground level and climbs a cleaned strip through the ivy in its lower section.

25 Turf 'em Off F6b+ 2014

18m An easy lower section leads to a worthwhile upper wall.

Little Plum Area

The big, steep, clean wall to the right holds some of the buttress's best routes. The first routes begin from a ledge directly above where the path leaves the main road. An easy scramble leads to a ledge and bolt belays. At the left-hand end of the ledge is:

26 Glue 'em Back F7b   2014
13m A short wall 6m left of *Dig Deep*.

27 There May Be Rubble Ahead F7b   2014
15m An unbalanced route: F6c with an English 6c move.

a Rubble Rouser, F7c+ (2014), starts up *There May Be*... to a faint break at 5m then moves right to finish up *Dig Deeper*.

28 Dig Deeper F8a   2014
15m Leave *Dig Deep for Victory* and leap over the bulge on the left.

29 Dig Deep for Victory F7c   2006
15m An intense climb. Lower-off just above the first break.

Dig Deep for Victory has several extensions: **a Do You Dig It?**, F7c+ (2014), continues into the groove of *Gerremdown* (pegs) then carries on directly over the roof. Some loose rock; **b My Middle Name is Rubble**, F7c (2015), climbs a parallel line just right; **c Easy Victory**, F7c (2015), links this into *Easy Skanking* via the girdle break.

30 Ozone Bozo F7c ★   1989
15m Short, but with some quality moves. Make crux moves leftwards to the base of the groove. Finish up *Dig Deep*... The original finish, up the flake, is dangerous.

31 Tollbar F8a+ ★★   2014
15m Straight up the wall from *Ozone Bozo*. Perhaps the best of the harder routes on this wall. **Photo on page 43.**

32 The Trouble With Rubble F8a ★   2013
12m The technically sustained excavations.

33 The Big Apple F8a ★   2014
12m A fingery "creation" with an exciting finish taking the blunt arête. Low in the grade. Finish at the first break.

There are two continuations to The Big Apple:

34 Golden Delicious F8a ★   2015
30m Step left for 2m, climb to the break, then over bulges, joining *Easy Skanking*. There is a project just right.

35 Crankerdown F8a ★   2007
12m A more direct line going directly to the break and over the bulges above (F7c in its own right).

The Big Apple can then be linked into the second pitch of *Little Plum* for a monster of a pitch, although it's still the same grade: **Big Plums**. F8a (2013), or into *The Lover's Leap* to give **The Big Leap Forward**, F8a (2013).

36 Easy Skanking E6 6b, 6a ★   1984
A bold route tackling the shallow hanging scoops.
1. 19m Pull up the initial scoop of *Little Plum*, clipping a high bolt, and then make a difficult move left. Committing moves lead into and up a shallow groove which eases towards the break. Peg belay on the left.
2. 17m Move back right and up to the break. Traverse left and cross the roof just to the right of *Gerremdown* (bolts), to finish rightwards up an easier corner and loose wall.

37 The Lover's Leap F7b+ ★   2002
15m A good but inconvenient pitch, best approached up *Little Plum*. Climb through the roof left of the top pitch of *Little Plum*, starting from that route's first belay. **Photo on page 70.**

38 Little Plum F8a ★★   1963/1981/1982
30m Jerry Moffatt's free ascent once gave one of the world's hardest routes and is still a big Stoney testpiece. Most only do the first pitch (F7c+). Enter the scoop and make very fingery moves first up and then right and out into a shallow groove (belay). Follow the groove to the break. Step left and tackle the huge roof by climbing slightly rightwards to reach a niche on the lip (F7b+).

39 Ming the Merciless F8a+ 2007

12m A very poor route. The bolted line right of *Little Plum* gives an intense little affair.

The next two routes start from a double-bolt belay on the ledge on the right. They are best done in a single pitch from the ground, via Higherlands or Lowerlands.

40 Virgin King F7b ★ ★ 2014

33m Perhaps the best of the recent development hereabouts, a mish-mash of four routes spanning a 30 year period now put together to create a very direct and logical pitch. Long - check your rope length. Climb easily to the ledge (via *Higherlands*). Climb to the first break. Continue slightly leftwards to the break of *Pendulum* and finish over a bulge, small groove and niche. **Photo on page 69.**

Virgin King supercedes **King of Ming**, F7b+ (2007), which itself superceded the older routes **Virgin on the Loose**, E6 6b (1984), and **Big Nose**, E4 6a (1985).

41 Flycatcher E5 6a 1977

37m A very bold route with pushy climbing, little protection and little respite. Start up *Lowerlands* to its belay. Climb the wall just right with fingery moves up and leftwards into the groove then onto a ledge (cams useful). Step right and climb a blackened flake to the main break. Move right and pull over the overhang into a finishing groove.

The next routes begin at ground level where a slabby lower wall has several bolt-lines leading to or past the ledge at 8m.

42 Higherlands F6a 2014

10m The short left-hand line to the ledge, starting 3m right of the ivy strip / shallow corner.

43 Lowerlands F5 2014

10m The short right-hand line starting from the left end of the higher, left-hand of two block ledges just to the right.

44 Lowlands F6c+ ★ 2012

20m Start from the lower, right-hand of the two block ledges. Climb the slabby wall to the ledge at 8m. Move left and snatch quickly up the fingery and reachy wall.

45 Dreamcatcher F6b+ ★ ★ 2001/2012

30m A great journey making the most of the tall wall. Follow *Lowlands*, to the ledge at 8m. Continue slightly rightwards past a break to eventually gain the main, girdle, break. Bust long, reachy moves over the impressive final overhang.

46 Cream Snatcher F6b ★ 2012

18m Climb the slabby wall 5m left of the arête to a the ledge at 8m. Continue up the delicate face to a belay.

47 Evasor VS 4b, 4c ★ ★ 1965

The most exposed VS in the Peak? A fine climb with amenable climbing throughout. Start just right of the arête right of *Cream Snatcher*.
1. 18m Better than it looks, and with reasonable, but spaced, protection. Climb slightly leftwards over a series of small ledges to reach a blunt rib. Steeper moves up this gain a tree belay.
2. 27m Continue to the main break then traverse left until below a steep groove. Pull over a small overhang into the groove and follow it rightwards in a fine position to the top.

48 Atropos HVS 4b, 5a, 5a 1967

1. 18m As for *Evasor*.
2. 30m Traverse a break out left, all at hand level, for 3m and then foot traverse it for a further 10m to a small ledge. A swinging hand-traverse leads left to a stance below *Chewemoff*.
3. 12m Traverse left around the arête to meet *Rippemoff* beneath its crux bulge. Avoid this by descending to a grass ledge and peg belay.

a Ployed, E4 6a (1977), took a line up the hanging bay to the right and has become very vegetated.

The next routes start in the last bay, just before the crag turns to ivy. There is a short low corner with stepped ledges on its left. Four Thousand etc. start up the stepped ledges and Now't About Change up the right wall of the corner.

49 Can't Stop Now F6c+ ★ 2013

18m Branch left from *Four Thousand* where a short hard section leads to a lower-off below the break.

50 Up Yours F7a 2014

28m Press on from the belay of *Can't Stop Now* to climb onto the upper wall. Cruxy.

51 Four Thousand F6c ★ ★ 2013

32m Gary Gibson's four thousandth new route! Start up the stepped ledges to a steepening. A technical wall leads to a break and a lower-off (F6a+ to here). Carry on up the upper groove and wall to the lower-off. A 60m rope just gets you to the ground.

52 Onwards and Upwards F6a 2013

15m Straight up from the start of *Four Thousand*.

53 Now't About Change F6b 2014

15m Start up the steep lower wall and continue with sustained climbing just left of the arête.

b The now-overgrown **Aquiline**, HVS 5b (1965), once lay to the right.

54 The Pendulum HVS 4c, 4c, 5a ★ ★ 1963

One of the great Stoney classics from an era when traverses were all the rage. A pleasant ramble in great situations. Start by scrambling up the descent path on the right of the crag. Break left from the main path and follow smaller tracks to a well-used entry point, quite high on the slope. Swing round to belay on the edge of the face.

Follow the main break with stances below *Little Plum* and *Chewemoff*. A final crux pitch leads to a belay above the yew tree below *Happy Wanderer*. Abseil off from here.

As well as The Pendulum there is also a more esoteric high left-to-right girdle. This is gained by traversing into the gully right of Compositae Groove.

55 My Girdle is Killing Me E4 6a, 5b 1967/1979

1. 33m Traverse right on poor rock past an old tree before stepping down into a faint groove. Continue via an intricate hand-traverse to a belay in the groove of *Helicon*. Several pegs and bolts help protect the pitch.

2. 33m Move up and make an exciting (especially so for the second) traverse right with the break at foot level into *Rippemoff*. Move down and continue around the arête to a yew tree. Traverse right on poor rock to follow the easy final wall of *Little Plum*.

Goddard's Quarry

A recently-developed wall giving a handful of vertical wall climbs. Good for a few quick F6s and F7s on a summer evening.

Conditions and Aspect
The wall lies in a north-facing bay and gets virtually no sun. Not much seepage. The rock is clean and solid. It is a bit bleak in winter.

Parking and Approach
Park in the large lay-by as for Stoney Middleton. Walk towards Stoney for 100m until opposite the garage, before Garage Buttress. Cross a stile by a wooden gate onto a quarry track (public footpath sign). Walk up the track for 100m and the wall is just ahead of you. 5 minutes.

1　Nematodes F6b　　　　　　　　　　2014
15m　The pleasant wall with a fingery finale from a ledge.

2　Crustacean F7a+　　　　　　　　　2014
15m　The face with a desperate boulder-problem crux. Very difficult to on-sight.

3　Brachiopods Bite Back F6b ★　　　2014
15m　Good climbing up the face with a hard start.

4　Pearls from the Shell F6a+ ★　　　2014
15m　The fine crack and corner line.

5　Red Mist F7a ★　　　　　　　　　2014
15m　Fine climbing up the reddened tower with a tough crux.

6　Corner, It Is F6b　　　　　　　　　2014
11m　Just that. Very 3D.

7　Corner, It is Not F6a　　　　　　　2014
11m　Just that, to the right.

Stoney West

Trad: 26 (S to E5)   **Sport:** 30 (F5 to F7a)
Aspect: South   **Sunshine:** From noon   **Season:** All year
Conditions: Sheltered, seepage-free, can be hot, leafy
Best for: Bolted wall climbs in the F6s   **Approach:** 15 minutes

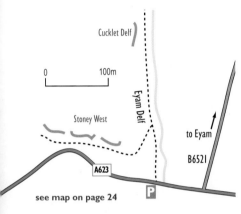

see map on page 24

This small and somewhat neglected crag last received attention in the early 1980s. Always a backwater, it fell into disuse for the following 20 or so years with little or no activity. It has recently received a full makeover with the addition of a number of sport routes together with a thorough tidy up of the traditional routes.

The Climbing
Stoney West offers a very pleasant and relatively sheltered venue with a number of worthwhile traditional and sport climbs that sit alongside each other. The climbing is akin to a mixture of Cheedale and Stoney Middleton where strong fingers and good footwork pay dividends. Recent traffic has cleaned the routes up a lot although there is still the odd loose hold.

Conditions and Aspect
The crag faces south and receives sun from midday and is a particularly useful venue in the winter, spring or autumn months. Its lofty aspect contributes to its quick drying nature but this means that it can sometimes catch a chilling wind.

Parking and Approach
Park on the side of the A623, between Stoney and Horseshoe Quarry on a muddy verge, just north of the Tarmac Quarry entrance, that itself is just north of the Eyam road junction. Please do not park in the quarry entrance.

Enter Eyam Delf through the gate on the opposite side of the road and follow the Eyam path for about 80m. Break left up the hillside on an indistinct path and then contour back around the shoulder to gain the right-hand side of the cliffs. Please do not approach the crag directly from the road.

Left Hand Buttress

Once you are under the crag, continue along below the initial walls, then under two seperate buttresses. The first of these is Central Buttress. The second, left-hand buttress, fifteen metres to its left, has an undercut base on its right.

1   Isolation F6b+   **2013**
10m   The short intense wall above an embedded flake.

2   Turkey Vulture Crack HVS 5b   **1960s**
21m   The crack and groove splitting the left-hand side of the buttress, gained from a flake on the left. Finish via the arête on the right or down from the tree on the left. **a** The direct start is 5c (1987).

3   Twang E3 5c ★   **1965/1976**
21m   A good route, though not always clean. From the flake, step up to the first break and traverse it rightwards (thread) where a tricky move gains an overhang. Pass this on the right and from a ledge finish up the arête.

4   Tequila Tory E6 6c ★   **1985**
20m   The blank wall bisecting the traverse of *Twang* has a fierce boulder problem (Font 7B+) to gain the break, thread. Hard moves gain another break (peg), where a tricky sequence up the blank-looking wall gains better holds leading to the top.

5   Arbeit Macht Frei E5 6b   **1984**
18m   Climb the thin groove on the nose of the buttress (old peg) to the end of the *Twang* traverse. Finish up the crack on the right-hand side of the buttress.

6   Let Your Guard Down F6c+ ★   **2013**
15m   A tricky starting bulge and excellent compact wall around to the right. The bolted line to the right is F6b.

a Devil's Eye, HVS 5a (1964), gains the crack of *Arbeit* via a traverse left from the grassy bank.

The small buttress to the right gives two mediocre routes: **Pile-up on the Dance Floor**, E4 6b (1988), climbs the centre of the buttress past a peg and **House on a Hill**, F6c+ (2013), the fingery little wall to its right.

Central Buttress

7 Can't Climb, Won't Climb F7a ★ 2013
15m The left-hand side of the buttress with pleasant face-climbing and a difficult bulge and short headwall.

8 Spiron HVS 5a ★ 1964
27m Circuitous but excellent. From the left-hand side of the buttress, gain the first break and then take a rising traverse right past a groove onto a ledge. Move up and then leftwards to finish via the arête of the buttress.

9 Northerners Can't Climb E5 6a ★★ 1981
21m A classic product of the Eighties when men were men and apparently Northerners weren't. Climb the thin crack and continue slightly rightwards via a shallow scoop to the break. Step left and launch over the bulges on reasonable holds until a pull left and then back right gains easier ground from the break above. Bolt belay.

10 Another Camden Day F6c+ ★★ 2013
15m The antithesis of adjoining routes. Climb the tricky wall to the right and continue up the blunt arête to the bulges. Steep pulls over this, all on good holds, lead to an exit alongside the belay.

11 Southerners Can't Climb E3 5c ★★ 1981
21m Another excellent pitch. Climb the thin groove on the nose of the buttress to a ledge. Move up into the black-ened alcove then step rightwards and up into the upper break. Bolt belays are available to the left or right.

12 Whisper F6c+ ★ 2013
15m A very bouldery start 3m to the right gains easier climbing via a faint groove and slab.

13 Elective Affinities E3 5c 1981
21m Start 5m right of *Southerners Can't Climb*. Follow a short groove and wall to a break. Traverse left to the arête and follow this to the top.

14 Joy or Despair F6a+   2013
15m The wall 2m to the right with a tricky start and enjoyable face-climbing above.

Around to the right is a bay of rock. The left-hand side of the face is marked by a vegetated crack at the back of an alcove.

15 Contemplation F6c+   2013
9m Very technical climbing to start then an easier finish.

16 Apparition F5   2013
9m Very pleasant climbing up a thin crack and bulge.

17 Superstition F6c+   2013
9m Another technical start on hidden holds leads to a thuggy finale.

18 The Seclusion F7a   2013
10m Fine fingery climbing on small holds. The bulge proves to be relatively easy.

19 No Greenwich Mean Time F6c+   2013
10m More fingery climbing with a complex sequence and tricky bulge.

20 The Thrill of the Chase F6b+   2013
11m Excellent face-climbing just right again to a shallow groove finale.

Julie White on Libation, F6b+ (this page).
Photo: sportsclimbs.co.uk.

21 In Conversation F6b   2013
11m A fine pitch with a technical sequence on the faint crack.

22 Libation F6b+ ★   2013
11m Perhaps the best of the bunch here? The faint crack with a very definite crux sequence from the initial break. **Photo opposite.**

23 An Illusion F6b   2013
12m Worthwhile climbing up the vague pillar.

24 Rainsong E1 5b   1977
18m Climb the groove exiting right into an alcove. Continue up the crack above to a grassy exit.

25 Late at Night F6b+   2013
15m Climb the thin crack in the face to the right then tackle the bulge and arête with gusto.

26 Dust F5   2013
15m The cleaned streak, finishing up a short arête and a prominent white groove. The wall 2m right is F6a.

Five metres to the right, **Postman's Meander**, D (1961), took a leftwards crack to an old tree and finished up the corner behind but has now been lost to the ivy.

Right-Hand Buttress

27 Suffocation F6a   2013
15m The clean line through the ivy, with some suspect rock, to a problematic move on the upper headwall.

28 Voices F6a+   2013
15m A direct line to the right with the hardest climbing on the steepest section.

29 Fred HVS 5a   2013
15m The crack just to the right to a bolt belay.

30 Eddie Cochrane F6b+   2014
15m The bolt-line right of the crack.

31 Setting of the Sun F6b ★   2013
15m An easier lower wall and pleasant climbing lead to a short difficult section above the third break.

Two older, bold trad routes (E4/5) originally climbed the rock covered by the next three routes. These have been retrobolted to give:

32 Satisfaction F6c ★   2013
18m A short difficult wall leads to easier climbing via a vague rib and a juggy bulge.

33 Don't Talk to Strangers F6c ★★   1988/2013
18m A boulder problem start gains better holds leading up the black streak to a good ledge. A strong pull rightwards leads to easy ground and the belay above.

34 Procession F6b+ ★★   1987/2013
18m A fine pitch. A boulder problem/long reach start gains better holds leading straight up the wall. A strong pull from a good ledge leads to good holds and the belay. **Photo on page 87.**

35 Perilscope F6c+ ★   1987/2013
18m Very fine climbing with a sustained lower section, definitive crux and juggy final bulge. F7a if started direct.

To the right is a prominent angled flake line beginning at 8m, below which is a less pronounced crack.

42 Bayliff VS 4b   1961
21m The straight crack. Take care with some fragile rock.

Bay Rum, VS 4c (1961), starts to the right and wanders across the face to finish up a thin crack on the right. It has been superseded somewhat by the next two routes:

43 No Finer Place F6a ★   2013
12m A great little route slap bang up the short wall.

44 Shake, Rattle and Roll F6b   2013
12m Overcome the low overhang by a stern pull and continue up the pleasant face above.

45 Before Too Long F6b ★   2013
26m Corner, roof and wall.

46 Long Enough F6c   2014
12m The rib and overhang.

47 Running Over HVS 4c   1970s
17m Climb the corner just left of the overhang, moving right via a crack to a finish over poor ground.

48 Pot Full HVS 4c   1961
18m The cracked groove in the left arête of the chimney.

49 Cave Crack S   1961
15m The chimney.

50 Little Moose E1 5b   1995
12m The right wall of the chimney, thread, to a convenient tree.

---

36 Horrorscope E3 5c   1970s/2013
21m Climb a crack and trend right to below the next overhang. Traverse left along the break to a small niche (peg). Climb the thin crack above to a niche and finish via the crack into a final short groove. **a Direct Start**: climb the blackened face (bolt) to a break (bolt). Swing left and up via a shallow groove to reach the peg of the original route, E3 6a (2013).

37 The State of the Nation F6c ★★   2013
18m A direct line from the foot of the initial crack, past the right-hand side of the hole, to a troublesome finale.

38 Swansong HVS 4c   1964
25m The right-facing flake. Gain the flake and follow it awkwardly past a tree onto the arête. Continue up this and the groove to the top.

Around to the right lies a prominent crack bounded to its left by a clean wall.

39 A Time and a Place F6a ★   2013
22m The arête to the left of the cleaned wall gives a fine climb. Finish rightwards at the top to the belay.

40 Deconstruction F6a   2013
21m A direct line up the centre of the wall to a finish in a small corner.

41 Got it Wrong F6a ★   2014
12m The bolt-line left of the corner.

The shallow groove just right again gives **Flaky Pastry**, S (1961); the wall right again is **Puff Pastry**, HVS 5a (2013); the left-trending flake is **Choux Pastry**, VD (2013); the cleaned wall to the right is **Pastry Roll**, E2 5b (2013).

Several buttresses run leftwards along the escarpment from the Left-Hand Buttress. These had been developed in the past but are now overgrown. Runnng left from the *Twang* area, the first worthwhile buttress contains some prominent cracked blocks: **Crazzled Cracks**, S (1960s), climbs the wall to finish up the obvious cracks; **Muscle-Cock Crack**, S (1966), takes the weakness in the right-hand side of the next buttress; **Clean Crack**, S (1960s), is the not-so-well named crack to the left; **90 Centimetre Diedre**, VS 4c (1966), climbs the ivy-covered corner and flake-crack on the next buttress; **Obvious Crack**, VS 4c (1970s), takes the obvious line right of the chimney-crack in the well-positioned buttress to the left; **Cray-Pas**, VD (1966), climbs the chimney-crack just left, finishing leftwards and **Patience**, S (1964), climbs the crack left of the ivy direct to the top. Left of a shallow gully is the final buttress: **The Grauncher**, VS 4c (1960s), is the right-hand crack followed directly; **Lefrack**, VS 4c (1960s) is the left-hand crack and **Benstirer**, VD (1966), is the obvious crack left of *Lefrack*.

Marcus Buckley enjoys the September sun on Procession, F6b+ (page 85). Photo Ian Carr.

Cucklet Delf

The valley that runs up from the Stoney West parking spot has a few bits of rock scattered around. The first, and best, is a small wall on the left side of the valley. The lower overhanging wall provides a bunch of steep, fingery eliminates. To find it, park as for Stoney West, go through the gate signed Eyam Delf, and follow the valley for 200m. The wall is 20m up on the left: see map on page 79.

Candy Store Rock, HVS 4c (1977), is the groove and bulge on the left.

1   The Far Sidle   Font 7A+
From the left, traverse to *Eye of Nowt* and finish up this.

2   Eye of Nowt   Font 6C
From a sitter, head upwards via a gnarly mono. Swing right to finish on good jugs. A leftward finish is **Amphibian Conceit**, Font 7A. Continuing into the undergrowth is **Cuckley Delf Eliminate**, HVS 5a (1977).

3   Alacrity   Font 7B
Make a big move to an excellent pinch. Make more moves to gain the top jug. A sit start is Font 7C.

4   Fingermuse   Font 6C
From a crimp, rock into the good hold at the overlap. Finish on jugs. A sit start, starting with the left hand on a small undercling and right hand on the ledge, is Font 7B+.

5   The Beckoning Thumb   Font 6C
Sit start just left of *Meander* and head for the top jugs.

6   Meander   Font 6C
The rightmost line, from a sitter.

7   Wayfarer   Font 7C
From the jug on the far right, traverse left to gain and finish up *Eye of Nowt*.

8   Pursuit of Alacrity   Font 7C+
As for *Wayfarer*, but finish up *Alacrity*.

9   All The Way   Font 7C
Link *Wayfarer* into a reverse of *The Far Sidle*.

Tomarwa Groove, E1 5c (1966), the pinkish groove and overhang on the right.

Across the valley is a twin buttress. **Snerp**, VS 4c (1966), is the leftmost groove; **The Trundler**, VD (1965), is the crack to the right; **Just Another Tricky Day**, E3 6a (1987), is the groove and roof to finish at the top of the next climb; **Allergy**, VS 4c (1966), is flakes just right. On the buttress to the right is **Left-Hand Crack**, S (1965); **Jungle Burger**, E1 5c (1988), the wall to the right; **Right-Hand Crack**, VS (1965) and **New Moon on Monday**, E3 5c (1988), the wall to the right to a bolt belay below the ivy.

Hidden Quarry

This is the huge quarry on the left-hand side of the road immediately alongside the hairpin bend just before reaching Horseshoe Quarry. It is most easily recognisable by the striking arête of the main buttress when approaching in the direction of Stoney Middleton from Horseshoe Quarry itself. Access to the quarry is currently denied.

Parking is somewhat limited although a small lay-by on the crown of the hairpin bend can be used – it is probably best to park as for Horseshoe Quarry and walk down to this point. From here a discreet entry into the quarry via a grassy hillside and fence gains access directly to the buttress. See map on page 24.

The first routes are situated on the face to the left of the large arête. **Sniffer Clarke**, HVS 5a (1973), is the right-hand of two cracks on the left-hand side of the wall; **Sit-in Wall**, F5+ (2012), is the wall immediately left of the arête; **Stand-Out Arête**, F6b (2012), goes right from the second bolt on *Sit-in Wall* to climb the arête and crack; **Christmas Crackers**, F6b+ (2012), tackles the right-hand side of the huge arête with a short crack and bulge to finish; **Big Chiv**, E3 5b (1973), is the huge hanging chimney crack to the right.

Horse-Thief Quarry

This is the small low-level quarry 200m after the hairpin bend and just before the right turn into Horseshoe Quarry. The golden wall has three routes: **Golden Brown**, E3 6a (1987), climbs the left side of the wall moving leftwards past a peg to a belay; **Ghost in the Machine**, E4 6b (1987), climbs the wall right of *Golden Brown* with hard moves to a peg belay and **Gothic Demarcation**, E4 6b (1987), climbs the rib right again moving leftwards to the belay of the previous route.

Golden Wall

A recent development. A quarried wall near the road. Can be a bit slow to dry. Park as for Stoney West. Walk towards Horseshoe Quarry for 300m, then the crag can be seen just on the right. See map on page 24.

1   Jumping Blacks   F6c+   2015
15m A difficult boulder problem start leads to easier climbing above the third bolt. The boulder-problem start can be done from a low start, from the low break, at Font 7A+; **Snail Male**.

2   The Blicks   F6b   2015
15m A technical rib and steep fingery finish.

3   Poison Flowers   F6a+   2015
15m The awkward wall. Enjoyable above the ledge. **Photo on page 7.**

4   Black Bryony   F6b   ★   2015
15m A fine pitch up the blunt rib and pleasant wall.

5   Blickin' 'eck   F6b+   ★   2015
15m An excellent wall climb.

6   Golden Wall Traverse   Font 7B
Start just left of the tree and traverse the break to the jugs at the bottom of *Poison Flowers*.

7   Undiscovered Blacks   F5+   2015
8m A short offering just right of the tree.

Horseshoe Quarry

Sport: 269 (F3 to F7b)   **Trad:** 25 (S to E4)
Aspect: All directions, mainly south-west   **Sunshine:** From late morning   **Season:** All year
Conditions: Very dry, sunny, not much seepage, sheltered, polished, sometimes loose
Best for: Lots of vertical sport climbs in the F6s   **Approach:** 5 minutes

Horseshoe Quarry (AKA Furniss Quarry) has the honour of being the most famous and popular quarry of its type in the Peak District. From the humble beginnings of 1985, when the quarry was first developed for its Main Wall attributes - good quality rock and long technical lines - it has now been developed into a very popular and multi-faceted venue.

Now worked out to its full potential, the quarry offers an array of routes so vast that it caters for almost every taste. The Main Wall routes have not changed their character (polish aside) but the surrounding cliffs have seen a number of new routes in the lower F6 grades and the slabby back walls offer a new dimension with a collection of much easier and longer sport routes.

The vast majority of the routes here are not on good rock. With the exception of the routes on the Main Wall, the solidity varies from friable holds (on the small scale) to sections which may well collapse after a bad winter. Care must be taken here as many routes away from the Main Wall, however easy, are NOT to be taken lightly and it is recommended that both leader and belayer wear a helmet for these. There have been some major rockfalls here and whole routes have been seriously affected.

Sport Climbing
A great crag for those operating in the F6a - F6c range, with a small number of F7s, as well as about 30 F4s and F5s. The majority of the routes are fairly technical wall climbs although there are a few overhanging climbs on Heart Buttress, as well as a number of slabbier climbs.

Note: Unfortunately the quarry has a few terrors where first ascensionists have taken the search for new rock and routes to a different level. Some hollow, and in places loose, rock still remains and these routes should be treated with caution and are marked as such in the text. However, as with all climbing, both climbers and belayers should be paying close attention at all times to ensure safety.

Traditional Climbing
Horseshoe Quarry has a long tradition of naturally-protected climbing. It was first developed at a time when placing a bolt only happened when there was no other form of protection available (and not always then); this resulted in bold trationally-protected routes, and routes with sportingly placed bolts.

Some of the older peg and bolt protected routes have been retrobolted somewhat. Most have been left with their original character. The quarry is also host to many fully traditionally protected climbs. These take the cracks and faces between the bolt routes, and often provide good climbing.

Conditions and Aspect
The walls face in 3 directions, so there will always be something in the sun or the shade. The majority of the routes face south-west and get sun for most of the day. The quarry takes virtually no seepage. Thanks to this it is an ideal winter, spring and autumn venue, especially if the sun comes out. However, it can feel chilly when a cold winter wind is howling around the quarry. In the summer months it can be a bit too warm in the full glare of the sun on the Main Wall, although this can be avoided by going there early or by going to one of the shadier walls.

Parking and Approach
See map opposite, and on page 24. The entrance to the quarry lies on the north side of the A623, 1km west of the Eyam junction (the B6521), just past a hairpin bend, and 1km east of the Foolow turn-off. Parking exists inside the quarry turn-off, just up a rough quarry track. There is more parking on a rough lay-by 50m up the road towards Foolow, and more again in a larger lay-by on the opposite side of the road. From any of these, follow the blocked-off quarry track through the trees to the crags.

Access

The majority of Horseshoe Quarry, barring areas around The Slabs and the Upper Bay, are owned and managed by the BMC. Obviously, this means there are no access issues. Those areas not owned by the BMC are in private ownership. Though the landowner Hancock (whose butcher's shop in Stoney has the best Pork Pies in the country) has never actually agreed to allow climbing on his land, no access issues have arisen in recent years.

It is worth noting that the BMC do not inspect bolts nor take responsibility for them. As with any climbing on fixed equipment, it is the climber's own responsibility to judge the safety of gear. The same goes for loose rock.

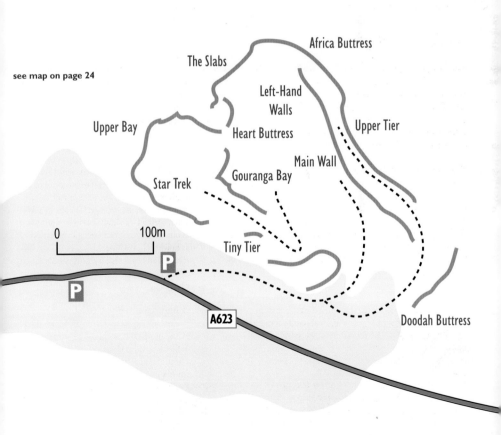

see map on page 24

Lower Left

The best feature to start from is the large slabby area at the back of the quarry (the Slabs). Left of this is the Heart Buttress and left again is a small sheltered bay.

Gouranga Bay

This slabby wall is situated directly opposite the Main Wall at the back of a recessed bay, and offers a few worthwhile morsels. The namesake route is the main prize. Good rock requiring good dry conditions. Not a winter or humid weather venue. The wall faces east and gets early morning sun.

1 NYD F6a+   2006
9m An isolated arête 30m left of the path and above the path up to the upper bay.

In the bay itself are:

2 Pig in a Poke F5   2010
10m A reasonably pleasant shallow groove.

3 Bad Boys Ink F6a   2001
10m A barely-worthwhile climb up the shallow groove.

4 Unruly Behavior F6a+   2001
9m A very minor route with two hard moves.

10 You Crack Me Up HVS 5a   2007
12m The straight jamming crack is a poor route.

11 Minnie Grip F7a   2006
10m The black face with two short technical sections.

12 Unhung F6a+   2010
11m The first pillar to the right of the angle of the bay.

13 The Fire Hang F6b   2010
11m The second pillar to the right of the main angle.

14 Hang Fire F6a   2010
12m The third pillar to the right of the main angle.

15 The Gobbler F5+   2010
12m The rib and jamming crack above a ledge.

16 Christmas Presence F6c   2005
12m The pillar. The finish has a sense of urgency.

17 Steeping the Goose F6c   2005
9m The left-hand line. Hard at the finish.

18 Turkey Shoot F6a+   2005
9m The centre of the wall gives a good yarding exercise.

The small isolated wall further right gives:

19 Farmer's Seed F6b   2011
9m The left-hand side of the wall with long a pull at
the top.

20 Chicken Feed F6a   2010
9m The wall and wide crack.

21 Top Gobbler F5+   2011
9m The right-hand side of the wall.

5 Treatment F6b   2001
12m Barely worthwhile. Don't use the crack on the left!

6 Therapy F6b ★   1992
12m The right-hand side of the smooth-looking black
face. Good moves, where a long reach helps.

7 Porgi Amor F6a+ ★   1998
12m The left-hand groove-line of two gives an interesting
challenge, especially in clipping the bolts.

8 Foreign Tongues F6a ★   2001
12m The right-hand of the two shallow groove-lines.

9 Gouranga (Be Happy) F6c ★   1998
12m Fine technical climbing but short lived. Tricky.

Heart Buttress

The only overhanging wall in the quarry. Rarely dry in the winter months or after long periods of rain. The wall faces east and gets some early morning sun.

22 Nine Eleven F6a   2010
12m   The shallow groove left of the arête to a rightwards exit.

23 Seven Eleven F6b   2008
12m   Good moves up the left-hand side of the arête.

24 Tors Colon F6c+   2001
12m   The arête is taken on its right-hand side after 5m. Sustained and fingery.

25 Vent Your Spleen F7b   1998
12m   A very bouldery start gives way to fingery and sustained upper walls.

26 Heart to Heart E4 6a   1986
12m   The straight crack varies from finger-width to hand-size. This is potentially a very good traditional climb, although the crack tends to be full of dirt.

27 Sliver F6c+ ★   1998
12m   When dry, this fine route gives a superbly sustained jug and jam fest.

28 The Stomach Pump F7b   1998
11m   The thin crack springing from the top of the pile of blocks. Desperate, but well-constructed!

29 Skin Flint F6c   1998
11m   Or flinted skin? The smooth-looking wall with a hard start and an airy, open finale.

30 Bad Blood F6b+   2010
12m   Swing right and up into the obvious crackline.

31 The Blood Bank F6b   2001
12m   This climb is gained from the top of the mud slope left of *Sharing Best Practice*. A hard start leads to easier climbing above.

32 There Will be Blood F6b — 2011
12m Swing right out of *The Blood Bank* to climb a short fine wall.

33 Taylor-Parkinson Gully IV, 5 — 1996
40m The mud and scree gully at the back left-hand side of the quarry. Originally done in 2 pitches. Climbed overnight in hard winter conditions, the ascensionists and all the equipment needed a bath afterwards. The crux is dry-tooling a short corner at 2/3rds height.

The Slabs

The vegetated-looking slabs have yielded a number of easier grade sport climbs in the F4 and F5 category. These have become quite popular due to their pleasant easier-angled nature, length and lack of such grades in the Peak District. The wall faces south-east and gets early morning and afternoon sunshine, and seems to be permanently sheltered from the wind.

WARNING: Some loose rock remains on these routes despite their popularity. Therefore wearing a helmet is strongly recommended. Some of these routes are longer than 30m meaning that you cannot lower back to the ground on a standard 60m sports rope. Please knot the end of your rope whatever its length.

34 Sharing Best Practice F6b — 2001
15m This prominent arête provides poor climbing.

35 Barney Rubble F5+, F5 — 2001
32m The left-hand line gives a poor climb. The route can be climbed in one or two pitches, stopping at the half-height ledge if so desired.

36 Chauvi's Slab F5, F5+ — 2001
32m Another route that can be split into two pitches, taking the right-hand and better of the two cleaned pillars. Feels a little bold due to the spacing of the bolts, despite the fact that there are 13 of them!

37 Stille Nacht F5+, F5 — 2007
35m The central line of the slab to the right with a one-third-height belay.

38 Trog F4, F5 † — 2000
38m A long two-pitch route based around the slabby wall system 8m to the left of the arête. Belay in a cave behind a tree. Needs more cleaning / traffic and hence an alert belayer. Currently stripped of gear.

39 Neanderthal F4, F5+ — 2000
38m A similar route to *Trog*, but slightly better, based around the prominent arête to the right of that climb. This route also needs an alert belayer.

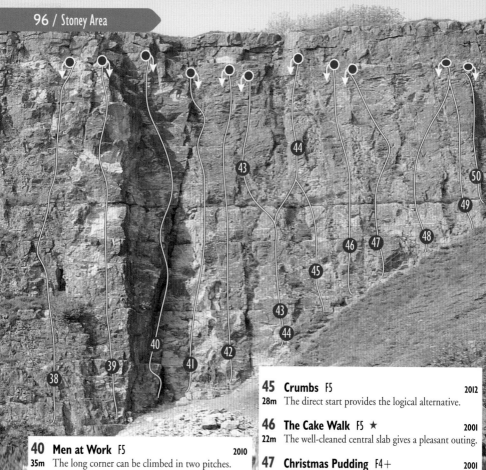

40 Men at Work F5 · 2010
35m The long corner can be climbed in two pitches.

41 The Quarrymen F6a · 2010
35m The wall and slab taken direct on the line of the bolts.

To the right of the main slab is a subsidiary set of slabs. These routes are by far the cleanest of the climbs on the slabs, and are getting better. However, the warnings in the introduction still apply.

42 Excavator F5 ★ · 1998
32m The best route on the slabs but you need a 70m rope to get back down the pitch in one.

43 Slab Cake F4+ ★ · 1998
28m The direct line up the strip of slab provides another pleasant outing. A 60m rope just suffices for lowering-off.

44 Spare Rib F4+ · 1998
28m This route takes the right-hand branch off the main line of *Slab Cake*, to climb a protruding rib.

45 Crumbs F5 · 2012
28m The direct start provides the logical alternative.

46 The Cake Walk F5 ★ · 2001
22m The well-cleaned central slab gives a pleasant outing.

47 Christmas Pudding F4+ · 2001
18m Identifiable by a prominent ledge at 4m. The slab above needs more cleaning.

48 Sago Slab F4 · 1999
15m The left-hand of the two strips of slab.

49 Dream Topping F4 · 1998
12m Pleasant and clean climbing up the right-hand strip.

50 Cinema Rage E1 5b · 1999
15m Climb the arête, avoiding the blank-looking start to the right.

51 Chocolate Blancmange Gully TD · 1982
50m This unique expedition takes the attractive mud slope. Climb the mud slope until progress is blocked by a suspect boulder. Climb onto this, then transfer to the right wall of the gully. Follow a series of delectable mud bands and rock steps, trending right, until a final corner/flake can be gained to finish. Has changed since the first ascent but worth recording for the hell of it.

Left-Hand Walls

These are the slightly recessed walls that sit to the left of the Main Wall. Here will be found a number of relatively poor routes and in some cases poor rock but mixed in amongst them are some good pitches. On a positive note, they do dry quickly. Afternoon and evening sun.

Africa Buttress

This is the first area, so called because it is said to be shaped like the eponymous continent. It also has the same colour as some of its deserts and a similar rock texture! The face consists of two walls, the lower providing a number of pleasant routes which give access to several more on the upper face (see the upper tier). As such, combinations give good two-pitch experiences. The lower face has a prominent left-hand arête.

1　**Out of Africa**　F6b　2002
11m　Reasonable climbing on the left-hand side of the arête.

2　**Madagascar**　F6a+　2002
11m　The right-hand side of the arête. Disappointing.

3　**Bird Island Pitch 1**　F6a　2002
12m　The main corner. A poor route but it does give easy access to the pitches above *Rainbow Warrior*.

4　**Seychelles**　F6b　2002
12m　A layback corner to a ledge and then a crack complete with overlap. Worthwhile, just.

5　**Rainbow Warrior**　F6c ★　1998
15m　A fine route based on the left-hand side of the lower rounded arête. Difficult at a thin crack low down.

6　**Weakened Warrior**　F6b　2005
15m　The rounded arête gives a reasonable pitch with a hard pull just below mid-height and a rounded finish.

7　**Sam in Your Eye**　F6a+　2008
12m　The wall on the right side of the arête to a crack.

8　**During the War**　F6a+　2009
12m　The crack in the left-hand wall of the corner.

9　**Before the War**　F5　2009
18m　The left-hand of two prominent corners.

10   Sahara F6c   2003
18m   The prominent arête has some hollow holds high up and may not be suited to those of a nervous disposition.

11   Union Jack F5   2009
18m   The right-hand corner.

12   African't F6b+   2006
18m   The cleaned wall and shallow groove lead on to the grey wall where a series of long moves reach the belay.

13   Desperate Dan F6b   2008
18m   Quite a good route up the newly-cleaned crack.

14   Fine and Dandy F6b   2008
18m   A zigzag line above the prominent cleaned scoop.

15   African F6b   2005
18m   The thin crack starting via a short arête.

16   Bloodguard F6c ★   1998
18m   A good pitch via a vague pillar and starting atop a mound of rubble. A short, difficult sequence.

17   Grab Your Mandrakes F6b ★   2002
18m   The right-hand side of the prominent arête and the wall above the roof. Worthwhile.

18   Tirfin USA F6a   2001
15m   The prominent corner leads to the belay of *Turf's High*. **a Tirfin Mandrakes**, F6a+ (2009), links the start of this with the finish of the previous route. Good moves.

19   Turf's High F6a+   2001
15m   The grey, slabby wall gives a couple of noteworthy moves.

20   Race of the Freuds F6b+   1999/2002
18m   The sinuous crack with an overlap that provides the crux moves. The slabby walls above lead to the belay.

21 Peckling Fever F5+ ★ 2000/2002
18m The short wall and crack lead to an final overlap.

22 Senter Home F6a 2001
18m The ramp / groove leads to an overlap. A difficult finish can be taken direct or to the right.

23 Tirfer Off F6a+ 2001
18m The shallow groove and slab immediately to the right.

24 Maillon Sunday F6b 2001
18m A rightwards, dogleg line with the crux after the second 'joint'. Easier above.

25 Bootiful Bernard Matthews F6b 1990
18m Climb the blunt rib to the right to reach a difficult ramp. Overcome the overhang on the left to reach the belay.

26 Nowt Taken Out F6a+ ★ 2011
18m The corner to a tricky finale leftwards. Worthwhile.

The next series of routes climb the white wall to the right. A distinguishing feature here is an obvious borehole.

27 Foul's Bane F6a+ 1998
15m Just right of the slim corner. Finish right of the roof to a belay above.

28 Drool Rock Worm F6b 1998
12m The slim wall to the left of the borehole leads to a belay below a tree.

29 Stonethroat F6b+ ★ 1998
12m The white wall to the right of the prominent borehole in the centre of the face. The best of the trio hereabouts.

30 Slay the Gray F6b 2006
15m The slim pillar gives a surprisingly good pitch.

31 Mr. Cellulite's Arête F6a+   2001
11m Reach dependent.

32 Bandolier F6a   2001
18m The rightwards-facing slim corner to the right.

33 Underslung F6b+   2008
18m The wall with a low crux and sustained interest above.

34 The Little Thin Mexican Across the Border
F6b   1994
18m The wall gains the left-hand side of a nose and an off-balance finale.

35 Desperate Measures F6b   2001
18m This route lies just left of a shattered section and has golden bolt runners. Harder climbing on the right-hand side of the sharp arête / nose. Finish as for the last route.

36 The Mexican takes Lexicon F6a+ ★   2003
15m A pleasant steep route on solid flat holds. A good warm-up.

37 Exceeding the Speed Limit F6b+   1993
18m Good moves high up. Pleasant.

38 Mind Your Head F6b+   2003
18m The name applies. Straight up the wall just to the left of a slim corner. Some hollow holds.

39 Desperate Housewives F6a   2006
12m The corner line. Still a little dusty.

40 Collared F6a   2002
12m The slightly steeper wall with a few fragile holds low down. **Photo opposite.**

41 Spare Rib F6b   2000
12m Much better. The gold-flecked wall behind an elderberry tree. A hard start leads to juggy climbing above.

42 Eddie McStiff F6a+ ★   2006
18m Climb the wall and shallow groove to the right. At its top swing up and left to a ledge and finish direct. Good climbing.

Collared, F6a (opposite). Photo: Mike Hutton.

43 Pelvic Thrust F6b 2002
12m The scarred wall to the right and left of the slim corner.

44 The Hippy, Hippy Shakes F6a+ 2008
15m The long slim corner to a high belay.

45 Due Care and Attention F6a 1987/2003
15m A short wall and groove / crack lead to an overlap. The steep crack above leads to the belay.

46 Any Old Iron F6a 2001
15m The short wall, flake and short arête above, all in the left-hand wall of a slim corner. Named from an old piece of ironmongery found in the quarry and now in the route!

47 Sunday Sport F6b ★ 1987
15m The slim, polished corner leads to a high belay.

48 Austin Powers F6b+ 2001
18m The groove in the arête, finishing via a hollow arête.

49 The Big Fat Texan on a Corner F6a+ ★ 1993
18m The centre of the clean white wall to the right. Not taken direct. Pleasant. **Photo opposite.**

Combining the start of *Austin Powers* along with the finish of *The Big Fat Texan on a Corner* gives the very cleverly titled **Austin Texas** (F6b), perhaps the best way up the wall.

50 He Seems So Sumo F6a 2004
18m Steep and sustained climbing on the borehole / crack.

51 Olive Oil F5+ 2001
18m A worthwhile wall-climb to the right and left of the main angle of the bay. Keep direct on the line of bolts.

52 Removal Men F6a 2001
18m Appropriately named. The large chimney in the back of the bay.

53 Some Place F6a+ 2001
18m The wider crack to the right followed by an arête and crack just to the left.

54 Sag Paneer F4+ ★ 2002
15m The crack in the left-hand side of the arête. One hard move.

The Big Fat Texan on the Corner, F6a+ (opposite). Photo: Neil Foster.

Sophie Whyte on Rain Dance, F6c (opposite page). Photo: Neil Foster.

The Main Wall - Megalithic Sector

The next section of crag, the impressive expanse of flat wall, provided the main interest of development in the mid-Eighties and still provides the quarry's best routes. Most of these may be found to be a little under-bolted by some modern standards but the angle of the wall gives many an opportunity to rest and consider one's options whilst climbing. Many of the routes have a good big feel about them.

The main features of the wall are a prominent borehole towards its right-hand side and an impressive crack towards its left. Old 'Climbing Prohibited' graffiti still adorn the walls but these are fading fast. The routes begin at the arête to the left.

The walls face south, and get afternoon and evening sunshine. They take virtually no seepage.

1 Pale Rider F6a ★   2001
15m   The left-hand arête of the main wall taken directly after the break. Using the crack to the right spoils the route somewhat (F5+). **Photo on page 106.**

2 Knight Rider HVS 5b/ F5+   1984
22m   Gain the crack on the right from the arête and follow it to a series of unstable blocks leading to the top. It is better to lower off from the belay of *Pale Rider*.

3 Rain Dance F6c ★★   1985
18m   Excellent face-climbing with a hard start and and a delicate rightwards traverse on the headwall. **Photo opposite.** There are two alternative finishes to this route: **a The Colostomy Finish**, F6c+ (1992), up the arête; **b Physical Fizz**, F6c+ (1986), a highly technical wall to the right, which is hard for the grade.

4 School's Out F6b ★   1985/2002
18m   A fairly tricky start via a faint rib gains a good ledge. The scoop above leads to a pleasant finishing crack.

5 Rotund Roolay F6b+ ★   1986
18m   Technical and surprisingly sustained in its upper section via a scoop and rib.

6 Waves of Mutilation F7a   1992/2002
18m   The wall to the left of a thin crack provides a desperate fingery sequence. Reachy.

Pale Rider, F6a+ (page 105). Photo: David Simmonite.

7 First Day of Winter HVS 5b   1986

18m The thin crack has an awkward start and pleasant climbing above.

8 Wall of Jericho F6b+ ★   1986

18m A hard start leads to ledges. The awkward and polished rib above provides the crux.

9 The Leading Line F6b+ ★   2001

18m The long 'galena-filled' crack gives a surprising find. Interesting manoeuvres and a long reach at the crux.

10 Say it With Flowers F6c ★   1986

18m The slim face gives a very trying move just above half-height.

11 Legal Action F6c ★★   1984

18m A sustained fingery face climb with loads of rests and a low crux. Start via a short, left-facing flake and continue direct. Excellent. The second bolt is hard to clip especially if you are short and risks a ground fall.

12 Run For Your Wife F6c+ ★★   1987

18m Another fine, intricate testpiece. The bulge above the rightwards-facing flake provides the difficulties. Climbing directly past the bolts above provides further entertainment.

13 Private Prosecution F6c ★★   1986/1998

18m Superb varied climbing. A new start, coupled with a technical scoop and airy finish on the headwall. Perhaps the best route on the wall?

14 Litany Against Fear F6c+ ★   1985 /2003

18m Starts by an elderberry bush. Straightforward climbing leads to a hard bulge and a new direct finish up the slab. The original and easier finish crossed the slab rightwards.

15 Megalithic Man F6b+ ★★   1985

18m The classic of the wall. Varied and intricate low down, leading to a superb slabby finish. Start via the orange patch; go leftwards through the triangular overlap and rightwards across the upper slab.

16 Megalithic Man Super-Direct F6c+ ★   1998

18m A harder finish with excellent, fingery moves.

17 Poisonality F7a ★   1991

18m The direct version of *An Ancient Rhythm*, with a well-defined crux section. The line climbs directly to a faint, leftwards-facing corner.

18 An Ancient Rhythm F7a ★   1985

18m A popular route. A cruxy lower section past the second bolt leads to a sustained thin crack above. Glassy and desperate in the sun.

Dave Barker on Demolition Man, F7a (opposite page). Photo: Neil Foster.

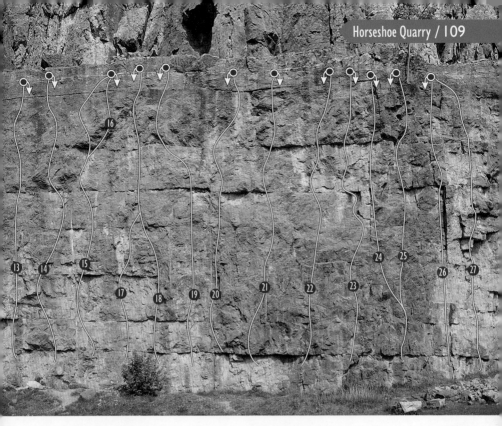

19   Demolition Man F7a ★   1986
18m A typical product of the mid 'Eighties. Scantily bolted with a fingery start and a blind, airy finish **Photo opposite.**

A good variation, **Ancient Man**, (2001), does the start of *Ancient Rhythm* then makes bold and committing moves directly to gain the finish of *Demolition Man*. F7a+, although with its run-out nature, it feels more like E5.

20   Shot Yer Bolt F6b+ ★   1986
18m The long borehole gives the start to one of the original routes on the wall. Where this ends, trend rightwards to a crux just below the belay. Polished. **Photo on page 113.**

21   Southern Man F7b ★★   1986
18m Classic fingery face climbing with a bold feel to it. The wall to the right of the borehole gives the line, the last 6m the entertainment.

22   Nice Face, Shame About the Ledge
         F6c ★   1985
18m Appropriately named. A tricky start followed by a thin slab leads to an airy finish via a faint flake.

23   Flatworld F7a ★   1998
18m A very good eliminate on the right edge of the wall. A trying and powerful crux repels many.

24   Lost Monolith F6b+ ★   1986
18m Easy ledges and a straightforward crack lead to a pleasant crux bulge. Good climbing after a scruffy start.

25   Screwy Driver E1 5b   1987
21m From the last bolt on *Lost Monolith*, move rightwards up a flake to a ledge.

26   Sound as a Carp E1 5b   2092
18m The shallow groove leading to bolts higher up. The route avoids the direct line.

27   Harvey Wallbanger F6c   2010
18m The blunt rib with very hard moves directly through the overlap. Using the crack out right makes it a more balanced route at F6b.

28   Spring Awakening E1 5c ★   1986
18m A straight thin crack on the right-hand side of the wall gives another good traditional route finishing at an obvious tree. Harder since the collapse of the pillar to the right.

29 Mutley Stole My Route Man F6b   2000/2008
18m   The edge of the wall taken via the left-hand side of a vague arête.

30 Winter Fingers F6b   2001
15m   Keeping right-hand of the line of bolts provides a tough and solid pitch for the grade.

31 Broken to Bits F6c+   2011
15m   A fragile line following a steep wall to a shallow groove.

32 Down to the Last F6b   2007
15m   The shallow groove gained by a short steep wall.

33 Fragmented F6c   2009
15m   The shallow groove, blunt rib and technical finale.

34 Mice Breaker F6b   2001
15m   A direct line up the wall has hollow holds throughout.

35 Finishing Off F6b   2008
18m   The left arête of the groove with a crux at the top.

36 Spectrophotometry E3 5b   1986
15m   The long V-shaped groove behind the bushes (peg).

37 Fifty Bolts to the Gallon F6a+   1998
15m   Keep to the arête low down.

38 Like Ice, Like Fire F6a ★   1986
15m   The groove and the thin flake give pleasant climbing to a tricky finish.

39 Galening Crack HVS 5a ★ ★   1986
15m   The best trad route in the quarry but you haven't many to choose from! The crack in the slim groove.

40 Compromise E2 5b   1997
15m   The shallow groove contains some old fixed gear.

41 Promises F6a+   2007
15m The rib taken directly with hard moves at mid-height.

42 The Rotten Word F6c+   1999
15m A surprisingly tough route straight up the wall.

43 Decayed Dance F6c   1999
15m Easy and relatively insignificant climbing leads to a fine headwall. Start to the left of the base of a pillar.

To the right is a large shattered pillar with an old traditional route on its left-hand side: Order Number 59, E2 5c (1986).

44 A Right Earful F6a+ ★   2001
15m The left wall of the large corner via cracks. The shallow groove above gives a hard finish.

45 Clean Your Mouth Out F6c   2001
15m The right wall of the prominent corner to the right leads to fine moves above the roof on the headwall.

46 The Dust Bunnies F6c+ ★   1998
15m A direct line up the wall to the right leads to a stopper move on the headwall. Telescopic arms or a contortionist manoeuvre would pay dividends.

47 Dalken Shield F6b ★   1986
15m A good route, though slightly bolder high up. The vague arête to the right, finishing via a steep headwall.

48 Hardcore, You Know the Score F6b ★   1992
15m The shallow groove behind the tree leads to a peculiar sequence through an overlap. Popular, hence the veneer.

49 The Director's Cut F6a+ ★   2003
15m Pleasant climbing squeezed onto the vague rib to the right. Finish at the belay of *Bladerunner*.

50 Blade Runner F6a+ ★   1986
15m A super little pitch due to its hint of boldness: three bolts in its length. The route takes the wall to the right via an obvious scoop. More like E2 5b.

51 Bruce's Bonus F6b   1996 /1998
15m The first line to the left of the corner provides a good introduction to the sport climbing hereabouts.

52 Do Androids Dream of Electric Sheep?
E2 5c   1985/2006
15m The corner leads to a rightwards line across the wall. Traditional gear. The direct finish is F6a+.

53 Rage F6b ★   2001
15m A direct line up the centre of the wall. Better than its right-hand neighbour.

54 The Running Man F6b   1991
15m A good pitch that is becoming less enjoyable due to polish, taking the crack 8m to the right of the corner. A troublesome overhang at half-height gives food for thought.

55 The Long Walk F6c   2010
18m The left-hand side of the arête with sketchy moves low down and a good finale.

56 The Dark Tower F6b+   2006
15m Climb the shallow groove to reach an overhang. A stiff pull with hard-to-see footholds provides the crux.

57 The Drawing of the Three F6b+   2008
18m An easy lower wall with a difficult overlap and a spicy finish.

58 Willie the Kid F6a   2001
18m Not brilliant. The large corner. At the roof, traverse a long way rightwards to reach the belay.

59 Calamity Jane F6b   2001
15m Climb the left-hand side of the arête forming the right-hand wall of the corner. Stiff in its upper half, over-bolted in its lower.

60 Jeff Garrett F6a   2001
15m The wall right of the prominent arête behind the tree.

61 The Dogs F6b+   2001
15m The shallow groove and wall above. Avoiding the edge of the wall makes it harder and artificial.

62 The Man from Delmonte – He Says "Yes"
HVS 5b   1986
18m Start from the base of the slope to the left of the cave.

63 Derailed F6b   2002
12m A short, hard wall to the left of the cave. A long reach helps, as do quick feet.

A climber enjoying Shot Yer Bolt, F6b+ (page 109), as the Red Arrows give a celebratory fly-past. Photo: Mike Hutton.

The next obvious feature is a prominent cave at 6m, the site of previous diggings by Geoff Birtles and Tom Proctor. After much excavation (see the pile of dirt underneath), Birtles got deep into the heart of Horseshoe. He was never the same again!

64 Passage of Time F6b 1993
12m   Easy climbing leads to the cave. The headwall above provides the entertainment.

Lower Tier - The Toilet Sector

The walls to the right provide a series of routes in the lower grades. The routes are the result of heavy excavation, so be careful with the holds.

65 The Sewer F6a+ 2003
11m   A crack with a short steep upper section.

66 Latrine F5 2003
11m   The shallow groove is pleasant enough.

67 Armitage F6a 2003
11m   An enjoyable face to the right.

68 Shanks F6a 2003
11m   The black groove, with loose holds .

69 Potty F6a 2003
11m   A poor route.

70 Psycho Ceramic F6a+ 2008
12m   A steep start and fingery overlap above.

71 The Bog F6a 2003
11m   A steep start leads to good holds leading up the wall above.

72 Twyfords F6a+ 2003
11m   The next route starts via a short groove. Care with the rock is required.

73 The Small Room F6a+ 2003
11m   A tricky little steep start gives way to some hollow holds above.

74 Thomas Crapper F6a 2003
11m   Perhaps the best route in this section, with easy climbing low down and a fine juggy roof finale.

75 Two Loos F4   2006
12m The shallow flake and groove give a pleasant pitch.

76 Montezuma's Revenge F6a+   1998
12m A relatively poor route with a hard section at half-height. For the man who has done everything?

77 Latrec F5   2006
11m A shallow groove just to the right moving leftwards to finish.

78 Toilet Graffiti F5   2006
11m Starts via a short orange corner to a steeper wall.

79 Toilet Humour F5   2007
11m A tricky start and easier above.

80 De Throne F5   2006
11m A shallow groove.

81 On Uranus F6a   2006
11m A shallow corner start and a juggy finish.

82 Eau de Toilette F6a   2006
11m Steep, with a difficult start to finish on the left-hand side of a nose.

83 Wipe it Clean F6a   2006
10m A steep start finishing via an overlap to the right-hand side of the nose.

84 Andrex F6b   2006
9m Hard start, then easy.

85 Easy Come, Easy Go F3   2007
8m Straightforward climbing after an initial pull.

86 Monster Traverse E3 6a   2011
A huge traverse of the walls at mid-height from right to left. Start up *Andrex* and finish at the mud slope on the far left. Done in 14 pitches, the hard sections are from *Willie the Kid* to *Blade Runner* (E3 5b) and from *Say it with Flowers* to *Wall of Jericho* (E3 6a).

Upper Walls

These are a collection of walls facing the Upper Tier, and on the same level. They are accessed by walking up the big ramp opposite the Main Wall. The first sector encountered is surprisingly small.

The Tiny Tier: One of the world's smallest pieces of rock sits just above the access ramp. There are three routes on it. **A Tracky Little Problem**, F4 (2001), is on the left, **Tracker Bar**, F5+ (2012), in the middle and **A Tracky Little Bleeder**, F5 (2001), is on the right.

Disney Wall: A small wall on the left, to the left of the larger grey wall. From left-to-right these are: **Mickey**, F3 (2012); **Minnie**, F3 (2012); **Daffy**, F4 (2012); **Goofy**, F4 (2012); **Donald**, F4 (2012); **Pluto**, F4 (2012).

Star Trek Wall

This is the long grey wall which lies a little further along the tier and contains a number of easier sport climbs of limited quality. The wall faces east and gets sunshine only in the early morning.

1 Gargle Blaster F6a   2001
6m The short tricky wall on the left-hand side of the face.

2 Uranus F3   1998
8m The left-hand crack, to the belay of the next route.

3 Luke Skywalker F4   2001
8m The right-hand crack.

4 Klingon F4   1998
8m Another faint crack.

5 Saturn's Ring F5   1998
8m The wall to the right.

6 Vogon F6a   1999
7m The best route on this wall.

7 Dr Who? F6a+   2001
7m Pass a prominent scar by hard moves.

8 Torchwood F6a+   2006
7m The wall to the right with a hard start.

9 Beam Me Across Scotty F5   2001
12m Traverse the wall from right to left.

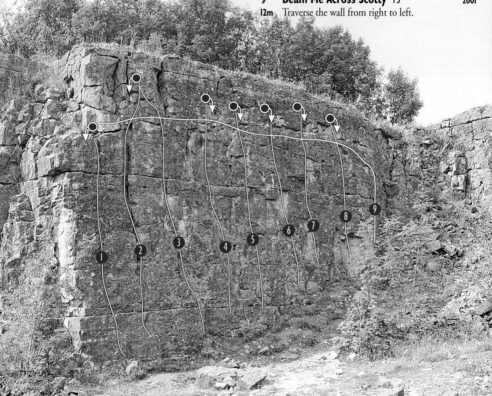

12 Statuesque F6b 2001

9m The thin crack system on the right-hand side of the wall. Again worthwhile.

The next routes are on the arête and corner just across the bay.

13 Mucker's Wall F6a 2001

10m The slabby wall.

14 Citizen's Arête F4 2001

10m The innocuous arête in the centre of the bay.

The final routes are based around the right-hand arête of the bay and the wall to its left.

15 Freedonia F6b 2006

10m A pleasant face tucked away in the left-hand side of the wall.

16 Drumming in a Lay-by E1 5b 1999

10m Climb the wall left of *Greeder*. Starting 3m to the left, climb a slight corner to breaks, move slightly right then back left to finish up a steep little crack.

17 Greedor E2 5b ★ 1999

12m The fine arête gives an good traditional route. Climb the thin crack in the lower wall to a break. Tackle the arête head on.

18 The Whinger F6a+ 2001

12m The right-hand side of the prominent arête. A poor addition which somewhat spoils the previous route.

19 Off Limits F6a 2001

12m From the ledge, climb the centre of the narrow wall to the right of the arête via a thin crack.

The Upper Bay

The next three routes are situated on a small wall to the right of the Star Trek Wall. The stumps of a butchered elderberry tree marks the wall.

10 The Libertines F6b+ 2006

9m The left-hand side of the wall with a hard start and extending bulge.

11 Taking Liberties F6c+ 2001

9m The centre of the wall leads to a very hard finish. Good.

The Upper Tier

Although the routes here are generally shorter, this is a super place to climb. There is a gentle atmosphere, without the attendant hordes of the lower tier. It is accessed by scrambling up the worn path in the banking, leading to the right-hand side of the walls. The walls face south, and get afternoon and evening sunshine. They take virtually no seepage.

Africa Buttress Upper

The next series of routes is gained from the ledge across the top left-hand corner of the wall. This can be gained from the routes below or via an abseil from the top. The routes here are short and relatively unworthwhile.

1 Elizabethville F6a 2002
9m The left-hand edge of the wall utilizing its left-hand arête. Tricky for 2m!

2 Burundi F6b 2002
9m Short but packs a punch. A very thin crack 5m to the right of the left-hand edge of the wall.

3 Townships F6c+ 2003
9m A short desperate sequence on the next little wall.

4   Victoria Falls F6a   2002
9m   The layback groove to the right.

5   Kariba F6a+   2002
10m   The steep crack has a hard move to gain a ledge.

6   Zanzibar F6b   2002
10m   A poor eliminate requiring a direct start. Step rightwards out of *Kariba*, move up, and finish almost on *Simonstown*.

7   Simonstown F6c+ ★   2002
11m   The rightmost route from a slightly lower ledge. One significant hard move in a fine position.

The next series of routes is situated above the ledge atop Rainbow Warrior. They can be gained via that route or others below.

8   Ring Thane F6c+ ★★   1998
12m   A super pitch, the best hereabouts. It takes the striking arête left of *Pretoria* and can be combined with the lower pitch of *Rainbow Warrior* to give one massive route.

9   Pretoria F6b+   2002
12m   The right-hand side of the arête forming the left-hand wall of *Mombassa*. Poor.

10   Mombassa F6a   2002
12m   The crack and corner above the lower walls.

11   Greenpeace F6a   1998
12m   The centre of the wall to the right of the corner.

12   Bird Island Pitch 2 F6a   2002
12m   The right-hand arête of the wall.

At the far left-hand side, the tier merges with the lower tier and a rope handrail leads across the ledge system to an area of cleaned ledges with a series of prominent grooves above. Here lies the first handful of routes.

13   Brew Thyme F6a   2007
15m   The crack right of the arête.

14   Thyme Out F6a   2007
15m   The wide crack and V-niche.

15   What's the Thyme? F6a   2007
15m   The next crackl just to the left of the corner.

16   Bridge Over the River Thyme F5   2007
15m   The main corner.

17   Bit of Spare Thyme F5+   2007
15m   The wall to the right of the corner, almost on the arête.

18   Fat Betty F4+   2007
15m   The easy corner.

19   Take Your Thyme F5+   2007
15m   The right-hand wall of the corner.

20 Porridge F4+   2007
15m The slim corner line to the left of the arête. Pleasant.

21 Crunch Yer Nuts F4   2010
15m The fine wide crack system.

22 The Soggy Bottom Boys F6b   2003
12m The right-hand side of a slim arête on the end of the tier. A couple of quite testing moves.

23 Man of Constant Sorrow F5+   2003
12m The left-hand side of a bubbly calcitic arête starting via a crack.

24 Big Rock Candy Mountain F6a ★   2003
12m The right-hand side of the calcitic arête gives a good little pitch with plenty of exposure.

25 Everett's Arête F6a   2003
12m The poor and insignificant arête to the right. One testing move.

26 Repulse F5   2009
11m The left-hand of two newly cleaned lines.

27 Prince of Wales F5+   2009
11m The right-hand line.

28 That Old DA Look F4   2011
11m The shallow groove and short bulge to the right.

29 FOP F6a   2003
12m The wall 6m to the right. Poor.

The Upper Tier

The remainder of the routes are situated on the upper tier proper. The first routes start on its left-hand side at a grassy ledge at 5m.

30 In the Jailhouse F6a   2005
10m Climb the short fingery wall to good holds. The overlap above is straightforward.

31 Po Lazarus F5+   2005
10m The crack and overlap just to the right.

32 No Way is Patience a Virtue F6b   1999/2001
11m The left-hand side of the wall with a tricky initial wall involving a fingery pull.

33 While the Cat's Away E3 6b   1986
12m Tackles the centre of the wall via a hard move past a lonesome bolt.

34 Oh Brother Where Art Thou? F6a   2002
10m The right-hand side of the wall above a ledge.

35 Dapper Dan F6a ★   2001
12m The arête to the right. Enjoyable open climbing.

36 Babe the Blue Axe F6a   2006
12m The wall gives a tricky start. Above, easier climbing leads to a steep finish.

To the right is an area of poor rock with an isolated arête in its centre.

37 The Cretan F6b+   2001
11m The arête mostly on its right-hand side to finish via a layaway edge - the groove on the left is not the route.

38 Corinthian Spirit F6a   2005
11m The crack to the right gives a pleasant pitch.

39 Theseus Saurus F6c   2001
11m A short wall leads to a ledge. The finishing wall is mean for the grade and the bolt feels awfully low.

40 It's All Greek to Me F6b   2001
11m The thin crack system directly past a ledge. The start and finish provide the difficulties.

41 The Minor Tour F6c+   2001
11m A very hard start to the left of the cave finishing via a short technical face. The start can be avoided on the right – **The Minor de-Tour**, F6c.

42 Olympiakus F6c   2009
12m Climb leftwards into the hanging groove.

43 Her Aklion F6c   2001
9m Innocuously situated above the cave. Thuggy climbing once the start has been negotiated.

44 Almost There F5   2006
12m The bubbly arête tucked away in the right-hand side of the bay gives steep moves on jugs.

45 Into the Labyrinth F5+ ★   1986
12m The central line of the pillar via a thin crack system. A good sport route.

46 By Zeus F6a+ ★   2002
12m   The pleasant arête has hard starting moves.

47 Spiteful Rain F5   2001
12m   The slim face to the right, starting up a groove.

48 Commiseration F5   2009
12m   The slim groove to the belay of *Spiteful Rain*.

49 Second Prize F5+   2006
12m   The slim pillar/face with an awkward start.

50 Tawny Owl Pie F5   2006
12m   The excavated groove exiting left and up to the belay.

51 The Owl F6c   2006
12m   The cleaned wall gives quite a good route.

52 White Dove E1 5b ★   1986
12m   The thin crack.

53 Nullo in Mundo Pax Sincera F6c+   1998
12m   A hard eliminate requiring a lot of discipline.

54 Supplementary Question F4   1986/2005
12m   The slabby corner gives a pleasant outing at the grade.

55 A Liberal Smear F6c+   2001
12m   Just what is needed for the crux moves at the top.

a **No Flair Blair,** E3 5c (2001), is the groove to the right.

56 Labour Relations F6c+ ★   2001
12m   The smooth slab taken direct.

57 Avoiding the Issue E4 6b ★   1999
12m   Climb the thin crack to the right until a bulge is
gained. Overcome this via a series of thin pulls (bolt) to
gain a lower-off just above.

58 PM's Question Time E3 5c ★   1986
15m   Follow *Avoiding the Issue* to the top of the crack and
then traverse carefully right for 5m. Now climb the shallow scoop and rib above (bolt) via a series of precarious
moves.

59 Booker Prize F5+   2009
12m   Climb the front face of the pillar.

60 Sir Pryse F6a+ ★   2001
12m   Pleasant climbing through the scarred overlap.

61 Oy Missus F6c   2001
12m   The left-hand side of the slab gives a slippery prize.
Hard to avoid the corner on the left. Verging on F6c+.

62 Mr. Blue Sky F7a ★   1986
12m   Very technical and slippery moves on the right-hand
side of the inset slab. Unusual.

63 Esso Blue HVS 5b 1986
13m Take the thin crack 3m to the left of the prominent arête to gain a slabby area. Finish as for *Mr. Blue Sky*.

64 Smoke Gets in Your Eyes F6b+ ★ 1985
12m The short arête is started on its left-hand side. Finish directly via a thin crack.

65 Esso Extra E2 5c 1986
16m Climb the groove on the right-hand side of the arête to gain the slab. Either finish up *Smoke Gets in Your Eyes* or move leftwards to the finish of *Esso Blue*.

66 Shell Super F6c 2008
12m A hard boulder problem if taken direct on the sidewall. Finish up *Smoke Gets in Your Eyes*.

67 Mumble Jumble F7a+ ★ 2001
12m An overhang! All hard moves surround this or do they? Keep to the centre of the pillar below and to the right of the corner to reach it.

68 Fargo F6a+ 2001
10m The straight thin crack. You can extend the route by swinging rightwards from the belay to join *Blue Sunday*.

69 Blue Sunday F6b ★ 1986
12m The centre of wall starting just to the left of a cave.

70 Do It Yourself F6c 2001
12m The very hard middle section may require telescopic arms. Keep direct to the line of bolts low down.

71 New Bolts and Yankees F6a 2009
12m A steep start with a crack above.

72 Kushti F6a 2002
12m The thin crack 8m to the right. Worthwhile. **Photo on page 125.**

73 Lovely Bubbly F6c+ 2001
12m Hard and technical moves at half-height.

74 Bimbo Strikes Again S 1985
15m Climb the prominent corner to the right and lower off from the belay of the next route. Dirty.

75 Slabby but Nice F6a 2006
15m The right-hand arête of the corner gives a pleasant climb with the difficulties concentrated into the last 5m.

76 Sam and Mary F5 2009
12m A crack to a steep finale.

77 Ma Marmalade F6a+ 2009
12m The left-hand arête of the groove to ledges and a tricky finale.

78 Slam the Jam F5   2003
12m   A prominent groove and jamming crack above.

79 Jam Slice F6b   2010
11m   The wall and shallow groove.

80 Don't Try This at Home F6b+   2009
15m   The face to the right. Hard finale, high in the grade.

81 Red Rum F5+   2010
12m   The corner to the right.

82 Nijinski E2 5b   1985
11m   The slim, slabby face. Move leftwards and then up from half-height. **Seated Moon**, E2 5b (2000), steps right and climbs the crozzles to the same belay. **The Easy Interloper**, HS (1986), is the wide crack to the right.

83 The Party Animal F6b   1986
9m   The arête taken on the right at the top (or left: F5+).

84 Café Bleu E3 5c ★   1985
10m   A little gem up the face. Tiny wires protect the start.

85 Dinky Toy F6c ★   1986
11m   A short pitch gives excellent fingery climbing.

86 Corgi Registered F6b   2005
11m   The arête on good hidden holds. Steeper than it looks.

87 Hornby F6a+   2009
9m   The steep wall with an overlap over to the right.

The Doodah Buttress

This is the buttress passed on the approach to the upper tier. It has become somewhat overgrown. **Slabbering Slab**, VS 4c (1986), is the leftmost corner; **Shetland Chimney**, VD (1986), is the groove to the right of the chimney; **Chicken**, VS 4b (1986), climbs to the left of a small pinnacle avoiding an overhang to its left; **Liquid Engineering**, E2 6a (1986), is the direct on this; **Little Damocles**, VS 4c (1986), is the groove to the right of the overhang; **Cob**, VS 4b (1986), climbs the flaky crack; **Footprint**, VD (1986), takes the wide crack; **Ol' Dirty Bastard**, E3 5c (1995), is the wall to its right; **Golden Tights**, VS 4b (1986), climbs the straight crack above an old tree stump; **Pot Washer's Wall**, HVS 5b (1986), is the straight crack to the right; **Hot Zipperty**, HVS 5a ★ (1985), is the best route here. Climb the thin twisting cracks and the rugosity-ridden wall to finish via a shallow groove; **Bimbo does Limbo**, E1 5a (2010), climbs the vague face just right; **Bimbo Has his Head Examined**, VS 4b (1986), climbs the groove to the right; **Golden Grockle**, E1 5a (2011), climbs the prominent rib to its right again; **Grockle's Gully**, VD (1986), climbs the obvious dirty gully to the right; **Gold Label**, VS 4c (1986), moves right out of the gully to climb the wall. The right-hand side of the buttress has five poor routes: **Nimbo Slab**, VS 4c (2012), climbs a slab and face left of the left-hand crack; **Bimbo on the Loose**, S (1986); climbs the left-hand crack, **Bimbo Drops his Codpiece**, VS 4c (1986), takes the next crack to the right; **Bimbo's Off-day Route**, VD (1986), is the next crack; **Bimbo's Arête**, VD (1986), is the arête on the right.

Kushti, F6a (page 123). Photo: Niall Grimes.

Tom's (Roadside) Cave

Bouldering: 9 (Font 5 to Font 8A+)
Aspect: South **Sunshine:** Not much **Season:** Spring to Autumn
Conditions: Shady, seeps in winter, ugly
Best for: A bit of dirty power **Approach:** Roadside

A little roadside grotto with a handful of filthy-hard problems. Seconds from the car park. The setting is not so great, but if you can ignore the aesthetics, then there are some great, hard problems here.

The cave was climbed on in the Eighties by Jerry Moffatt. Dawid Skoczylas rediscovered its potential in 2007 with *Andronicus* and *Hannibal*. Dan Varian added to the tally in 2010 with *Titus*, *King Cannibal* and *Tamora*.

The Climbing: Powerful limestone bouldering on roofs and lips. Best for harder stuff.

Conditions: Seeps in winter and after periods of heavy rain. Can be humid due to thick tree cover which prevents much movement of air. The trees make it shady.

Approach: The cave is on the side of the A623. It is on the same side as Horseshoe Quarry, about 60m up the road from the Horseshoe entrance/parking. There is a layby directly opposite. **See map on page 24.**

1 Back Wall Traverse Font 7A

2 Back Sitter Font 6B
A short problem from a sit-start.

3 Andronicus Font 8A
A brutal, sequency and gymnastic problem. Move up to the undercut at the back and contort out towards the pinch on the lip. Move up and rightwards to finish on the higher jug. **Photo opposite.**

4 Hannibal Font 7C
From a sitter, move up to the beak then gain and follow the lip leftwards, finishing on the upper jug.

5 Hannibal Corner Font 7B+
Follow *Hannibal* then move up the short corner.

6 Titus Font 7C
Jump to the lip-jug, move up to the higher jug, then traverse the lip leftwards to finish on the tree.

7 Tamora Font 8A+
The link-up of *Andronicus* into *Titus*. Very sustained.

8 King Cannibal Font 7C+
The obvious lip link-up of *Hannibal* into *Titus*.

9 Jugs Font 5
The warm-up.

Dawid Skoczylas on Adronicus, Font 8A+ (opposite page). Photo: Alex Ekins.

WATER-CUM-JOLLY

RUBICON / MOAT BUTTRESS / THE CORNICE / CENTRAL BUTTRESS +++

Katy Whittaker on The Sissy, F8a (page 160). Photo: Alex Messenger.

Litton Mill Approach: Upper Circle / Jackdaw / Ping Pong

Turn off the B6049 by the Anglers Rest pub and follow the small road along the River Wye as for the Raven Tor approach. A mile down this road, and 750m past Raven Tor, is a large car park on the left at the foot of Tideswell Dale. Park here. Continue on foot down the road to Litton Mill (no parking here). Enter the mill (between the two bollarded pillars). Walk down then veer right to cross a bridge and onto a large riverside path. This is the main access path for the crags.

Litton Mill Approach: Central Buttress Area

For Central Buttress, Mill Buttress, Church Buttress and Two Tier Buttress, park at Tideswell Dale as for the approach above. Walk towards Litton Mill and cross a bridge before the Mill. Follow the path as it zigs up onto the Monsal Trail. Turn left and follow this to the first tunnel entrance. Follow a small path that skirts the entrance on the left of the tunnel. Go up to cross a stile. As the main path goes uphill, follow a smaller track along the rim. Pass over two small rocky outcrops and, 50m before Central Buttress, drop down a small path to the river bank. Go left for Mill Buttress, right for Central Buttress. For Church Buttress, stay on the high path and drop down before the crag.

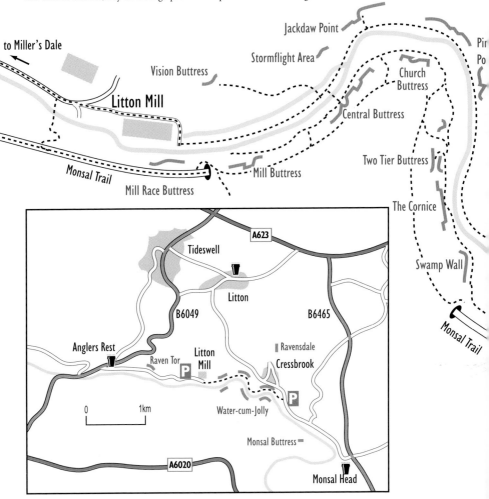

Cressbrook Mill Approach

Park on the roadside verge just outside Cressbrook Mill, which is just below Cressbrook Village. Follow the public footpath that runs to the right of the black metal fence, alongside the entrance to the mill. Follow this for 120m to arrive at the lake.

North Bank: Rubicon / Lammergeyer / Ping Pong

For crags from Rubicon, as far as Ping Pong and beyond, turn right and follow the path.

South Bank: Black / Moat / Cornice / Two Tier

For crags on the South Bank, from Black Buttress, to The Cornice and beyond, turn left and cross the bridge over the weir and go up the steps. At the top, turn right to contour along the exposed hillside on an indistinct path. See specific approaches in individual sections.

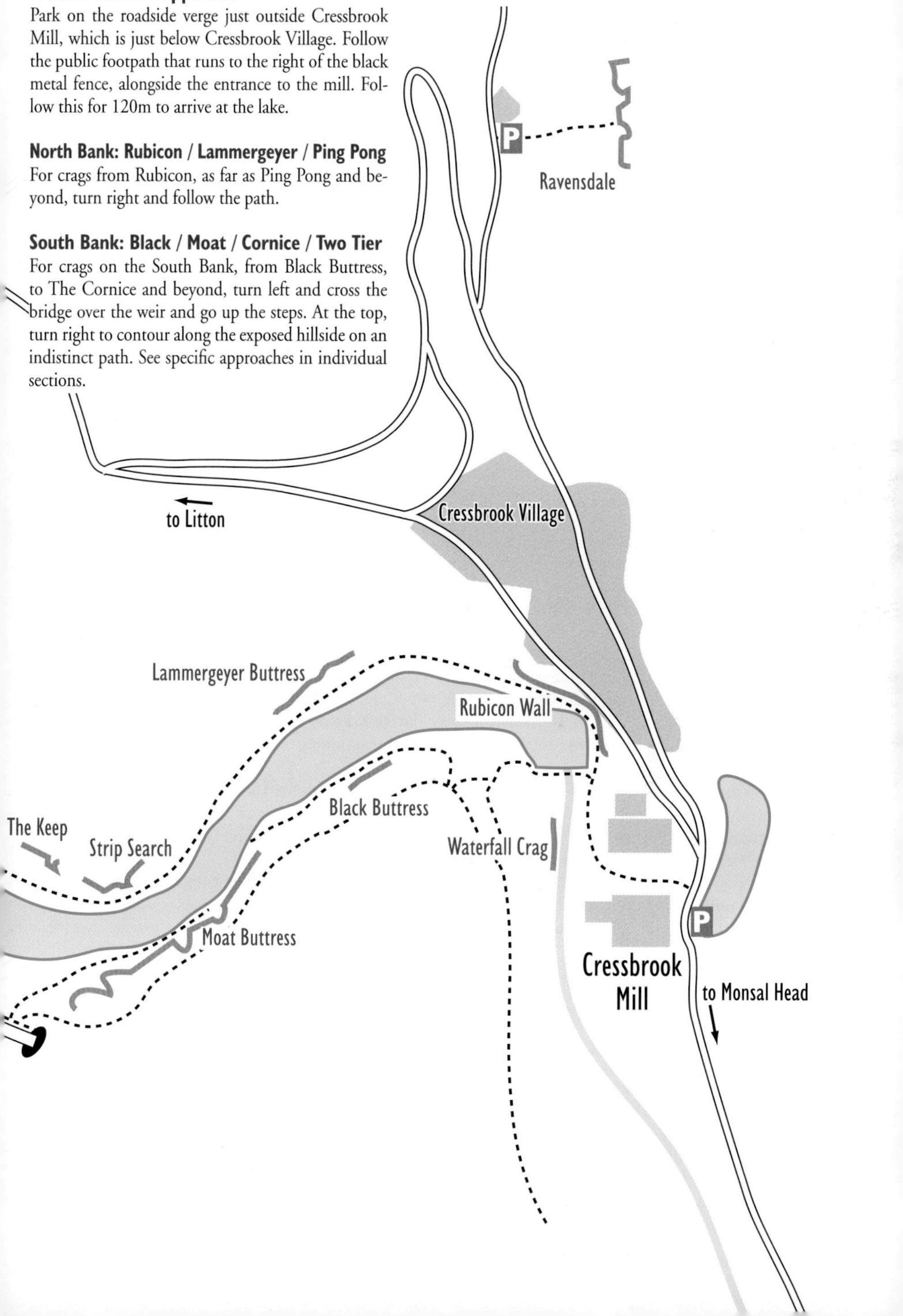

Ravensdale

to Litton

Cressbrook Village

Lammergeyer Buttress

Rubicon Wall

The Keep

Strip Search

Black Buttress

Waterfall Crag

Moat Buttress

Cressbrook Mill

to Monsal Head

Water-cum-Jolly Access Notes

Access to Water-cum-Jolly has been difficult in recent years following a change in the ownership of Cramside Wood. This part of the dale was purchased by the Derbyshire Wildlife Trust (DWT) from Cressbrook & Litton Flyfishers Club around 2008. Since this time, water bailiffs from the fishing club and DWT staff have challenged climbers in the dale. Despite a meeting with DWT in 2014 to try to resolve their concerns, they maintain their position of no permission for climbing.

Considering the long history of climbing here, with routes originally established in the 1930s and climbing having continued throughout the decades since, the BMC does not support a ban in Water-cum-Jolly. Below are some facts about access to the dale:

• The north bank of the river is owned by several different landowners and parts of this side of the river are the subject of current access disputes.
• The south bank of the river is privately owned and leased to two graziers. There is no formal access agreement here but climbing access has never been an issue.
• Vision Buttress is privately owned by one of the residents at Litton Mill. She does not allow climbing on the buttress and has been known to forcefully approach climbers with her (sometimes aggressive) dogs and ask them to leave.
• DWT have stated they do not permit climbing on their land in the dale. Given that the dale is not designated as Open Access under CRoW, should you choose to climb here, technically speaking you will be trespassing. This is a civil (rather than criminal) offence and it is unlikely that a landowner would pursue legal proceedings providing no damage was caused.
• Cramside Wood includes Jackdaw Point, Inch Test area (aka The Upper Circle), Ping Pong area, The Keep and Strip Search buttress. Within this area DWT ownership extends from the landward edge of the riverside path upwards.
• The riverside path is owned by the fishing club and is a permissive route across private land – there is no formal right of way here although it has been used by the general public for many years.
• Cramside Wood is a SSSI. The fact that a crag is situated within a SSSI does not mean it cannot be climbed on, with many of the UK's most well-known and used crags falling within SSSI boundaries. (The BMC itself owns several crags located within a SSSI, including the nearby Horseshoe Quarry). Providing climbing doesn't damage the interest features of a SSSI, there is no reason to ban climbing. If there are concerns that this may occur, an agreement can usually be made to avoid sensitive areas whilst allowing climbing to continue.
• Currently no rare species of bird nest in the dale. However, were this situation to change, the BMC would negotiate a reasonable temporary restriction on a case by case basis as we do elsewhere.
• Fishing in the river without a valid rod licence and membership to Cressbrook & Litton Flyfishers Club is a criminal act and were climbers to be implicated, would be a significant point of contention with fishermen in any future access discussions.
• Flooding can be a problem here. This is known about by the Environment Agency, but given that no property is threatened it is a very low priority issue for them.

If you do decide to climb in Water-cum-Jolly, please follow the guidelines below in order to prevent any impact upon other users and important habitats:
• Maintain a quiet and low-key presence whilst visiting.
• Don't disturb the fishermen and always remain polite when interacting with other people in the dale.
• Do not interfere with flora or damage property in any way.
• DWT have a legitimate concern about damage to limestone grassland vegetation below and above crags. This can easily be prevented by following the approaches described:

Jackdaw Point: approach via the faint path starting directly beneath the crag only.

Inch Test area (aka The Upper Circle): do not use the path up the scree slope on the right (facing the crag), instead use the faint path directly below the crag.

Cupid's Buttress (aka Ping Pong Buttress): a bolt lower-off has been installed as the descent path leads through a particularly sensitive habitat at the top of the crag. Please lower off rather than topping out and descending.

Central Buttress: two approaches are possible, either wading the river or dropping down using the path from the tunnel on the Monsal Trail. If wading the river, cross at the naturally formed bedrock weir. You may be challenged by a bailiff or member of the fishing club here but there are no issues with crossing at this point.

The Cornice: access to this buttress should be as quiet and discrete as possible as the bank on the approach to the crag provides good habitat for rare and easily disturbed wildlife.

The Upper Circle

Trad: 60 (VS to E6) **Sport:** 7 (F7a+ to F8a+)
Aspect: South-west **Sunshine:** Afternoon and evening **Season:** All year
Conditions: Sunny, quick drying, sheltered, sometimes overgrown
Best for: Classic sunny trad, E1 to E5; a savage redpoint, F7c to F8a+ **Approach:** 15 - 20 minutes

A fine string of buttresses run along the north bank of the Wye in the upstream reaches of Water-cum-Jolly between the hardcore sport climbs of Vision Buttress and the classic E1s on the Ping and Pong area. In-between is a wide range of mid-grade trad and tough sport climbs that will bring a smile to sun-loving wanderers.

The Climbing: The routes are steep and physical and there are plenty of starred classics to chew on.

Conditions and Aspect: The buttresses are mostly clean apart from a few seriously overgrown sections. The crags tend to be very sunny and sheltered and in many cases are a good bet for a spot of winter action. Quick drying.

Parking and Approach: See map on page 130. Crags are best gained from the Tideswell Dale parking / Litton Mill approach. Park at the Tideswell Dale parking and follow the path down to and through the mill. See the introduction to each buttress for its specific approach.

Vision Buttress

The first climbing is to be found on a small buttress named after its central route, Fawcett's breakthrough ascent from the early 1980s.

Approach: Follow the Litton Mill approach (**page 130**), through the mill and onto the riverside path. Follow this until opposite Central Buttress. A tree lies across a subsidiary brook of the main river. Walk across the tree and scramble leftwards up to the crag, about 100m away.

Access: Vision Buttress is privately owned by one of the residents at Litton Mill. She does not allow climbing on the buttress and has been known to forcefully approach climbers with her (sometimes aggressive) dogs and ask them to leave.

1 Sunshine Superfrog E6 6c   1987
18m A sustained and fingery exercise. The route has lost a number of holds and is overgrown.

2 The Vision F7c+ ★★   1962/1982
20m An extremely technical route that showed that Fawcett was still head and shoulders above his rivals at the time.

3 Knocked Out Loaded F7c ★★   1987
18m Follow *The Vision* then move out right and climb the bulging wall past three bolts to a lower-off.

4 Agrippa's Knees E6 6b   1962/1981
20m A serious route up the bulging arête on poor rock.

5 A Grippa Clippa F7a+   2011
12m The bulging wall right of *Agrippa's Knees*.

Stormflight Area

A minor area, majorly afflicted by vegetation.

Approaches

The base of the crags in this section suffer from lots of vegetation and brambles and routes are hard to reach. Four hundred metres from the mill and just past a metal bridge, a poor path leads back leftwards from a spring to the start of the Upper Circle. After 25m it passes under a small buttress situated opposite the metal bridge.

The undercut crack in the left-hand side of the buttress is **Bad Day**, VS 5a (1978), whilst the bulge taken on the left or right finishing via a thin crack is **Worse Night**, HVS 5b (1970s). Twenty metres to the right the pinnacle taken on its right-hand side: **Bakerloo**, HVS 5a (1977).

Just to the right of the pinnacle and above Bad Day is a steep wall holding:

6 No Strange Delight E4 6a 1986

18m Climb to the base of the leaning wall. Bold moves lead to a shallow depression and a pocket. Pull rightwards to reach back right for a sapling. Traverse left to exit.

Forty metres further to the right is a vertical, smooth wall.

The flake on the left of the wall is taken by **Chicane**, VS 4c (1977).

7 A Matter of Style E4 6b 1986

13m Climb just to the left of a sapling at the base of the wall moving rightwards to reach some good holds. A sneaky step right gains a thin crack. Pull up and leftwards to reach a second crack, crux, finishing more easily.

8 Stormflight E3 5c 1986

13m Climb to a ledge and flat hold above. Move left to the base of a thin crack and climb it to a prickly finale.

9 In the Shadows E1 5b 1986

10m From the flat hold on *Stormflight*, continue up the wall to another prickly finale.

10 After the Snow E2 5c 1986

13m Step right to a thread. Climb the wall rightwards to a second thread and finish more easily rightwards to a tree.

11 Random Factors Align E2 5c 1986

13m Move right to below a bulge and overcome this on tiny ripples to reach the finish of *After the Snow*.

12 Rippledom E1 5b 2011

12m The shallow, left-facing groove just to the right.

Twenty metres to the right again is a short wall:

13 Wolfen E2 5c 1979

12m Climb up to the hole, move right and follow a thin crack to finish.

14 Your Melon E4 6a 1983

12m Climb the bulging wall past a small square flake trending first right and then left to finish.

15 Life After Death E4 6a 1983

12m Climb up to the break 3m to the right and go leftwards, then step back right and finally straight up to finish just to the left of a tree.

16 Omah Gourd E1 5b 1985

12m The flake to the right. Lives up to its exclamation.

Jackdaw Point

The Upper Circle continues with a larger buttress 45m to the right. This is Jackdaw Point, and gives a score of mid-grade trad routes.

The Climbing
Technical traditional wall climbs on fairly good rock. A few of the routes rely on fixed pegs.

Conditions and Aspect
A sunny, south-facing crag. Fairly sheltered, so can be climbable in winter, but hot in summer. Generally clean and mostly solid.

Parking and Approach
See map on page 130. Park at the Tideswell Dale parking. Follow the Litton Mill approach along the main path by the river, then a small path directly to the main face.

17 Ground Control E2 5c   1985
15m Climb the corner to the left of a hanging flake. a **Stop the Pigeon**, E5 6b (1985), exits right from the groove past a peg.

18 Skyline Pigeon E4 6b   1985
12m Starting as for *Ground Control*, climb directly to the flake via a peg and blind bulge.

19 Armed with an Empty Gun E4 6a   1985
15m Climb the wall below the trio of cracks stepping left to a short thin crack. Move up to the left-hand of three cracks and follow this to a difficult and fragile finish.

The next six routes all lead to a ledge. There is a 5a finish up the wall but this is becoming overgrown. Most abseil off from the ledge.

20 Erithacus E1 5b ★   1977
18m Climb the wall to the cracks and follow these to a resting place. Traverse right along the flake to a belay.

21 Army Dreamers E2 5c ★ ★   1981
24m Climb the serious wall right of *Erithacus* to a peg, passing the bulge slightly leftwards to better holds. Trend rightwards to the ledge to finish direct up a cleaned wall. a **Final Sacrifice**, E1 5b (1985), is a variation finish taking a bulge and obvious line left of the ivy.

22 Fledgling Flakes HVS 5b   1976
24m Start in the centre of the buttress and climb the wall to the obvious flakes. Use these with care to go left then more easily right to gain the belay ledge. Finish as for *Erithacus* or *Final Sacrifice*.

23 Burning up Time E3 6a ★   1979
24m Starting 2m to the right, pass a 'nail' with difficulty to gain a small ledge. Continue up the wall (peg) to a hanging flake which leads to a ledge and a choice of finishes from a bolt belay on the right or via a ledge a little higher.

24 Nervous and Shaky E4 6a   1990
13m The wall to the right leads to the bolt belay.

25 The Fledgling VS 4c   1961/1962 - 1969
20m Climb the depression and continue over some loose blocks to the belay ledge.

26 Violation of Trust E3 5c 1985

6m A variation finish to *Fledgling Flakes* climbing the wall left of its top section on steadily improving holds.

27 Trial Run VS 4c 1976

13m The overgrown flake.

28 First Flight HVS 5a 1976

12m The shallow vegetated groove is gained via a bulge.

29 Palmolive E1 5c 1983

12m The pleasant wall to the right has one peg.

30 Endless Flight E1 5b ★ 1978

12m The flake crack and bulge.

31 Fear of Flying E1 5b ★ 1978

12m Climb the wall to reach a flake. From the top of this continue direct (peg) to finish.

32 Come Fly with Me E3 5c ★ 2011

12m The very pleasant blunt rib. Aptly named after some first ascent escapades!

33 Flight Path VS 4b 1976

12m The corner leads to a bulge and rightwards finish.

34 Victory Roll VS 4c 1976

12m Climb the flake and pass the overhang to the right.

The next three routes take a wall 25m to the right and have become completely inaccessible and overgrown: **Tiger by the Tail**, E3 5c (1985), climbs the centre of the wall; **Knightmare**, HVS 5a (1985), starts at the same point but moves left and then up and **Demon Striation**, E5 6b (1985), traverses right to climb the bulging wall.

Some 125m right again is an isolated buttress. **2001**, E2 5c (1978), climbs the centre of the buttress; **Eighe**, VS 4c (1978), climbs the wall 5m right and **Potential Orbit**, VS 4b (1980s), climbs the wall and crack 10m right again.

The next buttress 30m to the right contains several grooves, mostly overgrown and ivy-choked: **Space**, VS 4c (1976); **Oddity**, HVS 5a (1976), the next groove; **Daylight Robbery**, HVS 5a (1976), the next groove; **Possession by Design**, E4 5c (1986), a sentry box to the right exiting it rightwards; **Not for Hire**, E2 5b (1983), climbs the next groove; **Reach for the Sky**, E2 5c (1983), climbs yet another groove; **Crash Crazy**, E3 5c (1988), climbs the wall and bulge to the right.

To the right, past a clump of ivy, a more continuous section of rock appears. The first obvious feature 9m along this is a depression taken by *Groovy Baby*. To the left of this is a loose bulge taken by **Intuition**, E3 5b (1988), with an easier finish above whilst **Orchmire**, E1 6a (1987), climbs the loose wall via twin cracks 6m left of *Groovy Baby*.

Inch Test Buttress

The main event here is a bulge of white rock, home to a small number of very hard, fingery and worthwhile sport climbs. A clutch of testing trad climbs lie on either side.

It is fairly quick drying and is seepage-free and climbable in winter. Sheltered and sunny. Can be hot in summer.

Parking and Approach: See map on page 130. Park at Tideswell Dale. Follow the main riverside path for 500m. Approach directly up a small path to the main buttress.

35 Spiritualist E5 6a   1988
9m   Climb past a peg to reach an undercut in the roof above. The groove above (poor peg) leads to moves rightwards onto a slab.

36 Groovy Baby E3 5c   1976/1986
12m   The groove is gained by a short wall and soon eases.

37 Yankee Doodle E2 5b   1976
12m   Climb up to the roof and finish via a groove.

38 Hesitation Dance E5 6a   1988
8m   The small undercut flake and hanging groove.

39 Specialist E3 6c   1962/1982
13m   A desperate sequence of moves lead to an easier finish in the upper corner.

40 Pragma F7c+ ★   1964/1988
12m   The first of the desperates on the wall to the right. Possibly unrepeated and probably harder since hold-loss.

41 Eat the Rich F7c ★   1990
12m   The bulging wall and roof provide a stern test. Climb to the bolt under the roof; F7b+ to here. For the full tick pull round the roof to gain good holds. Reverse onto the last bolt to lower off: **photo on page 140.**

42 The Three Spheres F8b ★   2007
12m   The bulge to the right provides the toughest route on the buttress.

43 The Inch Test F8a+ ★★   1964/1989
14m   The original and best of the bunch with a very difficult clip at the crux.

Rupert Davies on Eat The Rich, F7c (page 139). Photo: Andy Newton.

At the right end of the bulges, a shallow weakness breaches the upper wall and has become covered in ivy; **Psychic Emulator**, E3 6b (1983/1986), climbs the wall 3m left of the lower weakness finishing rightwards into the groove; **Sour Grapes**, HVS 6a (1960s/1976), which gains the weakness by some very bouldery moves; **Splinter of the Mind's Eye**, E2 6b (1986), climbs the bulge 2m right and follows a shallow groove to finish as for *Sour Grapes*.

44 Sweet William E2 5c ★   1976
16m A thin crack leading to an overhang. Follow this and overcome the roof with difficulty.

45 Wandering Thoughts E1 5b   1986
25m Start as for *Dead Tree Groove*, but immediately step left from the slab and trend leftwards to finish left of the ivy.

46 Western Somoa E4 6b   1991
16m From part way up the slab to the right, step left to the right-hand side of the roof taken by *Sweet William*. Cross this to finish up the bold headwall.

47 Dead Tree Groove E1 5c ★   1960/1976
17m The slab taken direct leads into an awkward finishing corner (peg).

a Palace of Tyranny, HVS 5b (1979), is a poor route taking a direct line to the right of *Dead Tree Groove*.
b Trench Warfare, E2 5b (1988), climbs a shallow groove and bulge finishing rightwards, 3m to the right.

48 Sweet F.A. E1 5b   1976
15m From the foot of the shallow corner, trend up and left to finish via a shallow scoop.

49 Dead Tree Crack E1 5b ★   1960/1976
12m A surprisingly tough little route taking the shallow corner in its entirety.

Fifteen metres further to the right the crag reappears as a pillar with an undercut base. This can be reached directly via the scree slope directly above the weir.

50 Raptor on Ice E1 5b   1993
13m The thin cracks in the wall 2m left of the pillar.

51 Christmas Cracks VS 4c   1964
15m Move up to the base of the pillar and step left to follow a series of flakes into a small left-facing corner. This leads to a ledge on the right and a direct finish up the wall above.

52 Euroman HVS 5a ★   1979
15m Pleasant climbing up the groove right of *Christmas Cracks* leads to a pedestal. Finish via the pillar above.

53 Looking Good E3 6a ★   1990
15m The shallow groove and ramp gain a thin finishing crack. Avoiding a rest in *Euroman* increases the grade to E4.

54 Nidhögg Loves Jormangand E5 6a   1983
8m The short wall with a series of hard moves above a slot 4m to the right. It once had a peg (no longer in place).

Forty metres to the right is a sharp-edged arête directly above the weir. This is taken by **Axe Edge Buttress**, VS 4a (1957). **Axilla**, E1 5c (1981), climbs the crack and wall from the foot of the arête and **Cicatrix**, HVS 5a (1957), climbs a groove and jamming crack on the right-hand side of the buttress finishing via a short groove to a small tree.

Ping Pong Area

This is the collective name for three close-together but-tresses, named after the two great E1s in the centre of the walls. The area is quiet and good: well worth a visit.

The Climbing: Nice tall walls with technical routes and good protection.

Conditions: Clean and solid with afternoon sun.

Approach: Approach from either Litton Mill or Cress-brook Mill in about 20 minutes (**page 130**). A scree-ridden gully leads to the right end of the walls.

The Everglades

1   Going Bush E5 6c   1996
18m   The wall gives a serious lead with hard-to-place pro-tection. Two wires were pre-placed on the first ascent and cams provide additional protection. Bolt belay.

2   Jungle Jim E2 5b   1964/1976
20m   After a pleasant start this route degenerates into some serious climbing on poor rock. Follow the corner to the roof and swing right to climb the wall on hollow flakes.

3   Tree Dweller's Crack E3 6a   1984
20m   Climb the yew tree and tiptoe along a branch to gain a crack in the wall right of *Jungle Jim*. Follow this to the top (peg) and much poor rock.

4   Deception E4 6a ★ ★   1981
21m   A gem of a pitch requiring a cool head. Climb the wall and bulge right of the tree, peg and thread (have a look first to ensure they are in-situ), to the break. Move left and climb the wall to the insecure finishing groove.

5   Confidence Trick F7b+   2006
21m   The bulging arête, swinging left into the centre of the face. Desperate moves up this lead to easier ground. Take some wires to supplement the in-situ protection.

A simpler time. Graham Hoey, on a cold winter day in 1974, free climbing Ping, E1 5b (page 144). Photo: Mark Scott.

Cupid's Buttress

This is the next buttress situated 20m to the right. There is a bolt belay at the top of the wall. Please use this to lower off in order to avoid trampling around the top of the crag as it is a site of special interest to botanists. **The Ponger**, VS 4b (1976), trends left into a dirty finishing groove on the left-hand side of the buttress.

11 Ping E1 5b ★★   1959/1968 - 1969
21m Excellent, perhaps the best around. Gain the crack to the right of the arête and follow it past a small ledge to the top. (Please avoid the top of the crag by lowering off from a bolt belay). **Photo on page 143.**

12 Desmond Douglas E3 5c ★   1988
20m Worthwhile. From the tree below the centre of the buttress, climb the wall slightly leftwards to a prominent thin crack. Step left and climb the fine wall past a thread to a junction with *Ping*.

13 Ping Pong E1 5b ★★   1966/1969/1968 - 1969
21m Another quality climb. Gain the crack and its continuation flake to a tricky finish on the short bulging wall. Move left to lower off.

14 Pong HVS 5b   1959/1968 - 1969
21m Gain and climb the undercut corner to the right and be careful with some of the rock higher up.

The Creative Urge, HVS 5b (1969/1970s), climbs thin parallel cracks around to the right finishing to the right of the overhanging nose whilst **Virgin's Crack**, S (1959), is the crackline 3m to the right.

Psyche's Buttress

The relatively broken buttress on the opposite side of the gully to the right gives a number of poor routes: **The Arrow**, S (1959), climbs the left-hand of three cracks; **The Quiver**, S (1959), climbs the central crack; **The Sight**, S (1970s), the right-hand crack. To the right the rounded arête gives a wandering route: **Bow String Groove**, VS 4c (1961). Fifteen metres to the right is an ivy-covered rock tower. **Eros**, HVD (c.1957), climbs a rift to a hole and exits via a groove above; **The Fairy**, D (c.1957), passes through the hole to finish up a chimney beyond and **The Goblin**, HVS 5a (1976), climbs to the right of the pinnacle moving left from the chimney to finish via a scooped wall. A small isolated buttress to the right provides: **Apex Left Foot**, VS 4c (1987), which gains and climbs a flake rightwards from the left side of the buttress; **Apex Middle Foot**, S (1987), climbs the centre of the wall; **Apex Right Foot**, S (1987), climbs a groove on the right trending leftwards.

6 Rio Verde E4 6b ★   1984
22m Climb the shallow groove then swing left and up the bulging arête along a hairline crack, peg. Finish direct.

7 Matto Grosso Chimney VS 4c   1957/1977
24m The groove, finishing left.

8 Mandrake E5 6a ★★   1977/1981
24m A superb route in its upper reaches. Climb a thin flake crack to gain a good ledge. The crack in the wall above provides the meat of the route (peg) and gives sustained and strenuous climbing.

9 Christiliano Wall E4 6b   1984
24m From *Mandrake*, step right to follow a groove through an overlap. Continue in the same line to easier ground.

10 Marsh Dweller's Rib E3 6a   c.1959/1976
24m Climb the yew tree and gain the crack a.s.a.p. Disconcerting moves past the loose overhang lead to an easier finish.

The Keep

This area provides a handful of limited-quality pitches. The first route is situated on the left-hand side of the rounded buttress to the left of the pinnacle.

1   Small is Beautiful   F7c+   2006
15m   An easy start leads to a very bouldery bulge above the ledge and then easier moves to finish. **a** The right-hand finish, above the break, is a project.

2   Firelance   E4 6a   1987
18m   From a midway point between *Small is Beautiful* and a left-facing chimney flake to the right, climb the lower wall (peg) with intimidating moves to reach the ledge. Move left to finish via a bulge trending leftwards above.

3   Dawn Razor   E4 6a   1991
18m   Start just to the left of a thin crack. Climb the wall (bolt) to a half-height ledge and continue straight over the bulge above past two bolts to a bolt belay.

4   Early One Morning   E2 5b, 5c   1963/1983
1. 15m   Follow a thin crack to the break and traverse left to a belay below a hanging corner.
2. 8m   Pull into the corner and finish more easily.

5   The Keep   VD   c.1957
18m   Climb the deep chimney on the left-hand side of the tower and then the narrow wall on the right to reach the summit. From here leap onto the main cliff and amble to safety. The chimney can also be bridged at S.

6   Keep on Truckin'   HVS 4c, 4c   1976
1. 11m   Climb the crack to a break that is traversed to the right (thread) to reach a crack. Climb this to a stance.
2. 11m   Move right and pull over the final bulge to a crack. Escape by jumping to the mainland.

7   Convoy   E1 5a   1966/1976
22m   The loose flake on the right-hand side of the front face of the pinnacle leads to a ledge. Move left to finish as for the previous route.

Cry Tuff, E2 5c (1983), is the ivy-covered flake 6m right of the pinnacle; **Limited Edition**, E3 5c (1988), is the clean wall and bulge 7m right of *Cry Tuff*; **While Stocks Last**, E4 6b (1988), is the bulging wall 3m right again

Strip Search Wall

Forty metres right is an ivy-choked wall that houses a number of good routes. Two trees mark the base of the wall: **Summons**, E2 5c (1970s/1982), is a strenuous and serious wall behind the left-hand tree; **Nappy Squad**, E4 5c (1986), climbs the wall and roof right of the right-hand tree; **Dreams of Living**, E5 6b (1981), climbs the left-wards-leaning flake and roof 5m right of the right-hand tree; **Love is the Drug**, F6c+ (1990), is the wall to the right on disposable holds; **The Still Small Voice**, E3 5c (1970s/1981), climbs the shallow pocketed groove to the right and **Strip Search**, E2 5c (1983), climbs a shallow groove to the right passing to the left of an overhang.

Water-cum-Jolly History

The first recorded climbs in Water-cum-Jolly appeared in 1933 courtesy of Eric Byne and Clifford Moyer. *The Gully* 1933 and *Crystalline* were modest little affairs, but for their time were a rare excursion onto the serious medium of limestone which few pioneers were willing to explore. And it was Byne who, some twenty four years later, was indirectly responsible for the next phase of development in the valley when he mentioned its potential to Graham West, the leading light of the Manchester Gritstone Climbing Club (MGCC). After succeeding on the limited free-climbing possibilities available to them, the club enthusiastically took on the audacious aid-climbing challenges present in the Dale. From 1958 till 1970 Water-cum-Jolly became largely the preserve of the aid climber with the MGCC soon being joined by members of the Rimmon Mountaineering Club and the Cioch Club. Stand out routes from this period include West's *Nemesis*, Bob Dearman's *Convulsion*, Brian Moore's *Triton*, James Curtis's *Rubicon* and Bruce Andrew's *Basilisk*. All these routes were graded A3 and, given the equipment available, were extremely difficult and serious propositions.

By 1970 attitudes to free-climbing on limestone had changed. Al Evans and Keith Myhill showed the way with free ascents of *Sermon Wall* and *Ribcrusher Crack* (Evans) and *Ping*, *Ping-Pong* and *Knuckle Knocker* (Myhill). Their visionary approach was initially ignored however and it wasn't until 1975, with the arrival of Tom Proctor, that the ball really got rolling. Proctor initially stole a march with free ascents of *The Bellringer, Hemmingway's Horror, Vicar's Vertigo, Hairy Legs* and an almost free ascent (one aid-point) of the imposing *Behemoth*, a phenomenal effort made during a snowfall! However, competition was not far behind: Ron Fawcett and Pete Livesey, who had been previously working *Behemoth*, turned up only minutes behind Proctor and had to settle for a 'tidying up' the following week. By the end of 1976 over 50 routes had been added to the valley, some resulting from free ascents of old aid routes and others taking completely new lines. As well as Proctor and Fawcett, the main protagonists were Jim Cambell, Brian Cropper, Jim Reading, Con Carey and Pete O'Donovan. Although by no means the hardest new route, Chris Jackson's *Dragonflight* at Rubicon Wall was significant for showing that the seemingly blank rock here could be climbed free and hinted at the vast potential of the wall. Jackson also went on to highlight the possibilities of the loose Moat Buttress opposite with his ascents of the serious *Triton* and *Pirhana Wall*. On this occasion however, Jackson's example was not followed and the buttress remained neglected until the arrival of bolt protection.

Proctor's final significant contribution came in 1979, with his free ascent of *Rubicon*, one of the biggest limestone roofs to be free-climbed in Britain at the time. His cleaning of the route was described as somewhat overzealous but considering the fact that many of the holds Proctor left have subsequently dropped off, perhaps he can be forgiven! 1979 also saw Jim Moran and Geoff Milburn start their determined attempt to rid Central Buttress of its remaining aid points. After just a few months they opened up the buttress to free-climbing leaving *The Alien, War, Time Warp, Yankee Dollar*, and a direct start to *Behemoth*.

1981 saw standards rise further. Rubicon Wall was the perfect canvas for the wall-trained and technically brilliant Lee brothers, Dominic and Daniel. The previous year, Dominic had made a visionary attempt to add a free-climb to one of the most intimidating buttresses on Peak limestone – The Cornice. Using just one rest point he climbed what was later to become *Brachiation Dance* when Tim Freeman managed without in 1984. On Rubicon Wall, Daniel was responsible for *Bigger Splash, Jezebel* and the testing *White Bait*, while Dominic produced the then hardest move in the valley on *The Angler*. They were

Andy Pollitt. Photo: Richie Brooks.

Chris Jackson on The Creeper on Central Buttress (page 195).
Photo: John Atkinson.

not alone here however: Andy Barker found the frustrating *A Miller's Tale* while Fawcett also left his mark with *Honeymoon Blues, Jaws, and Pirhana*. Barker's regular climbing partner, Paul Mitchell, was incredibly prolific and was responsible for discovering and developing many buttresses throughout the dale. Across the valley from Rubicon Wall, Fawcett continued the development of Central Buttress adding *La Chute, Cool Hand Luke* and *White Fright*. Almost as hard was Dominic Lee's neighbouring *Leviathan*, while his brother Dan's *Agrippa's Knees* was the first route to tackle the impressive Vision Buttress and has probably yet to receive a second ascent. In 1982 Jerry Moffatt found himself *In Bulk* to leave one of the hardest routes in the Peak District at the time. All these climbs relied mainly on old and unreliable in-situ pegs or bolts and represent the highest standards of traditional climbing in Water-cum-Jolly to date with one exception, Malc Taylor's serious *Plectrum Maxilla Direct* climbed in 1991.

Things were about to change - slowly. Climbers were no longer happy to rely on 'old manky gear' and over the following years the hardest new routes increasingly utilised pegs and/or bolts to provide good protection. A significant portent was Fawcett's route on Vision Buttress in 1982 on which he placed 3 bolts and a peg. Originally given E6 7a, the route has now been rebolted and translated to F7c+ which places it alongside Moffatt's *Rooster Booster* at Raven Tor for the hardest sport route in the Peak District at the time.

For a while, the valley rested, but 1986 saw the start of a prolonged period of development which culminated in Water-cum-Jolly becoming home to some of the hardest sport routes in the Peak. On Rubicon Wall, Ben Moon extended Chris Gore's *Kudos* to produce *Hot Fun Closing*, the first sport route on the wall. Tony Ryan then stepped in and added *Caviar*, one of the hardest, most popular, F8a+'s in the Peak. As if this wasn't desperate enough, in 1987, a rapidly rising Moon climbed *Zeke the Freak* which at F8b was considered Britain's hardest route for a brief period. In 1995 Ruth Jenkins pushed forward the standard of women's climbing by redpointing *Zeke*, the first British female to a climb F8b.

The breaking of the dam in early 1988 provided light relief and much new rock when the whole of Moat Buttress became accessible. Little had been climbed here since Jackson's early forays, although Andy Pollitt had made a fine free ascent of *Excalibur* in 1986. Never one to miss an opportunity, Gary Gibson was first on the scene, but he was soon

Ruth Jenkins on Zeke the Freak at Rubicon (page 160). Photo: Jon Barton.

joined by a strong supporting cast including Chris Plant, Seb Grieve and Keith Sharples. *Moaterhead, Another Moatside Attraction, No Mud, No Thud, The Lady of the Lake* and *Moat Madness* being the best routes from this time.

Attention now shifted back to The Cornice. In 1986, Andy Pollitt had climbed *Empire Burlesque* at the 'easier' right-hand side of the buttress, but in 1989 he returned for a full frontal approach. His excellent *Rumble in the Jungle* (a free ascent of an old A4 aid route) was soon joined by a plethora of increasingly desperate, top quality sport routes up alarmingly steep territory. Few climbing venues have such a concentration of hard routes, nor such a collection of associated trivia. As Pollitt arrived to do '*Rumble*' he spotted visiting French superstar Jean-Baptiste Tribout 'walking' up 'his route'. Pollitt thrashed waist deep across the river to see Tribout sportingly grab a quick-draw below the finish. Ben Masterson's F8a, *Yorkshire 8b*, was a tongue in cheek wind-up of Yorkshire grading. *The Free Monster* reclimbed a short-lived route, The Tea Monster without its 'non-indigenous' hold. Robin Barker's *Albatrossity*, was a project of Andy Pollitt's which he had to abandon in order to grab a seat aboard the penultimate jet to Australia on which smoking was allowed! Simon Reed's own desperate direct on this was only added because Reed couldn't manage the 'easier' finish!

2001 was a relatively busy year for The Cornice. Keith Sharples added the excellent *The Auctioneer*, Steve McClure its hardest route; *Ape Index* and Reed the desperate *Monsterosity*. Other high-standard additions to the valley include Tony Coutts' desperates on Crunch Buttress from 1998/99, Andy Harris' *Barracuda* from 2007 and Rupert Davies' *Three Spheres* from 2007.

However, the hardest route in Water-cum-Jolly lies not on The Cornice but on Rubicon Wall. After a year of attempts John Welford, in 1995, succeeded on *The Bastard*, a free ascent of an aid route called *Free that you Bastards!*. Originally given F8c, it is now considered F8c+, and stands , with only one repeat from Steve McClure in 2001, as the hardest climb in the dale.

But the story doesn't end there. The Dale lay relatively quiet with the odd new route here ands there until in 2014, Gary Gibson took up the mantel of tidying up Central Buttress. Whilst undertaking this task he also managed to add a number of new routes of which *Une Jour Parfait, La Brute* and *C'est Plastique* are the best. The crag is now once again a major destination. Similarly, Kristian Clemmow's rejuvenation of Moat Buttress in 2013 has turned this forgotten and dusty crag into one of the valley's finest venues for climbers in the F7s. The future looks Jolly.

Graham Hoey

Below left: Ben Moon on Zeke the Freak from the front cover of On The Edge number 1. Photo: Richie Brooks.
Below Right: Ruth Jenkins. Photo: Jon Barton.

Lammergeyer Buttress

Trad: 8 (E5) **Sport:** 5 (F7a to F7b)
Aspect: South-west **Sunshine:** Evening **Season:** Spring to autumn
Conditions: Shady, quiet, neglected **Approach:** 12 minutes
Best for: Somebody who likes cleaning up old routes

These once clean walls provided a number of good, semi-sport climbs but they have since fallen into disrepair. All of the routes need re-cleaning and re-equipping. If done, it would once more provide a superb little venue. It lies 350m upstream from Rubicon Wall (**see map on page 130**).

The first route begins at the very far left-hand end of the buttress hidden under the ivy. **Zob**, E2 6a (1982), ascends the wall and overhang trending rightwards; **Part-Time Hobby**, E2 5b (1986), climbs the wall just to the right of the arête; **Aquarian Warriors**, E5 6b (1986), starts 5m to the right and climbs past a bolt and thread to finish round the roof; **On the Third Day**, E5 6b (1989), moves right from the break to finish as for *Mr Puniverse*.

1 The Lammergeyer Twins E5 6b 1983
14m A little gem when clean. Climb into the scoop and move out right to a 'peg'. Finish directly up the flake above with a certain amount of caution.

2 As Summers Die E4 6b 1989
11m Climb the wall by a series of gymnastic moves. Two bolts and two pegs protect.

3 One Way Reflection E5 6b 1986
14m Climb over the bulge and up the wall (bolt) making a long reach up right and then back left to finish via a short groove, threads for retreat.

4 Final Apocalypse E5 6a 1987
14m Gain an undercut and move leftwards to reach a flat hold from where better holds lead to the break. Follow this leftwards to a sapling which aids the finish. Two bolts and a thread en-route.

5 Mr Puniverse E5 6b 1989
12m From the second peg on *Myth...*, move up and left past a bolt and attack the bulge (peg) to reach a belay.

6 The Myth of Masculinity E5 6b 1985
14m The powerful flake gives a strenuous test with just sufficient in-situ protection.

Six metres to the right is another flake in the back of the alcove.

7   The Ego has Landed F7b   1989
12m   The bulging wall has two bolts and a peg before the final peg of *Myth...* is reached.

**8   The Amnicolist Spies on the
       Black Submarine** E4 6b   1985
13m   Hard moves up the flake lead to an easier finale out left.
a Periscope Voyeur, F6a (1985), gives a right-hand exit.

9   Living with a Porcupine F7a   1988
11m   Climb the scoop on disappointing holds to the second of two pegs. Pull leftwards to a thread and peg at the break and exit over the left-hand side of the overhang.

10   Tree Surgeon F7a+   1987
12m   Climb the wall and, after 3m, move left and up to a bolt. Continue up the wall to a break and exit rightwards.

11   Once Upon a Time E5 6b   1986
14m   The direct version of *Tree Surgeon* with a hard sequence of moves past a couple of bolts onto a pillar with a peg at its top. Finish on better holds.

12   The Fall F7a+ ★   1989
11m   Climb the wall past a peg to reach a bolt. Intricate and fingery moves enable the break to be reached, thread and peg. Pull over the bulge leftwards to a belay.

13   Vindicator F7b ★   1987
11m   The bulging wall via an obvious undercut and two bolts leads to the break. Pull directly over the roof to reach good finishing holds.

There is an old bolted project to the right again.

Thirty metres on, at the far right-hand end, is a white, ivy-covered, wall sporting a flake. **White Line Fever**, E2 5b (1986), climbs a short groove 3m left of the flake bearing left past a bulge into a V-groove above and **Paradox**, E3 5c (1986), climbs the flake trending rightwards above via a ledge and overhang adorned with a peg. Twenty five metres down the dale, **The Rabbit**, VS 5a (1970s), is a short route taking the wall next to the path and ending at a tree.

Ivy Buttress

A further 180m down the dale and 70m upstream from Rubicon Wall is this ivy-covered buttress which is again in need of an overhaul. It is easily identified by a rockfall at its centre.

Brief Scramble, E1 5a (1984), climbs the wall at the left-hand side of the buttress just left of some hanging corners; **A Trail of Destruction**, E4 6b (1985), climbs the left-hand of two bottomless corners; **Pig Pen Comes Clean**, E5 6c (1986), moves right from the previous route to tackle a bulge; **Clean Cut**, E4 6b (1985), takes the right-hand of two hanging corners; **Money for Nothing**, E3 6b (1985), climbs the bulge right of the tree finishing directly and **Jungle Ape**, E1 5b (1984), climbs a leftward slanting corner gained direct.

Rubicon Wall

Sport: 26 (F6b+ to F8c+)   **Bouldering:** 30 (Font 5 to Font 8B)   **Trad:** 29 (E2 to E7)
Aspect: South   **Sunshine**: From afternoon until evening   **Season:** Spring to autumn
Conditions: Sunny, quick drying, can be hot, showerproof, wet in winter, popular, polished
Best for: Hard sport (F7a to F8a+), trad (E5) and bouldering (Font 5 to 8A)   **Approach:** 5 minutes

This gleaming white wall above the millpond has been the subject of many climbers' attentions over the years. It is one of the 'Meccas' of Peak District climbing containing some valued testpieces amongst its routes and boulder problems.

The rock is generally good quality limestone low down but the upper walls do have a tendency to shed the occasional hold. Climbing here typically involves bearing down on small crimps up vertical or overhanging walls where good footwork on the inevitably polished holds is a necessity. Weaklings will have little success here, for Rubicon is a place where even the strongest come to get stronger. At times, especially in the heat, it can all feel just a little too desperate and success can prove to be frustratingly elusive. On these occasions it's best to just sit down and take in the sheer beauty of the setting: the swans and other wildfowl gracing the millpond and the rippled reflections dancing on the underside of Rubicon Roof. Suitably relaxed the moves will now flow more easily and the place will feel like heaven.

Please be courteous and respect all the other users of the path below the crag.

The climbing
Hard, fingery and powerful sport climbs, trad climbs and boulder problems. The sport climbs are better in the higher grades and many of them are historical landmarks of their era. Routes such as *Rubicon, Let The Tribe Increase, Hot Fun Closing, Caviar, Zeke the Freak* and *The Bastard*

were all pretty much state of the art for their time. They are still coveted redpoints.

The trad climbs, similarly, were big deals for their day. They remain stiff and typically bold and are rarely climbed. Any in-situ protection on these routes is often very old and although at first sight the chance of natural placements appears unlikely there are the occasional hidden slots which take small wires and cams. They are brilliant routes all the same, and very memorable.

The bouldering is powerful fingery cranking and success on a problem here is worth boasting about. Lots of eliminates are possible. Not generally very highball although the landing is hard.

Conditions and Aspect
A very sheltered, sunny venue. It faces south and the sun comes on from afternoon till late evening. Usually wet in winter and can get very hot in the summer sun. Fairly showerproof. Some seepage patches can remain in the alcoves for some time. The base, especially around Rubicon Roof, can get very boggy or even flooded in wet weather.

Parking and Approach
See map on page 130. Park at Cressbrook Mill. Follow the footpath and turn right to meet the crag.

1 Alimony F7b+ ★ 1994

7m A short steep desperate, climbing left of the crack over the bulges onto a ledge. The bulges above provide a few blind slaps and a painful finger lock. The bolted bulge to the right is a F7c project.

2 Honeymoon Blues E5 6b ★★ 1981

11m A classic tale of what (not) to do on your Honeymoon! Ron and Gill chose climbing. Take the bulges to the right via a scalloped lower wall and an infuriating bulge, thread. From the ledge, step left (peg) and pull rightwards over the bulges to a tree belay.

3 Salar F8a ★ 1992

10m A bouldery route, friendly for the grade for the tall. Follow the vague groove to a break. Move left and pass the bulge above. Judging by the original grade and bolt placement, one must assume that the first ascensionist levitated directly past the last bolt directly to the ledge at F8a+. The bulge can be avoided by traversing right from the first bolt into *Lapin*: **Dapper Slapper**, E3 6b (1984).

4 Slapin F7c 2011

10m Follow *Salar* to the break then slap in to the holds leading out right over the bulge.

5 Slapdasher F7a 2011

10m Climbs the thin wall to the right.

a Lapin, E3 5c (1970s), climbs the broken flake to the right and retreats from a tree stump.

6 Welsh Rarebit F6c 2012

10m The wall, keeping out of the flake for a tricky finish.

b The Blue-Eyed Myxamatoid, E3 5c (1985), climbs the non-descript wall right again.

7 The Brer Faced Cheek of It F6a 2013

10m The wall just to the right.

Returning to the water's edge, and starting a few metres right of the ivy-covered gully is:

8 Hare E3 5c 1970s

12m A wandering line past two overlaps, the first taken on the right and the second direct to finish up a loose corner. Some ivy will have to be cleaned off before an ascent can be made.

9 Changing Fortunes E4 6b 1988

12m A better challenge taking the wall just to the right past a solitary peg to finish via a flaky overhang above a ledge.

10 Chairs Missing E3 6b ★ 1981

12m Classic bouldering moves over the lower bulge to the right (peg) moving right to the ledge and a finish as for the previous route.

11 A Tall Story E5 6c ★ 1983

12m An absolutely desperate climb requiring a monster reach over the bulge 5m to the left of the flake of *Dragonflight*. A few easier moves above lead to the ledge and finish.

12 Dragonflight E3 5c ★★ 1976

13m The classic mid-grade Rubicon testpiece is a quick and rousing little thing. Climb the flake to get stood in the break. Step up and commit to the delicate slab (harder for the short) to reach easier ground and the ledge. Finish via the flaky bulge on the left.

13 Dragonflight Traverse Font 6B

A great, long slabby traverse with a few tricky sections. A nice way to enjoy the scene. Start just right of Dragonflight and finish on ledges on the left of the wall.

14 Jezebel E5 6a ★★ 1981

13m A sumptuous pitch requiring very strong fingers. The thin wall leads past a bolt slightly leftwards to a thin break. Traverse this rightwards to a tiny flake and follow it to a ledge. Finish up the wall above past two pegs.

15 Kingfisher E5 6c ★★ 1985

13m Very much the mantra of the crag, giving a full-on fingery nightmare. Having pre-clipped the bolt on Jezebel, climb the wall to its right to a pair of pegs. An outrageous move leftwards gains the finish of *Jezebel*.

16 Jaws E5 6b ★★ 1981

13m Beautiful wall-climbing but beware of sharks. The wall behind the tree to the right leads to a peg. Gaining a standing position provides the crux whilst the moves to gain the ledge are best done quickly. Finish via an unsound corner.

To the right lies the central alcove of the wall, the scene of some of its most fingery testpieces. On its left edge lies one of the cliff's more serious propositions.

17 Plectrum Maxilla Direct E7 6c ★ 1986/1991
13m Rubicon's hardest trad lead. Climb the wall to gain a conspicuously protruding peg in the bulging wall. Continue directly with some urgency but slightly less difficulty. From the ledge finish up the upper wall of *Jaws*.

18 Barracuda F8b 2008
14m A desperate sequence of moves diagonally rightwards across the wall. Painful holds heighten its difficulty.

19 Caviar F8a+ ★★ 1986
12m A big addition from the early days of Peak sport climbing, this intense sequence still doesn't get any easier. Boulder up the scoop to gain small holds by the second bolt (crux) and swing left and back right to gain the break. Pull over the bulge to complete the session. The start is sometimes bouldered at Font 7B.

20 Beluga F8a+ ★ 2008
12m After the first few moves of *Caviar*, tackle the fierce wall to its right.

21 Eugenics F8b+ 1993
12m A desperate sequence up the wall to the right, unrepeated since the loss of a hold. The grade is an estimation.

22 Let the Tribe Increase F8a ★ 1986
12m The first free route to breach this wall and an impressive achievement for its time. Short, hard and mean and a notch harder since the loss of a hold.

23 The Dangerous Brothers F8a 1987
10m The desperate little wall to the right measures up to the grade. **Dangerous Tribes**, F8a (2010), is the obvious link.

24 Too Old to be Bold F7c 1987
12m Another desperate though polished exercise up the wall. Short and powerful. **Sheer Travesty**, F7c+ (1989), for some reason, links the top of this with *Caviar*.

25 Coot E4 6a ★ 1981
15m Climb the undercut flakes just right of the tree with a certain degree of trepidation to gain a hollow jug. Fighting off the brambles above proves difficult for the break to be gained. Step right and either lower off or climb the top wall direct.

Kudos Bouldering

26 Piranha E6 6b ★★ 1981

15m A super route if one gets past the scary unprotected crux an uncomfortable distance above the ground. Climb the fingery wall past a short sharp flake to reach the break. Continue slightly leftwards via a better flake to a large ledge. Finish up *Coot* or lower off from a fixed belay.

27 Cora E6 6c 1986

15m The wall to the right is a desperate enigma. Things ease at the break.

28 White Bait E5 6c ★★ 1981

15m The original route of this section has a low crux but is quite sustained. Start with a desperate sequence of moves from the drill holes and a small flake to gain a break (peg). The bulge above is passed first rightwards then back left to a ledge. Finish leftwards, passing more pegs. **White Bait Start** is Font 7A.

To the right is a prominent hole in the wall at 6m.

29 Flaked Out Shake Out E4 6c 1987

15m Climb the wall to the left of this via an obvious flake, (thread) to a peg in the break. Move left and join *White Bait* to finish.

30 Pirhana Traverse Font 7A

Move left from the start of *A Miller's Tale* to holds at the start of *Coot*.

31 A Miller's Tale E5 6b ★★ 1981

15m A classic tale which has begun to shows its age. Boulder up to the hole and extend around the bulge above (peg). Follow the wall above, protected by fiddly wires and cams, with a spicy sequence to gain the ledge. From here, finish direct. Hard.

32 Hot Fun Closing F8a ★★ 1986

10m One of the many breakthrough routes on this wall. Extend *Kudos* (see next page) up the wall above.

33 An Even Bigger Tail F7b+ 1985

10m Extend the classic boulder problem (*A Bigger Tail* - see next page) up the wall. **Photo opposite.**

Water Bailiff, HVS 4c (1976), gains the break just to the right before traversing left for 5m to follow a shallow flake to the top and **Freewheeler**, HVS 4c (1976), climbs the wall and steep face 7m right again behind the ivy.

Emily Huzzard on An Even Bigger Tail, F7b+ (opposite page). Photo: Paul Evans.

Kudos Bouldering

The pride of Rubicon bouldering lies on the steep, barrel-shaped overhang to the right of the start to *A Miller's Tale*. There are many eliminates to be had but the main lines are solid natural lines of the highest historical pedigree. Fingery.

1   Miller's Tale Start Font 6B
The easiest of the classics on this wall. Font 6C from a sit.

2   Kudos Font 7B
Start from jugs and use sidepulls to gain flakes up and left. There's a 'Hard Way' and an 'Easy Way'. Both are the same grade. **Photo opposite**. A sit start is Font 7B+.

3   Kudos Traverse Font 7B
From the *Kudos* starting jug, pull up and right to the starting jug of *A Bigger Tail*. Follow this then move right to the finishing hold of *The Press*.

4   A Bigger Tail Font 7A+
Jump, or stretch, for a high edge then move right and up on edges to finish on a jug.

5   A Bigger Belly Font 8B
The desperate sit start to *A Bigger Tail* starting with a poor crimp for the right hand and a tiny dish for the left.

6   The Pinch Font 7B+
Start low on poor slopers and slap for the sidepull jug up and left.

7   A Bigger Splash Direct Font 7B
Start standing with a small right hand layaway and left on an undercut. Pull on and slap to and match the jug. **The Kneeling Start** goes from holds in the break below: Font 7B+.

8   Tsunami Font 8A
A sit start to 7, starting down and left with both hands in the slanting pocket.

9   Low Right Start Font 7C
Another sit start to 7, this time from the slots under *A Bigger Splash*.

10   The Press Font 7B+
Start standing with hands on two high opposing gastons (the left-hand one being the sidepull on *A Bigger Splash Direct*). Pull up, lock for a crimp then slap for the jug on *ABSD*. A **Kneeling Start**, from the rail, is Font 7C+.

11   Low Left Start Font 8A
A tough sitter comes in from the slanting pocket as for *Tsunami* and swings in to *Press Kneeling Start*.

12   Low Right Start Font 7C+
Start *The Press* from the slots under *A Bigger Spalsh*.

13   A Bigger Splash Font 7A+
Start from jugs then follow crimps and left-hand sidepulls up then left, aiming for the tiny groove below the high break.

14   A Bigger Prize Font 6C
The bulging wall from a sit start.

Mark Leach on Kudos, Font 7B (opposite page), resplendent in the height of 1980s fashion. Photo Richie Brooks.

Rubicon Roof Area

The first rock reached from the approach is characterised by the umbrella roof on the right. The first two routes are now ruined by ivy growth: **a Professor Kirk**, E5 6b (1983), takes the wall up to the roof, peg. Go left and over the roof past a flake and peg to the top. **b Maureen**, E4 6a (1983), went right and over the same roof.

34 Last but not Least F6c+   2010
12m A cleaned pathway through the ivy gives this route.

35 Sperm Worm E5 6a   1983
15m Climb up just to the right of a clump of ivy to a large ledge, pegs in the break above. Continue up the faint flake above to a break (peg) and finish rightwards across the overlap with a move back left to a tree.

36 Dumb Animal E5 6a ★   1988
16m From the ledge on *Sperm Worm*, trend rightwards on a series of layaways to reach a break. Continue past another break, steeping right to a difficult finish. Three pegs.

37 The Pinch Test F7c+   2009
12m The very bouldery wall, starting up the ledgy wall.

38 The Angler E5 6c ★   1981
15m From the large ledge, move up to a blanker section where desperate moves (two pegs), gain a flake seemingly an impossible distance away. From the top of this (thread and pegs) move left and finish direct past another thread.

39 The Sissy F8a ★   1989
15m The desperate wall, well suited to small fingers. Climb direct then swing right up to a tiny corner high on the wall. **Photo on page 128. c The Wimp**, F7c (2010), connects *The Sissy* to *The Angler* from the fourth bolt.

40 Zeke the Freak F8b ★★   1987
15m An amazing achievement for its day and a milestone in the development of Rubicon Wall. Climb the leaning wall with the difficulties centred on the mid-height bulge, where a couple of options provide success. Finish direct. **Photo on page 148.**

41 The Bastard F8c+ ★★   1980s/1995
15m One repeat in twenty years? The overhanging wall to the left of the cave is still a state-of-the-art examination in nasty crimps.

Traverses Area
Bouldering

42 No Jug, No Thug E5 6b ★   1983
10m An exposed route traversing the breaks. From the *Rubicon* belay, follow the break leftwards past a peg (and a bolt) for 4m to a flake, up which the route finishes.

43 Cruising the Seven Seas F7c ★   1989
16m Continues the traverse along the break from *No Jug, No Thug* with more difficulties leaving *The Sissy* and past *The Angler*. Once you reach the ivy, you now have the pleasure of having to reverse the experience.

44 Totally Awesome F7b ★   1991
15m At last something easier but it still packs a punch.

45 Rubicon F7a ★★   1960/1976/1979
15m The old classic of the crag gives an exhilerating ride through obscene steepness on (mainly) big polished jugs. **Photo on page 163.**

46 Zeitgeist F7b   1991
15m The roof to the right of *Rubicon* gaining it from the first bolt on that route and rejoining it just before the lip.

47 The Bomb is Coming E5 6b   1983
15m The initial bulge 5m to the right of *Rubicon* leads to a ledge. The overhanging scoop above is tackled head on for the prow above to be negotiated rightwards. A peg and a bolt protect the upper section.

Toenail Pie, E3 5b (1975), trends rightwards from the start of *The Bomb...* via an overhanging groove. **Debris**, E4 5c (1979), starts 3m to the right, moves leftwards to a thread and tackles the overhanging wall above via a shallow groove. **Small but Perfectly Formed**, F7a+ (2010), is the overhanging prow to the right again and underneath the ivy fronds reaching a jug above the 2nd bolt for the grade (F6c+ if you don't) whilst **Skippy the Bush Kangaroo Weird**, E3 6c (1983), is a short and desperate thin crack above a shelf just right again.

There are two other traverses on the wall: **Doing the Dirty**, E4 5c (1983), follows the break leftwards from *Water Bailiff* to finish up *Piranha* and **Crab Walk**, E2 5b (1967/1982), traverses leftwards from the large bedding plane on *Water Bailiff* to finish up *Lapin*.

Traverses Area Bouldering

The area under Rubicon Roof is good for a few easier problems and is often used as a warm up for the routes or harder bouldering. Also good for stamina traversing and link-ups. Very sheltered from the rain. Extremely polished and a bit rattly. In wet weather the ground underneath can become a suppurating bog.

1 Warm-Up Traverse Font 5
Traverse the juggy ledge from the far left as far as good holds below the sign.

2 Bulge Font 6A

3 Toenail Pie Font 5
The wall to the left of the sign.

4 Debris Groove Font 6A
The steep wall right of the sign.

5 Crimps and Pockets Font 6B+
The right side of the groove.

6 Peg's Path Font 6B
The left-hand line up the steep wall. Crimpy.

7 Font 6B
The right-hand line on the steep wall.

8 Font 5+
A short, steep couple of pulls to gain the right end of the shelf/ledge thing.

9 Flakes and Pockets Font 5+
Trend leftwards to the same finish as the previous problem. Photo opposite.

10 Top Traverse Font 5+
The easisest traverse of the three-level traverses, and a good continuation to the *Warm-Up Traverse*.

11 Middle Traverse Font 6A+

12 Low Traverse Font 6B+
The hardest of the three-level traverses, a crouchy classic on slots and crimps.

A link-up, going left along the *Low Traverse*, right along the *Middle Traverse* then left again along the *High Traverse*, to finish up *Debris Groove*, is Font 7B.

13 Porthole Traverse Font 7A
Start from the obvious hole and traverse left below the shelf. Using the shelf itself makes it slightly easier.

Alex Barber on Rubicon, F7a (page 161). Photo Paul Evans.

Waterfall Crag

This is the small steep crag on the left just after crossing the bridge over the weir. All the in-situ gear will need checking out as these routes have seen few ascents.

In The Flesh, E3 6a (1985), is 9m left of the bridge past three threads. Trend left after a hole. **Rapture**, E5 6c (1985), starts just right of the roof, 11m left of *In The Flesh*. Climb direct, swing left to a good hold, then up to another good hold. Move right to the roof and pull round to a ledge and short wall. **An Eagle Does Not Catch Flies**, E4 6a (1985), is the line of four pegs 15m left of the bridge. **No Fool Like An Old Fool**, E5 6b (1985), starts just left of *An Eagle*... Move right past two pegs to a short shallow groove. Climb this and exit right past a peg.

Black Buttress

This is the first buttress when walking upstream. It is an esoteric wall in a pleasant waterside setting. Steep wall climbs, with the odd loose bit. Fairly quick drying. Northwest facing; gets the evening sun.

Parking and Approach: See map on page 130. Follow the Cressbrook Mill approach to crags on the south bank. Cross the weir, follow the steps up and at the top, by a sign, turn right and contour along the slope on a small track. After 100m a vague path runs down to the water. Take this then turn left along the water's edge to find the crag. Ten minutes.

Confidence, HVS 5c (1981), is the leaning flake on the left of the buttress and **There is No Zen**, E3 6a (1983), the short technical wall 3m to its right.

1 Castration E2 6b 1983
14m The right-facing corner.

2 Millennium Doom F6c+ 1998
12m The wall and overlap with a tough finish.

3 Premature Arthritic Enjoys Dawn Chorus
E4 6c ★ 1981
15m The wall just left of a scoop (poor peg) to the overhang. Pass this (peg) to a short hanging corner.

4 Ichor E3 5c 1983
15m Climb just to the left of the scoop and traverse back right into it, direct is 6b. From the top of the scoop (peg) climb the wall and overhang finishing via a groove.

5 Ripples E1 5b 1981
25m Climb the flake crack to the right and move left to where a groove bisects the bulge. Follow this moving left again to a final corner/groove. Poor rock.

Moat Buttress Area

Sport: 4I (F6b to F8b)   **Trad:** 9 (E2 to E6)
Aspect: North-west   **Sunshine:** Evening   **Season:** Spring to autumn
Conditions: Quick drying, shady, not much seepage, some rainproof climbing, quiet, secluded
Best for: Fingery sport climbing, F7a to F8a   **Approach:** 15 minutes

Moat Buttress Area comprises Moat Buttress, Majorca Buttress and Crunch Buttress, forming a string of walls that hang over the mill pond. It has a chequered history. In 1988 the dam below Rubicon Wall broke and before its repair all hell broke loose from the climbing fraternity. The resulting frenzied activity saw routes going up everywhere with one activist being so keen to find a quick way down he fell from the top.

The crags have had a significant tidy up in recent years. Routes have been straightened out and regeared, new routes have been added and with a proper knowledge of what goes where and at what grade, the crag is now a great option for climbers looking for mid-grade clip-ups.

The Climbing
Mostly sport, with some trad. Better in the higher grades. Vertical or slightly overhanging climbs. Very fingery. Lots of the routes on the right have had a recent makeover.

Conditions and Aspect
The cliff dries fairly quickly after rain. The central section of the cliff does suffer from seepage, the right-hand side doesn't. Facing north-west it receives only evening sunshine and is sheltered. Some of the routes around Shearwater Buttress are flooded at the base and access to routes 3 (*Out of the Shadows*) to 10 (*Excalibur*) can vary a lot. Overall quite a dry crag with little seepage or humidity.

Parking and Approach
See map on page 130. Follow the Cressbrook Mill / South Bank approach. Cross the weir, and go up the steps and turn right to contour along the slope on a small track then take one of the following approaches:
For the Sheerwater Area, Routes 1 to 8: Follow the track rightwards from the steps for 100m then take a vaguer path downhill to the river. Follow it under Black Buttress to a high tide point at the end of the buttress.
For the rest of the crag: Continue along the upper track for 500m, cross a fence and drop down onto the Monsal Trail just as it exits the tunnel. Drop down the slope on the right and follow some indistinct paths down and right under Crunch Buttress and down to the river and to Excalibur Buttress.

Sheerwater   Excalibur   Moatorhead

tidal area

Sheerwater Area: The far left-hand side of the crag is marked by a collapsed tree. Here the water level varies but when it is at its usual low summer level the first five routes can just about be reached on foot.

1   Sheerwater E2 4c, 5b ★   1976
30m   An ingenious route, finding a way onto the face by an inventive and superb first pitch.
1. 15m   Traverse rightwards across the scalloped wall until a series of steeper moves lead to a ledge and peg belay.
2. 15m   Continue up to the bulge where good holds give access to a ledge above. Pull over the next roof to a fine groove finale. **Sheer Indulgence**, E2 5b (1988), climbs the wall 2m to the right finishing via a slight bulge.

2   Nude Motorcycle Girl F7a   1991
15m   The leftmost of the bolted lines provides a tasty morsel, especially in its upper half.

3   Out of the Shadows F7a+ ★   1988
15m   A harder prospect with difficult moves over the capping overhang. If the tide is high the upper section can be reached from the previous route.

4   Another Moatside Attraction F7a+ ★   1988
15m   Good. Climb the bolted line 5m from the water's edge via a difficult starting sequence until a good resting place is reached. The bulge and short wall on the left lead to a tree belay.

5   Moat Madness F7a+ ★   1988
20m   The rightmost bolt line that can just about be reached on foot. Start with a taxing series of blind moves. Step back left and pull over the final bulges on good holds.

The next three routes, due to the current state of the lake, can only be reached by dinghy, wading or abseil.

6   Sheer Power F7a+   1988
12m   Climb direct to the stance on *Sheerwater*.

7   The Lady of the Lake F7a ★★   1988
22m   A fascinating route up the impressive flake, enhanced considerably by the effort required to access it.

8   D.T.'s Route E5 6b ★   1988
22m   Use the start of *The Lady of the Lake* to gain and climb the crack to the right.

Emily Huzzard on Moat People, F7b+ (page 169). Photo: Paul Evans.

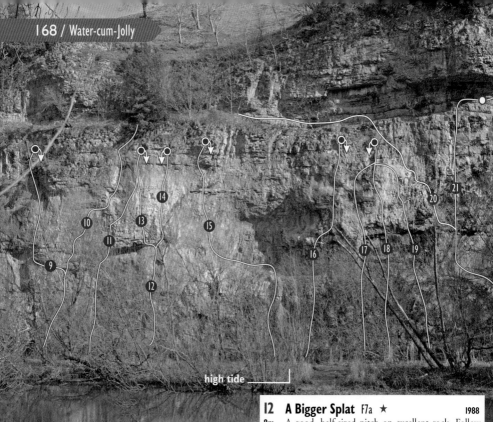

high tide

Excalibur Wall: If you plan to climb here, the water levels at Rubicon will give a good indication of what you can get on: when the path under *Rubicon* is dry it is possible to get to the start of *Excalibur* on foot; when the path is flooded it is still possible to get to *Moatorhead*.

9 Drawbridge Down When the Levee Breaks
F7c ★ 1988
22m The shallow groove at the left side of the buttress gives a tough pitch with sustained moves and a fingery crux section. Bring a good pair of wellies to get to the start.

10 Excalibur E6 6b ★★ 1967/1986
22m Talked about and revered for a number of years before its free ascent, when freed this route gave the best route on the buttress. The impressive flake system gives a superb and powerful pitch with a hint of yesteryear about it. It is mostly protected by pegs although some wires are needed. With these in place it is F7b+.

11 No Mud, No Thud F7b+ ★★ 1988
20m A hidden gem. The groove line to the right of *Excalibur* is very much its sport-climbing equivalent. Sustained, but with a very powerful crux passing the bulge.

12 A Bigger Splat F7a ★ 1988
8m A good, half-sized pitch on excellent rock. Follow the enticing flake-cum-groove line to halfway up the wall. Make sure to finish stood on the half-height ledge on the right for the tick. Reverse the traverse and descend from the twin bolts in the groove.

13 A Bigger Thud F7c ★ 2012
20m From the top of the groove of *A Bigger Splat*, shuffle left onto a narrow ledge and tackle the wall above.

14 Let the Tripe Increase F7c ★★ 1988
20m The logical extension of *A Bigger Splat* gives a great route with a very bouldery crux bulge. From the top of the groove, climb over the bulge (hard) and continue up the wall above. **Photo on page 170.**

15 All Hands to the Pump! F7c+ 2012
20m Solo onto the terrace via the easy crack on the right and start from the left-hand end of the terrace. Powerful climbing leads to a slight rest below the bulge. More tricky stuff leads to a jug and belay.

An old aid-route, **Digit of Derision**, A2 (1970/1986), took the old bolt line from the ledge. **Intercity Nova**, E4 6c (1988), is a short desperate route up the wall to the right.

Moatorhead Wall: The four routes to the right have had a makeover and have somewhat altered in grade and direction.

16   Moatorhead F7b+ ★   1988
18m A good, tough pitch via a shallow niche at three-quarters height. Be sure to milk that no-hands rest!

17   Coming up for Air F7c   1999
18m Far more complex in execution than the previous route but somewhat compromises the next line to its right in its central section. Harder and possibly unrepeated since hold loss.

18   Moat People F7b+ ★★   1988
18m A fine climb which steadily increases in difficulty the higher you go. Harder since hold loss. **Photo on page 167.**

19   Afloat in the Moat F6c+ ★★   1988
18m The final route of the quartet gives a quality route. Climb the shallow groove, steep breaks and delicate slab.

20   Piranha Wall E2 5c   1965/1976
20m Climb the wall from the left-hand end of the grassy ledge into the base of a corner. Move up onto the wall above and then take a leftwards line across the face to reach a tree belay on the terrace. From the belay, **Jaws II**, E4 6b (1966/1984), climbs the overhang and cracked wall to the left.

21   Triton E3 5c, 5a   1976
1. 27m From the top of the corner on *Piranha Wall*, move right and up a shallow groove exiting right to the ledge.

2. 9m Traverse across the ledge to gain and finish up the hanging groove on the right.

22   Two Sheep to Leicester F7a+ ★   1991
15m From the ledge, climb the hollow bulge moving left-wards onto a flake and thence a fine white wall above.

23   Searching for the Yeti F7b+ ★   1991
15m Break out right from the previous route to climb the steep arête. Harder since hold loss.

24   Moat Wall E5 6c   1965/1989
10m A desperate sequence over the bulge leads into the easier groove. Some very old in-situ gear helps protect.

25   Moat Race F6c+   1988
9m A short intense little sequence up the wall.

26   Moat Puddings E4 6a   1988
8m A poor little route over the roof to the right that was once protected by a single bolt, which fell out!

27   Castle Pudding E3 6a   1985
8m The final line on the wall via a short hanging corner just to the left of a tree abutting the cliff has 3 pegs in it.

28   Flying Dutchman F7c+ ★   1966/1988/1999
70m A right-to-left traverse of the cliff from just to the right of *Triton* along the horizontal break to reverse the final pitch of *Sheerwater*. A mixture of new bolts and old tat protects.

Ben Masterson on Let The Tripe Increase, F7c (page 170). Photo: Paul Evans.

Majorca Buttress

This buttress is immediately upstream from Moat Buttress, and only a short distance across the scree slope. It is passed under on the approach to Moat Buttress. The buttress has recently been given a makeover with some of the old trad routes being bolted as well as some new sport routes being added.

On the left-hand side of the buttress are: **Dirty Little Sheila**, 13m VS 4b, a short steep wall and scoop finishing via the cracked wall behind and **Wellington Route**, 13m VD, the corner some 15m to the right. The next route begins from a small alcove at the left-hand end of the face.

29 **You got no Reason** F7a   2014
9m A difficult and hollow bulge leads to an easier finish.

30 **Rhyme Crime** F7a+   1988/2014
13m Pull through the bulge above the alcove and continue up the short wall trending rightwards at the top.

31 **You got Rhyme** F6c ★   2014
9m Good climbing with a fingery start and good climbing above.

32 **Rhyme and Reason** F6c ★   1988/2014
13m Gain the shallow groove from the right and climb it moving right at the top onto the face leading to a tree.

33 **Reserve Judgement** F6c+   1988/2014
13m Climb directly before moving leftwards at the top.

34 **Happy Days** F6c+   1988/2014
12m The obvious undercut is gained via the wall below. Better holds above lead to a yew tree belay.

35 **Oh Dear!** F6c+ ★   1988/2014
12m The best line on the buttress takes a direct line to the yew tree via a series of flakes and corners and a steep exit.

36 **Four Men Tour** F6c   2014
9m A tough little start is rewarded with excellent holds above.

37 **Val de Mossa** F6c+   2014
9m Another tough start to a smart little wall.

38 **Blanca Expression** F7a   2014
9m The start is mean, the remainder barely less so.

39 **The Majorca Alternative** F7a   1988
9m The wall 4m left of a tree brushing up against the rock. A series of undercuts lead up the wall to a bolt belay.

40 **Costa del Jolly** F7a   2011
9m Just left of the tree.

41 **Wish you Were Here** F6b   2011
9m Just right of the tree.

Crunch Buttress

The imposing beak of Crunch Buttress has a series of very intense sport routes on excellent, compact limestone.

42 Do I? F6b+ 2014
10m The prominent flake with a butch exit.

43 Mission Impossible F8a+ ★ 1998
10m The leftmost line of the wall gives a pure test of finger-strength and endurance. A horrendously reachy lock-off to an awkward layaway provides the main difficulties.

44 Karma Killer F8b ★ 1999
10m Reach a poor mono off a poor undercut. Horribly difficult. **Photo opposite.**

The next 3 routes have a nasty habit of merging into one another and it is hard to determine which one is the parasite.

45 Agent Provocateur F8a+ ★★ 1998
10m Perhaps the best route here up the right-hand side of the nose of the streaked wall. Fingery bouldering leads to the break. Move left and make demanding moves to better holds.

46 Perfecto F7c+ ★ 1997
10m Although marginally easier, the line to the right allows an enormous rest in the break.

47 Trainer Tamer F7b+ 1997
9m A problematic wall gains a groove leading to the ledge.

48 Breakbeat F8a ★ 1998
17m A rather strange concoction traversing the face from right to left, beginning via *Trainer Tamer* and following the break to finish via *Mission Impossible*.

49 One on One F7a+ 1990
8m The final route of the group on the right-hand side of the wall. One bolt and a peg but no lower-off!

50 Under Western Eyes E4 6b 1962/1981
16m From just to the right, climb the bouldery wall (peg) via a shallow scoop to a ledge. Finish via the groove and overhang above.

From the ledge above the sport routes are: **Alligator Crawl**, A2 (1969), takes a thin wiggly crack in the roof and **The Crunch**, A3 (1967), which tackles the roof at its widest point.

Rupert Davies on Karma Killer, F8b (opposite page). Photo: Andy Newton.

Swamp Wall

A neglected and grotty series of buttresses with some abandoned trad climbs and a cleaner wall with three sport routes.

The Climbing: Unremarkable vertical sport climbs.
Conditions and Aspect: North facing. Very shady.
Parking and Approach: The routes are passed on the approach to the Cornice. Follow that approach to the Monsal Trail. Drop down before it re-enters the tunnel and bear left to reach the walls. **See page 130 and map opposite.**

The first routes on the wall as you scramble down the slope are now engulfed in ivy: **Solo in the Jungle**, E1 5b (1985); **Midden**, HVS (1985), and **Green Fingers**, HVS 5a (1985); the dirty chimney is **Hippo's Chimney**, HS 4b (1959). To the right, **Crocodile**, VS 4c (1959/1960s), wanders around via scoops and trees now covered in ivy.

On the front face are three sport routes:

1 Margins of my Kind F6b+   2011
12m Climb the faint right-facing groove and short wall.

2 Swamp Fever F7a+   2011
12m The technical and fingery face to the right with difficulties around the slight bulge.

3 Tsetse Piece F7a+   2011
12m Five metres right again the wall provides another fingery testpiece.

On the cleaner face to the right are: **Leprosy**, HVS 5a (1976), the rib on the left-hand side of the face. A short traverse left leads to a cracked overhang taken directly to the final groove; **Rainmaker's Rib**, VS 4c (1961), takes the rib direct to a ledge finishing via a crack on the right; **Lassa Fever**, HVS 5b (1965/1976), takes the groove, from the right, above a prominent yew tree; **Water Margin**, E1 5b (1965/1976), climbs a flake to gain the yew tree from where a diagonal traverse rightwards into the middle of a steep wall leads to good climbing to a break and then leftwards to a tree and an overhanging exit; **Liang Shang Po**, E1 5b (1976), begins below a sycamore tree on the right taking the wall until a traverse leftwards lead to a big ledge and finishing wall via a tree and shallow groove; **Green Monkey**, HVS 5a (1976), starts from a ledge halfway up the right-hand side of the buttress and climbs an overhanging wall to reach a break where moves left leadwards to a tree and finishing crack.

The Cornice

Sport: 23 (F6c to F8b+) **Trad**: 5 (E4 to E5)
Aspect: East **Sunshine**: Early morning **Season**: Summer and autumn
Conditions: Slow-drying, shady, cool, sheltered, popular, rainproof
Best for: Very steep, classy sport climbs F7b+ to F8b **Approach**: 20 minutes

This soaring sport crag is a much burlier and more biceps-intensive brother to Rubicon giving the dale its other classic venue for hard clip-ups. Roof is stacked upon roof giving a wave of routes from the mid-F7s to the mid-F8s. A brilliant crag when dry.

The climbing
Great, burly sport climbing over roofs.

Conditions and Aspect
The crag seeps badly all winter and dries out around April or May. Routes clean up pretty quickly once it dries although damp patches can linger. It gets hardly any sun and is great in hot weather. Tree-covered, so can be humid.

Parking and Approach
See map on page 130. Follow the Cressbrook Mill / South Bank approach. Cross the weir, and go up the steps to the track and turn right. Continue along the track for 500m, over a fence and down onto the Monsal Trail just as it exits the tunnel (as per Crunch / Moat Buttress).

Follow the Trail for 80m and, before it goes back into the next tunnel, follow a path down right, passing Swamp Wall just as you arrive by the water. Continue left on a path along the water's edge for 100m and cross a fence. The main crag lies just beyond.

Before the fence marking the left-hand side of the face are: **Alpha Groove**, VD (1960), a dirty groove on the left-above the fence; **Putty White Flesh**, E2 6a (1983), the groove above a ledge to the right with an old peg; **Sting in the Tail**, E4 6a (1983), traverses right along the ledge to a roof and tackles this to reach a corner above moving left and up to finish; **Morion**, E3 6a (1961/1984), begins just left of a patch of ivy to the right and climbs up to and over a small bulge to a break where it continues via a crack to a grassy finish via a thin crack in the centre of the face.

Crystalline, S (1993), climbs the slabby front face to a ledge, tree and finishing corner; **The Gully** (1933), S (1933), forms the left-bounding perimeter of the main face above and to the right; **Groundhog Day**, E4 5c (1995), traverses the central break; **The Cornice Traverse**, A3 (1969), traversed above the lip gained from a bolt ladder at the right-hand end of the cliff.

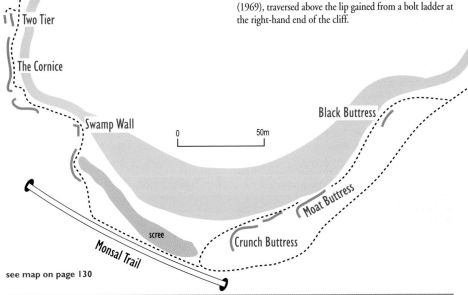

The left-hand section of the cliff is less steep than the main bulk of the crag, although it is still very bulging. The first four routes follow similar but not exactly the same lines as some trad lines. The trad climbs are: **Bandwagon on Direction**, E5 6a (1988), the wall immediately to the right of the gully; **The Bulge 1984**, E5 6a (1984), up the flake left of *A Major Moment*, then over bulges above; **Nothing to Help the Poor**, E5 6b (1984), which moved right at the break of *The Bulge 1984* to climb the wall above; **The Thatcher Years**, E5 6b (1988), a direct start to *Nothing to Help the Poor*.

1 The Workhouse F7a+ 2014
18m The leftmost bolt line with a steep finish.

2 Poorlaw F6c+ 2014
18m The slabby wall leads to a steep section.

3 A Major Moment F6c+ 2014
18m Start right of the flake and trend left to a lower-off in the scoop.

4 Supplementary Benefit F7a+ 2014
18m Slabby wall and steep bulge action.

5 Incapacity Benefit F7a+ ★★ 2006
15m Climb the wall to the bulge crossing it on its right, then skirting back left to a belay above.

6 The Dole: 1989 F7c ★ 1989/1990
18m Tackles the bulges in a direct line to a bulging finale. Extended by carrying on to the top of the crag. **The Enterprise Allowance**, F7c+ (1989), has an extra grade but no lower-off.

7 Yorkshire 8b F8a ★ 1989
20m The direct line, taking the left-hand branch of a pair of bolt lines. Usually finished leftwards at the top at this grade. The original line went rightwards at the top but, due to hold loss, is now a miserably fingery F8a+.

8 Ape Index F8b+ ★ 2001
20m The right-hand branch of bolts from the roof gives an even harder challenge.

9 The Weakling F7c+ ★★ 1988

20m Classic irony. The difficulties are at the initial over-laps and in getting established underneath the final over-hang. Dispatching this should not be taken for granted.

10 Brachiation Dance F7b+ ★★★ 1959/1984

21m The introductory route on this impressive wall. Climb the slab then overlaps above to reach the capping roof. Swing right and then make a crux throw out left to jugs and the top. Originally, for the true tick, you had to stand up over the lip, then jump off to dismount; scary. The modern method, lowering off the last bolt, is soft. **Photo on page** 4. A link-up, gaining the final overhang of *The Weakling* from this route, is **The Wee Cling**, F7c (2014).

11 The Free Monster F8a ★★★ 1990s/1991

18m A route with a chequered history. Climb the slab above the tree stump to a break from where a series of hard moves on small holds leads to the capping roof. This gives one testing move to finish, especially if you get your hands the wrong way round. **Photo on page 179.**

12 The Auctioneer F8a+ ★★★ 2001

18m An easy start just left of a bulge leads to a break. Continue slightly leftwards up the wall by a sequence of desperately-fingery pulls.

13 Rumble in the Jungle F8a+ ★★★ 1989

18m The right-hand branch of bolts weaving right to a prominent perched flake and then back left over the roofs to an impressive finale: a double-dyno over the capping overhang.

14 Barbarossity F8b ★★ 2010

18m From the big flake on *Rumble...*, move right before attacking the huge roofs directly above.

15 Monsterosity F8b ★★★ 2001

18m From the big flake on *Rumble...*, climb rightwards by powerful undercutting to finish via the final roof of *Albatrossity*.

16 Albatrossity F8a+ ★★★ 1992/1994

18m A superb test of strength. A fingery start leads up the wall to the flat overhang which requires a massive reach to pass it. From here continue direct to the final roof.

17 Superfly F8a+ ★★ 1995

18m Another power-packed pitch. A fingery start leads to easier climbing and the first roof. A flying leap leftwards over this leads to marginally easier moves above to the classic roof finale.

18 Superocity F8b ★★ 2007

18m The desperate direct line to the right.

19 Eclipsed F8b ★ 1999

18m A hard start to the right gives way to a desperate finish on a tiny pocket.

20 The Disillusioned Glue Machine F8a ★ 1989

15m Pull over the bulge 6m to the right and at the break step left before tackling the bulges and final roof direct. The use of a divided pocket and a crucial heel-hook pay dividends.

Mark Tomlinson on The Free Monster, F8a (page 177). Photo: Chris Lockyer.

21 Empire Burlesque F7c+ ★★ 1986

15m Although easier than the routes to the left, this is still not to be trifled with. Start up *Glue Machine* and gain access to a direct line over the bulges above. The crux is centred around the shallow scoop in the roof.

22 The Nasty Man F7c ★ 1998

15m A mean fingery start gains the break from where a step left leads into big undercut moves and a tiny edge to gain the finishing roof.

23 Goldcrest F8a 1999

14m Mean. From the break on *The Nasty Man*, make a series of very hard moves rightwards to gain the break under the final roof. This provides a very stiff test, especially if you can't use the helpful knee-bar.

24 Sirius F7c+ ★ 1989

14m The initial bulges, although tricky, only provide the taster for the desperate nature of the final roof. Tree belay.

25 Attila the Hun F7a+ ★ 1990

14m The undercut base proves tricky but the meat of the route surrounds the finale.

26 Catch the Rainbow F6c 2010

12m A worthwhile little route on the right-hand side of the wall and a useful warm-up pitch. Use the last bolt as a lower-off once you have passed it.

(1961/1962-1969), climbs the left edge of the slab to the right via a bulge moving left to a tree on the large ledge and finishes via slabs on the left until they steepen, then takes the easiest line bearing left to the top and **Dude's Route**, VS 4c, 4b (1961), climbs the groove on the right to the ledge and continues diagonally rightwards into a grassy groove which it follows to the top.

Two Tier Buttress

The upper of a two-level buttress to the right has had some sport routes added.

Parking and Approach: For the high level buttress containing the sport routes, follow the Cressbrook Mill / South Bank approach (**page 130**). Follow the approach for the Cornice (**page 175**) as far as the Monsal Trail. Instead of going right to the water as for the Cornice, continue through the trees, over a little fence and carry on the path above the Cornice until it opens out. The crag is just below and you pass it before doubling back down a little descent gully to it. To get to the low level buttresses, traverse right from The Cornice, scramble up a gully just beyond the Cornice.

On the initial buttress **Oscar's Groove**, HVS 4a,5b (1961/1976), is the vegetated face; **Last Chance**, VS 4a, 4b (1959), moves right from the terrace to climb a pinnacle.

Beyond a grotty gully is the lower tier of the two, with the following routes: **Flyaway Crack**, VS 4b (1959), an undercut groove on the left-hand side of the lower tier; **Lost Arête**, VS 5a (1966), is the rib above a head-height ledge just to the right. **Jumping Beans Wall**, VS 5a, 4b

1 Tierfull F6c   2014
8m   A bouldery start leads to an easier but steep finale.

2 My Tiers Led up to This F6b ★   2014
10m   A tough fingery start leads to a pleasant face.

3 Tiery Henry F6b ★   2014
10m   The best of the bunch via an easy face, bulge and slim arête.

4 Unde-Tiered F6c   2014
9m   The right-hand route has an ingenious crux and reach-dependant slab.

Witchcraft Wall

The first climbs are 80m from The Cornice. The wall is now ivy-covered, but originally held **Spellbound**, HVS 5c (1977), up the left-hand side of the wall; **Witchcraft Wall**, E3 6b (1960/1981), a short flake and bottomless groove 3m to the right; **Belladonna**, F7b (1989), up the centre of the wall; **Black Sabbath**, HVS 5b (1976), the right-hand side of the wall via a rib and cracks, which can be gained direct at 5c. A further 100m up the dale lies an isolated route on an undercut buttress up a prominent hanging groove gained via grassy ledges from the right: **Rock Bottom Groove**, VS 4c (1976).

Church Buttress

Trad: 11 (VS to E4)

Aspect: North   **Sunshine:** Early morning and evening   **Season:** Spring to autumn

Conditions: Shady, exposed, clean

Best for: A few secluded trad routes with an esoteric vibe   **Approach:** 20 minutes

A couple of buttresses that will give solitude seekers a handful of fun routes in the mid-grades. Steep trad, good for HVS to E2. Shady, fairly quick drying, fairly solid.

Parking and Approach: See map on page 130. Follow the Litton Mill Parking / Central Buttress Approach. Approach as for Central Buttress and follow the path along under that crag and along the slope to reach the buttresses.

Left-Hand Buttress

At the far left-hand side of the buttress is a wall with a small overlap at a gap in the ivy. **Sweet Surrender**, E2 5c (1987), passes an overlap finishing leftwards to a grassy exit; **Dreamy Intentions**, E2 5b (1987), makes difficult moves 3m to the right to gain an ivy-covered flake; **Open History**, E4 5c (1987), a bold little route up the bulging,

ivy-covered wall 5m to the right; **Queerboy**, S (1978), battles through the sycamore to the right finishing via a flake crack.

1   Northern Grit E1 5b   1976

15m   Pleasant. Climb the wall into a scoop which leads to an overhang. The left edge of this gives access to the top.

2   Vicar's Vertigo E2 5c ★   1959/1976

18m   Climb the wall and groove to the right with a series of bold moves to gain the capping overhang. Cross this leftwards to an easier finish.

3   Go Again E3 6a   1987

18m   Climb the smooth wall on small holds to a good hold. Easier moves lead to the break beneath the roof where a step right leads to the finish of the next route.

4   The Verger HVS 5b ★   1976
18m   The crack leads into a thinner crack to its left after 5m. Climb this direct to the finishing groove.

5   Sermon Wall VS 4c   1959/1970
18m   The starting crack of *The Verger* leads in its entirety to the break. Move left and finish up the groove or, not quite so fine, by moving right into a more vegetated exit.

Right-Hand Buttress

6   Ringmistress E1 5b ★   1987
14m   The fine scooped wall leads to an awkward final wall.

7   Ringleader E1 5c ★   1976
15m   The left-facing flake leads to an easier finale.

8   Ringmaster E2 5c   1959/1976
15m   The flake leads rightwards over the bulge and provides only a modicum of protection at the start. Above the bulge the crack eases. Finish via a crack on the right.

9   Confusion E4 6b ★   1970s/1981
12m   The innocuous scoop is gained by a desperate sequence. The exit is similarly perplexing before *Ribcrusher Crack* is gained for the finale.

10   Ribcrusher Crack HVS 5b   1959/1970
14m   The short corner. passing the overhang to its left in favour of the wall above.

11   White Riot E4 6a ★   1986
14m   The smooth wall behind the tree leads via a pocketed crack (peg) to the overhang. Pull over this and follow a thin crack to a tree.

Six metres to the right is **Corner Crack**, VD (1959); the left face of the pinnacle right again is **Drip**, S (1959); the crack on the right via a rightwards exit over the overhang is **Dry**, HS (1959).

Central Buttress

Trad: 46 (VS to E6)   **Sport:** 19 (F6c to F7c)
Aspect: North-west   **Sunshine:** Evening   **Season:** Spring to autumn
Conditions: Quick drying, lots of shade, big, impressive, quiet, some loose and overgrown climbs
Best for: Classic trad, E3 to E6, recent sport, F6c to F7c   **Approach:** 15 minutes

This towering crag is the largest and most imposing of the crags in the dale, its stark profile standing out against the grassy hillside. Seamed with cracks and grooves, despite the recent addition of a few sport routes, this cliff is the crucible of traditional climbing in the Dale.

A recent clean up in 2014, regearing and general sprinkling of TLC, has given this crag a long-needed rejuvenation. Loose rock has been removed, old gear replaced, lines straightened out and new routes added across the middle grades. While there might still be the odd tuft of grass or rattly hold, Central Buttress once again stands proud as one of the finest crags in the valley.

The Climbing
Long, steep walls with blockbusting trad routes that start around HVS, really come into their own about E2/3 and reach their peak around E5/6. There are a lot of seriously hard trad routes here. Some rely on old fixed protection. Whilst this is in the process of being replaced, many old pegs still exist.

There is a handful of sport routes mainly spread across the F7s. While not quite in the same league as the better trad routes they certainly turn the venue into a classy alternative to the more popular venues nearby.

Conditions and Aspect
Crag faces north-west and gets the evening sun in summer. It is quick drying and for most of the year suffers little seepage, even in winter. However, its shaded aspect means it is unlikely to become a popular winter venue. Care should be exercised as there is some loose rock.

Parking and Approach
See map on page 130. Follow the Litton Mill / Central Buttress approach. The traditional approach, Freddie's Weir, crossing the river to the base of the crag, has been discouraged recently by the local water bailiff (any damage to the weir will impact adversely on the habitat of the managed fish stock).

Ringing Chimney, D (1960s), bounds the left-hand side of the face and faces downstream.

Neil Foster on Behemoth, E5 6b (page 188). Photo: Keith Sharples.

1 Tiddle-de-Dum F6c   2014
12m A short difficult bulge leads to good holds.

2 Te Deum E3 5b   1976
5m Bold and dirty. Move up to the bedding plane then left to the overhang. Step right to a knobbly crack above the bulge and continue on loose rock via a bulge to a more solid exit on the finishing crack. Needs re-cleaning.

3 Hammy Hamster's Last Rites E2 5c ★ 1986
18m A crack leads to the bulge. Pull over it and swing left (peg) on undercuts into a short-lived crack.

4 Chiming Crack E3 6a ★   c.1958/1976
18m A worthwhile climb. From the bulge on the previous route, step right and move up to a niche at the base of a crack, tricky. Finish up this.

5 Dangerous Liaisons E5 6b ★   1990
18m A tough little cookie at the upper limit of its grade. Climb the wall past a peg to reach the large bulge. Pass this with difficuly (bolt) onto the headwall (bolt). Finish up a tricky thin crack.

6 Carillon Crack E3 5c ★   c.1958/1976
18m Climb up to the recess and pull through its left-hand side to reach a steep crack. Continue up this.

7 Silent Storm E5 6a   1987
18m Climb up to the recess, place a runner in the crack to the right, and step back down to climb the bulge on the left to reach a thin flake crack in the headwall. This leads past a vague scoop to easier ground.

8 Carol's Crack E3 5c ★   1976
18m Climb into the recess and climb the rib on the right into a steep crack and follow it to the top.

9 Hemmingway's Horror E2 5c ★   c.1958/1976
18m From the base of *Carol's Crack*, step right into the scoop and climb it before exiting up a flake.

10 The Importance of Being Ernest E4 6a 1985
18m Climb a large flake to a ledge and continue up a shallow groove to a peg at its end. Swing right and finish up a short but tricky headwall.

Sophie Whyte on The Treadmill, F7b (page 188). Photo: Dan Arkle.

11 The Bellringer E2 5b ★ c.1958/1975

18m From the top of the *Ernest* flake, traverse right then round the bulge to finish up a flake.

12 It Tolls for Thee F6c+ ★ 2014

16m A direct line with good moves and a high crux.

13 Vapour Stream F7a+ ★ 1986/2014

16m An old route straightened out to give a direct line with lots of disappointing holds.

14 La Belle Age E6 6b ★ 1986/2014

18m A bold and intimidating proposition with some spicy runouts above bolts. Climb directly past three bolts to the bulge (peg) into a shallow niche (bolt on the right). Climb this exiting it leftwards to finish up a short bulging crack.

The next four routes all use the prominent flake to start.

15 En Masse Descendre E6 6b ★ 1987

18m More bolted-but-bold climbing. From the top of the flake, climb up and left to a shallow groove (bolt). Climb the wall above the bulge leftwards to gain a series of good holds leading into a prominent finishing crack.

16 In Bulk E6 6b ★★ 1982

19m A breakthrough route of its era. Despite the loss of some old pegs the route is still adequately protected by wires. From the top of the flake climb up and left to a shallow groove in the bulge (bolt). Climb the groove, harder than it looks – and it looks hard enough – to reach a short, right-facing edge. From the top of this cross the smooth-looking wall leftwards to a series of finger slots and flakes leading to the top.

17 Leviathan E6 6b ★ 1966/1981

26m A terrifying route which has been the scene of one or two epic moments over the years. From the top of the flake, step right and locate a short flake in the wall above. Pull over the overlap and climb boldly up to the flake, creak, creak. Step right and up past a poor peg to easier ground and the crack above.

18 St Paul E2 5c ★★ 1960/1976

26m A classic of its genre, possibly the best E2 in the dale. From the top of the flake, walk right along the ledge to beneath a pair of cracks. Climb the bulging wall (bolt) to gain the cracks and follow them, sustained, to a good ledge. Finish up the easy corner.

19 Pauillac F7c ★ 1987/2009

20m An intense pitch up the shallow groove system. Start up the lower wall, the old direct start to *St Paul*, to join that route at the ledge. Step right and follow the grooved pillar with some very bouldery climbing.

20 Behemoth E5 6b ★★★ 1960/1976/1980

26m Mega! One of the great classics of Peak limestone and a milestone in any climbing career. The route was the subject of much competition for its first free ascent in the mid-seventies and is now a testament to those days. The initial crack is mean and leads to a ledge. (It can be gained from the start of *Pauillac* at a more amenable technical grade). Trend up and right to below the crack and follow it, straightforward at first and with a clutch of pegs, to gain the meat of the crack. This provides a stern test of jamming and laybacking until a slim groove is gained. This leads more easily to the top. **Photo on page 185.**

Yankee Dollar, E5 6b (1980), gained the groove right of *Behemoth* from that route at the level of a poor peg but has been somewhat superseded by:

21 That'll do Nicely E5 6b ★★ 1970/1989

24m Another excellent route which was originally protected by pegs, many of which have now disappeared. Start 2m to the right at a faint thin crack piercing the lower bulges. Climb the wall (two bolts) to a break and move up and left into a small hanging groove (bolt), above which lies a ledge. Move right (peg) and climb a thin crack (peg on the right) and bulge to a good hold at the base of a groove (peg on the left). Climb the groove (peg) to the roof and swing right and up via a hanging corner.

22 The Treadmill F7b 2009

17m A direct route up the pillar. Climb the fractured wall moving slightly leftwards into a shallow groove and then back right onto a ledge. Continue up the wall and flake above to the lower-off. **Photo on page 187.**

23 Fort Knox E5 6a 1983

22m Start below the left-hand end of a prominent overlap. Move up to a small ledge and then continue leftwards into a hanging groove. Climb this and the flake on its left to a break where moves right lead to an old peg. Move up to the bulge above (peg), and pull over it to a flake. Finish directly up the wall to a tree.

24 Fort Knox Direct F7b+ 2010

18m A direct assault of the wall outmoding the surrounding routes. Move up *Fort Knox* to the overlap and pull directly through it onto the wall above. This gives a challenging finale as it steepens for the lower-off to be reached.

25 The Troll E3 6a, 5a 1966/1976

1. 14m Move up as for *Fort Knox* and continue up the overlap. Move right under this swinging right at its end to pull over a bulge (peg) to a spacious stance on the obvious diagonal crack (*Crumbling Cracks*).

2. 28m Move out left to a shallow groove and finish via this and a crack above.

The next group of routes start at a lower level below the obvious entry into the large crack-cum-chimney.

26 Crumbling Cracks VS 4b   c.1957
26m Climb a hollow flake and larger one above to a ledge. Traverse left through the brambles into the chimney leading to the top.

27 Squatter's Rights VS 4c   1975
26m From the bramble bush of *Crumbling Cracks*, climb the huge flake to the right of the chimney finishing via the chossy gully on the left.

28 Warhead E4 6a ★   1967/1982
17m A good route although now somewhat superceded. From the base of the flake on *Squatter's Rights*, move right and enter the scoop above, exiting it rightwards (bolt) to a grass-choked crack. Follow this and the hollow groove above to the top.

29 My Fickle Resolve F6c+ ★   2014
20m The wall, intersecting *Warhead's* traverse.

30 Une Jour Parfait F7b+ ★   2014
21m A tough route, very bouldery. Go straight up from *My Fickle Resolve* to join *Warhead*.

31 Fire on Water E6 6b ★   1986
22m A trad-sport mix. After leaving *Alien,* the meat of the route is a bolt-protected F7b+. Follow the first section of *Alien* into the scoop. Continue slightly leftwards up the wall to a break. Move leftwards to a bulge and pass this with difficulty to a thin flake and continue directly up this and the wall above (wires handy) to a lower-off.

32 The Alien E4 6b ★★★   1967/1979
23m A true masterpiece of its genre plundering the scoop and wall above. Well-protected and on immaculate rock. Climb the vague crack into the scoop and step right before climbing the rib above. Move leftwards to a flake crack which leads rightwards past two pegs to some undercut holds in the bulge. Make a devitalising span leftwards over the bulge to a hidden hold at the base of a shallow scooped groove. Climb this to a lower-off just above the break. **a Aliens**, E6 6c (2000), climbs the wall to the right from where *Alien* crosses the overlap.

To the right and at a slightly lower level is an overhang at 5m with a striking rightwards-slanting crack above its right-hand side, the line of Knuckle Knocker.

33 White Fright E6 6b ★   1981
24m An impressive pitch tackling the shallow groove system in the white tower to the left of the crack system. Climb the wall to reach the slim overhang and cross it leftwards and move up to a ledge above. Pull up to the bulges above and follow them leftwards (peg) until it is possible to pull back rightwards into a shallow groove in the centre of the compact white pillar. Follow this more easily to the top.

34 Knuckle Knocker E3 5c ★★   1960/1970 - 1974
28m A very fine pitch at a more accommodating grade. Climb up to the overhang (peg on the lip), and traverse right before pulling over onto easier ground and a good ledge above. Continue up the sustained, well-protected crack above moving right at the top.

35 War E5 6a ★★   1979
28m A great route up the front of the white pillar. Nowhere desperate but tenacious route finding and gear placement is required. Climb the front face of the tower via a shallow depression to a small ledge below a bulge. Continue over the bulge (three pegs), onto the face above and at a break move left onto the arête. Follow this to a ledge and junction with the finish of *Knuckle Knocker*.

36 Freedom is Insane F7a ★★   2013
18m A surprisingly good find. Excellent rock and climbing. Climb the face to the right aiming for the ledge and bulge. Overcome this bulge by a series of tenacious moves before the technical wall above gives access to the belay.

Access to the next routes above is by way of a cleaned wall 8m to the right.

37 Hairy Legs E3 6a ★   1959/1976
19m The shallow groove in the right arête of the white pillar. Climb a vague groove right of the vegetation (bolts) to a ledge and move left below a slight bulge, possible belay. Pull over the overhang on the left into the shallow groove and crack and follow it (peg), to a lower-off at the break.

38 Aftervision E2 5c ★   1981
19m From the ledge and possible belay of *Hairy Legs,* ascend the tricky undercut flake over the bulge to an easier upper section, leading directly to the break and lower-off.

39 Déjà Vu F6c ★   2013
22m A good, long climb with an indistinct start but fine, sustained climbing above. Climb *Hairy Legs* to a small ledge. Overcome the bulge above by an extending move and continue up the wall and blunt rib above to a ledge. Pull out leftwards and finish up the short headwall.

40 Heatwave HVS 5a   1960s/1976
20m Climb *Hairy Legs* and continue directly into the square-cut groove. Follow this to a ledge on the right. Traverse right to a vegetated area and abseil off.

Robin Richmond on Fatal Attraction, F7a+ (opposite page). Photo: Andy Birtwistle

41 No Chains on Me F6c+ ★   2013
16m A fine little route. Take a direct line up the wall passing a small overlap, to gain a ledge. A series of technical and fingery moves lead into a slight groove where moves up its right arête gain jugs and the lower-off.

42 The Chain Gang F6c+ ★   1990
18m Start up *No Chains...* and continue up the wall into a hanging groove. Climb this to a lower-off.

43 Cool Hand Luke E5 6b ★   1981
20m Good, difficult climbing above half-height. Start up *The Chain Gang* and trend rightwards to a break. Move right and power into the flake above the bulge, peg. Follow this (peg) by a series of barn-door layback moves until the sanctuary of the ledge above is gained.

44 Disparagement E4 6a   1961/1969/1976
22m Follow *Cool Hand Luke* to the break and move right past its exit through the bulge until below the left-hand of two grooves. Gain and climb the groove by difficult moves through the overlap after which the climbing eases.

45 Time Warp E5 6a   1961/1980
25m Follow *Disparagement* and traverse right until beneath the rightmost groove, two pegs. Climb the groove by sustained layback moves past three pegs to a ledge at its top.

46 Escape Artist F7b   2014
25m The wall direct, briefly visiting *Cool Hand Luke*.

47 Fatal Hesitation F7b+ ★   1986/2014
20m A short powerful sequence leftwards leads to a good rest. Tricky moves lead over the bulge onto the excellent headwall. Originally gained from the right, the new start is called **Premature Evacuation**.

48 Fatal Attraction F7a+ ★★   1990
20m An excellent pitch with a fingery start and continuously testing climbing, trending leftward over the bulge onto the easier headwall. **Photo opposite.**

The link-up routes, starting up *Fatal Attraction* and finishing up *Fatal Hesitation*, and vice-versa, are both F7b+, although easier than *Fatal Hesitation*.

49 Sox E5 6a ★   1982

18m Climb the lower flake to a bolt and continue direct onto a block, good wires. Make a series of hard moves up onto the flake line and follow this to a bolt belay.

50 La Brute F7a+ ★   2014

18m A good sport route. Climb a fingery lower wall, followed by some stiff pulls to gain a break. Traverse right into a corner (*La Chute*) which is left directly by strenuous climbing to finish up *Sox*. Low in the grade.

51 La Chute E5 6b ★ ★   1981

22m The best of the bunch hereabouts. Pull up and move leftwards (peg) until beneath a short white groove. Climb this (bolt) and move left along the break (bolt) to some good footholds below a bulge. Pull over the bulge (bolt) onto the smooth, white headwall. Cross this diagonally leftwards to an easier finishing groove and bolt belay.

52 La Route E5 6a ★ 1985
20m From *La Chute*, continue up via a short flake crack. Swing right at the top of the groove and finish directly up to the tree and abseil point.

53 Coldity Groove E3 5c ★ 1964/1976
20m Start as for *La Route* but pull rightwards over the bulge to a ledge. The constricting groove above leads to a lower-off on the left.

54 Coldity Crack E1 5b 1964/1976
17m The clean shallow corner leads to a leftwards exit.

55 C'est Plastique F6c ★ 2014
16m A direct line up the compact wall bisecting *Plastic Wonder* to an interesting finale.

56 Plastic Wonder VS 4c 1970
17m The diagonal, stepped crack to the right.

57 Plastic Blinkers HVS 5b 1980s
15m Climb a crack up to a large flake. From the flake reach a large flat hold and finish direct to a tree.

58 Gwendoline HVS 5a ★ 1970
15m Climb the fine left-hand crack of a pinnacle moving left across the wall to a tree.

Orient Route, D (c.1957), is the right-hand chimney. The rib to the right is **China Rib**, VD (c.1957).

59 Dis-Orientated F6b+ 2014
9m The route to the right, behind the trees.

60 Strange Beings E4 6b 1986
9m From 4m up the chimney, move right along a break

and tackle the wall above (bolt) by a series of tense moves rightwards to an easier finale.

61 Being Strange! F7b+ 2013
9m Just that. The blank-looking wall is only possible for those with an almighty reach. Hideous.

62 Agent of Destruction E3 6a 1986
9m From 4m right of the chimney, follow a series of flakes to an undercut hold. Pull over into the scoop above and finish easily leftwards to a tree.

63 Slantered E1 5b 1987
12m The slanting flake crack eases above. Continue up the wall to a flake and traverse right to gain a tree on the right.

64 Mignonette E2 6b 1987
10m The wall to the right has difficult bouldery moves to begin. Easier climbing leads rightwards to the tree.

65 Mikado HVS 5b 1987
9m The wall below the tree of the previous routes.

66 Fools Rush In E1 5c 1986
7m Good climbing but now choked in grass. The centre of the wall (thread) leads slightly rightwards to a tree.

67 The Creeper E3 5c 1964/1982
140m Traverse the crag from the recess on *Carillion Crack*, mainly along the line of the bedding plane at one-third height, to eventually touch back down somewhere near *Coldity Crack*. **Photo on page 165.**

68 Emulator HVS (1pt) 5b 1968
80m A traverse of the rock, breaks, ledges and grass to finish up *Hairy Legs*.

Mill Buttress

Trad: 28 (VD to E4)

Aspect: North   **Sunshine:** Late summer evening   **Season:** Spring to autumn

Conditions: Shady, neglected, overgrown

Best for: Steep trad climbs with an esoteric flavour   **Approach:** 20 minutes

Mill Buttress has a lot of climbs, many of which have fallen into disrepair. For those that want something esoteric or a cleaning operation, this may well be the crag for you.

The Climbing: Trad routes on steep walls and cracks.

Conditions and Aspect: Sunless walls that don't seep much and dry quickly. A little scruffy.

Parking and Approach: See map on page 130. The best approach is to take the Central Buttress approach and follow the riverbank to the cliff.

At the left-hand end of the crag a small buttress with a curving crack gives **Ginza Crack**, S (c1957). Across the gully to the right the crag begins with a shallow corner.

1	**The Shield** HVS 5b	1976
2	**Pentagon Route** VS 4c	1959/1976
3	**Toe Tip Crack** HVS 5b	1976/1981
4	**Tip Toe Wall** HVS 5b	1959/1976
5	**Yukon Groove** VD	1976

6	**Flaked Out** E1 5b	1983
7	**Ikon Wall** VS 4b	1976
8	**Iconoclast** HVS 5b	1976
9	**Weaver's Wall** HVS 5b	1959/1976
10	**Drophammer** VS 4c	c1957
11	**Zero Option** HVS 5b	1965/1981

12	**Scoopy Little Number** EI 5b ★	1983
13	**Cricket, Lovely Cricket** HVS 5b	1983
14	**Out for a Duck** HVS 5b	1983
15	**Lengthening Shadows** VS 5a	1983
16	**Gardener's Question Time** HVS 5a	1983
17	**"I Can see How to Do It…"** EI 5b	1983
18	**Wee Douglas** EI 5b	1985
19	**Novelty** E3 6b	1993
20	**Strange Ways** E3 6a	1984

21	**One-Way Stretch** E4 6b	1984
22	**Two-Way Stretch** E2 5c	1984
23	**Alcatraverse** E4 6a	1984
24	**Hollow Way** E3 5c	1984
25	**Resin Erection Shuffle** EI 5a	1976
26	**Meddler's Wall** HVS 5a	1976
27	**Birthday Groove** HVS 5a	1976
28	**Thinfinger** HVS 5b	1976

Mill Race Buttress

This is situated behind Litton Mill and upstream from Mill Buttress. It is out of condition and access is not encouraged due to its proximity to residential properties. The following route are only included for completeness. The first routes climbs a pink groove 15m downstream from the toe of the buttress: **Will the Real Mill Buttress Please Stand Up**, HVS 5a (1986). **Vanishing Point**, E3 6b (1986), traverses the break rightwards from the toe of the buttress to climb the scooped wall through a small roof (peg) to gain easier ground. **Ostwald Bastable**, HVS 5b (1986), climbs the flaky crack to a bulge, moving left to a groove to finish.

The next two routes are situated directly behind Litton Mill. **Hamsters in Aspic**, HVS 5a (1986), climbs the groove down which you have to abseil; **Après le Deluge**, E4 6a (1986), takes a wandering line from the sycamore via a groove to gain the arête of the buttress.

Ravensdale

Trad: 68 (VD to E6)
Aspect: West **Sunshine**: Afternoon and evening **Season:** All year (bird restrictions in spring)
Conditions: Lofty, quick-drying, sunny, impressive, quiet, a bit loose and polished
Best for: Classic trad, VS - E1   **Approach:** 15 minutes

A large cliff with a host of traditional classics providing some of the best mid-grade, multi-pitch rock climbing on Peak limestone. A crag for adventurers.

The Climbing

Raven Buttress, the most prominent buttress in Cressbrook Dale, has routes of great length and character predominently in the VS to E1 grades whilst the walls around its smaller neighbour, Flying Buttress, provide a number of shorter single pitch routes with some particularly good crack climbs and one or two fierce technical testpieces. Polished rock does exist but it is really only a problem on a handful of routes. Care should be taken to avoid loose rock, particularly near the top of the cliff and on the less-travelled routes. Good belays at the cliff-top can be tricky to find but they do exist although they often require a little lateral thinking. Avoid damaging the wall and fence at the top of Raven Buttress. The ever-encroaching ivy has reclaimed a number of the more obscure routes although this may not be such a bad thing!

Conditions and Aspect

The cliff commands a magnificent, elevated position high above the eastern bank of Cressbrook Dale, overlooking Ravensdale Cottages and the wooded slopes beyond. Although it can be exposed to the elements, the cliff's lofty west-facing aspect ensures it recieves the evening sunshine and that it dries quickly after rain. Consequently, the cliff is ideal after a dry, sunny spell in winter, but is not a good venue on windy days.

Parking and Approach

See map on page 130. From the Cressbrook Mill parking for Water-cum-Jolly, take the right fork and continue uphill for 500m to enter a narrow lane on the right, signposted Ravensdale Cottages. This leads down to limited parking for six cars. Do not block the residents' access road or park in their allocated spaces. Go over a stile in the car park wall, cross stepping stones in the river bed (usually dry) and follow a steep path up the hillside to emerge, warmed up, below the main cliff of Raven Buttress.

Access

Ravensdale and its surrounding area is part of the Derbyshire Dales Nature Reserve and managed by Natural England. Bird restrictions may well be in place. Please observe these. For up-to-date info consult the BMC's RAD database.

Flying Buttress   descent
Rockbiter Wall
Left End   The Bay
Raven Buttress

Ian Carr on Via Vita, HVS 5b (page 209). Photo: Niall Grimes.

Left End

Where the approach path meets the cliff traverse left beneath Raven Buttress, and continue along a slight track before crossing a wire fence at a rickety stile. The path leads up and left to reach a buttress with a large through-cave. This is Flying Buttress and a good base for operations. One hundred metres left of the through-cave is an easy descent.

A short crack in the left edge of the buttress left of the descent is **Raven Crack**, VD (1970s). **Canopy Crack**, D (1960s), is the chimney crack; **Unpleasant**, S (1960s), is the crack 2m right; **True Lime**, VS 4b (1970s), is the short corner just right of the easy descent, traversing right below an overhang to an ivy-clad pedestal and finishing up the arête to the left.

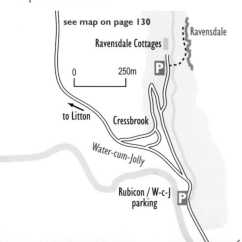

1   Bifurous Chimney VD   pre-1961
13m   A vintage struggle up the prominent chimney. **Pedestal Branch**, VD (pre-1961), traverses left at 4m to the pedestal to finish up a crack; currently overgrown.

2   Bifurous Corner VS 4c   1961
14m   The smooth corner leads to the *Bifurious Chimney*.

3   I Want Cookie E2 5b   2000
14m   Step right out of the corner and follow the crack in the steep wall.

4   The Bigot Direct E3 6a ★   1979
14m   The bulging crack is a strenuous struggle. **The Original Start**, HVS 5b (1976), reached this by a traverse right, just above an overlap, from 5m up the corner.

To the right, and now hidden beneath the ivy, lies **Forgotten Groove**, VS 4c (1964), **So-So**, (1960s) and **Ivy Corner**, HS 4a (1961).

Standing proud of the verdant growth is a clean tower.

5   Beachcomber HVS 5a ★   1978
19m   An elegant pitch up the front face of the tower. From the lowest point, climb up to a small overlap which is avoided on the left. Move back right and finish direct. The vegetated corner left of the tower is climbed by **Tower Climb**, VD (1961).

A variation on *Beachcomber*, **Beachy Hug**, E1 5b (1989), follows the left edge of the tower. **Tower Crack**, VS 4b (1960s), takes the crack in the right side of the tower.

Jim Symon on Tria, HS 4b (page 204). Photo: Paul Evans.

Flying Buttress

These are the steep walls and grooves that lie on, and either side of the detached pillar. The descent at the left end of the crag is recommended.

6 Bosky HS 4b 1978
16m A slim crack in the left wall of the V-groove.

7 Gruesome Groove HS 4a 1965
16m Ascend the V-groove, moving either left at the hanging flake or continuing direct up a crack and exiting left at the top.

8 Scorpion E3 6a ★ 1966/1970s
20m Thin and technical low down, rather worrying above. Gain a small niche 2m right of the V-groove then step right with difficulty onto a thin flake crack. Swing onto the right-hand side of the arête and finish carefully up this.

9 Gymnic HVS 5a ★★★ 1960
21m An old favourite that seems to be getting harder with every ascent. The difficult and rather slippery cracks give access to a fine groove. Exit either side of the overhang.

10 Freedom Slaves E6 6c ★ 1994
20m It looks impossible but... The open groove right of *Gymnic* leads to a large overhang. Pull straight over the overhang and finish up a blunt arête.

11 Cold Shoulder E1 5b 1981
21m Start up *Amain* but traverse left, above the overhang and around the arête onto a scooped face. Finish up the arête overlooking *Gymnic*.

12 Amain VS 4c ★★ 1960
21m A fine tussle with the wide hanging crack just right of the cave. After a strenuous start, which is not as bad as it looks, the corner above leads less urgently to the top. An alternative finish is possible up the big hanging flake on the left wall of the corner.

13 Russian Roulette HVS 5b ★ 1978
21m Between *Amain* and the arête is a thin crack. Follow the crack before striding right onto the arête at half-height. Take the arête on its left-hand side to the top

14 Looking at the Blue HVS 5b ★ 1979
19m The thin crackline just right of the arête gives nice technical climbing before a step left gains a small ledge on the arête at half-height. A bit of *Russian Roulette* should finish things off.

15 Impendent VS 4c ★★ pre-1961
18m A cracking pitch up the clean jamming crack in the outside face. A must for any gritstone-shy limestoner.

Ravensdale History

Early exploration at Ravensdale kicked off around 1958 with *Frore* by John Loy and Bill Woodward. In the summer of 1960, the main challenge of Raven Buttress was tackled by Dave Johnson and Dave Mellor who produced in quick succession *Medusa*, *Mealy Bugs* and *Delusor*. Later in September, the main prow of the buttress was ascended with some aid to give *Via Vita*. With this, Loy and Mellor had produced one of the hardest and most out-there limestone routes of the time.

1964 was a big year; *Mephistopheles* was climbed by Sheffield based Paul Nunn and Oliver Woolcock and *Conclusor* by Clive Rowland and Nunn. Both these lines were to become future classics.

1976 was a frantic year for aid reduction across Peak limestone. The plumb line here of *Via Vita Direct* was freed by both Steve Clegg and Chris Jackson, both operating separately around the same time. 1977 took Mike Browell

and Giles Barker *Round the Bend*, freeing the one of the few true aid routes on the crag. In the following year, Phil Burke and Keith Myhill added the hardest routes on the crag at the time, *Cut Loose or Fly* and Chris Jackson added the excellent *Rockbiter*.

Gary Gibson came onto the scene in 1979, adding a number of routes, *Bullets* and *Vintage Two* being the best. Ron Fawcett left his calling card in 1982 with the very hard and bouldery *Wilt*. The direct, *Alternative*, start being added in 1995 by Quentin Fisher, using his very long reach and well-honed bouldering ability. In 1984, Johnny Dawes, on a rare limestone first ascent, added the *Pagan Man*.

Nothing much has happened since. The crag remains the domain of the mid-grade limestone trad climber looking for a bit of exposure and polished excitement. Any fixed pegs have all-but gone together with lesser routes suffering from the creep of the ivy.

Clare Reading on Conclusor, HVS 5b (page 211). Photo: Neil Foster.

16 Shattered Crack S — 1959

18m This wide and not surprisingly shattered crack is started from a lower level and is not as bad as first appearances would suggest.

a Amnesiacs, E1 5b (2005), takes the cracks on the steep wall left of the cave leading to a gnarly tree. Retreat from this or face loose rock above.

17 Cave Corner S — 1959

12m The blocky corner is reached from the right.

18 Ash Crack VS 4c ★★★ — pre-1961

15m Brilliant crack-climbing despite the shiny exterior. Fortunately well-protected. **Photo opposite.**

19 Hydrolysis HVS 5b ★ — 1979

16m A neat technical eliminate up the thin crack and wall.

20 Tria HS 4b ★★ — 1960

17m The right corner of the recess, with some steep pulls. A good pitch even if it is a little 'glossy'. **Photo on page 201.**

The tree at the top of Tria gives a convenient abseil point. Please do not put your ropes directly around the tree.

21 Cut Loose or Fly E3 5c ★ — pre-1961/1978

18m Fine climbing and good rock, although maybe a little escapable. Great confidence is required in what lies above. Climb an awkward left-slanting crack for 6m until it is possible to swing right onto the wall via a hidden jug. Some surprising flakes above give access to easier ground.

22 Wilt E5 6b ★★ — 1982

20m Strenuous technicality but fairly well protected by small wires. Move right from the initial crack of *Cut Loose or Fly* to good holds. Traverse desperately right into the faint crack and climb it with urgency.

23 The Wilt Alternative E5 6c ★ — 1985

18m A desperate direct start, peg and thread runners.

24 Pagan Man E5 6b — 1984

18m Somehow find holds on the smooth scoop above the *Wilt* traverse.

25 Worry Wart E3 6a — 2000s

20m The blunt arête just right of *Wilt*. Pull over the bulge (peg runner on the right) and go steeply up to a good jug. Continue in the same line until the angle eases to an easier finish.

Ian Carr on Ash Crack, VS 4c (opposite page). Photo: Niall Grimes.

Rockbiter Wall: The wall on the front of the buttress.

26 Malpossessed El 5b ★ 1966
2lm A well-positioned struggle. Move up and right to a prominent block overhang. Pull round with difficulty and grope left into a thin groove. Bridge steeply up the groove to an easier but slightly loose upper section. Sustained.

27 Sneck El 5b 1970s
20m Climb up and left to below a small sharp groove in the overhang. Hard moves up this (peg) lead to easier but vegetated climbing. Finish over a small roof split by a crack.

28 The Watcher E2 6a 1980s
20m Two metres right of *Sneck* is slim groove in the overhang. Climb a tricky wall (two pegs) and go over the overhang to a vegetated finish.

29 Tank El 5b 1980
20m Start 3m right of *The Watcher* and 4m left of a prominent V-groove. Climb the wall to a bulge and turn this on the right by a short V-groove. Trend leftwards across the upper face to a grassy exit.

30 The Wick VS 4b 1966
20m A relatively clean and pleasant climb up the obvious pronounced V-groove.

3l Ice Cream Phoenix HVS 4c 1970
20m Fragile. Start 2m right of *The Wick*. Gain a narrow ledge and trend leftwards, up a shattered slab, to a vegetated finish.

The once-prominent flake system splitting the upper wall 8m right of *The Wick* is **Exfoliation**, VS 4c (1978).

Thirty metres right is an obvious gully giving an awkward descent. Ten metres to the left of this is a clean wall.

32 Troops of Tomorrow El 5c ★★ 1980
16m Follow a series of thin shallow cracks up the smooth wall just left of the cracks of *Rockbiter*.

33 Rockbiter HVS 5a ★ 1978
16m A neat, well-protected pitch up the obvious thin cracks in the centre of the wall. Belay a long way back.

34 Plaque Crack VS 4b 1960s
14m Start just left of the gully. Move up to and round the right side of the 'plaque' to an unstable finish.

The clean-cut groove immediately right of the gully is taken by **Gorrah**, HVS 5a (1960s), whilst **Begorrah**, HVS 5a (1960s), mounts a block 2m right then follows cracks to finish up *Gorrah*. Thirty metres right of the gully is a slab bounded on the right by a curving crack, **Sagittarius**, VS 4c (1960s), takes the steepening crack, past a block overhang, to finish slightly left.

The Bay

Up left of Raven Buttress is a vegetated bay. This contains some leafy cracks and only one really worthwhile route. For routes left of *Postern Crack*, approach by skirting left under the buttress on the main path and then back right, crossing a fence. For the *Y Chimney* area, approach direct.

35 Cracked Edge VS 4b 1960
18m Cracks 1m right of the arête lead to a ledge. The arête above is gained from cracks around to the left and followed to an unstable exit.

36 Round the Bend E3 5c ★   pre-1961/1977
19m The old aid route provides a good climb, sustained and nicely positioned. Start 2m right of *Cracked Edge* at a short corner. Go up the corner until a step left gains a thin crack. Climb the crack with increasing urgency to finish almost on the arête.

37 Hi-Fi VS 4c   1966
21m Go up the shallow groove then traverse right to a flake, possible stance. Follow the left-slanting corner to the top.

38 Boulder Problem VS 4c   1965
21m Climb the corner 8m right of the tree moving left to a second corner which leads into *Hi-Fi* and a common finish. A direct continuation of the second corner makes for a memorabile and loose alternative.

39 Metronome VS 4c   1965
21m The impending wide crack is a strong line. Start up the initial corner of *Boulder Problem*, step right and launch up the crack with conviction.

40 Postern Crack VS 4c   1960's
20m Start 3m right of *Metronome* on a higher ledge. Go directly up a wall to a crack which leads to a ledge. Finish via a yew tree.

41 Yew Cap VS 4c   1962
18m The shattered crackline just right is followed to the yew tree, using the right-hand corner in the middle section.

42 End of the Tour E3 5c †
17m A worrying pitch which has a few doubtful holds. Ascend the centre of the steep wall right of *Yew Cap*.

43 Y Chimney VS   1961
15m The chimney bounding the right-hand side of the bay. The steep right-hand crack makes for an exciting finish.

descent

Raven Buttress

The pride of Ravensdale. A towering buttress riven with cracks and grooves giving high-quality lines and some of the best VS / HVS adventures on Peak limestone. The rock is good, if a little polished. The climbs are often done with belays although, with careful ropework, can give tremendous 45-metre pitches; superb. The wide gully right of Raven Buttress contains a well-used descent path.

44 Myopia HVS 5b   1970
40m A scrappy line up the left side of the buttress leading to an all-out finish. Climb a line of broken grooves to a possible stance right of *Y Chimney* (4c). Take a line up the pillar above (two pegs) to unstable finishing cracks.

a The short clean crack in the wall right of *Myopia* is **Solitaire**, HS 4b (1960).

45 Conclusor HVS 5b ★★★   1959/1964
43m A tremendous, well-protected route, perhaps the finest on the cliff, that feels high in the grade. Start beneath the long slender groove in the left side of the buttress. The steep 4c corner leads to a small stance and possible belay. The fantastic slim groove above is climbed direct before an exit right leads into a wide finishing crack. A sustained pitch. **Photo on page 203.**

46 Hades E2 4c, 5b †   1965/1970s
Be prepared for fragile rock and copious vegetation and you won't be disappointed. Start 3m right of *Conclusor*.
1. 14m Climb the wall and two shallow grooves.
2. 32m Follow a flake crack to a pillar. Turn the bulge above on its left and enter a steep groove which leads to a tree. Take the left-hand groove to finish.

47 Delusor VS 4c, 4c ★   1960
A connoisseur's route with a devious start and a rewarding steep crack high on the wall right of *Conclusor*.
1. 13m Make a rightwards ascending traverse to a stance at the base of the groove. **b:** The direct start, a steep, undercut crack, is HVS 5b and makes a good start to *Via Vita*.
2. 32m Ascend the cracked groove, via a bulge, and continue up further grooves to a finish up *Medusa*.

48 Medusa VS 4b, 4b ★★★   1960
A lustrous classic taking the slabby gangway high on the cliff. The most popular means of ascent on the cliff. Start 3m left of a large tree.
1. 18m A deep stubborn flake crack leads to ledges. Step right and climb a fragile wall to a large pinnacle; belay.
2. 28m The crack behind the pinnacle is the key to gaining the slabby gangway. Follow this before a step left gains the final groove of *Delusor*.

49 Via Vita HVS 4c, 5b ★★★   1960/1970s
A well-travelled favourite that builds to a thrilling and well-protected finale up the prow of the buttress. Start as for *Medusa*.
1. 26m Follow *Medusa* onto its fragile wall and continue up the steep groove above to belay on *Medusa*.
2. 23m Go up the gangway for a few metres until a sensational swing right gains a small ledge. Getting established in the right-hand crack above proves trying. Once achieved, difficulties soon ease to a staightforward exit. **Photo on page 199**

There are two great variations on the second pitch:

50 Via Vita Direct E2 6a ★★   1964/1976
23m A ferocious little testpiece up the overhanging groove above and right of the stance. Enter the groove with great difficulty and follow it to rejoin the normal route.

51 The Sinister Finish E1 5b ★★   traditional
23m Low in the grade but equally fine. From the ledge before the crux, traverse left and climb a square-cut corner to easier ground.

52 The Edge of Insanity HVS †   1970s
45m A line up the crest of the buttress. Loose rock and plenty of exposure. Start at a shallow groove just right of *Medusa*. Climb the groove and vegetation to the *Medusa* pinnacle stance. Swing up and right onto the arête and climb a shallow V-groove. Keeping close to the overhanging edge, move up to a ledge. Step up, just right of the arête, until forced right to the foot of an obvious crack. Swing left and over the overhang to finish up a slight rib.

53 Mealy Bugs VS 4c, 4c ★★   1960
A highly enjoyable route, varied and well-balanced throughout. It tackles the prominent chimney / crack and then the large open scoop right of the crest of the buttress.
1. 22m Start in a small bay just left of the toe of the buttress. The chimney / crack leads awkwardly to a stance on a small terrace to the right.
2. 25m Go up the groove above the belay into a large slabby scoop. Cross this to an exposed finish up the prominent twisting crack on the left.

54 Mealystopheles HVS 5a, 4c ★   1965
A hybrid line with some worthwhile climbing. Start beneath a thin crack just left of the toe of the buttress.
1. 22m The crack leads up to the foot of a shallow groove. Ascend the groove, crossing a tricky bulge, and continue direct to reach the *Mealy Bugs* stance.
2. 24m Go up the groove of *Mealy Bugs* and into the open scoop. Traverse right around the rib (peg) into the prominent wide crack of *Mephistopheles* which is followed to its conclusion.

55 Bullets HVS 5a, 5b   1980

A direct eliminate with some taxing climbing. Start at the very toe of Raven Buttress.

1. 22m Climb a very shallow groove to a horizontal break. Step up and left onto a thin flake which leads leftwards onto an arête. Delicate moves up this and over a bulge gain the *Mealy Bugs* stance.

2. 23m Step onto the arête right of the *Mealy Bugs* groove and go up to a peg runner. The fragile bulge above guards entry into the wide finishing crack.

56 Mephistopheles E1 5a, 5b ★★   1964/1970s

The hardest of the big Raven Buttress classics with a tough, well-positioned crux. Start below a prominent wedged block just right of *Bullets* and 2m left of a thorn tree.

1. 22m Move up to the block and the horizontal break just above. Climb a thin crack and either continue direct or move right and go up to the terrace. Belay as for *Mealy Bugs*.

2. 23m Trend up and slightly right to the base of an obvious thin crack. Climb this and at its end move right and over a bulge into the easier, wider continuation crack.

57 Purple Haze El 5b, 5a ★★ 1970

Classic seventies rock! Excellent open climbing. Start behind a hawthorn tree.

1. 22m A thin flake leads up to an overhanging groove. Climb this with difficulty and continue up easier grooves to a belay on the terrace.

2. 23m Follow a wide crack to a yew tree. The fine wall above the tree is climbed, past a bulge, to a steep finishing corner.

58 Ploy VS 4c, 4c ★ 1964

A wandering line giving pleasant and varied climbing. Start beneath a corner a metre right of the hawthorn tree.

1. 23m Climb the corner and exit right into a niche. Follow the crack rising from the niche to the terrace and belay beside a wide flake crack.

2. 26m The flake crack leads to a yew tree. Continue easily up and right to a groove, possible belay, and climb this to a step left, peg runner. Go over a slight bulge to a direct and airy exit.

59 Frore VS 5a, 4c ★ 1958

The shallow groove 3m right of the hawthorn. The earliest recorded climb on the cliff.

1. 21m Gain a ledge below the groove and bridge intricately up it until a rightward-trending traverse leads to a tree in a grassy bay. Belay up and left.

2. 22m Trend easily leftwards, through the encroaching ivy, to a junction with *Ploy* and a possible belay. From a few metres up the groove of *Ploy* take a rightward-rising traverse line pleasantly to the top.

The overgrown rock to the right was taken by **Thyrsus**, HVS (1965/1970s).

60 Enigma HVS 5a 1965/1970s

20m A strenuous but worthwile pitch. Scramble in from the right. Climb a rib to a fragile flake, move left and ascend the steep wall past two pegs.

61 Vintage Two E2 5b ★ 1980

20m A cracking little pitch up the clean, smooth wall above the left-hand end of the terrace. Scramble in from the descent path on the right. Move up to a tree and follow a crack to a break. Climb up and left to a flake below a thin crack and follow this to the top, two peg runners. **For the Love of Ivy**, E3 6a (1986), is a direct start.

62 Paupericles VS 4b 1965

17m Slight. Start at a crack in the right edge of the buttress above the terrace. Climb the crack then traverse right to a tree, possible belay. Move left past a flake and finish up a groove.

64 Girdle Traverse VS 4c ★ 1964

This left-to-right traverse of Raven Buttress almost reaches mountaineering stature. Pitch 1 of *Delusor* (4c); belay. Follow the second pitch of *Delusor* to its junction with *Medusa*. Step right and swing right onto the exposed ledge of *Via Vita* (4c). Belay. Traverse right around the rib to join *Mealy Bugs* below its final crack. Cross the scoop and descend the slab/groove to a belay on the terrace (4c). As for *Ploy* but take a belay at the foot of the groove (4b). From the groove take the rightward-rising line of *Frore* to finish (4c).

65 Critical Town HVS 5a 1970s

55m A high level girdle from right to left. Start at the right end of the terrace at a thorn tree. Traverse left, below the overhang and past the flake on *Enigma*. Follow the break then drop down to a belay below pitch 2 of *Frore* (5a). Traverse around the arête into the scoop of *Mealy Bugs*. Continue the traverse, round the rib, to belay on the exposed ledge of *Via Vita* (4c). Reverse the *Via Vita* swing and traverse left to finish up the final crack of *Conclusor* (5a).

On no account should climbing take place on the buttresses right of the descent gully.

Crag X

Sport: 22 (F5 to F7c+)
Aspect: North-east **Sunshine:** Till 11am in summer **Season:** Sping to autumn
Conditions: Shady, some rain shelter, cold in winter, close to a busy road.
Best for: Short, punchy sport climbs, F6c to F7b. **Approach:** 10 minutes

A nice little crag with easy access and a pleasant aspect. The intricate character of the rock together with its compact nature makes this a worthwhile venue for an evening visit or in conjunction with another crag on the same day.

The Climbing
The routes are on slightly overhanging walls, with some roofs thrown in, and tend to be fierce and fingery. The rock is mostly good quality, and well-bolted.

Conditions and Aspect
The crag sits just up from the A6, nestled in thick trees. The setting is pleasant, but not peaceful, although thick foliage in summer helps help to keep the noise from the road down. It is best visited as an escape from the heat, making it less than ideal as a winter venue. Due to the overhanging nature and capping roof, the climbs can stay dry in light rain.

Parking and Approach
Park in the Monsal Dale pay & display car park on the A6. Walk towards Buxton, passing a bus stop at 200m, then at 400m, locate a red clearway sign (the 'X' of 'Crag X') on the left-hand side of the road. Strike straight up the hillside to reach the crag. Thrill seekers, the anti-walking lobby, and those unwilling to pay for parking, may wish to park just below the crag, on the Bakewell side of the sign (parking on the other side can result in a ticket).

1 Bag of X F6c+   1995
12m A poor route. From the right-hand side of the cave, climb the wall above to a difficult finale.

2 Xactly F6b   2011
12m A bulge, slab and leftwards moves through overlap.

3 X Box F6b   2011
12m An awkward lower bulge leads to a slab and overlap.

4 X Marks the Spot F5   1995
10m An easier line to the right of the huge hanging bush.

5 Ham and X F6b   2011
10m An easy start to a steep layaway finale.

6 Xtermination F6a+   2011
10m Climb to a ledge then the short technical wall above.

7 Xageration F6b   2011
10m An easy start over ledges leads to a technical finish.

8 In the X Team F6b   2011
10m An easy start leads to an intricate finish.

9 eXit Stage Left F6a   1995
11m A pleasant shallow groove rising from the centre of the platform.

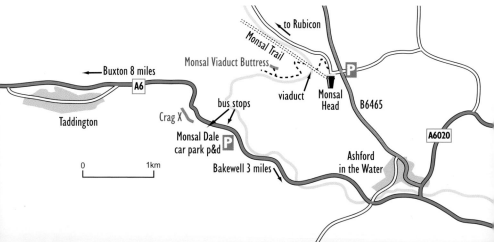

10 The X Files F6b+   1995
11m A tricky lower bulge just to the right.

11 Xtra Time F6b+   1993
11m The left-hand line from a bolt belay.

12 Red X F6c+ ★   1993
11m The best route from the terrace takes the right-hand side of the wall above the belay. Good sustained climbing.

13 Great Expectations F6c ★   1993
15m Varied face-climbing up the prominent hanging slab. Watch out for the finish which provides a sting in the tail.

14 Certificate X F7b ★   1993
15m A fine pitch. Easy climbing leads to the first break. Hard moves lead left through the scoop to a fingery and trying finish. Clipping the last bolt is the crux!

15 Malcolm X F7b ★   1995
15m A direct line up the wall with a fingery and technical section and a 'goey' finale.

16 Top MarX F7a+ ★   1995
12m The steep wall, with hard moves above the break which are best done quickly.

17 XXXX F7b ★   1993
12m The best route on the crag, climbing the compact grey wall above the break. Fine, sustained wall-climbing and low in the grade.

18 Little Blue Lies F7b ★   1995
12m High in the grade. The wall yields to a positive approach.

19 Y Should I? F7b+   1995
12m Hard moves through the bulge to the right precede a difficult move onto the slab. Hard to on-sight.

20 Xcursion F7c+   1997
11m A totally hideous problem through the bulge and up through the scoop above. Belay on the right.

21 X.T.C. F7a+   1995
10m A short, hard and innocuous crux over the bulge.

22 X Partridge F7a+   2011
11m The mean bulge at right-hand side of crag.

Monsal Viaduct Buttress

A small, steep, blocky buttress nestled in some trees near Monsal Head. Park at the junction, near the pub and hotel. Drop down footpaths to gain the Monsal Trail. Cross the viaduct and on the far side, drop down to the bank. Follow the river downstream for 150m. As the path goes into some trees, walk up the hillside on the right to find the crag (**see map opposite**). On the left of the crag is a stepped groove. **Blocky Balbao**, F7a (2013), enters this and traverses right to a steep finish; **The Blocky Road to Ruin**, F7b+ (2013), is the bulge to the right; **The Blocky Horror Show**, F6c (2013), is the groove on the right with a hard start.

RAVEN TOR AREA

RAVEN TOR / TIDESWELL DALE / BLACKWELL DALE +++

Ethan Walker on Kaaba, F8c+ (page 224). Photo: Jon Clarke.

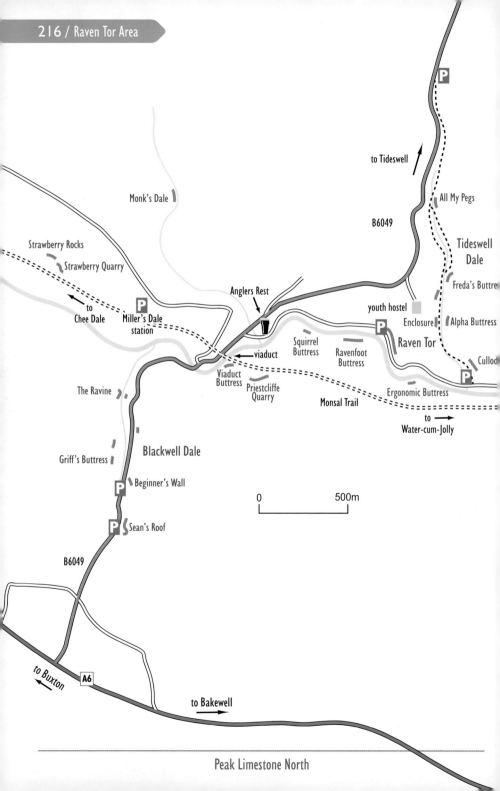

Monk's Dale

Strawberry Rocks

Strawberry Quarry

to Tideswell

B6049

All My Pegs

Tideswell Dale

Freda's Buttre

youth hostel

Enclosure

Alpha Buttress

Anglers Rest

to Chee Dale

Miller's Dale station

Squirrel Buttress

Ravenfoot Buttress

Raven Tor

Cullod

viaduct

Viaduct Buttress

Priestcliffe Quarry

Ergonomic Buttress

Monsal Trail

The Ravine

to Water-cum-Jolly

Griff's Buttress

Blackwell Dale

0   500m

Beginner's Wall

Sean's Roof

B6049

to Buxton

A6

to Bakewell

Peak Limestone North

Adie Jebb high on The Prow, F8a (page 222). Photo: Adam Long.

Raven Tor

Sport: 90 (F7a to F9a)   **Bouldering:** 70 (Font 6A to Font 8B+)
Aspect: South-west   **Sunshine:** Afternoon and evening   **Season:** Spring to autumn
Conditions: Sheltered, mostly rainproof, hot in the sun, winter seepage, polished, popular
Best for: Powerful and polished redpoints of the highest order   **Approach:** Roadside

Raven Tor is the crucible of sport climbing and limestone bouldering in the Peak District. For over thirty years it has been at the cutting edge of standards, both locally and nationally, and some of its routes laid claim to be the hardest in the world at their time. Today it is an essential proving ground for any serious climber in the country, and while it no longer attracts the cream of global superstars, when they do visit they tend to walk away empty-handed.

Its white walls host climbs that vary from gently overhanging to bastard bulges, from soaring to short and from hard to hideous. The Tor is criss-crossed with eliminates, link-ups and variations which sometimes blur the perceived boundaries between boulder problems and routes. Do not expect an easy time here.

A honeypot for fit climbers (who hang out on the left), for strong climbers (who hang out on the right) and for good climbers (who hang out in the middle).

The Climbing
A paradise for hard redpoints and training.
Routes: Powerful, crimpy sport climbing. Some routes up to 35m in length providing seriously pumpy leads. Others are shorter and are pure power endurance beasts while some are almost bouldering with a rope on. The crag has many proud lines and these are complemented by endless variants that weave in and out of them in search of more or less difficulty. A myriad of link-ups are possible.
Bouldering: Great for steep power problems, traverses and eliminates. As with the routes, these are a combination of good lines and eliminates. Generally very powerful and fingery. Sometimes highball. The landings are hard and rocky so a lot of pads are useful.

Conditions
Very sheltered. The crag faces south-west and gets the sun from early afternoon onwards. The rock can get greasy in the sun. Most of the climbing is rainproof, but seepage is a major problem in the winter months and the starts of many routes, particularly those on the left, can remain out of condition until late spring. In winter the low sun is often hidden behind the opposite side of the valley.

Approach
See map on page 216. The crag is roadside. Park in the bays at the left or right end of the crag (keeping completely off the road: it's a clearway). Consideration and courtesy should be extended to other users to maintain good relations. Inconsiderate parking in the past has threatened access to the crag and alternative overflow parking is available further down the road at the car park at Tidesewell Dale. This is only a pleasant 10-minute walk back to the crag. Miller's Dale, the valley that Raven Tor lies in, can be accessed by bus from Sheffield, Buxton and Chesterfield.

Access
Climbers should not leave ropes or quickdraws in place overnight. If you are staying overnight in a van, please leave a note to inform the water bailiff, as poaching is a problem here. Human excrement has been a problem in the past and it would be better if climbers could avoid causing a health hazard by thinking in advance or using the public toilets at Miller's Dale Station (open in the daytime).

The first two routes start high up on the grassy hillside on the left of the crag: **S.B.S.**, HS (1968), takes a groove, a short traverse and a chossy wall above; **The Flying Scotsman**, HVS (1973), continues the traverse of *S.B.S.* out towards the second pitch of *Mecca*.

At the base of the crag at its left-hand end is a narrow rock terrace. From here several routes start but unfortunately are often damp and dirty low down. To the left, **Arabian Nights**, E4 6b (1985), initially follows a line of ring bolts, then goes leftwards to a break and groove above. **Sheikh, Rattle and Roll**, F7b (1988), follows the above to the break then climbs straight up. Both of these are buried under ivy. **Koran Direct**, F7a+ (1985), takes the line of bolts whilst the parent route, **Koran**, E4 6a (1968/1982), wanders right into a loose scoop before traversing left along a break to rejoin the bolt line. Just left of a short crack is **Ayatollah**, F7a (1988), which takes a direct line into a shallow groove before a difficult bulge above the break leads to a belay. At present this route is partly de-equipped.

Steve McClure on Mutation, F9a (page 230). Photo: Keith Sharples.

1   Hubris   E5 6a   1956/1976/1980

22m   Partly bolted but still an adventure. Climb the crack and wall to a break. Surmount a loose bulge then follow a fragile upper wall protected by 'ring-pull' hangers. Finish at the break (poor belay) or, most sensibly, move right into *Indecent Exposure*. Seldom climbed and often dirty.

Variations to Hubris:

2   Austin Powers   F7a+   2011

24m   Start as for *Hubris* then move left with difficulty to reach flakes that lead awkwardly up to a break. Continue to the belay (as for *Ayatollah*).

3   Barely Decent   F7b+   2008

22m   Starting just left of *Indecent* is a difficult bouldery wall. Climb this until you are forced into *Indecent* at the first break. Move left and finish up *Austin Powers*.

Right again is a one-metre-high tree stump. This is all that's left of the legendary 'Indecent tree' up which many of the classics started. Since its demise all of the routes have gained a grade whilst some now start in different places altogether. The chopper's identity remains a mystery.

Accessing the routes is now a lot harder and arguably less pleasant. The groove above the stump is **Indecent Direct** while a more diagonal line leading into *Body Machine* is **Push Up**. They are both frequently wet although *Push Up* can sometimes be climbable when it looks soaked.

4   Indecent Exposure   F7c ★★★   1970/1982

27m   One of the best of the older classics giving sustained and fingery climbing all the way. The groove behind the tree stump leads past a break to undercut flakes. Follow these rightwards. Pull into a scoop then stride back left to the middle of the wall. A few quick cranks gain the girdle break. Once recovered, continue over the bulging wall then trend slightly rightwards to a rounded ledge. Tricky moves up the rib on your left gain a hanging belay.

Variations to Indecent Exposure:

A **Left-Hand Start** to *Indecent*, F7b+ ★★, follows *Hubris* to the break then moves right into the original. Apart from being easier it also stays drier than the normal *Indecent* start.

5   Balls Out   F7c   2013

26m   A direct version of *Indecent Exposure*. Where it moves right, climb over the bulge (bolt) and up the wall to rejoin and finish as for the original.

6   Indecent Exposure Pitch 2   F7a/E5 ★   1982

18m   The original route moved right to the belay of *Body Machine* from where the second pitch (from which the route gained its name) then swings out right along a break to the very exposed groove of *Proud Whore*). Great fun!

7   The Full Monty   F7c+ ★★   2005

30m   Extend *Indecent* by climbing up the rib to reach the left side of the roof. Pull rightwards in a sensational position on reinforced holds, then up to a ledge with an extended belay. Take care with the holds near the belay.

8   Introducing the Hardline According to Terrence Trout   F7c, F7c, F7b   1970s/1988

50m   Start up *Indecent* and belay at the break. Move right into *Body Machine* and follow this to the next break. Traverse right to join *The Prow*. Keep going right and drop down to *Mecca*. Finish as for *Freedom Fighter*.

9   O'Donovans Blind Variant   E5 6b   1983

26m   Link the easy upper crack of *Mecca pitch 2* leftwards above the traverse line of *Terrance Trout* via a rounded hand traverse to join *Indecent Exposure pitch 2*.

10   Body Machine   F7c+ ★★★   1984

25m   Ron Fawcett's stylish super-route is still one of the best pitches in the Peak. Long, pumpy and strenuous. Start at the tree stump and climb up and slightly rightwards to a break. Move right until a good hold can be reached. Move up and then make the legendary rockover rightwards to a good hold. Some more difficult climbing leads to the break (classic foot-jam rest). Crimpy pulls over the bulge are followed by a pumpy traverse right and final bulge. **Photo on page 243.**

Variations to Body Machine:

11   Half Decent   F7c ★★   2008

27m   A hybrid that gives balanced, sustained climbing. Fingery. Follow *Body Machine* to the first break then step slightly left to join *Indecent* at the crux. Finish up this route.

12   Unzipped   F8a ★   2012

27m   A link-up with some good moves but the new climbing is very squeezed-in. Follow *Half Decent* into *Indecent* then climb the fingery wall on fragile holds to join *Body Machine*. Follow this over its bulge then climb to the break and overlap above. Make a big reach to slopers then teeter up left to join *Indecent* at its last bolt and finish up this.

13   An In and Out of Body Experience   F8a ★★★   2007

33m   A quality extension. De-pump at the *Body Machine* belay then shuffle left until the steep wall above can be climbed to the roof. Difficult moves up and left over this lead into *The Full Monty*. Finish up this. Very exciting!

14 Body Builder F8a+ ★   2005
25m A short excursion leaving *Body Machine* at the girdle break and rejoining it above. Powerful, cruxy moves.

15 The Prow F8a ★★★   1963/1982/2003
35m Fawcett's masterpiece. Formerly climbed with two hanging belays but now bolted so it can be led in a single pitch on one rope with long slings. Follow *Body Machine* to the first break where a low traverse along a break leads past the *Revelations* belay. Above, a small flake is gained and exited with difficulty to a hole in the break (Pitch 1, F7b+ to here). Climb a tufa fin until a hard exit out right then back left leads into the large hanging groove and the *Body Machine* belay (Pitch 2, F7c+ to here). Climb the groove and make gymnastic moves in a wild position then trend up and right to a hanging belay. **Photo on page 217.**

Variations to The Prow:

16 The Crucifixion F8a ★★★   2006
35m A sensational endurance pitch despite some dubious rock. Follow *The Prow* to the shakeout at the base of the hanging groove. Step slightly right then pull over a small (possibly hollow) roof and plough up the awkward rib and wall. A crucifying move up left leads to better flaky holds above. Move left again to gain a hanging belay.

17 Proud Whore F7c+ ★★★   2003
36m One of the best routes of its grade in the country giving a long sustained pitch with a superbly-positioned finish. Follow *The Prow* to the top of the tufa fin. A difficult swing right leads to some hard pulls on pockets to reach a hanging groove. This leads to a belay on the ledge.

18 Brazen Strumpet F8a ★★   2006
42m Follow *The Prow* to the top of *Revelations*. A difficult traverse right leads to a fingery sequence to gain the girdle break. Go right to the top of *Mecca Extension* then pull up and left (crux) to meet *Proud Whore*. Move right up a tiny gangway then straight up the bulging wall to an awkward mantel to gain a large ledge and belay.

Back on ground level, just right of the tree stump:

19 Jehovahkill F8b+ ★   1993
10m Short, intense and 'ard! A selection of non-holds leads to the obvious single hold on the right and then still-tricky ground to gain the break and lower-off.

20 Revelations F8b ★★★   1965/1984
10m Iconic. Jerry Moffatt's freeing of the true start to *The Prow* gave the first 8 in the Peak. A desperate move gains the hanging groove where laybacking, kneebars, toe hooks – not to mention a no-hands rest – lead up and

right to a nasty little slab finish. The grade arithmetic is Font 7C-ish for the start followed by a F7c route = soft F8b. Maybe. **Photo on page 245.**

21 Rage F8b ★★   1992
27m Climb *Revelations* and continue up *The Prow* to the hole in the break. Pull over the bulge to gain and climb a thin flake. Continue up the wall to the pocketed break (almost joining *The Prow* below the groove) and then move left. A final hard move gains the *Body Machine* belay.

Variation to Rage:

22 Anger Management F8a+ ★★   2008
30m The superb final wall of *Rage* can be gained either via *The Prow* pitch 1 or via *Body Machine*, with an independent move right after the rockover to gain the flake near the top of *The Prow* pitch 1.

23 Rage into Crucifiction F8b ★★   2013
35m A tough, direct way up the cliff with lots of hard climbing. A slightly easier version, **Cross 'n Angry**, F8a+ (2013), climbs *Anger Management* into *The Crucifixion*.

24 Hubble F9a ★★   1990
10m THE hard route of the crag, and one of the most famous hard routes in the world. Massive in status and diminutive in stature, and considered to be Font 8B+. After 25 years repeats still make the news. No sneaky use of rope drag – the crag police are watching! A long stretch left to a blocky pinch leads back right to match undercuts via the infamous UK7b move. Press on to victory up mere F7c+ terrain. Adam Ondra didn't do it but suggested F9a. That's good enough for us. **Photo on page 247.**

25 The Whore of Babylon A0/F8a ★   1987
32m An unpopular oddity but a tremendous pitch despite the aid. Aid up *Hubble* and use a high undercut and climb the technical wall above to join and follow what is now *Brazen Strumpet* to the break. Finish up *Proud Whore*.

26 Brandenburg Gate project
10m If you thought the holds on *Hubble* were poor, glance right to where there doesn't appear to be any at all. All the moves have been done, and the route was nearly climbed by John Gaskins some time ago. There are two moves on it harder than the crux of *Hubble*.

27 Make It Funky F8c ★★   1993
13m A hard testpiece. From jugs just left of the start of *Mecca*, swing out leftwards to gain undercuts. Savage pulls here lead to another undercut and the infamous bolt-hole 'mono' move which leads out left to another undercut. Move up and then out right to finish at the *Mecca* belay. A direct start is possible but with no change in grade.

Variation to Make It Funky

28 Mega Whore F8c ★★   1998
30m A mega link taking *Make it Funky* into the old *Whore of Babylon*. Avoid the exit right into *Mecca* and continue up the *Whore...* Move right at the break to gain the *Mecca Extension* lower-off.

29 Mecca F8b+ ★★★   1960/1988
13m On your kneepads and pay homage. The compelling groove is one of the most sought after sport routes in the UK. The advent of kneepads has eased the route significantly, but it is still F8b+. Sustained and quite complex moves lead up the bulging wall that guards access to the groove. Once the groove is reached, either layback up the arête of the groove with a sense of history or use your kneepad to good effect. A final stretch left leads to a huge flake and the belay. **Photo opposite.**

Mecca Pitch 2, E2 5b (1960/1973), climbs the groove above the *Mecca Extension / Kaaba* belay then trends right into the wider grove.

Variations to Mecca:

30 Mecca Extension F8c ★★★   1998
25m The logical finish and worth F8a in its own right. From the *Mecca* belay flake, crimp upwards to a large sidepull pocket. Scuttle rightwards into a small right-facing flake. Power your way upwards to better holds and belay at the break. **See front cover.**

31 The Hajj F8c ★★   2004
25m From the belay flake of *Mecca*, move upwards as for the *Extension* until its traverse right. Step left and attack the blank black wall via a very bouldery sequence and some disappointing holds. Step back right at the top to the same belay as *Mecca Extension*.

32 Kaaba F8c+ ★★★   2004
25m The best and hardest of Steve McClure's *Mecca* variations. Climb *Mecca* until its final moves leftwards. Continue straight up to a small overlap. The next section is fiercely crimpy requiring a determined approach and high pain threshold. Battling through here leads immediately into the desperate last moves of *Mecca Extension* which will feel even harder than usual. **Photo on page 214.**

Neil Mawson on Raven Tor's ultra-classic Mecca, F8b+ (opposite). Photo: Tim Glasby.

Evolution

Chimes of Freedom

The Green Alternative

Weedkiller

Ben's Cave Bouldering

I Too Hard for Mark Leach Font 6C

The exit to *Ben's Roof*, starting on low jugs and finishing on a big jug at the start of the roof. Font 7A footless.

2 Ben's Roof Font 7C

A classic problem where the "rules" have been consigned to history <sigh>. Start part way in the cave on the right at a vague collection of holds. Climb upwards and backwards over the arch to plant yourself on the left side. Crimp out and leftwards and finish up *Too Hard...* A kneepad allows a good rest midway. Without this it's more like Font 7C+. **Photo on page 227.**

Variations: The right-hand, original finish follows the ordinary route but before moving leftwards, reach up and right to a crucial undercut in the roof and slap directly up to a sloper then the final jug; same grade. **Ben's Roof Extension:** you can start further back in the dark with feet on the back wall and hands on a slopey undercut pod: Font 7C+, or Font 8A without the kneebar rest coupled with a right-hand exit.

3 Sympathy in Choice Font 8A

From a sitter at the pillar of *Ben's Roof*, swing right to the lip using the crimps on *Keen Roof*, finishing right on a jug.

4 Keen Roof Font 8B

A modern testpiece. Start sitting beneath the left-hand wall halfway into the cave. Climb out into the pod in the centre of the roof then go direct to the lip before moving leftwards and up to the jugs under the top roof. An extension has been done from the start of *Ben's Roof*; harder but no change in grade. A still-lower start, as for *Ben's Roof Extension*, is **Belly of the Beast**, Font 8B+. **Keen Roof Stand Start** is Font 7A+. **Photo opposite.**

5 Fat Lip Font 8B

Steve McClure's crimpy meanie. Go from the stand start of *Cave Problem* to the lip, then head leftwards to the finish of *Keen Roof*.

6 Hook Font 7C

Climb up from the good lip hold on *Keen Roof* on small crimps avoiding better holds on the left.

7 Cave Problem Font 7B+

Brilliant. From a painful slot (often damp), pull out to a small crimp and tiny undercut on the lip and traverse right to finish up *Chimes Start*. The sit start is Font 7C.

8 Shades of Grey Font 7C

Follow *Cave Problem Sit Start* but instead of heading right to the *Chimes Start* jug, slap direct to the good hold next to the bolt on *Chimes Start*.

James Pearson on his his own modern classic, Keen Roof, Font 8B (opposite page). Photo: John Coefield.

9 Tumbleweed Font 7C+

Start as for *Cave Problem Sit Start*, follow *Weedkiller Traverse* in reverse to to finish up *Basher's Problem*. **Let's Get Ready to Rumbleweed**, Font 8A, links *Tumbleweed* to *Basher's Right-Hand*.

10 Chimes Start Font 6B

A burly pull to the big incut jug under the roof.

11 Converter Font 7C

From a sit-start on sharp pockets on the right, gain a pinch and undercut pocket. Reach the lip and finish on the *Chimes Start* jug.

12 Weedfiller Font 7B

An alternative finish to *Weedkiller Traverse* between the normal finish and *Basher's Problems*.

13 Basher's Problem Font 7A

The easiest of the cave's classics. From 3m left of the start of *Weedkiller Traverse*, use undercuts at the back of the bulge and head straight out via two two-finger pockets above *Weedkiller Traverse*, to finish at a flat hold over the lip. The left-hand method gets the left pocket with the right hand to reach left to a diagonal crimp. A right-hand method reaches up and right to a very sharp crimp before the final jug.

14 Basher's Right-Hand Font 7A+

Move right at the pockets and flake just below the lip, to finish on a good edge just above the next overlap.

15 Weedkiller Traverse Font 7B

A classic right-to-left traverse. Easy for the grade especially for the strong and thin fingered. Start matched on an obvious boss on the right edge of the cave then launch leftwards to gain and follow the obvious thin break to jugs. Finish up *Chimes Start*.

Variations to *Weedkiller Traverse*: **Weedkiller Footless** is Font 7C. Finishing as for *Shades of Grey* is **Wee Dimension**, Font 7B+. Doing it in reverse, from the jugs, is **Perverse Reverse**, Font 7B (it can also be finished into *Basher's Problem*: still Font 7B). *Weedkiller Traverse* there and back is **Killerweed**, Font 7B+. Back and there is **Perverse Killer** which unsurprisingly is also Font 7B+. *Killerweed Footless* has been graded Font 8A+. **Extended Weedkiller** (still Font 7B) starts 3m further right of the normal start on opposing sidepulls.

16 Weedkiller High Font 7B

Start on large holds just right of the normal start and take a higher line on pockets to the finish of *Basher's Problem*.

Michaela Tracy on the exit of Ben's Roof, Font 7C (page 226). Photo: Alex Messenger.

33 Evolution F8c+ ★★ 1995

13m "There are only 3 people who can hang on these holds – Me, myself and I." (Jerry Moffatt). A classic test of power endurance crimping. A long reach and fingers of steel might make the grade feel generous. Swing up and right to the lip. Crimp viciously upwards to a desperate lunge leftwards to a massive flake. From here scurry up a move or two to clip a high single bolt and lower-off. *Ben's Roof* has been linked into *Evolution* to give **Roofolution**, F9a.

Variations to Evolution:

34 Stevolution F9a ★★★ 2008

25m From the massive flake where *Evolution* ends, step leftwards and straight into *Kaaba*. An obvious and superb link-up, unrepeated at the time of writing.

35 Mutation F9a ★★★ 1998

20m Steve McClure's masterpiece of crimping remains unrepeated at the time of writing though not from want of trying (Chris Sharma: "I could never do this route.") Blast up *Evolution* to just before its desperate lunge. Instead, make a flying crossover rightwards to a half-decent hold. Press on upwards on crimps that would barely qualify as footholds, to a final tough rockover into the recess on the left of the *Chimes* belay. **Photo on page 11 and 219.**

36 Devolution F8b+ ★★ 2005

20m This is an easier alternative to *Evolution* escaping rightwards into *Chimes Of Freedom*. Climb *Evolution* around the bulge to the thin break. Then make a few moves upwards before escaping rightwards into the very good holds of *Chimes*.

Devolution has also been linked into *Waddage*, though the grade of that monster is still the same.

37 Chimes of Freedom F8a+ ★★★ 1982/1986/1990

25m Another classic. The *Chimes Start* boulder problem is extended leftwards across the lip of the roof. Several methods, none of them easy, lead past the lip to a good hold. The superb upper wall, whilst more amenable (F7b+/c), is still fluffable. Belay in the scoop on the left.

A seldom climbed second pitch continues up the wall to the break then left to the *Mecca Extension* belay. After a few moves up the corner, take a diagonal traverse to and over the obvious 'beak' of rock. E5 6b. Superseded by *Freedom Fighter*.

Variations to Chimes of Freedom:

38 Baby Chimes F8a ★★

9m An easier version, which lowers off at the break over the roof.

Weedkiller Chimes, F8b (1990), links *Weedkiller Traverse* into *Baby Chimes*. *Weedkiller Traverse* into *Full Chimes* is still the same grade. *Cave Problem Sit Start* into *Baby Chimes* is F8b+.

39 Freedom Fighter F8a+ ★★ 2013

27m A spectacular outing that takes *Chimes* to its logical conclusion. Follow *Chimes*, passing the belay, surmount the heavily-reinforced flake and press on to the break. The belay is just above the pointy nose on the skyline.

40 The Resistance F7c 2013

10m A short pitch, high on the crag, first climbed as an independent second pitch from the *Chimes* belay, most commonly used to provide link-ups. Make the first few moves above the break as for *Freedom Fighter*, then span out right and use some poor holds to reach a good undercut beneath the roof. Pull over and join the last route to finish.

Linking *Chimes of Freedom* into *The Resistance* is F8b. Linking *Right to Roam* into *The Resistance* is **Resistance is Futile**, F8a+ (2013). One of the few routes of the grade here that doesn't have a desperate move.

41 Waddage F8b ★★★ 2003

28m Follow *Chimes*, but instead of traversing left to the belay, continue to the break with one further hard move. From the break, most continue via a huge jump and a traverse right to a large ledge. Great fun.

42 Kristian's Traverse F8a+ ★ 2004

15m Also known as *Mecca Traverse*. Link *Weedkiller Traverse* into *Chimes*. From below the lip of the roof of *Chimes* move left across *Evolution* to finish by down-climbing the jugs at the start of *Mecca* onto the slab. It has also been linked into *Mecca*.

43 The Green Alternative F7c+ ★ 2007

7m Start as for *Chimes* but move right at the first jug and make some hard moves over the roof to the *Weedkiller* belay. **Photo on page 233.**

Variations to The Green Alternative:

Linked with *Weedkiller Traverse* is F8a (2010). Can be linked into *Chimes* via the break (**Chimes Alternative**, F8a, 2013).

44 Right to Roam F8a ★★ 2013

33m The line of least resistance at an amenable grade. Start up *The Green Alternative* and follow *Rooster Booster's* second pitch until a thin break is reached. Move left here into *Chimes* and follow this and *Freedom Fighter* to the top.

Ben's Cave bouldering

45 Weedkiller F7c+ ★   1984/1990
7m Pull over the low bulge just left of the corner then make some very taxing moves over the larger roof to reach a small flake. Up this more easily to reach the small ledge on the left. Distinctly harder for the short.

46 The Killer Strumpet F8a ★   2013
35m A long exciting link route. Up *Weedkiller* to the little ledge then continue up *Right to Roam* until about 5m above the *Cream Team Special* break. Move up and left into the groove of *Mecca's* second pitch then pull out left to finish up *Brazen Strumpet*.

47 Rooster Booster pitch 2 F7c   1982
25m The second pitch of the old testpiece is mostly climbed as part of many link-ups. Follow the groove, then follow sidepulls and crimps to arrive at the *Cream Team Special* break. Continue to a belay. There is some worthwhile climbing above on undercuts to the top of the crag but the original belay is very poor.

There are a variety of finishes leading off the small ledge where *Weedkiller* ends. All were originally started up *Weedkiller* but *The Green Alternative* is another option.

48 The Green Rooster F7c+ ★
25m Link *The Green Alternative* into *Rooster Booster* pitch 2.

49 Fowl Play F8a ★   2004
27m Well worth the journey. The ability to recover before the hard finish is key. Follow *Weedkiller* or *The Green Alternative* then continue up *Rooster Booster* pitch 2 to the top break. Move 2m left then pull over the bulge via a tiny overhung corner using very small crimps to reach better holds leading to the *Waddage* belay.

50 The Missing Link F8a   2007
22m A good direct route with a surprisingly sustained upper wall. Follow *Weedkiller* to the ledge then take the right-hand of the two grooves to a slight break. Steam straight up the wall above until a nasty traverse left leads to the break of *Rooster Booster* pitch 2, up which the route finishes.

51 Let's Get Naked! F8a   1987
25m Forgotten for many years but worthwhile. As for *The Missing Link* to the faint break then traverse right for a few metres. Pull into the slight depression above until a difficult last move to the break:

Let's Get Naked was originally climbed via an aided start to give **Jive Turkey**, F7b+. It can be started via *The Green Alternative* to give **Let's Get Green**, F8a.

52 The Exterminator F8a+ ★   2007
25m This mean wall is best climbed quickly. From the top of *Weedkiller*, swing out right and make some very thin moves up the wall above to a junction with *Let's Get Naked!* Follow this to the top.

53 Rooster Crossing F8c ★   2007
25m Straightens out *The Exterminator* to give a very direct line up the wall with a desperate bouldery start. Use an assortment of upside down holds and polished footholds on *Rooster Booster* to eventually hit the traverse line of that route at a good jug. Move straight up above that to join *The Exterminator* at its crux which is followed to the top.

54 Rooster Booster pitch 1 F7c+ ★★   1964/1982
15m An early free-climbing testpiece. Two pitches, although the first is popular in its own right. Steeply gain the leftward traverse along the break (as for *Sardine* etc.) and follow it leftwards with difficulty to slightly better holds and finally the *Weedkiller* belay. Reverse aid the route to clean it.

It is possible to take a second rope and continue up the top pitch, without weighting the belay, at F8a.

55 Tin Of F7b+ ★★   1988
20m The left-hand of the two easier classics at the Tor. Good sustained and fingery climbing. Do the juggy, thuggy start and leftward traverse of *Sardine*, then make some hard moves up a shallow groove to better holds. Continue weaving up the tricky wall to the break.

56 Crumblefish F8a   1995
20m Crumbly and poor. Some hard moves and harder for the short. As for *Tin Of* to a flat ledge then move out left with difficulty until it is possible to climb direct to the faint break on *Tin Of*. Finish up *Tin Of*.

57 Bullet the Blue Sky F7b+ ★   1987
22m Good climbing but very few new moves. Climb *Tin Of* to a foot traverse and continue left with difficulty to join and finish up *Let's Get Naked!*

58 The Grand Tour F7c ★★   2010
32m Something of an expedition covering some exposed ground. As for *Bullet the Blue Sky* until it joins *Let's Get Naked!* From here traverse left into *The Missing Link* until the break. Finish up *Fowl Play*.

Opposite page| Lucy Creamer on The Green Alternative, F7c+ (page 230). Photo: Alex Messenger.

59 Sardine F7b+ ★★ 1969/1981

20m Derided for its polish, this wandering line reeks of history and is an essential part of the Raven Tor experience. Move up and follow polished holds left, up and back right to a shiny ledge. Stand on the ledge with difficulty (crux) to reach good holds above. This sequence can be avoided by traversing right at a higher level at much the same grade. Continue, passing a fingery traverse right, to big holds up a flake leading to the top. A direct finish is possible above the start of the fingery traverse, no change in grade (1991).

Ello Ethique, F8a (1985), startsup *Weedkiller*, reverses *Rooster Booster* then joins and finishes up *Sardine*.

60 Another Toadside Attraction F7c ★ 1984

19m Well known for being bouldery low down and soft for the grade – no wonder it's so popular. Climb direct to *Sardine*, follow this through its crux, then swing up and out right to a small overlap. Difficult moves past this eventually lead to good holds and the last moves of *Sardine*.

Just right again and a few metres up are a line of small pockets in a faint flake.

61 In Brine F8a+ ★ 1987/2009

19m Fierce and fingery wall-climbing, significantly harder since hold-loss. A complicated sequence leads to the pockets. From the top of these very hard moves lead to an overlap and the relief of a good flat jug. Easier climbing up and then left leads to good holds and the belay.

Tomato Sauce, F7c (1990s), links leftwards into the crux of *Sardine* from the pockets.

62 Obscene Gesture F7c ★ 1982

20m A bolted version of an old trad route (E6) although in reality it only shares a couple of metres with the original, and the crux is different. Climb a flake to a ledge. Use *the* mono and move up and left to cross the bulge just right of *In Brine*. From here step right then finish direct to a lower-off. Can be started at the foot of *In Brine*.

63 Obscene Toilet F7c ★★ 2009

20m A deservedly popular link-up. From the small ledge on *Obscene*, move right to join *The Toilet* and finish up this.

The original **Obscene Gesture**, E6 6c (1982), continued by using the mono above the ledge to move right and then onto the slab above (bolt) up which the route finished.

64 The Toilet F8a ★ 1988

22m Up a short corner to a jug then out left to some positive crimps before a traverse left on terrible holds leads up to better ones. From here a massive reach or crank on crimps for shorties may gain some chunky undercuts and the upper slab to a belay at the break. **Toilet Gesture**, F7c+, links from the crux traverse left into *Obscene Gesture*.

65 The Call of Nature F8a ★★ 2009

20m Popular. From the positive holds on *The Toilet*, a hard rockover up and right leads to a further taxing sequence before better holds are reached. The wall above gradually eases.

66 Verbal Abuse E7 6b ★ 1984

20m One of the last surviving trad routes at the Tor: F7c+ on top rope! Pull into the groove and up this to a large undercut (two pegs). Hard moves up the wall above lead to a faint break (peg and small wire). Move up and right, quite tricky, to easier ground. Either continue to the break or move right to the belay of *The Flushings*.

67 Hot Flushes F8a 1994

17m As for *Verbal Abuse* to the large undercut then traverse right with difficulty to a small finger-hold. A sustained wall leads up and leftwards, eventually, to good holds. Slightly redundant after the addition of the following route.

68 Ring of Fire F7c+ ★ 2011

17m The best piece of climbing hereabouts giving a very sustained piece of climbing. Start as for *Verbal Abuse* but from the large jug move diagonally right at a lower level than *Hot Flushes* to a good sidepull. From here, press on up with some urgency to join and finish up *Hot Flushes*.

The Right End

To the right the crag changes character. The routes become shorter, the rock more compact and the starts significantly undercut. This makes the area a severe test of power and crimp strength with a strong collection of boulder problems and bouldery routes. The walls are relatively quick drying and can give dry climbing in the winter and in the summer the trees can offer shade to boulderers.

To help with route identification, see the Right End Bouldering section on page 239.

69 A Little Extra F7b+ ★ 1979

15m One of the first free routes at the Tor. From the boulder, jump to a polished jug and make hard moves up to another. Move awkwardly up to undercuts then escape up and rightwards. F7c with the Font 7A direct start.

70 The Flushings F7c ★ 1989

17m Quite a testing little route. As for *A Little Extra* to the undercuts then move out left into the final wall of *Hot Flushes*. Beware of rope drag.

Pinches Wall

Right End bouldering

71 Little Boots F7c ★ 2009
15m Start ss for *A Little Extra* to the first jug then make hard moves up and across *Cream Tea Special* to finish up *Boot Boys*.

72 Cream Tea Special F7b+ 1994
18m A strange mini-girdle. As for *A Little Extra* to the undercuts, step down and traverse right with difficulty before moving up and rightwards to the belay of *Out of My Tree*.

73 Hooligan F8c ★ 2003
12m Absolutely desperate! Being tall helps. The boulder problem start leads to relatively good edges. Sort your feet out and attack the hard wall above via some finger-ripping crimps that lead to easier climbing.

74 Boot Boys F8a+ ★★ 1987
12m A mean though satisfying pitch which is seldom climbed. Pop to the jug then use a mono (crux for the fat-fingered) to make a big pull to better pockets. From these, move out left to an undercut which is left with difficulty (crux for others), to reach a good finger-hold. Move left then easily to a belay.

75 Out of My Boots F7c 1998
10m Up to the jug as for *Boot Boys* then move out right and up with difficulty to reach the second jug on *Out of My Tree*. Finish up this.

76 Out of My Tree F8a ★ 1976/1987
10m Pockets to the right lead with difficulty to a jug. Contort up and left to a second jug from which easier slabby climbing leads to a belay.

77 Dialectics F8a+ 1993
10m From the first jug on *Out of My Tree* move right and up, crux, to better holds.

A few metres right is a short left-facing groove a few metres up.

78 Pump Up the Power F8a+ ★ 1987
9m Originally graded E6 6c and nowadays Font 7C+. Take your pick! Boulder up to the faint groove and climb it with great difficulty.

79 Rattle and Hump F8a ★ 1989
9m A difficult boulder problem leads to the jug. Exit leftwards from this with difficulty, harder for the short, and up to better holds. Head right to the belay.

80 Seraphim F8b+ ★ 2007
9m Looks squeezed in but feels independent once involved with the desperate sequences. Make the first move on *Wild in Me*, but where that route spans right, move left into extremely tenuous climbing on awful holds. Awkward and unforgiving all the way to the belay!

81 Wild in Me F7c+ ★ 1986/1993

9m A short, bouldery route with fluffable moves high up. Go from a low, right-facing flake up right to another flake. Stretch left to a crimp. Tricky moves above lead to easier ground.

A few metres right is a black flake.

82 Super High Intensity Body Building F7a 1986

8m A difficult move leads to the flake and then a jug. More hard moves lead to a belay above the grass. High in the grade. Sometimes referred to as "Super High Intensity Training". Work it out.

On the right, above a small parking spot, is the final wall.

83 Saline Drip E2 6b 1981

7m The thin wall leads to an easier, though bold, upper wall.

84 Cream Team Special
F7b+, F7a+, F7a+ ★ 1961/1976

The crag's main horizontal break gives a great line in a great position, but don't do it on a busy day! Usually done from right to left.

1. 20m Start up *Sardine*.
2. 20m Traverse the break until some hard moves lead to the belay of *Mecca Extension*.
3. 20m Continue in style to *Indecent Exposure*. Abseil off from here.

It is also possible to gain the fault line via a scramble with care along grass ledges.

85 The Ministry of Silly Walks HVS 5a 1979

100m Wanders in from the right then traverses grass and some good rock with an exciting finish up the final moves of *Mecca Extension's* second pitch. Probably never climbed since the first ascent?

Playstation Buttress

Fifty metres beyond the right-hand side of the Tor lies an unusual wave of limestone. This provides three routes: **Mortal Combat**, F7b+ (1998), the left-hand line via a shallow groove on the bulge; **Tomb Raider**, F8a (1998), the central line; **Gran Turismo**, F7b (1998), the right-hand line.

Adam Coefield on Rattle and Hump Start, Font 7A+ (page 240). Photo: John Coefield.

Right End Bouldering

The ever-bulging wall on the right-hand side is home to lots of burly classics. These are sometimes the starts of hard routes, and can go quite far up the crag.

Pinches Wall: The collection of polished crimps, bumps and ripples on the left-hand side is known as Pinches Wall. It is a museum to the obsession of generations of Raven Tor devotees and as such is riddled with revered eliminates and pointless gymnastics.

1   The Rib Font 6A+
The rib left of the wall to jugs.

2 Font 6A
The easiest line on Pinches Wall, from the big low sidepull, up on edges, to the rounded jug.

3   Verbal Abuse Start Font 6A+
The groove to jugs.

4   Little Extra Direct Start Font 7A
From a good slot in the break, reach high and left to a shiny crimp and go for a rounded jug up right. Match here, or continue to more jugs at Font 7A+. Alternatively, get the shiny crimp with the right hand and rock left to slots.

5   Undercut to Crimp Font 7B+
From low slots move into the obvious undercuts, then up to a high, slanting crimp and then left to the jug on *A Little Extra*. Doing the same but using the sloper just above the crimp is Font 7C.

6   Sidepull Problem Font 7C
From the slots, move out to a split-finger pocket, up to a crozzly sidepull with the right hand then back left to the jug via both the crimp and sloper. Using the undercut instead of the pocket is Font 7B+.

7   Pump up the Vallium Font 7C+
From a high pinch with the left hand and a poor undercut with the right, make a hard cross through to a crozzly undercut and follow crimps above to a high jug.

8   Wild East 8A+
Dyno from the start holds of *Pump up the Vallium* straight to a sika edge up right.

Right again are some obvious 'improved' holds a few metres up.

9   Hooligan Font 8A+
Pull on using a poor pinch for the right and a tiny undercut for the left. Slap for a small crimp, cross right for another crimp then gain better flakes.

10   Ben's Traverse Font 8A
From the pillar at the end of *Powerband* crab your way leftwards until the climbing gets easy. F8b route grade. In reverse is **Pocketrocity**, Font 8A.

11   Boot Boys Start Font 6C
Use big burly undercuts and pockets to gain a glued jug.

12   Out of My Tree Start Font 7B
Pockets and slots lead with difficulty to a jug.

15   Rattle and Hump Start   Font 7A+

From a square pocket and good edge, bust up right to small crimps and choose from a variety of equally frustrating methods to reach the jug in the groove. The 'hard way' starts just to the right on the first two of the higher line of slots and goes straight up to match the crimps without using the heel-toe on the left (Font 7B). **Photo on page 238.**

16   Powerhumps   7B

A classic extension to *Powerband*, gaining it from the slots on *Powerband*. Font 7B+ if linked into the hard way.

17   Powerband   Font 7C

A famous testpiece, first climbed by Jerry Moffatt in the face of some stiff competition. Hard for the grade, and harder again for those lacking wingspan. Start at a low horizontal hold with both hands. Move leftwards on slots with feet frantically clawing at the polished edges in the back of the scoop. Eventually a jug is reached before the final crux move using a shallow pocket to cross under and drop down to gain the pillar. **Photo below.**

13   Pump up the Power   Font 7C+

Boulder up to the short left-facing groove and leave it with considerable difficulty for a jug on the left.

14   The Steve Miller Band   Font 7C

Link left from the lip of *Pump up the Power* into the jug of *Out of My Tree*.

18   Blueband   Font 7C

Reverse *Powerband*. **Strict Blueband**, Font 7C+, eliminates the undercut slot (halfway along), the square pocket and the final pocket of the higher line of pockets to produce a fiendish dropdown move. In reverse with those rules it is also Font 7C+. **Bluehumps,** Font 8A, links *Strict Blueband* into *Rattle and Hump* 'hard way'.

Steve McClure on Powerband, Font 7C (above). Photo: Keith Sharples.

19 Influx Font 8A

Sit start with right hand in the undercut and left in the first of the pockets. Pull up to a crimp and sidepull just above then onto a crimp above. Match this to finish.

20 Kristian's Problem Font 7B

Compress up between the sidepulls on *Influx* and *Wild in Me*. Climb upwards past a high crimp to get established on the juggy flake above, on *Wild in Me*. **Stamina in Me**, Font 7C, links into this from the start of *Staminaband*.

21 Wild in Me Start Font 6C

Go from the diagonal flake to the sidepull jug up right.

22 Staminaband Font 8A

An extension start to *Powerband*, beginning about 8m to its right in a small groove just right of twin pockets. F8b+ route grade. In reverse, with the same rules (grab a local if unsure!) is **Contraband**, Font 8A.

The next problem is right of the tree and is essentially the hard part of the route of the same name.

23 Saline Drip Font 7A

A choice of multiple methods on awkwardly placed crimps lead to the jug. A sit start is 7A+.

24 Boyband Font 7C

From the large head-height jug to the right of the start of *Saline Drip*, traverse leftwards to finish at the start of *Staminaband*, hopefully without falling onto anyone's car bonnet or impaling yourself on the tree.

Link-ups: Which link-ups are given route grades and which are given bouldering grades is more a quirk of recent history than a conscious and logical distinction.

Staminaband/Pump up the Power (F8c+ or Font 8B) Made famous by Ben Moon's attempts on it as a training link, now established as a modern classic in its own right.

Powerband/Pump up the Power (Font 8A+) AKA Pump up the Powerband.

Staminahumps (Font 7C+) *Staminaband* into *Rattle and Hump* hard way. Possibly even better than *Staminaband*.

Should be Banned (Font 8A+) *Staminaband* into *Ben's Traverse*. Take a good book for the rest on the pillar.

Boyband/Staminaband (F8c+/F9a) You can put your book away for this one.

Out of Stamina (F8c or Font 8A+) *Staminaband* into the *Out of My Tree* boulder problem. No stepping left onto the pillar for a no-hands rest.

Boyband, Ben's Traverse, and then on into *Weedkiller Traverse* and eventually into the start of *Mecca* has been linked.

Raven Tor History

Chris Jackson and Geoff Birtles aiding The Prow (page 217). Photo: Bob Keates.

Raven Tor has been at the cutting edge of limestone free-climbing standards. in the Peak District since the early 1980s, taking that crown from Stoney Middleton. For decades it made the pace and over the years its walls hosted such triumphs as the hardest route in the country, the first F8b+ in the UK, the hardest route in the world, the first F9a in the Peak, among its many historic routes and boulder problems. While it has almost reached maturity, with few remaining gaps, its steep grey walls and polished crimps still present a challenge from which even the best in the world can still walk away empty-handed.

Like most limestone crags, it remained untouched up until the 1950s being too loose and steep to contemplate given the equipment available, the fitness and climbing style of the day. And again, like many such crags, it was the artificial climber who first looked to it for entertainment.

In 1956 Ron Hughes and John Hadfield started trying to aid-climb Raven Tor, ground up, hindered by loose rock. These first recorded attempts on the crag would come to fruition in 1957 when John Hadfield succeeded in aid-climbing *Hubris*, a vague crack on the left-hand side of the crag. The ascent was punctuated with several huge falls (including one that took in almost the entire height of the crag as Hadfield slipped whilst topping out on wet vegetation) and several changes in line as falls stripped both pegs and loose rock.

Raven Tor remained the preserve of the aid climber throughout the 60s and first half of the 70s. The Manchester Gritstone Club began attacks on the blank, overhanging central section of the crag in the late 50s. The aid climbers started out using

Ron Fawcett on Body Machine (page 220). Photo: Leo Dickinson.

pegs, threads, slings and the occasional "golo" (a short expandable peg placed in a hand-drilled hole) to pass blank sections, but the use of bolts gradually took off. *Mecca* was the first to fall in 1960, the culmination of the previous year's efforts, with the first 2 repeats taking 9 hours each. Other obvious weaknesses and features fell over the next decade: the *Girdle* in 1961, the Prow in 1963, *Brandenberg Gate* (approximately just right of where *Hubble* is now) in '66, and *Sardine* in '69.

In 1976 what was probably the first "free" route was climbed by Ron Fawcett, who tied a boulder to a tree and stepped off this to miss out the first overhanging and difficult section of the climb before free climbing to the top creating the *Perfidious Primate*. The boulder problem start to this route was later added by Andy Pollitt to create *Out of My Tree*. Fawcett later climb *Hubris* with one point of aid and girdled the high break to create the *Cream Team Special* but the big blank central walls remained the bailiwick of the aid climber. This began to change in 1981 when Fawcett returned and free climbed *Sardine* (previously a loose A3). This was the first major free route at the crag and it became a major testpiece over night.

In 1982, a young Jerry Moffatt began to give Fawcett some competition. After Moffatt climbed *Rooster Booster*, Fawcett followed up with *Indecent Exposure* and then *The Prow*. With modern grades between F7b+ - F7c+ these were almost the equal of cutting edge routes in Europe and America and Raven Tor began its long tradition of pushing free-climbing standards. In 1984 Moffatt climbed *Revelations*, the name reflecting what was becoming possible through dedicated training and a change in style.

Prior to *Revelations*, routes were yo-yoed, often on twin ropes, but after climbing with French climbers such as Jibe Tribout and the Le Menestrel brothers Jerry decided to climb *Revelations* in redpoint style, practicing the easier top section before attempting to climb through the boulder problem start. Revelations became an internationally desirable tick, but many climbers such as Jibe Tribout and Stefan Glowacz failed, presumably on the start that still shuts down many extremely strong climbers 30 years later. It must be noted however that the difficulty of *Revelations* has increased, (possibly by as much as 2 grades) due to changes to the holds. With *Revelations,* the often-damp crux slot became markedly worse when the edge crumbled after repeated drying with a blow-torch and then became even shallower when the back was lined with sika to prevent seepage. Incredibly, the route was soloed by Antoine Le Menestrel in 1985.

In 1988, on his last day before departing from the UK to take a job with Mammut in Switzerland, Martin Atkinson completed his 2-year project to free climb Mecca. The original intention had been to climb the full route, but after 2 years it was apparent that this was not going to happen soon and Martin was relieved to reach the halfway flake to create *Mecca, the Mid-Life Crisis*. At F8b+ this was the hardest sport route in the UK. Although Martin was super-fit from years of yo-yoing, success on *Mecca* was due to increases in boulder and finger strength generated from bouldering along the bottom of the crag, lapping problems such as Jerry Moffatt's *Powerband*. Raven Tor climbing is characterised by a short, steeply undercut lower section and small finger holds and it was the application of boulder strength to these sections that created the hard routes over the next decade.

Ron Fawcett. Photo: Geoff Birtles.

Jerry Moffatt. Photo: Richie Brooks.

Jerry Moffatt on Revelations (page 222). Photo: Neil Foster.

In 1990 the hardest route in the world came to the Tor. At its conception the route was an attempt to boulder through the previously aided start of the *Whore of Babylon*. Before completion several of the top climbers could do the moves, but the difficulty was in linking them. The 7 crux moves came together for Ben Moon relatively quickly and *Hubble* was born, the name suggested by Sean Myles. Ben considered *Hubble* to be a step up from his previous hardest routes such as *Agincourt* in the South of France (F8c) and he graded the route E9 7b, or F8c+, a world first. In 1991 Wolfgang Gullich climbed *Action Directe*, UIAA XI in Germany. After trying the route and almost succeeding, Ben stated that he considered the route to be the same grade as *Hubble*, F8c+. Over the years, *Action Directe* received a number of ascents from various globetrotting climbers and the grade settled as benchmark F9a, the first of the grade in the world. *Hubble* however had become the benchmark by which other routes were graded in the UK and the grade remained at F8c+ without question until Adam Ondra, despite failing on the route, commented after a quick visit that it was probably F9a (and therefore both the world's first F8c+ and F9a), with a Font 8B+ crux section. Almost 25 years later there are still few routes with Font 8B+ or harder climbing on them and Ben's put-down made shortly after Malcolm Smith's second ascent in 1992 that, "two years is a long time in climbing," has proved wrong.

After another long siege, Mark Pretty gave the crag its second F8c, *Make it Funky* in 1993. In 1995 Moffatt returned and climbed *Evolution*. The initial grade of F8c+ did not last long and it was quickly repeated and downgraded to F8c – it's fairly safe to say that (by modern standards) the mid-90s sport climbing scene in the UK was under grading at the cutting edge by a grade. *Evolution* is now considered F8c+.

In the late-90s, Steve McClure came to the Tor as a sport-climbing beginner but soon rocketed through the grades to climb *Evolution*. After extending *Make it Funky* and *Mecca* he began work on the extension to *Evolution*, the conditions necessary for success rendering his fingers, "as cold as pegs". *Mutation* was climbed in 1998 and graded F9a but this grade makes less sense as the years pass and the comparison routes get upgraded. It is unrepeated at the time of printing.

After *Mutation* the major gaps had been filled. However, the start to *Brandenburg Gate* remains unclimbed despite John Gaskins' efforts. Steve Dunning closed the blank section left of *Boot Boys* with *Hooligan* and Steve McClure linked every hard route into every other hard route as training for projects elsewhere. Mark Pretty also returned and began to climb every remaining unexplored foot of the upper walls, creating a spider's web of new routes and links. Down below, the bouldering (now an end in itself) was also pushed to the limits of the available rock. Gaskins completed Ben Moon's training project linking *Staminaband* into *Pump up the Power* at Font 8B/+ and James Pearson climbed directly out of the cave to create *Keen Roof* at Font 8B. In 2013, Chris Webb Parsons started at the very back of the roof, eschewed the available knee-bar rest and finished up Keen Roof, creating *Belly of the Beast,* Font 8C, later repeated with the knee bar at Font 8B+.

Rupert Davies

Ben Moon. Photo: Richie Brooks.

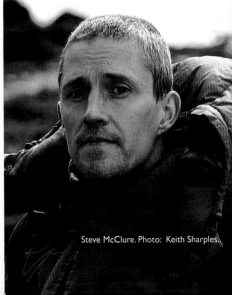

Steve McClure. Photo: Keith Sharples.

Ben Moon on Hubble, F9a (page 222). Photo: Steve Lewis.

Tideswell Dale

Trad: 58 (VD to E7) **Bouldering:** 13 (Font 5 to Font 7C+) **Sport:** 2 (F8a to F8a+)
Aspect: All directions **Sunshine:** All times **Season:** Spring to autumn
Conditions: Sheltered, esoteric, mostly clean, pretty location
Best for: Esoteric crag-hopping **Approach:** 1 - 20 minutes

This pleasant little dale, with a well-used public footpath running through, links the Tideswell Dale picnic spot with Miller's Dale. The climbs are generally fairly short, distributed over several buttresses on essentially good rock. From a climbing perspective, it is very unvisited. A nice place with lovely settings.

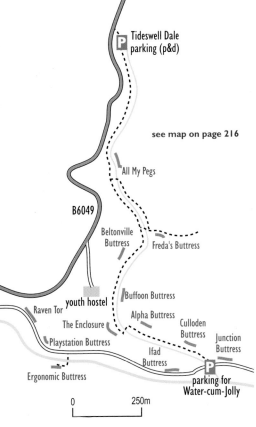

Tideswell Dale parking (p&d)

see map on page 216

All My Pegs

B6049

Beltonville Buttress

Freda's Buttress

Buffoon Buttress

youth hostel

Raven Tor

Alpha Buttress

The Enclosure

Culloden Buttress

Playstation Buttress

Junction Buttress

Ifad Buttress

parking for Water-cum-Jolly

Ergonomic Buttress

0   250m

The Climbing

Lots of small buttresses with pleasant climbs. Steep, fingery and technical routes.

Conditions and Aspect

Crags lie on both sides of the dale and face various directions so there is always some sun, if it's shining, and lots of shade. Most of the routes are fairly clean, apart from the now-overgrown Buffoon Buttress. Some loose rock.

Parking and Approach

Park at one of the two parking spots. The upper, Tideswell Dale parking (pay and display) or the lower, Miller's Dale parking, is 400m past Raven Tor.

All My Pegs

Approach in 10 minutes from the upper parking. There is a series of bulges just before the valley opens up. At the bottom of these is an overhanging crack. **All My Pegs in One Basket**, F8a (1991), is the pegged crack, finishing at a dodgy jammed nut belay. Two pegs.

Freda's Buttress

The best buttress in the dale. Clean and solid. It faces north and sits by a small steep path that breaks off from the main valley towards the plateau above.

1 Lee Perry Presents 'It's a Knockout' E1 5b 1997
12m Go up the prominent corner at the left-hand end of the crag (*Frolic*). Pull left over the bulge and climb the slab rightwards, finishing left of the tree.

2 Frolic VS 4c 1991
10m The slanting groove.

3 Freda HVS 5b ★ 1960s
16m Climb to the overhang, traverse right to a groove and follow this past an old peg runner to the top. The start is **Freda's Start**, Font 5+.

4 Freda Direct Font 6B
Ascend direct to *Freda's* final groove.

5 Infinite Suspense Font 7C+
A classic. Undercut up to a sloper and right-hand pinch, make a crux move to a poor edge, then press on to high jugs.

6 Skylarkin Font 7A+
Start on a thin left-hand undercut and a good right-hand undercut/sidepull. Leap to the juggy rail.

7 E.T. Bone Home Font7A
From jugs, climb directly upwards via a poor left-hand crimp and a high slopey right hand hold. Pull through to the good jug, as for *Skylarkin*.

8 King Louis Font 5
From the start of *E.T...*, climb rightwards to good holds.

9 More Glee in the Jungle Font 6A
The direct start to *King Louis*, off big undercuts.

10 Pedal to the Nettle Font 6C
From a sitting start, pull up past a flat hold and on to jugs.

11 Bum Note Font 5+
Climb up from low jugs.

12 Scroll Font 7A
Start up *Bum Note* and traverse left to finish up *More Glee...*

Continue along *Scroll* to finish up *E.T...* at Font 7B: **Space Invaders**. **Cripple's Crab**, Font 7A+, continues the traverse all the way to the left.

Buffoon Buttress

This lies further down the valley and is completely overgrown. It held: **Chinese Wall**, HVS 5b (1985), **Exiled Transformer**, E1 5b (1984), **Green Dragon**, E1 5b (1985), **Buffoon Crack**, VS 4c (1965), **China Crisis**, E2 5b (1985), **Annapurna South Face**, HVS 5b (1985), **Old Dog – New Trick**, E4 6a (1985), **Flags for Everything**, E3 5c (1985), **The Stone Leopard**, E5 6a (1985), **Ice Out in the Rain**, E1 5a (1985) and **Ice 9**, E2 6a (1985).

Alpha Buttress

Closer to the bottom of the dale, and just upstream from a little bridge, is a clean buttress, characterised by a shallow cave in its centre. It lies 5 minutes from the lower parking. **Débutant**, E3 5c (1985), starts up a short corner on the left of the buttress. Climb directly, finishing rightwards; **Dissident Aggressor**, E2 5c (1983), gains the short corner of the previous route then moves out right over the bulge and finishes up the crack to reach the trees; **Lost Ambition**, E2 5b (1983), starts 2m to the right, and 4m to the left of the cave. Climb to a good incut ledge. Either climb the groove or swing out left and gain the groove higher up. Finish up the pseudo-crack. **Survival Limit**, E5 5c

(1983), starts just to the left of the cave. Climb to a pinch and continue over two small roofs finishing leftwards up the steep headwall; **Close Enough**, VS 4c (1985), begins 10m right of the shallow cave where a groove is capped by an overhang at 7m. Climb to the roof, swing right on to the slab, then go up and left above the roof to finish.

Culloden Buttress

The next rock is 200m down the dale, very close to the car park. The left-hand side of the buttress is marked by **Wide Crack**, S (2014). To the right is a slabby-looking face with a thin crack in its left giving **The Neb Crack**, VS 4c (1960s); just right, **Sensation**, VS 4b (1960s), climbs another crack whilst the left-facing corner right again is taken by **Tideswell Cenotaph**, VS 4b (1976). This is guarded on the right by **The Hulk**, VS 4b (1976).

The next piece of rock gives three better pitches:

13 Trinig E1 5b ★
1960s/1976
12m A fine little route via the short bottomless corner and excellent prominent crack.

14 The Meanie E4 6a
1966/1980
15m Brutal by name and brutal by nature. The leaning thin crack to the right is deceptively strenuous and difficult.

15 Culloden F8a+ ★
1990
11m A desperate bouldery affair up the leaning face to the right.

Junction Buttress

Further to the right, a buttress overlooking the road has a smattering of pitches, which may prove more difficult due to encroaching vegetation and passing motorists. **In-slippy**, VS 4b (1966) and **Blackbirds**, VS 5a (1976), have now been overcome by ivy whilst **Custard**, E1 5b (1976), is the first noticeable crack. **Roobarb**, E2 6a (1976/1981), takes the next crack; **Tales of Pinkie Power**, F6c+ (1987), tackles the de-geared wall right again; **Blacksmith's Lactic**, E3 5c (1981), the final thin crack on the right.

Ifad Buttress

This is the first of the buttresses on the opposite side of the valley. It is just above a small parking spot, 40m before the larger car park. Here lie a number of little routes starting just beyond a layby at a slabby face: **Black Magic**, HVS 5b (1976), climbs the centre of this to a tricky finale; **White Magic**, HVS 5b (1976), tackles the steeper wall just right passing a peg and overhang; **Nowt Much**, VD (1976), tackles the left-hand side of the overhang 7m to the right via a finishing corner; **Particular Groove**, HVS 5a (1976), gains a V-groove above the overhang to the right; **Ifad**, E3 6a (1960s), climbs the thin cracks through the ivy-covered overhang right again; 3m right of *Ifad*, **Vanishing Resources**, S (1976), climbs a flake/corner; **Hairline Fracture**, E2 5c (1985), climbs the groove just right again with three slings; **Runaway**, E1 5b (1986), climbs the groove and crack 5m right again.

The Encolsure

The first rock on the left-hand side of the dale proper when approaching from the lower car park. **Breaking the Chain**, E3 5c (1985), climbs the wall left of the flakes, and follows the obvious line slightly rightwards to finish at a tree; **Still Life**, E2 5b (1985), takes the flake to its end, pulls round the bulge and climbs to the tree (as for the previous route); **Restoree**, E4 6a (1985), starts 2m right and climbs the wall to a bulge. Pull up and gain large sloping holds on the right, move back left then climb the wall to a small tree belay. Poorly protected; **Sanctuary**, E2 5b (1985), is 3m to the right of the previous route. Gain a short corner capped by a roof and exit leftwards using the handholds of *Restoree* as footholds. Finish as for *Restoree*.

To the right is a larger, towering wall, steep in its first half. **Chains**, E3 5c ((1985), climbs the wall on its left-hand side to a thread, then easier climbing leads to the top; **Self Control**, E7 6b (1985), takes the white streak in the centre of the wall, to the overlap. Make a hard move past this to an undercut from which the easier upper wall can be reached. Move right at the top to a tree. Unprotected.

Running Wild, E4 6b (1985), takes the wall on its right edge to a pillar. Using holds on the ramp to the left, make hard moves to gain better handholds (but not footholds) in the wall to the left. Continue left to finish at the tree of *Chains*.

Beltonville Buttress

This is high on the side of the dale, 300m past The Enclosure. It has a vague, central arête with a deep groove on either side. **Ode to Eric**, HVS 5a (1985), is the wall left of the left-hand groove; **Eric's Left Buttock**, VD (1985), is the deep left-hand groove; **Adrenaline Suspender Belt**, E1 5c (1985), is the arête. Make a difficult starting move round the overhang, keeping your foot off *Eric's Left Buttock*, then go more easily to the top; **Bastard Toadflax**, S (1985), is the pleasant hand-jamming crack, just to the right of the previous route; **Urtica Dioica** VD (1985), is the prominent groove just right, with a detached pillar in its right; **Bad Guts**, VS 5a (1984), is the groove to the right. Step right and finish up the arête; **Lanky Sod**, VS 5a (1984), follows the leftwards-slanting flake on the right to a small stance, then climb a wall above.

Miller's Dale South Bank Crags

The next crags are a series of small buttresses on the bank opposite Raven Tor.

Ergonomic Buttress

The most eastern of these, at the Litton Mill end of the bank, is quite good, and the most easily accessible. It lies just upstream of the bridge crossing the river downstream of Raven Tor.

Big Word Climb, VS 4b (1976), climbs a corner and crack on the left again; **Brand X**, HVS 5b (1980), takes the hanging flake on the wall to the left of the overhangs; **Ergonomic Buttress**, E3 5c (1960s/1976/1981), climbs the centre of the large overhang via a hanging corner via a leftwards traverse and groove above.

Raven's Foot Buttress

This buttress lies further down the valley, slightly upstream from and opposite to Raven Tor. It is best gained by following the riverbank upstream from the bridge just below Raven Tor.

The buttress is characterised by a long slim wall on its left-hand side with a large flake roughly 20m high in the centre of the face behind which is *Raven's Foot Chimney*. To the right of this the cliff gives a concave face with an open corner and an undercut, bulging wall to its right with three trees shrouding the middle to the right. **Yer Right Me Duck**, E3 5c (1991), takes a line behind the middle tree past two bolts and sling to a fixed belay; **Cuck the Duck**, F7b+ (1991), climbs the centre of the face past a preposterous boulder-problem; **Count Duckula**, F7b+ (1991), climbs the tough face left again; **White in the Face, Black in the Palms**, E5 6b (1986), climbs the angle of the bay exiting left along the break and over the bulge to a tree; **Where I Live**, E4 6b (1991), the fine, pleasant bolt-protected face to the left.

Alive She Cried, E2 5b (1963/1983), climbs a thin crack right of the crack on the right-hand side of the huge flake finishing via a steep groove (peg); **Raven's Crack**, VS 4c (1963), climbs the crack on the right-hand side of the flake, finishing via loose rock above a pinnacle; **Raven's Foot Chimney**, VD (1961), climbs the chimney forming the left-hand side of the flake. **Raven Loonie**, HVS 5b (1984), climbs the crack system just to the left and starting at a higher level. The direct start is 5a.

The long wall to the left contains a myriad of problems: **Sex-Crazed Gorilla**, E2 5b (1984), takes a flake, overlap and groove; **Raven Bonking**, E3 6a (1984), climbs the wall 2m to the left to a tree; **Kuwait and See**, E5 6b (1991), climbs the wall 4m left again past in-situ gear; **No Short Coutts**, F7b (1991), climbs the wall and desperate overlap left again; **The Power to Heal**, F7a (1989), climbs the wall 2m left again; **Stony Ground**, E4 6b (1991), tackles the short wall and bulge left again; **Silk Coutt**, E3 6b (1991), is the final problem route on the left.

Slip and Slime Buttress

Another 100m up the river is a small buttress: **Slip and Slime**, E1 6b (1985), is the thin crack splitting the bulge on the left; **Stuff of Dreams**, HVS 6a (1985), is the crack and leftwards-facing corner to the right; **No Strange Delight**, E1 6a (1985), climbs the hanging corner on the right

Squirrel's Buttress

A small but classy wave of limestone with a handful of powerful testpieces including one of the best Font 7Cs in the Peak.

The Climbing
Powerful bouldering on lovely big holds on steep, clean limestone. Problems from standing and sitting.

Conditions and Aspect
North-facing and very shady. Thick tree cover in summer. Sheltered. Seeps in winter.

Parking and Approach
From the Anglers Rest, walk down the road towards Raven Tor for 100m, and the buttress can just about be spotted across the river. Ford the river direct to the buttress. Another possible approach is to cross the bridge by the pub and walk down the bank but the vegetation is abominable here. See map on page 216.

Twenty metres left of the main buttress, a wall runs up to the crag. On the left of this is **Beat the Gun**, E4 6a (1985). Gain a scoop below the roof, cross this (peg on the left), and continue (passing two more pegs). **The Staircase**, VD (1960s), is the staircase just right of the wall.

1 **Old-Fashioned Hot Air Balloon** Font 7A+
The left arête. Traverse left to escape.

2 **Peeled Baby** Font 7A+
The narrow wall between the groove and the arête finishing right on jugs.

3 **Paradox Wish (AKA The Groove)** Font 6C+
The groove to finish right on jugs.

4 **Hand Candy** Font 7C
The right arête of the groove, starting on a pocket. A sit start is possible from a jug and crimp down left but this doesn't add much.

5   Candy Floss Font 7B+

Start *Hard Candy* from sitting, and link this into the top section of *Candy Kaned*.

6   Hard Candy Font 7C+

Link *Candy Kaned* into *Hand Candy*.

7   Candy Kaned Font 7C

Mega classic. Start sitting, with right hand on a jug and left on a small white crimp, and slap up using sidepulls and crimps to finish with hands on the ledge. The standing start is **Down Like a Rock**, Font 7B.

8   Candy Man Font 7C

Start standing, with your left hand in a good pocket. Move up then head left to the ledge. **Candy Man Sit Start**, Font 8A, starts with a high right-hand undercut and a left-hand crimp just above.

9   Midget Gem Font 7B

The short grey wall to the right of *Candy Man*. Start with a left-hand gaston and right hand in a small pocket. Make a big move to the ramp and finish up this to join the other problems at the ledge.

10   Hero's Challenge Font 6B

Traverse the lip from the right to finish on the ledge.

The groove on the right is **Red Squirrel**, HVS 5b (1985).

Slow Water Tor

This crag is 400m upstream from Litton Mill, almost directly opposite the entrance to Tideswell Dale. **Slow Water Girdle**, VS 4c (1973), traverses the obvious break 7m above the river from right-to-left. On the upstream end of the tor an obvious groove goes through a large black overhang. The left-hand finish is **Ellis Needham**, VD (1973), and the right-hand finish is **Robert Blincoe**, S (1973).

Viaduct Buttress

This is the small, somewhat hidden buttress situated directly under the viaduct. It is reached by crossing the footbridge opposite the Angler's Rest and meandering upstream. **A Clip in Time**, E4 6b (1983), climbs a left-leaning flake on the left of the buttress and crosses the bulge with difficulty (peg). **Mister Blister**, E6 6c (1986), climbs the desperate roof 7m to the left past three pegs and an in-situ nut.

Priestcliffe Quarry

This and other gloomy quarries are high on the hill overlooking Miller's Dale and are clearly seen from the Tideswell road. The crag takes a good deal of drainage and the climbs are dirty, with a quantity of loose rock. It does have a grade VII icicle, in the right conditions. Approach along the Monsal Trail from Miller's Dale station. Pass a sign indicating the public footpath to Taddington and go up some rough stone steps past a notice indicating that you are entering Derbyshire Wildlife Trust's Miller's Dale Quarry Nature Reserve.

Monk's Dale

From the church, behind the Angler's Rest, follow the path up this little dale. After a stroll of 10 minutes a small buttress will be seen on the left. The buttress is in an area of outstanding beauty. All the routes have now retreated behind the vegetation and are best left that way.

Strawberry Rocks

A forgotten crag with some loose rock. The crag is reached from the old Miller's Dale station Pay and Display carpark in about 10 minutes. Follow the old railway track past the disused concrete lime kiln and branch off right along an overgrown path into the quarry. The crag forms the left-hand wall of the quarry and is well hidden behind the mostly harmless vegetation.

The routes, from, let to right, are **The White Wall of Impending Doom**, VS 4b (1966), **Fallen Dead**, HVS 5c (1984), **Delusions of Hell**, E1 6a (1984), **Kerouac** Crack, VS 4b (1990), **Improved Groove**, VS 4c (1965), **Walking Dead**, HVS 5b (1984), **Fried Parrot Groove**, HVS 5b (1965), **Nabeel**, E1 5b (1990), **Dingle**, VS 5a (1965), **Wolfsbane**, E3 6a (1984), **The Dharma Bums**, E2 5c (1990), **Hyperbole**, VS 4c (1965), **The Big Sur**, VS 4b (1990), **Andy Bean**, E2 5c (1984), **Tarantula**, VS 4b (1965), **Zombie Master**, E2 6a (1984), **Power Wars**, E4 5c (1984), **Loremaster**, E1 5b (1984), **Double Negative**, E3 5c (1984), **The French Connection**, E3 5b (1991), **Active Terrorist**, E4 5c (1984), **Pincer Attack**, HVS 5a (1984), **Tactical Withdrawal**, E1 5b (1984), **Frontal Attack**, E2 5c (1984), **Rinceworld**, E2 5c (1984).

Strawberry Quarry

Approach (with caution) as for Strawberry Rocks. It is the first large area of rock, set well back on the right in a quarry on the right-hand side of the railway line just before the lime kiln. NOTE: The DWT does not want any climbing on the cliff.

Blackwell Dale

Sport: 10 (F7a+ to F8a+)   **Bouldering:** 64 (Font 6A to Font 8A+)
Aspect: East and west   **Sunshine:** Varies - all day   **Season:** Spring to autumn
Conditions: Traffic-y, shady, sometimes slow drying
Best for: Short, steep, powerful quick hits F7c to F8a+, Font 7A to 8A+   **Approach:** Roadside

Blackwell Dale is the home of a classy collection of small buttresses that line the road as it threads its way up the hillside from Miller's Dale up towards the A6. Throughout its length it is littered with numerous small buttresses and walls that have, over recent years, become very popular to the bouldering fraternity. There are also a small number of good-quality sport routes, also of a very bouldery nature. Overall, this is a great spot, offering some easily accessible routes and problems of excellent quality.

Conditions and Aspect
A good summer venue. The road runs roughly north to south and with crags on either side there is a choice of morning or evening sun. On the other hand, the narrow nature of the tree-filled valley can provide welcome shade. Trees and the valley means there is lots of shade. The problems seep in winter and some of the buttresses, especially Sean's Roof, are slow to dry. Lots of the problems are steep enough to offer good rain protection. The Sean's Roof and Red or Dead areas are 'very roadside' and the traffic noise can be intrusive.

The Climbing
Most of the routes are extremely fingery and bouldery in style. The bouldering is fairly hardcore in nature with lots of burly, fingery problems. These are sometimes very low-ball, especially on parts of Sean's Roof, but are the rest are of a good height and with good landings.

Parking and Approach
See map on page 216. There is a layby under Beginner's Wall, serving that crag and the Griff's Buttress area. If coming from Litton/ Raven Tor direction, it is on the left, a kilometre after you pass under the railway viaduct near the Anglers Rest. The crag is 25m away up the hill on the same side. For the Griff's Buttress area, park here and cross the road and drop down to the valley below.

Sean's Roof / Roadside Wall parking is 200m uphill, again on the left. It is obvious by the low dark roof that overhangs the layby.

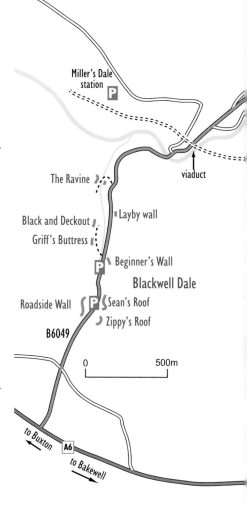

see map on page 216

Emlyn James on Young, Gifted and Black. Font 7A (page 263). Photo: Jon Fullwood.

Layby Wall

A little wall by the first shallow layby after the bend. All the problems are graded for not using footblocks. **See map on page 254**

1 Part-Timer Font 7B

Sit start at the far left of the wall on good ledges. Swing rightwards with some hard moves to gain and finish up *Forager*.

2 Forager Font 6C

Sit start at the left end of the steep section (right hand undercut, left hand sidepull) and power upwards.

3 Sidewinder Font 7A+

Sit start as for *Dances With Wool*, but traverse the lip left and finish up *Forager*.

4 Dances With Wool Font 7A+

In the centre of the steep section, sit start (start left hand sidepull) to the lip, then a hard move to get stood up.

Beginner's Wall

Quality power-based sport climbing and a dozen fingery problems. **See map on page 254**

5 The Midges Bite Back F7a+   1989

10m A series of testing overlaps left of the cleft.

6 Citadel E1 5b   1970

12m The leaning cleft is an old-style grovel and grope.

7 O'Leanna the Butler Dunn It! F7c+   1995

10m A very hard boulder-problem just right of the crack leads to a flake line.

8 A Bit on the Side Font 7A

From the same start as *Recreational Violence*, move out left for good holds, then back right to the same finish.

9 Recreational Violence Font 8A+

Climb the grey streak, using a right hand undercut and left hand crimp to dyno directly for the slopey jugs. A left-hand version is Font 8A. This takes the crimp with right hand and goes left to another, then on to the top. Stay right of the good holds to the left.

10 The Love of Money is the Root of All Evil
F8a+   1998

10m More hideous climbing to the right leads via a lurch/jump to gain the flake. The problem start is Font 7B.

11 Aurora Font 7C

The wall to the right of the groove. Sit start, and head left and up the imposing overhanging wall, via a heel hook, sidepulls and crimps to gain the obvious two large edges.

12 Short Problem Font 7A

From sitting, climb to the left end of the juggy ledge.

The next routes all start by gaining the ledge at 3m.

13 Fossil Wall F7c ★★   1986

10m The original classic. From the left end of the ledge, undercut up left to gain the flake. Up this, then back right via a crack with a big move to gain the final crack.

14 Let's Get Physical F8a+ ★★   1988

10m Perhaps the best here? Fine bouldering up the steepest part of the wall. The original version goes up from the left end of the ledge with hard moves to reach a pocket by the bolt. Finish up the right side of the prow. Rarely repeated.

15 Let's Get Physical Right-Hand F7c ★ 1988

10m A more popular version moves up off the ledge as per *Beginner's Wall* then reaches left to the pocket by the bolt

16 Let's Get Fossilised F7c+ ★   2009

10m Link the *Right-Hand* version into *Fossil Wall*. Linking the original into *Fossil Wall* is as yet undone.

17 Beginner's Wall F7b+ ★★   1984

8m A cool route with powerful moves. Gain the ledge and move off the right side to climb the steep wall on pockets.

18 Man of Steel Font 7B

Start sitting, hands on good holds, and climb up to the spikey jug, staying right of the crack.

19 Swing Time Font 7A+

Start as for *Man of Steel* and move out right to a sidepull jug, then back left to the same finishing jug.

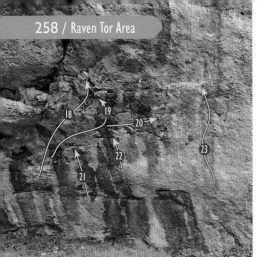

20 It's a Traversty Font 7B

Start as for *Swing Time* and continue traversing into *Neil's Wall* finish.

21 Advanced Training Font 7C+

Sit start on tight pockets. Pull up to a shallow vertical slot with a crimp above it, then on to the middle hold on *Swing Time*. Finish as for *Man of Steel*.

22 Mike's Problem Font 7C+

Pull on with poor crimps and lurch for the *Swing Time* spike. The sit start is Font 8A.

23 Neil's Wall Font 7B+

A fingery classic. From opposing crimps / gastons, slap the jug, then continue upwards to a tricky match on the slopey ledge. Font 7C from a sit.

24 Neil's Wall Right-Hand Font 8A

A hard eliminate. From a sit start, move up and use the right-hand triangular crimp from the original for the left hand and a toe hook out right, heading for a slot.

25 Middle-Aged Spread F7b+   1988

8m   The wall to the right with a variation, starting on the right, moving left, up then back right to the belay. Going direct, **A Big Slap**, is the same grade.

Around to the right is an overhanging corner by some old sawn-off stumps. **Elephants Never Forget**, E2 6a (1983), climbs a short flake and arête, peg, whilst **Ivory Poacher**, E3 6b (1983), climbs straight up past the peg.

The Amphitheatre: Further up, before Sean's Roof, is a little amphitheatre of rock. There is a roof on the left. **Roof Left**, Font 6A, climbs the left side of the roof. **Back in Black**, Font 7A, is the centre of the roof from jugs.

Sean's Roof

The next parking bay up the dale hosts a score of problems on fingery bulges. These vary in stature from 'lie-down starts', all the way through local classics up to Jerry Moffatt highballs. The crag is very slow to dry and is a slimy pit in the wetter seasons. However, the problems are popular when in condition. Not much sun.

26 Uno Font 6A

Sit start the bulge left of the crack.

27 Wedgie Font 6B

Sit start from the crack. Aim for jugs above.

28 Bungle Font 6C

Lie-down start. From low holds hit the crack jug. Finish at the protruding jug up and right.

29 Somebody's Head Font 7A

Lie-down start on low holds to finish on the protruding jug.

30 Orange Si Font 7B

Lie-down start from a low line of crimps and head up via small crimps to a good jug.

31 Twice a Slice Font 6C

Sit start from the low break and head up to the next break, then jugs.

32 My Friend Flicka Font 7B

Sit start from two crimps either side of the groove crack, gain the crack hold and flick for the top jugs.

33 Witchettygrub Font 7B+

Sit start from the low crack-jug and pull up and left to gain holds on the bulge. Reach a right-hand crimp and power up to lip-holds then a jug just above and right.

34 Fudge Font 7A

From the low crack jug, use holds on *Witchettygrub* and *Don't Jump* to gain the *Witchettygrub* jug.

35 Don't Jump Font 6C

Sit start from the low crack-jug and head straight up to edges. Make a tricky move to gain the jugs.

36 Pushmepullyou Font 6B+

Start as for *Don't Jump* and climb up via layaways and a slopey hold to gain the jugs up and slightly right. A sit-start from poor crimps just right is Font 7A+.

37 Me Eyes! Me Eyes! Font 7C

Sit start on the low jugs of *Don't Jump* and follow the in-termittent seam/break to join *Paint It Black* at the top.

38 Byker Groove Font 7C

The groove. Sit start on the left end of the starting rail of *Paint It Black* and pull straight up the groove to finish at the grass line on an obvious juggy right-facing flake hold.

39 Paint It Black Font 7C

The steep prow is a classic, the most sought-after tick in the dale. From a low sit start on the horizontal rail, work directly up the prow on crozzley crimps to the slopey break, stretch left to undercuts and use these to reach over the capping roof to a finishing hold.

40 Back to Black Dyno Font 7B+

A big dyno from the break on the prow of *Paint it Black*. Stretch out right to a crimp and throw for a jug over the lip. Linking this into the start of the problem gives **Paint it Black Direct**, Font 7C+.

41 Back to Black Font 8A

From a crouch on a wavy crimp right of the arête, pull left to gain *Paint it Black*, then finish as per the dyno.

42 Working 9-5 Font 8A+

Start sitting and make a hard move to gain the wavy crimp of *Back to Black*. Climb into the *Paint it Black* and finish as for that. A crouching start, from the wavy crimp, is Font 7C.

43 Sean's Roof F8b+ ★ 1995

8m   The central line on the cave, bolted standing on the roof of a Peugeot 205 GTi, is now commonly climbed as a hard highball above several mats at Font 8A+. Follow the line of bolts through the left side of the roof to finish matched on the large hold by the last bolt with feet off. The last move is definitely the crux without a rope.

Dole Technician, E4 6a (1983), climbs the right-hand side of the cave via a large pocket reached from a small tree on the right.

The low flat wall 15m right of the cave holds:

44 Uptown Beaver Font 7A
Sit start the left end of the wall. A fingery pull up and left leads to good holds.

45 Plaster Lank Font 7A+
Start sitting in the centre of the wall, just as the overlap starts to curve upwards. Slap to a good dish with the right hand and continue upwards. A right-hand version gets the dish with the left hand and uses good holds out right at Font 6C.

Zippy's Roof

The final climbing on this side of the dale lies on a not-so-obvious roof almost directly above Sean's Roof. This would be a good bouldering spot were it not for the steep landing.

46 There's Method to my Madness F7b+ 2012
10m The bulging wall on the left.

47 More Hunky than Funky F7c ★ 2012
10m The central line finishing on a large jug.

48 Zippy's Roof F7b+ 2012
10m The short, intense bulge at the right side of the wall.

Roadside Wall

The short walls opposite Sean's Roof have great rock and a handful of fine, harder problems. Clean and seepage free. The walls get afternoon and evening sun. **See map on page 254**

49 Jugs Font 6A+
From the juggy ledge on the left side of the wall, climb to the break.

Red or Dead, Font 7A+ (opposite page). Photo: Alex Messenger.

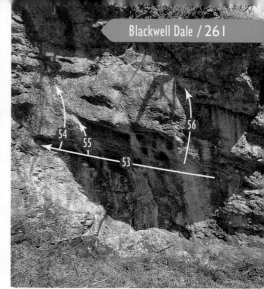

50 Free Range Abattoir Font 7A+

From the slopey ledge, power upwards to a fingery finish. Font 6C from standing. A lower start, from the break under the roof of the cave and moving left into the original, is Font 7B+.

51 Red or Dead Font 7A+

From the slopey ledge, move right to a pocket, then continue up. Font 6C from standing. **Photo opposite.** The lower start is **Any Hole's A Goal**, Font 7C.

52 Top Shop Font 7B+

From a low flat hold on the right, traverse left to finish up *Red or Dead*. There is also a couple of higher variations, all at the same grade. Gaining and finishing up *Free Range Abbottoir* is Font 7B: **Deranged Abbott**

53 Jerry's Traverse Font 7A+

A classic. Starting on the right, traverse left on excellent holds to jugs. Same grade either way.

54 Spock Font 7A

Start just left of the crimps on *Jerry's Traverse*. Pull up to a pinch, then trend up and left, to a small crimp and a couple of slopey pockets. Left again to a sidepull, up to the spok hold, then finish left and up to the thin sharp flake.

55 Vulcan Font 7B

From the first crimps on *Jerry's Traverse*, reach into a deep pocket then trend leftwards into. Finish up this.

56 A Lack of Colour Font 7B

A good problem with a poor landing. Blast straight up the groove to finish on jugs at the top of the crag. Linking the traverse (in either direction) into this is Font 7B+.

Griff's Buttress Area

See map on page 254. This collection of small steep buttresses offers more typical Blackwell Dale bouldering – low starts and powerful fingery steepness – albeit in a more gentle setting. They lie about twenty metres back from the busy road and a shading of trees keeps it a bit quieter. Griff's Buttress is clean and the other buttresses will clean up with more traffic. They get morning sun but are quite shaded by trees. They seep in winter.

Park as for Beginner's Wall. About 30m down the road a small track runs towards the dale. Follow this, carefully crossing the fence, and up to Griff's Buttress.

Griff's Buttress: This is just behind the trees. There is a bolted project up the wall left of the groove of *Mint Sauce*.

57   The Flake   Font 6B
The flake, from a burly sitter, to jugs below the little roof.

58   Ru's Traverse   Font 8A+
Sit start on the left, left of the undercut bulge, and traverse the lip rightwards to finish up *Ovine*.

59   Mint Sauce   Font 7C
Climb into the groove and follow it to a highball finish. The sit start, off a big right-hand pinch, is Font 7C+.

60   Ovine   Font 7B
The buttress classic. Start with a left-hand slot, right hand on a pinch. **Photo on page 264.**

61   Ovine Low Left   Font 7C
A low left start to *Ovine* starting with the left hand on the incut edge, right hand next to it on anything. Make a big move to the right-hand sloper then cross into the slot and finish up *Ovine*.

62   Mutton Busting   Font 8A+
A Peak power classic. The sit start to *Ovine*. Start low on two crimpy ears with a heel/toe on the bulge at the back. Pull up into the stand start.

63   Bovine   Font 7B
Sit start on the right of the low cave of *Mutton Bustin'* and make a big move to a large flat hold. Finish slighty left (virtually on *Ovine*) on crimps. A more independent finish gains the slot out right before finishing direct on crimps - same grade.

64 Lovine Font 7C
Start on *Bovine*, match the good left hold after the initial slap, span left into the starting slot on *Ovine* and finish up this.

65 Griff's Traverse Font 7C
Start from a sitter and traverse the break into *Ovine*.

66 Up Font 6B
A long move over the bulge from slots.

67 Unstatic Font 7C
Use two tiny crimps to dyno for the break.

68 Shelf Problem Font 5
Move up from the sidepull to the shelf. Font 5+ from a sitting start.

69 Font 6A
Crimp up from the spiky jug to the shelf.

70 Font 6C
From the spike jug, climb up and right on slopers and finish matched in the unhelpful depression.

71 Font 6B+
Up from the low jug into the unhelpful depression.

Black and Deckout Buttress: This lies just downhill.

72 Black is the Colour Font 6A
Starting from the flaky crack on the far left of the buttress, span out to a crack in the wall on the right and a solid finish.

73 Young, Gifted and Black Font 7A
From the base of the flaky crack, climb out to a finger jug on the high prow on the right, before pulling back left to topout. A lovely highball on pristine rock. A slightly less exciting left-hand variant, making a huge crimpy lock straight up the wall, is Font 6C+. **Photo on page 255.**

74 Black & Deckout Font 7A+
Climb the highest section of the front face, starting at a good left-hand layaway slot. Finish up an easy groove to tree.

75 Whoa Black Betty Font 7C
Gain the prominent hole via an almighty slap from the obvious layaway and a choice of poor right handholds.

76 Blackhole Font 6B
Gain the hole at 3m, starting from twin pockets.

Four metres right of the big hole the buttress is steeper and lower.

77   Black Magic   Font 7A+
Start on undercuts and reach a good slot with the left hand then continue direct.

78   Cross & Blackwell   Font 6B
The farthest right problem on the butress. Sit start at a short crack and follow a ramp till stood over the bulge.

79   Black by Popular Demand   Font 7A
Sit start left left of *Cross & Blackwell* on a pinch and an undercut. Slap to middle of ramp and topout (get stood over bulge) rightwards.

The Ravine

This is at the lower end of the dale where the road takes a sharp rightwards turn, when travelling from the A6 and veers from the dale. Scramble down below the chevrons that mark the bend. **See map on page 254.**

A buttress on the far side of the stream gives **The Enchanted Place**, HVS 5a (1977) taking a right-to-left traverse above the overhangs and **Bossyboots**, S (1977) taking the groove below the finish of the traverse.

Little Jordan, HVS 5a (1998), from a tiny cave right again climb right through overlaps then back left to a shield and finish up a pillar.

The first buttress reached is Streamside Buttress. **Commit Dirty Act**, E2 5b (1998), goes from the large tree on the left to traverse a break right to gain a final corner, then an overhang above; **Elvis Gets My Bus**, E2 5c (1998), the discontinuous flakeline left of centre to pockets and a corner; **Powerful Torches Officer**, E2 5c (1998), an obvious groove to a break, then strenuous traverse to finish of previous route; **Hot Thighs**, VS 4c (1977); as the previous route but trend right to folow an obvius groove; **Jubilee Groove**, VS 4c (1977), the groove 4m right; **The Idol**, HVS 5a (1977), the slab and arête right of *Jubilee Groove*; **Bone Idol**, HVS 5a (1998), the arete of *The Idol* on its right-hand side moving left to a tree to finish.

On the buttress with the large roof are two test-pieces of a different culture. **Big Youth**, E4 6b (1981), starts via a crack and moves right across the roof past a peg whilst **Big Daddy**, A3 (1988), takes the rib and bulges to the left. Further right is **Little Wimp**, HVS 5b (1981), the rib in the centre of a wall to finish in a groove.

Michaela Tracy on Ovine, Font 7B (page 262)
Photo: Alex Messenger

CHEE DALE

The Embankment / Max Wall / Cornice / Chee Tor / Two Tier / Long Wall / Plum Buttress +++

Chris 'Gus' Hudgins on Lightweight, F7c, at Two Tier Buttress (page 373). Photo: Adam Long.

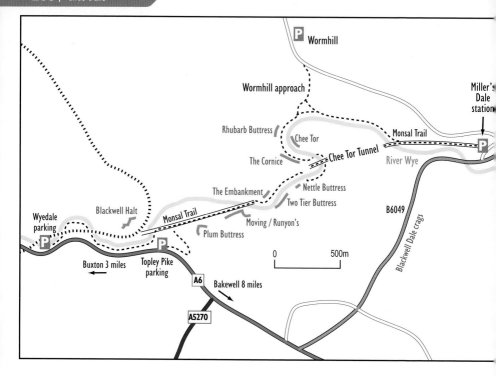

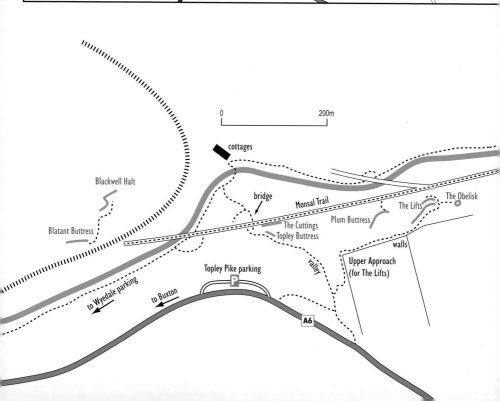

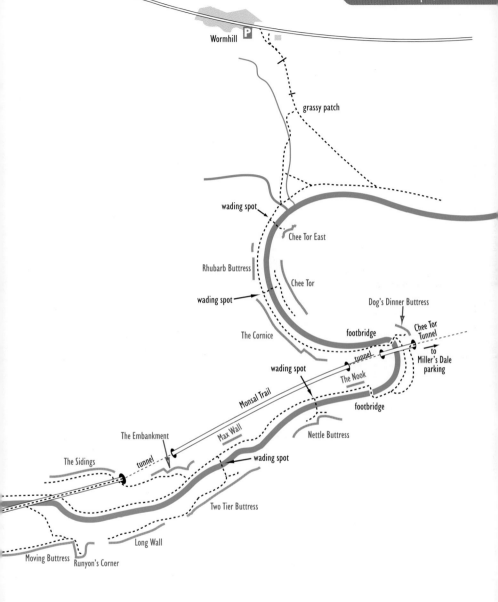

Wormhill

grassy patch

wading spot

Chee Tor East

Rhubarb Buttress

Chee Tor

wading spot

Dog's Dinner Buttress

The Cornice

footbridge

Chee Tor Tunnel

to Miller's Dale parking

wading spot

tunnel

The Nook

Monsal Trail

footbridge

Max Wall

Nettle Buttress

The Embankment

The Sidings

tunnel

wading spot

Two Tier Buttress

Moving Buttress

Runyon's Corner

Long Wall

Chee Dale is one of the great climbing areas of the Peak District with an eclectic mix of magnificent traditional climbs, state-of-the-art sport routes together with a mix of downright and bizarre esoteria. There is no doubt that the place has been transformed over the past few years as a nationally, if not internationally, recognised playground for sport climbing, harbouring some of the best climbs of their type in the region.

Conditions

The cliffs face in a variety of directions and many of them can be ideal venues in the spring and autumn months when you want the sun's rays on your back. Conversely, in the summer months when the sun's heat is at its highest, many of the faces provide shade and can give an ideal climbing venue when the crags are dry. Some of the crags suffer from seepage during the winter and as a result some of the climbs can be dirty even halfway through the summer.

Parking and Approach

Venues can be accessed from several parking spots as detailed below. Some of the approaches to crags involve wading across the river. Wellies or flip-flops will make this more pleasant. The three main parking spots are:

Topley Pike

This is the best approach for The Sidings, The Embankment, Max Wall, Two Tier, Long Wall, Runyon's Corner, Moving Buttress and Plum Buttress. The large lay-by off the A6, 3 miles west of Buxton. Follow the footpath, which starts from the eastern (uphill) end of the lay-by and leads into and down a small valley (or veer off right for The Lifts). A gap in the wall at the bottom of the valley gives access to the Monsal Trail, the old railway track. Turn left here for Blackwell Halt and Blatant Buttress or right for the main Chee Dale crags.

Miller's Dale Station

This is the pay & display parking on the Monsal Trail. Drive along the B6049 then take the small road that angles off towards Wormhill, 200m west of the overhead railway viaduct After 100m there is a car park and old station on the left. Park here. Follow the Monsal Trail for 1km, the last 400m being through Chee Tor Tunnel. The trail emerges from the tunnel and crosses a viaduct, but for crag access at this end of the dale, leave the trail as soon as it emerges from the tunnel.

Turn left and go through a gap in the wall and follow a path as it drops down to meet the main riverside path. For Nettle Buttress and The Nook, go left (upstream), and cross a footbridge to arrive at The Nook. Nettle Buttress is a little further on, on the opposite bank, accessed by wading.

For The Cornice, Rhubarb Buttress and Chee Tor, drop down to meet the main riverside path and turn right (downstream). Follow the path under the viaduct and cross a footbridge over the river. The Cornice is the first crag you meet and a little further on is Rhubarb Buttress. On the opposite bank, is Chee Tor, accessed by wading.

Wormhill

The old approach to the Chee Tor end of the dale, before Chee Tor Tunnel was re-opened, was via the village of Wormhill. Park in the village on roadside verges. At the south end of the village is a footpath signposted Chee Dale. Follow this path for 300m, through two gates. After the second gate carry on down to the river and turn right. along the waterside path to walk under Rhubarb Buttress after 600m. This approach for Rhubarb, Chee Tor and The Cornice takes about the same as the Topley Pike approach, but it's pretty uphill at the end of the day.

Access and Conservation

The BMC supports your right to climb on all the crags in Chee Dale. However, whilst the valley has a long and significant climbing history dating back to the 1930s, it is also internationally important for its crag flora and steep grassland as well as a very popular area for walkers. Therefore all climbing must take place in a way that protects the environment and respects all other users.

Please observe the following points:

Chee Dale is a SSSI with a high level of legal protection under European law. However, this does not mean that climbing is banned: responsible climbing will not compromise the area's special features.

Only approach the crags by the means described in the Chee Dale general introduction and in the individual crag introductions.

Do not leave in situ gear on bolt hangers overnight.

Do not obstruct paths with belongings or when belaying. This is a particular issue at the Cornice where the path is very close to the crag and can become difficult for walkers to pass.

Do not remove vegetation.

No further development of new buttresses or currently-unclimbed sections of crag.

Ben Bransby on Mad Dogs and Englishmen, E3 5c, Two Tier Buttress (page 373). Photo: David Simmonite.

Blatant and Blackwell

Sport: 43 (F5+ to F7b)
Aspect: South / South-east **Sunshine:** All day **Season:** Year round
Conditions: Sunny, quick drying, clean, midgy
Best for: Low to mid-grade sport in a dry, sunny land **Approach:** 10 minutes

These are two crags lying near the railway line at the head of Chee Dale. They both offer a good collection of F6 routes. Blackwell Halt gives good, long mid-grade sport climbing on solid rock, set peacefully in a pretty meadow giving splendid views down Chee Dale. Blatant Buttress lies only two minutes away giving more varied climbing, with the added attraction of quarry trains rumbling underneath every now and then.

The Climbing

Blatant Buttress is a steep wall of grey limestone, where the better routes are generally in the higher grades. With its grooves, ramps and walls, it manages to give a good variety of styles, despite being quite small. The main wall of Blackwell Halt is deceptively steep and provides a welcome number of high-quality middle-grade sport climbs of a similar style: technical and fingery with the occasional good resting place.

Conditions and Aspect

Both are fairly quick-drying venues with good sunshine and are a good bet for the early spring months and even in winter during a good dry spell. Blatant Buttress: The buttress dries very quickly and faces into the sun for most of the day. In the winter and early spring months the sun dips below the skyline relatively early and makes the crags a cold venue. The walls take little seepage except after deluges of rain. Blackwell Halt: The walls dry relatively quickly in the spring months and stay dry in light rain. They get the sun from early morning until about 3pm but can become midgy on a summer's evening or in humid weather.

Parking and Approach

Note: The approach to these crags demands the crossing of railway lines that are still frequently used. It is important to pay the utmost care when crossing these.

See map on page 268. The Traditional Approach: Follow the Topley Pike approach as far as the Monsal Trail at the bottom of the hill. Turn left through an old gate, crossing a bridge over the River Wye, then through some trees to reach a 'live' railway track. Blatant Buttress is on the side of the track, 50m to the left; for Blackwell Halt, cross the track immediately and with care, and scramble up banking behind a yellow sign to reach the quarry. Walk-in: the approach takes just over 10 minutes, although it's just over 15 to get back out again, so save some energy for that hill.

Alternatively, park further down the hill at Wyedale parking (pay & display, or park just outside the quarry across the road), and follow the Monsal Trail along the tranquil river for a few hundred metres until it leaves the riverside and climbs up by the third railway bridge. This is the bridge mentioned for the above approach.

Access

No access problems have occurred although it cannot be emphasized enough that Blatant Buttress lies on a live railway track and caution should be exercised at all times.

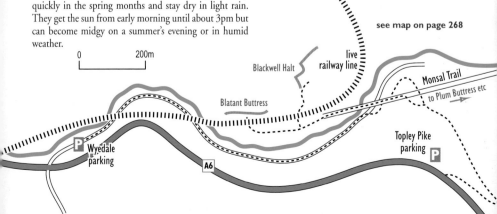

Emily Huzzard on Mega Byte, F6b (page 277). Photo: Paul Evans.

Blatant Buttress

The wall faces south getting late morning and afternoon sun.

1   Chug, Chug, Chug F6b+   2006
15m   One hard move and a horrible mantelshelf at the top.

2   For the Good of the Cause F5+   1998
18m   Climb a faint rib and ledgy corner.

3   Close to the Edge F6c   1998
18m   Climb the left wall of the corner to finish up the wall above, as directly and as closely as possible to the arête.

4   Every Breath You Take F6c   1998/2006
18m   Spaced bolts but not runout! Start up the layaway edge and finish up the right-hand side of the arête. The best route on this part of the buttress.

5   Eye Catching Cod Piece F6b+   1998
18m   With a crux crossing an overhang above the black patch.

6   Pipistrelle F6a   1998
18m   The rib and groove finishing up the wall above the ledge.

7   Rave On F6a   1998

8   Chill Out F6a+   1998
18m   Average climbing saved by some good final moves. Ledges lead to a pleasant slabby finish.

9   Feel the Beat F6b   1998
18m   Tricky moves to enter a vague groove. A zigzag line on the slab gives another good finish.

10   Emission Control F7a+ ★   1998
18m   The steep and fingery wall leads into *Feel the Beat*.

11 Good Vibrations F7a+ ★   1998
18m   A very fingery wall leads into an excellent shallow and technical groove.

12 Wobbly Wheels F7b ★   2009
18m   Branch right out of *Good Vibrations* to climb the centre of the wall. Reachy.

13 Loco-Motion F7a ★   1998
18m   The wall just left of the ramp leads to a hard finishing wall on hidden holds.

14 Love is a Swallow F6a+   1998
18m   The wall above the ramp. Steep at the finale.

15 The Runaway Train F6a+   2006
18m   Pleasant climbing up the lower wall to a few fingery moves on the face above.

16 Came Down the Track F6b ★   2006
18m   The steep wall with a fine sequence towards the top.

17 One Track Offensive F6a   2009
18m

18 Burning Rails F5+   2009
15m   The wall on the right, to a steep finish.

At the far right-hand side of the cliff is another buttress with three routes:

19 Puffing F6b+   2009
15m   The left-hand side of the wall.

20 Steaming F6b   2009
15m   The cracks in the centre of the wall.

21 Sidetrack F6c   2009
15m   The steep, right-hand side of the wall.

Blackwell Halt

Walk down the track for 50m to a yellow sign, and then scramble up the bank. The first routes are on the subsidiary wall in front of the main wall. The walls faces south-east, and gets the sun until about 3pm.

Sid's Wall: An aperitif for the main wall, this subsidiary wall consists of a fine juggy headwall with a lower smoother section which provides the main difficulties.

22	**Byte Size** F6b		2007
23	**Ernie** F6c+		1995
24	**Defrag** F6c+		1995
25	**A Soldier's Diary** F6c		2007
26	**Anoraks and Trainspotters** F6b		1995
27	**Micro-nerd** F6b+		1995
28	**Nerd the Absurd** F6b		2007

Main Wall: This is the larger wall to the right. All of the routes have a similar feel to them but offer, in the most part, excellent climbing for those operating in the lower end of the sport-climbing grades. The first routes start from the platform.

29 Micro Chip F6c+   1995
9m   The compact wall. Short and intense.

30 Modem F6a+   1995
9m   The easier wall to the right leads directly to the tree. A good warm-up.

At a lower level is:

31 CD Romp E2 5c   1995
15m   The corner to finish up the crack above the ledge.

32 Arapaho Connection F6b+ ★★   1995
15m   The best route on the crag. Starting just right of the corner, the wall and overlap give fine sustained climbing.

33 Hard Drive F6c ★   1995
15m   A tricky start leads to the centre of the wall above.

34 Mega Byte F6b ★   1995
15m Gain a ledge then continue direct. **Photo on page 273.**

35 Gopherspace F6b   1995
15m Take a small roof on its left-hand side.

36 Windows 95 F6a+ ★   1995
15m The roof, taken centrally, and delightful wall above.

37 Falling Icons F6b   1995
15m The right-hand side of the overlap. A tricky move / long reach on the upper wall lie in wait.

38 She got the Bosch, I got the Drill
    F6b ★   1995
12m From a short way up the slope on the right, climb the wall to a ledge and finish directly above. Reachy.

39 Waste Bin F6a+   1995
12m Climb the right-hand side of a vague groove to a roof.

40 The Hacker F6b+   1995
12m The left-hand of four routes, with two hard moves.

41 E Mail F6b   1995
12m Fingery.

42 She Mail F6b   2007
12m A tricky fingery wall above the ledge.

43 No Mail F6a   2009
12m A pleasant face leads to a groove on the right-hand side of the wall. Move left to the belay.

44 Surfing the Net F6c   1996
25m A mid-height girdle traversing the wall from left to right. Climb to the second bolt on *Modem* then traverse right, clipping 11 bolts en-route, to lower off *E Mail*. A medium nut is useful for the section leaving *CD Romp*.

The Sidings

Trad: 24 (VS to E5) **Sport:** 6 (F6b to F7c+)
Aspect: South **Sunshine:** From mid-morning **Season:** All year
Conditions: Sunny, fresh, clean, seepage-free, quiet
Best for: Esoteric, fingery trad; winter sun **Approach:** 15 minutes

This is the first section of cliff encountered on the left-hand side of the Monsal Trail when approaching from the Buxton end of the Dale. It is conspicuous by its bright colour when the sun glints against its surface and has the distinct advantage of drying very quickly after rain. In fact, it is one of the very few sections of cliff that can be climbed upon during the winter months.

The Climbing
Intricate face climbing, mostly of a traditional nature with the occasional fixed point of in-situ gear. There are also a handful of very short sport routes which are not akin to the quality of other such sport routes in the Dale.

Conditions
Very sunny, open, clean and quick drying. Not popular.

Approach
See map on page 268. Approach from Topley Pike parking. Gain the Monsal Trail. Turn right and after 800m, just before the first tunnel, hop over the fence to access the main area.

The first group of routes are situated on a rather neglected crag some 150m to the left of here on a small isolated buttress some 50m up from the river. The first route has been climbed 30m to the left of this on a debris-ridden buttress: **A Dude Called Deborah**, HVS 5c (1990), provides a short face climb; **I Love My Pigeon**, HVS 5a (1990), is situated to its right.

Humiliation Buttress: On the buttress to the right: **Spank me Senseless with a Red Herring**, VD (1995), is the poor wall at the left-hand side of the buttress. The wall to the right contains three routes: **Humiliation**, F7a (1995), is the left-hand of the three sport pitches moving right to finish; **Honorary Slate**, F7b+ (2010), is the smooth wall right of *Humiliation*; very bouldery; **Kick the Bucket**, E2 5b (1990), climbs the centre of the wall via a groove moving left at the top to reach a tree belay; **Get Down and Bark, Bitch**, F6b (1996), is the right-hand of the three sport routes via a blunt rib.

The next two routes are situated on an isolated high buttress roughly 100m to the left of the end of the main crag and on the upper tier. This is gained by a careful scramble up the scree slope to a jutting nose of rock.

1 Glasswegian Kiss F7c+   2011
10m   The feisty bulge on the left. **Photo opposite.**

2 Strawberry Kiss F7b   1996
10m   The impressive bulge with three bolts.

Rupert Davies on Glasgwegian Kiss, F7c+ (this page). Photo: Andy Newton.

Main Crag: The majority of the good climbing is to be found on the first walls you come to.

3 Up the Creek E5 6a   1984
11m The thin crack complete with a peg shows little evidence of popularity, probably due to its looseness.

4 Hupsters F7a   1994
10m A desperate little sequence up the blank-looking wall to the right. Innocuous it may be, easy it is not.

5 Fizzy F6c+   1991
10m Polished rock and tiny holds to the right give another test of mettle.

Quidnunc, F6a (1988), traverses this wall from right to left.

The wall to the right contains three pleasant routes when clean:

6 Tetse HVS 5a   2012
12m The left-hand side of the face with good moves and an exit requiring care.

7 Firefly E1 5b   1977
12m This route takes the central line via a faint thin crack in the centre of the wall to another 'careful' exit.

8 Mosquito E2 5c   2012
12m The right-hand side of the wall gives its best route and best exit.

Strawberry Kiss

Two Tier

Main Crag

Moving Buttress

The Obelisk

Humiliation Buttress

Monsal Trail

Six metres to the right the rock begins to improve, providing a better selection of routes.

9 Dusty Lusty E2 5b 2013
12m The wall immediately to the left of a prominent flake leads boldly to easier ground and a finishing slab.

10 Sleepers VS 4c 1977
11m The obvious crack from the back of a shallow alcove. The curving flake to its left can be used as a variation start.

11 Lust in the Dust E1 5b 1985
12m Gain a short, steep crack with a long stretch. A difficult stretch, harder for those short of valuable inches, gains better holds leading to a tree.

12 Platonic Desire E2 5c 1987
11m The wall to the right and just to the left of a prominent crack has an old thread runner.

13 Spring is Here HVS 5a 1985
12m A shallow groove, the right-hand of two, gains a small overhang and a leftwards finish. Take care with the hollow finishing holds.

Two minor offerings take increasingly vegetated lines to the right: **Crabs**, VS 4c (1977), follows a thin bulging crack and **Snoozin**, S (1977), is a thinner crack just to the right again.

The next piece of rock provides The Sidings' most significant routes on fine rock with a technical feel to them:

14 Binge Drinker HVS 5a ★ 2013
12m A short flake leads to good holds and a recess just right of a tree. Move out to the right and climb straight up on good holds. Worthwhile.

15 I Drink Therefore I Am E4 6b ★ 1982
12m The blank-looking wall gives a series of tricky moves. Climb up to clip a peg right of the line before retreating back to the floor. Now climb the intricate wall to its left before moving slightly to the right passing a second and very comforting peg, to reach a crack. This leads easily to the yew tree.

16 The Dukes of Hazzard E5 6c ★ 1982
12m An 'on-off' series of moves via the groove / scoop to the right leads to a desperate finale. Escaping rightwards does not provide the same rewards or the same grade – E4 6b! At last the correct spelling!

17 County Time E4 5c 1999
12m Bold and intricate face-climbing to the right with difficult-to-place small wire protection and relatively few features, save the odd micro-flake. Tough on the mind.

18 A Touch Too Much E1 5b 1982
14m Pleasant moves on the vague arête to the right, passing a faint bulge slightly leftwards but unfortunately soon petering out.

19 Puffing Billy VS 4b ★   mid-1960s
12m The pleasant shallow groove and crack leads to a yew tree.

A poor route, **Sign of the Times**, VS 4c (1979), begins via the prominent flake to the right before quickly escaping left and up via a vegetated wall and faint groove.

20 Sprint Start E1 5a ★   1979
12m A prominent layback flake, with tricky gear, leads onto a fine headwall with a profusion of good, though hidden, holds.

21 Lethal Dose E3 6a ★   1977
12m The classic of these walls. A thin crack to the right of *Sprint Start* gains an undercut flake slightly to the right. An extending reach into the scoop and hasty exit give food for thought, leading to an easier finish.

22 Fame but no Fortune E2 5c   1983
12m The face, attempting to avoid the clutches of the tree, lead onto a flake. Step left and up to finish.

The crack containing the tree gives **Fireman's Frolic**, D (post-1970).

On the buttress directly above this area lies the hidden **Limited Edition**, E2 5b (1990), which takes the left arête to a break along which it moves right before an exit on pockets is made.

23 The Invisibles E2 5b   2013
15m Climb up to a roof and bypass this to the left to reach the slabby face above. Pick a way up this finishing via vegetated ground.

24 Visible Void E1 5a   1984
12m A fine grey wall and flake crack attains the overhang. Move right to avoid this and then up to finish.

25 Voidless F6b ★   2013
12m A fine little route bisecting *Visible Void* via an excellent lower wall and easier climbing above the overlap.

The solitary blank face on the tier above the one described gives **Human Fit Tailors**, E1 5b (1999), which takes a leftwards line of holds and a bulge above a niche.

Returning to the railway track and immediately to the left of the tunnel entrance, a combination of rock types here gives an unusual pitch.

26 Lateral Passage VS 4b   post-1970
21m Climb the left-hand corner of the tunnel entrance to reach a large grassy platform – nick-named the Waiting Room. Finish via a vegetated flaky corner above.

27 Unzipping the Wild Physique VS 5a 1970s
8m Another unusual gritstone pitch and with bolts! The right-hand arête of the tunnel entrance gives the line and the controversy. **Photo opposite.**

Jon Winter on Unzipping the Wild Physique, VS 5a (opposite page). Photo: Ian Parnell.

Stone the Loach, F7c (opposite page). Photo: Michael Watson.

The Embankment

Sport: 30 (F6b+ to F7c) **Trad:** 5 (E1 to E5)
Aspect: South **Sunshine:** Morning to late afternoon **Season:** Spring to autumn
Conditions: Sheltered, sunny, some seepage, open; an early drying crag
Best for: Cranky sport climbs, F7a to F7c **Approach:** 20 minutes

One of the more popular sport crags in the Dale thanks to a good range of routes on steep, clean rock. The climbs are fingery and powerful with interesting moves. A good crag to visit early in the season as it is a quick dryer.

The Climbing
Overhanging fingery sport climbing in the F7s. Powerful. The holds are unfortunately of the 'stuck on' type and consequently have a habit of becoming unstuck. Perhaps for this reason the routes aren't quite as classic as those on crags such as Two Tier.

Conditions
Open and sunny, getting sun morning and afternoon. Sheltered. Some seepage, but often dries out earlier than other nearby crags. A little polished.

Parking and Approach
See map on page 268. From Topley Pike parking, drop down to gain the Monsal Trail. Turn right and after 800m, just before the first tunnel, drop down and right on a small path to the crag.

Above the left-hand of the three ramps is a large grassy platform known as The Waiting Room. Gain it by scrambling up one of the ramps. The wall above gives: **Attack the Ghost**, HVS 5a (2008), the leftmost line, **Bone and Globe**, HVS 5a (2008), in the centre, and **Rampant**, S (1976), on the right.

1 The World According to Tommy Trout
E4 6a   1988

20m A bold route, with one lonely bolt. Climb to a slanting flake and pull leftwards over the bulge (bolt) into a prominent recess. Exit the alcove rightwards to finish at a tree. Step right to the lower-off.

2 Hungry Eyes F7a+ ★★
1982

20m Superb climbing with a beefy crux. Climb the wall to reach the flake. (The original line took the flake in its entirety.) From a good resting place, strenuous moves gain a good hold. Step left and climb the headwall. There is a poorer left-hand variant moving leftwards through the bulges at a lower level.

3 Beef It F7b ★
1987

16m Follow *Hungry Eyes* to an undercut rest on the right. Steep and fingery moves first up and then rightwards lead to a final steep pull to the belay.

4 The Secret Gudgeon Society F7b ★ 1987

16m The vague, rightward-trending line is gained directly by a short fingery wall.

5 Stone the Loach F7c ★
1988

15m A route that embraces all that is typical of Chee Dale sport climbs. The centre of the bulging wall has long fingery pulls and one not-so-natural hold. Above the break, the difficulties ease off. **Photo opposite.**

6 Mind of a Turbot F7b ★
1987

13m The wall gives a fingery exercise. From the obvious break, move left and then up to jugs and the bolt belay.

7 The Man Who Fell to Earth F6c+ 1989

12m The short wall with the difficulties centred on the half-height bulge.

8 Arachnothera F6b+
1976/1996

18m Climb the groove and exit directly with a fingery pull. The left-hand finish at the roof is F6b.

9 Prawnography F6c   1996
14m Direct and pleasant wall-climbing right of the groove.

The wall to the right has a series of fingery testpieces.

10 Bream in Black F7a ★   1987
14m Escalating difficulties. Gain a shallow depression. Exiting this rightwards is not as straightforward as it looks, and is getting harder thanks to hold-loss.

11 Breamtime F7a+ ★   1987
14m The central line of the wall. A hard move gains a slim overlap. Overcoming this leftwards provides the second crux of the route.

12 The Barracuda Bass Sound F7a+ ★ 1987
14m A non-descript line just right, with some good climbing. It gains the same overlap as *Breamtime*. In this case finish directly through its right-hand side.

13 No Hiding Plaice F7a ★   1987
14m The wall leads into a thin, bulging crack. At first straightforward, this gives a taxing finish.

14 Whiting on the Wall F7c   1995
14m The direct line, starting up *Sturgeon*, gives perhaps the hardest sequence on the wall.

15 Sturgeon in the Cupboard F7c ★ ★ 1987
14m The classic route of this section of cliff, although the debate about its grade lingers on. It takes a reverse question mark line with a final exhausting pull rightwards to the belay. F7b+ if you have spent too long on the campus board! **Photo opposite.**

Dominic Lee on Sturgeon in the Cupboard, F7c (opposite page). Photo: Neil Foster.

16 The Black Widow E1 5b 1976

18m The bulging corner is one of the few routes on this crag for those seeking something from the old school. Unfortunately, you'll probably have to fight through the surrounding bushes to access it first.

17 Silence of the Clams F7a+ 1991

18m Climb the wall to gain a flake crack and the fish's tail. Exit directly around the difficult bulge.

18 Future Paradox E3 6a 1984

20m Gain the right-hand side of the fish's tail and follow the groove to a bulge. Either finish directly, the original route, or move left to the belay of *Silence of the Clams*.

19 Over the Rainbow Trout F6c+ ★ 1987

11m Start slightly left of a rib and gain the face above. Tricky moves right and then up lead quickly to the belay.

20 Night of the Guppy F7b 1988

10m Powerful and blind climbing combine to make this a tough flash. Tackle the bulges to the right directly.

21 Lamprey on Ice F7a+ 1999

10m Still no respite. Gain the left arête of the corner by a series of awkward moves. Avoid the corner by taking a direct line on the rib to reach the belay.

22 The Red Spider E2 5c 1975

20m Gain the hanging corner and, once reached, avoid the capping overhang to its right in favour of a shallow finishing groove.

23 The Zander Welfare Club F7b ★ 1987

16m Make difficult moves over a bulge onto the rib. Once gained, the overhang soon comes to hand. Finish directly through this to belay.

The Web, A3 (1960s), is an old aid route tackling the bulges to the right and still repels free-climbing attempts.

To the right, a long undercut section of cliff provides a stiff barrier to access the walls above.

24 Red Snapper Meets the Dogfish F7a+ 1999

15m Unlikely moves lead through the bulge into a depression. Good holds on the right-hand side of this lead to the belay.

25 Name that Tuna F7c 1988/1999
16m At the right-hand side of the bulges, a tiny groove gives its only identifiable feature. Gaining this proves desperate and finishing directly gives a fitting climax. More Font 7B+ than F7c!

26 Garfish Serenade F7a+ 1999
18m The vague blunt rib forming the right edge of *Name that Tuna* provides a problematic eliminate.

27 The Open Secret E5 6b ★ 1983
18m Classic, in the old style, and undeniably clean. Move up to the remnants of a tree stump and make difficult moves into the groove (bolt). Once gained, the climbing gradually eases.

28 Fragile Earth E5 6a ★ 1983
18m A nerve-jangling exercise on the wall 3m to the right. Climb to the break and follow a series of thin flakes slightly leftwards to where an long reach gains jugs. Somewhat relieved, finish via easier climbing on the upper wall. Good small wires protect, as long as you can hang on to place them.

29 Something Fishy F7c ★ 1992
18m The wall provides a severe test of your finger strength, with its Font 7C crux.

The bulging wall to the right is again being consumed by ivy. At its right-hand side a shallow hanging scoop peeks out.

30 Fishing Without a Licence F7c ★ 1989
18m Gain the scoop by baffling moves. Once gained, yet more hard moves lead to the belay.

31 Barefoot in a Pool of Sharks F7b+ ★ 1987
15m A fine line breaching the clean bulging wall. It can suffer from seepage but once dry provides a fine testpiece. Gaining the overlap proves difficult enough while leaving it will bring a smile to the face of the rockover experts amongst us.

32 Kiss the Mackerel F7c 1999
15m Desperate in two stages. If your reach challenges you, then don't challenge it! Consider the idea of the name?

33 The Life of a Stickleback F7b+ 1987
15m A very difficult starting sequence out of the alcove gains marginally-easier climbing above. More Font 7A+ than F7b+.

34 Minnows as Substitute for White Bait
F6c 1999
15m An interesting concoction designed to allow easier access to the belays of this section of crag and hence the opportunity to clean or view the routes below. From a starting point almost at the top of the slope to the right, swing merrily onto and along the break until a tricky finale gains the belay of *Fishing Without a Licence*.

Johnny Reay on Max to the Wall, F7a+ (page 294). Photo: Michael Watson.

Max Buttress

Sport: 22 (F6a to F7c+) **Trad:** 6 (HVS to E6)
Aspect: South-east **Sunshine**: Morning
Season: Spring to autumn **Approach:** 20 minutes
Conditions: Sheltered, fairly quick drying, popular
Best for: Pumpy sport, F6c to F7b

AKA Riverside Buttress. This is the next buttress downstream from the Embankment and is situated adjacent to the river. It has become very popular over recent years after the bolting of the majority of its pitches although two good traditional lines remain.

The Climbing
Great for sport routes in the mid-sixes to mid-sevens. The steep, water-worn rock gives predictably powerful and intense routes that will reward quick thinkers. A few old, bold trad climbs for scare-heads.

Conditions
Sheltered. Quite a lot of tree shade. The crag gets some morning sun. Some seepage in winter although it can dry out earlier in the year than most and may even give climbing in the winter. Some seepage on *Max Head Room* and *Max 'is Wall* after rain. Becoming a bit polished.

Parking and Approach
See map on page 268. From Topley Pike parking, gain the Monsal Trail and follow it for 800m and break off right before the first tunnel as for The Embankment. Drop down the slope to the riverside path and follow it downstream for 100m to the crag.

The left-hand side of the buttress is bounded by a steep earthy slope descending from the railway line. Just up from the base of this are two poor sport routes: **Mix and Match**, F6b (2002), the left-hand line and **Maximum Potential**, F6b (2002), the right-hand line. The easy but vegetated chimney at the foot of the slope gives **Maxi**, HVS 5a (1979), the roof being avoided by a traverse to the right to reach a tree belay.

1 Pepsi Max F6c   1999
15m The wall and problematic roof 3m right of the corner.

2 Max Factor E2 5b ★   1982
20m Very pleasant climbing with poorly-protected moves low down. Climb the wall from a small ledge at 2m, into a shallow left-facing groove. Reach the overlap, traverse right for 3m and pull through the overlap to gain a belay.

3 Max Head Room F7a ★★   1985
20m Intricate, fingery face-climbing leads directly from the small ledge to the final moves of *Max Factor*. Popular.

4 Max Wall E5 6a ★   1979
20m The antithesis to the sport climbs hereabouts and therefore sadly neglected. Climb to a small right-facing groove. Swing left and make precarious moves up the somewhat lonely wall to reach the second of two breaks. The finish is easier but vegetated.

5 Max Pax 'em In F7a+ ★   1991
20m A difficult sequence through the bulge.

6 Max 'is Wall F6c ★★   1985
20m Climb a bulge and wall to gain a small ledge. Step up and then right before tackling the excellent headwall. **Photo opposite.**

7 Lunatic Fringe F6c+ ★   1985
20m The difficult bulge leads onto the diagonal ramp. Pull left over a bulge to join the finish of *Max 'is Wall*.

8 Max Pact F6b   1985
20m Gain the ramp directly, or from the right at F6a+. Climb the wall above and move slightly left from a break before finishing up the headwall. The ramp, finishing left of *Max 'is Wall*, is **Black Max**, E1 5b (1977).

9 The Max Works F6c+ ★★   1983
20m A super little route trending rightwards to gain an arched overlap. Pull over the bulge to reach the belay.

10 Incandescent Courage E6 6a   1984
20m A bold direct line to the arched overlap, gaining *The Max Works* from the initial vague break.

Steve Franklin on Max 'is Wall, F6c (opposite page). Photo: Paul Evans.

11 Max to the Wall F7a+ ★★   1985
20m Take a direct line up a faint streak and through an
overlap to the belay. Low in the grade. **Photo on page 290.**

12 Max A Million F7b ★   1985
20m The infamous reach-route; you've either got it or
you haven't. Climb the wall and bypass the hard move by
a long reach or levitation. Above it eases considerably.

13 Afterlife E6 6b ★   1983
20m Bold but rewarding. Climb the green streak on
sloping and unhelpful holds to reach the overlap, threads.
Overcome by this a very fingery sequence. Rarely climbed.

14 Maxonomy F7a+   1991
20m A contrived line to the right, which attempts to
avoid *Afterlife*. Stay on the line of the bolts to reach the
bulge. This again provides the crux.

15 The Max Museum F7b ★   1985
20m Getting harder and more intense. The improbable
wall to the right on small sharp holds requires a determined approach.

16 Maxwell House F7b+ ★   1991
20m More of the same to the right. Clipping the second
bolt is as hard as doing the moves!

17 Rough Justice F7c 1991
18m Another desperate bouldery sequence direct to the finish of *Maxwell House*.

18 A Bigger Max F7b+ 1985
18m The wall above the second stepping stone requires ability and trust in your mate's belaying skill.

19 The Max They Love to Hate F7b ★ 1991
18m The fingery wall above the stepping stone. Pick a day when the footpath is quiet.

20 Dream Thief F7a 1986
18m The bulge and wall, just to the left of an undercut groove, lead to the second break. Swing left and up to the belay of the previous route.

To the right, a series of forgotten routes penetrate the lower bulges and walls above: **Orgasmus Maximus**, HVS 5a (1979), takes the undercut shallow groove; **Maxative**, E3 5c (1985), is the wall 3m to its right; **Max's Mum**, E3 6a (1985), tackles the bulge to the right again, thread and peg; **Micromax**, E3 6a (1985), begins from the 7th stepping stone to overcome the bulges above; **Dinosaurs Don't Max**, E4 6b (1985), is a boulder-problem through the bulge to the right and marked by a single bolt.

To the right, and across the widest part of the roofs, are five excellent routes. The requirement for 'low tide' is a priority considering the need to allow walkers to pass.

21 Tyrannosaurus Max E3 6a ★ 1985
10m From the stepping stones, pull over the bulge to reach the main overlap. Swing left and power over the bulge (peg) to gain the tree.

22 Let the Max Increase F7b ★ 1991
10m Move up to the centre of the roof and follow a leftwards line along the lip until its apex can be gained.

23 Crankus Maximus F7b+ ★ 2011
10m The direct finish to *Let the Max Increase* proves good fun. Down-aid the route to prevent getting wet.

24 Maximuscle F7c+ ★ 2011
10m Swing immediately right from the start of *Let the Max Increase* and cross the roof to finish on a tree root. Down-aid to retrieve the gear.

25 Maxing Around F7a+ 1991
10m A direct assault on the flat roof to the right. Powerful.

The Nook

Sport: 12 (F7a to F8a+)   **Trad:** 3 (E3)
Aspect: South   **Sunshine:** Little sun   **Season:** Summer
Conditions: Quite seepy and dirty in early season, slow to dry, shady
Best for: Redpointing roof warriors   **Approach:** 25 minutes

A hooded little crag where the difficulty of its routes impressively outweighs their diminutive size. Desperately-fingery walls lead to hideous roofs and bulges and this is surely the playground for the campus boarders and cellar dwellers of today's generation.

The crag remains wetter than most crags for most of the year and once it dries can need a bit of a cleaning. In 2014 it got a major overhaul with much cleaning, rebolting and sorting out of lines by Kristian Clemmow, Paul Freeman and Mark Pretty. It receives little sunlight despite facing south.

The Climbing
Short and powerful climbing on bulges and roofs.

Conditions and Aspect
Prone to seepage in the winter and spring and initially dirty when it dries. Very shady. Nice setting just beside the river. Good in hot, dry years when the crag dries and gets cleaned early.

Parking and Approach
See map on page 268. It takes about 25 minutes from Miller's Dale or Topley Pike.

At the left-hand side of the wall where the main bulk of the roofs run out is a hanging shallow groove. To the left of this the banking begins to increase. **Perverted Mind**, E2 5c (1983), climbs into the vegetated groove from part way up the slope and exits the overhang into the undergrowth; **Fuckpig**, E2 5c (1979), climbs the wall 2m to its right once again exiting the capping overhang rightwards and **Eddy's First**, E2 6a (1983), gains the hanging groove with difficulty and exits as for the previous route.

1   The Dukes of Earl (Grey) F7c   1994
12m   The left-most of the bolted routes requires careful placement of the feet. A big ape-index helps.

2   Michael Foot Jam F7c+ ★★   1989
12m   The left-hand side of the main prow gives The Nook's best climb. The clue is in the name.

3   A Cure for Foot Jams F7b+ ★★   2014
12m   A new take on a neglected pitch. The big juggy roof provides a great overhanging testpiece, starting up *Michael Foot Jam*.

4   A Cure for Arapiles F7b+ ★   1985
12m   The older roof pitch begins as for *Kalymnos 8a* then moves left to finish up *A Cure for Foot Jams*.

5   Kalymnos 8a F7a+ ★   2014
12m   Good juggy climbing joining *Santiano* in the large recess.

6   Santiano F7a+ ★   1979
12m   Another rusty trad climb rejuvenated in 2014 to give a punchy sport climb.

7   A Mighty Wind F7b+ ★   2014
10m   The short and steep roof.

8   The Storm F7b+ ★   1982
12m   Another renowned testpiece from the early-Eighties across the stepped roof. **Rock Umbrella**, E6 6b (1982), took a line leading up and left through the roof but it has shed holds and the gear is in a very poor state.

9   A Bit of Nooky F8a ★   1989
12m   The steep initial wall with desperate moves leads to better holds. A final hard move gains the belay.

10   The Lockless Monster F7c+ ★★   1989
12m   The better of the harder routes with desperate moves past the third bolt to land you in a niche. Finish by moving out to the left. There are two bolts from an abandoned project in the bulge just to the left of this.

11   Theoria F8a+ ★   1990
10m   A true cellar-problem just left of the tree. The start is hideous: above is marginally less so. Exit the niche rightwards.

12   There's Life in the Old Log Yet F7c ★ 1993
10m   The desperate wall and tiny groove just to the right of the tree. Downclimb the tree to retreat.

The walls to the right contain some routes which would be good highballs if the tops were clean.

13   New Enemies E3 6b   1979
8m   Gain the groove via a series of sloping holds.

14   Powerplay E3 6b   1987
7m   Climb the bulge and faint rib 2m to the right.

15   Zebedee's Got Syphilis E3 6b   1979
7m   The bulge and rightwards-leaning ramp 2m to the right again.

Chee Dale Sport Climbing History

In the late 1970s and 1980s, activists had begun to focus on the limestone crags lining the Derbyshire Dales. Action was centred on free-climbing old routes that had previously used some form of aid. At the same time, British climbers were migrating away from a summer of storms in the Alps to explore the bolted climbing of Southern France: the Verdon and Buoux areas in particular.

Consequently, climbing ethics in the early-Eighties were undergoing a metamorphosis from a pure bottom-up trad approach. A combination of frigging and resting on the rope, gaining ground and protection, was slowly being overtaken by the European redpoint style of ascent.

These influences and new techniques began to be tested on areas of rock in the Dale that were devoid of natural and peg protection. Pushing the envelope at the time was a small handful of individuals who chose to place the odd bolt to supplement the existing peg or natural protection. An early exponent of this was Ron Fawcett who, in 1982 and with just two bolts, forced his way up *Tequila Mockingbird*. The development from the yo-yo, rarely pulling the rope, to the flash or redpoint was in line with the modernisation of the protection styles in the dales.

This did not to go unnoticed by a young and impressionable Gary Gibson, who began to add the odd bolt on relatively easier climbs around the Dale. His view was

quite clear; he had seen others do it to achieve their goal at a higher level, so why not at his level.

The defining moment of this era came in 1983 when Gibson plunged himself into a major controversial debate by bolting a line on The Cornice that had hitherto not been done as an aid route. *Clarion Call*, the name intending to provoke a call to arms, became instantly popular but provoked outrage in some areas of the climbing community. Never before had anybody challenged the ethical boundaries so much. Later, the bolts were removed and the route re-led as a serious and unpopular route on poor pegs by Nick Dixon. After this, the arena settled back temporarily into a confused ethical position, but Peak District limestone climbing was never to be the same again.

Clarion Call had been a bold statement but it was too early for the majority of climbers to accept its status and for a period of time new routes returned to the minimalist ethic of having only the occasional bolt. However, as more climbers visited European sport destinations it wasn't long before up-and-coming climbers started to add fully fledged sport climbs of their own. A prime example of this was Ben Masterson's *Boo* on Chee Tor, a fully bolted climb on a smooth grey wall, adjacent to traditional climbs. Similarly, Jerry Moffatt's free ascent of *Orange Sunshine* on Two Tier initially relied upon a mixture of old and new bolts, but was essentially a sport route. These were followed by Chris Gore's *The Ogre*, again on one of Chee Tor's unclimbed walls.

Around this time, the British 'E' Grade system began to struggle to describe the difficulty of the hardest sport routes with the restrictive limiting grade of E6/E7 6c. Experience has shown that this could have meant anything from F7b to F8a. Cheap flights and fuel, together with settled winter weather abroad encouraged more and more climbers to taste the delights of France and Spain. Thus the French grading system which supported the redpoint approach took hold initially in the Peak, but soon spread across the rest of the UK.

Joining the early fray was young Mark (Zippy) Pretty who was to play a major role in the sporting activities of the Dale later in the Nineties and Noughties. He added a number of fingery desperates perhaps most notable of which was the F8a, *Unleashing the Wild Physique* in 1986. Slightly later came *Bored of the Lies*, F7b+, a route named in direct reference to a controversial bolting episode across the river on Chee Tor.

Gary Gibson. Photo: Ian Smith.

Ben Masterson making the first ascent of Boo (page 333). Photo: Keith Sharples.

In 1986 Simon Nadin applied his not-inconsiderable talent to add three classics: *The Sea is a Brown Paper Bag, The Tier Drop Explodes* and in 1987 the even more impressive *Gonads*, all on Two Tier. Around the same time, Gibson tapped into the wealth of opportunity by climbing the first sport routes on The Embankment, the pick of the crop being *Sturgeon in the Cupboard*. In 1988 Chris Plant added a significant pointer to the future when he beefed up The Cornice's overlapping walls to give *Powerplant* (the must-do F8a) and Mark Pretty added *That Was the River* and *This is the Sea*, also on The Cornice.

These were just pockets of development rather than a whole-hearted approach. This slow, nervous acceptance of bolted climbing changed forever with a big bang in 1989. More and more climbers had decided, rightly or wrongly, that this was the way forward and portable cordless power drills had become more commercially available making the whole process much 'easier' than the manual tap-tap, star-drilling method. Sport routes were developed throughout the Dale by a small but dedicated band of devotees, the dry spell of weather creating a friendly but very competitive environment. The result of this activity was a major step forward for the Dale, if not in standard, certainly in the volume of sport climbs being done. '89 was indeed an important year.

Things started off quite slowly due to the wet spring but when the rock finally dried out, the Dale became a hotbed of competitive activity. Long Wall saw a batch of routes, the best being Chris Hardy's *Kiss Me Hardy* and Keith Sharples' *Jungle Rock*, whilst The Nook captured the imagination of the campus boarders: John Hart coming up trumps with *Lockless Monster* and Mark Pretty, *A Bit of Nooky*.

Whilst these were excellent offerings it was The Cornice that saw the most impressive events. Sean Myles lay down his first calling card with the wickedly fingery *Four Door Dostoyevsky* and Ben Moon demonstrated his bouldering prowess on *Masculine Power Trip*. Alongside this came Pretty's *Mescaline Power Trip* and Malc Taylor's *Feminine Ego Trip*. Not to be left out, Jon de Montjoye completed the well-named, *Whose Line is it Anyway?*, just before he emigrated to France.

The most impressive event was Sean Myles' free climbing of the aid route *Monumental Alabaster* to create the pertinently named *Monumental Armblaster*. This was a true marker for the future.

Throughout the rest of the Nineties the pace slowed, but some landmark routes were nevertheless picked off. Seb Grieve delivered a major challenge in the form of *K3*. Likewise, John Hart delivered his *42*, named after his age when he climbed it (or was it the 'meaning of life'). Ruth Jenkins added *De Vine*, the hardest female first ascent in the Dale. Chris Wright climbed the superb duo of *Lightweight* and *Minos*, on Two Tier Buttress, as well as a batch of routes on both The Cornice and Long Wall.

Graham Hoey on Systems Malfunction, F7b, on Two Tier (page 361). Photo: Ian Smith.

Malcolm Taylor on Monumental Armblaster, F8b, on the Cornice. (page 308). Photo: Keith Sharples.

Gibson continued to add routes throughout the Dale but the main focus in the latter part of the Nineties came from the extremely talented Steve McClure who breached the huge roof on The Cornice to give the Dale its first F8c, *Dreadnought*, the hardest route in the Dale. He also added *Asian Shadow Player* to the right-hand side of the same wall. This complemented Seb Grieve's earlier technical masterpiece, *Love Amongst the Butterflies*. McClure also came up with *Malcolm X* alongside *Monumental Armblaster*. This flurry of development brought the 1990s to a close.

Following all this activity, development in the new century was slow. The top climbers refocused their attentions on Hard Grit, with bouldering taking centre stage. However, what little development that occurred did involve some extremely difficult climbing. Two Tier Buttress received attention, initially from Alistair Hannah who in 2002 discovered the worthwhile F8b *Hardcorejunkie*. Rupert Davies took up the challenge of the walls to the left of *Countdown* to give *Kali Yuga*, also F8b in 2003 followed ten years later with *Flow* as a neighbouring twin. Both of these had been abandoned projects.

The main event of 2004 was when Kristian Clemmow finally freed the *Spider* on Plum Buttress. The last aid point only being eliminated 17 years after Andy Pollitt's nearly free effort, albeit using a slight variation in line.

The Cornice was at the centre of attention as some last great problems awaited an ascent, perhaps due as much to the wet summer conditions as to the limited number of climbers who wanted to do them. Clemmow continued his interests on The Cornice with *Snatch*, F8b in 2003 and *32*, (Clemmow's age at the time), F8b+ in 2007. Then in 2005, Steve McClure crimped the desperately thin F8c of *Somehow Super*, essentially bringing the decade to a close.

Good dry conditions arrived in 2010 and Kristian Clemmow reappeared on The Cornice scene to deliver an F8b in the form of *Bricktop*. This was followed by the extremely fingery *Barney Ragin'* by James Mchaffie. In the following year, yet more hard routes fell: Clemmow was back for *Clematis* and the widest part of the Big Roof, *Gran Techo* whilst Bob Hickish succeeded on *Techno Prisoners*.

Whilst not strictly sport climbing, it is worth mentioning the extreme boulder-problem traverses of Dog's Dinner buttress. *Pedigree Chum* at F8c+ and *Finest Pedigree* at F9a+ are phenomenal tests of finger strength and stamina. Both tie for being the longest 'routes' in the Dale. The former, by Paul Smitton avoids a seemingly blank section by climbing alarmingly high in its final third. Whereas the latter, by Steve McClure, qualifies for being one of the hardest pieces of climbing in the country at the time of writing.

It could be said that the Dale is now largely worked out, but one or two major gaps remain. These will be the challenges of the future as more and more climbers begin to climb the ninth grade.

Gary Gibson

Mark Pretty. Photo: Richie Brooks.

Sean Myles. Photo: Richie Brooks.

Dave Pegg on R 'n P. on the Cornice (page 316). Photo: David Simmonite.

The Cornice

Sport: 77 (F6b+ to F8c) **Trad:** 20 (VS to E6)
Aspect: North-east **Sunshine:** None **Season:** Summer
Conditions: Shady and cool, tree-covered, sometimes humid, slow drying, rainproof
Best for: Powerful, top class redpoints, F7a to F8b+ **Approach:** 20 minutes

In many ways this is the *piece de resistance* of Chee Dale sport climbing, with a collection of magnificent routes on overhanging walls, overlaps and roofs. The only detraction is the length of time it takes for them to dry out. When they do, the cliff provides a fantastic venue for mid-to-high grade sport climbs. It is ideal in the summer months when it receives little sunshine and it can be refreshingly cool being close to the river.

The Climbing
A very steep crag giving predominantly hard sport climbing. There are some classy trad climbs but ascents are infrequent. Brilliant in the mid and upper grades; The F7s are generally considered warm-ups here. Routes have varying character. A few short power-bulge type routes on the extreme left; a bunch of F7c to F8c roof climbs right of this; classy leaning walls with longer routes in the F7s and easier F8s. Biceps-busting undercutting testpieces on the right-hand side and vertical, fingery and highly technical old-school bum-spankers on the extreme right. Many of them are classics of their grade in the Peak.

Conditions and Aspect
The crag resembles a seaweed farm for most of the winter and often into the spring. Indeed, some years it barely dries out at all. Routes usually begin to dry in late spring. In early season, the more that people abseil down routes with a brush and remove dust and slime, the quicker they will be in condition. So be public-spirited and bring a soft brush.

Once dry and clean, routes stay in good condition. It is a great summer crag thanks to a shady aspect and nearby river to keep things cool. It will stay dry in the rain, although humid days lead to condensation. It is generally busy when in condition.

Parking and Approach
See map on page 268. Approach from Miller's Dale station in about 20 minutes.

Access
Walkers pass very close to the cliff. Please be polite and do not block the path with gear or belaying practices.

Ethan Walker on 32, F8b+ (page 315). Photo: Jon Clark.

Power Trip Wall; The leftmost end of the crag sports a bunch of bouldery routes. However, it is rare to find dry conditions. **Ophelia's Lob-elia**, F7b+ (1989), climbs the shallow groove above the left side of the stepping stones.

1 Forehead Trombones F7b+   1989
12m The flake-groove gives relatively straightforward climbing to a hard long lurch over its capping bulge.

2 Sharp Practice F8a+ ★   1995
12m Start as the stepping stones run out. The desperate leaning wall leads to sloping holds at the lip of the bulge. Pulling onto the face is easier said than done. A link-up, **Trombone Practice**, F8a (2014), requires a big span left at the bulge to join *Forehead Trombones*.

3 Masculine Power Trip F8a+ ★   1989/1994
15m One of the first routes to breach this section of cliff and a testament to Ben Moon's bouldering ability. Very powerful and fingery moves lead up the seam to a rest below the upper bulge. This ain't easy either.

4 Mescaline Power Trip F8a ★   1989
15m Another desperate exercise, requiring a pile of boulders to reach the first holds. Hard, fingery moves lead to a teetering rockover onto the face. The bulge above is marginally easier than its masculine neighbour.

5 Wright On F8a ★   1994
14m Hard, bouldery moves straight from the ground. Crossing the roof needs a fair degree of improvisation before the belay of *Taylor Made* is gained.

6 Wright to Left F7c ★   1995
18m Gain the groove as for *Taylor Made*. From here, traverse leftwards across the sandwiched slab, mainly with hands in the roof, crossing the existing routes, with the occasional resting spot, until a lower-off can be gained at the left-hand side of the roof.

7 Taylor Made F7c ★★   1989
14m Hard moves to leave the ground below the hanging groove followed by better holds to enter it. After taking a good breather, make difficult moves to gain the lip of the roof before unusual hanging and slapping moves lead leftwards and up to the belay.

8 Feminine Ego Trip F7c+ ★   1960s/1989
10m The right-hand exit from the groove has a particularly trying sequence to reach a flake. Hard for the short. A **Strict Left-Hand Finish**, F8a (2014), moves out left to the sloping shelf to campus up the wall, keeping clear of the jugs in the groove.

A desperate project starts just to the right.

Rupert Davies on Nemesis, F8a+ (page 308). Photo: Stuart Littlefair.

To the right, an arching groove bends rightwards across the crag. This is the line of Monumental Armblaster.

9 Nemesis F8a+ ★★★   1994

15m A major classic breaching the leaning tower of rock. From the foot of the arching groove, make a couple of improbable moves leftwards to get established on the wall. Continue the cranking via edges and flakes to gain the upper bulge. A lunge/jump lands a good jug. Gain the flake and the final headwall leading to a short finishing corner. **Photo on page 307.**

10 Clematis F8b ★★   2011

15m Climb to the high niche of *Nemesis* and leave it either directly or leftwards. Both methods are equally difficult, particularly when pumped. Get the jugs at the top of the crag then reach back down for the belay.

11 Bricktop F8b ★★★   2010

18m Power-endurance at its best. After doing the crux of *Nemesis*, burl out to the right and, using edges, climb the mean wall above.

12 Monumental Armblaster F8a+ ★★★   1989

20m The awesome leaning groove provides a major classic. Sean Myles' free ascent of the old aid line was the route that pointed the way to the harder possibilities of the crag. The entire pitch provides a very sustained stamina exercise. The final bulge, although height-dependent, provides a fitting climax to a magnificent route. **Photo on page 301.**

13 Malcolm X F8b+ ★★   1999

20m The counter-line through *Monumental*. Gain the flake under *Monumental* by testing moves and follow it leftwards and then up into the groove. Leaving this and heading leftwards across the bulge and wall provide the real meat of the route before the *Bricktop* belay is attained. It is also possible to link this with the finish of *Monumental* to give **Malcom Armblaster**, F8b ★★ (2010).

14 Last Eggs Before the MI F7c+   1991

20m Start as for *Malcolm X* and follow the rising flake to a belay below the roof. A long-standing project aims to link this into *Monumental*.

Stone Elworthy on The Jug Jockey, F7c+ (page 310). Photo: Paul Bennett.

15 Gran Techo F8b ★★★ 2011
20m Climb the wall to the roof. An improbable sequence leads to the lip. A final stiff move deposits you onto the "slab". A few delicate shuffles along the ramp lead to a rest point before the final pull to the ledge and *Jug Jockey* belay.

16 Techno Prisoners F8b+ ★ 2011
20m The super-reachy direct finish to *Gran Techo*.

17 The Jug Jockey F7c+ ★★★ 1990
20m A Sharples masterpiece, one of the best F7cs in the Dale. Gaining the lip is relatively straightforward. However, from here the problems really come to light: **photo on page 309.**

18 Easy Rider F7c+ 2011
22m From under the roof on *Jug Jockey*, go right to exit via an easier headwall. Potentially loose and dangerous.

19 Dreadnought F8c ★★ 1999
20m An awesome route providing one of the hardest roof problems around. Climb the wall and cross the roof, past the enormous ring bolt. The crux upper wall awaits.

20 Roof Warrior F8a ★★★ 1991
20m A magnificent route with three distinct cruxes. Climb the wall with a difficult start to a knee-bar just below the lip of the roof. Hard moves over the lip, centred on a letter-box hold in the wall, gain a prominent flake. This leads more easily to the belay.

21 Cry of Despair F7c ★★★ 1990
20m Classic stuff. Exasperated redpointers will know the name well. Sustained and fingery climbing gains the groove. Hard moves lead to a resting place before the final obstacle, the overhang.

22 That Was the River F7b+ ★★ 1988
15m The arching overlap provides a superb and pumpy pitch. Gaining it is the main crux but keep some reserves for the final draining stretch.

23 Rapid City F8a ★ 1990
15m The direct version of *That Was the River*. Desperate in humid conditions. The upper roof is quite unstable, so it might be a good idea to lower off below it.

24 Streamline F7c+ 1994
12m A fingery eliminate; possibly unrepeated since hold-loss.

25 This is the Sea F7c+ ★ 1988
12m Desperate moves gain a very shallow left-facing groove. This, although easier, requires some degree of concentration until a junction with *That Was the River*.

26 Old Man River F7b ★★ 1986
15m A superb route, finding a way up the impressive wall. Follow flakes to a respite. Gain a jug then make complex moves left to the belay of *That Was the River* or finish direct at F7b+, (1995). A possible link into the next route is: **Dirty Old Man**, F7c ★★ (2010).

27 The Naive and Sentimental Lover
F7b+ ★★   1989
16m Superb moves on the headwall. Follow *Up the River...* to good holds above the overlap. Move up and left and climb the vague flake and short difficult wall.

28 Up the River Without a Paddle
F7a ★★★   1984
18m The classic warm-up for the harder routes on the crag but magnificent in its own right. Pull over the two overlaps to gain a good hold. The upper wall, although steep, is littered with excellent holds leading rightwards.

29 Snails of the Riverbank F7b ★★   1986
16m Another fine climb when dry with two hard overlaps and a fingery wall. Climb the lower wall with a sharp pull over the overlap to the second overlap. An unlikely sequence gains gradually improving holds up the headwall.

30 Zippy Stardust and the Spiders from Mars
F6b+   1976/1983/1995
23m Start below a step in the mid-height overlap. Climb the wall on good holds to reach the overlap. A few difficult moves gain the upper wall and easier climbing. Often filthy.

31 The Monday Club F7a   1989
23m A fine top wall but the lower wall is often very dirty. Follow a direct line up the wall passing two overlaps.

32 Trampled Underfoot F7a ★   1989
23m A better right-hand variant to *The Monday Club*. From beneath the first overlap, move right and pull over into a corner. Pass the roof above to the right, to a thin crack above.

33 Gardener's Question Time F7a   1994
12m A difficult lower wall, often damp and greasy, leads to the left-hand side of the overlap. Pull over this on large holds to finish via a shallow groove. Aptly named.

34 Rue Morgue F6c ★   1979
20m One of the old traditional routes of the cliff can now be done as a sport route. Start by a flake leaning against the cliff. Climb the wall past a flake and small overlap, with one awkward move to gain the roof. Traverse left for 5m before turning the overhang into the shallow groove of *Gardener's Question Time*.

35 After the Goldfish F7b ★ 1986
20m A direct finish to *Rue Morgue* with some difficult moves to dispatch the overhang. A long reach helps.

36 Crowd Control F7c ★ 1989
20m Climb a slim pillar to the overlap. Overcoming this is the crux but the rounded nature of the climbing above adds a new dimension to limestone faith-in-friction.

37 Une Crime Passionnel E4 6a ★★★ 1982
22m A trad classic; almost a sport route but you need a few small wires for the top wall. Climb the shallow depression with a hard move directly past, or just to the right of, the first bolt to gain a niche below the overlap, Pass this to the left to a crack leading up the headwall. **Photo opposite.**

A Basic Problem of Power, E6 6b (1989), takes a direct line to the right taking the overlap and 'shield' directly.

38 Fey E4 5c ★ 1980
22m An old classic, superb when clean. Climb to a short right-facing groove then gain and follow the flake.

39 War Memorial F6c+ ★ 1983
22m A good climb, often used as a warm-up. The wall is followed to a bulge, then tricky moves into the finishing flake of *Fey* (large wire useful).

40 Succubus F7b ★★ 1994
22m A fine pitch with a frustrating and difficult crux at the bulge, taken on sloping holds. Hard to flash.

41 Shazam E4 6a ★ 1976/1982
22m The thin crack gives way to a bulge. The difficulties in passing this are short-lived. Trend right to the belay.

42 Martial Music F7a+ ★★ 1983/1984
22m The first of a trio of excellent face-climbs, with a difficult move low down and a tricky top bulge.

43 Clarion Call F7a ★★★ 1983
22m The original bolted classic of the early-Eighties gives a pushy pitch for the grade. Climb the intricate wall to the first overlap. Bypassing this is tricky and becoming worn. The final overlaps require a determined effort.

44 The Poppy Fields F7b+ 2004
22m A tight eliminate. Pull left over a bulge then over the overlap. Keep out of *Clarion Call*, to the top. Blinkers needed at this grade, more like F7a+ otherwise.

Tim Lounds on Une Crime Passionnel. E4 6a (opposite page). Photo: Mark Rankine.

45 Armistice Day F7a ★★★ 1984
22m Another early classic which weaves its way up the wall past several overlaps.

46 Whose Line is it Anyway? F7b ★★★ 1989
22m Harder than its neighbours and at the upper limit of the grade. A difficult move low down is often avoided by a detour to the right. The finish remains frustrating.

47 Big Store E5 6b ★ 1984
23m Climb the shallow groove to where it becomes an overlap. Long moves leftwards and then back slightly right lead onto a short headwall and belay above.

48 The Egyptian Bizarre E5 6b 1989
22m The direct finish to *Big Store* past two bolts. Starting up *Big Zipper* and stepping left at the bulge turns it into a fully fledged sport route (F7b).

49 Hawaii Five-O/Ali F7b+, F7a ★ 1989
63m A traverse starting up *That Was the River* to its last bolt then right to belay on *Rue Morgue*. Carry on, descending *Une Crime Passionnel*, then on, passing the niche on *Clarion Call* to lower off *Egyptian Bizarre*.

50 Tour de France F7a 1983
35m Gain the base of the groove on *Fey* then traverse right, as for *Hawaii Five-O*, to the belay of *Egyptian Bizarre*.

51 Big Zipper F7a+ ★★ 1986
20m Good climbing with a tough, pumpy finish. Climb the lower wall to reach a bulge. Force rightwards then make a hurried exit on rather disappointing holds to reach the belay. **Photo on page 317.**

52 Beezlebub F7b+ 1996
18m Tackle the upper bulge of *Big Zipper* directly.

53 Bored of the Lies F7b+ ★★ 1986
20m A fine route with a bizarre series of moves to avoid *Big Zipper*. Climb the blunt rib to reach *Big Zipper*. Make difficult moves right and slightly downwards until a swift pull brings the belay within reach. The more natural line, finishing up *Big Zipper*, gives a well-travelled F7b.

54 Ouijaboard F8a ★★ 1997
20m A hard and fingery route up the blank-looking grey wall to the right, starting up small crimps and undercuts, to finish as for *Bored of the Lies*. A very difficult sequence to unlock since every combination is desperate.

55 Four Door Dostoyevsky F8a+ ★★ 1989

17m The meat of this tough pitch, the shallow curving groove/depression midway up the wall, gives hideously thin climbing. Sharp.

56 Powerplant F8a ★★★ 1988

17m The classic of its grade in the Dale. The difficulties are centred on the overlap at two-thirds height, made somewhat easier thanks to kneebars/pads. Climb to the strip roof and make crux moves rightwards. The upper wall is brilliant. A project has been bolted directly up the wall.

Powerpants, F8a (2011), links the start of *Powerplant* into *Devonshire Arms*.

57 Devonshire Arms F8a+ ★★ 1997

18m The wall to the right is even more powerful, with even more technicalities thrown in for good measure. Passing the third bolt is the crux and passing the fifth bolt is debilitating. The good news is that the last stretch is relatively straightforward. Nails for the grade.

58 K3 F8a+ ★★★ 1994

19m Another classic of its genre said to require more effort than climbing the famous 8,000-metre peak: that is minus the oxygen and Sherpas. Start 5m to the right and move up to the bulge. Lots, and lots, and lots of undercutting leftwards leads onto the headwall which still provides a few nervous moments.

K5, F8b (2011), starts up *K3* but when you get to the 'pancake', undercut left into *Devonshire Arms* then left again into *Powerplant* above its crux. Finish up this.

K2, F8b+ (2011), continues from *Powerplant* across *Four Door Dostoyevsky* to the belay of *Bored of the Lies*.

59 42 F8b ★ 1995

19m An even more direct line than *K3* at the very upper limit of the grade. It takes *K3*'s starting difficulties before ploughing out right via a series of undercut holds. Marred by the unsightly glue streaks. Named after the age of the first ascensionist.

60 32 F8b+ ★★ 2007

20m Desperately fingery and powerful. Difficulties start at the first roof. Either use raw power or a contorted egyptian to gain an unhelpful sloper. All that remains is an infuriating move to gain the relative sanctuaty of *R 'n P*. Also named after the age of the first ascensionist. **Photo on page 304.**

61 R 'n P F8a+ ★★★ 1990
21m Said to be the best line on this section of cliff. Follow a leftwards line through the overlaps onto the headwall. This is slightly easier but still notoriously stubborn. **Photo on page 303.**

62 Snatch F8b ★★★ 2003
22m Brilliant climbing. From above the first bulge on *R 'n P*, continue directly up the thin wall.

63 Barney Ragin' F8b+ ★★ 2010
23m Sustained and fingery with no rests. Start up *R 'n P* then break out right at the bulge to a good slot. From the slot, hard climbing leads into *Love Amongst the Butterflies*.

64 Love Amongst the Butterflies F8b ★★ 1996
21m Superb technicalities, the antithesis of the climbs to the left. From just right of a tree stump, take a leftwards line and pull over bulges to a rest on the impressive slab, or is it? Climb the desperate wall above past a prominent undercut.

65 Asia Shadow Player F8b ★ 1997
20m A sort of direct finish to *Love Amongst the Butterflies* gaining it from the 'rest' on that route and climbing the slightly harder wall to its right.

66 Somehow Super F8c ★ 2005
20m Redefines the meaning of the word 'nails'. The ghastly wall gained from the start of *Love Amongst the Butterflies*.

67 Unleashing the Wild Physique
F8a ★★★ 1986
20m A brilliant technical exercise taking a bold, sweeping line. Climb to a small hole, step left and arc leftwards across the wall to gain some thin flakes/undercuts. Climb slightly rightwards to reach a small ledge.

68 Cosmopolitan F7b+ ★★ 1984
20m The first breach of the wall. The original runout has been tamed by a new bolt near the top. From the small hole, tackle the bulge directly. Move slightly left into a depression and exit leftwards to the belay.

69 Cordless Madness F7c ★★ 1989
20m The hideously thin direct finish to *Cosmopolitan* which is showing signs of wear. Where *Cosmopolitan* moves left, step right and climb the wall passing a small overlap.

70 Mandy F7b+ ★ 1986
20m A very fingery series of moves out of the right-hand side of the hole leads to a jug. Once established on this, easier climbing leads rightwards up the wall to the belay.

71 Flowers in the Dirt F7b ★ 1989
20m A direct and fingery line to the right with a slightly bold central section. The crux around the second bolt can be very frustrating and after the third bolt some may choose to place some small nuts for protection.

Natalie Bennett on Big Zipper, F7a+ (page 314). Photo: Paul Bennett.

72 The Third Order F7b ★ 1985

20m Gain the niche and make desperate moves to exit it onto the wall above and some respite. Continue directly, finishing via a thin crack and a few more technical moves.

73 Loco F7b+ ★ 2001

20m Even harder climbing, with a reach-dependent crux breaches the wall 2m to the right. Once you have landed on the slab, the upper wall proves to be a breeze.

74 Too Pumpy for Grumpy F7b+ 1989

20m A hard lower wall.

75 Further Adventures in Greendale
F6c+ ★ 1989

20m A fine wall-climb with tricky moves over a bulge low down and a fingery finale. Hard for the grade.

76 The Cruel Sea E5 6a ★ 1982

27m A big sweeping line from right to left across the face with some good climbing. Climb the hanging groove of *Old Man's Gambit* to its end and then traverse leftwards across the face, with a step down towards the end to gain a flake. Finish up this (peg).

77 Old Man's Gambit E2 5c 1976

25m The hanging groove demarcating the right-hand side of the face gives a pleasant pitch when clean, which it usually isn't. At its end move left and up the wall with a certain amount of trepidation.

78 The Corniceman F7a+ ★ 1986

20m A good and popular route. Climb the wall right of the flake by a sequence of fingery moves to an easing in angle. Finish slightly leftwards over the upper bulges.

The walls to the right have returned to nature, much to the delight of the land owner (the Derbyshire Wildlife Trust) who would like things to remain this way. The next routes are included purely for information purposes only.

Jelly Fingers, HVS 5a (1979), gains the rock from the top of the tree and moves up to good holds before traversing left to exit via a corner. **Vandal**, VS 4c (1979), climbs the wall slightly leftwards from a vegetated block 2m to the right. **Whitebeam**, E1 5c (1979), climbs directly up the wall to the right to finish via a rightwards curving groove. **Disgusted of Tunbridge** Wells, HS

4a (1979), climbs the wall 3m right of the ash tree to the right.

To the right, the walls rear up again and have a slightly cleaner profile.

79 Chapter and Verse F6b
12m A direct line up the clean face to the right.

80 Ezekiel Stool E1 5b   1979
20m Climb the wall to the right of the ash tree to gain a good left-facing flake. Move slightly left to a good hold and then trend back rightwards via easier climbing and obligatory vegetation to the top.

81 Um Bongo E4 6b   1986
20m The smooth-looking wall 2m to the right has two old bolts and leads to a lower-off. No skulking off to the right.

82 Led up the Garden Path E1 5b   1985
10m The shallow corner to the right has now returned to its original garden state.

83 Percy's World F6c+
11m A short intense affair to the right.

84 Flash Harry E4 5c   1985
13m The wall to the right provides a bold and fingery pitch with a peg. Good holds are somewhere beneath the vegetation.

85 Too Jugless for Douglas E4 6b ★   1985
12m A super little pitch, although the in-situ gear could do with replacing. Climb the shallow groove just to the right of a tree past a peg and bolt to the bulge. Pass this via a long stretch and two thread runners above.

86 Subversive E2 5b   1985
9m The steep flake to the right gives a pitch requiring much more urgency than the grade may suggest.

87 Bombardier F6c+
11m The blunt rib to the right with a technical finale.

Fibrin, VS 4c (1979), climbs the rib and prominent flake to the right whilst **Rinky Dinky**, E1 5c (1985), climbs the thin crack around the corner to a junction with *Fibrin*.

88 The 'too small for the tall' Wall E5 6b 1986
12m The desperate smooth-looking wall to the right requires a telescopic reach and no little technical ability. A ring peg runner shows the way.

The wall to the right appears to be a forgotten project. The final three routes are situated on an undercut buttress 6m to the right.

89 The Snap F7a
9m A short steep bulge with hard starting moves.

90 Mike's Bike and the Collar-bone Experience
F7b+   1989
12m The left-hand of the two lines of bolts provides the route and no little effort is required in its short length.

91 Skin-Flick F7c+   1989
9m The right-hand line is a truly hideous problem requiring the ability to hang on to 'match-sticks'.

Rhubarb Buttress

Sport: 20 (F6b+ to F8a+) **Trad:** 5 (E1 to E4)
Aspect: East **Sunshine:** Morning **Season:** Summer
Conditions: Shady, slow-drying, dusty, not popular
Best for: Esoteric mid-grade walls **Approach:** 20 minutes

A long wall of generally good rock with some sections of flora; this is due to it receiving very little in the way of sunshine and remaining damp for long periods during the winter months. When dry, it gives a number of reasonable mid-grade sport climbs which can be climbed in light rain because of a helpful tree canopy.

The Climbs

A score of sport climbs mainly in the mid-grades with a couple of harder offerings. Mostly vertical or slightly overhanging walls. Some unpopular trad routes too.

Conditions

Slow-drying. Shady. Best in a good summer. Can be a little dirty. Some routes are overgrown.

Approach

See map on page 268. Rhubarb Buttress lies a hundred metres down from the Cornice and almost opposite Chee Tor. The rightmost routes are immediately above the path.

The first routes begin at the extreme left-hand end of the cliff where the banking disappears and just to the right of a mossy ramp.

1 The Way of the Gone Wives F6b+   1998
12m An easy lower wall is followed by a thin flake on the upper section of the wall.

2 Custard Pie in Your Eye F6c   1998
12m Climbs a shallow groove and bulge directly to a tree.

3 Cry Havoc F6c   1998
11m The short wall finishing via the scooped groove.

4 Fallout Zone F6c   1998
11m Start behind a large tree. Climb the wall on small holds moving slightly left from the break to finish over the bulges at the top.

Augustus Carp, E1 5a (1979), is the large flake to the right and has become in need of a good clean.

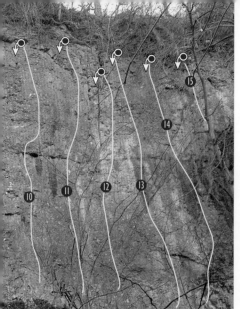
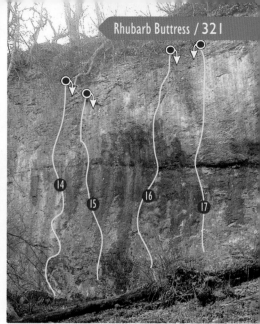

5 Gaseous Exchange F6c+ ★ 1998

12m Probably the best route on this section. Climb the shallow groove to reach a small overlap. Zigzag through this to gain the upper wall which gives a delightful climax.

6 Chemical Weapons F6c+ ★ 1983/1998

12m The delicate lower wall, bulge and technical wall.

7 Rhubarb, Rhubarb, Rhubarb F6b+ ★ 1998

12m Climb to the break. The blunt rib above the overlap gives something to aim for and all on positive holds.

8 Semolina Sunday F7a 1998

12m The wall leads to a squeezed-in finish to the left of a groove.

To the right the routes have become overgrown: **The Bee's Knees**, E1 5a (1979), the wall and **A Laugh a Minute**, E1 5a (1979), the groove gained from *The Bee's Knees*. **No Laughs**, E5 6a (1982), is the groove direct.

9 The Garlic Twist F6b+ 1998

12m A direct line via a slight bulge.

10 Brief Camouflage F6c ★ 1982

14m Originally a traditional route but since being bolted it has proved more popular. It takes a direct line up the centre of the wall and concentrates its technicalities from the break onwards. Good.

11 The Day of the Long Knives F7b+ ★ 1989

15m A very technical wall climb. From 5m up *Brief Camouflage*, move rightwards up the wall to reach the break.

Hard and technical moves on hidden holds lead up the smooth wall to eventually land you on a small ledge. There is no belay at present so you have to finish upwards.

12 Feline Fine F6c ★ 1998

15m A pleasant and technical face-climb climbing the lower wall and keeping out of the shallow groove.

13 The Fat Ginger Cat F7a+ ★ 1989

18m Starting just to the right of the thin crack of *Feline Fine*, climb the difficult and technical wall to reach the now much thinner break. A long reach and strong pull brings better holds and the lower-off slightly to the right.

14 Turbo-Charged Monster Mouse F7a+ ★ 1986

18m The centre of the smooth-looking wall taken direct gives another fine pitch. The difficulties are less than its neighbour but the route just about merits the grade.

15 Thrash Your Woodie F7b 1989

18m Tackles the right-hand side of this slightly barrel-shaped wall with an easy start but difficult bulge and final fingery pull.

16 Me Tarzan F7b+ ★ 1989

15m At a slightly higher level 5m to the right, cross the roof by a desperate pull into the hanging shallow groove.

17 De Vine F8a ★ 1995

15m Even meaner. The impressive bulge and scoop to the right, left of the dangling and even more impressive ivy strands.

The next series of routes are situated at a slightly higher level and 30m to the right. A prominent overlap guards entry to the upper walls. These overlaps, whilst festooned with old and rotting gear, also contain some rare plants. Don't climb here. For the record:

Zebedee Visits the Clinic, E6 6b (1986), tackles the bulge which leads onto the rounded right arête of a prominent scoop via a bolt and two pegs. Situated 8m to the right is **Blue Arsed Fly**, E6 6b (1986), the desperate bulge marked by a long sling on an old peg. There is another peg at the lip. **The Rainmaker**, F7b+ (1989), has a desperate entry into the shallow hanging scoop.

To the right, as the low overlap begins to peter out, are a small number of old traditional routes.

18 Bloodworm E3 6a 1982
15m Climb the wall past a thread to reach the break. The groove directly above provides an easy but dirtier finish.

19 Blood Lust E2 5c 1978
18m Climb the lower bulge leftwards into a red streak and follow this on better holds to reach the break. Stand up and reach right to gain a flake which in turn leads to the top.

20 Bad Blood E5 6a 1982
20m A bold proposition with superb moves but limited protection. Gain a good flake at 2m then trend leftwards

across the wall via a series of shallow hollows to reach the break. Move right along this to a thread runner and then climb the blunt arête above before moving back leftwards across the wall. **a** This can be gained direct, **Bad Blood Direct**, E5 6c (1982).

21 Blood Transfusion E4 6b ★ 1989
18m A hard direct start to reach the first thread runner of *Bad Blood* by two distinct hard sections, bolt.

Further right, a fine grey wall close to the river's edge does offer two pitches on clean, compact limestone.

22 Lady's Fingers F7b ★ 1998
14m The left-hand line of two sport routes provides technical and fingery climbing up the left-hand side of the face.

23 The European Female F7a ★ 1983
14m The fine grey face to the right has a technical lower bulge and excellent moves above. The meaning of the name has taken on more relevance since the first ascent.

Three other vegetated routes exist here: **Moonflower**, E4 6a (1990s), the wall starting 3m to the right of *The European Female* via a scoop and scooped wall; **Naiad**, E1 5b (1976), climbs the wall two metres to the right via the easiest line and **Nip in Nippon**, E1 5b (1985), climbs a shallow scoop on the walls three metres to the right again.

Chee Tor East

Trad: 8 (E2 to E4) **Sport:** 2 (F7c to F8a+)
Aspect: North-east **Sunshine:** None **Season:** 1984-1985
Conditions: Filthy
Best for: People with a brush **Approach:** 25 minutes

A sadly out-of-condition crag whose routes were once classics. Many of these have now returned to a lichenous state and most routes will require significant cleaning before an ascent. It lies 80m downstream from the main crag. Derbyshire Wildlife Trust have requested that no further gardening be carried out to the left of *The Glorious Ninth* or to the right of *White Death*: the star ratings and grades are for the cleaned-up versions of the routes.

The only approved access to the cliff is by wading across the river. This is best done by finding a narrowing in the path just after crossing the footbridge on the approach from Wormhill, or just after the rock step beyond Rhubarb Buttress and descend down to the river.

Next, E2 6b (1986), climbs the small buttress at the foot of this descent and is identifiable by a peg.

The left-hand side of the crag is composed of two long and prominent grooves. **The Stripper**, HS 4b (1976), climbs the wall and crack system to the left of the vegetated gully at the left-hand side of the face.

1 The Glorious Ninth E4 5c ★ 1984
15m A once-good little route taking the overhanging groove.

2 Flying Circus E2 5b 1976
18m From 6m up *The Glorious Ninth*, move right onto its right wall to finish in the jungle.

3 Too Tame for the Trouble E5 6a 1983
17m The rickety and poorly-protected wall five metres to the right. Move rightwards across the half-height bulge to finish via a slim groove to the left of the main groove of the cliff.

4 White Life E4 6a ★★ 1976
18m The superb central groove gives a classic of both its type and its era with excellent bridging moves and just-about-adequate protection.

5 Blanc de Blanc E4 6a ★ 1984
19m Slightly harder and more worrying than *White Life*. From the thread runner on *White Life*, move right and up into a shallow groove (peg) which gives a worrying few moves.

6 Kumquat F8a+ ★★ 1997
18m Great when clean. The central arête of the crag and its adjoining white wall give a route of superb quality and difficulty. It takes a line from the right with a hard start to the break.

7 White Out E4 6a ★ 1983
19m To the right of the wall a flake leads to a good small ledge. Gain the wall to its left and continue directly (peg) where a hard move gains better holds to the top.

8 White Death E4 6a 1983
18m The surprisingly strenuous but well-protected crack to the right yields to a determined approach.

9 Truffles F7c 1999
18m Start at the base of the dirty crack of *Freedom Fighter*. Swing up and left to a flake. Climb this and continue to the break. Climb the smooth wall above, up and left to a flake and finishing corner.

Freedom Fighter, VS 5a (1976), climbs the obvious crack and groove to the right whilst **Risty Frog**, VS (1976), takes the crack and flake right again.

Chee Tor

Trad: 92 (VS to E7) **Sport:** 11 (F6c+ to F8a)
Aspect: West **Sunshine:** Afternoon **Season:** Spring to autumn
Conditions: Quite shady and cool, dirty in early season, can be leafy and humid in summer
Best for: Classic trad, VS to E5; technical sport climbing F7c+ to F8a **Approach:** 25 minutes

Chee Tor is the great bastion for traditional climbing in the dale, home to some of the best limestone routes in the Peak, if not the country, with *Tequila Mockingbird* and *Mortlock's Arête* being of national significance.

The routes here have lots of character. They mostly follow strong lines with technical and pumpy wall-climbs on well-featured but low-friction rock. Flakes, cracks, grooves and arêtes abound as well as smooth walls in-between.

The Climbing
A mixture of superb walls and shallow grooves. Although seemingly featureless and intimidating on first sight, closer inspection reveals a host of pockets and thin cracks which provide the lines, and much needed, though often hidden, protection.

Classic traditional climbing abounds, usually protected by a myriad of small wires, thin threads and the odd slippery cam. Strong fingers and good footwork pay dividends, especially on some of the more popular routes that can feel a bit polished especially in the heat of summer. Keep chanting the mantra, a weighted foot never slips!

In recent times a number of sport routes have been added. These are normally very hard and limited to the wall left of *Mortlock's Arête* and the bulges above the girdle break. Additional bolting of the lower walls is discouraged.

Quite a few routes rely upon limited, but key, in-situ gear. Like-for-like replacement is encouraged; light or white coloured threads should be used where possible.

A number of the routes finish at the girdle break, from where it is normal practice to either lower off or abseil back to the ground, sometimes omitting the upper pitch but more importantly avoiding the vegetation.

Conditions and Aspect
The tor catches the sun from late morning till late afternoon, after which time the sun creeps up the walls.

In a good year the crag can dry by March or April, but if you are visiting in early season be warned: holds and ledges can be covered in accumulated leaf mulch and cracks can have dandelions growing from them. Your experience will be greatly enhanced if you can abseil down your intended line from an adjacent route with a nut key and a soft brush and give it a spring clean.

The base of the crag can be damp and muddy after wet weather, so a mat or towel will be found useful. In humid weather, the summer tree cover can make the starts of the routes quite damp. It may be best to try another venue when these conditions prevail.

Approaches and Access
See map on page 268. Approach from Miller's Dale station or Wormhill. From below Rhubarb Buttress, opposite the left-hand end of the crag, wade the river crossing the island to dry land beneath the wall containing the classic routes of *Sergeyenna* and *Hergiani*.

1 Scratch Your Eyes Out E3 6a 1986
18m Untravelled and overgrown. Take a direct line above the water's edge. Retreat from a bolt belay (if you can find it).

2 Shake Hands with the Octopus E5 6c 1986
18m A rarely-repeated route with an intense series of moves low down and a tricky finish. Starting just to the right of the water's edge, climb a very technical wall (peg) directly past a faint break to the upper more prominent break. The wall above (peg and thread) provides a stubborn sequence in order for the bolt belay to be gained.

3 White Gold F7a ★★ 1960s/1982
20m Great climbing. Climb the shallow groove and bulge to reach a break. A loop leftwards is followed to the next break, where a nifty traverse back right gains a flake groove and butch finish. **a** Straightened-out is harder at F7b.

Ben Bransby on The Golden Mile, E5 6b (page 334), one of the great E5s on Peak limestone. Perfect rock, big history and superb moves all make it a cherished tick. Photo: Ian Parnell.

Matt Pickles on The Ogre, F8a (opposite page), an early bolted addition to Chee Tor's fine walls, and still a good tick today. Photo: Adam Long.

4   Nobody's Hero E5 6b   1984
20m   Worthwhile but unloved. From high in the groove, move right before climbing the technical wall past a flake and thread to the break (peg). Move right again (thread) before exiting via a thin crack through a bulge.

5   The Myrmidon E5 6b   1984
18m   A very fine technical effort, especially at the second crux. Climb the thin crack via a tricky rockover to a respite at the break. Swing left (peg) and scratch frantically up via the shallow scoop into the trees.

6   Fatty Manwell and the Paranoid Oysters E4 6a   1984
15m   Climb the thin crack (thread) and shallow groove until a rightwards escape gains vegetation.

7   Koroblin E1 5b •   1965
23m   The corner. Not to be cleaned or climbed.

8   The Ape Escape E4 6a •   1984
23m   From part way up, *Koroblin*, move right and follow the shallow rightwards trending scoop/groove to gain the arête. Not to be cleaned or climbed.

9   The Ogre F8a ★★   1986
15m   The red-flecked sidewall gives an exquisite pitch with numerous intricacies. The climbing, which is always technical and fingery, takes a slightly leftwards line. Harder for the short. **Photo opposite.**

10   Igor F7c   2010
10m   A companion route to *The Ogre* though much shorter and with a rather pokey feel to it.

To the right and just to the left of the vague arête is a shallow hanging groove in the wall which has unfortunately become very lichenous.

11   Kriklet's Cancer E6 6b   1984
15m   Entry into the groove is relatively straightforward but the exit rightwards is not. The difficulty is particularly enhanced by the nature, or lack, of its original in-situ gear.

The walls to the right improve in stature and provide a series of classic lines in the low to mid E-grades that are much sought-after by the traditional climber.

12 Tec E1 5b 1978
23m An indistinct line just to the right of the arête. Trend leftwards to reach a thin crack splitting a small overlap (peg) leading to a vegetated ledge. Finish via the left-hand of two grooves.

13 Oblomov E2 5c 1965/1976
22m A pleasant pitch, hardest lower down. Climb the wall via an indistinct crack, thread and tree stumps. At its end, move left and up to finish via a V-shaped groove.

14 Two Sunspots E2 5c ★★★ 1980
22m Something of a classic, providing fine wall-climbing with short difficult sections. Follow an indefinite flake to reach a shallow scoop and respite (threads). A few tricky moves leftwards (don't go too high – 6a) onto a good flake allows the obvious crack and bulge to be climbed. Take care stepping left under the capping bulges, to a steep finish.

15 Midnight Summer Dream E5 6a ★★★ 1983

23m A very fine route. Sustained climbing with reasonable gear and an urgent finish. Low in the grade. Climb a hollow lower wall to a leftwards-trending crack. At the top of this (bolt) step slightly left and pull awkwardly over a bulge onto a thin flake (thread). Follow this to reach the capping bulges, and left to the finish of *Two Sunspots*.

16 Midnight at the Oasis E6 6b 1992

23m A technical, airy eliminate. From the bolt on *Midnight Summer Dream*, climb carefully rightwards, all a bit insecure, to reach a peg a precarious distance above. Continue direct to finish.

17 Blind Alleys E4 5c ★ 1980

25m From the top of the crack on *Midnight Summer Dream*, traverse precariously rightwards to gain a good hold on *Sergeyenna*. Follow this route to the roof which is overcome with a thuggish pull (peg).

18 Sergeyenna E2 5b ★★★ 1976

30m The classic of the wall with sustained moves and good protection. Start up the thin crack system and continue up a fine wall to the overlaps. Traverse awkwardly rightward under these to their end. Make a final precarious move around the roof into the finishing groove, with inevitable rope drag. Low in the grade when clean and dry.

Climbers on Two Sunspots, E2 5c, (opposite page), one of the wealth of great routes in the E1 to E3 range at Chee Tor.
Photo: Mark Rankine.

To the right, a prominent flake crack ends at 8m to give a small ledge atop a pinnacle. The next route starts 5m to the left of the crack.

19 Heart of Darkness E3 5c ★   1980

23m Takes a line through *Sergeyenna* on great holds and rock to give a worthy pitch. Climb the left-hand side of the pinnacle before stepping left and climbing up into a scoop. Exit carefully from this to reach the bulge. Move left to a strenuous sequence over the roof to the trees.

20 Hergiani E2 5b, 4c ★ ★   1965/1970s

1. 23m Follow the crack up the right-hand side of the pinnacle. Step right and make a couple of fingery pulls up into a shallow groove. Continue up into the trees.
2. 22m Seldom climbed: the shallow groove system above.

21 Absent Friends E3 5c ★ ★ ★   1979

25m The quality keeps coming. Sustained wall-climbing with adequate protection. Climb the wall to reach a series of thin flakes. Step left under a slight bulge and pull through its left-hand side somewhat urgently to gain better holds and a rest above. Move right then continue up more easily to reach trees. The belay is to the right.

Pete Livesey attempting Mortlock's Arête, E4 6a (page 333). Photo: Geoff Birtles.

22 A Widespread Lack of Imagination E3 6a 1985

15m From the bolt belay at the terrace, climb the faint groove (thread) by some technical moves and finish from the break via a bulge.

23 Nostradamus E1 5b ★ 1970

22m A nice introduction and customary warm-up. Climb the lower wall making a tricky move into the groove (peg). Follow a shallow groove stepping right to a final steep pull to a bolt belay at the break.

24 Rave On E3 5c ★★ 1976

22m The rightwards-trending flake gives a strenuous, well-protected pitch with the crux at the top. **a** A direct start provides scary entertainment at E4 5c.

To the right lies the most impressive section of wall on the crag and one of the foremost climbing venues in the Peak District. Revered for many years until the first breakthrough of free climbing was made by Tom Proctor in the late-Seventies, this wall now plays host to a hatful of impressive pitches and is the home of one of the most significant achievements of the early-Eighties: Tequila Mockingbird.

25 Boobs F8a ★★ 1988/1996

20m The first of a series of impressively thin routes on the big flat wall. The route features a continual sequence of very hard moves for almost its entire length, eventually joining the next route for its finish.

26 Boo F7c+ ★★ 1985

21m Fine technical climbing, although a little unbalanced with just one particularly hard section. Climb relatively easily to just above the second bolt. An intense sequence, trending slightly leftwards, leads to better holds. **Photo on page 299.**

27 Tequila Mockingbird E6 6c ★★★ 1982

25m A truly significant route which epitomizes the era of its creation, when bolts were permitted only as a last resort. The wall has changed a little over time – some holds have come off the start – but it remains a true milestone in the history of Peak limestone climbing. The limited in-situ gear of just two bolts and two pegs provides a mind-numbing and fingery experience. F7c if the first bolt is pre-clipped (but you'll need a very long stick).

28 Basic Channel F8a ★ 1998

23m Another very fingery route on the fragile walls to the right. Desperate for those of limited stature. Lower off from twin bolts at three-quarters-height or continue via *Eyes of Fire* with a few small wires.

29 Eyes of Fire E6 6c ★★ 1984

23m The final route of the quintet on this magnificent wall should not be underestimated. Start below the left-hand of two cracks on the rounded arête to the right, the right-hand being *Mortlock's Arête*. Climb the left-hand crack to join that route. Traverse strenuously leftwards onto the face and just before you meet *Tequila Mockingbird* (bolt), climb straight up via a series of short-lived but very fingery moves past limited small-wire protection.

30 Mortlock's Arête E4 6a, 6a ★★★ 1962/1976

A must-do classic of Peak Limestone. The striking line up the prominent arête gives sustained climbing with two cruxes. One low on the first pitch and a boulder problem on the second.

1. 25m Climb the very thin crack. At its top, make a difficult pull leftwards into the main line. Follow this with particular difficulties where it bulges to gain easier ground and a tree belay.

2. 15m The groove above is gained by a trying move over the bulge and eases rapidly. There is sometimes an abseil point on a tree to the right. **Photo on page 331.**

The next group of routes lie on the walls to the left of the upper pitch of Mortlock's Arête. These can be gained either from the first pitch of either that route or Rave On, or by abseiling in from above - not easy to locate.

31 The Freeman Trap F6c+ 2009

12m The bouldery wall.

32 Mantrap F7b+ 2010

12m The central line with a frustrating bulging start.

33 The Poverty Trap F7a+ 2010

12m A bouldery bulge and wall.

34 The Freedom Trap E5 6a ★ 1984

18m A sadly-overlooked pitch on the technical wall and flake with three pegs.

35 Books on the Bonfire E6 6b 1988

15m Bold and intimidating climbing high on the cliff requiring a certain cool. Start from a thread belay in the break to the right of *Mortlock's Arête*. Move over the bulge (bolt), swinging leftwards to a good flat hold. Stand up on this before trending slightly leftwards to reach the upper break. Move left, with some relief, to gain and finish up *Mortlock's Arête*.

36 The Golden Mile E5 6b ★ ★ ★   1980

23m A major wall-climb classic, one of the finest in the area. High in its grade and requiring a certain tenacity in route finding. Climb the shallow groove in the centre of the wall and exit rightwards to a rest. Swing diagonally back leftwards and up to a good thread, usually in place, below a small white ledge. Gain a standing position on this (crux) and a reasonable rest on the left. Swing up and right to a flake using a naughty hold and sprint up to the break. Swing left to belay. It is possible to traverse left and down to abseil from the top of pitch 1 of *Mortlock's Arête*. **Photo on page 325.**

37 The Dream Mile E5 6b ★ ★   2010

43m Though eliminate in nature, this fine route gives a full-height experience on immaculate rock with good protection. From a few feet up *Apocalypse*, move up and left to a small ledge shared with *The Golden Mile*. Hard moves lead to easier though sustained climbing and eventually the girdle. Continue into the top pitch of *Apocalypse*.

38 Apocalypse E4 6a, 5c ★ ★ ★   1976

A must-do classic frightener. The reputation of this route's top pitch and its lifting wires is legendary.

1. 22m Climb the large corner and wall to its left, which has a finger-pulling crux, to reach a belay in the break.

2. 18m Swing left and over the bulge into the hanging flake/groove. Follow this, intimidating but straightforward. Grit your teeth and swing left along the top break to join *Mortlock's Arête* and subsequent relief. There is sometimes an abseil point on a tree above. **Photo on page 346.**

Rab Carrington on Meditation, E1 5b (page 337). Photo: Neil Foster.

39 Alfresco HVS 5b, 5b   1960/1970s

One of the original ways up the face and a worthwhile challenge at the grade.

1. 25m From part way up the main corner, swing right into a prominent crack and follow this, awkward at first, to reach the break.

2. 16m Unfrequented. Move left until above the corner and pull awkwardly over the overlap into a decaying groove.

40 Suddenly E5 6b ★   1983

23m A sadly-overlooked pitch with a good upper section which may need recleaning and the peg replacing. Climb the technical wall right of the main angle of the bay to reach a prominent crack, that of *Alfresco*. Step up and then left onto a tufa pillar and follow this with some urgency (peg) to the break.

41 One Night E1 5b   1983

10m A better alternative finish to *Alfresco*. Pull directly over the bulge from the stance of *Alfresco* into a pleasantly-exposed and easier shallow groove.

42 Less Than Zero E3 5c ★   1978

23m A good little route with just one short section of bold, fingery climbing. Climb the shallow groove to a thread. From this, move left to a flake and make a tricky move over a bulge to gain better holds. Continue more easily to the break and belay. Abseil descent.

43 Meditation E1 5b ★★★ 1977

27m A superb route with pleasantly sustained climbing on fine rock. Climb the shallow groove as for *Less Than Zero* then make an intricate traverse right (thread) followed by moves up on good holds to gain a white scoop. Cross this rightwards past a bulge to gain the girdle break and belay. Abseil descent. **Photo on page 335.**

Dandelion, E1 5b (1984), is an eliminate line to the right.

44 Valentine E5 5b, 6b ★ 1970/1982

A disjointed route with a frightening upper pitch due to the state of the bolts. Pitch 1 gives a good E1.

1. 25m Climb the wall onto a glacis with two saplings. Step left and up into the open scoop of *Meditation* via a bold sequence of moves. Move left to a tree and continue up the wall to a thread belay at the break. Abseil descent unless you wish to take on pitch 2!

2. 28m The top pitch climbs the broad open scoop above the break with a series of 'ring-pull' bolt hangers.

45 Approaching E3 5c ★★ 1983

23m A cool route with very good climbing. Climb the wall (thread) to gain a flake leading leftwards into the scoop. Avoid traversing too high (more like E4). Exit leftwards from this into a short groove leading to the finish of *Meditation*. **The Messiah**, E4 6a (1989), is a direct finish up the arête left of the groove of *Ceramic*.

46 Ceramic E4 5c ★★★ 1976

23m A beautiful route taking the cleanly-sculptured white groove. The slight polish enhances its boldness. Start directly below the groove and climb relatively easily up to and into it. Exiting leftwards from its top provides the technical difficulties together with a certain feeling of insecurity. The scene of many flights.

47 Ceramic Extension E5 6a ★★★ 1982

43m The superb wall above the break gives a brilliant and committing finish. If you found the groove okay, then go for it. From the threads in the break, pull over the bulge onto the wall and traverse scarily right clipping a (poor) peg with some relief. Now pass it rightwards in favour of the large flake which gives an easy finish in a fine position.

48 Terrorcotta E6 6c 1998

43m A very bold offering squeezed onto the rock right of *Ceramic*. From the base of the groove, arrange some poor protection, step right and climb the fine wall, gradually easing, to reach the girdle break. Pull straight over the bulge on poor sloping holds and gain the peg on *Ceramic Extension*. Finish easily up the large flake above.

49 Laughing E6 6b ★★ 1985

23m A fine bold pitch, taking the hanging white wall to the right of *Ceramic*. Climb the wall 5m to the right to reach a bulge above an easing in angle. Pull over the bulge, then swing left to below the wall (bolt). Climb the centre of this, hard at first and rather boldly above to reach better holds leading to the break.

50 Splintered Perspex E3 6a ★★ 1981

23m A super stylish route at the grade. Climb the wall to the left of the flake to reach a good rest on a small ledge below the white wall. Move slightly rightwards and climb the groove slightly leftwards past a peg before continuing directly to the break.

51 A Nasty Farming Accident F7b 1996

12m From the belay of *Splintered Perspex*, climb the bulge and shallow groove to a lower-off. Enigmatic by name and style.

52 Great Central Route E2 5b, 5c ★ ★ 1963/1970s

An old classic of the crag with a particularly trying move on the second pitch.

1. 25m Climb the flake/groove moving rightwards to a small tree. Swing right again to the base of a large flake. Climb this to the break. A good (but shiny) HVS pitch.

2. 20m Step left and pull through the large bulge with difficulty, peg. Finish up the impressive groove above.

53 Of Youth E3 5c ★ 1981

23m Worthwhile. Climb the wall trending leftwards to gain a small tree. The wall above this gives excellent and bold climbing to reach the break.

54 Rattle and Role E3 5c ★ 2006

23m Climb the very shallow groove past a tiny thread and crux bulge. The upper shield is taken slightly leftwards.

55 Shake E1 5b ★ 1971

23m Trend rightwards to gain the flake and follow it to the break; placing gear and climbing at the same time can provide a genuine source of amusement for any onlookers.

56 Highway 57 E1 5b 1977

25m Moves right from the flake of *Shake* after 10m to climb the wall to the right.

The next two routes start from the girdle break at the Shake belay.

57 Captain Ahab F7a+ 2011

15m Climb the tricky bulge and upper wall above.

58 The Body Line E4 6a 1966/1983

15m The scoop above is out of condition and best avoided.

59 Two Generations E6 6b ★ 1985

25m An unfrequented route with a bold and tricky start. Climb to a small flake at 5m and arrange some runners. Steep right, thread, and embark on a series of very fingery moves to gain a flake. Continue slightly rightwards past a small groove to easier ground leading to the break.

60 Autobahn E5 6b ★ ★ ★ 1981

25m Fun, fun, fun! One of the harder classics of the crag and Peak District limestone. Superb climbing mixed with good but hard-earned protection. Pumpy. Start below the leaning pink-flecked wall. Climb to a leftwards-leaning flake, sprouting a small thread. Climb this, then make awkward scary moves up to a small bulge and runner placements. Pull left over this to a small ledge and relief. The wall above quickly relents.

61 Lily Street E5 6b ★ 1986

20m Another worthwhile route with a well-defined hard section. Climb the wall 3m right of *Autobahn* to reach an old thread. Move slightly left and up to a bulge (thread) and make very extending moves, reach-dependent, to gain the traverse of *Queer Street*. Finish easily up the wall above.

62 Queer Street E3 6a ★★★ 1966/1971/1984

25m A great old classic with superb climbing on a prominent flake. Only a determined approach will reap rewards. Climb the initial groove, stepping left into the main flake. This leads frantically to a thread, where a second step left lands you on a small ledge. Climb the easier face above to a tree belay. **a** It is also possible to finish directly from the thread at the same grade but with trickier moves.

63 Moby Dick F7b+ 2011

12m The bulge above the *Queer Street* belay provides a short sharp shock to the system.

64 42nd Street E3 5c ★★ 1971

23m Another very fine and popular pitch with a tricky start and bold moves above. Climb slightly leftwards with a fingery pull to a break and stand up to an easing in angle. Trend rightwards below the white wall to gain a good hold and then climb the vague blunt rib above and slightly leftwards to better holds.

The next two routes start from the 42nd Street belay.

65 Theology F7c ★★ 1996

18m Fingery, even more so since the loss of a crucial hold. Climb the impressive and exposed bulging arête to finish via the thin crack of *Duel in the Sun*. Low in the grade.

66 Duel in the Sun E5 6b ★★ 1983

18m A brilliant, if short, punchy pitch. From the belay, step right and pull over the bulge into a scoop, peg. Move up and leftwards to a good flake hold, then step right and pull over a bulge using a hidden hold followed by a hard move to gain the break. Move left and finish via a thin crack.

67 Hatred E4 5c ★ 1982

23m Despite being something of an eliminate, this still provides a good pitch. Climb the shallow groove and, avoiding the traverse right of *Sunny Goodge Street*, continue straight up the vague rib above. Good climbing with only a modicum of comforting protection.

68 Sunny Goodge Street E2 5c ★ 1977

25m A very worthwhile pitch with short-lived but airy difficulties. Climb the shallow groove of *Hatred* before moving rightwards to reach a prominent flake. Climb this and where it ends continue directly to the break.

Chee Tor Right-hand

69 The Last Laugh (Tigon) HVS 5a 1970/1971
25m The overhang and groove. The crack on the left gains a short wall leading to ledges at the break. Overgrown.

70 Lom Attack E4 6a 2011
25m From a glacis, tackle the bulge on the left-hand side of the scoop (peg) to reach a tree. Continue up the easier blunt white rib above to a thread and belay on the right.

71 Sellar Dweller E4 6b ★ 2011
20m A surprising find. Enter the scoop to the right (peg) via a difficult, short-lived sequence. Pull over a slight bulge to better holds which lead directly to a tree belay.

72 Pink Panther E5 6a 1981
20m A serious and unpopular pitch. The bulbous wall is climbed past a couple of pockets and an undercut, which offers the only hope of protection.

73 Grinning Chimney E1 5b, 4a 1961/1970s
1. 20m Climb the overhung recess beneath the vegetation past a rotten peg to gain trees at the half-height break.
2. 18m Traverse right to finish up a narrow chimney.

74 Hooligans E3 5c 1989
23m Climb the hooliganized wall 3m right of the overhung recess.

75 Match of the Day E3 5c ★ 1976
23m A fingery pitch up the centre of the buttress. Climb the wall moving slightly rightwards to gain a short flake. Climb this with difficulty, and then continue more easily via a larger flake to the terrace.

76 Goal of the Month E2 5c ★ 1984
23m A fingery pitch straight up the wall past two threads and a series of tricky moves.

77 The Chopper VS 5a ★ 1964
27m The thin polished crack left of the groove has a few hard moves. Step left and climb the easier flake.

78 Sleepwalkers HVS 5a, 5b 1976
1. 22m The vegetated groove all the way to the girdle.
2. 12m The overhanging wall directly behind the belay.

79 Pleasant Dreams HVS 5b 1976
23m From 5m up *Sleepwalkers*, move right above the lower overlap (peg) and up onto the face. Finish up the shallow groove. **Advanced Warning**, E3 5c (1984), tackles the lower bulge directly to gain the shallow groove.

80 Rape E2 5b ★ 1965/1976
23m The red-streaked wall gives a super little pitch. Hard for the grade and difficult to protect. Move left across the lower wall to reach a thin, slightly rightwards-trending crack. Follow this to gain easier ground and the break above. The second pitch is overgrown.

81 Grapple and Grope E5 6a 2011

23m From a short way up *Gulle Gulle Groove*, step left onto the wall and, after a tricky technical sequence, climb boldly up (peg) to better holds. Pull up and slightly rightwards to follow a shallow groove exiting rightwards.

82 Gulle Gulle Groove VS 4c ★★ 1965

23m The prominent rightward-trending groove gives an enjoyable pitch with a bit of everything.

A stout tree to the right marks the left-hand side of a fine grey wall and a trio of excellent little pitches.

83 Flycatcher E1 5c ★ 1977

23m Climb the wall behind the tree to reach a flake, then move slightly left and up to the base of a wall/nose. Climb rightwards to finish up a crack to the rake. Very pleasant.

84 Snap Dragon E5 6b ★ 1984

23m A tough cookie, with difficult-to-place protection, an issue that fully enhances the flavour of the route. An excellent testpiece. From the flake on *Flycatcher*, move up and slightly right to a thread. Continue slightly leftwards up the wall above with a series of slaps to gain holds a long, long way above. Sidle up to the break above.

85 Leering Wall HVS 5b ★★ 1965/1970s

23m A fine route. Climb up to the prominent overlap and make a series of difficult moves rightwards either high or low to gain a standing position on a good hold followed by a thin move to a tree. Finish more easily up the open scoop above.

86 Dagenham Dave E1 5b 1979

23m Worthwhile although slightly contrived. Climb the wall, just left of an easier line of holds, and cross a slight bulge leftwards to a ledge. Step left and climb a shallow groove to gain the girdle break.

87 Clive's Route VS 4c 1965

23m The easier line of holds just to the right, avoided by *Dagenham Dave*, finishing slightly rightwards up a scoop to reach the trees.

88 Switch E2 6a 1985

11m The wall past a faded thread and with a clearly identifiable on/off crux.

89 Changeling E4 6a 1984

15m A short difficult route taking a slight depression in the wall. The finish slightly to the right is now vegetated.

90 Doggy Style E4 6b 1991

10m The unattractive wall just to the left of the groove with two bolts.

91 Doggone Groove VS 4b 1961

1. 23m The polished yet enjoyable groove.
2. 17m Traverse right for 5m and follow a clean corner until a further traverse right gains the finishing groove.

92 What Aches E3 5c 1985

12m Bold climbing via the vague rib 3m to the right of *Doggone Groove*. Finish rightwards to a tree belay.

93 Otaix E1 5b 1983

15m The grubby wall to the right directly to the tree.

94 Negative Earth E1 5b 1985

12m Five metres to the right, climb the slabby wall leftwards to finish up a short steep headwall.

Girdle Traverses

95 Tropic of Cancer E1 5a, 5c, 4c, 5a 1980

An esoteric offering taking the upper horizontal break from left to right starting from the terrace above the first pitch of *Hergiani*.
1. 24m Climb a crack to reach the horizontal break and traverse this rightwards for 10m to reach a rotting peg. Continue rightwards to belay alongside a small tree.
2. 27m Continue into the corner and move across this to reach a groove and cross the arête beyond to a thread. The right wall provides an awkward move and leads onto a small ledge and tree belay.
3. 24m Move down and rightwards to reach a smaller tree just beyond some flakes. Continue on to a tree belay.
4. 27m Move down to reach *Great Central Route* and cross the corner of this to reach a tree. Hand-traverse rightwards (peg) to reach a tree belay in a gully. Abseil off.

96 Pheasant Plucker E2 5b, 5c, 5c, 4c 1976

A low-level right-to-left traverse.
1. 11m Follow *42nd Street* to belay in a white depression.
2. 21m Traverse leftwards past the thread on *Queer Street* to reach a small ledge. Continue the traverse until a short descent is possible. Move leftwards and then ascend to reach a small sapling on *Of Youth*.
3. 24m Traverse leftwards across the slabs, beyond the groove of *Ceramic*, descending slightly to reach *Valentine*. Finish as for the first pitch of that route. A good pitch.
4. 26m Traverse leftwards to gain the top of the smooth groove of *Apocalypse* and continue around the arête to reach a tree belay at a lower level – the final section of this pitch is as for the final pitch of *Chee Tee Girdle*.

97 Rasputin E2 5a, 5b 1973

A rising left-to-right traverse of the *Sergeyenna* walls.
1. 27m Climb *Oblomov* to reach the base of the thin crack. Traverse right and ascend beyond saplings to reach a thread on *Sergeyenna*. Step down and traverse right to belay atop the pinnacle on *Hergiani*.
2. 40m Climb the thin pocketed crack to reach a peg and ledge. Gain the sapling to the right, then move up and across *Nostradamus* to reach a second tree emanating from behind a large block. Step down before moving around a rib, and then continue on vegetated holds to gain the tree belay atop *Tequila Mockingbird*. Abseil.

98 Blind Spot E4 6a 1986

30m A higher and better alternative to *Rasputin*. From the higher of the two tree stumps on *Oblomov*, traverse horizontally rightwards past a peg to reach the bolt on *Midnight Summer Dream*. Step down and continue rightwards to reach *Sergeyenna*. Continue the traverse of that route into *Absent Friends*. Finish up that route.

99 Chee Tor Girdle VS 4b, 4b, 4a, 5a, 4c ★ ★ ★ 1964

A classic voyage traversing most of the crag, traditionally
from right to left along the major bedding plane. A complete adventure at the grade. A lot of the route is littered
with threads that provide ample protection and belays.

1. 30m Follow *Doggone Groove* to the break and belay.

2. 42m Left along the break via a series of good ledges before an awkward descent leads to a ledge. Continue back
up and leftwards to belay in a large tree-filled bay.

3. 33m Continue leftwards to a large yew tree.

4. 36m Continue leftwards until tricky moves crossing the *Ceramic* groove lead to a belay just before the prominent corner.

5. 26m Move into the corner, and then sprint leftwards in
a magnificent position until the angle relents. A short descent leads down to a tree belay. Abseil from here. Abseil
virgins beware – it's quite steep. **Photo this page.**

Big air on Chee Tor Girdle, VS 5a (this page), where wild moves across E4 country provides a sense of urgency.
Photo: Ian Parnell.

Graham West aiding the first ascent of The Big Plum on Plum Buttress (page 402). Photo: Tom West collection.

Chee Dale Trad Climbing History

Probably the first route of any significance to be climbed on the River Wye crags was *The Stalk*, led sometime between 1955 and 1957 by Harold Drasdo. Although only Very Severe, at 27m it was one of the longest routes in the Peak on one of its most impressive buttresses. It was inevitable that a direct assault on the front of this buttress should attract attention. Drasdo's partner on *The Stalk*, Gordon Mansell, made the first attempt which nearly ended in serious injury as all his pegs in the roof 'unzipped' and he crashed into the lower wall. It wasn't until 1960 that *The Big Plum* was eventually aided by Graham West and Barry Roberts at the second attempt. At A3 it was described at the time as 'the longest vertical route in the Peak District and without doubt one of the most magnificent climbs to be found in Derbyshire'.

In the early sixties, the Dale became the haunt of the Manchester Gritstone Club who developed a large number of relatively easy, but almost exclusively, free climbs – a rarity for limestone which still had a reputation for seriousness and looseness. Two of the best routes from this period are *Whistling Crack* climbed in 1960 by Jack Arrundale and *Doggone Groove* added by Malcolm Baxter the following year.

This activity soon attracted the attention of the Cioch Club and in1964 Chris Jackson and John Atkinson added *Chee Tor Girdle*, a remarkable free ascent of an intimidating line for the time. The same year, Tony Howard opened up people's eyes to the potential of the Dale with his two pitch offering: *The Chicken Run*. This bold ascent was eclipsed, however, by Bob Dearman's audacious journey up the loose, ridiculously exposed upper wall of Plum Buttress.

Sirplum, his solution of this futuristic challenge, using just a few pegs for aid and little protection, stands as a defining moment in the history of limestone free-climbing.

By 1971, improved technology, fitness and confidence on limestone led to a significant rise in standards. Chee Tor still had few free climbs and was the ideal backcloth for this development. Tom Proctor, climbing with Chris Jackson, added *Queer Street* and *42nd Street*. Those first tentative probes indicated the superlative quality of the big, seemingly-impossible smooth walls. People sat up and began to take notice, and before long other climbers were attracted to the acres of free-climbable rock in the Dale. One of these was Gabe Regan who had a particular fondness for Chee Dale. In 1974, at just the age of 17, he free-climbed an old aid route *Wedgeway*, pointedly renaming it *Freeway*. One year later he introduced The Embankment to this 'new wave' with a free ascent of *The Red Spider*.

By 1976 he had the bit between his teeth and almost single-handedly set about rebranding Two Tier Buttress from the preserve of the aid climber to one of the best free-climbing areas in the Wye Valley. Pitch one of the hard aid route, *Avernus*, was to be liberated, which he renamed *Isolate*. Next came *Mad Dogs and Englishmen*, which, although not at the cutting edge, followed an intimidating line through some unlikely territory.

In July, he added *Ceramic* to Chee Tor, a very bold route with the frightening prospect of a 40 foot fall from the crux. Even more impressive, however was his virtually free

Tom Proctor on Santiano at The Nook (page 297). Photo: Geoff Birtles.

Ron Fawcett on the upper pitch of Apocalypse, E4 5c, on Chee Tor (page 334). Photo: Geoff Birtles.

ascent (1 point) of *Darl* to leave one of the boldest and hardest routes in the Dale at the time. Despite all this, the talking point of the year was Proctor's free ascent of the stupendous *Mortlock's Arête*, possibly the finest line on Chee Tor and one of the best routes of its grade in the country. At around the same time, grit legends Steve Bancroft and John Allen added *Apocalypse*, a massive route of its day and the only route to get E6 in the legendary Recent Developments guide from 1977.

Meanwhile, Chris Jackson and Bob Conway pottered, climbing many minor routes, plus two major routes in 1979 which opened up possibly the second hardest limestone cliff in the Peak, The Cornice. *Rue Morgue* was led by Jackson and Conway added *Fey*.

The early Eighties saw two of Britain's finest climbers push standards further still. In July of 1980, Pete Livesey did his hardest and best route on Peak limestone, *The Golden Mile*. By 1982 Livesey's protégé Ron Fawcett had acquired a formidable reputation as one of the best climbers in the world, and at Chee Tor, he left his mark. He added the tough classic *Autobahn* in 1981, then the following year upped the stakes another level. The smooth wall left of *Mortlock's Arête* had been tried by a few to no avail. Adding two pegs and two bolts, Fawcett produced his *Tequila Mockingbird*. The magnitude of the challenge was obvious and few criticised Fawcett for his use of the bolts. It is now recognised as one of the few E7s on Peak limestone, but it wasn't the first.

That prize goes to *Ninth Life*, on Two Tier Buttress. It was initially attempted by a young Jerry Moffatt, in early 1982, who fell from close to the top and decked out. Although badly shaken, Moffatt survived to fight another day but was beaten to the first ascent by Jonny Woodward.

At the same time Gary Gibson continued to add to the tally of climbs in the Dale. Between 1980 and 1985 on Chee Tor alone he added twelve routes up to E6 among them such classics as *Two Sunspots*, *Approaching* and *Midnight Summer Dream*. On other crags, climbs such as *Multiplex* (Long Wall) and *Une Crime Passionnel* (The Cornice) from the same era went on to become trad classics.

1984 saw the first appearance of Simon Nadin in Chee Dale, with the devious *Flight of Icarus* on Two Tier and the frightening, alluring *Eyes of Fire* on Chee Tor. Both routes were given E6, but they represent the lower and upper limits of the grade respectively. Dougie Hall is one of the few climbers to have repeated *Eyes of Fire* to date, and it was by mistakenly 'repeating a route' in 1984 that he added the third and last E7 to the Dale; Dave ('The General') Lee's Nettle Buttress project became *General Incompetence*. By now, more and more new routes were being bolted, and although given traditional grades were eventually to be recognised as sport routes and in most cases have now been fully rebolted. With a final few splutters, most notably Neil Foster's superb *Sloe Gin* in 1987, the era of hard traditional routes on Peak limestone was drawing to a close, and sadly, the flame of traditional limestone development went out.

Graham Hoey

Pete Livesey. Photo: Richie Brooks.

Gary Gibson on the first ascent of Multiplex, E4 6b, Long Wall (page 379). Photo: Gibson collection.

Dog's Dinner Buttress

Trad: 8 (E1 to E5)   **Sport:** 6 (F6b to F7c)   **Bouldering:** 10 (Font 6A to F9a+)
Aspect: South-west   **Sunshine:** From afternoon   **Season:** Spring to autumn
Conditions: Dry, clean on sport and boulder routes, leafy, sheltered
Best for: Fingery bouldering, monster traverses, fingery sport   **Approach:** 15minutes

An obscure buttress despite easy access, clean rock and a variety of challenges. The entire length of this crag is also slightly undercut which has made it a frequently visited spot for its bouldering.

The climbing
The most notorious challenges on the cliff are the two versions of the monster boulder-problem traverse which weigh in at route-grade F8c+ and F9a+. Lots more up-problems here giving fingery cranking in the high Font 6 to mid Font 7 range on good rock with reliable conditions. As well as that there are fine sport climbs on good rock, mostly in the F7s. Some of the trad climbs rely on old fixed pro which is not above suspicion.

Conditions and Aspect
Sheltered. Quite sunny, although trees give lots of cover to the lower half in summer. Very quick drying and doesn't take much seepage. The upper section, which is trad, is overgrown..

Parking and Approach
See map on page 268. Exit Chee Tor tunnel, go left and follow the path to reach the riverside path, go right toward the Cornice and just before the footbridge, scramble up scree to the crag.

One hundred metres downstream from the main buttress, an isolated route, **Dogfight**, F7c+ (2011), tackles the desperate leaning wall to a jug above the belay bolts.

On the far left, **Carcass**, HVS 5c (1981), gains a jug on the grey wall and finishes via a slab and crack; **Renascent Ability**, VS 6a (1983), climbs the wall and crack.

1   Muscae Volitantes   E4 6b   1982
18m   Follow flakes with a difficult move until better holds are gained as the angle relents. Move left and climb up via a short vertical crack in the slabbier wall.

2   Scooby Snack   F7a+   2011
10m   A short bouldery wall leads to easier face climbing.

3   Tail the Dog   F6b   2014
12m   A short problem start leads to a pleasant face.

4   Wag the Dog   F6c   2014
12m   The short steep face to an easier wall. Good.

5   Dog's Day Route   E1 5b   1961/1976
20m   Climb the wall just right of the flake and follow it to gain the overlap. Continue along this, until after 6m a shallow niche can be gained and a finish made.

6 Turkey Lurking F7b ★ 2010
12m A boulder-problem start 5m to the right, moving rightwards gains a position below the strip overlap. Desperate moves through this lead to the face above, where the upper overhang proves relatively straightforward.

7 Baffled by Waterwings E4 6b ★ 1987
12m A good route, with a bouldery crux. Make powerful moves over the initial bulge, aided by a small boulder to start, to gain a ring-peg slightly to the left. Follow the slabby wall more easily to the overlap and pull over this on small holds to gain the second overlap. Pull over this to reach an in-situ belay.

8 Learning to Swim E4 6b ★ 1987
12m The right-hand line has a similar start 3m to the right, gaining a peg slightly to the left. Continue directly above over the first overlap to reach the second, larger overlap. Move leftwards over this to gain the belay of the previous route.

9 Hot Dogger E4 5c 1961/1981
12m A bold undertaking considering both the nature of the rock and lack of protection. Climb the shattered flake just to the right to gain the large overlap with some relief. Pull straight over the overlap (peg) to reach a flake and degenerating finish (this is the finish of *Sick with Fear*).

10 Dog Dirt F7c ★ 2014
9m A desperate little pitch up the slightly-impending wall by very bouldery moves.

11 My Dog Dill E5 6a ★★ 2011
12m A superb recent addition, devoid of the vegetation and with a certain aura to it. Start 5m left of the foot of the scree slope on the right at a good hold below a faint green streak. Pull up to the hold, bolt above, and follow a series of flakes leftwards into the centre of the wall, peg. Climb the grey face to meet the overlap and pull over this (peg) on good holds and with a mighty lurch to reach a bolt belay. Spoiled somewhat by the bolts to the left.

12 Go Cat F7a ★★ 2010
12m From the start of *My Dog Dill*, climb straight up the mottled and crozzly wall to gain the roof. Gain holds on the lip, move slightly to the right and pull over to the lower-off.

13 In the Drink F6c+ ★ 1987
12m A good little pitch. Takes the grey face from the foot of the scree slope exiting right over the capping overhang.

14 Cat Lick F7b 2010
12m A desperate boulder problem gains easier climbing leading to the overlap. Pull straight over the bulge to the lower-off. F7a if the start is avoided on the right.

15 Little Curver El 5a, 5b ★   1972/1973

An interesting excursion across the face, utilizing the flake and overlap to great effect.

1. 28m Follow the flake from the right-hand edge of the buttress and traverse it to gain a belay in a hanging corner.

2. 22m Continue leftwards around a corner and cross the slab to reach another hanging corner. Move left around this before finishing leftwards into undergrowth.

16 Sick With Fear El 5b   1990s

12m A good way of finishing *Little Curver* more directly. From the centre of the large roof, pull straight over (peg) to reach a good flake and easing finish.

17 Pedigree Chum F8c+

An outrageously long and hard boulder-problem traverse, given a sport grade due to its sustained, route-like nature. Start on the far left and shuffle all the way right. Move up to the high break for the final section. **Photo below.**

18 Finest Pedigree F9a+

The hardest piece of climbing in Chee Dale. The lower, harder finish to *Pedigree Chum* stays low all the way to the end.

Paul Smitton on his own mega-creation, Pedigree Chum, F8c+ (this page). Photo: Rob Clifton.

Karen Whitehouse on Subterra, F7b, on Nettle Buttress (page 355). Photo: Neil Foster.

Nettle Buttress

Trad: 9 (E2 to E7) **Sport:** 20 (F6a to F7c+)
Aspect: North **Sunshine:** Evening **Season:** Summer to autumn
Conditions: Slow drying, dirty in early season, shady, quiet, good rock
Best for: A classy redpoint in the F7s or a cool E5 **Approach:** 20 minutes

A fine buttress presenting a curtain of grooves and bulges. The routes are sometimes dirty, sometimes good and, in a handful of cases, utterly brilliant. The best routes, sport and trad, tend to be tough. Not a particularly popular venue as there are only a few quality routes at any grade.

The Climbing
Mainly vertical wall-climbs often following groovy features. Fingery and very technical. Lots of E5s here, some great, some poor.

Conditions
A slow-drying crag which is well-shaded. Gets the evening sun and makes an ideal summer or autumn venue.

Approach
See map on page 268. The quickest approach is from the Miller's Dale station car park, or a little longer from Topley Pike. Wade the river directly to the crag. The river is chilly on the feet, or refreshing in the heat.

The left-hand side of the buttress is marked by a lessening in height and a large beak of rock to the left of a wide bay with some detached blocks sitting at its foot. Around to the left of this is a wall of reasonable rock covered in a veneer of white lichen. This wall contains four routes:

Back to Basics, F6c+ (1999), tackles the prow at its left-hand side; **Basic Logic**, HVS 5c (1984), gains the crack to the right with a difficult start; **Personal Voyage**, F7a (1999), is the best route directly up the wall to the right; **Journey's End**, E2 6b (1984), climbs the chimney crack to the right, with a difficult start.

Returning to the beak of rock at the left-hand side of the crag is **Totonic**, F7a+ (1998), a poor route avoiding the roof on the right and **Snail Mail**, F6b (1998), a relatively disjointed route up its right wall. **Schickster Groove**, E1 5c (1964), climbs the corner to the right complete with threads and lots of vegetation.

1 Harmonious Harmonica 7a 1998
12m The vague arête gives a contrived pitch,

2 Symmetrical Systems F6b 1998
12m The slim corner. Retreat from a tree.

To the right is a broad scoop just to the left of the arête of the wall.

3 Balanced Ballistics F6b ★ 1983
15m Climb the scoop by a series of pleasant and balance-orientated moves.

4 Suryanamasker E5 6a 1984
15m The shallow groove in the arête requires hard moves to get established in it and even harder moves to quit it. Lots of old pegs.

5 Long Dead Train F7b ★ 1998
18m The arête is taken via a series of fingery moves on small crimps. **a** Gaining it via the direct start (Font 7A) ups the ante a bit to F7b+.

6 Stuffed Badger E5 6b ★★ 1982
20m The proud groove is a classic product of the Eighties combining steep and difficult climbing with only a modicum of fixed protection. Gain the break and swing right to gain an old thread. A series of bouldery moves lead up to, then past, a bolt until a swing left gains a ramp. More delicate climbing leads up the rounded groove to the top. **b** The direct start is **Brock the Start**, Font 7B.

7 Summer Wine E5 6a ★★★ 1983
18m *Badger's* little brother is even better. Classic climbing with sustained moves and just-adequate protection. From the left-hand of two large blocks, swing left along the break and move up to reach a shallow scoop, peg. Move slightly left before a sequence of steep moves on good small holds leads to a final difficult section to reach the top. **c** The direct start is Font 7A.

8   The Eve Syndrome   E5 6c   ★   1989

16m A variant on *Summer Wine* with harder moves past a bolt. From the peg on *Summer Wine*, step right and move up into the shallow hanging groove, bolt. Hard moves above this past a jutting hold (peg) soon gain easier ground.

9   First Light   E2 5b   ★★   1976

18m A gem. From the left-hand block pull up onto the wall to reach a good ledge. Excellent, thin moves along the rightwards-slanting groove eventually lead into a small red groove and a belay on a small tree.

10   Epidavros   F6c   ★   1982

15m Now bolted this gives good climbing with hard moves before and after *First Light*. Climb a crack to the right of the blocks and pull over the bulge into a scoop with the ramp of *First Light* just above. Pull out left and up to the belay.

Rob's Dilemma, VS 4c (1964), climbs the starting crack of *Epidavros* before swinging right and up the obvious continuation crack.

11   Light Ideas   F6c+   ★   1998

18m Something of a warm up for the harder routes. Climb the wall just to the right of *Rob's Dilemma* and continue over the break onto the headwall. This gives intricate moves to a perplexing finish. Can be greasy due to condensation in summer which makes it almost un-climbable.

12 Sravandrabellagola F7b ★   1998

15m The left-hand side of the roof is gained via the lower groove. The roof itself requires a sequence of powerful pulls on flat holds to reach the belay.

13 Esmeralda F7c ★   1998

15m A very impressive pitch. Climb the wall right of the groove to reach the roof. Hard and powerful moves lead leftwards through this to the belay. Most attempts end in defeat. A long reach really helps. It is also possible to link this with the finish of *Stung*: **Esmerunga**, F7c.

14 Stung F7b+ ★★   1998

18m A superb creation combining sustained climbing with great moves on a fine line. Climb the initial wall as for *Esmeralda* to the roof and step right. After a fingery pull, pursue a leftwards line on the lip of the overhang to gain good layaway edges. Continue up and slightly rightwards to finish to the left of a shallow V-groove.

15 Major Incontinence E5 6c ★   1988

20m Somewhat overshadowed by its neighbours, this route has a lot to offer, in particular one very hard move. Follow *Stung* to the overlap, then swing right and up onto a ledge. A difficult sequence past a bolt gains the flake and groove. Easier climbing leads to the top.

There is a bolted project to the right.

16 General Incompetence E7 6b ★★★ 1984

20m A classic of its genre with a spectacularly amusing history, especially so since its first ascensionist had thought it had already been done! Archetypal climbing from one of the era's unsung heroes. Climb the wall 5m left of the main corner to a break, peg. Move boldly up the wall before uncertain moves lead left to grasp the flake. Climb this exiting deftly rightwards, still tricky, to finish. Possibly E8, and reputedly F8a on top-rope!

17 Toys for the Boys F7c+ ★★ 1994
20m Almost as good as 'the General' but its complete antithesis. The sheer black wall to its right leads to a technical feast of moves on a varied series of holds – not all are what they seem however. **Photo on page 356.**

18 No Light E3 5c ★★ 1960s/1976
20m The corner has just what it takes. Well-protected climbing, interesting moves and a steep difficult ending.

19 Subterra F7b ★ 2002
18m The vague pillar to the right houses a surprisingly good addition with a difficult series of moves to exit the shallow scoop at the top of the wall. **Photo on page 351.**

20 Terra Incognito E5 6b ★ 1983
19m Superb when clean; it often isn't. Climb the wall and gain the break. Above lies a thin flake/groove which in turn leads to a difficult series of moves to pass the bulge (peg) to gain a tree belay.

21 Gobblin' Women F6b+ ★ 1999
18m The steep wall and shallow groove/flake to the right has a hard start.

22 Fish-u-Like F6b 1999
18m Right again. Climb the wall via a sharp edge and short slabby wall above and to the right.

23 Fishlock F6b+ ★ 1998
16m Climb a shallow scoop.

24 Kakaho F6a+ 1998
16m Follow a shallow left-facing groove and flake. The finish provides the difficulties.

25 Cock a Hoop F6a 2002
15m A short though amenable pitch following a shallow groove onto the headwall.

26 Bursting Out F6c 2002
15m The pleasant and technical open scoop to the right. Finish leftwards.

The walls to the right bear the remnants of three old traditional routes all covered by Ivy. **Hyperon**, E3 5c (1984), follows a rightwards-slanting flake; **Glory Road**, HVS 5a (1984), is the next flake and **Hyperactive**, E2 5c (1984), is the ivy-covered groove, exiting left.

The Upper Tier

Beyond a short gully, an upper tier continues rightwards to eventually join up with Two Tier Buttress at its left-hand end alongside *Home from Home* and above Waterline Buttress. This section of rock is best described under Nettle Buttress as it is from here that the easiest access can be gained. Fifty metres along the tier an area of compact grey limestone can be seen. This houses four good little routes.

27 War Locks F6c+   2001
9m   A bouldery wall and bulge soon gain the belay.

28 Pulsar F7a ★   1984
11m   A wall and fine shallow groove give an esoteric gem.

29 Birthday Boy F7b+   2001
11m   The wall and bulge lead onto the smooth headwall.

30 Magician's Enemy F6b   1984
11m   Tackles a wall and bulge on the right. Worthwhile.

Situated 20m to the right on a prominent red buttress: **Backstreet Vogue**, E3 6b (1990), gives a boulder-problem start and an awkward move over a bulge (bolt).

Fifteen metres right and just to the right of a tree-filled recess is **Pain and Pleasure**, E5 6b (1983), which climbs a shallow groove that is hard to enter (thread).

Neil Kershaw on Nettle Buttress's prime sport tick, Toys for the Boys, F7c+ (page 355). Photo: Adam Long.

Two Tier Buttress

Sport: 70 (F6a+ to F8b+) **Trad:** 26 (HVS to E7)
Aspect: North-west **Sunshine**: 3pm till sunset **Season:** Spring to Autumn
Conditions: Quick drying, clean, classic, solid, popular
Best for: Top-quality sport, F7a to F8b **Approach:** 20 minutes

Brilliant. Two Tier Buttress is the best of the crags in the upper section of Chee Dale. Its impressive barrel-shaped front together with its excellent rock and open nature give it an atmosphere unsurpassed in the Peak District.

The Climbing
Most people come for the sport climbing, although there are a bunch of trad routes here which are classics of Peak limestone. The routes mainly take faces and grooves on slightly leaning walls. Fingery, technical, sustained and pumpy.

Conditions
The crag stays out of any sunshine until around 3pm in the summer months, dries very quickly after rain and, even in the winter months, can have areas of rock that take very little seepage. Unfortunately, areas of rock, such as those in the *Mad Dogs* and *Open Gate* area can have seepage after spells of heavy rain.

Parking and Approach
See map on page 268. Park at Topley Pike. Approach as for the Embankment, then drop down to the riverside path below. Cross the river just before Max Buttress by using the weir. At 'low tide' this can be crossed easily. When the water is a little higher you will have to wade.

Waterline Buttress

A neglected little buttress tucked in alongside the water's edge with routes of a bouldery nature. Because of issues regarding the flora and fauna on this section of cliff, climbers are requested not to climb here.

For the record, **Down Some Lazy River**, E4 6b (1985), jumps for a hold on the lip of the overhang 7m left of the main arête of the buttress and proceeds over a series of bulges to a short finishing groove; **Tomorrow's Dream**, E5 6c (1983), tackles the desperate bulge 2m left of the arête and continues direct via the horizontal breaks (thread) to reach the 'hanging gardens of Babylon' finish; **Cabbage Disease**, E5 6c (1985/1990), climbs the rounded bulging arête with a distinctive crux section at two-thirds height and **The Immunity Syndrome**, E4 6a (1983), follows the shallow groove on the right-hand side of the arête moving left from the top of the groove to finish.

A major scarefest from the pre-sport-climbing era in Chee Dale, Jordan Buys on Ninth Life, E7 6b (page 366).
Photo: Mike Hutton.

Open Gate Area

A fine big wall with a fistful of long sport climbs in the mid grades. Very enjoyable, with a airy, open feel.

1   Home from Home   E4 6a   1988
10m   A tricky sequence rightwards gains a good hold and ledge. Stand on the ledge and move back left and up to a tree belay. The direct is easier (still E4 6a, 1989).

2   Another Brick in the Wall   F7b+   1990
11m   The leftmost line of bolts; a very hard sequence.

3   Osher, Osher, Osher   F7a+   1985
12m   A very fingery lower bulge leads onto an easier wall.

Just to the right is a project. Right of this is:

4   The Bride and Groom   F6c+   1990
12m   The best of the short routes hereabouts. A bulge and face which gets easier the higher one progresses.

5   The Burqa King   F7b   2001
15m   The bulge and smooth-looking wall to the right of a prominent flake gives a deceptive pitch.

6   The Incredible Pierre   F7a+   ★   1985
15m   Superb moves leftwards over the bulge leads onto the wall. One hard move remains.

7   Short Sharp Shock   F7c+   ★   1987
22m   The headwall proves a desperate affair, much changed due to hold loss. Climb the easy lower wall to the break and then take the wall via the left-hand line of bolts.

8   Pour Dill   F7c   ★   1999
22m   Marginally better than the previous route but more left-arm work than right. The route takes the right-hand line from the half-height break. In memory of the first ascensionist's dog.

9 Open Gate F7a+ ★★★ 1985
22m A classic. The upper wall requires a cool head despite the bolts. Follow the crack then the airy headwall above the break.

10 Case Adjourned F7a ★★ 1985/1989
22m Quality. Climb the blunt arête to reach the break. The headwall is pushy but always on good holds.

11 Smelting Pot F6c+ 1982/1999
22m Climb the wall, moving away from the groove until the break is reached. A few stiff pulls lead to the belay.

12 Thoth E1 5b, 5a 1964/1965/1970s
A big route although often dirty.
1. 15m Climb the corner with a steep start.
2. 21m Enter the flake and crack directly and follow its curving line first left and then up into vegetation.

13 Cockerel Cry F6c+ ★ 2002
25m Climb the right-hand wall of the corner, slightly contrived, to a ledge. Tackle the short steep wall on the left crossing the large overlap with one final steep pull.

14 Jackson's Browned Off F6c+ 1999
12m A direct line, starting from the edge of the platform. Detouring out right and back left reduces the grade a little.

15 Running on Empty E5 6a 1981
12m From the end of the platform, swing dangerously out right and once established step right again before finishing directly. No in-situ gear at this grade.

Three routes spring from the platform above Jackson's Browned Off and can be reached from that route, Thoth or the first section of Cockerel Cry.

16 Just Pullet F7a+ ★ 1999
15m The exposed and open left-hand arête yields to a determined approach and gives an exciting experience.

17 Evidently Chickentown F7c ★ 1999
15m The central line requires a very powerful approach. Climb to the left of the bolts initially, and then directly to reach a bottomless finger-crack. Extremely reachy.

18 Poultry in Motion F7b+ 2001
15m The right-hand line requires a few hard pulls to get established on the wall which quickly eases.

19 Mega-Bites F7b 2001
15m A good power problem to the right taking a direct line above a stump.

20 Systems Malfunction F7b ★★ 1985
12m A super roof problem on which a long reach helps. Climb the blunt rib to the left of the open scoop to gain the roof properly. Hard moves across the stepped roof and over the lip lead to easier climbing above. Photo on page 300.

21 Reboot F7c+ ★ 2012
12m Tackle the bulge to the right. Much like its harder neighbour the use of knee-pads may be beneficial.

22 Titter Ye Not F8a ★ 1990
12m A direct assault of the *Offal* roofs gives a testing pitch. Perhaps eased a little with the use of knee pads.

23 Offal E3 6a ★ 1982
27m Climb the open scoop and traverse right before tackling the stepped roof above (peg) to gain the slabby face. Take a direct line up this to gain the terrace.

24 Waffle F7b+ 1999
12m Cuts through *Offal* like butter. Climb the arête to meet the overlaps part way along *Offal's* traverse. A difficult series of moves may land you on the face above.

25 Ghee Force E4 6a 1991
18m A contrived addition with a short difficult section linking *Malnutrition* to the finish of *Offal*, bolt.

26 Malnutrition E3 6a ★ 1976
25m A classic product of the pre-bolt era. Climb the corner and swing right onto a ledge. Reach the overlaps and cross the roof on large flat holds. Move slightly to the left and finish up a scoop to a tree belay.

27 Isolate E3 6b 1976
18m Climb the technical wall to reach a small ledge. Move up to the roof before traversing right underneath it to gain the arête. A short wall leads into the capping vegetation.

28 Stolen Fruit E4 6b ★ 1980s
27m A curious but fine addition. From the small ledge on *Isolate*, traverse along the first break to gain a large thread. Now climb the technical and intricate wall above to reach the top or retreat from a bolt belay.

Orange Sunshine, F7c+ (page 365). Photo: Adam Long.

Jon Garside on the crag's classic F7b route, Daylight Robbery (page 366). Photo: Mike Hutton.

29 Hunger Strike F6c+   2013
16m The wall. Where it meets the *Stolen Fruit* traverse, move up and slightly left and pull over the small awkward roof.

30 Split Infinity E4 6c   1985
20m The corner has an utterly heinous start. Exit as for *Isolate*.

31 Nerefaun E4 6c   1984
20m From 3m up *Split Infinity*, hideous boulder-problem moves lead up a rounded arête. From its top, climb the fine compact wall to reach the finish of *Isolate*.

32 Stogumber Club F7c+   1996
15m A short desperate sequence on tiny flakes. After the main break is gained, move right and up to the belay.

33 Entree F8a+ ★★   1990
15m A superb route aiming for the shallow groove midway up the wall, guarded by a desperate, and fingery boulder problem (Font 7C).

34 Kali Yuga F8b ★★★   2003
16m One of the most impressive pitches in the Dale on superb rock up the centre of the buttress. The line is obvious but so too are the difficulties.

35 Flow F8a+ ★★   2013
16m A great route packing it in on its lower half. It gets close to *Countdown* at one point but avoids holds on that route.

36 Countdown F7b ★★★   1981
22m One of the true classics of the Dale taking the long shallow groove in the centre of the buttress. The majority of the difficulties are centred on the bulge at 5m although the finish provides a fitting climax.

37 Darl F7a ★★★   1976/1981
25m The classics keep on coming. Gain the layaway crack in the bulge with difficulty and follow it to an impasse. Moving up and left across the slabby wall is easier said than done and hindered by the polished nature of the rock.

38 Why Me? F7c+ ★★   1986
15m A very hard route requiring steel fingers up the bulging wall. The aim is to gain and use the obvious undercut.

39 Orange Sunshine F7c+ ★★   1984
16m A landmark in the development of Chee Dale free-climbing which focused attention on the blanker areas of rock. It takes a steep and desperate line on the nose of the buttress and is not over-endowed with fixed protection. **Photo on page 363.**

40 Boring F7b+ 1989
18m A poor and unpopular attempt to climb the wall left of the shallow groove but having to use it for some of its length.

41 Ninth Life E7 6b ★★ 1982
22m The infamously-bold shallow groove proves to be the antithesis of the sport routes on this buttress. Gaining the groove is difficult; the remainder only relents towards the top but has a dearth of protection throughout (sky-hook useful). **Photo on page 359.**

42 Daylight Robbery F7b ★★ 1989
22m The vague pillar looks unlikely but due to holds on its right-hand side, almost in *Ra*, it proves to be just about feasible. Keep cool on the pumpy headwall. **Photo on page 364.**

43 Ra E4 6a 1971/1976
25m The tight V-groove gives a short but intense little exercise.

44 The Cruise Brothers F7a+ 1987
15m The first of a series of marginally easier sport routes. Climb the intricate wall by a series of powerful layaway and undercut moves.

45 Luck be the Magic Number F7b 2012
12m The faint rib with a hard start past the second bolt.

46 Some Coincidence F7a+ ★ 1986/1999
15m A testing route which, if taken direct, is difficult for the grade. From the low ledge, pull up the wall and move left and then direct to eventually reach better holds. Trend rightwards across the wall to reach the belay.

47 Rising Sap F6c ★ 1999
15m An eliminate start (F6b+ if you use the shallow groove on the right) leads to good climbing above. Pull straight up the wall as for *Some Coincidence* and move slightly right before climbing direct onto the white wall. Easier climbing follows a slim ledge.

48 Osiris E1 5a 1971
21m The shallow rightwards-trending groove gives a good pitch with limited protection.

49 Subterfuge F6c ★ 1981
15m Cross the tricky bulge to gain a blunt rib. Follow this more easily to the belay. Reachy.

50 Quality Control F7a ★★ 1985
15m The best route hereabouts. Climb the bulge to reach the right-hand side of a scoop. Climb the right edge of this and follow its lip leftwards to gain the belay.

51 Nogads F7b+ ★ 1988
15m A hard fingery start over the bulge leads to technical moves to gain a bulge. Pulling through this requires concentration as it proves harder than it looks. The short may prefer to finish as for *Quality Control* at a still worthwhile F7b.

52 Blockhead F7b+ ★ 2001
10m The short and intense fingery exercise taking the left edge of a shallow depression.

53 Reasons to be Cheerful F7b+ ★ 1985
11m Another vicious little exercise taking the right edge of the depression. Passing the overlap proves to be the hardest section.

54 The Inbetweenies F7a+ ★ 1999
11m The wall proves marginally easier until the short headwall is reached.

55 Wot a Waste? F6c+ 1982
11m The shallow groove system proves perhaps the final strong feature of the wall.

56 Tippers F7a 1999
10m The short desperate wall has one hard move.

57 Tip Dollar F6a+ 2012
10m The blunt arête.

To the right the cliff continues to decrease in size, not least because of the encroaching vegetation.

Billericay Dicky, E1 5b (1985), climbs into a scoop exiting left; **Clever Trevor**, HVS 5a (1985), moves right and up out of the scoop; **The Great Escape**, S (1986), moves right out the vegetated gully to climb the wall and **The Trap**, VS 4a (1964), climbs the vegetated gully.

Upper Tier

The tier of crag above *Subterfuge* gives one of the best areas of rock in the dale. A perfect setting in which to work out those sequences in peace.

Approach: To get to the cliff, follow the grassy diagonal ramp to the right of the Mad Dogs area, which can be particularly nasty after wet weather and due to its nettle-infested nature. At the top, traverse across the top of the buttress to a gully below a small rock wall. Abseil from the chains down *Sibser* to the terrace below. To retreat from the terrace, abseil off the chains below *The Tier Drop Explodes*.

At the far left-hand end, where the terrace runs out is:

58 Laurels for Hardy F7b+ ★   1992
18m   A good intricate pitch springing from a single bolt belay on the terrace. Move left from the belay and climb the hollow wall past some good holds higher up to reach a tree belay.

59 In Tiers F8b+   2009
11m   Desperately thin climbing leads up the wall just to the right of the big roof. On the first ascent the first two bolts were pre-clipped.

60 Darl Pitch 2 F7b ★   1965/1981
12m   Climb the flake crack and at its end make a series of difficult moves to gain the break. The belay lies up the groove above.

Six metres to the right is a line of rotting ironmongery. This is the scene of the finest challenge in the Dale for which Bob Dearman offered free beer for a lifetime to its conqueror. No suitors have yet dealt a free blow to Orange Sunshine Pitch 2, A3 (1970).

61 Hardcorejunkie F8b ★   2001
18m   The desperate starting wall leads to a jug. Above lies further hard moves to the break. The finishing bulge proves relatively straightforward.

62 Welcome to My World F8a ★ ★   2009
16m   An excellent route with superb fingery moves throughout. A reachy start leads to the first jug on *Hardcorejunkie*. Climb the blank wall up and right to gain the break and then a short groove to the belay.

Just to the right a line of bolts marks a desperate project.

63 The Curse of the Mummy F8a ★   1976/1986
15m   The hanging scoop and wall has now been rebolted. Either finish directly (trad) or much better via the upper section of *A Vision of Loveliness*.

64 A Vision of Loveliness F7c+ ★ ★   2000
22m   A superb route taking the fingery lower wall via a series of glued-together holds. Above the break don't be deceived into thinking it is any easier.

65 A Picture of Perfection F8a ★   2009
22m   A bouldery start which shares a few holds with the

Access from
Mad Dogs gully

Abseil from here to escape

route to the right. At the break briefly traverse leftwards then up the bulge to finish up the last few moves of *A Vision...*

66 The Sea is a Brown Paper Bag
F7b+ ★★★ 1986
22m Immaculate: top quality and top of the grade. The route of the wall with superb crimpy face climbing. Climb the technical scoop and flake above to the break. A few steep moves gain access to the thin finishing moves and a useful root to gain the belay. **Photo on page 370**.

67 Recycled F7c ★★ 2009
22m A variation finish to *The Sea...* Climb that route until over the bulge above the break, then make a hard move leftwards to gain two pockets. Continue straight up via a thin seam to the belay of *A Vision...*

68 The Tier Drop X-plodes F7c+ ★ 1986
20m A hard move on the lower wall climbed via the cream-coloured streak gains the roof. Cross this in superb fashion to gain the belay.

69 Reward F7b ★ 1991
20m The blank-looking wall gives a thought-provoking exercise. The roof above requires a single-minded approach.

70 Monster Mouse Resurgent F6c+ ★ 1991
18m A shallow groove, roof and open groove.

71 Aggrieved F6c+ 1999
15m The wall to the right, gained from *Monster Mouse* gives a good few moves.

72 Disjointed Might E5 6a 1986
15m The obvious reddened flake and disjointed crack to the right past a poor ring-peg.

73 Sibser F7b+ 1991
15m The desperate technical wall to the right.

There are two magnificent traverses with an impressive combination pitch linking them both.

74 Communication Breakdown F7c+ ★★ 1997
30m Climb *Darl Pitch 2* to the break and then follow this rightwards to the belay of the *Curse of the Mummy*, 15 bolts.

75 Nervous Breakdown F7b+ ★★ 1996
25m Begin by climbing *Reward* to gain the break and then follow this leftwards to a belay atop the *Curse of the Mummy*, 14 bolts.

76 Total Breakdown F7c+ ★★★ 1999
45m Combines the two pitches by starting up *Communication Breakdown* and following this past the belay and reversing *Nervous Breakdown* to finish over the roof of *Reward*. Have you got enough clips? You need at least 30, so give your mates a call.

Mark Pretty on the classic Upper Tier route, The Sea is a Brown Paper Bag, F7b+ (page 369). Photo: Ian Parnell.

Mad Dogs Area

The rightmost buttress continues the quality with a great mix of sport and trad classics.

Rock Follies, E1 5a, 5a (1976), climbs the poorly protected and rounded front face of the buttress and a groove to the terrace.

77 The Chicken Run HVS 5a, 4b ★   1964
A classic from the halcyon days of the first forays onto limestone in the 1960s.
1. 18m Climb the shallow corner and trend slightly right before continuing straight up to a belay off to the left.
2. 15m Traverse right across the break to exit into a vegetated area. Descent is via the diagonal ramp or abseil.

78 A Rooster in the Hen House F6b+   2002
25m A sport route mirrors the start of *The Chicken Run* before veering off slightly to the right to finish via a short wall above a large flake.

79 Goldfinger E2 6a ★   1970/1976
32m A technical start up the grey wall (bolt) gradually relents for a resting place below a large flake. Climb the flake, swinging left at its top to finish up *A Rooster...*

80 Flight of Icarus E6 6b ★★   1984
33m An impressive product of Simon Nadin's early years showing remarkable route finding coupled with a requirement for his renowned coolness. Follow *Goldfinger* to the bolt, then climb slightly to the right via a shallow groove to a slight easing in angle. Move carefully rightwards until below a small overlap and small wire protection. Pull over and continue slightly leftwards (good runner placements) to below the final overlap. Cross this to a bolt belay above.

81 Aberration F8a ★★   1988
35m A long diagonal line with a steep start and technical traverse. From just above the bolt on *Goldfinger*, traverse carefully rightwards, crossing *Minos*, and make a hard move to arrive just to the left of the belay on *Gonads*. From here continue directly to reach the belay.

82 Minos F7c+ ★★★ 1996

25m A magnificent route with a depressingly difficult start. From 6m to the right of *Goldfinger*, cross the initial bulge by a series of very hard moves to get established on the wall proper. Move slightly left into a shallow scoop and then up to gain a slim overlap. Pull over this, stepping back to the right and up via a faint rib, gradually easing, to gain the break. Pull up and leftwards to reach the belay.

83 Celebration F7c ★★

35m A link-up for those people who find the start of *Minos* just a little bit too brutal. Follow *Aberration* to the rest on *Minos* then finish as for that route.

84 Buster F8b ★ 1997

18m Tackle the centre of the bulging alcove via a series of difficult moves to join and finish up *Gonads*.

85 Gonads F8a+ ★★ 1987

26m An impressive achievement in its day, still revered today: a testament to Simon Nadin's ability. Start below a prominent flake. Pull desperately over the bulge, or sneak in from the right after a couple of moves up *Lightweight*, before pursuing a diagonal leftwards line across the lip of the alcove to gain the bottom of a shallow groove. The groove, still tricky, gives the finale.

86 Ultralight F8b ★ 2000s

20m Tackle the wall directly above the start of *Gonads* by a desperately fingery sequence to finish at the belay of *Seven Pounds Overweight*.

87 Seven Pounds Overweight F7c+ ★ 1986

25m A climber's motto? A route somewhat superseded by its neighbours but still maintaining its difficulty and aura even today. Pull over the initial bulge as for *Gonads*, and then trend diagonally rightwards into a leftwards-facing flake. Move up this before undercutting the overlap leftwards to gain a belay at its end.

88 Lightweight F7c ★★ 1995

20m The super direct version of *Seven Pounds Overweight* gains the leftwards-facing flake of *Spizz Energy*. Follow the overlap leftwards to finish as for *Seven Pounds Overweight*. Much the more popular of the two routes. Can also be finished up *Spizz Energy* at a hard F7b+. **Photo on page 266.**

The undercut section of the lower wall diminishes in stature to give an easier-angled face, still in the vertical, consisting of two prominent rightward-trending flakes in its lower half.

89 Spizz Energy E5 6b ★★★ 1980

22m A Ron Fawcett classic encapsulating everything that is good about mixed-protection routes. Start below a rightward-leading flake. Climb the technical wall (peg and bolt), to reach the flake. Delicate moves left and down from this lead onto a leftward-facing flake. This leads to an overlap, where a difficult pull and rockover (bolt and peg) gain a respite. Finish slightly rightwards to a bolt belay.

90 A Touch of Class E5 6a ★ 1989

22m Hybrid it maybe but good it remains all the same. Follow *Spizz Energy* into the rightwards-leading flake and continue up this until a step right leads onto a grey slab. Pull over the overhang (peg as for *Mad Dogs and Englishmen*) onto the slab above and finish directly by a couple of delicate moves.

91 Spazz Energy F7a+ ★★ 2001

22m An interesting concoction interspersing the traditional routes hereabouts to find an independent sport line. It takes a direct line up the wall to reach the rightwards overlap. Above this a short difficult section gains holds on the right before a difficult step back left and up gains the belay. Thought by some to be better than *Spizz...*

92 Mad Dogs and Englishmen E3 5c ★★★ 1976

25m The classic route of its grade in the dale, a route to do in the full sun. Short hard sections are intermingled with superb moves, mostly of the delicate variety. Climb the right-hand flake line and, from a ring-peg, move left to the left-hand flake. Move up to the overlap (peg) and step left and over, crux, onto a small ledge on the slab above. Tiptoe gingerly rightwards into a scoop up which the route finishes. **Photo on page 271.**

93 Machineries of Joy E1 5b, 5b ★ 1976

1. 25m Climb the flake line up which *Mad Dogs...* begins to gain the overlap. Traverse right beneath this (peg) to gain the terrace after a step up.
2. 18m The shallow groove above and to the right of the diagonal ledge system, gained from the left.

94 Ape Index E6 6c 1982

18m The name says it all. A desperate reach through the overlap above the start of *Machineries of Joy* (peg) gains the headwall and another desperate move to get established over the lip.

95 Within Reach F6c 2004

12m A short technical face-climb to the right and starting three metres from the right edge of the wall. The belay lies just over the overlap.

Vista Buttress

This is the tier to the right of the approach to the Upper Tier. Climbing in this area is discouraged for environmental reasons and much of the in-situ protection has been removed. The only really climbable route is **Machineries of Joy (pitch 2)** E1 5b, which takes the shallow groove on the left, gained from the left. For the record, the routes running right from *Machineries...* were: **Speedmetal Bedmoshin'**, F6b (1991); **Big Jesus Trashcan**, F6c+ (1990); **Superstring**, F7c (2006); **Dizzy**, F7c+ (1994); **Eggs, Bacon, Coffee and Suicide**, F7b (1989); **Decade to Decayed**, F6c+ (1989); **Kill your Television**, F6c (1991).

Long Wall

Sport: 31 (F6b+ to F8a)   **Trad:** 15 (HVS to E6)
Aspect: North-west   **Sunshine:** From 3pm   **Season:** Summer, autumn
Conditions: Slow-drying, shady, sheltered, sometimes dirty
Best for: Quality summer sport, F7a to F8a   **Approach:** 25 minutes

A myriad of shallow grooves, overlaps and bulges with a steepness that belies its apparent shortness. For this reason nearly all of its sport routes are in the seventh grade. The climbing is epitomised by the short powerful and fingery variety rather. Less classic than Two Tier but still very good: some of the routes here are among the best of their grade in the dale.

The crag was given a makeover by Kristian Clemmow in 2014, replacing old bolts and lower-offs, straightening out lines, re-establishing routes that had suffered from significant hold-loss and tidying up old projects.

The Climbing
Steep and bulging sport climbing. Powerful, technical and fingery climbs that pack a lot of punch into their short length. Some of the best slab/wall climbing to be had on limestone (after the starting bulges have been breached!)

Conditions
A slow drying crag with a much shorter season than its neighbour, Two Tier, having more tree cover and getting much less sunlight. However, the right-hand side of the crag dries much quicker than the left-hand side. The crag is in the shade until about 3pm in the summer months. A good choice in high summer. Dank in winter. When the routes dry out they can remain dirty until cleaned so consider bringing a brush early in the season. Very sheltered. Some rain cover but not as much as Two Tier.

Parking and Approach
See map on page 268. The only approved approach to Long Wall is via Two Tier Buttress. Follow the approach to this and follow the track rightwards to the crag.

Thirty metres left of the main section of Long Wall, and passed on the approach, is a barrel-shaped buttress.

1   Ethical Nightmare E3 6a   1982
12m Climb a shallow grey scoop via a short bouldery sequence. Where the cliff turns to vegetation, traverse right to finish via a short shallow groove.

2   Barney E2 5b   1982
12m The centre of the buttress via a small flake to finish via the red-stained shallow groove.

3   Super Orchic F7b   1994
12m The right-hand side of the buttress provides quite a vicious technical exercise on what appears to be a completely smooth section of rock.

The next routes are 30m right, starting left of a square recess.

4   Columnus F7b+   1996
15m The hanging arête, starting behind the trees, provides a difficult and fingery exercise.

5   Banana Republic E3 5c   1983
18m The hanging corner is gained by a tricky and devious entry from below and to the left. Exit left at the top into the undergrowth.

6   In Merittville E3 5c, 6a, 5a   1984
62m A strange route providing a tour of the wall from left to right in three pitches. From the groove of *Banana Republic*, traverse right into *Berried* (belay). Continue along the break into an obvious recess (belay). The corner above leads to the belay of *Kiss Me Hardy* on the left.

To the right, three sport routes tackle the lower wall and prominent capping overhang. These often suffer from seepage for a long period of time but when dry (and clean) give worthwhile routes.

7   The Orange Order F6c   2000
18m   The first route to the right of the hanging corner is something of a space-filler with a few good moves.

8   Orange Free State F6b+ ★   1996
18m   The central line is much better and despite a steep starts saves its crux until the end.

9   Berried F6c   1996
20m   The right-hand of the three routes gives much harder moves to and over the roof. It also has more intricate difficulties on the lower wall.

The previous two routes supersede the route Voyage to Nowhere, E2 5b (1983).

The routes get harder and better as the wall begins to steepen.

10   Black Rights F7b ★   1996
20m   A subtle technical line following a vague rib. Surprisingly hard and difficult to work out.

11   High Society F7a+ ★★   1984/1999
20m   A super little route. Amenable, technical and sustained with fine moves throughout. From above a bush, take a direct line up the wall to reach an overlap. A tricky and blind sequence through this soon leads to the belay.

12   Kiss Me Hardy F7a+ ★★★   1989
20m   A classic route giving sustained fingery climbing. Start 2m right of the yew and take a direct and engrossing series of moves up a shallow scoop with a long reach through the final bulges. The first bolt is very hard to get to: clip stick recommended.

13 Kiss My Arcy F7b ★★ 1999
20m Harder than *Hardy* and hardly any less good. The initial bulges are fingery and the rockover above provides the crux. Thereafter the difficulties relent.

14 Demystified F7b+ ★ 1986/1999
22m A short and intense pitch with a very reachy crux section centred on the bulge at 6m and using a very distant hold. **Mystical Attainment**, E6 6b (1986), started up this route before moving left into the finish of *Kiss My Arcy*.

15 Mouldwarp Wall F7c+ ★ 1993
22m A very good route when in condition. A reachy or powerfully bunched sequence is required to gain a layaway below the overlap. Move right on undercuts and tackle the fine bulging wall above. Move left and teeter onto the slab to the belay. At the time of writing the first bolt is missing and there is no belay.

16 Brothers in Arms F7b+ ★ 1989
20m Aim for the hanging scoop and gain it via a series of undercuts and a desperate rollover move: whatever your height, there are a few sequences that prove effective.

There is a line of old project bolts between Brothers in Arms and Rouge Total.

17 Rouge Total F7b 1991
20m A tough sequence to get established on the upper wall via a series of rightward-leading flakes.

18 Total Rock F7c 2003
20m Another desperate sequence over the bugles on undercuts and small incut holds.

19 Jungle Rock F7b+ ★ 1989
20m If you are into undercuts and powerful pulls, this route can't fail to please. After a low crux it eases with just enough bite to maintain interest. Head through the bulges, aiming for a shallow right-facing groove. The upper bulge is straightforward.

20 Some Things Change F7b+ ★ 1996
20m A powerful sequence and, more importantly, a massive span passes a bulge to gain the white sheet of rock. Atop this, step left to finish as for *Jungle Rock*.

21 Fatal Attraction F7a ★★ 1989
20m The warm-up for the wall, but no pushover. A fine and sustained pitch with the difficulties centred on the final bulge. Cross the bulge 2m left of the shallow hanging groove and climb a right-facing flake to the overlap. Surmount this with a sense of urgency.

Chain of Command, E4 6b (1982), gained the flake of *Fatal Attraction* from the right and at its top moved left beneath the overlap to gain the finish of *Jungle Rock*.

22 Lucky Finger F7b ★   1996
20m The vague arête provides a stern test. Gain it via a short wall and follow it to the bulge. A long reach off a small layaway gives access to crux moves to gain the belay.

23 Monopedagogue E3 5c   1979
24m Entry to the corner is bold and tricky. Once gained it proves to be well-protected. Exit left at the top.

24 Rolling Stone E4 6b   1990
22m Cross the initial bulge leftwards into a scoop (peg). Continue onto a slab and faint groove, junction with the next route, and follow it to the roof. Cross this on good holds to reach the belay (missing at the time of writing).

25 The Balancing Act F7b ★   1999
22m Cross the bulge with difficulty to gain a blunt rib. This leads to the slabby area of rock beneath the roof, which is crossed to reach the belay (missing).

26 Trick Show F7b+ ★   1982/1999
22m A direct line up the centre of the bay. The start, via a couple of bulges and a slight depression, gives a very

complex series of moves. Once a ledge is gained, easier climbing leads to the roof which provides a fitting finish.

27 Casamance F7a+ ★   1991
18m Cross the lower bulges slightly rightwards to a ledge. The wall above leads to the roof which is quite tough.

28 Macumba F7a+ ★   1991
18m A sort of right-hand and easier version to *Casamance* via the odd-looking nose of grey rock to its right. Once deposited on the ledge, finish as for *Casamance*.

29 Freeway HVS 5a   1966/1974
18m The large corner provides a classic of its type but is rarely climbed. Exit rightwards at its top.

30 Titanic F7b+ ★★   2013
18m The old project up the leaning prow now gives one of the best routes around at the grade. Climb up to the crack. Move out onto the leaning wall and jump and crank your way to the top. Harder for the short.

31 Big News Man Mouth F7c ★★   2013
18m A recent rock fall has made way for this superb link on much improved rock. Follow *Titanic* to its crux and dip around the arete onto the sustained headwall shared with *North Atlantic Drift*.

32 North Atlantic Drift F8a ★★ 2013
20m Quality. Start up *Atlantic Realm* before powering leftwards across the lip in an *R 'n P* fashion. The headwall will provide ample opportunities to spit the unfit off.

33 Atlantic Realm F7c+ ★★ 1990/2013
18m A good route which has been resurrected from the rubble to give a harder and more solid version. Climb into the corner and aim for the distant jug out right via a series of chunky moves. A final awkward pull onto the headwall leads to an easier, but still tricky, haul to the belay.

34 Gob on the Mountain F7c 1988
19m The leftmost line on the front wall. Gain a thin break and make hard moves past an 'ear' of rock to reach a large flake way above. Move left into *Atlantic Realm*. Essentially superseded by the next route.

35 Gobstopper F7c ★ 2013
18m A more direct finish to *Gob on the Mountain* gives a better, more independent route.

36 Meterol F7b+ ★★ 1996
19m Tiny holds and sustained difficulties. Climb the wall just to the left of a long shallow groove. From the break, move slightly rightwards to gain a good hold. Trend slightly leftwards up the wall past a tiny spike hold to gain another jug at the end of the hard section of climbing. Finish up the wall above trending slightly rightwards.

37 Breathless E7 6c 1987
20m An old testpiece from the pre-sport era, it currently feels more like a badly-bolted F7c+. Hold-loss has created deck-out possibilities from the second clip. Climb the wall behind the tree to the break (peg). Step up (bolt on right) and run it out diagonally leftwards (serious) to a shallow groove (bolt). Continue right of the shallow groove to either find a belay above or traverse right and up to finish as for the next route.

38 Cathedral Taste F7c ★ 1996
20m This meaty route offers a short sequence of hard climbing before the slabby wall is gained. Climb the wall to get established on the slab. Climb this directly (peg) finish at a tree belay after an awkward bulge.

39 A Bout de Soufflé F7c ★★ 1996
18m The last of the hard routes. From the break make a very powerful move crossing into the glued undercuts. More hard moves follow before a welcome rest on the slab above. The last two bolts try to force a very unnatural finish (maybe due to hold-loss). Best to move right then back left to the not-so-easy finishing bulge.

40 Multiplex E4 6b ★★ 1982
22m The original route of the wall and still one of its best. Pass the right-hand side of the arch to gain holds above, and then swing quickly leftwards, first up and then slightly downwards onto the slab. Technical moves up this

lead to a left-facing corner and a rightwards exit into the jungle above. Alternatively, make tricky moves left to the lower-off on *A Bout de Soufflé*. **Photo on page 347.** The direct start is **Smutt**, E5 6c (1987).

41 Child Lock F7a+ ★   1990
11m The direct finish to *Multiplex* via the hard slabby wall.

42 Hot Panties F7a ★   1987
11m Another finger-ripping testpiece at the grade. Climb the steep and fingery wall, always trending rightwards on tiny incuts to a final strong, long pull onto easier ground.

43 Steaming Strides F7a+ ★   1996
13m The left-hand finish to *Hot Panties* from its second bolt gives a very technical sequence and one which is un-usual for limestone. Suited to the 'converted' gritstoner!

44 Nookie Bear F7a   1996
11m Three hard moves on the wall 2m to the right on 'tinies' may lead to split fingers.

45 Child's Play E4 6a   1990
11m This route climbs the left-hand side of a shallow re-cess and requires one or two good wires despite a jutting peg. Move back left to gain the belay of *Nookie Bear*.

Twenty metres right, a white pillar stands out from the rock. **Shaka**, VS 4c (1966/1976), climbs the vegetated slab and shallow groove on its left-hand side.

46 Gooseberry Pillar E5 6a   1996
18m From 6m up *Shaka*, move right around the arête and climb the front face of the pillar slightly rightwards. Continue up to the break in unnerving fashion and finish up the headwall moving leftwards to gain the rib.

47 The Gobbler HVS 5b   1979
18m Climb the bulge and slab trending leftwards, just to the right of the pillar.

Ten metres right there is a smooth wall, just left of a prominent pillar of rock.

48 Odd Day Wall E2 5c   pre-1961
12m The faint, incipient crack on the left-hand side of the wall can be climbed with difficulty. It doesn't let up until the overhang is gained. At this, move left and finish via a faint rib.

49 Skid Marks E3 6b   1987
12m The centre of the smooth-looking wall to the right gives hard moves to gain the break and a lower-off.

50 Odd Day Crack VS 4c   pre-1961
12m Climb the crack to the right until it is possible to move right onto a flake cloaked in vegetation. Finish di-rect if you can. Continuing direct up the corner to the break and finishing around the small overhang in favour of a finishing groove gives: **Dirty Deeds**, E1 5b (1983).

Runyon's Corner / Moving Buttress

Trad: 55 (S to E6) **Sport:** 37 (F6a+ to F7b+)
Aspect: North **Sunshine:** Summer evenings **Season:** Spring to autumn
Conditions: Runyon's is a sunless and sometimes dank corner; Moving Buttress is open and exposed but with some vegetation
Best for: A fun trad day VS to E1, with the odd sport hit **Approach:** 20 minutes

A continuous series of walls with two distinctly differing characters. The Runyon's Corner area is a shady nook that is home to a hotchpotch of short sport climbs in the lower and mid-ranges, as well as the odd overgrown trad route.

As the rock swings round the corner, Moving Buttress presents a long run of open, exposed walls hosting a good mix of trad and sport climbs. Nowadays it has become somewhat neglected and is showing signs of vegetation. However, this is not the case on the better routes and a good day can be had here in the HVS/E1 grade.

The Climbing

Runyon's Corner offers a dozen short fingery sport climbs on the F6/F7 border. The routes on Moving Buttress are taller and more technical with the best climbs taking well-defined cracks and grooves as well as some harder, fingery wall-climbs.

Conditions

Runyon's Corner is a large bay of rock formed by two walls covered, in places, with dense vegetation. It can remain damp early in the year or after rain. It only receives morning sunshine and can provide a welcome respite on warm days. This section of cliff is one of the most unpopular in the dale: the old traditional crack climbs may in themselves be unclimbable due to the nature of their exits. The base can get very nettley in summer.

Moving Buttress receives the sunshine in the summer months from about 4pm onwards. It is exposed, and dries relatively quickly after rain. Some seepage remains during the winter months and after longer spells of rain.

Parking and Approach

See map on page 268. There is only one permitted approach. A small track leaves the Monsal Trail at a stile, about 40m east of the viaduct. Follow this uphill (quite vegetated in summer) to arrive below Moving Buttress. A little track leads leftwards to gain the rock at the main arête of the wall (*Never to Look Back*). DWT requests that the cliff not be reached from either The Lifts or Long Wall.

The first routes at Runyon's Corner are situated 40m left of the main bulk of the crag on a buttress behind an impressive tree. **Louie the Lug**, VS 4c (1970s), takes the left-hand crack; **The Sky**, VS 4c (1970s), follow a shallow groove, crack and wall; **Nicely Nicely Jones**, VS 4b (1976), climbs the shallow groove and crack direct from the start of *The Sky*. The next routes are situated across a grassy slope at the left-hand side of the crag on a broken wall with three cracks: **Big Nig**, S (pre-1961), **Upstate Red**, S (pre-1961) and **The Weeper**, HS 4a (pre-1961).

The Upper Tier: This section of cliff is situated above the *Decapitator* area and offers a number of relatively insignificant routes of an even more esoteric nature than those on the lower section of cliff. This wall is best gained via the easy chimney to the left of *Louie the Lug* and traversing back to the right.

Brandy Bottle Bates, S 4a (1970s), takes the crack to the left of a smooth-looking wall; **Nighthawks at the Diner**, F7a (1991), climbs the smooth-looking wall finishing leftwards from the break; **Shred Your Stick**, F7a+ (1991), climbs the next wall 12m to the right and just to the left of an obvious chimney; **Soupbones Chimney**, VD (pre-1961), takes the chimney; **Hot Horse Herbie**, HS (pre-1961), moves right out of the chimney to climb an ivy-riddled crack.

upper approach

Plum Buttress

Monsal Trail

Runyon's Corner

The left-hand side of the crag proper, to the right of the poorer rock previously described, provides a compact wall of good rock with a number of reasonable pitches. Their shortness in some cases belies their difficulties.

1 Watch this Space F6c **1995**
10m A short technical exercise gives a pleasant pitch.

2 The Decapitator HVS 5b **1976**
18m The prominent flaky crack leads to an old peg and thread runner. Move slightly right to gain a faint groove which in turn leads to a small ledge. Unfortunately the vegetation above may prevent you from achieving your goal.

3 Roberts Roberts F7a+ ★ **2011**
12m Climb the crack and tackle the bulges direct with difficulty to reach a lower-off just beneath the vegetation. Good climbing.

4 Local Vortex E3 6b **1984**
18m The vaguer of the two cracks is gained by a series of difficult moves. Once a thread has been gained the difficulties ease somewhat but the vegetation does not.

5 Kill the Bill F7b+ **1990**
13m The most technical of the pitches. Yet to be rebolted.

6 Overslapped F7a ★ **1995**
13m The best of the bunch on the slightly bulging wall.

7 Slappy, Happy, Chappy F7a **2011**
12m The twin overlaps give good moves.

8 Thundertrapped F7a **1996**
13m A short, sharp shock via the overlap.

9 Overclapped F7a+ **1995**
12m A tough little cookie. Underestimate it at your peril.

10 Megaflapped F6c **1996**
12m Climb via an overlap and a difficult move on the upper wall before the wall diminishes in height.

11 Runyonectomy F6b **1996**
10m A poor short route.

Waldo Winchester, VS 4a (1976), takes the main angle of the bay and is best left to the climbing vegetation. **More than Somewhat**, S (pre-1961), climbs the right-hand side of the block right of the corner and again has 'matto grasso' above.

12 The Jury's Out F6c ★ 1995
16m The pillar 8m right of the angle of the bay gives a good, technical but slightly unnerving lead.

Big Butch, VS 4c (1976), follows the first crack to the right of the pillar.

13 Seldom Seen VS 4c pre-1961
20m Climb the prominent corner crack to reach an overhang. Strenuous moves, using all that is available, give an entertaining crux.

14 Nathan Detroit VS 4c 1976
16m The groove, overhang and continuation gained via a faint arête.

15 Community Service F6c+ ★ 1995
15m Much better. Climb the sustained wall 5m to the right into a series of leftward-leaning flakes. Exit these rightwards to gain a thin crack which leads to a good hold and moves rightwards to finish.

16 Open Verdict F7a+ ★ 1995
15m A bouldery start 5m to the right gains a thin break and another series of difficult moves into a thin crack. The belay lies just above with a mid-height crux. At the top end of the grade.

To the right are two prominent cracks, the left-hand one barely reaching the ground.

17 Smash, Bang Wallop E1 5b ★ 1979
22m Climb the right-hand crack to a break, then traverse

a thin break leftwards (peg) into the crack. This gives fine climbing via a bulge until the vegetation is reached. The direct start is E2 6a.

18 In the Defence F6c+ 1996
14m An awkward pitch taking a direct line up the pillar to the right with a scary final clip followed by the crux.

19 Harry the Horse HVS 5a pre-1961
20m Climb the right-hand crack and its right-hand wall into a shallow groove. Once out of this, somehow negotiate the vegetation above. The direct version of the crack is **Big Daddy**, HVS 5a (1979).

20 The Fifth Amendment F6c ★ 2011
12m The centre of the pillar just right with a technical lower section. Pleasant.

Spanish John, VS 4b (pre-1961), is the next crack to the right and **Little Isadore,** S (pre-1961), is the crack almost in the corner of the bay via a small cave. The short steep wall of good rock to the right gives two routes:

21 For the Prosecution F6c+ 1996
9m The poor left-hand line.

22 Witness This F7a 1996
9m An intense sequence on the right-hand side of the sidewall.

23 The Plea F6a+ ★ 2011
12m The excellent front face leads to a short wall and bulging finish.

Frankly Ferocious, VS 4c (pre-1961), takes a bulge and V-shaped groove to an awful finish; **Educated Edmund,** VS 4c (1970s), climbs the left wall of the corner 5m to the right finishing via the right-hand of two cracks.

24 Guilty F6c 2011

12m Difficult moves gain a short groove and ledge with an easier finish.

Red Nosed Pollination, VS 4c (1979), climbs the left-hand of two cracks to the right; **Regrets Groove**, VS 4b (pre-1961), climbs the right-hand of the two cracks finishing up the corner and vegetation above and **Mindy's Route**, VS 4b (pre-1961), climbs the shallow groove and crack 9m to the right and just left of a compact white wall. Returning almost to the right-hand arête of the wall where you gained access to the crag, it presents probably its best section of rock with a handful of routes to match:

25 No Intent F6b+ 1995

13m Just to the right of the vegetated crack, climb the wall and shallow right-facing groove/flake on the left-hand side of the wall. Exit with difficulty.

26 As Loose as This? F6c+ ★ 1987

13m Solid! A better route than once thought to be. Climb the wall 3m right of the shallow groove/flake with sustained interest to a belay just above the break.

27 In the Stox F7a ★ 1996

13m A sustained pitch with no single hard move, slap bang up the centre of the wall.

28 Stax a Time F7b 1996

13m A hard pitch with a peculiar crux around mid-height. The bolts are spaced low down but should not prevent you from getting to the meat of the pitch.

29 Never to Look Back F7b ★★ 1991

12m The classic of the area and you have passed it to get to the rest of the routes! The arête dividing Runyon's Corner from Moving Buttress provides a sustained affair with a number of tricky moves. Photogenic: **photo opposite.**

Gary Gibson on Never to Look Back, F7b (opposite page). Photo: Ian Parnell

Moving Buttress

The best form of retreat is by abseil from one of many trees lining the terrace.

30 I Had a Black Shirt F7a   1996
12m A vague and slightly contrived line to the right of the arête gives a rather squeezed-in, but worthwhile pitch. The majority of the difficulties are found above half-height.

31 Protest and Survive E4 6a ★ ★   1982
20m A typical product of its era with intricate face-climbing combined with a paucity of protection. Climb the face to the left of the prominent wide crack aiming for a right-facing flake. Scamper up this to the break and exit directly onto a short grassy wall.

32 Whistling Crack HS 4b ★ ★   1960
20m Another classic of its era, reminiscent of a big gritstone line. The wide crack provides the challenge.

33 Gander Meat E6 6c ★ ★   1984
22m A mega test of finger strength, with F7c climbing and good, but desperate-to-place, small wires. Climb the wall starting 5m right of *Whistling Crack* on small pockets, passing a buried peg, to a finger-wrenching sequence of moves to reach the break. Finishing left from the peg via a thin crack gives a slightly easier alternative at E5 6b.

34 Meat and Two Veg F7b+ ★   1984
22m The series of thinner pockets leads to a final definitive crimp-nasty finish. AKA Foie Gras/Dope.

35 Spirit of the Age E5 6a   1985
20m The shallow white scooped groove requires a bold approach since the gear is very limited.

36 Autonomon HVS 5b ★   1976
20m An easier line of good quality. Climb a series of vague 'steps' to reach a short steep wall leading to a grassy ledge. Exit via the grassy groove slightly to the left.

37 Automaton F7a   2002
15m A blunt pillar provides a fingery test with a move rightwards above the break to reach the belay.

38 Monoton VS 4b   1966
20m The pleasant shallow groove gains the horizontal break after a move left. Finish via the grassy groove above.

39 Vibrator E1 5b ★ 1976
25m Climb the thin crack and from where it ends, make a tricky sequence of moves slightly rightwards via the slab to reach the grassy ledge. Finish via a thin crack and groove 2m to the right.

40 Witch in Stitch F7b ★★ 1986
18m The desperate wall yields to ability and the luck required to 'land' a hold above the second bolt. Finish via the clean white wall to the left of the grassy ledge.

41 Soft Shoe VS 4c 1976
22m Climb the cracks via a bulge to reach the grassy ledge. Traverse right for 3m and finish above a tree via a wide crack. The direct finish is HVS 5b (1979).

42 Shapeshifter HVS 5a 1979
18m Climb the wall slightly rightwards to reach a tree. Finish via the wide crack as for *Soft Shoe*.

43 Transit Groove VS 4c 1960s
18m From the base of the prominent crack, move left and up onto a small ledge. Climb the shallow groove above finishing via the crack behind the tree.

44 Escort Crack VS 5a 1979
22m The crack with a distinctive hard move to gain a tree. Move slightly rightwards into a groove and then swing right again to finish via a hidden shallow groove.

45 Thin Lizzy HVS 5b ★★ 1979
22m A superb pitch with plentiful protection and all on a fine line. Climb the shallow right-trending groove to reach a break. Move right and pull over the bulge to gain the wall above. The obvious groove provides the finish.

46 Swinging Wall VS 4c 1965/1969
27m Climb the crack and pillar above to reach the break. Traverse left to gain a tree and utilize the finish of *Escort Crack* to procure an exit.

47 A Man Called Horse F7b+ 1990
20m A desperate little pitch on small fragile flakes. Climb the left-hand side of the white wall past three bolts to a resting place at the break. Pull over the bulge leftwards to gain a bolt belay.

48 Dynamic E1 5c ★ 1976
20m The shallow groove system bounding the right-hand side of the wall has a technical entry. From the grassy ledge finish direct and more easily.

49 A Farewell to Arms E3 6a 1982
20m The left-hand crack. Harder than it looks.

50 Nettle Wine E3 6a 1982
20m The right-hand crack.

51 Still Wall VS 4b 1960s
20m A shallow groove; somewhat overgrown.

52 Orchrist VS 4c 1970s
20m A fine little pitch with an unfortunate finish. Climb the shallow groove system in the left-hand wall of the main grey groove.

53 Osculation HVS 5a ★ 1965
25m The fine grey groove gives excellent climbing with a relatively unvegetated exit. **Oscillation**, VS 4b (1965/1970), provides a poor variation traversing right out of the groove via a horizontal break to finish via a subsidiary groove to its right.

To the right, the continuity of the rock re-emerges with a fine lower section of clean white limestone. Unfortunately, there is also a complement of fragile rock.

54 Yuk E4 6b 1986
12m The shallow groove leads to improving holds before a move left leads onto the arête and groove.

55 Wise Up! Sucker E4 6b 1989
9m The wall has two bolts, a difficult rockover and little to merit it.

56 Your Rotten Thoughts F7a 2002
10m Another route of little merit save for two very hard moves on the small wall.

57 Priming the Pump E4 6a 1965/1982
25m The thin, leaning crack has been the scene of many battles both in its aided and free form. Seldom visited.

58 Oh No! It's the Wall-to-Wall Birthday Party
F7a+ 1990
12m The desperate crack and bulge yield to a very determined approach. Retreat from old threads in the break.

59 Fresh Jive F7c 1996
10m A desperate sequence past three bolts. Retreat from the last bolt if you can!

60 Shaking Crack E1 5b ★ ★ 1960/1976
25m The superb, left-trending crack is a mirror to *Priming the Pump*, but provides a popular pitch with sinking protection. From the ledge finish via a crack to gain a tree.

61 Big Boned Backside Melon F7b+ 1996
25m A finger-shredding micro-climb tackling the nasty bulge. Three bolts, the last being used as the means for retreat.

62 Suicide's Reprieve E4 6a 1984
25m A good, though bold, little route. Climb the thin crack springing from a small alcove to reach the break, finishing via a crack to reach the terrace.

63 Dangleberry VS 4c ★   pre-1961

35m A fine pitch that is well worth seeking out. Climb the prominent groove above the block and from the black niche swing leftwards along the break to gain a small ledge after five metres: possible belay. Continue up the crack above to the terrace. **Monkey Wall**, VS 4c (1960s), provides a finish above the terrace by climbing the vegetated wall to a tree and rightwards exit.

64 Mackenzie Frenzy E3 5c   1987

15m From part way along the traverse of *Dangleberry* climb the white wall above a peg to reach a groove and easier finish.

65 Thor's Hammer HVS 5a ★ ★   1960s/1970

25m From the black niche on *Dangleberry*, swing up and leftwards onto the imposing black flake in the arête. Climb this in a strenuous fashion and, from its top, move gradually rightwards to reach the terrace. It is also possible to gain the flake via a thin crack in the lower arête at HVS 5b.

66 Socialism E3 5c ★   1982

25m Climb the blackened slab to the right of *Thor's Hammer* to reach the overlap. Gaining the thin flake in the arête to the left proves tricky as does climbing it.

To the right, another series of grooves pierce the face ending in a prominent corner complete with a wide crack.

67 Colon HVS 5b ★   1962

27m Climb a faint rib in the wall to gain an overhang at eight metres. Traverse left to enter the largest groove in the wall. This gives excellent and well-protected climbing to a tree belay on the terrace.

68 Thin Thin Groove VS 4b ★   pre-1961

25m Another enjoyable route. From the overhang on *Colon*, pull over the overlap to gain the thinner groove. Continue up this until an exit leftwards from its top gains the terrace.

69 Calvi Corner S   pre-1961
28m The wide crack and corner.

70 Behaviour of Fish E4 6b ★   1986
12m Follow the curving flake to the right of *Calvi Corner* moving leftwards from its top to a small ledge, peg. The smooth-looking wall above is tackled rightwards by some technical moves to reach a bolt belay.

71 Forgotten Dream E5 6b ★   1986
12m Climb the thin, now ivy-covered, crack 5m to the right to gain the white wall (peg). Hard moves via an undercut hold and small flakes gain a bolt belay.

72 The Roaring Forties E3 5c ★   1983
28m Another route being suffocated by vegetation. An easy crack just to the right, and just to the left of a shallow white groove gains the bulge. Pass this with a long reach on a good flake (peg) to gain easy vegetated ground. Finish rightwards.

73 Quake HVS 5b ★   1965/1977
26m A super little route taking a direct line up the shallow groove system to the right, easing as you progress. This in turn leads to a tree suitable for abseil retreat. Essentially the direct start to *Vibration*.

74 Vibration HVS 5a ★ ★   1966/1976
28m Excellent. Climb the leftward-trending flake-cum-groove (thread) leading into the shallow groove of *Quake*.

75 Family Fortunes F7a+ ★   1997
15m A modern concoction amalgamating two routes. From the thread on *Vibration*, climb directly up the sustained and fingery face above, gradually easing, to a bolt belay. **The Price of Fame**, E4, 6b (1985), gained the same upper wall by moving rightwards from a slightly higher point up *Vibration*.

76 Pushed to the Hilti E4 6a   1989
23m Takes a direct line from the start of *Vibration* with two bolts higher up. Wires will be required well in advance of these and make it an airy proposition.

77 Shock the Monkey E4 6a   1965/1982
33m The leftwards-arcing crack at the right-hand side of the wall is festooned with rotting ironmongery and threads. Nowhere easy and distinctly unnerving.

78 Gibbon Take F6c   1997
11m A minor morsel at the right-hand end of the wall gives a hard start and has few memorable qualities.

79 Moving Buttress Girdle El 5b 1969/1976/1980

68m A fine expedition in the traditional mould contouring the entire length of the buttress via the obvious break which is gained from *Calvi Corner* and followed leftwards. Take your belays as you see fit, the route finishing up *Mindy's Route* just inside Runyon's Corner. The in-situ gear is untrustworthy!

Railway Buttress

This is the small and relatively insignificant buttress tucked in alongside and to the right of the first railway bridge. Its bulging and relatively short nature provides a number of bouldery routes. Unfortunately, its lack of popularity has lead to the routes returning to vegetation once more. The central feature of the wall is a pink, left-facing groove, taken by *Pink*.

The Trainee, F7b+ (1991), tackles the groove and overlap to its left 6m to the left of *Pink*; **Wye Train**, F7b (1991), has a very technical start through the bulge just right of *The Trainee* leading to easier climbing above. **Pink**, E1 5b (1983), is the groove, which would be worthwhile if clean; **Tunnel Vision**, F7b+ (1991), tackles the short wall and nasty bulge, complete with hollow block, to the right of *Pink*; **Loco Motif**, F7b (1991),

is the best of the bunch through the centre of the bulge to the right and merits attention; **Steam Train**, F7b (1997), requires some very long reaches to cross the bulge to the right; **The Railway Children**, F7a+ (1991), is the penultimate line to the right, again with a worthwhile and fingery sequence; **One Track Mind**, F7a (1991), tackles the bulge and short headwall at the far right-hand side of the buttress.

The Obelisk

An isolated monolith of little distinction containing a sextet of routes of little worth. Approach from the Third Lift. **Heathenism**, VD (pre-1961), is the centre of the wall facing the hillside and is also the best means of descent; **Idolatry Wall**, S (pre-1961), takes the wall just to the left of the left-hand arête of *Heathenism*; **Paganism**, S (pre-1961), tackles the crack to the left of *Idolatry Wall*; **Tosser's Wall**, HVS 5a (1976), tackles the valley side face of the pinnacle; **Anarchism**, VS 4a (1979), takes the wall facing down the valley and is pretty appalling; **Fetish Cracks**, VD (pre-1961), takes the cracked face of the wall opposite *Heathenism*.

Runyon's Corner / Moving Buttress

The Lifts

Trad: 22 (S to E5)   **Sport:** 23 (F6a+ to F7b)
Aspect: North   **Sunshine**: From 4pm   **Season:** Spring to autumn
Conditions: Exposed, quick drying
Best for: A random Chee Dale adventure   **Approach:** 15 minutes

A seldom-visited escalator of exposure. Three floors of limestone that rise in quality from fairly poor on the ground floor to tolerably flaky on the second up to esoterically worthy on the top floor. There can be a lot of ivy about and the rock isn't always perfect but still, it will deliver a rewarding day out to climbers who like their entertainment a little left-of-centre.

The Climbing
A side-by-side mixture of traditional crack and groove climbs with a fair selection of vertical sport climbs.

Conditions
Exposed and fairly quick drying. Some routes are completely overgrown but others are quite clean. Some loose and flaky rock. Evening sun.

Approach
See map on page 268 and photo on page 380. Follow the approach from Topley Pike parking. From part way down the valley below the parking, a steep path rises up the right flank. Follow this to the top then follow the wall

left for 30m then right around the corner. Keep following the wall and after about 100m another wall joins it on the right. At this point there is a tree on the left, on the edge. This is directly above *Ragged Arête*. About 50m past this, on the far side of the 'headland' you will find a gully. Go down this and take the first track on the left for the Third Lift and the lower one for the Second Lift.

The First Lift

The poorest of the three could have been a valuable sport-climbing venue had bolting here not been banned. Three routes are overgrown: **Fire Dance**, HVS 5a (1977), the left side of the wall; **Sun Dance**, HVS 4c (1977), takes a line 5m to the right; **Rain Dance**, HVS 4c (1976), is up the wall 4m to the right.

1   Generously Cut Trousers S   1970s
15m   Worthy of any horticulturist's attention, the chimney can only be described as one of its type. A full wetsuit may be useful unless it's in the driest of condition.

The Second Lift

Mostly sport climbs of limited value and more appropriate for those seeking solitude. To get there, scramble down the gully just beyond the crag, passing the track to the Third Lift, and on to the next track. **See photo opposite.**

2 Mississippi Burning F7a   1997
12m A hard sequence where a long reach helps.

Black Mamma, VS 4c (1977), is the first crack.

3 Tricky Dicky F6c+   1997
12m A couple of good moves centred on a glued-on hold.

4 The Black and White Minstrel Show F7b   1991
12m Desperate. Not reclimbed since hold-loss.

5 Rustie Lee F7a+ ★   1991
12m The best route on the buttress via a shallow scoop which leads to an airy finish.

6 Daddy's Riding the Range F7a+   1997
12m A hard sequence utilizing a couple of unnatural holds, is gained by a 'balls-out' start.

7 Close Control F6b+   1983
12m The wall and groove on the left side of the arête.

8 White Riot F6a+   1997
12m The face right of the arête is better than it looks.

9 Phase Contrast E1 5b   1979
12m A series of thin flakes yields to a precarious sequence.

Massa, HVS 4c (1977), is the left-hand of two cracks whilst the right-hand crack is **Rastus**, HVS 4c (1977).

10 Iron Filings F6c   1997
12m The left-hand line of three without utilizing the crack. Good.

11 Steel on Steel F7a   1982/1997
12m The centre of the wall has a hard entry sequence over the initial overlap.

12 Mettle Fatigue F6c   1997
12m The right-hand line; good moves with a tricky exit.

The Seventh Veil, VS 4c (1978), is the crack to the right; the wall right again is **Pop the Rivet**, F6a+ (1997).

The Third Lift

The upper lift is by far the best of the trio and has an array of routes both in the lower end of the traditional spectrum as well as a series of sport routes from the late Nineties. The rock here is predominantly of a high quality, although some of the routes tend to have a flaky texture to them whilst the added bonus of masses of exposure certainly adds to the atmosphere.

Black Leg Groove, VS (1960s), tackles a grassy ramp on the extreme left-hand side of the buttress whilst **Fingerpops**, F7b+ (1997), provides two desperate moves on nondescript pockets to the right.

13 Crank it Up F6c+   1987
12m The centre of wall gives good moves and a sharp intake of breath.

14 An Uplifting Experience F7a   1997
12m The wall without resource to the flake on the right. F6c if you do use it.

Eight metres to the right, the wall increases in height and provides a number of easier grade traditional routes. On the left-hand side of the wall a thin groove pierces the face.

15 The Hunter House Bust HVS 5a ★   1983
15m Climb the groove zigzagging around to find the easiest line. Excellent climbing.

16 Get Lifted E1 5b ★ 1998
17m Another good little climb. Move up the groove for 2m and exit right round the arête to climb the front face of the wall. An alternative start gains the route from the shallow groove to the right.

17 Cetswayo VS 4b ★ 1966
18m A real gem of a pitch gaining the shallow grey groove 3m to the right before taking a cunning diagonal line across the wall to its right to reach a tree. Exit via the groove above.

18 No Hammer Involved HVS 5a ★ 1998
18m Starting 2m right of *Cetswayo*, pull directly over the overlap and then climb diagonally leftwards crossing the traverse of that route.

19 The Hoochie Koo HVS 4c ★ 1978
18m Another great little climb tackling the open groove to the right and finishing just to the right of a tree.

20 Firefly Crack VS 4c ★ 1960s
18m A good route climbing the impressive crack.

21 Access All Areas F7a+ ★ 1997
18m Sustained and fingery climbing on the vague blunt rib gives a good but slightly contrived pitch.

22 Elephant Talk F7a+ ★ 1987/1997
18m Climb the centre of wall to gain an undercut flake. Move slightly to the left and tackle the wall above moving rightwards to easier ground.

23 Hamish F7a 1995
18m An intense fingery exercise climbing the blunt rib.

24 Five Miles High F6c+ ★ 1997
18m The hanging groove gained with a hard entry. The groove and wall above are easier and lead leftwards to the belay.

To the right, a black groove stands proud on the front face of the buttress.

25 The Black Adder E1 5b 1983
18m Once the groove is gained, move left and follow the undercut flake to its end. Finish above or lower off the bolt belays to the left.

26 The Black Edge E1 5b ★ 1964/1976
18m An intimidating pitch for the grade via the black groove. Approach it with trepidation but once gained it provides easier and better-protected climbing.

27 Thrills and Spills E5 6a 1983
18m Even more frightening since the in-situ pegs were removed. Climb the fragile wall to reach a blackened bulge. Difficult bold moves lead blindly over the bulge to gain the hanging groove up which the route finishes.

28 All Fall Down F7a+ 1995
20m Challenges the front face of the buttress to give a sustained and fingery pitch with the odd friable hold. The spacing of the bolts makes for a spooky experience.

29 High Scream Sunday F6c+ ★★ 1997

20m A very photogenic pitch tackling the arête, moving leftwards at the top to a shallow groove.

30 Disraeli Gears E1 5a ★ 1978

20m The superb thin crack in the right wall of the arête. Start up the corner to the right before traversing into the crack after 5m.

31 Succulent Corner S pre-1960

20m The wide corner crack provides a route in the 'old style'.

32 The Sting HVS 5b ★ 1970s

20m From part way up *Succulent Corner*, move right to climb the hanging corner.

33 The Siberian Hamster F7a ★ 1995

20m The arête to the right gives a sustained and technical exercise.

34 Fawlty Towers E1 5b 1978

20m Climb the faint ivy-covered crack in the face to the right to gain the break. Pull leftwards over the bulge to climb the upper face in a superb position.

Tikka, VS 4a (1964), traverses across the buttress from *The Sting* to finish via the vegetated corner.

The path to the right begins to drop away and has been engulfed by a large area of ivy. Progression along this requires careful negotiation in order that you don't end up in a hundred metre tumble.

Cohesion Cracks, VS 4b (1960s), has now been lost to the ivy and climbed a groove to the left of a tree to a ledge. The crack above led to a wizened tree from which the route finished via a wide crack on the right. **The Taboo Finish**, VS 4c (1970s), finished via another crack from the ledge, if you can find it!

35 Chagrin E2 5b ★   1970s
25m Nearly lost to the ivy but it may be gone by the time you get there. Climb the gap in the ivy to finish via the hanging groove and a steep finishing wall, two pegs. Very good, when clean.

Eight metres to the right is a prominent vegetated corner.

36 Philadelphia E1 5b ★   1983
25m Climb the wall 3m left of the corner to a bulge. Step right, move up and climb a series of thin cracks to an awkward exit. **Philadelphia Direct**, E3 6a (1987), climbed direct to the left of the bulge to gain the original finish.

The Tendril, S (pre-1961), takes the vegetated corner crack and **Burlesque**, S (pre-1961), the next corner to the right which is also very vegetated.

37 The Eye Line E2 5b   1982
21m Cross the wall to the right of *Burlesque* to gain an obvious pocket – the Eye. Finish up the arête to a bolt belay.

38 Eye Shadows E4 5c ★   1982
18m Excellent face-climbing taking the series of thin flakes in the arête directly below the Eye to the finish of the previous route.

39 All Made Up F7a+   1995
18m A contrived pitch tackling the right-hand side of the blunt arête by as direct a line as possible and not by straying off to the left.

40 Powder Puff F6b   1995
12m A hidden warm-up style route on the left-hand side of the gully wall to the right.

To the right lies a leaning pinnacle.

Tokyo Wall, S (pre-1961), climbs the left edge of the pinnacle.

41 Uninspired E3 6a   1997
12m The front face of the pinnacle gives good traditional climbing.

42 Pinnaclised F6c   1997
12m The right-hand arête is gained from the start of *Uninpsired*.

Façade, VD (pre-1961), is to the right of the pinnacle.

Twenty five metres to the right lies an obvious gully. The next route, the best hereabouts, might be best gained by abseil. See approach info for location.

43 Ragged Arête S ★★   pre-1961
18m A classic of its type, climbing the steep jug-filled left arête of the gully.

Run Ragged, VD (1998), climbs the gully/crack.

Plum Buttress

Trad: 15 (VS to E6)   **Sport:** 15 (F6b to F8a)
Aspect: North-west   **Sunshine**: From late afternoon   **Season:** All year
Conditions: Clean, exposed, quick drying, little seepage
Best for: Brilliant mid-grade trad and fresh sport, F6c to F8a   **Approach:** 15 minutes

Plum Buttress is the first major buttress that you encounter when entering the Dale from Topley Pike, sticking out above the path like a gigantic, arrogant chin, daring you to take a swipe. Its great brooding hulk presents an impressive welcome to the valley.

This is one of the great traditional bastions of the Dale with sought-after classics in the VS/E1 range. These provide great lines with unprecedented exposure for their height. They are complemented by some medium and high grade sport routes that cover equally impressive, but steeper ground.

The Climbing
Mixed traditional and sport climbs. The defining characteristic of the crag is exposure, with harder climbs tackling overhangs and easier climbs weaving around them.

Conditions
The buttress faces north-west and receives late afternoon sun. It takes little seepage during the winter months. Clean and exposed. It may be climbable year round.

Parking and Approach
See map on page 268 and photo on page 380. Approach from Topley Pike parking via the Monsal Trail. Cross the fence at a stile directly under the main crag and follow a short path to the base.

Jake Young on Sirplum, the most exposed E1 on Peak limestone (page 404). Photo: Michael Watson.

Rob Grant on Scratch Race, F7a, (opposite page) one of the batch of shorter sport climbs to the left of the main prow area of Plum Buttress. Photo:Dan Arkle.

At the far left-hand end of the buttress is a small wall tucked away from the main bulk of the crag.

1   Cupid Sails F6c   2013
11m   The left side of the face with a short tricky section.

2   Eros Goes to Durham E4 5c   1986
12m   Climb directly up the wall via a scoop, zigzagging left and right past a thread and bulge to the top.

3   Piccalilli Circus F6b   2013
12m   The right-hand line gives a short, worthwhile pitch.

To the right is a steep wall with horizontal breaks. The next route starts on a ledge high on the left.

4   Sans Identity HVS 4c, 5a   1966
40m   From a grass ledge on the left, trend right to the ledge (belay). Continue up to a finishing groove. Overgrown.

5   Less of Your Lip F7b+   2012
12m   From the left end of a grassy ledge, climb up to a break and make hard moves around the finishing bulge.

6   Liposuction F7b+   2012
15m   Climb easily onto a ledge and from the 3rd bolt, best pre-clipped, move left and tackle the daunting overlap.

7   A Bit Lippy F7b+   2012
18m   From the start of *Liposuction*, climb straight up to the overhang and overcome this. Step right and up.

The next three routes start from the same spot.

8   A Bit on the Side F6c ★   2012
18m   Climb easily up and branch leftwards via an overlap and good little wall to the belay, as for *A Bit Lippy*.

9   My Secret Life F7a ★   1987
18m   A sketchy old trad climb, now bolted to make a better sport route. The bulging lower wall is festooned with good holds, the central bulge providing the crux.

10   The Wilderness Years F7b+ ★   1987
22m   An impressive and difficult line, directly up the left-hand side of the arête of the buttress. Trouble is centred around a half-height bulge. Some fragile rock low down.

11   Scratch Race F7a ★   1982
22m   An impressive line with some good moves and a short powerful crux section which just succeeds in climbing the impressive rounded arête of the buttress: **photo opposite.**

12   The Massive F6b+ ★   2012
25m   The right-hand side of the main arête with a few isolated hard moves and good rests in-between.

13 The Stalk VS 4c ★★★ 1955
27m A classic of the dale. The imposing corner provides a superb introduction to limestone climbing in the lower grades. Gain the corner directly over cleaned ledges. Blast up it, escaping left at the top to a fixed belay and abseil point on blocks.

14 Sparta in His Eyes E1 5b 1979
32m A pleasant face-climb. Climb leftwards over vegetated rock to a grassy ledge. Continue slightly rightwards via a scoop heading straight for the break. Exit left.

15 Giants F6c ★★ 2012
30m A fine addition. The lower wall is technical with fine climbing and the upper roofs are littered with jugs and jams.

16 Gigantic F6c+ ★ 2013
35m A right-hand variation on *Giants*. From the large break pull up onto the hanging wall and then right into *Victoria*. Swing right as for *Victoria* and then finish up the short upper arête of *Mrs. Brown*. Very exposed!

17 Victoria E3 5a, 5c ★ 1964/1971
Long ignored due to rotting gear, a recent repegging has rejuvenated the climb.
1. 23m Climb leftwards via a series of grassy ledges until a V-shaped groove leads to a belay.
2. 25m Move up and gain the hanging recess above the break by an unnerving swing left, then escape it rightwards onto the wall above. Finish up the wall slightly leftwards with relief.

18 Mrs. Brown F7c 2011
30m Climb the wall to the left of the central groove to reach the break (F6c to here). Step left and pull over the initial bulge as for *Victoria* but swing immediately out right and up with difficulty until easier ground is reached and a bolt belay. Out there!

19 Damson in Distress F7c ★ 2011/2014
40m The sport version of *The Big Plum* misses out the VS sections in favour of harder, bolted climbing. Start up *Mrs. Brown* then drift up right to the roof. Battle up this then finish rightwards into the final section of *The Spider*. Take care on the upper section – some loose rock.

20 Raisin Roof E5 6b ★ 1982
48m The first clean breach of the main overhangs is an intimidating prospect. Climb *The Big Plum*, passing a possible belay, to the main break. Move left for 4m to a break in the bulge. Tackle this head-on to reach a resting ledge. Step right to finish up *The Big Plum*.

21 The Big Plum F7c / VS ★ 1960/1983
48m The main break in the left-hand side of the roofs was, for many years, a much sought-after free line but once achieved its popularity has waned. Still, it remains a significant problem. The F7c bit is the short roof section with a VS bit above and below. Climb the central groove (VS 4c), passing a possible belay, to gain the main break. Confront the obvious weakness through the stepped roof on unhelpful holds (very reachy). Belay immediately above the roof. Continue up the VS groove to a tree belay on the penultimate terrace. A finish can be had up the arête above in a fine position. **Photo on page 334.**

Mid-grade adventurers could fill their boots with exposure by doing *The Big Plum* and aiding the roof section at a hearty VS/A1.

The next two routes start from a grassy ledge a third of the way up the first pitch of Sirplum. Although the climbing to get there is relatively easy, it might be wise to bring some trad gear and lead this section.

22 The Spider F8a ★★★ 1968/1987/2004
35m An awesome route finally free-climbing the central line through the great prow of the buttress which had attracted the eyes of many over the years. Cruxy, wild and with some good rests. The modern all-free version skirts around the aid move from 1987's nearly-free version. From the grass ledge, move left and up via the blackened streak to gain the first overlap. Pull over this and continue over the centre of the great overhang to its lip and some degree of respite. Continue up the front face of the buttress to a lower-off.

23 Chip off the Old Block F7c+ ★★ 2012
35m A great link-up. Follow *Sloe Gin* to the post-crux rest then launch out leftwards to join *The Spider*.

24 Sloe Gin F7c ★★ 1987
35m A very fine route skirting the right-hand side of the prow with some sensational moves and positions. Start at the same ledge as *The Spider*. Move up right and climb the brown streak to the main break. Stretch across the lip and pull over it into a niche. Continue to the next good break (that of *Aplomb*) and a thread. Pull up the wall above to gain *Sirplum*. Lower off threads at this point or continue up one of the easier routes (gear required).

The original version of this (E6 6b, 6a) took a different line after the initial bulges. Gain the *Aplomb* break as per the version above then move left to a hanging belay where it meets *The Spider*. Pull over the bulge as for that route then move right to climb the flaky arête (old pegs) to join and finish up *Sirplum*.

25 Sirplum El 4c, 5b ★★★ 1960s

One of the true classics of Peak District limestone, coupling magnificent positions and climbing at a relatively amenable grade. As popular now as it ever was and just as intimidating for both leader and second alike.

1. 27m Follow the series of grassy ledges then continue rightwards on a vague line to exit directly via a shallow scoop onto the terrace – the perfect perch from which to enjoy the antics of your leader.

2. 33m Surmount the bulge just to the left of the belay (crux). After considering the needs of your second, pursue a diagonal line leftwards across the wall on good holds to a pillar and huge thread. Continue leftwards in a fantastic position and all on excellent holds to gain and climb the finishing groove on the edge of nothing. Belay well back on the terrace above. A 45m abseil rounds off this nerve-jangling experience. Summit baggers may wish to continue up the arête above as for *The Big Plum*. **Photo on page 399.**

26 The Plum-Line Finish El 5b ★★ 1976

27m A variation on the original taking a direct line over the overhang and up the wall directly above the huge thread on the second pitch.

27 The Defector E2 5c 1979

27m Another variation. From the pillar before the giant thread, climb a crack to the overhang. Pulling over this gives a hard move to a detached block. Finish via the groove slightly to the left.

28 Peggy Sue El 5a 1976

25m From the half-height belay of *Sirplum*, pull over its crux bulge and follow the flakes up the left wall of the shallow corner above to the top.

The Little Prune, HVS 5b (1979), climbed the wall right of the groove above *Sirplum's* first belay but is overgrown.

There are three magnificent girdles, one of which provides one of the best routes of its grade in the Peak.

29 Sarin HVS 4c, 5a, 4c, 4c, 5b ★ 1968

A girdle of the lower half of the buttress with a few good sections of climbing. If the first two pitches are overgrown then start up *The Stalk*.

1. 20m As for the first pitch of *Sans Identity*.

2. 23m Traverse the break rightwards, some vegetation, to belay part way up the corner of *The Stalk*.

3. 26m Move up *The Stalk* for 5m and then traverse right across the wall to the stance of *The Big Plum*.

4. 16m Pull up to follow the slabby ramp to the stance on the terrace as for *Sirplum*.

5. 30m Pull over the crux bulge of *Sirplum*, then trend rightwards via a ramp to a grassy exit.

30 Aplomb El 4c, 4c, 5a, 4c ★★ 1968

A twin to *Sarin* but at a higher level and with some superb positions.

1. 30m Climb *The Stalk* to the belay.

2. 17m Move up the grassy wall behind the belay before moving rightwards onto rock at a spike. Traverse right across the very lip of the roofs to the belay on *The Big Plum*.

3. 30m Step down before traversing the very front of the buttress via a wide break and in a truly stunning position to meet *Sirplum* at its pillar.

4. 20m Continue the traverse into a shallow groove and follow this to the top or, better, finish up *Sirplum*.

31 The Plum Buttress Super Indirect
El 4c, 5a, 4c, 4c, 5a, 5a ★★★ 1970s

A magnificent route sampling every delight on the buttress and at a reasonable grade. Both leader and second should be competent. Do pitches 1 and 2 of *Sarin* then the remainder of *The Stalk*, then pitches 2 and 3 of *Aplomb* followed by the remainder of pitch 2 of *Sirplum*.

Ugly Wall

A poor wall high on the hillside right of Plum Buttress containing: **Ugly**, E2 5a (1979) , a shallow groove; **The Ugly Sister**, VS 4c (1960), a groove to the right; **Uglier Still**, HVS 5a (1960), a crack. Eighteen metres right are: **Romeo's End**, VD (pre-1961), a chimney; **Jularet**, VS 4a (1960s), the right arête gained from the chimney.

The Cuttings

Several poor routes were climbed around the rock and railway cuttings that hem the Monsal Trail just after the bidge. These include: **Crow's Nest**, S, **Black Hole**, VS, **Cropper's Scoop**, VS; **Honking Corner**, VS; **Three Tree Slab**, D. All 1976. The best route takes the man-made arête at the Topley Pike end of the south wall, just left of the prominent slab:

I Finnieston Ferry El 5b 1976

18m Climb the arête and the wall above, right then left.

Topley Buttress

This is behind trees and thorns at the bottom of the approach valley, just before reaching the Monsal Trail. **New Route Nausea**, HS (1980s), is left of *Cowslip*; **Cowslip**, HVS 5b (1976), is the groove on the left; **Crime**, E3 6a (1979), is just right of centre. **Little Big Climb**, F7a (1987), is just right and **Double Topley**, F7a+ (1991), just right again.

THE BUXTON AREA

Harpur Hill / Smalldale / Staden Quarry / Deepdale +++

Downtown, F6b, Harpur Hill (page 487). Photo: David Simmonite.

A climber catches the late light of a summer evening on Smalldale's Soggy Biscuits, F7b+ (page 417). Photo: Niall Grimes.

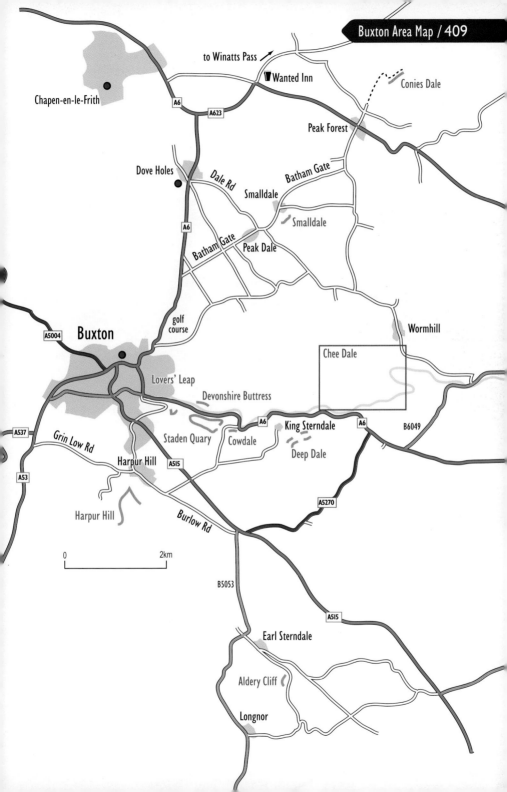

Conies Dale

Bouldering: 12 (Font 6B to Font 7C+)
Aspect: West-north-west   **Sunshine:** Summer afternoon and evening   **Season:** Summer to autumn
Conditions: Secluded, sheltered, summery, fresh, seepy
Best for: Fun, low-to-mid Font 7s in a nice spot   **Approach:** 20 minutes

Steep limestone bouldering in a lovely spot. A collection of basic steep problems in an unusually open setting for Peak District limestone. An ideal destination for aspirant 7th graders, or a change of scene and some volume for the hardcore. A good place to go on a fine summer evening to give your biceps a bit of exercise.

There are problems on either side of the ones documented. However, these are poorer and for ecological reasons are best left alone.

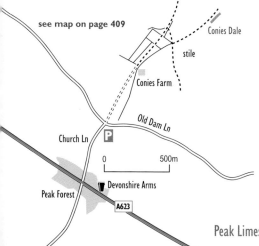

The Climbing: Non-eliminate problems on good rock. Holds are mostly weathered features – slopers, pinches, crimps – a refreshing change from the usual rattly Peak limestone. Problems start from the low break and end at about 4m. The rock continues, but deteriorates. Great landings, mostly flat and grassy. Lots of link-ups possible. See peakbouldering.info for more.

Conditions: Only climbable during the drier months due to seepage from the starting break. If Blackwell Dale is seeping don't bother. Best on a summer evening.

Parking and Approach: Climbers are asked to follow the approach detailed below. Taking short-cuts across fields and damaging walls will jeopardise access. Only cross walls at stiles. Crossing one fence just before the crag is unavoidable however.

At the traffic lights in Peak Forest, turn up Church Lane and park at the junction. Follow a track opposite Church Lane towards Conies Farm, on the right after 400m. After the track stops, a public footpath continues through two fields. In the third field there is a stile in the bottom right-hand corner of the field (the corner nearest the parking). Once over the stile, follow a wall up the valley, carefully crossing a fence, to arrive at the crag.

1 Big Fat Conie Font 7B
Start just left of *Conie Yeboah* and traverse to *Conie Lamiche*. Finish up this.

2 Conie Yeboah Font 6C+
Sit-start on two good starting holds in the break and head directly up via a fingerslot. Finish on a hidden jug up and right.

3 Conie Toutts Font 7A
Sit-start immediately right of the rock pile and climb the roof via a fingery sidepull for your right hand.

4 Conie Lamiche Font 7A
Sit-start at the right-hand end of the rock pile – a couple of handy slots in the ledge – and climb out passing crimps and a pair of 'ears' to a sticky-out jug.

5 Beak Forest Font 7C+
From the ledge, powerful moves on slots and slopers eventually gain jugs.

6 Conie Ferrino Font 7B
Do one move of *Beak Forest* then shuffle left through *Conie Lamiche* to finish up *Conie Toutts*

7 Conie Island Elephant Font 7A+
From an undercut (right hand) just above the break, reach a slopey pinch and trend left to crimps and slots and a big slap up and left to a good hold.

8 Conie Simpson Font 7A+
From the same start as the previous problem climb more direct/slightly right to edges and slots and eventually jugs.

9 Conie Lamprecht Font 7A
Reach out right from the undercut to a nice right-hand pinch and up good edges to jugs.

10 Conie Musselbrook Font 6C+
A big span off an awkward/painful undercut. Very reachy. This was done originally at Font 7B by using a pair of very slopey horizontal pinches to gain the jugs. Eliminate but much nicer than the reach method.

11 Conie Pepperoni Font 6B
A big move to a big 'burger' hold and up to jugs.

12 Conie Whitehouse Font 7A+
Start up *Conie Pepperoni* and, after the dyno, move left to finish up *Conie Lamprecht*. A good independent line.

Jon Fullwood and Ned Feehally at Conies Dale. Photo: Adam Long

Smalldale

Sport: 61 (F5 to F7b+) **Trad:** 12 (HVS to E2)
Aspect: North **Sunshine:** After 5pm **Season:** Spring to autumn
Conditions: Generally shady, seepage-free, cold in winter, unique location
Best for: Great tall vertical sport climbs, F6b to F7a+ **Approach:** 7 minutes

Smalldale should be hellish, but instead attracts a loyal following from climbers who can tell quality. Tall, leaning walls with long routes in the F6 and low F7 range will soon make you forget any aesthetic qualms you might have had about Smalldale. This is a quality venue.

The crag's setting can initially seem off-putting as you walk through a works yard specializing in the repair of buses and lorries, and a huffing and puffing that comes from mysterious sheds at the back of the yard makes it sound like they also do a bit of work on the odd dragon. However, while this may not be solitude and natural beauty, it is, like many of the quarries in this guide, another unique setting. The owner of the yard is friendly, although he does think climbers are mad. Be sure to make him aware of your arrival.

The Climbing
Mostly sport climbing. There are over 50 routes, mainly in the F6 range, but with a dozen high-quality F7s. All long single pitch climbs, up to 20m, on good quality rock. The routes are mainly wall climbs, but many are based around arêtes and cracks, offering varied climbing with lots of character. The crag has had a handful of traditional climbs added over the years, mainly taking the major cracks.

Conditions and Aspect
The cliff faces north-west and only gets any evening sunlight from roughly 5pm onwards. In the wintertime this can be a cold and inhospitable place but in the summer months it provides a welcome retreat from any cliffs roasting in warm sunshine. It provides an ideal evening venue. Seepage does affect the main wall after rain but does not affect routes too adversely in the summer months.

Parking and Approaches
See map on page 409. From just outside Smalldale village, a gravel track leads into the quarry. Do not park on this road but on the grass verge of the next tarmacadam road leading to the brick works. Walk through the small lorry park below the crag to reach its far left-hand end - please treat the owner with a degree of courtesy and inform him of your presence. He is friendly, although due to break-ins he has had to acquire a rather large dog, and in his own words, "There's nothing that dog would like more than to tear a few lumps out of you!".

From the parking, the routes can be accessed in a few minutes by walking across the yard and carefully crossing the wire fence in the corner. Track right to the main wall.

Access Issues
The crag is on private land and access depends on maintaining a good relationship with the landowner. Careful parking and courtesy are crucial.

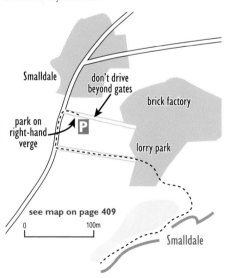

Smalldale

don't drive beyond gates

brick factory

park on right-hand verge

P

lorry park

see map on page 409

0   100m

Smalldale

A climber high on When Reason Sleeps. F7a+, (page 417). Photo: Niall Grimes.

First Walls

To the left of the prominent white Main Wall the cliff slants up and to the left and forms a cliff at right angles with a steep grassy bank running below it. Where this levels out a tier of rock runs leftwards to form a smaller cliff of good rock.

1   Beastiality F6a   2008
9m   The leftmost line via an isolated pillar.

2   Killer Bee F6c ★   2007
9m   Very technical moves on the face.

3   The Ladybird Killers F6c   1995
9m   Another technical route.

4   Six Bee or Not Six Bee F6c+   1995
9m   Hard and technical. You decide the grade?

5   Bee Movie F6a+   2007
9m   A direct line up the slightly easier face to the right.

6   To Bee a Star F6a   2007
12m   The left-hand side of the pleasant, taller face has a steep finale. **Comedy Club**, HVS 5a (1996), is the thin crack between *To Bee a Star* and *Terry and June*.

7   Terry and June F6c   1996
11m   The thin crack leads to an intricate finish.

8   Scott's Wall HVS 5a   1985
12m   Climb the prominent crack in the centre of the wall.

9   Tawk the Squawk F7a   2007
11m   The left-hand side of the sharp-edged arête.

10   Squawkietawkie F7a   1995
11m   The sharp-edged arête. A difficult entry via twin overlaps leads to a delicate climax.

11   Can'tgetmyfix F6c+   2007
12m   The thin crack in the grey tower to a finish on its left-hand arête.

12   Obelix F7a+ ★   1995
12m   The impressive grey tower taken centrally. Fingery climbing with some intricate final moves.

13   Getafix F7b ★   1995
15m   The right arête of the tower is airy above a box-shaped recess and difficult in its top half. Well worth seeking out and low in the grade for the tall.

14   Play it Again, Sam HVS 5a   1985
16m   The major square-cut corner.

15   Reservoir Frogs F6c+ ★   1995
18m   Excellent wall-climbing with sustained difficulties intermingled with the occasional rest.

Getafix Wall

This is the left flank of the main face as it rises up the slope. The main, left-facing part of the wall is east-facing and only receives sunshine during summer mornings. The smaller area at the top gets some evening sun.

The Main Wall

The gleaming white wall is the showpiece of the crag and provides a good number of tall, sustained climbs. The routes are solid and have a big airy feel to them, sometimes bordering on a trad vibe. This is a perfect venue for a summer evening or one of those sultry days we so often get in Britain. It faces north-west, takes little seepage and receives sunshine after 5pm.

16 First Offence F7a ★★ 1985
18m The impressive arête gives superb climbing in a fine position and requires a long reach at the crux.

17 When Reason Sleeps F7a+ ★ 1995
18m The wall right of the arête. It has a tricky start and a bold bit at mid-height followed by first-rate climbing on the upper section: **photo on page 413.**

18 Stainsby Girls F7a+ ★ 1985/1995
15m Gain an angled overlap directly via an elongated gash and follow it to a trying exit. An old classic, yet a little disappointing compared to its neighbours.

19 Virtual Insanity F7b ★★ 1995
18m Superb fingery climbing aiming for a left-facing flake at 12m. Started direct and culminating in a slightly disappointing finish on the arête, the only drawback on an otherwise great climb.

20 Soft Centre F7a+ ★ 1995
18m A tall pitch up the centre of the face via a shallow groove in a black streak. Gaining the overlap proves to be the crux. Above the overlap, the groove gives easier climbing to a steep finish.

21 Lies and Deception F7a ★ 1995
18m The smooth-looking wall gives fine climbing to the overlap. Once above this, follow the wall to the right of the groove with a baffling crux move: **photo on page 451.**

22 Summat Outanowt F7a ★ 2007
18m The long slim groove, the left-hand of two, gains the roof. Difficult moves over it lead to a fine headwall.

23 Lost Contact F7a+ ★★★ 1985
18m A great pitch. The shallow, left-facing groove and thin crack provide airy and sustained climbing towards the top. Low in the grade.

24 Soggy Biscuits F7b+ ★★★ 1993
18m A brilliant pitch taking the wall and vague pillar. Steep and sustained climbing leads to a final difficult sequence above the penultimate bolt: **photo on page 408.**

25 Can Boys F7a ★★ 1986
18m The original offering hereabouts is a sustained and fingery face climb. The 'traditional' spacing of the bolts can make it feel bold.

26 Can't Girls? F6c+ 2007
18m A pleasant face-climb squeezed into a tight space with a tricky finish on the compact headwall.

27 Little Lady E2 5c 1985
18m The thin crack and wider crack just to the left.

28 Bedlam F6c+ 1995
12m The penultimate route of the wall, started high on the right, gives a bold-looking pitch. Good face-climbing.

29 Noisy Neighbours F7a 2008
15m A difficult little route squeezed onto the face to the right. Some hard and fingery moves but short-lived.

Bosch Wall

The next group of routes are situated on a wall at a slightly higher level 30m to the right.

30 Bish, Bash, Bosch F6b 2007
6m One hard move on the leftmost line.

31 Bolt 45 F6a+ 1997
6m The third line from the right has spaced bolt runners.

32 Bosch Spice F6b 1997
8m Again, sportingly bolted, this line is the best route on the wall.

33 Eight till Late F6a 2008
9m The right-hand line.

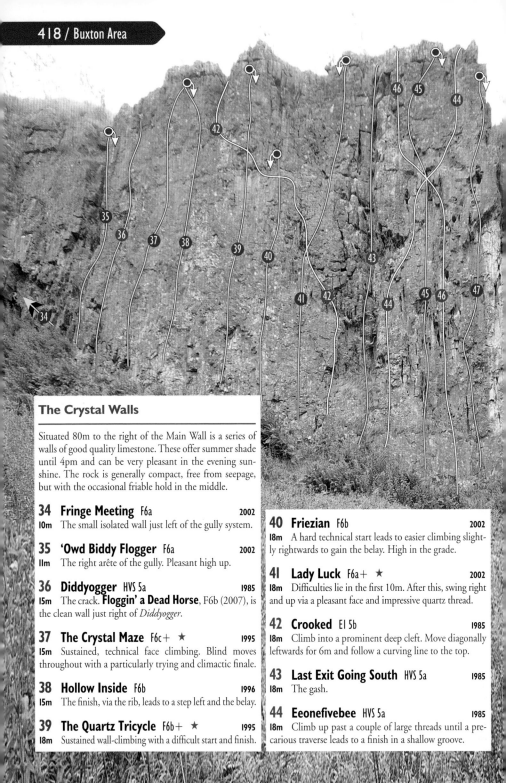

The Crystal Walls

Situated 80m to the right of the Main Wall is a series of walls of good quality limestone. These offer summer shade until 4pm and can be very pleasant in the evening sunshine. The rock is generally compact, free from seepage, but with the occasional friable hold in the middle.

34 Fringe Meeting F6a 2002
10m The small isolated wall just left of the gully system.

35 'Owd Biddy Flogger F6a 2002
11m The right arête of the gully. Pleasant high up.

36 Diddyogger HVS 5a 1985
15m The crack. **Floggin' a Dead Horse**, F6b (2007), is the clean wall just right of *Diddyogger*.

37 The Crystal Maze F6c+ ★ 1995
15m Sustained, technical face climbing. Blind moves throughout with a particularly trying and climactic finale.

38 Hollow Inside F6b 1996
15m The finish, via the rib, leads to a step left and the belay.

39 The Quartz Tricycle F6b+ ★ 1995
18m Sustained wall-climbing with a difficult start and finish.

40 Friezian F6b 2002
18m A hard technical start leads to easier climbing slightly rightwards to gain the belay. High in the grade.

41 Lady Luck F6a+ ★ 2002
18m Difficulties lie in the first 10m. After this, swing right and up via a pleasant face and impressive quartz thread.

42 Crooked E1 5b 1985
18m Climb into a prominent deep cleft. Move diagonally leftwards for 6m and follow a curving line to the top.

43 Last Exit Going South HVS 5a 1985
18m The gash.

44 Eeonefivebee HVS 5a 1985
18m Climb up past a couple of large threads until a precarious traverse leads to a finish in a shallow groove.

45 Just Passing Through F6a ★ 2002
18m A direct line right of the chimney to a difficult finale. Can you pass through the cave? Only slim Jims need apply.

46 Socket Set VS 4c 1985
18m The vague crack. Often overgrown.

47 Sock It To 'em F5+ ★★ 2002
18m Great rock and climbing. Takes a direct line just left of the crack dividing the buttresses. Nowhere difficult.

48 Stone the Crows F6b 2002
20m This is the first line to the right of the wide fissure. A series of cracks and a wall lead to the 'crows nest'. The final tower provides a finely-positioned finish.

49 Blockheads F6c 2011
20m A long line via a short wall, groove and headwall.

50 Learn the Lingo F6c ★ 2002
20m A long sustained pitch. Not too hard but makes the grade due to the blind nature of the climbing.

51 Mr. Love Pants F6b+ ★★ 2002
18m The right-hand branch from *Learn the Lingo*. Again fine rock and climbing sticking direct to the line.

52 Shanacie F6b ★★ 1985 / 2002
20m Great climbing; direct, sustained and satisfying to finish up the obvious short hand-crack. Hardest low down.

53 Riding the Bullet F6c ★★ 2002
20m Super technical climbing with two distinct crux sections at the start and finish on the fine headwall.

The Ubiquitous, E1 5b (1985), took a vague line left of the cave using sections of the next route.

Going Straight Wall

The larger wall provides longer and better routes. A great place to climb in the summer months as sunshine glints the walls from 4pm onwards. The routes can feel hard, fingery and technical on first acquaintance. The square adit (mine entrance) gives a landmark for the routes.

54 Open Season F6b ★ 2002
20m Pleasant climbing with a low crux. Enjoyable face-climbing leads to a finish via the right-hand crack.

55 More Chattery Teeth F6b ★ 2002
15m A tricky lower wall leads to steep jug-pulling to gain the belay.

56 Upminster Kid F6b 2002
20m Ascend the wall and slim tower using holds slightly left. Swing right to join *Going Straight* before the final tower.

57 Going Straight F6c ★★ 1985
20m Superb sustained climbing leads to a finish up the obvious tower.

58 Friend 15 F6a+ 1985
15m Direct climbing via a box-shaped recess and the odd fragile hold.

59 Shame on You F6a+ 2002
15m Direct climbing via a short ramp and steep little wall. Worthwhile.

60 The Awesome Foursome F6b+ 2007
9m Short and hard.

61 Single Decker F6a+ 2003
9m A very short route on the right-hand side of the wall. One hard move.

62 Triple Sec F6b 2002
20m An easy wall leads to a ledge – care with rock here. The wall above has worryingly hollow holds. The final pillar gives pleasant enough climbing if you get that far!

63 More for Four F6b 2012
20m Climb easy ground and a thin crack in the face to a ledge. Overcome a short wall to the half-height ledge and finish up the pleasant arête above.

64 Double Wammy F6b+ 2002
20m A route tackling both tiers. The steep lower wall is mainly juggy. The upper wall gives fine climbing to a difficult finish, taken direct.

65 Single Malt E2 5b 2002
15m Climb the wall right of *Double Whammy* (clipping the first bolt on that route) to a jamming crack and wedged block overhang. Climb the wall above directly to a tricky exit onto the large ledge. Now follow the superb crack splitting the right side of the upper wall.

Continue walking (60m or so) to the right to the final bay. This has a mixture of traditional and bolted pitches.

66 Slim Jim F5 2012
12m The left-hand line of the face gives a few good moves.

67 Fat Cat F5 2012
12m The right-hand of the two lines.

To the right is a bay of fragile rock at half height.

68 Too Fat to Tag E1 5b 2002
16m At the right side of the bay is a cleaned wall split by a series of discontinuous cracks. Climb this trending slightly left towards the top. Pleasantly sustained.

69 Too Thin to Chin E1 5b 2012
16m Gain a series of thin cracks 5m to the right and follow them to exit just left of a tree.

70 Anorexic Text E1 5b 2012
16m A slightly more worrying start just to the right leads into a series of more comforting cracks finishing past the tree.

71 Fix on the Mix F6b 2012
10m A tricky few moves to the right lead into a vague crack system and belay above.

72 Greet the Tweet F6a+ 2012
9m A short tricky start at the right hand side of the wall.

Devonshire (Beerhouse) Buttress

Sport: 20 (F6a+ to F7b)
Aspect: South   **Sunshine:** From late morning   **Season:** All year
Conditions: Sunny, clean, dry, open, fresh
Best for: A quick sport hit, F6b to F7b   **Approach:** 6 minutes

This is a pleasant little crag with an open aspect and good, quickly drying nature. It is a good venue for a quick visit, as it is easily visible from the road to check conditions, and the walk-in is very short. There are not a lot of routes, but it will easily reward one or two evening visits.

The Climbing
There are twenty routes in the F6s and low F7s on steep natural limestone. The nature of the climbing lends itself to short technical testpieces on small holds.

Conditions and Aspect
After long spells of wet weather the cliff can take some seepage, although this is not too severe, and due to its exposed and sunny aspect, can easily be dry at the end of the winter. The rock is clean and sound.

Parking and Approach
This is relatively straightforward. There is a concrete 'bridge' just off the A6 with parking for a couple of cars.

It lies a mile from the Morrisons roundabout on the outskirts of Buxton and 2.3 miles from the Topley Pike parking. From the parking, skirt round the fence and continue up to the live railway line. A tiny path goes up into the trees then contours right to the crag.

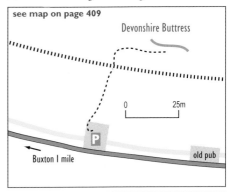

1 The Grape and Rye F6b+   2006
9m   The centre of the micro-wall on the left.

2 Banarama F6b+   2006
9m   The vague blunt rib to its right.

3 Nice Melons F6b   1997
11m A poor route up a rib and short bulge.

4 Gimme Shelter F7a   1997
11m Tackles the capping roofs by two hard moves.

5 And the Roof Fell In F7b   1997
11m Well-named. It is based round a short and very
hard section over the right-hand side of the capping
overhang.

6 Infantada F6b+ ★   1997
11m Another blunt rib to and over a bulge. Intricate.

7 Last Man First F7b ★   1997
12m A technical start leads to an excellent upper section.

8 Chain Reaction F7a   1997
12m A blunt rib leads to fine moves rightwards over the
small overlap. Best gained from the next route.

9 Jewfish F7b ★   1997
12m The desperately crimpy direct start to *Chain Reaction*.

10 Jihad F7b ★   1997
12m Marginally easier than *Jewfish* but still hard to flash.

11 Here F7a ★   1997
12m Fingery face-climbing with blind moves on hidden holds.

12 We are not Alone F6c+   1997
12m The rightmost route before the step-up. Good.

13 Little Brown Men F6c   1979/1997
12m The thin and technical wall.

14 Clotted Cream F6a+ ★   1979
12m A fine warm-up straight up the centre of the white
wall above the step-up in the path. A little gem.

15 The Age of Reason F6b+ ★   1997
12m The shallow white groove finishing up a compact face.

16 Savage Girth F6b+ ★   1997
12m Fingery from the word go. A shallow groove and rib.

17 Idiot Nation F7a   1997
12m A series of very bouldery moves lead to a shallow
crack on the left-hand side of an open groove.

18 It's Uranus F7a   1997
9m   Two desperate moves up and over a bulge.

19 Mercury Dripping F6c+   1997
9m   More bouldery action to the left of a scoop.

20 Men are from Mars, Women are from Venus
F6c   1997
9m   A route through the scoop. Again, bouldery.

Deep Dale

Trad: 120 (D to E5) **Sport:** 19 (F5+ to F7c+) **Bouldering:** 8 (Font 6B+ to Font 8B+)
Aspect: All directions **Sunshine:** All day **Season:** Spring to autumn
Conditions: Quiet, wooded valley, wet in winter **Approach:** 6 - 20 minutes
Best for: Hard bouldering; forgotten low and mid-grade trad and sport climbs in a beautiful place

A peaceful limestone dale containing an abundance of untraveled mid-grade sport routes and low- to mid-grade trad climbs as well as a few top-end boulder problems. There are no great routes here but an abundance of okay ones whose nobility is raised by their beautiful location.

A few of the buttresses here have become overgrown due to lack of traffic. When this is the case they have been given less detailed treatment. Please don't do any aggressive gardening to bring these back into condition (see Access and Conservation notes).

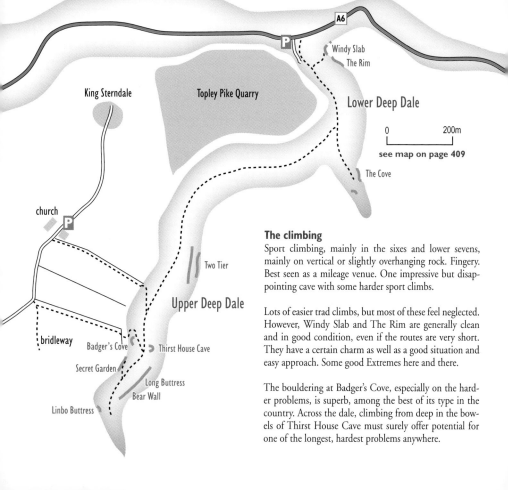

The climbing

Sport climbing, mainly in the sixes and lower sevens, mainly on vertical or slightly overhanging rock. Fingery. Best seen as a mileage venue. One impressive but disappointing cave with some harder sport climbs.

Lots of easier trad climbs, but most of these feel neglected. However, Windy Slab and The Rim are generally clean and in good condition, even if the routes are very short. They have a certain charm as well as a good situation and easy approach. Some good Extremes here and there.

The bouldering at Badger's Cove, especially on the harder problems, is superb, among the best of its type in the country. Across the dale, climbing from deep in the bowels of Thirst House Cave must surely offer potential for one of the longest, hardest problems anywhere.

Conditions and Aspect

Crags are situated on both sides of the dale, and consequently climbing conditions vary. In the summer, access to the routes will closely acquaint you with the healthiest specimens of nettle and chickweed (particularly below Long Wall). The Secret Garden buttresses are steep, quick-drying and get the sun until the early afternoon; it may be possible to climb here during rain. On the opposite side of the dale, the Long Buttress climbs get the afternoon and evening sun but are more prone to seepage. Badger Cove seeps badly in winter but can stay dry in the rain.

Parking and Approach

There are two approaches: the Topley Pike approach, best for the crags in the Lower Dale, and the King Sterndale approach, best for the Upper Dale. One can easily walk between the two in fifteen minutes.

Topley Pike parking: Park in a bay on the Buxton side of the entrance to Topley Pike Quarry on the A6. Follow the footpath signed for Chelmorton from the entrance to the quarry. Windy Slab and The Rim are just above the start of the path, which itself leads directly to The Cove.

King Sterndale parking: Park near the church and old school house. Parking is limited so please be considerate. Follow the footpath starting opposite the church. The path leads to the edge of the dale then zigzags down to cross the stream near Thirst House Cave (15 minutes). For Badger Cove and Secret Garden, a quicker approach is possible but more awkward to find. Follow the bridleway from the bend, 100m before the church, through two close-together gates. Cross the fields to the dale, alongside the wall and through one further gate, to reach a wall. A gap in the wall, 20m from the corner of the field, leads into the trees. Badger Cove is directly below you at this point. To access it, drop down to the edge and walk 15m left, looking out, where a fixed rope leads down a very steep slope to a rough path. The nervous will want to use a harness on this. Badger Cove is reached easily from here. An exposed path leads to the Secret Garden. 10 minutes.

Access and Conservation

The dale has been acquired by Derbyshire Wildlife Trust because of its outstanding natural value. It is a protected prime site of international importance. The Trust would prefer it if there was no climbing here at all but is prepared to accept low levels of activity on established routes. It is vital that if this concession is to be maintained there is no damage to vegetation – this includes grasses, ferns, mosses and lichens as well as more showy flowering plants. Scree slopes in particular are vulnerable and must always be left undisturbed as they host a special and fragile flora. Be particularly careful not to damage vegetation in wet areas, including where abseil descents / lower offs follow their line.

Lower Deep Dale

This is the smaller valley that runs up from the A6.

Windy Slab and The Rim

This is a string of small (ranging from 8 to 15m high) buttresses perched high on the rim of the dale. Despite losing out in the stature stakes, they have a certain charm and attraction especially for lower-grade climbers seeking to tick a lot of routes. The rock is good and the setting lofty and fresh (albeit a bit road-noisy). They get the afternoon and evening sun. To approach, simply scramble up the very steep hillside directly to them in a breathless 5 minutes from the Topley Pike parking.

Windy Slab: This is the little square buttress on the edge of the rim with a narrow grey slab pointing down toward the parking. The first route is on another buttress 15m left of the slab, on the A6 side of the ridge. **Viv Stanshall**, E2 5b (1997), climbs the left-curving undercut flake. On the main buttress, still on the A6 side, **D'Artagnan**, VD (1960), climbs the groove above the tree, 5m left of the arête, finishing via a slab; **Rubber-Tummy**, E1 5b (2000), climbs the short wall and rib above a ledge just right; **Aramis**, VD (1960), climbs the chimney, crack and corner 1m to the right; **Porthos**, S (1960), is the leftwards slanting crack/chimney; **Snails on Strike**, E2 5b (1999), climbs the arête of the narrow grey slab, gained via the left-hand sidewall; **Very Windy Slab**, VD (1960), climbs the centre of the grey slab; **Windy Slab**, S (1960), climbs the right-hand edge of the slab; **Worm War**, E2 5c (1999), climbs leftwards across the steep right wall facing the quarry finishing up the face right of the arête moving rightwards; **Big Ears' Crack**, HVD (1960), is the crack up the right side of the wall.

The Rim: At a higher level and over to the right, the next four buttresses together comprise The Rim.

Bypass Buttress: The first buttress is just right of the descent gully, and has a rightward slanting crackline below a blunt hanging arête on the left-hand side of the front face. **Brutal Brutus**, VS 4b (1960), the steep crack to the overhang which is passed on the left; **Egg Bag, Bag Egg**, E1 5b (1997), tackles the blunt hanging arête direct; **Gentleman Jim**, VD (1960), a short groove on the right-hand side of the buttress passing an overhang on the right or left; **Rambler's Arête**, VD (1960), is the arête 4m right; **Bypass**, D (1960), is the crack in the slab behind the tree, finishing rightwards or hand traverse into the corner. Seven metres right of the corner is a small cave below a crack. **Floating Rib**, VD (1960), is the rib to the left of the cave; **Ostrich's Throat**, S (1960), climbs out of the cave to follow the crack directly.

Reet Treet Buttress: The next buttress is the highest on The Rim. **Egg an' Onion Crack**, VS 4b (1960), a steep crack on the left side of the upper wall; **A Reet Treet**, VS 4c (1960), is the lower wall to a ledge then swing right into the fine steep jamming crack. Follow this moving left at the overhang to easier ledges; **The Direct Start**, HVS 5b, provides a couple of hard pulls over the bulge to gain the main crack; **Second Lesson**, E2 5c (1977), gains a groove on the nose of the buttress by a diagonal leftwards line and finishes right; **Right Slab**, D (1960), is the slab right of the corner.

Tower Buttress: To the right is a twin-towered buttress, divided by a square corner. **First Day Tower**, HS (1960), is the front face of the left-hand tower; **Second Day Crack**, S (1960), is the corner; **Lazy Day**, VS 5a (pre-1960), is the indefinite crack just right of the corner, finishing over a small overhang; **Third Day Tower**, E1 5b (1960/1969), is the peg-scarred crack up the centre of the right-hand tower; **Alan's Secret Drum Frenzy**, E1 5b (1997), the right-hand arête of the tower direct; **Pauline's Date with Deryck Guyler**, VS 4c (1997), moves rightwards from the arête to follow a flake and crack on the sidewall of the tower; **Early Bird Wall**, VD (1960), is a thin crack and shallow groove in the buttress 10m to the right; **Getting Into Ivy**, VS 4c (1995), is the face and overhung leaning crack on the buttress 5m to the right leading to ivy-covered rock.

Blueberry Tower: Further right is another large tower, the last of any size on The Rim. **Face the Blueberry**, VS 4b (1995), takes the steep cracks on the left of the buttress via a ledge and cracks on the left; **Blueberry Tower**, S (1960), is a narrow slanting groove and slab above; **Pay and Dismay**, VS 4c (1997), is the arête and right-hand face.

The Cove

About 300m from the road, the main valley curves round to the right behind the quarry workings. A side-valley continues to the left; two minutes walk leads to Thunder Buttress on the left. Approach: 6 minutes.

Lesley's Tower, VS 4b (1999), the wall and face of the pinnacle 20m left of Thunder Buttress; **Thunder Buttress Route**, S (1960), a short corner/groove via a rib and traverse right to a block and crack; **The Primrose Path**, HVS 4c (1977), a short corner/groove to the rake, continuing rightwards to the top of *Old Nick*.

1   Bob Slopes F6c+   1995
12m   The innocuous looking wall has a difficult start.

2   The Beast F7b+   1995
12m   Hard moves on the initial pocketed wall.

3   The English Impatient F7b ★   1997
13m   A difficult wall on pockets, undercuts and crimps.

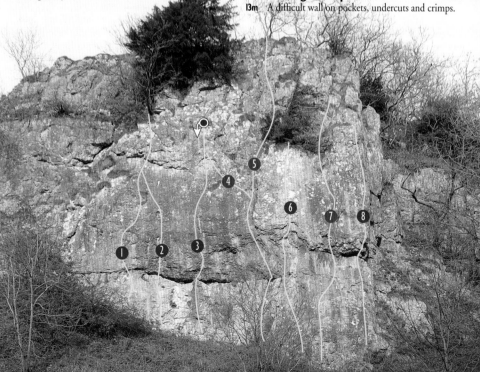

4 Nicodemus El 5c 1999

20m After pulling over the overhang on *Old Nick*, move left to follow an arching undercut flake to a peg. Either climb directly over the overlap to the lower-off on *The English Impatient* or continue diagonally left to a tree belay (easier).

5 Old Nick El 5b 1979/1983

18m The obvious crack splitting the overhang is followed to a finish up a steep slab.

6 Instrumentally Yours F7a 1997

12m Climb the wall to the right (peg) to gain good undercuts, Friend 2. Move up and left to good holds then finish direct. 2 bolts, tree belay.

7 Thunder Wall E3 6a 1967/1983

22m Trend rightwards up the lower wall to the thin crackline splitting the bulge. Pull over with difficulty then boldly climb the wall above, moving leftwards to a yew tree. A corner leads easily to the top, or the lower-off on the next route.

8 The Edge of Donnybrooks F7a 1995

16m The wall, bulge and overlap give a bouldery route.

Jack Frost, HVS 4c (1960), follows the right edge of the wall via an overhang and crack; **Thunder Chimney**, VD (1960), is the easy but dirty chimney to the right.

On the opposite side of The Cove is a slabby buttress next to the path. A pointed boulder below the centre of the buttress is a useful landmark. Five metres to the right is; **The Krab on Your Sac Says Weth**, HVS 5a (1999), climbs a short steep groove on the left side of the arête swinging right and up via an arête; **My Brain is Up to No Good**, E2 5b (1999), is the gently overhanging arête; **Polymath**, HVS 5a (1985), climbs an obvious groove to an overhang pulling over to a wide finishing crack; **The Fop**, HVS 5b (1985), climbs the wall and flake crack just to the right; **Nancy Boy**, HVS 5b (1985), climbs directly from the pointed rock passing a sapling and moving slightly left at a bulge before traversing right across the slab to finish up a crack in the arête; **Town Hall Clerk**, D (1978), the deep crack 7m to the right.

Upper Deep Dale

The main dale holds the majority of the climbing. All these crags are best approached from King Sterndale.

Two Tier Buttress: About 1km up the main dale from the quarry is an outcrop on the left in two tiers. The lower tier consists of four isolated towers, each with VD routes on their front faces. The upper tier has a few short but worthwhile routes on the left-hand buttress. **Clackers Broke My Glasses**, E2 5c (1999), climbs the steep left-hand sidewall on perfect rock; **Hangman**, VS 4c (1960), climbs past a hole to gain the prominent undercut crack which splits the left-hand buttress; **Toby, King of Wardlow Mires**, E2 5b (1997), moves out rightwards from *Hangman* to climb the gently overhanging face just right of the arête. Further right is a wall with two grooves. The left-hand one is; **Ash Gash**, VD (1960) and **Foxhole Groove**, VD (1960), the right-hand groove.

Approximately 150m farther 'upstream' the dale takes a leftward bend, just beyond which is the obvious Thirst House Cave on the left. Before reaching Thirst House Cave there are some broken slabs, the second and most solid one being climbed on its left-hand side by **Penny Bubbly**, VD.

Thirst House Cave: Sweet Sweet Bulbs, HVS 4c (1999), takes the easy-angled groove /corner that bounds the left side of the cave; **Ain't Built for Goin' Naked**, E3 5b (1999), climbs the wall and steep groove 4m left of the cave entrance and **Too Mellow to Bellow**, E5 6a (1985), is the steep groove just left of the cave entrance past some pegs.

9 Thirsty Work F7b 1995

11m A steep and fingery line.

10 Pow Wow F7c+ 2003

12m The steep central line is powerful.

11 Unquenched F7c 1999

12m A desperate bouldery sequence.

Zowie Pop, E1 5a (1985), climbs the front face of the pillar right of the cave entrance and **Gam**, HVS 5a (1985), climbs the right-hand corner of the cave.

Long Buttress

The next major section of rock. Descent is either by abseil, lower-off, or a descent gully at the left-hand end between *Goalie Wag* and *Three and In*. The first buttress encountered has a loose overhanging front face and a prominent arête on the right: **Apple Scrumping**, HS 4c (1999), climbs the fin starting on the right and finishing direct above the ledge; **Goalie Wag**, E1 5a (1999), climbs the next tower to the right; **Three and In**, E1 5a (1999), is the next tower 15m to the right via a crack and wall. Another 10m right is a more substantial buttress:

12 Yus Yus E2 5b   1999
13m The left-facing corner finishing with a blind move up to easier ground where it peters out.

13 Out Of Touch E3 5c   1985
13m The thin crack gained via a rising leftwards line.

14 One Night Stand E1 5c   1985
13m Climbs directly up the more amenable system of thin cracks on the right-hand side of the buttress, past a bulge and moving left to a tree belay.

Megsy, HS, the two trees in the groove 3m to the right have grown a lot bigger; **Stowaway**, VS 4b (1997), starts 3m right and follows a block, short wall and layback crack finishing via a short corner; **Welfare Orange**, HVS 5b (1999), climbs the small pillar to the right with steep

finishing moves; **Ha'penny Tray**, VD (1999), is the old-fashioned corner 6m to the right; **Coltsfoot Stick**, E1 5c (1999), climbs the compact wall to the right finishing via a thin crack right of a corner; **Get It Wired**, F7a+ (1997), is the desperate thin crack 2m to the right; **Scent of Spring**, HVS 5b (1982), the arête just to the right is good and **Hazy Day**, VS 4c (1982), climbs the small tower 5m to the right via a diagonal line of weakness.

Past an area of broken rock is a series of grooves:

15 Deep Thought HVS 5a   1982
11m The first steep groove to a grassy finish.

16 The Hair Bear Bunch E1 5a   1999
11m Climb the wall, trending leftwards towards the left side of the overhang. Overcome the bulge on the left via a deep incut flake crack. Finish direct.

17 Deep Throat HVS 5a   1982
11m The second groove; steep, sustained and strenuous.

18 Larium F7a   1997
11m A good climb up the rounded pillar to the right.

19 Antidote E3 5c   1980
11m The shallow groove is short, sharp and technical.

20 Vulture's Crutch HVS 5a   1979
15m The corner crack is followed to the roof. Move leftwards below this then finish up a steep flake crack.

The next routes are on more unreliable rock and have a pioneering feel to them. **Classical Gas**, VS 4b (1979),

climbs the shallow groove to the right reached from the previous route; **Knee Trembler**, VS 4c (1979), moves right from a tree in a small cave tackling the bulge and groove on the arête to the left; **Alexander Beetle**, HVS 5a (1979), climbs a groove moving right over the bulge; **A Private Cosmos**, E1 5b (1979), climbs a wall and crack 3m to the right; **A Poke in the Eye with a Sharp Stick**, E1 5b (1979), traverses right from *A Private Cosmos* to a tree and crack above.

Bear Wall

The wall right of Long Buttress, gained by an easy scramble.

21 The Bear Necessities F7a 1997
12m Has a short technical crux.

22 Bear Faced Cheek F7a 1997
12m The blank central section is best climbed quickly.

23 Bear It All F7a+ 1997
12m The most difficult sport route on the wall. Very demanding moves above the break leads to jugs.

24 Bearly F5+ 1997
12m A crack/groove above a weakness in the overhang.

25 Bearing All F6b 1997
12m The wall to the break. The hanging flake leads to good holds. Pleasant.

26 Water Method Man E3 5c ★ 1988
13m Boldly climb the wall to a bolt, pull over the bulge, thread, then step left to the finishing crackline.

27 Setting Free the Bears E4 6a 1988
13m Follow the previous route over the bulge and then boldly climb the right side of the smooth wall past a peg.

28 Emmaline E1 5c 1979
13m Climb past 2 bolts to a ledge. Continue up the bulging groove with a hard move past a pocket to gain the crack up and left.

29 Palestine F6c 1997
13m A devious but pleasant sport route borrowing the start from *Emmaline*.

30 Happy Humphrey HVS 5a 1979
14m Climb a shallow groove in the lower wall 3m to the right to a weakness in the bulge. Traverse 2m left along the ledge to a crack and follow this to the top.

Linbo Buttress: A little further up the dale where it bends round to the left is a small buttress on the opposite side of the dale. It has a few short routes. **Isolation Personified**, VS 4b (1997), climbs the small pinnacle to the left of the buttress; **Garden Shades**, HVD (1997), is a straight crack on the left side of the buttress; **Candy Wreath**, VS 4b (1997), is the flakeline on the left side of the buttress; **Linbo**, F6a+ (1997), climbs the left-hand side of the buttress; **Dog-calming Influence of Maltesers II**, E1 5b (1999), climbs the centre of the buttress; **Shades of Distinction**, F6a (1997), climbs the right-hand side of the buttress, using the right arête.

Secret Garden

A good wall on the west side of the dale. It is best gained by a grassy bank at its left-hand side.

Up and left is a small buttress between two gullies: **Chalk Boycott**, VS 4b (1999), follows this centrally then slightly leftwards to finish on the arête.

31 Little Weed E2 5c 1979
12m The bottomless groove is entered with difficulty. Sustained climbing up the wall and cracks above.

32 Costa Del Soul F6c+ 1997
12m Difficult climbing up the front of the buttress.

33 The Mosquito Coast E5 6a 1997
12m Climb the face moving left at the top to a tree belay.

34 Bill's Crack HVS 5a 1977
12m Trend rightwards up the lower wall until below a hanging crack which is climbed with interest to a big tree.

35 Ben's Groove VS 4c 1979
13m Start at a slight corner. Climb the lower wall to a break then move left to meet *Bill's Crack*. Trend rightwards to enter the groove and follow it to the top.

36 Admit You're Little E2 5c 1999
13m From the break on *Ben's Groove*, move up and right over the overlap. Move right to climb the arête.

37 The Abbey Habit El 5c 1982
12m Surmount the bulge with difficulty, move slightly right and continue up a short crack and wall above.

38 Half Way Crack E2 5c 1977
13m Ascend the steep lower wall to the break, pass the bulge with difficulty and finish up the crack. **Half Raped Wall**, E3 5c (1999), breaks out right from the niche and up the impressive wall to a finishing crack.

39 The Bird Cage F7a+ 1997
15m Climb the wall to a tree lower-off. Very reachy.

40 Valley of the Birds F7a+ 1997
15m Sustained climbing up the right side of the wall.

41 Tom's Off Day Route E2 5c 1979
15m Climb the lower wall to a ledge, traverse left and use hidden flake holds to gain the groove. Climb this to the top. **Future Selves**, E1 5b (1999), tackles the bulge direct from the ledge and finishes via a blocky groove.

42 Just Say No HVS 5a 1999
12m Climb the lower wall, over a small overlap then the featured slab on hollow-sounding rock, to a tree belay.

43 Holiday Home for Pets Pie Company
HVS 5a 1979
11m A shallow groove. Over the bulge on good holds then technical moves above. Move right to a lower-off.

44 Quiet, Shhh, Hush F6c+ 1997
11m Climb the wall moving left to a lower-off.

45 Midge Dance E3 5c 1979
17ma An exciting route. Climb direct to a protruding peg, rightwards below the overlap, then back left to an under-cling. Gain and finish up the flake.

46 Touch and Go / Secret Agenda F6b+ 1979/1997
18m The prominent groove and cracks gained direct with a hard move at the overlap. Move leftwards to a tree belay.

47 Robin Hood El 5b 1978
23m Start just to the right and climb the left side of a short wall to a short groove and left-facing corner which bounds the left side of the pillar. Finish via a crack.

48 Pillar Torque F6b 1997
23m Climb the lower wall direct to the break at the base of the pillar. Step right and follow the right-hand arête.

49 Tourist Groove HVS 5a 1978
20m The groove bounding the right side of the buttress.

Badger Cove

This cave high on the valley side holds some of the Peak's hardest boulder problems as well as a few neglected trad routes. For the direct aproach, see the introduction. It seeps in winter, stays dry in the rain and gets morning sun.

There are some routes on the left of the cave. **Rated X**, E2 5c (1985), takes the groove. **Blue Adept**, E4 6b (1985), starts 3m right and climbs past a small flake and block to a break, shallow groove and exit rightwards. **Forging the Chain**, E4 6b (1985), climbs the wall 3m right attacking the steep wall above to a groove on the right.

50 Crack Fox Font 6C
From a stand start, follow the break rightwards to finish over a bulge on hollow jugs; highball.

51 Urban Badger Font 7A+
Follow the crack to finish on hollow jugs over the bulge. This is essentially the start of **Figment of Imagination**, E4 6a (1985), which then moves left across the roof (2 threads) to an easy corner and exits left along the break.

52 Dandelion Mind Font 8B+
A class problem from Dan Varian, that requires pure board-style power. From a stand start, using the perfectly formed undercut pocket and the slot above, climb up and left to join and finish up *Crack Fox*.

53 Bewilderness Font 8B+
Start as for *Dandelion Mind* but from the pinch bust out

right and up using holds that get progressively smaller the higher you go. Take a spotter with you on this one as it tops out up the gully! **Photo opposite.**

The bulges to the right hold a couple of open projects.

54 Thread Nicole Font 7C
Starting in the back, work your way upwards through the various ramps and ledges. Often dirty. The upper section, climbed as a route, past two threads, is **Doggy's Roof**, E3 6a (1985).

55 Rampant Rabbit Font 7C
A highball with long moves. Cross the roof to join and finish up *Bewilderness*.

56 Curry Badger Font 6B+
From a sit, hands on the flat hold, climb up to finish in the cave.

57 Badger, Badger, Badger Font 8A
A classic at the grade. Start on the jug, finish at the hole above the cave.

58 Sheepish Font 7A+
Start 1m right of *Badger...* and head up direct to good holds high up after a slopey fight over the bulge.

Made You Look, You Dirty Duck, E1 5a (1999), from the right-hand side of the cave, climbs left, up and above.

Dan Varian on his own problem, the mighty Bewilderness, Font 8B+ (opposite page). Photo: Adam Long.

Craig-y-Biceps

Sport: 25 (F6a to F7c+)

Aspect: North   **Sunshine:** Very late summer evening   **Season:** Sumer and autumn

Conditions: Shady, seeps in winter and after rain, nettly and planty in summer

Best for: Quick, steep summer sport in the F7s   **Approach:** 3 minutes

A short, steep roadside crag with a load of intense, steep sport climbs where big arms are a major advantage.

The Climbing: Steep and powerful on natural limestone. Generally harder routes with some easier versions have recently been added to the wings. The name sums it up.

Conditions and Aspect: Some seepage in winter and after prolonged periods of rain can sometimes be cloaked in (easily removed) chickweed. It is best visited after a good dry spell later in the season. Beware the thick nettle growth on the approach to the crag.

Parking and Approach: Park in the village of Cowdale, as for Staden Quarry (page 434) and walk back down the twisty road to the crag.

1   Suck yer Thumb F6b   2010

2   Held her Head F6b   2010

3   She didn't Ken F6b+   2010
12m   The bolt line. The crack just right is **Mega Midgebite Massacre**, E1 5b (1991).

4   J.L.N.O.E. F7b+ ★   1991
12m   A short intense sequence over the bulge.

5   Much Monkey Magic F7a ★★   1983
12m   The overhanging crack feels very tough for its grade although it is well worth the effort. Superbly named.

6   Otto di Catania F7a+ ★   1991
12m   The imposing bulge. Gaining it is tricky, and passing it may require a flying leap or just brute force.

7   Blazed but Amazed F7b+   1991
12m   Stiff moves gain the break. Step right and make hard moves over the main bulge to reach a shallow groove above.

8   Meandering Peace Meal E5 6b   1988
11m   Gain and climb the crack. Needs rebolting.

9   The Philandering Sons of Magic Women
F7a   1991
11m   The twisting crack is gained and followed strenuously.

10   A Wild Man from Way Back When
F7a+   ★   1991
11m   A power-packed pitch over the bulge and overlap.

11   Duelling Biceps F7a   1988
11m   A short, powerful pitch via the box-shaped recess.

12   A Woman in Wellingtons F7b   1998
11m   The powerful bulge via a reconstructed hole. Hard.

13   Wet yer Whistle F7b+   1995
12m   The powerful bulge with a very painful glued hold.
Good, despite this, and high in its grade.

14   The Main Motor Mile F7a+ ★ ★   1982
12m   The original route, and still the classic of the crag. The
finger-crack yields to brute force and ingenuity. You may
have one of these, but what's the chance of having both?

15   Pingham's Route F7c+ ★   1995
12m   The square-cut roof is taken at its centre. Fingery
moves gain it and a gymnastic sequence leads over it.

16   Pinging in the Rain F7c+ ★   2011
12m   Start up *Pingham's Route* and finish up *Laughing...*

17   Laughing at the Rain F7c ★ ★ ★   1995
12m   One of the best short hard routes in the Peak. The
prow is gained by a powerful sequence and provides a jug-
fest above, assuming of course you have the stamina.

18   Mesmerised F7b ★ ★   1987
12m   The large hanging corner gained by a series of gymnastic moves leftwards over the roof below.

19   ET F7c ★   2011
12m   The desperate roof crack.

20   You Know UFOs F7a+ ★   1991
11m   An easier, right-hand exit.

21   Euphoric F7a   1995

22   Pneumatic F6c+   2010

23   Ecstatic F6b   2010

24   Fantastic F6b   2010

25   Traumatic F6b+   2010

26   Check Out F6a ★   2010
11m   The bulge leads to jugs, a crack and fine finish. Excellent.

27   New Nomad F6b+ ★   2010
11m   A tricky little bulge and crack to an overhang.

28   Napped a Nod F6a+   2010

Staden Quarry

Trad: 140 (HS to E6)
Aspect: Mainly north   **Sunshine:** Not much   **Season:** All year
Conditions: Shady, mostly clean, can be a bit 'planty', quiet
Best for: Classic summer trad, HVS to E2   **Approach:** 8 minutes

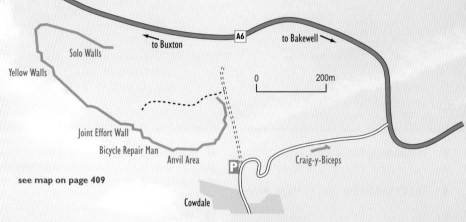

Solo Walls

Yellow Walls

to Buxton

A6

to Bakewell

0   200m

Joint Effort Wall

Bicycle Repair Man

Anvil Area

P

Craig-y-Biceps

see map on page 409

Cowdale

Staden Quarry is a wonderful crag. You'll have a great time and you'll always come back for more. The best routes are sustained and technical affairs up strong natural lines. The quarry is tranquil and green and also perfectly shady in a Buxton heat wave. It's common to climb more routes in a day at Staden than at any other limestone crag and to never climb anything other than starred routes The addition of many new lines in the outlying, occasionally esoteric, areas of the quarry have added further excitement and quality.

The Climbing

Technical sustained walls, cracks and slabs on great sound rock, especially on the popular venues. The less popular areas of Staden may need a dose of common sense and an ability to tread carefully as they have had relatively few ascents. Routes are generally well-protected, although some (e.g. *Welcome to Hard Times*) can feel very bold, but mostly you can push yourself in relative safety at this crag. Do not assume all pegs mentioned in the text are in-situ. There are a few bolt belays and lower-offs.

Neil Mawson on Cathy's Clown, E2 5c (page 445). Photo: Tim Glasby.

Conditions and Aspect

Various parts of the quarry face in various directions. The most popular areas are north-facing, making it a perfect venue on a hot day. The Solo Wall area gets sun for much of the day meaning it's ideal when there's a chill in the air, and part of Yellow Walls gets sun in the afternoon. Early in the season, routes may need some cosmetic attention to remove dandelions but this is easily done en-route.

Approaches and Access

Turn off the A6 at a small road on the apex of a bend (signed 'Unsuitable for HGVs'). This junction is 2km (1.6 miles) from Morrisons roundabout on the edge of Buxton. Wriggle up this little road, passing Craig-y-Biceps on the left, to arrive in the tiny village of Cowdale. Park at the bend, just where the quarry track starts. Follow the track, past a couple of gates, then into the quarry. Please park carefully and be very courteous to local residents.

Access

The landowner of Staden Quarry has banned climbing. This is not a ban that the BMC support. However, challenges seem rare. If you are approached and asked to leave, please do so courteously. Check the RAD on the BMC website for updates on this situation. It is worth noting that local residents have no issues with climbing in the quarry.

Left-Hand Walls

A few newly-developed walls are on the far left, starting with the Freezone wall. This area is split into two, the left-hand bit being more substantial, the right-hand area only just qualifying as routes but providing five quick hits.

1 Conspiracy Theory E2 5b   2010
15m   A bold start up a dirty slab to better climbing on the upper tower.

2 One Foot in the Cave E3 5c ★   2010
15m   Climb the slabby face to gain a ledge below an arête. Bold but fine moves up this lead to the top.

3 Down to the Armpits E2 5b ★   2010
15m   Good climbing. Climb the groove and bold face to a prominent wide crack which climbs like it looks.

The next five routes are all similar and short-lived lines. There are bolt belays on the grassy terrace at the back of the finishing ledge.

4 Monochlor E1 5c   2010
7m   Climb the vague left-facing corner, before breaking out right onto the face to finish up the thin crack. Bolt belay.

5 Slap on the Pyro HVS 5b   2010
7m   The thin crack with a technical start.

6 Corniche VS 4b   2010
7m   The wide, central crack to a bolt belay at the back of the ledge.

7 Don't Forget the Freezone E1 5b ★   2010
7m   The thin crack a few feet to the right.

8 Salactol E1 5b   2010
7m   The right arête to the belay off to the left.

Neil Mawson on Bimbo the Exploding Lorry Driver's Gulch Eliminate, HS 4b (page 440). Photo: Tim Glasby.

9 Locks, Box and Barrel VS 4c ★ 2010
13m   Steady climbing up the slab on the left of the recess.

10 Boxed In E2 5c 2010
11m   The apparently unattached block that is halfway up the route should be treated with a great degree of caution.

11 Thinking Outside the Box E3 5c ★ 2010
11m   The right arête of the recess. Two pegs protect the hard moves up the blunt rib to the easier cracks above.

12 X-Box HVS 5a ★ 2010
12m   The arête finishing via a crack.

13 Open the Box HVS 5a ★ 2010
12m   The cracked wall.

14 Little Boxes on a Hillside E1 5b ★ 2010
12m   Bypass the right-facing flake to finish on the arête.

15 Box Number 7 E2 5c 2010
13m   Crimp up the steep face to some wide cracks. Move right to finish up *Boxing Clever*.

16 Boxing Clever E1 5a ★ 2010
15m   A fine route. Climb the face just left of the railway track and continue straight up the left-hand side of the arête to a ledge. Continue boldly up the arête.

The slabby rock to the right provides three reasonable routes: **a Forbidden Rib**, E2 5b (2010), up the bold blunt rib finishing up the upper slabs of the next route; **b The Dead Parrot Sketch**, VS 4c (2010), the left-hand of the two cracks and slab above; **c The Ministry of Silly Walks**, VS 4b (2010), is the thin crack past a small sapling finishing via shallow grooves.

Anvil Wall: A nice, but not always easy, slab.

17 Tout Comprendre HVS 4c 1981
14m   The arête is pretty bold. Often soloed, though that doesn't mean you should! Sneak warily up the left side of the arête, pulling round to more exposure higher up.

18 Je ne Comprendre Pas E5 6a 2010
14m   A hard eliminate up the right-hand side of the arête joining *Tout Comprendre* in its upper reaches.

19 Game of Chess E5 6b ★ 1976
16m   "Chess is mental torture." – Gary Kasparov. A big reach makes the first crux easier, but might not help on the second! Side-runners will likely prevent a ground fall, but will also reduce the grade... but not by much.

20 Hammer into Anvil E2 6a 1976
16m   A good micro-route, with the difficulties concentrated into a few moves around the niche and overlap.

21 Nice 'n' Sleazy E2 5b ★ 1979
14m   The line of least resistance based around the overlap and faint crack. A good route which needs lots of commitment. **a** The direct start is unprotected E4, and certainly 5c.

22 96 Smears E5 6c 1991
12m   The hardest moves in the quarry and that most unusual of things: a limestone smearing testpiece.

23 Rupert Bear Goes Hiking VS 4c 1974
12m   The left-hand crack.

24 Bimbo the Exploding Lorry Driver's Gulch Eliminate HS 4b ★ 1974
11m   The right-hand crack. **Photo on page 439.**

25 Beau Jest E2 5a 1976
12m The very bold arête. The block that once provided runners is no more and the route may still be undergraded.

Three routes climb the back wall of the descent route. **a Get Your Clarks On**, HVS 5a (2010) is the thin crack, overlap and headwall; **b The Stig**, E2 5c,(2010), the face via thin crack; **c Stig of the Dump**, E1 5a (2010), the thin crack. Two cracks snake up the sidewall of the main area: **d Emblem Embargo**, HVS 5a (2010) and **e Somebody's Trademark**, HVS 5a (1979).

Bicycle Repair Man Wall

A fine slab, home to a good set of climbs. The diminishing remains of the old bike were still at the foot of the eponymous route in 2014.

26 Silent Manoeuvres E4 5c ★ 1980
18m Precariously climb the right side of the arête with a tricky move to get to the final break. Superb technical moves with no gear but the merest hint of escape for the optimistic and/or terrified.

27 Telescopic Demand E3 5c ★ 1979/1981
18m Tricky climbing that is often tamed by high side-runners. The sinuous crack is gained from *Swan Song* via an enormous reach for a jug. At E3 a very high side-runner is used in *Swan Song*, otherwise E4. **a** The direct start is bold, technical and fingery – stern E4 6a (or E3 with the very high side-runner).

28 Swan Song E1 5b ★ 1983
18m A lovely and enticing line making a beeline to a junction with *Bicycle Repair Man* at one of the finest holds on Derbyshire limestone before finishing directly.

29 Bicycle Repair Man E1 5b ★ ★ ★ 1979
20m A great route. A hard move at the top of the initial crack leads to lovely, technical and well-protected climbing. Continue ever upwards passing a mega hold. Finish via the wide crack just right.

30 Top Gear E5 6b ★ 2010
19m A devious eliminate with some good and very bold climbing. Climb straight up the wall right of *Bicycle Repair Man* to reach a ramp leading into that route. Step right and make desperate moves over a tiny overlap and continue carefully to the top.

31 Charas E1 5b ★ 1969/1977
20m Battle past the tree then tackle the finger crack and the easier groove above. A fine route if you like poor footholds and perfect runners but not everybody's cup of tea.

32 Mosaic Piece E4 5c ★   1981/1985
20m The face would be quite steady with a few nice runners, but guess what? You're on your own, buddy. A high
side-runner reduces the seriousness (and the E grade). **a** A
direct start is even more bold at E5 5c.

33 Wipe Out E3 5b ★   1979/1994
20m Initially technical, then simply bold, bold, bold, but
never harder than 5b. **b** A necky direct start is possible at
E4 5c.

A girdle of sorts, **Action Potential**, E4 5c (1983), started
up *Wipe Out* and eventually, having crossed *Charas* and
Bicycle Repair Man, finished up the arête of *Swan Song*.

34 Paraplege E3 5c ★★   1979
20m A route which still causes furrowed brows regarding
the grade. Let's just agree that some may feel this rather
easy for E3. Protection is adequate if enough micro wires
are carried but the route does have a bold feel.

a Amatarasu, VS 4c (1969/1970s), is the scruffy groove
behind the tree. There are four routes to the right of the
tree, two of which are very overgrown at the time of writing: **b My Tulpa**, E2 5c, (1981), the arête; **c Titanic
Reaction**, HVS 5a (1978), the thin cracks in the tower
to the right; **d Insidious Iceberg**, VS 4c (1978), is the
turf to the right; **e Down She Goes**, E3 5c (2010), is the
bold arête; **f Slipping Blocks**, VS 4c (2010), climbs the
wall and cracks 5m right.

Gary Gibson on Liquid Courage, E1 5b (page 445). Photo: Ian Parnell.

Joint Effort Wall

The showpiece of the quarry. A tall, rugged slab, which, at the right-hand side, is steeper and forms a fine calcite-encrusted wall. With the addition of eliminates in the 1990s it's become rather crowded, though virtually all of the routes contain good climbing. Some of the newer ones require blinkers and the old routes are generally the best.

Up and left is a bay. There are three routes here and all have bolted lower-offs: a **Hard Shoulder to Cry On**, E1 5b (2010), takes the main corner; b **Middle Laner**, E3 6a (2010), goes up the right wall; c **Curb Your Passion**, E3 6a, (2010), is the right arête mainly on the left.

35 Hell Driver HVS 4c   2010
24m Follow the thin crack up the left-hand side of the slabs to a wide crack finish.

36 Traffic Cops E2 5b   2010
24m Takes the bold slab direct to a grassy ledge. Climb the shallow grooves above, very bold, to a good ledge below a prominent corner, peg. Climb the left arête of this and swing back right to gain cracks leading to the top.

37 Fiat HVS 5a   1966
24m A serious route. Follow the crack and bulge to a niche, then finish up *Xenophobia*.

38 Wooden Leg E2 5b   1973/2010
25m Climb the steep wall on disconcerting holds to gain a ledge. Climb the face above via the faint crack. At the overlap traverse right and finish as for *Xenophobia*.

39 Xenophobia E1 5a ★   1978
25m An unjustly neglected and slightly bold route, though less so if all the opportunities for protection are taken (*Suscipiat* is close on occasions and the route is graded assuming that advantage of this is taken for gear).

40 Suscipiat VS 4c ★★   1966
25m After starting up the flutings there are lots of interesting positions and rock on this fine route. **Photo on page 449.**

41 Sunai E1 5b ★★   1997
25m A very worthwhile line with a bold start to a black wall, continuing via some great climbing through a niche. It is rather more independent than it might at first appear to be, although for the grade you'll have to be disciplined about not putting gear in *Suscipiat*.

42 The Nails E1 5b ★★   1969/1970s
25m The vague crack finishing up the white groove. The finish is always thought-provoking even with the peg in

place. **Variation**. A finish up the black slab above and left of the final groove (as for *Soft Times*) gives a fine and more balanced route at HVS 5b ★★.

43 Soft Times E1 5b ★   1994
25m A good eliminate between *Welcome...* and *The Nails*. Finishing up *The Nails* maintains the grade but is bolder

44 Welcome to Hard Times E2 5c ★★ 1978
25m Very fine face climbing. Follow a line more or less up the centre of the wall to the bulge. Pass this with interest on the left to reach a horizontal break, good gear and a finish up the groove of *The Nails* (or if not feeling bold, move right to finish up *Joint Effort*). a **The Direct Finish**, E3 5c (1983), leaves the parent route at the horizontal break and balances straight up the slab - very bold and the scene of many impressive whippers.

45 Joint Effort HVS 5b ★★★   1969/1970s
27m An excellent route following a natural line up the sinuous crack that runs the full height of the face. A steep and technical start leads to easier climbing up the pleasantly sustained rock above. Take a few slings for threads and be prepared for the odd tricky move high up.

46 Badlands E3 6a   1994
25m A bold-ish eliminate with consistent climbing between *Captain Reliable* and *Joint Effort* to an impasse at a bulge. Step right and finish via *Captain Reliable*.

47 Captain Reliable E2 5c ★★   1978
25m Good runners and easy climbing lead you up the garden path to some tough moves up and right, not forgetting a tricky and valuable runner almost mid-crux. Continue more easily, though the top section is still a little tricky.

48 Private Gripped E6 6b ★   1986
25m Hard, very runout, but not deadly. Follow *Captain Reliable* or *Badlands* to the bulge. Move left and climb the desperate upper wall.

49 Cross Purposes HVS 5b ★   1980
35m A rising diagonal line starting 3m right of *Captain Reliable* and finishing up the arête of *Xenophobia*.

a **Extra Effort**, E2 5c (1994), is an eliminate between *Captain Reliable* and the groove; b **Investal**, HVS 5a (1969), is the groove; c **Clowning**, E2 5b (1994), follows the arête to the right and joins *Cathy's Clown*.

50 Cathy's Clown E2 5c ★★★   1981
25m Superb sustained climbing which is both technical and precarious despite the steepness. Follow discontinuous cracks over a bulge to a standing position in a break

below a second bulge. Cross the bulge and, with relief, reach a scoop on the left which leads quickly to easy ground. **Photo on page 437.**

51 Cathy's Clown Right-Hand E3 5c ★ 1992
25m Follow *Cathy's Clown* to the break then move right to the orange patch and head straight up – bold.

52 Liquid Courage E1 5b ★★ 1979
25m Sustained, strenuous and high in the grade. Climb a scoop to the bulges (harder than it looks) and power diagonally right over these to a deep crack. Place runners, summon courage and climb forcefully to easy ground. **Photo on page 443**

The Left-Hand Finish joins the previous route at E3 6a (1988); **Waterloo Road**, E1 5b (1979), is a poor route crossing the face to finish up *Fiat*; **X Certs**, E1 5c (1981), diagonals to the groove of *The Nails*; **Sound as a Trout**, E3 5c (1988), starts up the corner right of *Liquid Courage*, pulls left on to the wall and then climbs direct.

The right-hand side of the wall has a prominent pinnacle with a striking arête. **Bladerunner**, E2 5b (1995), climbs it on its left. On its right it is HVS 5a. To the right of the pinnacle a high-level wall provides two routes: **One Second**, E5 6b (1991), climbs a bold little wall to the left of a wide crack with an easier finish whilst **If Nine Were Ten**, E4 6a (2008), climbs the wall to the right past two pegs.

Psycho Area: This is the more broken area to the right. The safest way to approach the next five lines is from above. The slope below the routes is steep, slick and littered with big, loose blocks. Abseil in, and clip into the abseil rope too. The most notable feature is the tower of *Psychological Warfare* which starts halfway up the slope 75m right. The first route is 20m left of the tower, below a cliff-edge tree.

53 Psycho Babble E2 5c — 2010
10m The slim black face has a few hard moves to gain a large block.

Next, on the tower itself is:

54 Psychological Warfare E4 5b ★ — 1983
12m A bold affair that begins safely enough up the crack in the front face but which then steps right and climbs almost directly up the tower with zero gear. The sense of exposure is heightened because the route starts so high off the quarry floor. If you muff the top moves make sure your belayer is willing to fling themself down the slope.

55 Complete Psychosis E3 5c — 2010
12m From the top of the initial crack of *Psychological Warfare*, overcome low hard moves to a bold finale.

56 Psycho Symmetry F6b+ ★ — 2010
12m The fun, bolted face to the right gives a fine pitch with a possible wire/cam placement at two-thirds height.

Psycho Flake, HVS 5a (2010), toughs its way up the flake and crack to the right.

The next two routes are in isolated grooves and shallow corners roughly 150m to the right. **Throwback**, VS 4c (1979), is a wide crack in a right-facing corner. **Broken**

Hammer, HS 4a (1979), is somewhere to the right. The original description talked of a groove past a diamond-shaped hole.

Yellow Wall Area

This is the long, high stretch of walls on the far right of the quarry, with many routes hidden behind trees and decades of mystery. Tales of climbers attempting them but never being seen again are rife; it is the Bermuda Triangle of Derbyshire. It contains a number of good routes for the VS/HVS leader, all of which are short-lived but fairly engrossing. There is a vague Pembrokesque feel to the lines, but unless global warming really gets going you probably won't get cut off by the tide. Setting up an abseil to get back to the foot of the crag makes your day much more enjoyable.

a Tyred Out, E5 6a (2010), ascends an isolated arête. After a scrappy start, launch up the arête in a bid for glory. Generally bold, with a peg on the headwall before a final stretch to a bolt belay. Returning to the main crag: **b Pig Sick**, VD (1979), is the short blocky corner; **c Snap, Cackle, Drop**, HVS 5b (2010), takes the face.

57 Hit the Deck but Don't Run E2 5c ★ — 2010
12m Start up a very thin crack to gain a horizontal break. Excellent moves up the face above gain another break and easier ground.

58 You're Closer than you Think! HVS 5a ★ — 2010
12m A punchy route up the groove and monster flake. Come on arms, do your stuff!

59 One Step from Earth VS 4c — 1978
12m The pod is sometimes a little sandy, but don't let that put you off. Worthwhile.

60 Don't Look Back E2 5c 2010

12m The thin crack gives hard moves until it widens to a more accommodating size and leads into a tight, right-facing groove.

61 Halcyon Drift HVS 5a 1978

12m A varied line via cracks and a corner at the left-hand end of the chunky overhang.

62 Great Expectations HVS 5b ★★ 1979

12m Superb moves up a superb crack are a fine way to surmount the overhang; properly marvellous.

a Rising Potential, VS 4b (1979), climbs the left-slanting crack; **b Ground Zero Man**, VS 4c (1978), is the wide crack with cheeky hand stacks required to make progress.

63 The Romans are Coming E2 5b 2010

18m Climb easily over ledges until moves slightly right gain a right-facing flake. Pull onto the front face and climb this with good low runners, until a thin pull gains a ledge, more gear and a simpler finish. **c Roman Numeral X**, E4 5b (1979), is the big, bold arête, gained from the left. Harder and more serious since a rockfall in the early 80s and to date has not been led.

The next routes are behind the trees at the very far end of the quarry. They are obscured for much of the summer which may affect the climbing, however, the rock on the six hard routes is clean and free of lichen.

64 Cocoa Pops E2 5c ★ 2010

18m A good find. Climb the thin crack in the left-hand side of the wall to a break. A few strong pulls gain a thin crack leading to a ledge and an easier finish.

65 Fruit and Fibre E2 5c 2010

18m Climb the centre of the wall, initially bold, to gain a small ledge. Continue direct on better holds and with good gear to a ledge and finishing crack.

66 Special K E2 5c ★ 2010

18m The faint white groove and wall leads past a peg to gain a thin break. Continue more easily, with good holds arriving before the finishing crack.

There are four recorded routes in the lost world of this next section all of which are good training for Stannington Ruffs: **a Kellogs Are On Strike**, VS 4c (1979), climbs the mucky face. The next three routes climb lines based around the large, central flake: **b The Heron**, VS 4c (1979), is the left-facing death flake; **c Boomerang**, VS 4c (1979), climbs a wall; **d Giant Staircase**, HS 4a (1979), is the right-facing death flake.

The slightly hidden wall to the right gives three routes.

67 Cheat E2 5c ★ 2010

15m From a ledge on the left of the face, climb the crozzly crack until a long move where it runs out reaches good holds and a shorter crack above.

68 Black Jack E4 5c 2010

15m The centre of the wall provides straightforward but bold moves. It shares a low first peg in a thin break with *Three Card Trick* before negotiating its way up the centre of the face to the ledge and respite.

69 Three Card Trick E5 6b 2010

15m Climb the right-hand side of the wall by a series of very fingery moves past 3 pegs to gain good holds after a fraught move for a hidden jug.

The Solo Area

This is the sunniest bit of Staden, containing some surprisingly good and bold routes that are certainly worth coming here for. There are multiple stake belays along the top of the crag as well as a good path. The first four lines take natural features: **a Solar Plexus**, VD (1978), the arête; **b Diaphragm**, VS 4b (1979), the cracked wall; **c Friendly Local**, S (1979), the ramp and corner; **d Generosity Exists**, HS 4a (1979), the cracked groove in the arête.

70 Sun Crack HS 4a ★ 1977
10m The enjoyable steep crack. **e Olotson**, S 4b (2014), climbs the groove and wide finishing crack to the right.

71 Flying Solo E4 6a ★ 2010
10m The arête with a tough and bold section above a break; **f Solo**, HS 4a (1966 and the first route at Staden), is the next corner; **g Fixation**, HS 4c (1969/1978), traverses from the tree on *Solo* to finish up *Emergency*.

72 Distant Thunder E1 5c ★ 2014
10m The centre of the wall, stepping in from the corner, to finish as for *Emergency*. Well protected on the crux.

73 Emergency E2 5a ★ 1978
10m An excellent and really bold route on good rock balancing its way up the arête; a spicy little gem.

Two routes attack either side of the overhang: **h The Orange Throated Gonk**, VS 4b (1974), on the left and **i Baang**, VS 5a (1969), on the right.

74 Frozen Assets HVS 4c ★ 1974
10m Another good route, climbing the rib and arête to the right of the overhang. Quite bold climbing with just enough in the way of holds and gear to give it the grade.

75 The Soloist E2 5c ★ 2010
10m A technical pitch up the middle of the fine grey wall.

76 Oh Solo Mio HVS 5a ★ 2010
10m Another fine climb with some good, crisp moves. Avoid straying onto the arête.

The crag now degenerates before rallying slightly for the last three routes. The main reference point is a single railway line sticking over the edge of the crag with a prominent groove below. Twenty metres to the left of this is an isolated wall behind a large tree.

77 Princess of the Streets HVS 5b ★ 1978
12m An easy groove leads to the foot of the wall proper. Climb this centrally by excellent moves.

The shallow groove and fluted cracks 10m right give **Solar Wall**, HVS 5b (1977); ten metres right, **Solar Groove**, VS 4c (2010), is the groove system leading to the railway track.

Staden Lower Quarry

An unvisited crag that is on the track connecting the quarry with the A6. The routes, running left to right, are: **Leningrad**, E1 5b (1983); **Route 1**, HVS (1978); **Death's Retreat**, E4 6a (1983); **Soft Mick**, E3 5c (1978/1983); **Bandobrass Took**, E3 5c (1983); **Taxing Times**, E3 5b (1983); **Indictment**, VS 4c (1966); **Leper's Groove**, VS 4c (1966); **Marmoliser**, HS (1966); **Invisible Lights**, E5 6a (1983); **Silent Fear**, E3 6a (1982); **Levant**, E2 5c (1983); **Ephemeral Groove**, HVS 5a (1966); **Before the Storm**, E3 6a (1983); **Restive Being**, E1 5b (1982); **Progression**, HVS 5a (1983).

Suspiciat, VS 4c, (page 444). Photo: David Simmonite.

Buxton Area Climbing History

The early forays into the quarries were fairly sporadic affairs with Graham West being the first to venture into Harpur Hill for his *Seven Deadly Virtues*. A little later, in the mid-60s, a group headed by Bob Dearman and Bob Toogood came for a few visits and found a number of routes, the best of which was *Seven Deadly Sins*. In the late-60s Dearman returned, this time with Paul Nunn, to plunder the fine walls of Staden Quarry with the classic lines of *Welcome to Hard Times* and *The Nails*, both with a bit of aid.

Climbers in the the 1970s were slow to focus interest in the quarries, although a batch of classic traditional lines were plundered by an ever increasing band of climbers interested in new routes.

In the late-70s and early-80s the theme continued, but the pace accelerated with the arrival of a climber whose appetite for new routes was to have a significant effect on the area's developments over the following 35 years. Gary Gibson first applied himself to Staden and accounted for a plethora of routes with *Liquid Courage*, *Wipe Out* and *Paraplege* being the pick of the bunch. During this period, one of his climbing companions, Mark Walton, picked a plum on a coin toss with the now classic *Bicycle Repair Man*. Phil Burke popped in with two gems in the form of *Cathy's Clown* and *Captain Reliable* whilst local Buxton activists Simon Nadin and Richard Davies climbed a bunch of routes in the lower quarries. Davies also snapped up *Private Gripped*, a scare-fest on the main upper Staden.

It was also around this time that Gibson discovered the potential of the small but very overhanging crag in Cowdale that was nick-named Craig-y-Biceps by one magazine editor. Gibson added two superb overhanging jug-fests in the form of *The Main Motor Mile* and the aptly named *Much Monkey Magic*.

As things quietened down for Staden, it was Smalldale that was to become the focus of attention in the mid-eighties. Chris Jackson, Bob Conway and Senan Hennassy took advantage of the unexploited opportunities to create *Going Straight*, *Stainsby Girls* and *First Offence* to name but three. Shortly after, Neil Foster added *Can Boys*, a fine bold achievement and Bill Wintrip finished the spree with *Lost Contract*.

A new style was to burst upon the scene at Harpur Hill in 1994 and was not to go unnoticed by the trad brigade. Nadim Siddiqui and Bill Birch had seen the potential for developing the crag into a sport-climbing venue and established a whole batch of excellent pitches across the grade range. *Power of Soul*, *Ratline* and *Cairn* were relatively high grade sport routes of impeccable quality, breaching areas of rock with very limited scope for traditional protection. Siddiqui and Birch didn't leave it there though and made every attempt to provide a sport-climbing amenity with routes across the whole grade spectrum. More easily accessible were *Coral Seas*, *Rocky Variations*, *Apollo Creed*, *Face Value* and *El Camino Real* and many more.

However, a number of climbers took exception to the bolting of easier lines, which they saw as the 'thin end of the wedge'. Shortly after the dust settled, these climbers, headed by Colin Foord and Ken Wilson, were up at the crag removing almost all of the fixed equipment in an attempt to maintain the traditional values of the crag. A small handful of routes were climbed without bolts and the cliff lay quiet once again.

Siddiqui by this time had transferred his interest to Smalldale. Whilst enlisting the help of Jim Burton, he also casually invited Gibson along, expecting an even battle for new routes: how wrong he was to be. Over a five week period, Gibson set to task with a plethora of new routes, the best being *When Reason Sleeps* and *Lies and Deception*. Burton captured *Soft Centre*, a somewhat bold trad line but Siddiqui came up with the prize of the bunch with *Virtual Insanity*, a classic line at a tough grade.

Meanwhile, Gibson had also been active at Craig-y-Biceps coming up with a gem of a pitch in *Laughing at the Rain*, whilst Paul Ingham climbed the very impressive roof to its left with *Pingham's Route*.

As 1998 came around the area was showing signs of being worked out save for the outstanding issue of Harpur Hill. Gibson eventually decided to revisit the crag for another look and undertook the regearing of some routes whilst tapping the potential of the remaining areas of cliff. Initially tackling the upper tier with a group of worthwhile routes including *The Prophecy*, *Four Telling Tales*, *Over the Hill*, *Exclusion Zone* and *Bag of Bones*, he has since gone on to develop the whole area of cliffs surrounding the hillside, some good and some definitely average.

And that's about how things have remained since. The controversies over bolting routes has settled somewhat and more routes have been added, mainly through Gibson's obsession with new-routing. This has made the area relatively popular but rarely will you see crowds adorning the cliffs, save for a warm summer day in Staden or a balmy September evening at Harpur Hill.

Clare Reading on Lies and Deception, F7a, at Smalldale Quarry (page 417). Photo: Neil Foster.

Lovers' Leap

Sport: 10 (F6a+ to F7b)

Aspect: North-east and south-west   **Sunshine:** Little   **Season:** Spring to autumn

Conditions: Ugly, shady, wooded, sheltered, humid

Best for: A quick hit for sewage workers   **Approach:** 1 minute

The name might conjure up a higher expectation than the venue delivers. This small and relatively insignificant crag lies on the outskirts of Buxton adjacent to the A6. It is a relatively inconspicuous venue with easy access, the routes only being 100m from the parking spot. When the foliage is down in the spring months and after a relatively dry period, it can provide a worthwhile hour or two of climbing.

The Climbing
Steep vertical walls and a few short powerful problem-style routes. Fingery climbing predominates.

Conditions and Aspect
The tight nature of the ravine allows the venue very little sunlight and it can be damp in humid weather or after rain. Best in spring and autumn.

Parking and Approach
Take the A6 out of Buxton and approximately 700m after the small roundabout by Morrisons will be seen a tiny layby/parking area on the right-hand side of the road. The entrance to the Leap is alongside this. The parking is 500m from a larger layby on the left if travelling towards Buxton from Topley Pike.

Buxton

Morrisons

sewage works

A6

0   250m

see map on page 409

Lovers' Leap

Left-Hand Side

The first group of routes is situated on the first wall on the left-hand side of the ravine.

1   Rat's Rally F6c   2011
12m   The short wall and hanging groove in the left-hand side of the wall.

2   The Falling F7a+   2011
15m   The centre of the smooth wall gives a fingery affair and may live up to its name.

3   Down in the Sewer F6a+ ★   1979
15m   Well worth doing. The central flakeline gives a neat little pitch.

4   Z.C.T. F6b   1979
15m   The right-hand side of the wall.

Fifty metres further up the dale will be seen a short, undercut wall.

5   Flushed Out F6c+   2011
9m   A short desperate start then jugs.

6   Blocked Flue F7b   2011
9m   Utterly desperate moves to the right reach a vague flakeline.

Right-Hand Side

The right-hand side of the ravine offers four routes.

7   Moss Marathon F6a   1997
10m   The flat mossy wall.

8   Mozzy Marathon F6c+   2011
10m   The short powerful arête and hard-to-reach crack.

9   My Life Led up to This F6c+   2011
10m   A short fingery wall.

10   My Wife Led up to This F6b+   2011
10m   The rightmost route.

Ashwood Dale

The dale running south-west from Lovers' Leap has had a number of routes added to its walls over the years, both on the roadside crags and above the railway. In the case of the routes above the road, these have been subjected to major clearance and stabilization over the past few years and are therefore unrecognizable from their original forms. The one route that lies above the railway is in fact illegal to access.

Harpur Hill

Sport: 287 (F4 to F7b+) **Trad:** 60 (S to E4)
Aspect: East, west and north **Sunshine:** Main area gets evening sun **Season:** Spring to autumn
Conditions: Exposed, quick-drying, industrial, not always solid, quiet
Best for: Doing lots of F5s and F6s **Approach:** 10 minutes

This complex area of quarries is one of the best and most popular of its type in the area with a host of routes in the low- to mid-grades. They reach up to a maximum height of 25m, on limestone which varies in character from typically quarried on the lower tier through to a more abrasive type on the upper tier where the quarrying has exposed large tracts of calcite-encrusted rock, almost natural.

As with all quarry climbing, extra vigilance regarding loose rock should be exercised whilst both climbing and belaying.

The Climbing

Harpur Hill exceeds Horseshoe Quarry in the number, and range of its mid-grade sport climbs. Well over 200 climbs provide varied climbing and cater for all grades up to the low F7s.

There are almost 60 traditionally protected climbs in the quarry. Apart from a few on Papacy Sector, these recieve little attention.

Conditions and Aspect

The individual sectors present a variety of orientations and it is possible to climb either in the shade or in the sun. The main faces face north-west, and get the sun later in the day. The crag can be windy, but again, shelter can often be found.

Parking and Approach

Note: Parking is limited in this area and there have been issues with security guards. For this reason please park carefully. There are three possible car parks:

Industrial Estate parking: From Harpur Hill village, take Grinlow Rd for 250m and turn into the industrial estate. Wind uphill to a sharp bend after 300m. Continue

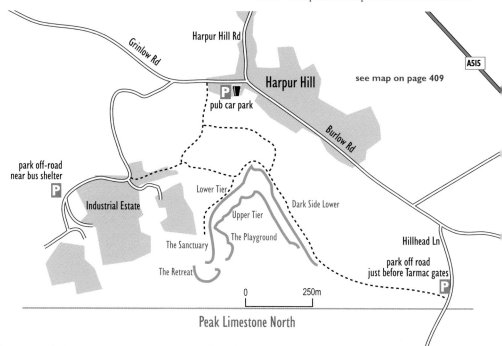

Peak Limestone North

for 200m past the go-kart track on the right to a bus stop on the left. Careful parking here off the road has room for 6 cars. Walk back to the sharp bend and go through a metal gate to follow a footpath along the edge of a field. After 200m go up the banking on the right to gain the main quarry track leading to the rocks. 10 minutes.

Pub parking: Park on the road alongside the Parks Inn and walk up Fiddle St and into the fields behind the houses. Here a public footpath leads across the fields that joins the previous approach just before the banking. Alternatively you can go left to the College Buttress and Dark Side Lower.

Hillhead Lane parking: Take this small road off Burlow Rd, at the south end of the village. Follow it for 200m to park on the verge before the Tarmac sign. Follow the bridleway to Dark Side Lower. 15 - 20 minutes to the Dark Side Lower.

Access Issues

There is no formal right to climb here. If you are approached by the landowner and asked to leave, please do so courteously.

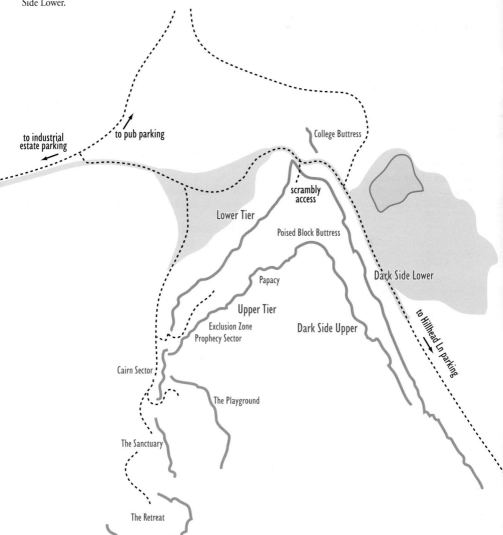

Peak Limestone North

Dark Side Lower

This is the lower of the two tiers on the north-east side. These walls get the morning sun. Approach: If coming from the industrial estate or pub approaches, skirt left round from the Lower Tier and follow the main track. This leads along the bottom of Dark Side Lower.

Racetrack Player Area: This is the area of cliff at the extreme left-hand end of the tier. It offers a number of pleasant enough pitches usually enhanced by the young locals hurtling around on motorbikes, hence the name. The first two routes are situated on a small, scruffy looking wall at the far left-hand corner of the quarry. This is to the left of a prominent grey pillar with three routes on it. **Skid Pan Alley**, F5 (2008), takes the slabby face direct and **Penelope Pit Stop**, F5 (2008), climbs the clean wall with a central bulge to its right. Worthwhile.

1   Pole Position F6a+   2008
11m   Straightforward slab-climbing with a difficult overlap on the left-hand side of the grey pillar.

2   Checkered Flag F5+   2008
11m   Pleasant face-climbing up the centre of the pillar.

3   Peter Perfect F5   2008
11m   The easiest and best on the slab finishing on the arête.

The next routes are 20m right.

4   The Whacky Races F5   2008

5   The Silver Stone F6a   2008
11m   The arête in the bay 10m to the right has a tricky start.

6   Long Playa F6a+   2008
11m   Intricate face-climbing starting via a blunt rib.

7   Dodgem Central F6a+   2008
11m   The centre of the overlap on buckets.

8   Life's a Drag F6a+   ★   2008
11m   The best sport route here via an arête and overlap on jugs.

9   TT Special F5   2008
9m   A short slabby face with a rib starting at a higher level.

10   Brands Hatched F6a   2008
9m   Thin face-climbing with a technical start.

11   Trick Cyclist F6b+   2008
10m   A short slab and technical finale above the scoop.

12   Speed Freak F6b   ★   2008
10m   The varied right-hand line.

13   Lap Times F5+   2008
10m   A pleasant arête with a reachy bulge.

14   Screaming Target E3 6a   ★   2002
14m   Climb the centre of the slab easily to good protection in a break. Enigmatic moves lead to the overlap and more protection where a pull over on a flat hold leads to the easier upper wall.

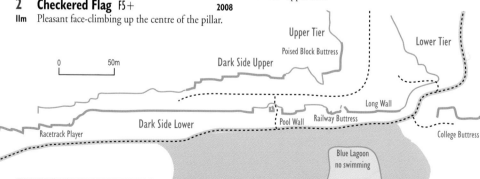

15 Boneman Connection E2 5c 2002
14m Climb a crack just left of the arête with a hard move to a break. Move left to gain the continuation corner. Unfortunately the crux may be avoided if the arête is used.

16 Fist to Fist is Done VS 5a ★ 2002
14m The fine arête is started on the right with a swing round to climb the left-hand side and front face.

17 Mikey Dread HVS 4c 2002
14m A few metres over to the right is an obvious corner with an overhang. Follow the crack-system and leaning groove in the left wall.

18 Scientist E1 5b 2002
14m The corner/groove is steep and sustained.

19 Speed Trials F7a 2008
12m A technical face with a powerful overlap sequence.

20 Quads F5 2008
9m The right arête of the face.

On an isolated face, 50m right is:

21 High Impact F6a+ 2008
10m The centre of the face.

Pool Wall Area: This is the section of cliff facing the pool. Left of the leftmost buttress are four routes. From left to right: **In Isolation**, F6a (2009), slim face to rock scar; **Strange Concept**, F4 (2009), easy but pleasant black face; **Can't Pin it On Me**, F6a (2009), left-hand arête of pinnacle. A crack on the front face of the pinnacle provides **Positive Discrimination**, VS 4c (1986).

To the right the fine gray face provides a number of excellent routes on superb quality limestone reminiscent of Staden Quarry. In many ways the routes are just as good but many have had only a handful of ascents.

22 Grow Fins E2 5b ★ 1999
18m The arête. Start at the left end of the wall and make a few steep moves up and left to gain the arête. This is followed with interest to a crux layback section at the top.

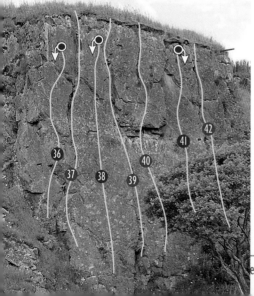

23 Cats 23 HVS 5a 1986
18m The crack, gained leftwards from a detached block.

24 Tricycle Man E2 5c 1986
18m Climb the crack and from a hole at 6m move right and finish direct up the headwall via a thinner crack.

25 Get Peddling F7a ★ 2008
18m A technical and reachy start on a rib leads to easier and enjoyable face-climbing.

26 Face Value E3 6a ★ 1986
18m Climb the thin crack into a prominent sentry box and continue via the thin crack above into the centre of the wall. Move right here to finish direct up its centre.

27 A Dip in Turquoise Nonsense E3 6a 1998
18m Almost as good. Climb the centre of the smooth-looking face to the right (bolt) past a thin break and balancy moves to reach the main break. Finish as for *Face Value*.

28 Faces in the Mirror F6c+ ★ 2008
18m A fine direct line left of the obvious crack.

29 College Crack E1 5b 1986
18m The jamming crack splitting the centre of the face.

30 Permutation Wall HVS 5b 1986
18m A disjointed crackline and ramp from half-height.

31 Balance of Probabilities F6c ★ 2008
18m The arête taking the overlap on the left.

32 Upthrutch HVS 5b 1986
18m The groove and crack 5m to the right until moves left gain the ramp. Once on this, move back right and climb the grassy headwall.

Eight metres to the right is a prominent hole.

33 Diamond Wall E2 5b 1986

18m From the hole, climb slightly rightwards to reach a grassy diagonal crack. Move leftwards up this and so to the top.

34 Pool Hand Fluke F6b 2009

15m A pull onto the face with short technicalities above.

35 More Pool You F6b 2009

15m Another steep pull onto a wall then a face above.

Railway Buttress: The next buttress is situated 20m to the right and has a piece of track sticking out at the top.

36 Sleeping Sickness F6a 2007

11m A slim groove and short wall on the left.

37 Narrow Gauge S 1986

8m The flake crack on the left-hand side of the buttress.

38 My Bed's Downstairs F6a 2007

15m The pleasant face left of centre of the buttress.

39 Wide Gauge VS 4c 1986

18m The prominent wide crack just to the right.

40 Railroaded HVS 5b 1986

18m The thin crack is a much more pleasant proposition, the overhang proving relatively straightforward.

41 Sleep On It F6b 2007

12m The slim wall with a tricky start and central section.

42 Just the Ticket VS 4b 1986

12m The wide crack using the railway track with trepidation.

Long Wall Area: This is the long wall to the right which extends almost to the cut-through when walking from the main lower tier.

43 Regulo Mark 6 F6b 2007

11m Tricky moves above both the first and second ledges.

44 Easy on the Gas F5 ★ 2007

11m Easier with one awkward move at the top.

45 The Pillar Talk F6a+ ★ 2007

11m A fine wall taken direct to a tricky finish.

Malaido, HVS 5a (1986), climbs the thin crack in the wall, moving left via the ledge to the top and **Malaise**, HVS 5a (1986), follows *Malaido* to the faint break and moves right to finish.

46 The Pillar Walk F5+ 2007

11m The pillar and crack via a two-thirds-height ledge.

47 Addit and Scarper F6b 2007

11m The cracks lead to a technical headwall.

48 You've Addit F6a ★ 2007

11m Twin thin cracks lead to an easier headwall.

49 Addit Enough F5+ ★ 2007

11m Begins just right of the adit (cave).

50 Addit Pillar F6a+ 2007

11m The thin pillar on the wall to the right.

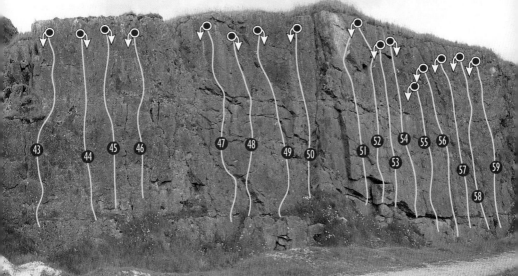

51 Flexor Hallucis Longus F6a 2007
IIm The arête to the right finishing via a final bulge.

52 Long Walk off a Short Pier F6a+ 2007
IIm Start via a prominent block trending leftwards to a difficult move on the headwall.

53 Tooooo Long F6a ★ 2007
IIm Starting via the crack right of the block.

54 Longevity F6a 2007
IIm The blank-looking face to the right gives a myriad of holds with a tough pull over the overlap at the start.

55 Long Time No See F6a ★ 2007
IIm Starts via a crack; pleasant face-climbing above.

56 The Long Walk F6b ★ 2007
IIm A difficult lower bulge leads to face-climbing above.

57 So Long, Farewell F6a 2007
IIm Start just right of a crack.

58 Belonging F5+ 2007
IIm A pleasant face with good climbing.

59 Doh F6b ★ 2007
IIm A short technical lower wall above the 'Homer block', always trending leftwards.

College Buttress: This buttress is situated at the right-hand end of the lower tier, to the right of the cut-through and facing the pool. It consists of a bay of rock with some excellent sport climbs and four long-neglected but worthwhile traditional climbs.

60 Old Fiends F6c+ 2006
IIm The wall above a bulge on perfect rock.

61 Carvery F6a+ 2006
IIm A calcite crack leads to a delicate face. Can be dusty.

62 The Wrong Unconquerable F6b ★ 2006
12m A classic crack on unusual rock to a fine finale on a layback flake. "It's the same as *Left Unconquerable* but the other way around."

63 Fartless F7a+ 2006
12m A short tricky section low down followed by a hard fingery sequence on the upper wall. Very bouldery (Font 7A).

64 Strap a Doc to Me F6b 2006
10m The unusually fluted face on the right. Worthwhile.

65 The Gypsy Kings F6c ★ 2006
12m An isolated arête between faces with fine climbing. Unusual.

66 Gooncrack F6b+   2007
10m The crack in the sidewall with a definite crux section.

67 Forfeit or Doom F6b+   2007
12m The arête with some good climbing above the pinnacle.

68 Meshrug a My Shoulders F6b   2009
12m The face above the right-hand side of the pinnacle on the ledge.

69 Profitless F6b ★   2006
12m Balancy face-climbing above the prominent ledge leads to a strenuous finale via a crack in the overlap.

70 Merry Pheasant E1 5c   1986
12m Thin grassy cracks to the right lead to another crack through the overlap.

71 Moontalk F6b+   2006
12m Technical face-climbing with a short hard section on the grey wall leads to tricky final moves on the headwall if the ledges to the left are avoided.

72 Frantic Manoeuvres E2 5c ★   1986
12m Fine climbing to the right via a ramp to a ledge. Finish via a short crack and thread (not in place).

73 Bonedigger E1 5b   1986
12m The prominent thin crack in the wall is unfortunately full of grass at the moment.

74 Prefect Day F6b ★   2006
12m Pleasant face-climbing with tricky moves over the final steepening.

75 Silently Sprung F6b ★   2011
12m The face and arête just to the right again.

76 Thirty Nine and a Half Steps E1 5b   1986
12m Vegetated rock to the right leads onto the left-hand side of the upper face.

77 White Wind F6a   2006
12m The final section of the face gives enjoyable climbing.

Dark Side Upper Tier

This is gained by either of two scrambles, one going up left of the first routes on the lower tier, the other up the steep grassy banking left of Cairn Sector.

Towards the left-hand side of the face, as the cliff diminishes in height, is a small bay followed by a grey wall just beyond. To the left of this are a number of very short sport climbs: **This is the End**, F5+ (2010), face with cracks; **The End is Nigh**, F5 (2010); slim face and arête; **Ending Now**, F6a (2010), arête; **Euroman Endeth**, F4 (2010), face on 'bobbles', **Endeth**, F5 (2010), slim face.

The next buttress 30m to the right gives: **It has to End Somewhere**, F6a (2005), slab trending leftwards to lower off; **Will it Never End**, F4+ (2006), left pillar; **Is this the End?**, F5 (2006), the central wall; **Coming to an End**, F6a+ (2006), the slim pillar; **End Games**, HVS 5a (2006), the crack on the sidewall to the right.

1 In My Darkest Hour F5   2008
11m   The left-hand side of the face.

2 Endsville F6a   2002
11m   The centre of the flat wall has a fingery finale.

3 Centreville F6a   2006
11m   The thin crack system just to the right.

4 Preston North End F6a   2006
11m   The thin crack to finish just left of a block

5 Will They? F5   2011
10m   The slim wall just left of the arête to the right.

6 People Will Talk F5   2002
11m   The pleasant arête gives enjoyable climbing.

7 The Parting of the Lips F5   2002
11m   The thin crack above the ledge.

8 Ear to Ear F6a   2002
12m   The face to the left of the twin traditional cracks.

9 Uncreased VS 4c   2002
12m   The left-hand and wider crack of two to the right.

10 Hairline VS 4c   2002
12m   The right-hand of the two cracks gives a better route.

11 The Mouth Waters F6c ★   2002
12m   The centre of the face. Excellent balance-climbing.

12 I'm a Port Vale Dribbler F6a   2010
11m   The slim pillar in the right-hand side of the bay.

13 George Stark Calling F6a+   2002
12m   The sharp arête tucked into the right-hand side of the bay. Climb it on its left-hand side.

To the right is a prominent protruding face which contains the next couple of routes.

14 Stark Disbelief F6c+   2002
15m Easy cracks lead to a blank-looking face. The holds may be subject to change whilst you are climbing this route!

15 The Dark Half F6b ★   2002
15m The prominent right-hand arête saves its difficulties for the moves off the half-height ledge.

16 Graveyard Blues F6b   2002
11m An isolated arête gives balancy moves at half-height.

17 In Stark Contrast F6c   2002
11m The high-level black wall. Technically excellent to the break. Steeper though easier above.

18 Ghost Writer F5+   2011
11m The pillar using a wide crack.

19 Under the Lifeline F6b   2010
11m The front face of the pillar to the right.

A wall set back at a slightly higher level gives:

20 Over the Deadline F6b   2002
11m The left-hand line on the wall provides its best route. Fingery moves at half-height.

21 Automatic Writing F6a+   2002
11m The centre of the wall passing a grassy ledge.

22 Fool's Stuffing F6b   2002
11m The right-hand side of the inset wall. Avoiding the chimney may prove difficult.

23 Pillar of Wisdom F6b   2002
11m The left-hand of three pillars. Start atop the grassy ledge system.

24 Invasion of the Creepazoid F6c+   2002
18m A scary pitch via the central pillar. Fingery and reachy. Start atop the insecure blocks.

25 Later that Night F6b+   2002
18m The right-hand of the three pillars with hard moves past the first two bolts. Use the crack on the left for a short section at mid-height.

26 The Coming of the Sparrows F5+   2002
15m The slab right of the prominent corner is hardest at the start. Keep to the line of bolts.

27 Flight of the Finches F6c   2010
15m Technical lower face and the pillar above.

28 Stop the Pigeon F6b+ 2002
11m Excellent moves. Technical climbing up the black slab ends atop an obvious pillar.

29 Pigeon Couped F6b 2014
18m A good route taking a thin crack with a hard move low down and easier climbing to the hand crack above.

30 Ken Dodd's Dad's Dog's Dead HVS 5b 2002
11m The wide crack leads to the belay of the next route.

31 Gathering Darkness F6c+ 2002
11m Climb direct up the smooth-looking slab to the right. A long reach may be essential. Unnerving.

32 A Trip on the Dark Side F6b ★ 2002
18m A long route up the centre of the wall. Good moves throughout with the difficulties around the 2nd bolt. **Photo opposite.**

33 Feel my Presence F6b+ 2002
16m Start via the corner before swinging right and up the satisfying arête. Better than it looks.

34 Tapenard F6a+ 2010
15m The face finishing leftwards above half-height.

Around to the right of the protruding buttress is an alcove and four pleasant routes.

35 Wild Olives F6b+ ★ 2002
18m Good wall-climbing above the alcove to the left. A long reach helps over the main overlap. Try to stay on the arête at the top.

36 Gorignak F6b ★ 2002
18m By starting through the prominent overhang to the right, the walls above give further good climbing. The crux lies at the top.

37 Galaxy Quest F6a ★ 2011
18m The long crackline and rib gives fine climbing.

38 Omega 13 F6a+ ★ 2002
18m A long sustained wall-climb to the right finishing via an obvious arête.

39 Dr Lazarus F6a+ 2002
11m A wide crack leads to a difficult rightwards exit.

Oliver Branagan on A Trip to the Dark Side, F6b (opposite page). Photo: Liam Dobson.

The Lower Tier

The lower tier is the first rock encountered upon entering the quarry. Although the routes might lack definition and stature compared to those on the upper tier, their friendly nature makes them a good starting point. The routes begin with a long groove line in the arête 20m to the right of the cut-through path: **Thank You Grooves**, F5 (2009).

Anarchy Sector: Situated in the far left-hand end of the lower tier this area offers a compact grey wall with excellent rock and a couple of titbits to its left. The cliff can have a very damp base after rain. To the left of a short arête is a wall at a slightly higher level: **Wallaclism**, F6b (2009), takes a leftwards line from a grassy ledge and **Arteaclism**, F6a+ (2009), climbs the sharp arête.

1 Overbored F5 2001
9m The short arête with an impressive borehole.

2 Getting the Groove F6a 2001
12m The lone groove further right, starting with an awkward corner.

3 Mine Anarchy F6a 2001
12m The pillar and wall above on sloping holds, all on the main black wall.

4 Only Ken's Anarchy Will Do F6b 2001
11m Climb direct to the left-hand side a of small overlap. Technical between the 1st and 2nd bolts.

5 Always Break the Rules F5+ 2001
10m A direct line with sustained moves on perfect rock.

6 Snap Decision F5 2001
11m The right side of the wall moving left to the belay.

Candy Sector: A longer section of wall with a handful of better routes. A good place to tick a lot in a very short time although some routes may feel very similar.

7 The Candy Man F6a+ ★ 2001
11m The final calcite-ridden slab gives an agreeable route, much like its right-hand twin.

8   Flossy's Slab F6a+ ★   2001
11m   Pleasant slab-climbing on the calcite to the right.

9   Toy Story F6a   2001
11m   Easier climbing from the left-hand side of a pancake of rock leads rightwards to the belay.

10   Suck on This F6a+   2001
10m   Strike direct through the obvious ledge system to climb the wall above. Hard starting moves.

11   Jelly Beans F6a+   2009
10m   The wall above the right-hand side of the ledge.

12   Smartie People are Happy People F6a ★ 2001
10m   The centre of the pleasant black wall with enjoyable moves. Can be made harder by sticking strictly to the line of bolts.

13   Candy Store F6a   2001
10m   Climb the right-hand arête of the black wall.

A prominent crack lies just to the right. The next route starts just right of this.

14   Tempting Children F6c+   2001
11m   Climb the difficult hanging groove above the ledge to the right.

15   Would You Like a Sweetie? F6c ★ 2001
11m   The best route on the sector. Climb direct via the slabby wall and overlap.

16   Bolts R Us F6a+   2001
11m   The arête to the right taken on its left-hand side and finishing via the face above. Worthwhile.

17   Sing for Your Dinner F6b+   2001
11m   From the base of a depression to the right trend leftwards across the wall.

To the right are three short and relatively uninteresting routes: **Do Little**, F6a (2006); **Playground Bully**, F6b+ (2006); **The Sweat Shop**, F6a (2006).

18   Totti for England F4   2006
11m   Pleasant climbing on an isolated slim slab.

Totty Sector: A nondescript wall in the centre of the lower tier. It offers a handful of easier routes and can be identified by a small, round cave at its foot.

19 A Bit of Totty F6a   2001
12m A short pillar and the steeper wall above. The best route on this section of cliff.

20 Top Totty F5+   2001
12m A leftward-rising line with sustained climbing.

21 Jelly Tots F4+   2001
9m The easy thin crack in centre of the wall.

22 Tiny Tots F5   2001
11m The better, left-hand, of two lines via a scoop.

23 Teeny Tots F5   2001
11m The rightmost line of the wall keeping to the rib.

Sumo Sector: Situated towards the right-hand side of the lower tier and opposite the entrance into the quarry, this area gives a broad selection of routes in the lower sport climbing grades and two tastier and harder morsels. The wall dries quickly.

24 The Jap's Eyes are on You F6b+   2001
10m The tricky wall keeping leftwards on the upper section.

25 Outside Tokyo F6b   2001
12m Start up the leftward-facing flake and go over the bulge. From the ledge easier climbing ensues.

26 Nagasaki Grooves 2 F6b   2001
12m The groove and flake with an awkward bulge provides the right-hand start.

27 Sumo F7a ★   2001
12m Hard, technical climbing. Keep to the overhung blunt arête to the right. Easier climbing from the ledge leads to the belay.

28 A Nip in the Air F6b   2001
11m The thin crack in the left wall of the obvious corner gives a sporting finale.

29 Geisha Grooves F6a   2001
11m The corner with good moves. Exit left to the belay.

30 Saweno Gancho F6c+   2001
12m The vague arête has blind and fingery moves.

31 Setting Son F6a   2001
11m The enjoyable shallow groove.

32 The Golden Goose F5   2002
12m A longer and easier route over ledgy ground.

33 **Hong Kong Fewy** F6a   2002
33 **Hong Kong Fewy** F6a   2002
9m   One hard move on the left wall of a low-level rib.

34 **The Rising Sun** F5+   2001
9m   Another short route via the blunt arête, with a hard initial move. Perfect rock.

35 **Kamikaze Clone** F6a+   2001
11m   Climb the right-hand side of a low-level rib, then the right-hand side of the short arête above.

36 **Shang-Hai** F6b   2009
12m   The lower wall right of the crack with a steep finale.

37 **Riding Shogun** F6b   2001
12m   The pillar to the right.

Further right are four more routes.

38 **Fuji Fantastic** F6a   2006
12m   A steep slim wall.

39 **Picture This** F6a+   2008
11m   The pleasant slim pillar.

40 **Jokoharma** VS 5a   2006
11m   A flake crack in a scoop 12m to the right.

41 **The Bullet** F7a   2006
11m   The difficult wall to the right.

The Upper Tier

Poised Block Buttress: The leftmost buttress. The left-hand section is known as Nidge's Wall which can be gained by easy scrambling up to its left-hand side from below.

1   What's the Paint? F5   2006
15m   The left-hand line with the hardest moves low down.

2   Pity the Graffiti F5   2006
15m   A long rib with a steep pull over an initial bulge.

3   Set Fred Free F6a   2006
15m   The wall right of a grassy corner, to a steep finale.

4   Wilky's Revenge F5+   2006
15m   The central line gives the best of the easier pitches.

5   Making Plans for Nidge F6b   2006
15m   Takes a line through the left-hand side of the alcove and past Nidge himself.

6   Helzapoppin' F7a   2006
15m   A superb stamina exercise through the centre of the alcove and over the roofs above. Doesn't let up.

7   Right Said Fred F6b   2006
15m   Climbs over the right-hand side of the roof.

Zebedee and **Greensleeves,** both VS (1960s), took the right side of the wall, although their lines are unclear.

8   Coyote Club F6a   2006
15m   Takes the left-hand side of the low wall and can be used to gain routes on Nidge's Wall.

9   Wile E. Coyote F6a ★   1999/2014
15m   Excellent face-climbing via a runnel and easier face above.

10   Beep Beep F6a+ ★   2014
15m   A tricky overlap leads onto excellent face-climbing.

11   Road Runner F5 ★   1999/2014
15m   A very pleasant face-climb, now more direct with fine open climbing.

12   Running for Cover F5+ ★★   2014
15m   A fine direct route with a tricky upper crux.

13   The Run Off F4   2014
15m   The final route on the face.

The Crazy Pinnacle: This is roughly 50m to the right and sitting at a slightly higher level. **Slob Team Special**, HS (1979), climbs the left-hand groove on the front face of the pinnacle and **Crazy Pinnacle Face**, HS (1960s), climbs the right-hand groove finishing via the arête.

Dave Smith on Full Frontal, F6c+ (page 477). Photo: Niall Grimes.

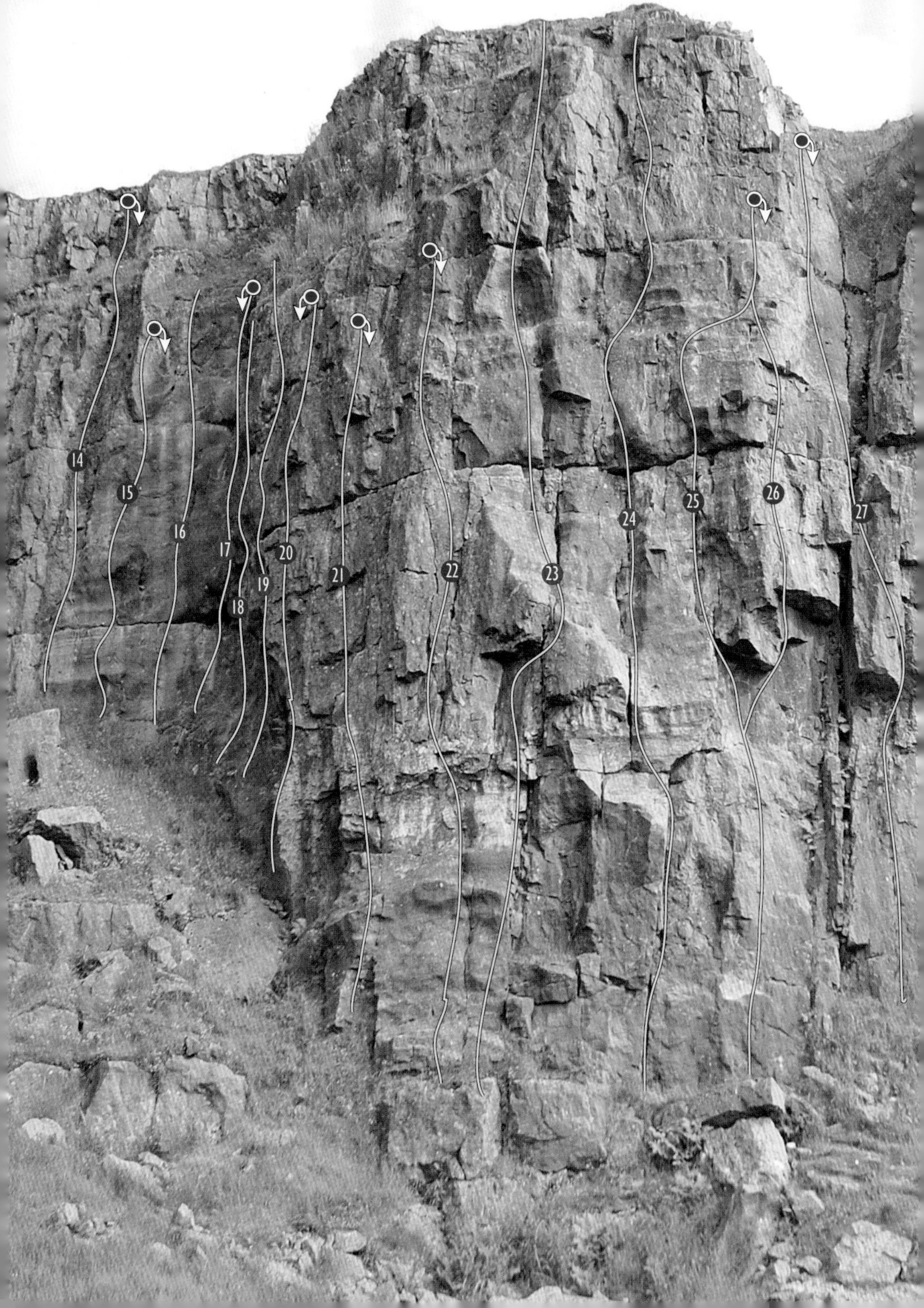
14
15
16
17
18
19
20
21
22
23
24
25
26
27

Papacy Buttress: The first buttress developed on the cliff both traditionally and as a sport climbing venue. Long routes abound in the mid to high F6s with a very pleasant feeling of exposure accompanying them. Here, sport and trad live happily together. The trad lines should not be overlooked. The right-hand side of the face receives the sunshine from around 2.30pm in the summer but can feel uncomfortably cold in breezy conditions.

14 Angleterre F5 2009
10m The rib and shallow groove up the gully on the left-hand side of the face.

15 This England F7a+ 1998
12m The hard, blank-looking face with fingery moves. A long reach helps.

16 Pleasant Valley Sunday E1 5b 1998
12m The crack to the right gives pleasant climbing after a tricky start.

17 Upthrutch VS 4c 1960s
12m The water-washed crack. Vegetated.

18 Grit Arête F7a 1998
12m Very rough rock and unusually rounded moves on the blunt arête.

19 Snake Eyes E3 5c ★ 1998
12m The snaking crack. Good.

20 Strangled at Birth F6c ★ 1998
14m A tucked-away route, with fine face-moves on rough black rock. Swing left around the arête then step right onto the wall. Urgent moves leftwards lead to an easier finish above the break.

21 Sincerely Yours F6b ★ 2006
18m Very pleasant face-climbing with an easy start and tricky central section.

22 I'm in the Sin Bin F6a 2006
18m Thin cracks and a shallow groove to finish.

23 Sin City E1 5b 2006
25m After a short grassy crack, climb the hanging groove above the bulge passing an overlap to a ledge and break. Finish directly up an excellent steep, thin crack.

24 Seven Deadly Sins HVS 5a ★★ 1966/1967
25m A classic traditional line. Climb into a corner and exit quickly left onto a ledge. Continue up the shallow groove and crack to a break and bulge. Overcome this directly – not on the left – to gain better holds in the prominent finishing groove. Take care with the final holds.

25 Coral Seas F6a ★★ 1994
18m A high-quality line of considerable merit. Take the initial rib direct before transferring left. A tricky bulge then leads to a rightwards exit across the finely positioned slab.

26 Avarice Allsorts F6c+ ★ 1998
18m The roofs that *Coral Seas* avoids, taken head-on. The upper arête is superb.

The next routes lie right of the wide crack, **Lust**, VS 4b (1966).

Dan Osbaldeston on Rocky Variations, F6b+ (page 477). Photo: sportsclimbs.co.uk.

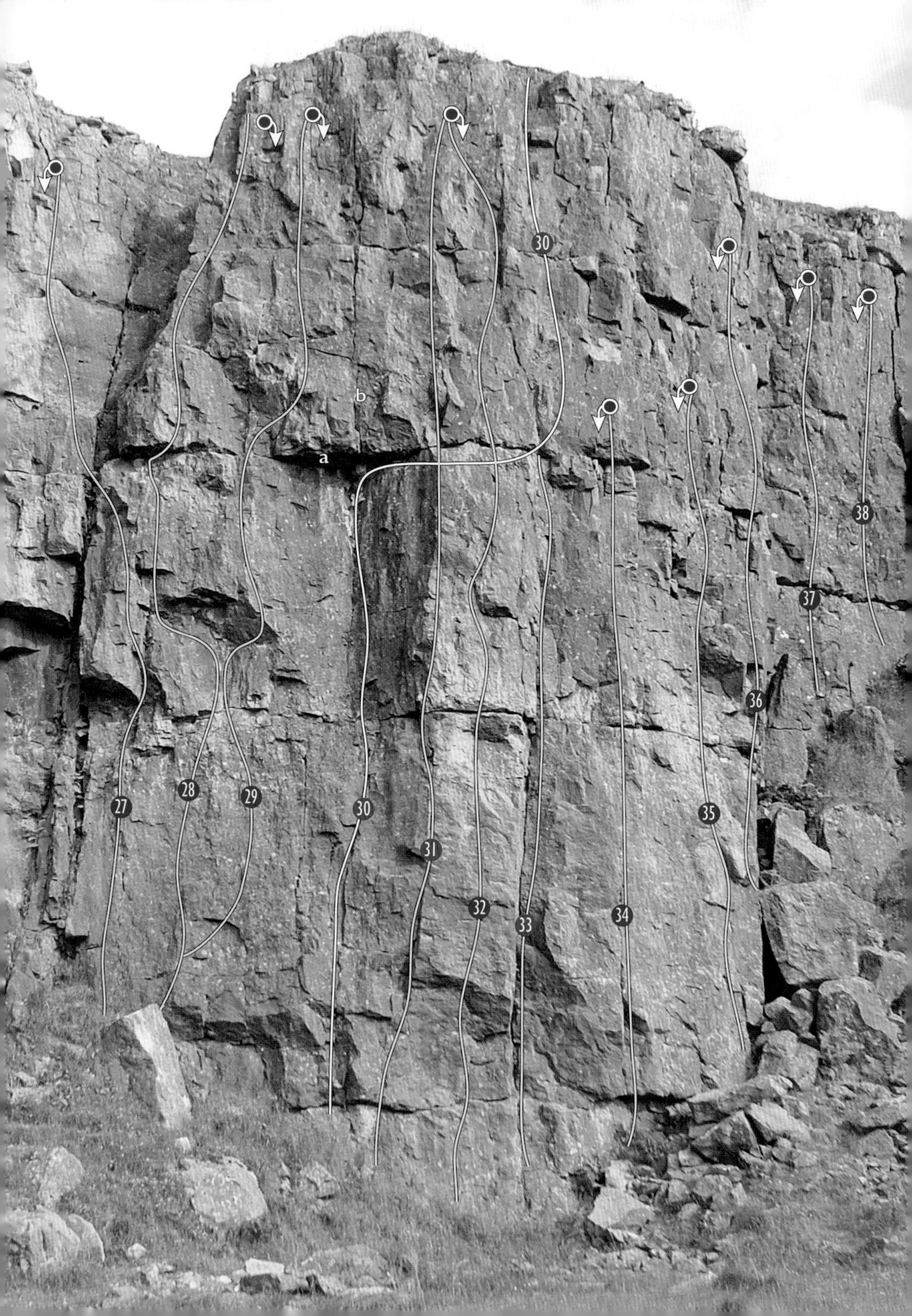
30
b
a
38
37
36
27
28
29
30
35
31
32
33
34

27 Ask Mr. T. for Tea F7a 2011
20m A line with hard moves to meet *Rocky Variations*. Finish by stepping left and climbing the left side of the runnel.

28 Rocky Variations F6b+ ★★ 1994
20m The left-hand of two fine pitches beginning atop a grey block. Sustained, though never too hard. Exit the scoop leftwards and take the overhang above from the right. **Photo on page 474.**

29 Apollo Creed F6b ★★ 1994
20m The right-hand twin provides a hard move exiting the right-hand side of the scoop. More rests accompany this route.

30 Seven Deadly Virtues E1 5b ★★ 1960s
30m A good climb. Gain the groove and follow it to the overhang. Avoid this by a surprisingly long traverse to the right. Finish up a shallow groove. Worth bringing a trad rack for. **a One Deadly Variant**, HVS 5b (1960s), avoids the capping overhang by a move left and follows the scoop and wall above. **b Luddite Thought Police**, E3 6a ★★ (1994), takes the roof and subsequent crack direct.

31 Penal Servitude E2 5b ★ 1994
28m Climb the arête of the open groove, mainly by its left-hand side, gaining it via a thin crack. Once the mid-height break is gained, continue directly and delicately up the face above to gain the top via a shallow arête.

32 Full Frontal F6c+ ★★ 1994
22m A great route taking the central pillar. Most avoid the hard start by sneaking in from the right. There is then a mid-height crux. **Photo on page 465.**

33 El Camino Real E1 5b ★★ 1994
30m The prominent cracked groove to the right gives superb and well-protected climbing. Where it begins to run out, carry on up the much shallower continuation groove with much less comforting protection.

34 Power of Soul F7b+ ★★ 1994
18m A faint, thin crack with very hard moves past the third bolt. Needs cool conditions.

35 Dementia Normale F6a 1998
18m A way of not doing *Power of Soul* on-sight. A pleasant crack and groove to its right leads eventually to a belay above. **Photo below.**

36 The Last Straw F6b 2001
18m Appropriately named. A thin crack is hardest low down.

37 Figure of Law F7a ★ 1998
15m A hidden gem taking the towering wall at the top of the gully. Hard above the third bolt.

38 I am the Law F6b+ 2006
12m The thin cracks are gained by a difficult manoeuvre.

Dimentia Normale, F6a (this page). Photo: Ian Parnell.

Exclusion Zone Area: Good rock on the bolted routes. The wall containing *The Exclusion Zone* is the first to receive any sunshine on the upper tier - about 2pm.

39 Danny Cool F5   2009
9m The slim rib leading up and to the left.

40 Cool Danny F6b   1998
12m Tackle the strip overhang direct to reach the face above.

41 Ta Jim E1 5b   2001
18m Climb the left of two grooves exiting with caution.

42 Getting the Groove E1 5b   2001
18m The right-hand groove is better but also loose.

43 Screaming Wheels F6b+ ★   1998
15m A finely positioned arête taken direct at the start. Keep to the arête higher up. Named after the local race track.

44 Swain's World F6b ★   2006
15m Fine exposed climbing just right of the arête of the buttress. Steep, urgent but juggy. **Photo opposite.**

45 No Man's Land F6c   1999
18m The left-hand branch off *The Exclusion Zone* with a bouldery start and harder finale. Can be mossy high up.

46 The Exclusion Zone F6c ★★   1998
18m The centre of the west-facing wall gives a superb pitch on surprising holds. Take care clipping the first bolt.

47 The Iron Curtain F6b ★   1999
18m An easier alternative to the previous route with pleasant sustained moves leading to a steep finale. Not quite as fine, but still very worthwhile.

48 Lachesis E1 5a   1970s
18m The corner via numerous loose blocks.

49 Mouse Hunt F6c   1998
18m A hard start and excellent, though runout, upper wall.

50 Slowly, Slowly Catch a Monkey F6a+ 2009
18m The groove followed by thin crack and pillar.

51 Thing Thang F7a   1998
11m The better of two short routes to the right.

Ian Carr on Swain's World, F6b (opposite page). Photo: Gary Gibson.

52 Thang Thing F7a 1998
11m The right-hand, poorer line for puerile tickers only.

53 Slab de Lune F6a+ 2011
15m The centre of the slab gives good climbing when clean.

54 Master of a Lune F6b 2009
15m The slim face to the right.

55 Sack of Stones F6b+ ★ 1998
15m A hard start if taken direct. Easier above via a thin crack finish. F6a+ using the left arête.

56 Bag of Bones F6a+ ★★ 1998
15m A sustained face-climb just left of a block. Excellent.

57 Plate of Scones F6b+ 2006
15m A surprising find with a trying crux from the ledge.

58 Sara Laughs F6b 1998
15m A technical wall above the centre of the lower ledge.

59 Tenth Heaven F6b 2008
15m A pleasant technical face leading to an easy crack.

60 Calci Mauve F6b ★★ 1998
20m A long Portlandesque route beginning up the front face of a pillar, building up to a very fine finish on beautiful calcite-covered rock. Avoid the wide crack on the right.

61 Glas Double F7a 1999
20m The desperately fingery right-hand variant.

62 Flakey Pastry HVS 5a 2006
20m The fine flake crack in the corner leads to a lower off.

Prophecy Buttress: The cliff receives sunshine from late afternoon and on a fine summer evening you can be setting off on your last route at gone 10pm. What pleasure!

63 Over the Hill F6c ★★ 2001
18m A classic thin-crack climb leads to an overlap from where good, open face moves lead to the top.

64 Nostalgia E4 6a ★ 1998
22m The snaking crack. May soon be bolted at F6c+.

65 The Omen F6b ★★ 2006
20m The long crack and groove gives a fine outing.

66 Yogi Bear F7a ★ 1998
18m The blackened face with intricate moves on hidden holds. The face above is taken just to the left of the bolts. Easier for the tall.

67 Four Telling Tales F6c+ ★★ 1998
18m The thin crack and left-hand side of the arête. Balance and friction climbing at their best.

68 The Talisman F7a ★ 1998
18m The right-hand side of the arête. Hard above the fourth bolt with 'barn-door' moves to gain *Four Telling Tales*.

69 Bleingassen F6b+ ★ 2006
20m The long shallow groove finishing via the arête and a ledge at the top. Has a short hard section after 9m.

70 The Oracle F7b ★ 1998
11m Super-technical face-climbing up the short, blank-looking face.

71 The Prophecy F7a ★★ 1998
20m The original route of the wall and a classic if the line is adhered to. The lower wall is taken direct up the line

of bolts. A hard bulge and long reach gain the break. The upper arête is taken direct and is fairly 'out there'.

72 Supernatural F6a ★★ 2006
20m A superb new addition taking the long thin crack to a hard finish. Well worth seeking out.

73 The Indian Cottage F6c+ 1998
12m An arête and blocky overlap provide two good moves.

74 I Predict a Roti F6a 2009
20m A long route following the scoop and flying arête.

75 Aloo Gobi F6c 1999
11m A short hard route via an overlap and wall.

76 Pappadum Groove F6a 1998
9m A short shallow groove of little quality.

77 Quartz Initial F6b 1998
9m A one move wonder up the very short arête.

Z Victor I, HVS 4c (1960s), gains the cave up via the groove of *Duma Key* and exits it on the left via a groove.

78 Duma Key F6a   2009
18m A blocky start leads to a steep finger-crack finale.

79 Viagra Falls F6c+ ★   1998
15m A hard start over the bulge to the left of the crack in the slab to the right leads to enjoyable face-climbing right of the flake. The upper overlap provides a thuggy finish.

80 Different Season F6a ★   1998
15m The thin crack with an airy start. Sustained.

81 Apt Pupil F6c ★   1998
18m Escalating difficulties on the lower face right of the crack lead to a trying overlap and airy moves to gain the belay.

82 In the Gravy F6a ★   1998
20m A long pitch using the summit of the pinnacle gives enjoyable face-climbing above.

83 From Cradle to Grave F6c ★   1998
20m The sidewall left of the corner. Taken direct, especially at the top, gives a route high in its grade. Slinking off left does not count.

All Souped Up, VS 4c (1999), is the corner.

84 Calcite Claws F6c ★   1998
11m A great little pitch which belies its length. Take the arête to the right head on.

85 So Veneer F6b   1999
11m Two difficult moves on the right-hand side of the arête lead to the belay of the previous route.

86 The End F6a   2001
9m Appropriately named. Hard at the start.

Mark Rankine on Cairn, F7a (page 485.). Photo: Rankine collection.

Cairn Sector

The best section of the lower tier, this area of crag can be found at its right-hand end, just to the right of the access path to the upper tier. It contains one of the cliff's classics in the form of a striking, eyelash flake and a number of other worthy routes. These walls dry very quickly, catch any wind that's going and receive the sun's rays from about 2.30pm onwards in the summer.

1 Inconsiderate Blinking F6a+   2002
11m   Situated on the left-hand fringe of the wall is this obvious arête gained via a tricky start.

2 Hey Diddle Diddle E1 5b   2003
15m   The jamming crack to the right leads to moves right to gain the lower-off of the next route.

3 Unilateral Thinking F6c   1999
12m   A short, steep wall and vague arête to its right complete with an array of calcite features.

4 Collateral Damage E3 5c   1999
12m   The crack. A steep exit gains the belay of the next route.

5 The Light F7a ★   1998
12m   Fine climbing. The centre of the white wall.

6 Take Flight F7a   2002
12m   The thin crack and arête are harder than they look.

The next three routes make great second pitches to *The Misfits* and *Hissin' Sid*. Gain them by scrambling carefully up the gully, rope in-situ, to below the left-hand side of the arête where there is a bolt belay.

7 Buxton Goes French F6b+   1994
12m   The slim face between the two wide cracks. Avoid touching the two cracks. F5+ if you don't!

8 Outer Limits F6b ★   1994
12m   A superb little pitch taking the left-hand side of the arête. Photogenic at 9.30pm on a summer evening.

9 The Twilight Zone F6a+ — 1994
11m The right side of the arête is surprisingly problematic.

10 Argy Bargy F5 — 2006
11m Pleasant climbing on the left-hand side of the face.

11 The Misfits F6a — 2002
15m The pillar and short headwall. Limited quality.

12 Hissin' Sid F6b — 1994
15m A difficult overlap and the pleasant wall above.

13 Slippery Bill HVS 5a — 1994
15m A vague shallow groove line.

14 Ratline F7b+ ★★ — 1994
12m A desperately thin, thin crackline. May seem easier on a redpoint but does not on-sight! Superb moves.

15 Cairn F7a ★★★ — 1994
12m A true classic taking the prominent angled flake. Gaining it and finishing direct provide the main difficulties. **Photo on page 483. a Stealth**, F7a ★ (1994), is a sharp and painful right-hand finish.

16 Two Cave Gully VS 4b — 1960s
12m The dirty corner via a traverse above the overhang.

17 Great White F5+ ★ — 1994
12m Pleasant slab-climbing above the overlap. **Orca**, F6b (1994), climbs direct over this.

18 The Naked Spur F4+ ★ — 2002
12m A pleasant pitch up the sharp right arête of the slab.

19 Assault and Battery F6b+ — 2002
10m A short fingery exercise in the back of the bay.

20 Trial and Error F7a+ — 1994/2012
10m The overhanging arête. Above the ledge, finish direct via easier but still technical climbing. Good moves.

21 Senile Delinquents F5 ★ — 1994
15m A flake and crack finishing via an overlap.

22 Cabin Fever F6b — 2003
15m The crack, roof and short wall.

23 Fred Flintstone VS 4b — 1994
10m The left side of wall with a peculiar 'worm' feature.

24 Barney Rubble VS 4c — 1994
10m The crack in the centre of the wall climbed direct.

25 Yabba Dabba Doo VS 4b — 1994
10m A direct line via a large hole to the right.

26 Breakfast at Safeways F6b — 1994
10m The left-hand side of the slab, with a high first bolt. Becoming a little slippery.

27 99p Special F6a+ — 1994
10m Start up the thin crack and finish up *Food for Sport*.

28 Jam Butty Mines Crack VS 4c ★ 1966
12m The obvious slanting crack with a tricky start.

29 Food for Sport F6a 1994
10m The pleasant right arête of the wall.

30 Over Easy F6b 2008
10m The right-hand side of the arête proves quite tricky.

31 Bluto HVS 4c 1960s
12m The broad groove to the right, avoiding a precarious
block on the left in favour of the arête and groove.

Avarice, VS 4b (1966), climbs the right-hand groove.

32 Full Set F6a+ 2006
10m Technical face-climbing on the right-hand side of
the wall. Blinkers essential.

Gluttony, S (1960s), climbs the groove further right.

33 Short Sport F6b 2010
8m The short face to the right has three bolts. The arête
to the right is **BYGOF**, F6a (2011).

The Sanctuary

This offers a number of shorter and easier routes on
excellent compact rock. It faces south-west, is relatively
sheltered and receives sunshine from midday onwards although seepage will be a problem after long spells of rain.

The best approach to this cliff is by descending the slope
below the end of Cairn Sector, behind the concrete posts
alongside *Breakfast at Safeways*, and walking leftwards,
facing out. The first five routes lie on a wall at the left-hand
side of the crag. These are nothing more than fillers-in.

1 By Caesarean F5+ 2002
10m The first wall taken direct. Some crunchy bits.

2 New Arrivals F6a 2002
10m Starting up the rib gains the previous belay.

3 Expecting F4+ 2002
10m Marginally better. A vague leftwards groove line.

4 Induction Program F5 2002
10m A steeper line, though no less juggy, to the right.

5 Premature F6a 2008
10m The line to the right.

6 Safe Haven F5+ 2001
18m The first of a trio of longer routes just right of a grassy flake. Some hollow holds exist, so be careful.

7 The Hollow Man F5+ 2001
18m A better and more direct line to the right to finish via an easier slab.

8 The Christian Salvage Man F6a ★ 2001
18m Named after the local security guard that you may meet. The better of the longer routes here. A small pillar and bulge lead to jug-pulling up the wall and a crack to finish.

9 Which Depp-Artment F6a+ 2001
11m A short route taking an awkward bulge.

10 Ichabod F5 2001
11m An easier line on the wall to the right with a problematic finish.

11 Sleepy Hollow F6a ★ 2001
11m A fine steep little pitch taking the vague blunt arête in the centre of the grey face on exquisite holds.

12 Bonny Helena F5 2011
11m Squeezed in but good, just to the right.

13 Gone for a Tim Burton F5 2001
11m A direct line up the jug-filled wall.

14 The Height Below F4+ 2002
11m Even easier up a brown streak left of a wide crack.

15 The Sanctuarian F6c 2001
11m Gains the left-hand side of the prominent overlap, with an evil crux over it.

16 For Haven's Sake F6b ★ 2001
11m The first of a fine trio of routes to the right.

17 Downtown F6b ★ 2001
11m Climb a wall to finish in a shallow groove: **Photo on page 406.**

18 What Lies Beneath F6b 2001
11m The wall, with an excellent finish.

19 Haven or Hell F6a+ 2002
9m The isolated pillar with surprisingly steep moves.

The Playground

This is the area of cliff around to the right of and slightly up from Cairn Sector. It forms a perfect grassy bay with a number of small walls of excellent rock. The bay gets the sun and due to its sheltered nature can be an excellent venue during winter and spring.

1   Edge Play F5   2007
10m   The left-hand wall of the slim groove.

2   Play Corner VS 4c   2007
1m   The narrow corner.

3   Play Doh F6a   2007
10m   The right-hand wall of the groove with a tricky start.

4   Sons of the Desert VS 4c   2002
9m   The small buttress to the right via a crackline in the arête and then a niche and groove above.

5   Helter Skelterer F6a+   2008
11m   A pleasant face above a tricky start.

6   Duelling Trousers HVS 5a   2002
11m   The wide crack and flake just right.

7   Pachucho Cadaver F6a ★   2000
11m   Follow a corner to an exit rightwards below the impressive steep headwall. Follow the centre of this to difficult finishing moves up the central shallow scoop. Super rock and excellent moves.

8   Hard Player F6b+ ★   2007
11m   The steep nose with a big rockover move.

9   I'm not a Player F4   2007
11m   The shallow groove and crack.

10   Playground Attraction F7a+ ★   2008
11m   A very technical crack and face.

11   The Hex F6c+   2008
11m   The tricky crack soon eases.

12   Ripsaw F7a   2008
11m   The pleasant blunt arête. Move right to belay.

13   Terror of the Towers F7a+ ★   2008
11m   The desperate face.

14   E for Friction E1 5b   2000
11m   The obvious, leftward-angled crack gained via a short vertical crack below. Tape up for this one, it bites!

15 Whose is Casey? F6a 2002
11m The slim face with a tricky central section.

The cracks to the right are: **That Ball, Love**, VS 4b (2000), and the corner on the right is **Clackers Sprained my Knackers**, S (2000).

16 Leben Tod F6a+ 2001
9m The left-hand side of the slim arête.

17 Spinball Wizard F6b 2008
9m The flat front face.

The next group of routes can be found on a series of pillars to the right.

18 Hamlet Prince of Players F6a+ 2007
9m The steep front face of the first pillar using the right arête.

19 William's Plays Shakespeare F6a+ 2007
9m The face and arête with a steep finale.

The crack is **As You Like it Played,** HVS 5a (2007).

20 Flog the Lume F6a 2008
9m The face using its right-hand arête.

The corner is **Much Ado about Playing**, S (2007), and the left-hand side of the cracked wall is **Taming of the Shrew'd Player**, HVS 5a (2007).

21 A Comedy of Played Errors F6a+ 2007
9m The arête with a high first clip and steep moves.

22 Did Romeo Play F4 2007
9m The easier arête.

23 With Juliet F6a+ 2007
9m The arête in the back of the baywithout the crack to the left.

The arête is **Othellow, Player of Venice**, E2 5c (2007), and the corner and roof to a slab is **Play it Again Sam**, E1 5b (2007).

24 A Merchant Played in Venice F4 2007
9m The arête on the right.

The Retreat

A newly-developed cliff with a a handful of short traditional routes and a larger number of sport routes. Access to these is by dropping down to The Sanctuary and following a vague path up into the basin of rock. It is very shady and gets some sun late in the evening in summer.

1 Clean Team F5+   2014
11m A slim cracked face to the left of the small bay.

2 Mean Team F4   2014
11m An easy slab with a tricky start. Stay out of the crack.

3 Cart the Wheel F6a   2014
11m A good little route with a tricky/long reach start.

4 Jamma yer Hut F6a+   2014
11m The thin crack in the wall.

5 Slip yer Foot F6a+   2014
12m The short groove and crack to the right. Better.

6 Bust yer Gut F6b+   2014
12m Just that. Thrash the arête to a finale on *Slip yer Foot*.

7 Unfinished Business F7b ★   2014
12m The left-hand side of the jutting prow. Start up the layback crack and launch, literally, up the left-hand side of the arête. Harder for the short.

8 Fin de Siecle F7a ★★   2014
12m The right-hand side of the arête of the prow. Great climbing in an out-there position.

9 Combien de Siecles? F7a+ ★   2014
12m The centre of the wall to the right beginning with a short jamming crack. Just one l-o-n-g reach or levitation. How many?

10 Irrational F7a+   2014
15m The left-hand line on the lower wall to the right. A slight thrash to get to. Use the left-hand arête of the corner. The finish is tough.

11 The Butch Master F6b+ ★   2014
15m The imposing layback to the right gained by a small gully and wall. The name should give you a clue.

12 Retro Rockets F6c+ ★   2014
18m A short, steep and hard wall leads to great climbing on the leaning headwall.

13 Let it Go F6c ★ 2014
18m The easier, although still steep, wall to the right. Finish first left then right of the arete.

The next group of routes are situated on the walls over to the right. These are much more overhanging than first appearances might suggest.

14 Gullied F5 2014
11m Pleasant climbing up an arête and pillar.

15 The Gully Folk F6b 2014
10m The left wall of the gully via a thin crack. Contrived but worthwhile.

16 Sub-Atomic F7a 2014
10m The mean wall just right of the gully.

17 Atomic Tommy Cooper E2 5c 2002
10m The wall via an undercut flake. Bold but good.

18 Clay Man VS 4c 2001
11m The prominent wide crack, the left-hand of two.

19 Dog Canute E1 5b ★ 2001
12m The superb jamming crack to the right.

20 Yardcore E3 5c ★ 2002
12m The bold arête, starting on its right-hand side.

21 Shardlowcore F5 2014
9m A short affair right of the gully.

22 No Retreat F6a+ 2014
10m The arête with a fingery finale.

23 Beat Retreat F6b ★ 2014
12m The wall. Steep, but jugs, jugs, jugs.

24 Couples Retreat F6b+ 2014
12m The crack gained via a difficult entry from the right.

25 Retreaty F7a 2014
12m The mean wall. Contrived but good.

26 VLC F6c 2014
12m The crack. All is not what it seems and if only you knew the meaning!

27 SLF F6a+ 2014
12m The wall to the right with a very peculiar hold.

28 MLT F4 2014
12m The final route of the wall via steps and a long move.

Aldery Cliff

Trad: 45 (D to E3)
Aspect: South-east **Sunshine:** Till mid-afternoon **Season:** All year
Conditions: Sheltered, friendly, some polish, vegetation and loose rock in sections
Best for: Mid-grade slabs on cool days and summer evenings **Approach:** Roadside

A sunny wooded quarry in the midst of some of the Peak District's best scenery. Aldery Cliff is an unusual and rightly popular crag with many memorable slab climbs, from the lower grades, to a few steeper testpieces. It is highly recommended for experienced climbers operating up to mid-extreme, but take care with novices.

Since the BMC has taken over ownership of the crag, there has been extensive work on tree management, clearing the summer brambles and nettles that used to blight the crag and the installation of a safety cable along the crag-top and down the descent path.

Whilst cleaning and checking routes for this guidebook, a significant number of new routes were put up and old routes were rescued, making it well worth a return visit for those who are familiar with the crag.

Warning: Aldery Cliff has some areas of very unstable rock as described in the text (especially the bulges on the far right of the crag). It also has some friable and loose rock on routes and ledges so be attentive when leading and belaying, especially on the less well-travelled routes.

Conditions and Aspect: It is fairly quick-drying on the clean lines. It gives welcome shade on a summer evening. The slabby classics, although a little polished, haven't been ruined by traffic and the steeper climbs, having something of a reputation, can be almost pristine.

Care is required on the exposed crag-top path and descent after rain as it can become dangerously slippery, as can the longer routes with muddy topouts. Alternative descents are by abseil from equipped trees/stumps, sometimes half-way up the crag, to avoid the occasional unpleasantly vegetated and friable second pitches. Some of the lesser climbs also suffer from loose finishes and vegetation.

The Climbing: There are about sixty routes from Diff to the mid-Extremes with the best being long classics on good rock, mainly protectable, although the harder routes tend to be bolder.

Parking and Approach: Situated on the valley side of the minor road heading south-east from Earl Sterndale, towards the hamlet of Crowdecote, at the junction with the B5055 Longnor Road. It sits opposite the distinctive ice-cream-cone property of High Wheeldon (that contains the Neolithic site of Fox Hole Cave). The walk-in is one of the shortest in the Peak with the car park directly below the crag. Belaying from the car is possible but not compulsory. There is room for about six cars, if parked considerately, although blocking folk in shouldn't be a problem, because they will never be far away.

A walk down the hill after a bus to Earl Sterndale is the best public transport option. The Quiet Woman pub is a good post-crag stop off, with excellent pork pies.

Access: The crag is owned by the BMC. Care must be taken not to damage boundary walls and fences. If the parking is full, please park considerately ensuring you don't block the road or gates. Always shut the gate.

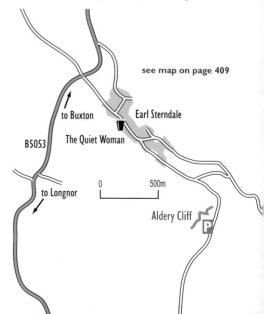

see map on page 409

Fran Santos on Surface Plate, HVS 5a (page 499). Photo: Eric Andrew.

Left-Hand Walls

On the far left is a gated cave entrance in a corner. The first route takes the left-hand crack left of the cave; its original direct exit is now very loose and overgrown:

1 Sword and Stone E2 5c 1985
12m The steep, thin crack to hands on a ledge, then traverse a break rightwards, across the corner, to a ledge-belay on the right. It is possible to continue on loose rock and vegetation above the belay, or escape by abseil, using saplings down and right, or from the stump up and right.

2 The High Crusade E2 5c 1985
10m Make surprisingly pressing moves diagonally up the right-hand crack and above the corner to the ledge-belay on the right.

3 Hidden Corner VS 4b 1960s
10m Pass ominous blocks up the corner to the previous belay; not for the faint-hearted. The bold VS 4b arête just right is friable and best avoided.

4 Best Forgotten Groove HVS 5b 2012
11m Ten metres right, the left-facing groove direct to the ledge. Lower off from the tree stump above.

5 The Constant Gardener HVS 5b 2012
11m The wall between *Best Forgotten Groove* and *Therianthropic*. A technical start up the centre of the wall, then cracks to a steep finish; lower off the stump above.

6 Therianthropic HVS 5b 1974
12m The wide crack has a hard finish. The old finish up the easier but broken wall above is bold and usually overgrown, so most will lower off the stump.

7 Jackorner VS 4c ★ 1974
15m Pull out a plum with this testing steep corner at the top of its grade. Traverse left up the broken wall to the tree stump lower-off or continue up the broken arête and vegetation above.

8 Perrin's Arête E2 5c ★ 2012
12m The arête left of *Cooper's Route*. Steep fingery climbing direct up the arête, from its left. Lower off from the tree. High side-runners in the crack to the left at this grade.

9 Cooper's Route E3 6a ★ 1960s/1977
12m Intimidating moves with fiddly pro to enter the hanging crack, then finger-lock up to glory. A real test-piece (for all but the tall). Lower off from the tree. **Lethanol** is E2 5b (1979), the serious wall to the right.

10 November Wall E2 5b ★ 1977
14m The delightful wall to the right on holds that just keep coming, unlike the protection. Super-fun but super bold, so no place for ditherers. The dirty left-slanting crack just right is **Symphonic Crack**, S (1979).

11 Carmel E1 5b 2012
15m A technical eliminate immediately left of *Timber* (HVS with a side-runner) requires care with the odd suspect hold and can get overgrown. Best finished at the tree stump.

12 Timber VS 4c 1974
15m If clean, the crack system gives worthwhile climbing to the same stump. Watch out for a wobbly suspect block.

Left-Hand Walls   Mitre Area   Ash Tree Area   Right-Hand Walls

13 Rentaghost S 4b 1974

15m The next crack also has a hard start and a wobbly block. Dirtier and usually more vegetated than *Timber*.

The overgrown rock to the right once hosted: **The Clone of Jeremiah**, VS 4c (1979), the thin crack; **Nazi Baby**, S (1979), the horrible gully and **Lost Thread**, HVS 5b (1970s), the crack on the right to *The Arête*.

The Mitre Area

14 The Arête E1 5b ★★ 1959

20m A brilliant climb with a technical start leading to a committing crux on fiddly gear, that many climbers baulk at, and another hard move above. Especially tricky for the short but tamed a little by micro-cams.

15 Mitre Crack VS 4c ★★ 1959

20m Good holds and good protection as you zigzag up this delightfully sustained route. An absolute must for visiting VS leaders.

16 Chance in a Marillion E3 6a 1986

20m A tasty slab eliminate with a crimpy midway crux and a delicate finish; spaced but good gear and escapable.

17 The Cardinal VS 4c ★ 1959

20m Less sustained than its neighbouring crack but with almost gritstone character. Work your way up and right into the corner and climb this to a well-positioned and polished exit. **a The Actress**, HVS 5b (1985), is a direct boulder problem start.

18 The Bishop HVS 5b ★★ 1960s

23m Tricky off-balance movement at the start (the slippiness indicates countless climbers not thinking about footwork), leads to easier moves up into the corner and a junction with *The Cardinal*. Just below the top, take the break out right in a superb position onto the cracked slab and follow this to the ledge.

19 Arch Bishop E2 5b ★   traditonal

25m The hanging arête left of *Sycamore Crack*. Start as for Sycamore Crack, traverse the horizontal break left, arrange gear and go for it on thin moves up the arête. Exciting stuff!

20 Sycamore Crack HS 4c   1959

23m A good start pulling out of the overhanging recess normally leads to disappointment. The cracked slab above is normally dirty, vegetated and home to vicious biting ants.

To the right, **Jeremy's Jungular Jaunt**, S (1979), and **Jackdaw Gully**, HD (1959), are both overgrown. The clean slab to the right again has nice rock and the first two climbs are recommended. They are often finished at the tree stump but the solid arête above is good fun.

21 Carmen Jones VS 4b ★   1959

25m The delectable arête gained diagonally from the start of *Carmen*, with a committing crux to reach the upper ledge. **a** A direct start up a groove is 5a (if clean).

22 Carmen VS 4b ★   1959

25m A pleasant start with helpful holds next to the crack almost lulls you into a false sense of security but the foot-traverse right and the left-slanting crack above soon return you to reality, hopefully not with a bump! The more direct crack to the tree gives a beefier variant at VS 4c ★.

23 Deceptor HVS 4c   1973

23m Follow the diagonal crack right of *Carmen*, then go up and pass an undercut flake on its left and trend slightly right above on suspect rock. A finish into *Carmen* gives a good VS.

24 Carmen Mirander E1 5b   2012

25m Start as for *Deceptor* but climb the right-hand crack to the break and then up the slab (small wires) to the overlap. Go direct over this and up the rib above to lower off roots (or climb vegetated friable rock above): **photo on page 501.**

25 Sans Nom VS 4b   1960s

27m Gain and climb the hanging crack left of the gully to continue in the same line on sometimes dirty and slightly suspect rock to an exit crack.

26 Lizzie HVS 5a   2014

27m A fun climb up the narrow slab between *Sans Nom* and the gully, on nice rugosities to an overlap and a finish up twin diagonal cracks. Avoid loose blocks in the gully.

Warning: The gully to the right, **Central Gully**, HS (trad), has seen the removal of large amounts of dangerous rock but the line still has loose blocks. **a** To the right, the sidewall via a creaky flake to a cave and out right and up cracks is **Black Country Rock**, HVS 5a (1979).

Ash Tree Area

The slabs to the right give the most popular climbs on the crag.

27 **Ash Tree Arête** S 4a
1960

20m From a ledge on the left, 7m above the mossy lower section, pull boldly onto the arête and either climb the groove and crack above or more easily follow steps and ledges looping right to *Ash Tree Slab*. Good when clean.

28 **Anti-Digestant** E1 5a
1979

25m A bold technical eliminate up the slab left of the corner to a ledge. A crack retains some interest above before easier ground is reached.

29 **Ash Tree Slab** HS 4b ★
1959

25m A slippery crux start in the left-facing corner with fiddly protection. Pleasant well-protected climbing follows cracks above to a groove and a finish up the groove just left of the upper arête. Lower off from a tree on the next ledge up. The route originally finished up the arête direct at HVS 4c.

30 **The Nonsense Man Start** VI 5b

The centre of the shield of rock, trending slightly left-to-right. Many variations are possible. Continuing up between *Ash Tree Slab* and *Nettlerash* to gain (crux) and finish up the top slab arête gives a fun E1 eliminate.

31 **Nettlerash** VS 4c ★
1959

30m The crack where a distinctly tough and polished sequence at about 5m raises the heart-rate. Enjoyable climbing leads to a crux on the steepening headwall and a potentially friable exit. A rightly popular alternative moves left to the finish of *Ash Tree Slab* at a nicely balanced HS 4b ★ ★. **Photo on page 498.**

32 **Broken Toe** HVS 5a ★
1960s

30m Good moves at the top of the grade on the bold lower slab; steeper but more straightforward on dirtier ground above.

Lynn Robinson on Nettlerash, VS 4c (page 497). Photo: Dan Lane.

Climbing the pleasant slab just right of *Broken Toe*, from the same start is **Venom**, E2 5b (1981); the same start to cracks and a groove give **Formic**, VS 4c (1981); the left-facing groove, crack and middle groove above is **Yukio**, VS 4c (1979), a good climb when clean; next up, **Awkward Corner**, VD (trad), gives a useful way to the tree: well-named and poorly-protected so not a beginner's lead.

Warning: The second pitches in the bay above *Central Arête* have some large suspect blocks and given the position (above a popular area and the parking) are best avoided.

33   Central Arête HVD   1959
17m   A pleasant, ledgy climb turns a little nasty near the top so teeter left, a little boldly, into the gully. The direct finish is a good but heart-in-mouth VS 4b. Most lower off the tree as the second pitch is harder and overgrown.

34   Janbaloo HVS 5b   1978
15m   Good moves with spaced protection on the lower slab and a bold-feeling finish up the arête (side-runners in *Surface Plate*). A direct finish up the slab is E1.

35   Surface Plate HVS 5a ★   1959/1960s
15m   A clean, interesting and bold route. The polished crack leads to the ledge and hard moves above, with the added excitement of a stretch at the top. **Photo on page 493.**

36   Clothesline HVD 4a ★   1959
17m   The corner system gives the best lower grade route on the crag: initially easy but soon increasing in challenge to a fine finish up the diagonal crack (do you prefer balance or jams?). The dirty corner exit is the same grade but unsatisfying. Most lower off a tree at the ledge, as the upper pitch is poor, friable and overgrown.

37   The Fly HVS 5a   1977
20m   Climb *Clothesline* for 3m, then gain a hanging groove on the wall (easier from further up *Clothesline* or from *The Spider*). The moves up the groove are reachy and not as well protected as you'd like; micro-wires useful.

38   The Spider VS 4c   1959
20m   Climb the broken groove just right or the arête to the top of the groove. Make an awkward step left onto the nose and go up to the tree stump; take care with the odd suspect hold. A HS 4b variant goes direct.

39 **Burst** El 5a   1979

25m Climb the corner then teeter up and left to the arête. A nice eliminate, **Inset Slab**, E3 6a (early 2000s), takes the narrow slab direct, crossing *Burst*, to complete the slab above a pedestal, then joins *The Bender* traverse to finish on the top slab, right of the arête.

40 **The Bender** HVS 5a ★   1978

35m Expedition time! Follow a scoop awkwardly to the terrace and from 4m up the groove, break left up the shallow diagonal corner to a ledge. Swing right around the arête and finish up the crack on the right.

41 **Terrace Wall** VS 4b ★   1959

35m A good exploratory climb. Follow the initial arete to the terrace. From here either take the slabby right-slanting groove on the left, or a flaky crack just left of the right-hand overhang. Finish up a broken corner system where an in-situ lower-off may avoid a muddy exit slope. **a** A much better finish, **Terrace Wall Direct**, VS 4c ★ (2014), takes the wall above the groove direct, past an old tree stump to a break, then steps right and up the slab to finish left of a slanting groove in an excellent position.

42 **A Question of Palance** VS 4b   1979

30m The groove in the lower wall and the short right-facing corner lead to testing moves through bulges. Finish up *Terrace Wall* or better, the *Direct*.

43 **Right Arête** HS 4a   1960s

30m Pleasant climbing up the ledgy arête with a bold mantel on the last step (S 4a if you bypass this on the right). Loose scrambling above, so many will lower off at the small tree or escape left.

44 **Hard Labour** El 5a   2013

15m Don blinkers and follow the unprotected drainage line up the left of the slab next to the arête, move right at the break (big cam) into a vague scoop (possible in-situ thread) and a lovely easing but very bold finish, trending slightly right above. High in both grades. Lower-off just above the top of the slab.

45 **A Pig in the Middle** E2 5c ★   1990s

15m A beautiful test of nerve, high in the grade. Head up the centre of the slab, trending slightly right. A clean and technical start leads to the break (big cam just left) and a testing finish, via a hole, up the convex rock to the right of *Hard Labour*. A nice combo, **Yellow Blanket** E1 5a ★ (1990), starts immediately right and finishes as for *Hard Labour*. **Gardener's World**, HVS 5a (late-1990s), takes the far right of the slab, then moves out right to pockets, and trends back left above. All these finish at the same lower-off.

Warning: The overhangs on the right of the crag have been assessed for stability and are extremely unstable. Avoid totally.

A poor **Girdle Traverse**, VS (1960s), is almost certainly best forgotten.

Rick Gibbon on Carmen Mirander, E1 5b (page 496). Photo: Dan Lane.

THE CASTLETON AREA

WINNATS PASS / CAVE DALE / BRADWELL DALE +++

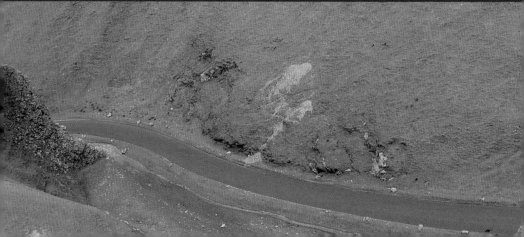

Jon Winter high above Winnats Pass on the lofty Matterhorn Ridge, VD (page 505). Photo: Ian Parnell.

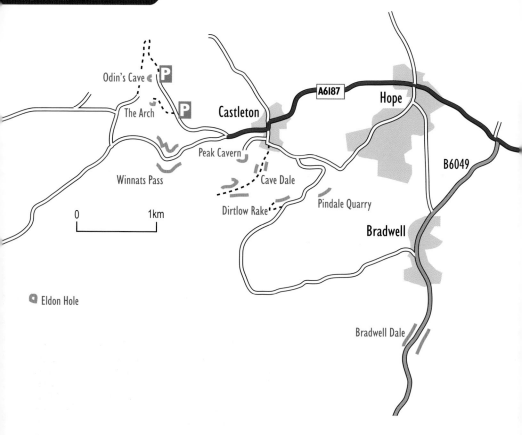

The Castleton Area

A limited chapter covering the esoteric crags centred on the villages of Castleton and Bradwell in the Hope Valley. The climbing is concentrated in and around the three dales leading back towards the core of the limestone countryside. These are Winnats Pass, Cave Dale and Bradwell Dale.

Winnats Pass

Winnats, or Windgates as it is also known, is the steep limestone gorge running east-west from Castleton towards Chapel-en-le-Frith containing the diverted A6187. The area is very popular with tourists as it provides access to both Peak and Speedwell Caverns. It is also very popular with walkers. The pass itself was probably formed by the collapse of a cave system that has left some very

steep crags on its south side and more open ridges opposite on the north side. The grassy slopes on the south side run straight onto the road below giving the crags a very exposed feel. The land is owned by the National Trust who does not wish the area to be used by climbers. Due to the potential danger and hazards to other users of the area, climbing on the south side is not encouraged nor recommended. The route descriptions on the south side are therefore recorded for completeness.

Winnats Pass South Side

The south side contains two high level crags on the rim of the gorge, Shining Tor on the left and The Shield on the right. Both are approached from the top as the wet grassy slopes below the crag are lethal and contain rare Ferns and Bryophytes (mosses). Please do not climb here.

Shining Tor: Shining Tor is the left-hand of the two buttresses on the southern skyline.

1   Rite of Way   F7b ★★   1985
25m The left-hand side of the wall, starting up a thin crack then moving right to a line of less-ancient bolts higher up the wall. Needs rebolting though a new belay was added in 2014.

2   Forgive My Trespasses   F7a+ ★★   1988
25m Start 4m right of *Rite of Way*. A butch start on undercuts and layaways leads to easier climbing up the line of a faint groove. Traverse left to join and finish as for *Rite of Way*. Needs rebolting.

3   Berlin Wall   E4 5c ★★   1988
20m The green wall to the left of *Kaiser Bill* has pegs. Climb easily to a ledge, then take the thin crack on the right and move left at its top. Move back right to reach a ledge and follow a ramp leftwards to a loose finish. A good well positioned route, but probably never repeated so would need a brush.

4   Kaiser Bill   HVS 5a   1969
25m From left of the cave, climb up to a traverse right at 8m to gain a crack. Take the crack, passing the cave to a rightwards exit.

5   Do Up Your Flies   E5 6b   1970s/1985
25m Start 3m to the right of a small cave. Decaying in-situ gear marks the way.

6   Womb with a View   E4 6b   1969/1988
25m Start 10m to the right of the cave and climb a shallow corner-cum-groove.

The Shield: Three hundred metres further up the rim of the pass is a shield-shaped undercut buttress.

7   Ginger Man   HVS 5a   1969
25m The left-hand side of the face contains a groove. Climb this, moving right around the overhang, to a small ledge. Gain the lip of a hole with difficulty then finish up a shallow loose groove.

8   Pint of Blood   E2 5b   1969/1974
20m Start on the right and gain a ledge at 5m. Continue up the shallow groove stepping right into a crack. Follow this to the top.

9   Burning Giraffe   A1   1970s
25m Start to the right of a black circle on the right wall. Using pegs, follow the horizontal weakness round the arête into *Pint of Blood*. Finish up this.

Winnats Pass North Side

This is characterised by the two rocky ridges that run from the rim down to the road. The lower one, *Elbow Ridge*, runs to the roadside by a bend. Seventy metres uphill is;

10   Matterhorn Ridge   VD ★★★   pre-1910
70m A well-travelled classic of the Peak. Wet or dry, day or night, summer or winter, take your pick. **Photo on page 502. Matterhorn Face**, HS 4b (1970s), traverses left onto the face after a few metres of the ridge then finishes left again. **Cave Wall**, HS 4b (1960s), starts just right of the cave in the front of the buttress and climbs direct to the ridge.

11   Elbow Ridge   D ★   pre-1910
60m Less classic but a good baby brother. The ridge that runs right down to the bend.

Tourist Buttress: The lump of grassy rock by the road, near the bottom of the hill. It contains **Tourist Crack**, VD (pre-1930), on the left and **Tourist Wall**, S (pre-1930), on the right.

The Arch

A small cave-like feature with a few steep, fingery problems. Visible from a distance, but hidden from closer angles. To approach, head west out of Castleton. Where Arthurs Way (the Winnats Pass road) turns left, continue for 700m to park on the roadside near Treak Cliff Cavern. Follow signs to the cave, up steps and right along a footpath. Pass the cave entrance and continue for about 150m and, by a large hole, turn left and go up the hill to the crag.

1   Grass Dynamique   Font 7B+
On the far left, step up on the slab to reach high undercuts. From these, swing out to a good hold round the arête, then head towards a good jug.

2   Cry of the Beholder   Font 7A
Start undercutting a large pocket in the back left of the undercut feature. Contrive a sequence to a jug higher up the wall, then hold the swing and finish on jugs above.

3   Sight Beyond Sight   Font 7B+
Start undercutting a large pocket in the back right of the undercut feature. Using a small pocket and crimp, power out to a flatty on the lip. Finish on a jug just above.

4   Dot the Eyes   Font 6C
From a sitter on the right, traverse left to the finishing jug of *Sight Beyond Sight*. Traversing beyond this is possible, but the rock is dodgy.

Odin's Cave

A unique subterranean vault containing a hard, funky classic. It is fairly underground, is pretty dark and weatherless. It can be dry in winter, or indeed at any time, but can suffer from condensation in warm, humid weather.

To approach, head west out of Castleton. Where Arthurs Way (the Winnats Pass road) turns left, continue for 1km until the road is gated. The cave entrance can be seen on the left, 30m away.

I   The Dark Room   Font 8A
Cool roof climbing involving some lateral thinking, based around the horizontal break/weakness on the left side of the cave. Sit start on the low pillar at the left end. Move up and traverse right using kneebars to finish matched in a jug in the hole on the right.

2   Short Circuit   Font 7A+
Sit start on large holds at the back of the cave and head to the finishing holds of *The Dark Room*.

Peak Cavern

Peak Cavern cave entrance, also lovingly known locally as 'The Devil's Arse' is the tourist centrepiece of Castleton. The large crag that forms the entrance to the show cave has been climbed upon over the years, but only by invitation / permission. There are four routes, three aid and one free. To approach, follow signs from Castleton.

The following route was climbed for a BBC documentary in 2011. It was equipped, cleaned and climbed over a number of days and is most likely to be unrepeated.

I   Ring of Fire   F7c+, F7a, F7b+, F7b   ★ ★ ★   2011
100m Probably the longest up-route in the Peak, climbing the left-hand side (looking in) of the massive cave entrance in four pitches. Gradually traversing out towards the headwall using a combination of bedding planes and water-worn features.

2   Original Aid Route   A2 (not equipped)   1981
In 1981, Ian Buster Wright and Rob Harrison bolted the first ascent of Peak Cavern roof. Although at the time it was the longest roof climb ever, it was based upon the agreement that the ~250 bolts would be stripped to prevent any further ascents. Since then, public-access restrictions have inhibited further opportunities for play. However, John Harrison (the cave owner) allowed Dave Williams to create two additional routes.

3   The Roof   A2   ★ ★   2007/2008
This route starts approximately 2m to the left of the culvert/bridge at the back of the cave.

50m Follow the bolts up the back wall. After about 25 bolts there is a possible escape. Continue along the roof for another 15 bolts to a second possible escape route. Instead of escaping, follow the bolts and eventually you'll come to the lip and a chain lower-off. Seven moves higher, there is an even more comfortable chain lower-off. Rivets and bolts continue to a third lower-off further up the front wall; it is 30m to the ground from here. More bolts and rivets will take you to a final lower-off near to a tree, 50m of climbing off the deck.

Note: Two moves before the lip, there is a line of 14 bolts continuing down to a lower-off on a ledge. This can act as a third escape route for *The Roof* or a means of doing the routes the other way around; preferably if you wish to do the routes there and back. It's a good idea to go front-back-front, starting from this ledge, as you'll get more light.

4   Violin Solo   A2   ★ ★ ★   2011/2012
This route starts approximately 10m to the right of the final steps.

50m After finding the first bolt, lean across the gap and begin. Follow the bolts to the left and after ~20 you'll get on the roof proper. Follow the bolts towards the front of the cave until you join *The Roof*, approximately 20m from the lip. *The Roof* goes right as *Violin Solo* goes left. When you reach the lip, you can either: continue up the headwall on bolts and rivets finishing up the final few feet of *The Roof*, or, a bolt and a couple of rivets and you are back on *The Roof*. *Violin Solo* is arguably the better of the two routes as it is more sustained, has longer reaches and is inescapable without the sacrifice of gear.

It is approximately 100m from the beginning of *Violin Solo* to the lower-off ledge. In addition, there is 25m between the lip and the top lower-off on the front-wall.

Both routes are thoroughly good fun especially if you do them there and back. If you would like to do them, speak to John Harrison or a member of staff at the cavern. As climbers are guests please be respectful to tourists by keeping noise to a minimum whilst tours are on and refraining from bad language. This way we can build and maintain a good relationship between climbers and the cave.

There is a line of bolts going up to, and into, the large hole in the centre of the roof. This is primarily for cave exploration but makes a pleasant aid-route in itself.

Cave Dale

Cave Dale lies immediately south of Castleton and is overlooked by Peveril Castle. Outside of school holidays or weekends, parking is available in the village. Otherwise park in the large pay & display car park in the village, or on the roadside towards Winnats Pass. The dale is approached in about 10 minutes from the village where a sign-posted path leads up a steep narrow ravine that opens out into the dale. The dale is very popular with walkers and not so popular with climbers. Consequently the routes can be loose and overgrown. There is some bouldering in the dale, some of which is described below.

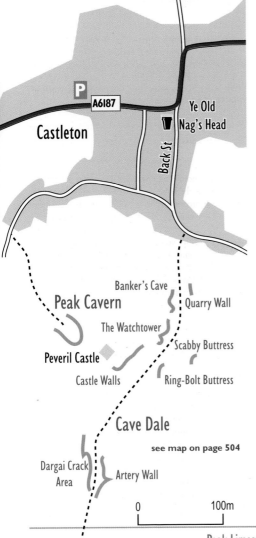

The climbs are described firstly, on the left, as you walk up the dale and then back down the dale again on the opposite side.

Cave Dale East Side

Quarry Wall: As you enter the dale there is a gate, the first routes are to be found on a small quarried wall approximately 25 metres further up on your left.

1   Dancing the Hard Bargain El 5c   1984
9m   Follow the short leftward leaning groove to a finish up the wall.

2   Alpha VS 4b ★   1960s
10m   The twisting crack just to the right.

3   Dobbin HVS 5a   1984
10m   The easier-than-it-looks wall from left to right.

4   Beta VS 4c   1960s
10m   The fingery right-hand crack.

About 50m up the dale, up the hillside before Ring-Bolt Buttress, is a large broken buttress. **Scabby Buttress**, VD (1961), follows the easiest line up this.

Ring-Bolt Buttress: This is the steep buttress right by the path, 60m after entering the dale.

5   Mr Jagger's Warning E3 6a ★   1980s
10m   The scoop, just to the left of the central rib, is climbed on small pockets to a ledge. The steep wall above is taken on large holds (peg). Belay well back on a stake.

6   Mundgripe E4 6a ★   1987
15m   Start to the right of the large bolt at a flake. Climb two large flakes to reach a ledge (bolt) and pull over the roof (peg) to finish up the wall above. Stake belay.

7   Ring-Bolt Buttress HVS 5a   1960s
15m   Take the awkward crack to the right to the overhang. Traverse rightwards to a break in the overhang where the top can be gained. **Barfleur**, VD (1960s), is the scrappy crack on the right of the buttress.

Artery Wall: A hundred metres up the dale the footpath becomes hemmed in by walls on either side. The tall, right wall holds *Dargai Crack*. The left walls are less imposing. The first climbs come out of a cave tucked in a groove:

8   Moaning Groove S   1961
15m   From the small cave, climb the steep left-hand side of the cleft.

9 The Artery VS 4c   1960s
12m   From the same cave, take the line up the right-hand side of the fault. Hard to start.

The walls to the right are overgrown. They contain: **Friction Wall**, HS 4b (1960s), **Curving Crack**, S (1960s), **Green Groove** S (1960s), **Scoop and Corner**, VS 4c (1960s), **Scoop Wall**, HS 4b (1960s), **Sycamore Groove**, HS 4b (1961), **V Groove**, D (1960s).

White Ridge Crawl, VD (1961), is up the left-hand-side of the ridge that starts halfway up the hillside; **The White Mane**, VD (1961), is the groove in the front.

Cave Dale West Side

The rest of the climbs are on the right-hand side of the dale, starting opposite *Artery Wall*.

Dargai Crack Area: This is named after the ground-breaking climb in the bay. There are some climbs on the slabby walls to the left: **Slab and Cleft**, HS 4b (1960s), starts from the right end of the slab and climbs a V-Groove above; **Jaggered Crack**, HS 4b (1960s), is the crack in the wall 3m to the right, with a jaggered rock at the top; **Exide**, VS 4c (1960s), starts 2m to the right and climbs direct to a small recess. Finish straight up.

10 A Friendly Chat with a Hungry Ghost
E3 5c ★   1986
15m   A stunning and unusual line, with climbing to match. Follow the steep corner on big scoops and pockets.

11 Goldfinger HVS 5b ★   1960s
15m   Start to the right of the lower overhang at the foot of *Dargai Crack*. Climb diagonally up and left. The upper overhang is taken via a good crack.

12 Dargai Crack VS 4b ★   1898
15m   One of the first routes on Peak limestone. Charge up the crack directly, passing a tree. If the finish is vegetated, then a cleaner, slightly harder finish is to step left and finish as for Goldfinger: **Dargai Variant**, VS 4c (1960s).

Some routes lie to the right but suffer from vegetation: **Ivy Groove**, VS 4c (1960s), pulls over the overhang just to the right onto the wall above. Climb the wall and groove; **Flim**, VS 4c (1960s), starts 3m to the right and climbs diagonally leftwards up the smooth slab on the right-hand end of the overhang to a weakness just to the left of the upper overhang; **Flam**, VS 4c (1960s), takes the right-hand edge of the slab to a slight groove in the arête between the twin caves above; **Peak Climb**, VD (1960s), climbs the vegetated weakness leftwards above a cave, hidden up and round to the right.

About 15m right is a grey wall facing down the dale.

13 Belvedere E3 5c   1984
15m   The slab and wall left of *Phone Home.*

14 Phone Home E3 5b   1980s
15m   The line of flakes on the right-hand side of the wall.

Zorbit, HS 4b (1960s), is on the overgrown buttress below and left of the castle.

Castle Walls: These are the now-overgrown walls under Pevril Castle. **The Keep** and **Keep Cleft** have both been obliterated by a rock-fall. **Keep Arête**, VD is the rib to the right of the rock-fall; **Jailer's Groove**, S (1961), climbs the groove just right. Both have horrendously grassy finishes and the whole area is best avoided. Around to the right is a bottomless groove. This is climbed by **Jailer's Crack**, HVS 5a (1961); the right-hand start 4m to the right is **Jailer's Wall**, HVS 5a (1961); **Terrace Wall**, VD (1960s), is the wall 10m to the right; **Castle Groove**, HS (1960s), is the wall right again.

Watchtower Area: The watchtower is the tall, steep buttress beside the path.

15 The Watchtower HVS 5a ★ ★   1961
20m   From the lowest point of the buttress climb directly over a small overhang to a stance and possible belay. Follow the flake crack to the left, to a recess around the arête. Move left for 2m and climb direct to finish, the crux of the route.

16 All Along the Watchtower E3 5c ★   1985
18m   Follow *The Watchtower* to its stance then climb directly up a hard-looking wall past a bolt and peg.

Banana, HS (1960s), goes from the same starting point and climbs climb directly up to a short ramp. Follow this to finish up the right-hand side of the tower; **Pock Wall**, HVS 5a (1960s), is a poor route that starts around the corner to the right in a recess. Climb the line of pockets leading left finishing through the ivy.

In the bay to the right is a section of short, steep rock.

17 The Letterbox E1 5c   1980s
12m   Climb the overhang directly to finish up a groove on the right.

18 Runts Grunt Stunt E4 6b   1980s
12m   Start slightly to the right of *The Letterbox.* Some of the original pegs may no longer be in place. Start below a peg. Climb the overhang past another peg trending slightly leftwards passing a further peg to finish. Pumpy.

19 Monkey on Juice E6 6c 1988
15m Move rightwards across the bulge left of *Belial*. Small wires protect.

The significant bulge to the right holds **Belial**, a rusty A2 (1960s). However, two sport climbs have been bolted and remain unclimbed. When either of these are completed, especially the right-hand line, they will earn the title of *The Hardest Route In Cave Dale*, and put the valley back on the map for the first time since 1898.

20 Mr Lewis's Blasting Company E4 5c 1988
15m Climb the wall right of *Belial* past a bulge (peg). Traverse left and finish up the wall and over another bulge. Bolt belay on the ledge above.

21 Piton Route HVS 5a 1960s
12m Climb the wall just left of the next route.

22 Puttrell's Crack VD ancient
12m Follow that crack 7m to the right of *Belial*. **Puttrell's Arête**, VD (trad), climbs the very loose arête to the right.

Banker's Cave: Further down the valley is an amphitheatre containing a cave. Most of the routes here are overgrown. The first two routes start by this cave: **Banker's Climb**, VD (1960s), goes from the cave onto a short wall then a further wall on the left to finish; **Borrower's Climb**, HS (1960s), climbs from the right of the cave past a bush to finish at a small tree. At a lower level and to the right is a deeply undercut nose: **Crack and Nose**, VS 4c (1960s), climbs a crack and wall above. **The Gangway**, Mod (1960s), takes the diagonal cracks. The final two routesnm nm,.,., to the right are completely overgrown. These are **Thin Crack,** HS (1960s), and **Chastity,** VS 4c (1960s).

23 Sheep Shifter Font 7B
This is the first rock on the right when entering the dale. Climb the 45 degree wall on the right of the amphitheatre from a sit start to a (glued) finishing jug. The block on the left is out.

Pindale Quarry

A miserable pit. The two recorded routes, **Balbus**, HVS 5b and **Fear and Loathing (In Las Vegas)**, HVS 4c, are based around a projecting buttress at the back.

Dirtlow Rake

A great big dusty slot in the ground. An odd beast with unusual and highly-featured rock and lots of potential. It currently has a Font 7C+ lip traverse, From Dirt Grow the Prowess, by Dan Varian.

To find it, see maps on page 504. In Castleton, turn up Back Street by Ye Old Nag's Head, then out Pindale Rd. After 250m, take the right fork in the road. Follow this for 900m until a drivable track angles off on the right. Park here. Follow the track for 100m, and the crag is visible on the right.

Bradwell Dale

The rocks lie on either side of the road just south of Bradwell. Often dirty. These were, starting on the east side, **Balcony Climb**, HS, **Hanging Garden**, VS, **Ratten**, HVS, **Mignon**, HVS, **Cake Walk**, HS, **Cave Crack**, VS, **Angled Buttress**, S, **Stack Wall**, HS, **Dysoning**, D, **Roof Route**, HS, **Scoop Route**, VD, **Bulging Wall**, S, **Flip Side**, S, **Pinnacle Route**, HS, **The Nose**, S, **The Platband**, HS, **Two-Tier Climb**, HS, **Direct Route**, VS, **Indirect Route**, HS. On the west side are: **Chockstone Crack**, S, **Elderberry Crack**, S, **Funf**, VS, **Flake Crack**, VS, **Recessed Corner**, VS, **The Steps**, VD, **Two Step**, HS, **Broken Crack**, HS, **Dragon's Back**, VS, **Dragon's Side**, VD, **Amphitheatre Wall**, VS, **Lefty**, HS, **Righty**, VS. All developed in the 1960s.

Eldon Hole

Eldon Hole can be found on Eldon Hill north of Peak Forest. This gash in the ground used to be feared as the entrance to a bottomless pit or even to Hell itself. It is still a dangerous place! Popular with cavers, not so with climbers. However, one adventure route has been climbed and recorded on the obvious wall.

1 Independence Day E5 6a 1989
36m One of the most esoteric climbs at the grade in the Peak District. Abseil in from two concreted-in posts in the right-hand side of Eldon Hole. Belay on a 3 bolt belay on a ledge, remembering to tie a knot in your ropes, as the hole is very deep!

Climb the wall underneath the abseil via an obvious flake to finish directly up the headwall. Originally protected by pegs and bolts, that were subsequently removed.

Graded List: Trad Climbs

Ald – Aldery Cliff; **Central** – Central Buttress, WcJ; **Cave** - Cave Dale; **Chee** – Chee Tor; **Church** – Church Buttress, WcJ; **Dog's** – Dog's Dinner Buttress, Chee Dale; **Jackdaw** – Jackdaw Point, WcJ; **Lifts** – The Lifts, Chee Dale; **Moat** – Moat Buttress Area; **Moving** – Moving Buttress, Chee Dale; **Nettle** – Nettle Buttress; **Ping** – Ping Pong Area; **Plum** – Plum Buttress; **Raven** – Raven Tor; **Ravens** – Ravensdale; **Rubicon** – Rubicon Wall; **Sidings** – The Sidings; **Staden** – Staden Quarry; **Stoney** – Stoney Middleton; **Two Tier** – Two Tier, Chee Dale; **West** – Stoney West; **Win** - Winnats Pass

E7

General Incompetence (Nettle)
Verbal Abuse (Raven)
Ninth Life (Two Tier)
Plectrum Maxilla Direct (Rubicon)

E6

Tequila Mockingbird (Chee)
Eyes of Fire (Chee)
In Bulk (Central)
Helmut Schmitt (Stoney)
Scarab (Stoney)
Excalibur (Moat)
Easy Skanking (Stoney)
Leviathan (Central)
Flight of Icarus (Two Tier)
The Big Plum (Plum)
Piranha (Rubicon)
Laughing (Chee)
Gander Meat (Move)

E5

The Dream Mile (Chee)
Duel in the Sun (Chee)
Kingfisher (Rubicon)
Hysterectomy (Stoney)
The Golden Mile (Chee)
A Miller's Tale (Rubicon)
Menopause (Stoney)
Wilt Alternative (Ravens)
Autobahn (Chee)
Four Minute Tiler (Stoney)
Black Kabul (Stoney)
Stuffed Badger (Nettle)
Northerners Can't Climb (West)
Behemoth (Central)
My Dog Dill (Dog's)
Kink (Stoney)
Emotional Rescue (Stoney)
Raisin Roof (Plum)

That'll do Nicely (Central)
Ceramic Extension (Chee)
Summer Wine (Nettle)
Sox (Central)
Spizz Energy (Two Tier)
La Chute (Central)
Wilt (Ravens)
Honeymoon Blues (Rubicon)
Circe (Stoney)
Jezebel (Rubicon)
Traffic Jam (Stoney)
Mandrake (Ping)
Kellogg (Stoney)
Midnight Summer Dream (Chee)
War (Central)
La Route (Central)
White Bait (Rubicon)

E4

Apocalypse (Chee)
Mortlock's Arête (Chee)
The Alien (Central)
Millionaire Touch (Stoney)
Oliver (Stoney)
Adios Tango (Stoney)
Speed Kills (Stoney)
Our Father (Stoney)
Bitterfingers (Stoney)
Kelly's Eye (Stoney)
I Drink Therefore I Am (Sidings)
Cardiac Arrest (Stoney)
Colonel Bogey (Stoney)
Wee Doris (Stoney)
Cabbage Crack (Stoney)
Ceramic (Chee)
Pickpocket (Stoney)
Protest and Survive (Moving)
Special K (Stoney)
Deception (Ping)

E3

Boat Pusher's Wall (Stoney)
Jasper (Stoney)
Welcome to Hard Times Direct (Staden)
Queer Street (Chee)
Bubbles Wall (Stoney)
Mad Dogs and Englishmen (Two Tier)
Gesemini (direct) (Stoney)
Splintered Perspex (Chee)
Cut Loose or Fly (Ravens)
No Light (Nettle)
Southerners Can't Climb (West)
Approaching (Chee)
A Friendly Chat with a Hungry Ghost (Cave)
Carillon Crack (Central)
Telescopic Demand (Staden)
Paraplege (Staden)
Carol's Crack (Central)
Knuckle Knocker (Central)
42nd Street (Chee)
Absent Friends (Chee)
Dragonflight (Rubicon)
Rave On (Chee)
Scoop Wall (Stoney)
Scorpion (Ravens)
Round the Bend (Ravens)

E2

John Peel (Stoney)
Cock-a-Leekie Wall (Stoney)
The Flakes Direct (Stoney)
Gollyberry (Stoney)
Two Sunspots (Chee)
Dies Irae (Stoney)
Cathy's Clown (Staden)
Helicon (Stoney)
Welcome to Hard Times (Staden)
First Light (Nettle)
Rippemoff (Stoney)
The Soloist (Staden)
Emergency (Staden)

Vicar's Vertigo (Church)
St Paul (Central)
Captain Reliable (Staden)
Army Dreamers (Jackdaw)
Via Vita Direct (Ravens)
Hergiani (Chee)
Arch Bishop (Ald)
Great Central Route (Chee)
Lucy Simmons (Stoney)
November Wall (Ald)
Bingo Wall (Stoney)
Alcasan (Stoney)
Carl's Wark Crack (Stoney)
Double Scotch (Stoney)
The Flakes (Stoney)
Windhover (Stoney)
Mani (Stoney)
Armageddon (Stoney)
Sergeyenna (Chee)

E1

Dead Banana Crack (Stoney)
Ping Pong (Ping)
Inquisitor (Stoney)
Solitaire (Stoney)
Sunai (Staden)
St Peter (Stoney)
The Arête (Ald)
The Slurper (Stoney)
Easy Action (Stoney)
Sprint Start (Sidings)
Meditation (Chee)
Charas (Staden)
Sirplum (Plum)
Aplomb (Plum)
Liquid Courage (Staden)
Ringmistress (Church)
Bicycle Repair Man (Staden)
Ping (Ping)
Troops of Tomorrow (Ravens)
The Sinister Finish (Ravens)
The Nails (Staden)
Mephistopheles (Ravens)

HVS

Via Vita (Ravens)
Medusa (Stoney)
Conclusor (Ravens)
Great Expectations (Staden)
The Bishop (Ald)
Purple Haze (Ravens)
The Pendulum (Stoney)
Bullets (Ravens)

Binge Drinker (Sidings)
Leering Wall (Chee)
Rockbiter (Ravens)
Thin Lizzy (Moving)
Thor's Hammer (Move)
The Watchtower (Cave)
Fe Fi Fo Fum (Stoney)
The Hunter House Bust (Lifts)
Joint Effort (Staden)
Padme (Stoney)
The Hoochie Koo (Lifts)
Gymnic (Ravens)

VS

Gabriel (Stoney)
The Pearly Gates (Stoney)
Chee Girdle (Chee)
Sin (Stoney)
The Stalk (Plum)
Aurora (Stoney)
Suscipiat (Staden)
Amain (Ravens)
Froth (Stoney)
Impendent (Ravens)
Ash Crack (Ravens)
Glory Road (Stoney)
Mitre Crack (Ald)
Mealy Bugs (Ravens)
Nettlerash (Ald)
Dargai Crack (Cave)
Puffing Billy (Sidings)
Alpha (Cave)
Gulle Gulle Groove (Chee)
Medusa (Ravens)
Carmen (Ald)

HS

Terrace Wall (Ald)
Whistling Crack (Move)
Tria (Ravens)
Rosehip Wine (Stoney)
Sun Crack (Staden)
Nettlerash left-hand
   finish (Ald)
Ash Tree Slab (Ald)

S

Ragged Arête (Lifts)

VD

Clothesline (Ald)
Tiger Trot (Stoney)
Matterhorn Ridge (Win)

D

Elbow Ridge (Win)

Mod

Mineshaft (Stoney)

Graded List: Sport Climbs

Beer – Devonshire (Beerhouse) Buttress; **Biceps** – Craig-y-Biceps; **BB** – Blackwell / Blatant; **Black** – Blackwell Dale; **Central** – Central Buttress, WcJ; **Chee** – Chee Tor; **Cornice - Chee** – The Cornice, Chee Dale; **Cornice WcJ** – The Cornice WcJ; **Crag X** – Crag X; **Dog's** – Dog's Dinner Buttress, Chee Dale; **Emb** – The Embankment; **God** – Goddard's Quarry; **Harpur** – Harpur Hill; **Horse** – Horseshoe Quarry; **Inch** – Inch Test Buttress, WcJ; **Long** – Long Wall; **Lover's** – Lover's Leap; **Max** – Max Buttress; **Moat** – Moat Buttress Area; **Moving** – Moving Buttress; **Nettle** – Nettle Buttress; **Plum** – Plum Buttress; **Raven** – Raven Tor; **Rhubarb** – Rhubarb Buttress; **Rubicon** – Rubicon Wall; **Runyon's** – Runyon's Corner; **Small** – Smalldale; **Stoney** – Stoney Middleton; **Lifts** – The Lifts, Chee Dale; **Nook** – The Nook; **Tideswell** – Tideswell Dale; **Two** – Two Tier Buttress, Chee Dale; **TTB** – Two Tier Buttress, WcJ; **Vision** – Vision Buttress; **West** – Stoney West

F9a+

Finest Pedigree (Dog's)

F9a

Mutation (Raven)
Stevolution (Raven)
Hubble (Raven)

F8c+

The Bastard (Rubicon)
Evolution (Raven)
Pedigree Chum (Dog's)
Kaaba (Raven)

F8c

Hooligan (Raven)
Rooster Crossing (Raven)
The Hajj (Raven)
Dreadnought (Cornice - Chee)
Mega Whore (Raven)
Make It Funky (Raven)
Mecca Extension (Raven)

F8b+

Sean's Roof (Black)
Jehovahkill (Raven)
Seraphim (Raven)
Mecca (original method) (Raven)
Barney Ragin' (Cornice - Chee)
32 (Cornice - Chee)
Malcolm X (Cornice - Chee)
42 (Cornice - Chee)
Techno Prisoners (Cornice - Chee)
Mecca (modern method) (Cornice - Chee)

F8b

The Three Spheres (Inch)
Superocity (Cornice WcJ)
Karma Killer (Moat)
Gran Techo (Cornice - Chee)
Snatch (Cornice - Chee)
Kali Yuga (Two Tier)
Bricktop (Cornice - Chee)
Zeke the Freak (Rubicon)
Monsterosity (Cornice WcJ)
Rage (Raven)
Love Amongst the Butterflies (Cornice - Chee)
Waddage (Raven)
Clematis (Cornice - Chee)
Barbarossity (Cornice WcJ)
Revelations (Raven)

F8a+

Devonshire Arms (Cornice - Chee)
Monumental Armblaster (Cornice - Chee)
Freedom Fighter (Raven)
Chimes of Freedom (Raven)
Four Door Dostoyevsky (Cornice - Chee)
Nemesis (Cornice - Chee)
R 'n P (Cornice - Chee)
Let's Get Physical (Black)
Culloden (Tideswell)
Boot Boys (Raven)
Superfly (Cornice WcJ)
Mission Impossible (Moat)
Pump Up the Power (Raven)
Gonads (Two Tier)
Flow (Two Tier)
Agent Provocateur (Moat)
Albatrossity (Cornice WcJ)
Theoria (Nook)
Rumble in the ungle (Cornice WcJ)
Caviar (Rubicon)
The Inch Test (Inch)

K3 (Cornice - Chee)
Tollbar (Stoney)
Auctioneer (Cornice WcJ)
Entree (Two Tier)
Anger Management (Raven)

F8a

The Sissy (Rubicon)
The Ogre (Chee)
A Bit of Nooky (Nook)
The Spider (Plum)
Let the Tribe Increase (Rubicon)
Hot Fun Closing (Rubicon)
Out of my Tree (Raven)
Right to Roam (Raven)
The Crucifixion (Raven)
Yorkshire 8b (left-hand) (Cornice WcJ)
Brazen Strumpet (Raven)
The Prow (Raven)
North Atlantic Drift (Long)
Welcome to My World (Two Tier)
Roof Warrior (Cornice - Chee)
An In and Out of Body Experience (Raven)
Powerplant (Cornice - Chee)
Boobs (Chee)
Little Plum (in one pitch) (Stoney)
Unleashing the Wild Physique (Cornice - Chee)
Ouijaboard (Cornice - Chee)
Salar (Rubicon)
The Call of Nature (Raven)
The Big Apple (Stoney)
Aberration (Two Tier)
Free Monster (Cornice WcJ)

F7c+

Weedkiller (Raven)
Wild in Me (Raven)
Minos (Two Tier)
Orange Sunshine (Two Tier)
Why Me? (Two Tier)
The Weakling (Cornice WcJ)
The Vision (Vision)
The Lockless Monster (Nook)
Chip off the Old Block (Plum)
Total Breakdown (Two Tier)
Atlantic Realm (Long)
Toys for the Boys (Nettle)
Easy Rider (Cornice - Chee)
The Jug Jockey (Cornice - Chee)
Boo (Chee)
A Vision of Loveliness (Two Tier)
Body Machine (Raven)
Rooster Booster (pitch I) (Raven)
Proud Whore (Raven)
The Full Monty (Raven)
Empire Burlesque (Cornice WcJ)
Michael Foot Jam (Nook)

F7c

Let's Get Physical Right-Hand (Black)
Fossil Wall (Black)
Cry of Despair (Cornice - Chee)
Eat the Rich (Inch)
There's Life in the Old Log Yet (Nook)
Taylor Made (Cornice - Chee)
Damson in Distress (Plum)
Recycled (Two Tier)
Knocked Out Loaded (Vision)
A Bout de Soufflé (Long)
Big News Man Mouth (Long)
Theology (Chee)
Celebration (Two Tier)
Let the Tripe Increase (Moat)
Fishing Without a Licence (Emb)
Esmeralda (Nettle)
Sloe Gin (Plum)
Obscene Toilet (Raven)
Pauillac (Central)
Half Decent (Raven)
Indecent Exposure (Raven)
Lightweight (Two Tier)
Cordless Madness (Cornice - Chee)
Sturgeon in the Cupboard (Emb)
Stone the Loach (Emb)
The Grand Tour (Raven)
Laughing at the Rain (Biceps)
Another Toadside Attraction (Raven)

F7b+

Titanic (Long)
Meterol (Long)
The Sea is a Brown Paper Bag (Two Tier)
The Naive and Sentimental Lover (Cornice - Chee)
That Was the River (Cornice - Chee)
Beginner's Wall (Black)
Moat People (Moat)
No Mud, No Thud (Moat)
Cosmopolitan (Cornice - Chee)
A Cure for Foot Jams (Nook)
Bored of the Lies (Cornice - Chee)
Stung (Nettle)
The Storm (Nook)
A Little Extra (Raven)
Sardine (Raven)
Tin Of (Raven)
Crankus Maximus (Max)
The Lover's Leap (Stoney)
Ratline (Harpur)
Brachiation Dance (Cornice WcJ)
Soggy Biscuits (Small)
Une Jour Parfait (Central)

F7b

Succubus (Cornice - Chee)
Beef It (Emb)
Max A Million (Max)
The Max Museum (Max)
Systems Malfunction (Two Tier)
Kiss My Arcy (Long)
Old Man River (Cornice - Chee)
Certificate X (Crag X)
XXXX (Crag X)
Getafix (Small)
Virtual Insanity (Small)
Virgin King (Stoney)
Southern Man (Horse)
Snails of the Riverbank (Cornice - Chee)
Daylight Robbery (Two Tier)
Whose Line is it Anyway (Cornice - Chee)
Subterra (Nettle)
Countdown (Two Tier)
Never to Look Back (Moving)

F7a+

Spazz Energy (Two Tier)
Incapacity Benefit (Cornice WcJ)
Big Zipper (Cornice - Chee)
Open Gate (Two Tier)
The Main Motor Mile (Biceps)
Hungry Eyes (Emb)
Martial Music (Cornice - Chee)
Kiss Me Hardy (Long)
Kalymnos 8a (Nook)
Breamtime (Emb)
High Society (Long)
Max to the Wall (Max)
La Brute (Central)
Fatal Attraction (Central)
Access All Areas (Lifts)
Emission Control (BB)
Lost Contact (Small)
Mumble Jumble (Horse)

F7a

Much Monkey Magic (Biceps)
Armistice Day (Cornice - Chee)
The Lady of the Lake (Moat)
Scratch Race (Plum)
Rubicon (Rubicon)
The Siberian Hamster (Lifts)
Darl (Two Tier)
Fatal Attraction (Long)
Can Boys (Small)
Cairn (Harpur)
Clarion Call (Cornice - Chee)
Quality Control (Two Tier)
Go Cat (Dog's)
Case Adjourned (Two Tier)
The Prophecy (Harpur)
White Gold (Chee)
Up the River Without a Paddle (Cornice - Chee)
I Hate You (Stoney)
Bream in Black (Emb)
Loco-Motion (BB)
Fin de Siècle (Harpur)
First Offence (Small)
An Ancient Rhythm (Horse)
Red Mist (West)
Max Head Room (Max)

F6c+

Community Service (Runyon's)
Cockerel Cry (Two Tier)
Light Ideas (Nettle)
In the Drink (Dog's)
Gaseous Exchange (Rhubarb)
Red X (Crag X)
Further Adventures in
    Greendale (Cornice - Chee)
It Tolls for Thee (Central)
The Max Works (Max)
Oh Dear! (Moat)
Monster Mouse Resurgent (Two Tier)
Five Miles High (Lifts)
War Memorial (Cornice - Chee)
No Chains on Me (Central)
Ring Thane (Horse)
Another Camden Day (West)
Run For Your Wife (Horse)
My Fickle Resolve (Central)
Afloat in the Moat (Moat)
Full Frontal (Harpur)
High Scream Sunday (Lifts)
Lunatic Fringe (Max)
Megalithic Man
    Super-Direct (Horse)
Over the Rainbow Trout (Emb)
Four Telling Tales (Harpur)
Reservoir Frogs (Small)
Avarice Allsorts (Harpur)
Labour Relations (Horse)

F6c

You got Rhyme (Moat)
A Bit on the Side (Plum)
The Jury's Out (Runyon's)
Legal Action (Horse)
Rising Sap (Two Tier)
Going Straight (Small)
Epidavros (Nettle)
Max 'is Wall (Max)
C'est Plastique (Central)
The Exclusion Zone (Harpur)
Déjà vu (Central)
Rhyme and Reason (Moat)
The State of the Nation (West)
Brief Camouflage (Rhubarb)
Don't Talk to Strangers (West)
Rue Morgue (Cornice - Chee)
Giants (Plum)
Hard Drive (BB)
Learn the Lingo (Small)
Over the Hill (Harpur)

Private Prosecution (Horse)
Would you like a Sweetie? (Harpur)
Riding the Bullet (Small)
Subterfuge (Two Tier)
Four Thousand (Stoney)
Rainbow Warrior (Horse)
Rain Dance (Horse)

F6b+

The Massive (Plum)
Procession (West)
Rocky Variations (Harpur)
Orange Free State (Long)
Dreamcatcher (Stoney)
Megalithic Man (Horse)
Gobblin' Women (Nettle)
Libation (West)
Rhubarb, Rhubarb, Rhubarb (Rhubarb)
Arapaho Connection (BB)
Shot Yer Bolt (Horse)
The Quartz Tricycle (Small)
Mr. Love Pants (Small)
Rotund Roolay (Horse)
Bohemian (Stoney)

F6b

Balanced Ballistics (Nettle)
Tiery Henry (TTB)
Calci Mauve (Harpur)
Mega Byte (BB)
Cream Snatcher (Stoney)
Apollo Creed (Harpur)
Came down the Track (BB)
The Omen (Harpur)
A Trip on the Dark Side (Harpur)
Shanacie (Small)
Prefect Day (Harpur)
Doh (Harpur)
Hardcore, You Know the
Score (Horse)
Speed Freak (Harpur)
Blue Sunday (Horse)
Downtown (Harpur)
Rage (Horse)
Sunday Sport (Horse)
Brachiopods Bite Back (God)
School's Out (Horse)
Before Too Long (West)

F6a+

Windows 95 (BB)
Bag of Bones (Harpur)
Life's a Drag (Harpur)
Down in the Sewer (Lover's)
Lady Luck (Small)
The Plea (Runyon's)
Clotted Cream (Beer)
The Big Fat Texan on a Corner (Horse)
Porgi Amor (Horse)
The Candy Man (Harpur)
Eddie McStiff (Horse)

F6a

Coral Seas (Harpur)
Check Out (Biceps)
Dapper Dan (Horse)
Big Rock Candy Mountain (Horse)
Supernatural (Harpur)
Like Ice, Like Fire (Horse)
No Finer Place (West)
Foreign Tongues (Horse)
Pale Rider (Horse)
Got it Wrong (West)

F5+

Running for Cover (Harpur)
Sock It To 'em (Small)
Peckling Fever (Horse)
Addit Enough (Harpur)
Into the Labyrinth (Horse)
Peckling Fever (Horse)

F5

Excavator (Horse)
Senile Delinquents (Harpur)
Excavator (Horse)
Road Runner (Harpur)
Easy on the Gas (Harpur)

F4+

Sag Ponir (Horse)

F4

Luke Skywalker (Horse)

F3

Uranus (Horse)

Index

A

A Basic Problem of
Power 312
Abbey Habit 431
Aberration 371
A Bigger Belly 158
A Bigger Max 295
A Bigger Prize 158
A Bigger Splash 158
A Bigger Splash Direct 158
A Bigger Splat 168
A Bigger Tail 158
A Bigger Thud 168
A Big Slap 258
A Bit Lippy 401
A Bit of Nooky 297
A Bit on the Side 256, 401
A Bout de Soufflé 378
Absent Friends 330
Access All Areas 395
A Clip in Time 253
A Comedy of Played
Errors 489
Acrophobia 30
Action Potential 442
Actress, The 495
A Cure for Arapiles 297
A Cure for Foot Jams 297
Addit and Scarper 459
Addit Enough 459
Addit Pillar 459
Adios Tango 64
A Dip in Turquoise
Nonsense 458
Adrenaline Suspender 250
A Dude Called Deborah 279
Advanced Training 258
Advanced Warning 340
Aerospace 37
A Farewell to Arms 387
Afloat in the Moat 169
African 98
African't 98
A Friendly Chat with a
Hungry Ghost 508
Afterlife 294
After the Goldfish 312
After the Snow 135
Aftervision 190
Agent of Destruction 195

Agent Provocateur 172
Age of Reason 423
Aggrieved 369
A Grippa Clippa 134
Agrippa's Knees 134
Ain't Built for Goin'
Naked 427
Alacrity 88
Alan's Secret Drum Frenzy 426
A Laugh a Minute 321
Albatrossity 178
Alcasan 66
Alcatraverse 197
Alexander Beetle 429
Alex it was Really Nothing 72
Alfresco 336
Ali 314
A Liberal Smear 122
Aliens 190
Alien, The 190
Alimony 153
A Little Extra 234
Alive She Cried 251
All Along the Watchtower
508
Allergy 88
All Fall Down 395
All Hands to the Pump! 168
Alligator Crawl 172
All Made Up 397
All My Pegs in One Basket 248
All Souped Up 482
All Systems Go 36
All The Way 88
Almost There 121
Aloo Gobi 481
Alpha 507
Alpha Groove 175
Always Break the Rules 466
Amain 202
A Major Moment 176
A Man Called Horse 387
Amatarasu 442
A Matter of Style 135
A Mighty Wind 297
A Miller's Tale 156
Amnesiacs 204
Amnicolist Spies 151
Amphibian Conceit 88
Amphitheatre Wall 509
An Ancient Rhythm 107

Anarchism 391
A Nasty Farming Accident 337
Ancient Man 109
Andrex 115
Andronicus 126
An Eagle Does Not Catch
Flies 164
An Even Bigger Tail 156
Anger Management 222
Angled Buttress 509
Angler, The 160
Angleterre 473
An Illusion 83
An In and Out of Body
Experience 220
Annapurna South Face 249
Anoraks and Trainspotters 276
Anorexic Text 421
A.N.Other 56
Another Brick in the
Wall 360
Another Camden Day 81
Another Moatside Attrac-
tion 166
Another Toadside Attraction 234
Antidote 428
An Uplifting Experience 394
Any Hole's A Goal 261
Any Old Iron 102
Anything Corner 55
Ape Escape 327
Ape Index 176, 373
Apex Left Foot 144
Apex Middle Foot 144
Apex Right Foot 144
A Picture of Perfection 368
Aplomb 404
Apocalypse 334
A Poke in the Eye with a
Sharp Stick 429
Apollo Creed 477
Apparition 83
Apple Scrumping 428
Approaching 337
Après le Deluge 197
A Private Cosmos 429
Apt Pupil 482
Aquarian Warriors 150
Arabian Nights 218
Arachnid 31
Arachnothera 285

Aramis 425
Arapaho Connection 276
Arbeit Macht Frei 80
Arch Bishop 496
A Reet Treet 426
Arête, The 45
Arête, The 495
Argy Bargy 485
A Right Earful 111
Armageddon 63
Armed with an Empty
Gun 136
Armistice Day 314
Armitage 114
Army Dreamers 136
A Rooster in the Hen
House 371
Arrow, The 144
Arteaclism 466
Artery, The 508
Ash Crack 204
Ash Gash 427
Ash Tree Arête 497
Ash Tree Slab 497
Asia Shadow Player 316
Ask Mr. T. for Tea 477
As Loose as This? 384
A Soldier's Diary 276
Asparagus 45
Assault and Battery 485
As Summers Die 150
As You Like it Played 489
A Tall Story 154
A Time and a Place 85
Atlantic Realm 378
Atomic Tommy Cooper 491
A Touch of Class 373
A Tracky Little Bleeder 116
A Tracky Little Problem 116
A Trail of Destruction 151
A Trip on the Dark Side 464
Atropos 76
Attack the Ghost 285
Attila the Hun 180
Auctioneer, The 177
Augean 55
Au Gratin 47
Augustus Carp 320
Au Revoir Monodoigt 36
Aurora 66, 256
Aurora Arête 66

Austin Powers 102, 220
Austin Texas 102
Autobahn 338
Automatic Writing 463
Automaton 386
Aux Bicyclettes 46
Avarice 486
Avarice Allsorts 473
A Vision of Loveliness 368
Avoiding the Issue 122
Awesome Foursome 420
A Widespread Lack of
Imagination 333
Awkward Corner 499
Axe Edge Buttress 141
Axilla 141
Ayatollah 218

B

Babelicious 58
Babe the Blue Axe 121
Baby Chimes 230
Babylon By-Pass 58
Back in Black 258
Backstreet Vogue 356
Back to Basics 352
Back to Black 259
Back to Black Dyno 259
Bad Blood 94, 322
Bad Blood Direct 322
Bad Boys Ink 92
Bad Day 135
Badger Badger Badger 432
Bad Guts 250
Badlands 444
Baffled by Waterwings 349
Bag of Bones 480
Bag of X 212
Bakerloo 135
Balanced Ballistics 352
Balance of Probabilities 458
Balancing Act 377
Balbus 509
Balcony Climb 509
Balls Out 220
Balthazaaaaah 52
Banana 508
Banana Republic 374
Banarama 423
Bandobrass Took 448

Bandolier 100
Bandwagon on Direction 176
Banker's Climb 509
Barbarossity 177
Barefoot in a Pool of
  Sharks 289
Barely Decent 220
Barfleur 507
Barney 374
Barney Ragin' 316
Barney Rubble 95, 485
Barracuda 155
Barracuda Bass Sound 286
Basher's Problem 229
Basher's Right-Hand 229
Basic Logic 352
Bastard, The 160
Bastard Toadflax 250
Bayliff 85
Bay of Pigs 52
Bay Rum 85
Beachcomber 200
Beachy Hug 200
Beak Forest 411
Beam Me Across Scotty 116
Beanstalk 55
Bearing All 429
Bear It All 429
Bearly 429
Bear Necessities 429
Beastiality 414
Beast, The 426
Beat Retreat 491
Beat the Gun 252
Beau Jest 441
The Beckoning Thumb 88
Bedlam 417
Beef It 285
Bee Movie 414
Beep Beep 470
Bee's Knees 321
Beezlebub 314
Before the Storm 448
Before the War 97
Before Too Long 85
Beginner's Wall 256
Begorrah 206
Behaviour of Fish 390
Behemoth 188
Being Strange! 195
Belinda 53
Belladonna 181
Bellringer, The 188
Belly of the Beast 226
Belonging 460

Beluga 155
Belvedere 508
Ben 46
Bender, The 500
Ben's Groove 430
Ben's Roof 226
Ben's Roof Extension 226
Benstirer 86
Ben's Traverse 239
Berlin Wall 505
Berried 375
Best Forgotten Groove 494
Beta 507
Beta Blocker 33
Bewilderness 432
Bicycle Repair Man 441
Bifurous Chimney 200
Bifurous Corner 200
Big Apple, The 75
Big Boned Backside
  Melon 388
Big Boris 51
Big Butch 383
Big Chiv 89
Big Daddy 264, 383
Big Ears' Crack 425
Big Fat Conie 411
Big Fat Texan on a Corner 102
Big Jesus Trashcan 373
Big Leap Forward 75
Big News Man Mouth 377
Big Nig 381
Big Nose 76
Bigot Direct 200
Big Plum 402
Big Plums 75
Big Rock Candy Mountain 120
Big Store 314
Big Word Climb 251
Big Youth 264
Big Zipper 314
Billericay Dicky 367
Bill's Crack 430
Bimbo does Limbo 124
Bimbo Drops his Codpiece 124
Bimbo Has his Head
  Examined 124
Bimbo on the Loose 124
Bimbo's Arête 124
Bimbo's Off-day Route 124
Bimbo Strikes Again 123
Binge Drinker 281
Bingo Wall 53
Bird Cage 431
Bird Island Pitch 1 97

Bird Island Pitch 2 119
Birthday Boy 356
Birthday Groove 197
Bish Bash Bosch 417
The Bishop 495
Bit of Spare Thyme 119
Bit of Totty 468
Bitter Fingers 55
Black Adder 395
Black and White Minstrel
  Show 393
Blackbirds 250
Black Bryony 86, 89
Black by Popular Demand 264
Black & Deckout 263
Black Edge 395
Blackhole 263
Black Hole 404
Black is the Colour 263
Black Jack 447
Black Kabul 36
Black Leg Groove 394
Black Magic 250, 264
Black Mamma 393
Black Max 292
Black Power 64
Black Rights 375
Black Sabbath 181
Blacksmith's Lactic 250
Black Teddy 61
Black Widow 288
Bladerunner 445
Blade Runner 111
Blanca Expression 171
Blanc de Blanc 323
Blazed but Amazed 434
Bleingassen 481
Blickin' 'eck 89
Blicks, The 89
Blind Alleys 329
Blind Spot 342
Blinkers 44
Blocked Flue 453
Blockhead 367
Blockheads 419
Blocky Balbao 213
Blocky Horror Show 213
Blocky Road to Ruin 213
The Blood Bank 94
Blood Diamond 34
Bloodguard 98
Blood Lust 322
The Blood of an Englishman 55
Blood Transfusion 322
Bloodworm 322

Blue Adept 432
Blue Arsed Fly 322
Blue Banana 68
Blueband 240
Blueberry Tower 426
Blue-Eyed Myxamatoid 153
Bluefinger 53
Bluehumps 240
Blue Sunday 123
Bluto 486
Boat Pusher's Wall 51
Bob Slopes 426
Body Builder 222
Body Line 338
Body Machine 220
Bog, The 114
Bohemian 71
Bolt 45 417
Bolts R Us 467
Bombardier 319
Bomb is Coming 161
Bone and Globe 285
Bonedigger 461
Bone Idol 264
Boneman Connection 457
Bonny Helena 487
Boo 333
Boobs 333
Booker Prize 122
Books on the Bonfire 333
Boomerang 447
Boot Boys 236
Boot Boys Start 239
Bootiful Bernard Matthews 99
Bored of the Lies 314
Boring 366
Born Again 54
Borrower's Climb 509
Bosch Spice 417
Bosky 202
Bossyboots 264
Boulder Problem 207
Bovine 262
Bow String Groove 144
Boxed 440
Boxing Clever 440
Box Number 7 440
Boyband 241
Brachiation Dance 177
Brachiopods Bite Back 78
Brandenburg Gate 222
Brands Hatched 456
Brand X 251
Brandy Bottle Bates 381
Brassiere Strap 45

Brava 35
Brazen Strumpet 222
Breakbeat 172
Breakfast at Safeways 485
Breaking the Chain 250
Bream in Black 286
Breamtime 286
Breathing Underwater 64
Breathless 378
Brer Faced Cheek of It 153
Brew Thyme 119
Bricktop 308
Bride and Groom 360
Bridge Over the River
  Thyme 119
Brief Camouflage 321
Brief Scramble 151
The Brighton Line 53
Brock the Start 352
Broken Crack 509
Broken Hammer 446
Broken to Bits 110
Broken Toe 497
Brothers in Arms 376
Brown Corner 27
Bruce's Bonus 112
Brutal Brutus 425
Bubbles Wall 36
Bubbles Wall Direct 36
Buffoon Crack 249
The Bulge 1984 176
Bulging Wall 509
Bullets 210
Bullet, The 469
Bullet the Blue Sky 232
Bum Note 249
Bungle 258
Burlesque 397
Burning Giraffe 505
Burning Rails 275
Burning up Time 136
Burqa King 360
Burst 500
Bursting Out 355
Burundi 118
Buster 372
Bust yer Gut 490
Butch Master 490
Buxton Goes French 484
By Caesarean 486
BYGOF 486
Byker Groove 259
Bypass 425
Byte Size 276
By Zeus 122

C

Cabbage Crack 27
Cabbage Disease 358
Cabin Fever 485
Café Bleu 124
Cairn 485
Cake Walk 509
The Cake Walk 96
Calamity Jane 112
Calci Mauve 480
Calcite Claws 482
Call of Nature 234
Calvi Corner 390
Came Down the Track 275
Can Boys 417
Candy Floss 253
Candy Kaned 253
Candy Man 253, 466
Candy Store 467
Candy Store Rock 88
Candy Wreath 430
Canine of Brine 46
Canopy Crack 200
Can't Climb Won't
Climb 81
Can'tgetmyfix 414
Can't Girls? 417
Can't Pin it On Me 458
Can't Stop Now 76
Captain Ahab 338
Captain Reliable 444
Carbon Neutral 34
Carcass 348
Cardiac Arrest 33
Cardinal, The 495
Carillon Crack 186
Carl's Wark Crack 36
Carl's Wark Traverse 36
Carmel 494
Carmen 496
Carmen Jones 496
Carmen Mirander 496
Carol's Crack 186
Cart the Wheel 490
Carvery 460
Casamance 377
Case Adjourned 361
Castle Groove 508
Castle Pudding 169
Castration 164
Catch the Rainbow 180
Cathedral Taste 378
Cathy's Clown 444
Cathy's Clown Right-Hand 445

Cat Lick 349
Cave Corner 204
Cave Crack 85, 509
Cave Problem 226
Cave Wall 505
Caviar 155
CD Romp 276
Celebration 372
Central Arête 499
Central Gully 496
Centreville 462
Ceramic 337
Ceramic Extension 337
Certificate X 213
C'est Plastique 195
Cetswayo 395
Chagrin 397
Chain Gang 193
Chain of Command 377
Chain Reaction 423
Chains 250
Chairs Missing 154
Chalk Boycott 430
Chance in a Marillion 495
Changeling 341
Changing Fortunes 154
Chantrelle 60
Chapter and Verse 319
Charas 441
Chastity 509
Chauvi's Slab 95
Cheat 447
Checkered Flag 456
Check Out 435
Chee Tor Girdle 343
Chemical Weapons 321
Chewemoff 72
Chicane 135
Chicken 124
Chicken Feed 93
Chicken Run 371
Childline 35
Child Lock 379
Child's Arête 35
Child's Play 379
Chill Out 274
Chimes Alternative 230
Chimes of Freedom 230
Chiming Crack 186
China Crisis 249
China Rib 195
Chinese Wall 249
Chip off the Old Block 402
Chockstone Crack 509
Chocolate Blancmange

Gully 96
Chopper, The 340
Choss 64
Choux Pastry 86
Christian Salvage Man 487
Christiliano Wall 144
Christmas Crackers 89
Christmas Cracks 141
Christmas Presence 93
Christmas Pudding 96
Chuck Berry 30
Chug Chug Chug 274
Cicatrix 141
Cinema Rage 96
Circe 61
Citadel 256
Citizen's Arête 117
Clackers Sprained my
Knackers 489
Clarion Call 312
Classical Gas 428
Clay Man 491
Clean Crack 86
Clean Cut 151
Clean Team 490
Clean Your Mouth Out 111
Clematis 308
Clever Trevor 367
Clive's Route 341
Clone of Jeremiah 495
Close Control 393
Close Enough 250
Close to the Edge 274
Clothesline 499
Clotted Cream 423
Clowning 444
Cob 124
Cock a Hoop 355
Cock-a-Leekie Wall 45
Cockerel Cry 361
Cocoa Pops 447
Co-Conspirator 32
Cointreau 48
Coldity Crack 195
Coldity Groove 195
Cold Shoulder 202
Collared 100
Collateral Damage 484
College Crack 458
Colon 389
The Colostomy Finish 105
Coltsfoot Stick 428
Columnus 374
Combien de Siecles? 490
Come Fly with Me 138

Coming of the Sparrows 463
Coming up for Air 169
Commiseration 122
Commit Dirty Act 264
Communication Breakdown 369
Community Service 383
Complete Psychosis 446
Compositae Groove 68
Compromise 110
Conclusor 209
Confidence 164
Confidence Trick 142
Confusion 183
Conie Ferrino 411
Conie Island Elephant 411
Conie Lamiche 411
Conie Lamprecht 411
Conie Musselbrook 411
Conie Pepperoni 411
Conie Simpson 411
Conie Toutts 411
Conie Whitehouse 411
Conie Yeboah 411
Conspiracy Theory 438
Constant Gardener 494
Contemplation 83
Contraband 241
Converter 229
Convoy 145
Cool Danny 478
Cool Hand Luke 193
Cooper's Route 494
Coot 155
Cora 156
Coral Seas 473
Cordless Madness 316
Corgi Registered 124
Corinthian Spirit 121
Corner Crack 183
Corner it Is 78
Corner It is Not 78
Corniceman, The 318
The Cornice Traverse 175
Corniche 438
Cosmopolitan 316
Costa del Jolly 171
Costa Del Soul 430
Countdown 365
Count Duckula 251
Country Rock 496
County Marin 52
County Time 281
Couples Retreat 491
Cowslip 404
Coyote Club 470

Crabs 281
Crab Walk 161
Crack and Nose 509
Cracked Edge 206
Crack Fox 432
Crankerdown 75
Crank it Up 394
Crankus Maximus 295
Crash Crazy 138
Cray-Pas 86
Crazy Pinnacle Face 470
Crazzled Cracks 86
Cream Snatcher 76
Cream Team Special 237
Cream Tea Special 236
Creeper, The 195
The Creeping Flesh 28
Cretan, The 121
Cricket Lovely Cricket 197
Crime 404
Crimps and Pockets 162
Cripple's Crab 249
Critical Town 211
Crocodile 174
Cropper's Scoop 404
Cross & Blackwell 264
Cross 'n Angry 222
Cross Purposes 444
Crowd Control 312
Crow's Nest 404
Crucifixion, The 222
Cruel Sea 318
Cruise Brothers 366
Cruising the Seven Seas 161
Crumblefish 232
Crumbling Cracks 190
Crumbs 96
Crunch, The 172
Crunch Yer Nuts 120
Crusade 494
Crustacean 78
Crux, The 46
Cry Havoc 320
Cry of Despair 310
Cry of the Beholder 505
Crystalline 175
Crystal Maze 418
Cry Tuff 145
Cuckley Delf Eliminate 88
Cuck the Duck 251
Culloden 250
Cupid Sails 401
Curb Your Passion 444
Curry Badger 432
Curse of the Mummy 368

Curving Crack 508
Custard 250
Custard pie in Your Eye 320
Cut Loose or Fly 204

D

Daddy's Riding the Range 393
Daedalus 30
Daffy 116
Dagenham Dave 341
Dalken Shield 111
Damocles 27
Damson in Distress 402
Dances With Wool 256
Dancing the Hard Bargain 507
Dandelion 337
Dandelion Mind 432
Dangerous Brothers 155
Dangerous Liaisons 186
Dangerous Tribes 155
Dangleberry 389
Danny Cool 478
Dapper Dan 121
Dapper Slapper 153
Dargai Crack 508
Dark Half 463
Dark Room 506
The Dark Tower 112
Darl 365
Darl Pitch 2 368
D'Artagnan 425
Dawn Razor 145
Daylight Robbery 138, 366
Day of the Long Knives 321
Dead Banana Crack 55
The Dead Girls 27
Dead on Arrival 34
Dead Parrot Sketch 440
Dead Tree Crack 141
Dead Tree Groove 141
Death is Part of the
Process 32
Death's Retreat 448
Debris 161
Debris Groove 162
Débutant 249
Decade to Decayed 373
Decapitator, The 382
Decayed Dance 111
Deception 142
Deceptor 496
Deconstruction 85
Deep Thought 428
Defector, The 404

Defrag 276
Déjà Vu 190
Delusor 209
Dementia Normale 477
Demolition Man 109
Demon Striation 138
Demystified 376
Derailed 112
Deranged Abbott 261
Desmond Douglas 144
Desperate Dan 98
Desperate Housewives 100
Desperate Measures 100
De Throne 115
Devil's Eye 80
De Vine 321
Devolution 230
Devonshire Arms 315
Dialectics 236
Diamonds and Rust 34
Diamond Wall 459
Diaphragm 448
Diddyogger 418
Did Romeo Play 489
Dies Irae 61
Different Season 482
Dig Deeper 75
Dig Deep for Victory 75
Digit of Derision 168
Dinky Toy 124
Dinosaurs Don't Max 295
The Director's Cut 111
Direct Route 509
Dirty Deeds 379
Dirty Little Sheila 171
Dirty Old Man 310
Disappointment 27
Disgusted of Tunbridge 318
The Disillusioned Brew
Machine 31
Disillusioned Glue Machine 178
Disjointed Might 369
Dis-Orientated 195
Disparagement 193
Disraeli Gears 396
Dissident Aggressor 249
Distant Thunder 448
Distinction 430
Dizzy 373
Do Androids Dream of
Electric Sheep? 112
Dobbin 507
Dodgem Central 456
Dog-calming Influence of
Maltesers II 430

Dog Canute 491
Dog Dirt 349
Dogfight 348
Doggone Groove 342
Doggy Style 341
Dog's Day Route 348
Dogs, The 112
Doh 460
Do I? 172
Doing the Dirty 161
Do It Yourself 123
Dole: 1989 176
Dole Technician 259
Do Little 467
Dome's Groove 32
Do Nothing 60
Don't Forget the Freezone 438
Don't Jump 259
Don't Look Back 447
Don't Talk to Strangers 84
Don't Try This at Home 124
Dot the Eyes 505
Double Scotch 48
Double Topley 404
Double Wammy 421
Do Up Your Flies 505
Down in the Sewer 453
Down Like a Rock 253
Down She Goes 442
Down Some Lazy River 358
Down to the Armpits 438
Down to the Last 110
Downtown 487
Do You Dig It? 75
Dragonflight 154
Dragonflight Traverse 154
Dragon's Back 509
Dragon's Side 509
Drainpipe Groove 32
Drawbridge Down When
the Levee Breaks 168
Dreadnought 310
Dreamcatcher 76
The Dream Mile 334
Dreams of Living 145
Dream Thief 295
Dream Topping 96
Dreamy Intentions 182
Drink and Be Merry 31
Drip 183
Dr Lazarus 464
Drool Rock Worm 99
Drophammer 196
Dross 64
Drumming in a Lay-by 117

Dr Who? 116
Dry 183
D.T.'s Route 166
Dude's Route 181
Due Care and Attention 102
Duel in the Sun 339
Duelling Biceps 435
Duelling Trousers 488
Dukes of Earl (Grey) 297
Dukes of Hazzard 281
Duma Key 482
Dumb Animal 160
Dump 441
During the War 97
Dust 83
The Dust Bunnies 111
Dusty Lusty 281
Dynamic 387
Dysoning 509

E

Early Bird Wall 426
Early One Morning 145
Ear to Ear 462
Easy Action 31
Easy Come Easy Go 115
The Easy Interloper 124
Easy on the Gas 459
Easy Rider 310
Easy Skanking 75
Easy Victory 75
Eat the Rich 139
Eau de Toilette 115
Eclipsed 178
Ecstatic 435
Eddie Cochrane 84
Eddie McStiff 100
Eddy's First 296
Edge of Donnybrooks 427
Edge of Insanity 209
Edge Play 488
Educated Edmund 384
Eeonefivebee 418
E for Friction 488
Egg an' Onion Crack 426
Egg Bag 425
Ego has Landed 151
Egyptian Bizarre 314
Eighe 138
Eight till Late 417
Elbow Ridge 505
El Camino Real 477
Elderberry Crack 509
Elective Affinities 81

Elephants Never Forget 258
Elephant Talk 395
Elizabethville 118
Ellis Needham 253
Ello Ethique 234
Elvis Gets My Bus 264
E Mail 277
Emanon 35
Emblem Embargo 441
Emergency 448
Emission Control 274
Emmaline 429
Emotional Rescue 27
Empire Burlesque 180
Empty Cartridge 71
Emulator 195
Enchanted Place 264
Endeth 462
End Games 462
Ending Now 462
End is Nigh 462
Endless Flight 138
End of the Line 53
End of the Tour 207
Endsville 462
End, The 482
English Impatient 426
Enigma 211
En Masse Descendre 188
Enterprise Allowance 176
Entree 365
Ephemeral Groove 448
Epidavros 353
Ergonomic Buttress 251
Eric's Left Buttock 250
Erithacus 136
Ernie 68, 276
Eros 144
Eros Goes to Durham 401
Escape Artist 193
Escort Crack 387
Esmerunga 354
Esso Extra 123
ET 435
E.T. Bone Home 249
Ethical Nightmare 374
Eugenics 155
Euphoric 435
Euroman 141
Euroman Endeth 462
European Female 322
Evasor 76
Everett's Arête 120
Every Breath You Take 274
Everything 249

Eve Syndrome 353
Evidently Chickentown 362
Evolution 230
Excalibur 168
Excavator 96
Exceeding the Speed Limit 100
Exclusion Zone 478
Exfoliation 206
Exide 508
Exiled Transformer 249
eXit Stage Left 212
Expecting 486
Extended Weedkiller 229
Exterminator, The 232
Extra Effort 444
Eye Catching Cod Piece 274
Eye Line 397
Eye of Nowt 88
Eye Shadows 397
Eyes of Fire 333
Ezekiel Stool 319

F

Façade 397
Faced Cheek 429
Faces in the Mirror 458
Face the Blueberry 426
Face Value 458
Fairy, The 144
Falling Icons 277
Falling, The 453
Fallout 30
Fallout Zone 320
Fall, The 151
Fame but no Fortune 282
Family Fortunes 390
Fantastic 435
Fargo 123
Farmer's Seed 93
The Far Sidle 88
Fartless 460
Fatal Attraction 193, 376
Fatal Hesitation 193
Fat Betty 119
Fat Cat 421
Fat Ginger Cat 321
Fat Lip 226
Fatty Manwell and the
    Paranoid Oysters 327
Fawlty Towers 396
Fear and Loathing (In Las
    Vegas) 509
Fear of Flying 138
Feel my Presence 464

Feel the Beat 274
Fe Fi Fo Fum 55
Feline Fine 321
Feminine Ego Trip 306
Fetish Cracks 391
Fey 312
Fiat 444
Fibrin 319
Fifth Amendment 383
Fifty Bolts to the Gallon 110
Figure of Law 477
Final Apocalypse 150
Final Sacrifice 136
Fin de Siecle 490
Fine and Dandy 98
Finest Pedigree 350
Fingal's Cave 46
Fingal's Flue 46
Fingermuse 88
Fingerpops 394
Finishing Off 110
Finnieston Ferry 404
Fire Dance 392
Firefly 280
Firefly Crack 395
The Fire Hang 93
Firelance 145
Fireman's Frolic 282
Fire on Water 190
First Day of Winter 107
First Day Tower 426
First Flight 138
First Light 353
First Offence 417
Fishing Without a Licence 289
Fishlock 355
Fish-u-Like 355
Fist to Fist is Done 457
Five Miles High 395
Fixation 448
Fix on the Mix 421
Fizzy 280
Flake and Pillar 36
Flake Crack 509
Flaked Out 196
Flaked Out Shake Out 156
The Flakes Direct 63
Flakes, The 63
Flakey Pastry 480
Flaky Pastry 86
Flared Beginnings 32
Flash Harry 319
The Flashing Fisher 48
Flatworld 109
Flavour of the Month 53

Fledgling Flakes 136
Fledgling, The 136
Flexor Hallucis Longus 460
Flight of Icarus 371
Flight of the Finches 463
Flight Path 138
Flip Side 509
Floating Rib 425
Floggin' a Dead Horse 418
Flog the Lume 489
Flossy's Slab 467
Flow 365
Flowers in the Dirt 316
The Fluff Pirate 68
Fluffy Roo Meets the
    Woodentops 68
Flushed Out 453
Flushings, The 234
Flyaway Crack 181
Flycatcher 76, 341
Flying Circus 323
Flying Dutchman 169
Flying Scotsman 218
Flying Solo 448
Fly, The 499
Food for Sport 486
Fools Rush In 195
Fool's Stuffing 463
FOP 120
Fop, The 427
Forager 256
Forbidden Rib 440
Forehead Trombones 306
Foreign Tongues 93
Forfeit or Doom 461
Forging the Chain 432
Forgive My Trespasses 505
Forgotten Dream 390
Forgotten Groove 200
For Haven's Sake 487
For Men Tour 171
Four Minute Tiler 72
Four Telling Tales 481
Four Thousand 76
Fowl Play 232
For the Good of the Cause 274
For the Love of Ivy 211
For the Prosecution 383
Fort Knox 188
Fort Knox Direct 188
Fortune 27
Fossil Wall 256
Foul's Bane 99
Four Door Dostoyevsky 315

Foxhole Groove 427
Fragile Earth 289
Fragmented 110
Frankly Ferocious 384
Frantic Manoeuvres 461
Fred 84
Freda 248
Freda Direct 249
Freda's Start 248
Fred Flintstone 485
Freedom Fighter 230, 323
Freedom is Insane 190
Freedom Slaves 202
Freedom Trap 333
Freedonia 117
Freeman Trap 333
Free Monster 177
Free Range Abattoir 261
Freeway 377
Freewheeler 156
Fresh Jive 388
Friction Wall 508
Friend 15 420
Friendly Local 448
Friezian 418
Fringe Meeting 418
Frisco Bay 52
Frolic 248
From Cradle to Grave 482
From Here to There 55
Frore 211
Froth 54
Frozen Assets 448
Fruit and Fibre 447
Fuckpig 296
Fudge 259
Fuji Fantastic 469
Full Frontal 477
Full Monty 220
Full Set 486
Funf 509
Further Adventures in
    Greendale 318
Future Paradox 288

G

Gabriel 46
Galaxy Quest 464
Galening Crack 110
Gam 428
Game of Chess 440
Gander Meat 386
Gangway, The 509
Gardener's Question Time

197, 311
Gardener's World 500
Garden Shades 430
Garfish Serenade 289
Gargle Blaster 116
Garlic Twist 321
Gaseous Exchange 321
Gaspera 61
Gathering Darkness 464
Geisha Grooves 468
General Incompetence 354
Generously Cut Trousers 392
Gentleman Jim 425
George's Groove 50
George Stark Calling 462
George's Wall Dyno 50
Gerremdown 72
Gesemini 51
Getafix 414
Get Down and Bark 279
Get It Wired 428
Get Lifted 395
Get Peddling 458
Get Six into the Mix 30
Getting Into Ivy 426
Getting the Groove 466,
478
Get Your Clarks On 441
Ghee Force 362
Ghost in the Machine 89
Ghost Writer 463
Giants 402
Giant Staircase 447
Gibbon Take 390
Gigantic 402
Gimme Shelter 423
Ginger Man 505
Ginza Crack 196
Glas Double 480
Glaswegian Kiss 279
Glorious Ninth 323
Glory Road 58, 355
The Glory Trail 58
Glue 'em Back 74
Gluttony 486
Go Again 182
Goalie Wag 428
Goal of the Month 340
Gobbler, The 93, 379
Gobblin' Women 355
Goblin, The 144
Gob on the Mountain 378
Gobstopper 378
Go Cat 349
Going Bush 142

Going Straight 420
Goldcrest 180
Golden Boy 27
Golden Brown 89
Golden Delicious 75
Golden Gate 53
Golden Goose 468
Golden Grockle 124
Golden Lips 34
The Golden Mile 334
Golden Tights 124
Golden Wall Traverse 89
Goldfinger 371, 508
Gold Label 124
Gollyberry 30
Gonads 372
Gone for a Tim Burton 487
Good Vibrations 275
Goofy 116
Gooncrack 461
Gooseberry Pillar 379
Gopherspace 277
Gorignak 464
Gorrah 206
Gothic Demarcation 89
Got it Wrong 85
Gouranga (Be Happy) 93
Grab Your Mandrakes 98
Gran 310
Grand Tour 232
Gran Turismo 237
Grape and Rye 423
Grapple and Grope 341
Grass Dynamique 505
Grauncher, The 86
Grave Snatcher 33
Graveyard Blues 463
Great Central Route 338
Great Escape 48, 367
Great Expectations 213, 447
The Great Leveller 55
Great White 485
Greedor 117
Green Alternative 230
Green Crack 37
Green Dragon 249
Green Fingers 174
Green Monkey 174
Greenpeace 119
Green Rooster 232
Greensleeves 470
Greet the Tweet 421
Griff's Traverse 263
Grinning Chimney 340
Grit Arête 473

Grockle's Gully 124
Groovy Baby 139
Groper, The 46
Grotty Totty 71
Ground Control 136
Groundhog Day 175
Ground Zero Man 447
Grow Fins 458
Gruesome Groove 202
Guilty 384
Gulle Gulle Groove 341
Gullied 491
Gully Folk 491
Gully, The 175
Gwendoline 195
Gymnic 202
Gypsy Kings 460

H

Hacker, The 277
Hades 209
Hair Bear Bunch 428
Hairline 462
Hairline Fracture 250
Hairy Legs 190
Hajj, The 224
Halcyon Drift 447
Half Decent 220
Half Way Crack 431
Ham and X 212
Hamish 395
Hamlet Prince of Players 489
Hammer 50
Hammer into Anvil 440
Hammy Hamster's Last
 Rites 186
Hamsters in Aspic 197
Hand Candy 252
Hang Fire 93
Hanging Garden 509
Hangman 427
Hannibal 126
Hannibal Corner 126
Ha'penny Tray 428
Happy Days 171
Happy Humphrey 429
Happy Wanderer 71
Hard Candy 253
Hardcorejunkie 368
Hardcore You Know the
 Score 111
Hard Drive 276
Hard Labour 500
Hard Player 488

Hard Shoulder to Cry
 On 444
Hardy, Kiss Me 375
Hare 154
Harmonious Harmonica 352
Harry the Horse 383
Hart Attack 33
Harvey Wallbanger 109
Has She Been? 35
Hatred 339
Haven or Hell 487
Haven't Got a Cluedo 46
Hawaii Five-O 314
Hazy Day 428
Heart of Darkness 330
Heart to Heart 94
The Heat 27
Heathenism 391
Heatwave 190
Height Below 487
Held her Head 434
Helicon 72
Hell Driver 444
Hell Hath No Fury 34
Helmut Schmitt 27
Helter Skelterer 488
Helzapoppin 470
Hemmingway's Horror 186
Her Aklion 121
Hercules 55
Here 423
Hergiani 330
Heron, The 447
Hero's Challenge 253
He Seems So Sumo 102
Hesitation Dance 139
Hex, The 488
Hey Diddle Diddle 484
Hidden Corner 494
Hi-Fi 207
Higherlands 76
High Impact 457
High Scream Sunday 396
High Society 375
Highway 57 338
Hinges 53
Hippo's Chimney 174
The Hippy Hippy Shakes 102
Hissin' Sid 485
Hit the Deck but don't
 Run 446
Holiday Home for Pets Pie
 Company 431
Hollow Inside 418
Hollow Man 487

Hollow Way 197
Holly 35
Holy Schmitt 27
Home from Home 360
Honeymoon Blues 153
Honeysuckle Lane 47
Hong Kong Fewy 469
Honking Corner 404
Honorary Slate 279
Hoochie Koo 395
Hook 226
Hooligan 236, 239
Hooligans 340
Horizon 45
Hornby 124
Horrorscope 85
Hot Dogger 349
Hot Flushes 234
Hot Fun Closing 156
Hot Horse Herbie 381
Hot Panties 379
Hot Thighs 264
Hot Zipperty 124
House on a Hill 80
How it Be? 30
How the Hell 34
Hubble 222
Hubris 220
Hulk, The 250
Human Fit Tailors 282
Humiliation 279
Hunger Strike 365
Hungry Eyes 285
Hunter House Bust 394
Hupsters 280
Hydrolysis 204
Hyperactive 355
Hyperon 355
Hysterectomy 64

I

I am the Law 477
I Can see How to Do It 197
Icarus 28
Ice 9 249
Ice Cream Phoenix 206
Ice Out in the Rain 249
Ichabod 487
Ichor 164
Iconoclast 196
Idiot Nation 423
Idolatry Wall 391
I Drink Therefore I Am 281
Ifad 250

If Nine Were Ten 445
Igor 327
I got the Drill 277
I Had a Black Shirt 386
I Hate You 72
Ikon Wall 196
I Love My Pigeon 279
I'm a Port Vale Dribbler 462
I'm in the Sin Bin 473
Immortal Combat 64
Immunity Syndrome 358
I'm not a Pla 488
Impendent 202
Importance of Being
 Ernest 186
Inbetweenies, The 367
In Brine 234
In Bulk 188
Incandescent Courage 292
Incapacity Benefit 176
Inch Test 139
In Composite 68
Inconsiderate Blinking 484
In Conversation 83
In Corpus 64
Incredible Pierre 360
Indecent Direct 220
Indecent Exposure 220
Independence Day 509
Indian Cottage 481
Indictment 448
Indirect Route 509
Induction Program 486
Infantada 423
Infinite Suspense 249
Influx 241
In Formalin 32
In Isolation 458
In Merittville 374
In My Darkest Hour 462
Inquisitor 61
Insidious Iceberg 442
Inslippy 250
In Stark Contrast 463
Instrumentally Yours 427
In the Defence 383
In the Drink 349
In The Flesh 164
In the Gravy 482
In the Jailhouse 121
In the Shadows 135
In the Stox 384
In the X Team 212
In Tiers 368
Into the Labyrinth 121

Introducing the Hardline 220
Intuition 138
Invasion of the Creepazoid 463
Invisible Lights 448
Invisibles, The 282
I Predict a Roti 481
Iron Curtain 478
Iron Filings 393
Irrational 490
Isolate 362
Isolation 80
Is this the End? 462
Is Ya Alright? 30
Is Ya Ready 30
It has to End Somewhere 462
It's All Greek to Me 121
It's a Traversty 258
It's Uranus 423
It Tolls for Thee 188
Ivory Poacher 258
Ivy Corner 200
Ivy Grotto Direct 55
I Want Cookie 200

J

Jackdaw Gully 496
Jack Frost 427
Jackorner 494
Jackson's Browned Off 361
Jaggered Crack 508
Jailer's Crack 508
Jailer's Groove 508
Jailer's Wall 508
Jam Butty Mines Crack 486
Jamma yer Hut 490
Jam Sandwich 48
Jam Slice 124
Janbaloo 499
Jap's Eyes are on You 468
J. Arthur 30
Jasper 27
Jaws 154
Jaws II 169
Jeff Garrett 112
Jehovahkill 222
Jelly Beans 467
Jelly Fingers 318
Jelly Tots 468
Je ne Comprendre Pas 440
Jeremy's Jungular Jaunt 496
Jerry's Traverse 261
Jewfish 423
Jezebel 154

Jihad 423
Jive Turkey 232
J.L.N.O.E. 434
John Peel 28
Joint Effort 444
Jokoharma 469
Journey's End 352
Joy or Despair 83
Jubilee Groove 264
Juggernaut 46
Jug Jockey 310
Jularet 404
Jumping Beans Wall 181
Jumping Blacks 89
Jungle Ape 151
Jungle Burger 88
Jungle Jim 142
Jungle Rock 376
Jury's Out 383
Just Another Tricky Day 88
Just Passing Through 419
Just Pullet 361
Just Say No 431
Just the Ticket 459
Just What the Doctor Ordered 35

K

K2 315
K3 315
K5 315
Kaaba 224
Kaiser Bill 505
Kakaho 355
Kali Yuga 365
Kalymnos 8a 297
Kamikaze Clone 469
Kariba 119
Karma Killer 172
Keen Roof 226
Keen Roof Stand Start 226
Keep Arête 508
Keep Cleft 508
Keep on Truckin' 145
Keep, The 145, 508
Kellogg 62
Kellogs Are On Strike 447
Kelly's Eye 53
Ken Dodd's Dad's Dog's Dead 464
Kick the Bucket 279
Killer Bee 414
Killer Strumpet 232
Killerweed 229

Kill the Bill 382
Kill your Television 373
King Cannibal 126
Kingdom Come 62
Kingfisher 154
King Kong 66
King Louis 249
King of Ming 76
Kink 61
Kinky 62
Kiss Me Hardy 375
Kiss My Arcy 376
Kiss the Mackerel 289
Klingon 116
Knee Trembler 429
Knightmare 138
Knight Rider 105
Knocked Out Loaded 134
Knockin' on the Bread Man's Door 71
Knuckle Knocker 190
Koran 218
Koran Direct 218
Koroblin 327
Krab on Your Sac Says Weth 427
Kriklet's Cancer 327
Kristian's Problem 241
Kristian's Traverse 230
Kudos 158
Kudos Traverse 158
Kumquat 323
Kushti 123
Kuwait and See 251

L

La Belle Age 188
La Belle et la Bete 72
Labour Relations 122
La Brute 194
Lachesis 478
La Chute 194
Ladybird Killers 414
Lady Luck 418
The Lady of the Lake 166
Lady's Fingers 322
Lammergeyer Twins 150
Lamprey on Ice 288
Lanky Sod 250
Lapin 153
Lap Times 456
Lard Wall 30
Larium 428
La Route 195
Last but not Least 160

Last Chance 181
Last Eggs Before the M1 308
Last Exit Going South 418
Last Laugh 340
Last Man First 423
Last Stand 59
Last Straw 477
Late at Night 83
Lateral Passage 282
Later that Night 463
Latrec 115
Latrine 114
Laughing 337
Laughing at the Rain 435
Laurels for Hardy 368
Lazy Day 426
The Leading Line 107
Learning to Swim 349
Learn the Lingo 419
Leben Tod 489
Led up the Garden Path 319
Lee Perry Presents 'It's a Knockout' 248
Leering Wall 341
Lefrack 86
Left-Hand Crack 88
Lefty 509
Legal Action 107
Lengthening Shadows 197
Leningrad 448
Leper's Groove 448
Leprosy 68, 174
Lesley Ann 45
Lesley's Tower 426
Less of your Lip 401
Less Than Zero 336
Lethal Dose 282
Let it Go 491
Let's Get Fossilised 256
Let's Get Green 232
Let's Get Naked! 232
Let's Get Physical 256
Let's Get Physical Right-Hand 256
Let's Get Ready to Rumbleweed 229
Letterbox, The 508
Let the Max Increase 295
Let the Tribe Increase 155
Let the Tripe Increase 168
Let Your Guard Down 80
Levant 428
Leviathan 188
Liang Shang Po 174

Libation 83
Libertines, The 117
Lies and Deception 417
Life After Death 135
Life of a Stickleback 289
Life's a Drag 456
Light Ideas 353
Light, The 484
Lightweight 373
Like Ice Like Fire 110
Lily Street 339
Limited Edition 145, 282
Linbo 430
Liposuction 401
Liquid Courage 445
Liquid Dream 35
Liquid Engineering 124
Litany Against Fear 107
Little Big Climb 404
Little Blue Lies 213
Little Boots 236
Little Brown Men 423
Little Capucin 34
Little Crack 36
Little Curver 350
Little Damocles 124
Little Extra Direct Start 239
Little Isadore 383
Little Jordan 264
Little Lady 417
Little Moose 85
Little Plum 75
Little Prune 404
The Little Thin Mexican Across the Border 100
Little Weed 430
Little Wimp 264
Living with a Porcupine 151
Lizzie 496
Local 448
Local Vortex 382
Lockless Monster 297
Loco 318
Loco Motif 391
Loco-Motion 275
Lom Attack 340
Long Dead Train 352
Long Enough 85
Longevity 460
Long Playa 456
Long Time No See 460
Long Walk 460
The Long Walk 112
Long Walk off a Short Pier 460

Looking at the Blue 202
Looking Good 141
Looking Through Gary
  Gibson's Eyes 45
Lost Ambition 249
Lost Arête 181
Lost Contact 417
Lost Horizon 46
Lost Monolith 109
Lost Thread 495
Louie the Lug 381
Love 489
Love Amongst the Butterflies 316
Love is a Swallow 275
Love is the Drug 145
Lovely Bubbly 123
The Lover's Leap 75
Lovine 263
Lowerlands 76
Lowlands 76
Low Right Start 158
Luck be the Magic Number 366
Lucky Finger 377
Lucy Simmons 58
Lucy Simmons Variation 58
Luddite Thought Police 477
Luke Skywalker 116
Lunatic Fringe 292
Lust 473
Lust in the Dust 281

M

Machineries of Joy 373
Mackenzie Frenzy 389
Macumba 377
Madagascar 97
Mad Dogs and Englishmen 373
Made You Look 432
Magician's Enemy 356
Maillon Sunday 99
Main Motor Mile 435
Majorca Alternative 171
Major Incontinence 354
Make It Funky 222
Making Plans for Nidge 470
Malaido 459
Malaise 459
Malcolm X 213, 308
Malcom Armblaster 308
Malnutrition 362
Malpossessed 206
Ma Marmalade 123
Mandrake 144
Mandy 316

The Man from Delmonte —
  He Says "Yes" 112
Mani 44
Man of Constant Sorrow 120
Man of Steel 256
Mantrap 333
Man Who Fell to Earth 285
Marasmus 35
Margins of my Kind 174
Marsh Dweller's Rib 144
Martial Music 312
Masculine Power Trip 306
Massa 393
Massive, The 401
Master of a Lune 480
Master of Tides 46
Match of the Day 340
Matricide 72
Matrix 72
Matterhorn Face 505
Matterhorn Ridge 505
Matto Grosso Chimney 144
Maureen 160
Max A Million 294
Maxative 295
Max Factor 292
Max Head Room 292
Maxi 291
Maximum Potential 291
Maximuscle 295
Maxing Around 295
Max 'is Wall 292
Max Museum 294
Maxonomy 294
Max Pact 292
Max Pax 'em In 292
Max's Mum 295
Max They Love to Hate 295
Max to the Wall 294
Max Wall 292
Maxwell House 294
Max Works 292
Mealy Bugs 209
Mealystopheles 209
Meander 88
Meandering Peace Meal 435
Meanie, The 250
Mean Team 490
Meat and Two Veg 386
Mecca 224
Mecca Extension 224
Meddler's Wall 197
Meditation 337
Medusa 51, 209
Me Eyes! Me Eyes! 259

Mega-Bites 362
Mega Byte 277
Megaflapped 382
Megalithic Man 107
Megalithic Man
  Super-Direct 107
Mega Midgebite Massacre 434
Mega Whore 224
Megsy 428
Melting Pot 66
Membrane 64
Memnon 64
Men are from Mars 423
Men at Work 96
Menopause 64
Mephistopheles 210
Merchant Played in Venice 489
Mercury Dripping 423
Merry Pheasant 461
Mescaline Power Trip 306
Meshrug a My Shoulders 461
Mesmerised 435
Messiah, The 337
Me Tarzan 321
Meterol 378
Metronome 207
Mettle Fatigue 393
The Mexican takes Lexicon 100
Mice Breaker 110
Michael Foot Jam 297
Mickey 116
Micro Chip 276
Micromax 295
Micro-nerd 276
Midden 174
Middle-Aged Spread 258
Middle Laner 444
Midge Dance 431
Midges Bite Back 256
Midget Gem 253
Midi 34
Midnight at the Oasis 329
Midnight Summer Dream 329
Mignon 509
Mignonette 195
Mikado 195
Mike's Bike and the Collar-
  bone Experience 319
Mike's Problem 258
Mikey Dread 457
Millennium Dome 164
Miller's Tale Start 158
The Millionaire Touch 27
Mindblind 53
Mind of a Turbot 285

Mind Your Head 100
Mindy's Route 384
Mine Anarchy 466
Mineshaft, The 55
Minestrone 45
Ming the Merciless 76
Mingtled Wall 54
Ministry of Silly Walks 237, 440
Minnie 116
Minnie Grip 93
Minnows as Substitute for
The Minor de-Tour 121
The Minor Tour 121
Minos 372
Mint Sauce 262
Minus Ten 48
Minus Wall 48
Misfits, The 485
Missing Link 232
Mission Impossible 172
Mississippi Burning 393
Mister Blister 253
Mitre Crack 495
Mix and Match 291
MLT 491
Moaning Groove 507
Moat Madness 166
Moatorhead 169
Moat People 169
Moat Puddings 169
Moat Race 169
Moat Wall 169
Moby Dick 339
Modem 276
Mombassa 119
Mompesson Rich Pickings 35
Monday Club 311
Money for Nothing 151
Monkey on Juice 509
Monkey Wall 389
Monochlor 438
Monopedagogue 377
Monosod 50
Monoton 386
Monster Mouse Resurgent
369
Monsterosity 177
Monster Traverse 115
Montezuma's Revenge 115
Monumental Armblaster 308
Moonflower 322
Moontalk 461
More Air Than Chocolate 36
More Chattery Teeth 420
More for Four 420

More Glee in the Jungle 249
More Hunky than Funky 260
More Pool You 459
More than Somewhat 382
The Morgue 33
Morion 175
Morning Crack 34
Mortal Combat 237
Mortlock's Arête 333
Mortuary Steps 33
Mosaic Piece 442
Mosquito 280
Mosquito Coast 430
Moss Marathon 453
Moss Side 47
Mottled Wall 54
Mouldwarp Wall 376
Mouse Hunt 478
Mouth Waters 462
Moving Buttress Girdle 391
Mozzy Marathon 453
Mr. Blue Sky 122
Mr. Cellulite's Arête 100
Mr Jagger's Warning 507
Mr Lewis's Blasting
  Company 509
Mr. Love Pants 419
Mr Puniverse 150
Mrs. Brown 402
Much Ado about Playing 489
Much Monkey Magic 434
Mucker's Wall 117
Multiplex 378
Mumble Jumble 123
Mundgripe 507
Muscae Volitantes 348
Muscle-Cock Crack 86
Mutation 230
Mutley Stole My Route
  Man 110
Mutton Busting 262
My Bed's Downstairs 459
My Brain is Up to No
  Good 427
My Dog Dill 349
My Fickle Resolve 190
My Friend Flicka 259
My Girdle is Killing Me 77
My Life Led up to This 453
Myopia 209
My Personal Pleasure 53
Myrmidon, The 327
My Secret Life 401
Mystical Attainment 376
Myth of Masculinity 150

My Tiers Led up to This 181
My Tulpa 442
My Wife Led up to This 453

N

Nagasaki Grooves 2 468
Naiad 322
Nails, The 444
Naive and Sentimental Lover 311
Naked Spur 485
Name that Tuna 289
Nancy Boy 427
Napped a Nod 435
Nappy Squad 145
Narrow Gauge 459
Nasty Man 180
Nathan Detroit 383
Naze 35
Nazi Baby 495
Neanderthal 95
Neb Crack 250
Negative Earth 342
Neil's Wall 258
Neil's Wall Right-Hand 258
Nematodes 78
Nemesis 308
Nerd the Absurd 276
Nerefaun 365
Nervous and Shaky 136
Nervous Breakdown 369
Nettlerash 497
Nettle Wine 387
Never to Look Back 384
New Arrivals 486
New Bolts and Yankees 123
New Enemies 297
New Moon on Monday 88
New Nomad 435
New Route Nausea 404
Next 323
Nice Face Shame About the Ledge 109
Nice in Nice 62
Nicely Nicely Jones 381
Nice Melons 423
Nice 'n' Sleazy 440
Nick 427
Nicodemus 427
Nidhögg Loves Jormangand 141
Nighthawks at the Diner 381
Night of the Guppy 288
Nijinski 124
Nimbo Slab 124

Nine Eleven 94
Ninth Life 366
Nip in Nippon 322
Nip in the Air 468
Nip Zip Diddly 55
Nobody's Hero 327
No Chains on Me 193
No Finer Place 85
No Flair Blair 122
No Fool Like An Old Fool 164
Nogads 367
No Greenwich Mean Time 83
No Hammer Involved 395
No Hiding Plaice 286
No Intent 384
Noisy Neighbours 417
No Jug No Thug 161
No Laughs 321
No Light 355
No Mail 277
No Man's Land 478
No Mud No Thud 168
Nonsense Man Start 497
Nookie Bear 379
No Rantzen 35
No Retreat 491
North Atlantic Drift 378
Northerners Can't Climb 81
Northern Grit 182
Nose, The 509
No Short Coutts 251
Nostalgia 480
No Statesman 46
Nostradamus 333
No Strange Delight 135, 251
Not for Hire 138
Nothing to Help the Poor 176
Novelty 197
November Wall 494
No Way is Patience a Virtue 121
Nowt About 55
Nowt About Change 76
Nowt Much 250
Nowt Said 44
Nowt Taken Out 99
Nude Motorcycle Girl 166
Nullo in Mundo Pax Sincera 122
NYD 92

O

Obelix 414
Oblomov 328
Obscene Gesture 234
Obscene Toilet 234
Obvious Crack 86
Odd Day Crack 379
Odd Day Wall 379
Oddity 138
Ode to Eric 250
O'Donovans Blind Variant 220
Offal 362
Off Limits 117
Of Youth 338
Ogre, The 327
Oh Brother Where Art Thou? 121
Oh Dear! 171
Oh No! It's the Wall-to-Wall Birthday Party 388
Oh Solo Mio 448
Okra 55
Old Dog — New Trick 249
Old-Fashioned Hot Air Balloon 252
Old Fiends 460
Ol' Dirty Bastard 124
Old Man River 310
Old Man's Gambit 318
O'Leanna the Butler Dunn It! 256
Olive Oil 102
Oliver 27
Olotson 448
Olympiakus 121
Om 44
Omah Gourd 135
Omega 13 464
Omelette 44
Omen, The 480
Once Upon a Time 151
One 'ard Move 27
One Deadly Variant 477
One Foot in the Cave 438
One Night 336
One Night Stand 428
One on One 172
One Step from Earth 446
One Track Mind 391
One Track Offensive 275
One Way Reflection 150
One Way Stretch 197
Only Ken's Anarchy Will Do 466
On the Third Day 150

On Uranus 115
Onwards and Upwards 76
Open Gate 361
Open History 182
Open Secret 289
Open the Box 440
Open Verdict 383
Ophelia's Lob-elia 306
Oracle, The 481
Orange Free State 375
Orange Order 375
Orange Si 258
Orange Sunshine 365
Orange Throated Gonk 448
Orang Utang 27
Orchmire 138
Orchrist 388
Orgasmus Maximus 295
Orient Route 195
Original Aid Route 506
Oscar's Groove 181
Oscillation 388
Osculation 388
Osher Osher Osher 360
Osiris 367
Ostrich's Throat 425
Ostwald Bastable 197
Otaix 342
Othellow 489
Otto di Catania 434
Ouijaboard 314
Our Father 64
Outer Limits 484
Out for a Duck 197
Out of Africa 97
Out of My Boots 236
Out of My Tree 236
Out of My Tree Start 239
Out of the Shadows 166
Out Of Touch 428
Outside Tokyo 468
Overbored 466
Overclapped 382
Over Easy 486
Overslapped 382
Over the Deadline 463
Over the Hill 480
Over the Rainbow Trout 288
Ovine 262
Ovine Low Left 262
'Owd Biddy Flogger 418
Owl, The 122
Oy Missus 122
Ozone Bozo 75

P

Pachucho Cadaver 488
Padme 44
Paganism 391
Pagan Man 204
Pain and Pleasure 356
Paint It Black 259
Paint it Black Direct 259
Palace of Tyranny 141
Pale Rider 105
Palestine 429
Palmolive 138
Pappadum Groove 481
Parachute 47
Paradox 151
Paradox Wish 252
Paraplege 442
Parr Kor 47
Particular Groove 250
Parting of the Lips 462
Part-Time Hobby 150
Part-Timer 256
The Party Animal 124
Passage of Time 114
Pastry Roll 86
Patience 86
Pauillac 188
Pauline's Date with Deryck Guyler 426
Paupericles 211
Pay and Dismay 426
Pearls from the Shell 78
The Pearly Gates 46
Peckling Fever 99
Pedal to the Nettle 249
Pedestal Branch 200
Pedigree Chum 350
Peeled Baby 252
Peggy Sue 404
Peg's Path 162
Pelvic Thrust 102
Penal Servitude 477
Pendulum, The 77
Penelope Pit Stop 456
Penny Bubbly 427
Pentagon Route 196
People Will Talk 462
Pepsi Max 292
Percy' World 319
Perfecto 172
Perilscope 84
Periscope Voyeur 151
Permutation Wall 458
Perrin's Arête 494

Personal Voyage 352
Personified 430
Perverse Killer 229
Perverse Reverse 229
Perverted Mind 296
Peter Perfect 456
Phase Contrast 393
Pheasant Plucker 342
Philadelphia 397
Philadelphia Direct 397
Philandering Sons of
  Magic Women 435
Phone Home 508
Physical Fizz 105
Piccalilli Circus 401
Pickpocket 51
Picture This 469
Pigeon Couped 464
Pigette 500
Pig in a Poke 92
Pig Pen Comes Clean 151
Pig Sick 446
Pile-up on the
  Dance Floor 80
Pillar of Wisdom 463
Pillar Talk 459
Pillar Torque 431
Pillar Walk 459
Pinch Test 160
Pinch, The 158
Pineapple 68
Ping 144
Pingham's Route 435
Pinging in the Rain 435
Ping Pong 144
Pink 391
Pink Panther 340
Pinnacle Route 509
Pinnaclised 397
Pint of Blood 505
Pipistrelle 274
Piranha 156
Piranha Wall 169
Pirhana Traverse 156
Piton Route 509
Pity the Graffiti 470
Plaque Crack 206
Plaster Lank 260
Plastic Blinkers 195
Plastic Wonder 195
Platband, The 509
Plate of Scones 480
Platonic Desire 281
Play Corner 488
Play Doh 488

Player of Venice 489
Playground Attraction 488
Playground Bully 467
Play it Again Sam 414, 489
Pleasant Dreams 340
Pleasant Valley Sunday 473
Plea, The 383
Plectrum Maxilla Direct 155
Ploy 211
Ployed 76
Plum Buttress Super-
  Indirect 404
Plum-Line Finish 404
Pluto 116
PM's Question Time 122
Pneumatic 435
Pocketrocity 239
Pock Wall 508
Poisonality 107
Poison Flowers 86, 89
Po Lazarus 121
Pole Position 456
Pollyanna 45
Polymath 427
Pong 144
Ponger, The 144
Pool Hand Fluke 459
Poorlaw 176
Poppy Fields 312
Pop the Rivet 393
Porgi Amor 93
Porridge 120
Porthole Traverse 162
Porthos 425
Positive Discrimination 458
Possession by Design 138
Postern Crack 207
Postman's Meander 83
Potential Orbit 138
Pot Full 85
Potty 114
Pot Washer's Wall 124
Poultry in Motion 362
Pour Dill 360
Poverty Trap 333
Powder Puff 397
Powerband 240
Powerful Torches Officer 264
Powerhumps 240
Power of Soul 477
Powerpants 315
Powerplant 315
Powerplay 297
Power to Heal 251
Pow Wow 427

Pragma 139
Prawnography 286
Prefect Day 461
Premature 487
Premature Arthritic Enjoys
  Dawn Chorus 164
Premature Evacuation 193
Press, The 158
Preston North End 462
Pretoria 119
Price of Fame 390
Priming the Pump 388
The Primrose 426
Prince of Wales 120
Princess of the Streets 448
Private Gripped 444
Private Prosecution 107
Procession 84
Professor Kirk 160
Profitless 461
The Profusionist 32
Prolapse 30
Promises 111
Prophecy, The 481
Protest and Survive 386
Proud Whore 222
Prow, The 222
Psychic Emulator 141
Psycho Babble 446
Psycho Ceramic 114
Psycho Flake 446
Psychological Warfare 446
Psychopath 30
Psycho Symmetry 446
Puffing 275
Puffing Billy 282
Puff Pastry 86
Pullemdown 72
Pulsar 356
Pump Up the Power 240
Pump Up the Power 236
Pump Up the Vallium 239
Purple Haze 211
Pursuit of Alacrity 88
Pushed to the Hilti 390
Pushmepullyou 259
Push Up 220
Puttrell's Arête 509
Puttrell's Crack 509
Putty White Flesh 175
Pygmies Walk Tall 48

Q

Quads 457
Quake 390
Quality Control 367
Quarrymen, The 96
Quartz Initial 481
Quartz Tricycle 418
Queerboy 182
Queer Street 339
Question of Palance 500
Quidnunc 280
Quiver, The 144

R

Ra 366
Rabbit, The 151
Race of the Freuds 98
Racial Harmony 64
Rage 112, 222
Rage into Crucifiction 222
Ragged Arête 397
Railroaded 459
Railway Children 391
Rainbow Warrior 97
The Rainbow Woman 53
Rain Dance 105, 392
Rainmaker's Rib 174
Rainmaker, The 322
Rainsong 83
Raisin Roof 402
Rambler's Arête 425
Rampant 285
Rampant Rabbit 432
Random Factors Align 135
Rape 340
Rapid City 310
Raptor on Ice 141
Rapture 164
Rasputin 342
Rastus 393
Rated X 432
Ratline 485
Rat's Rally 453
Ratten 509
Rattle and Hump 236
Rattle and Hump Start 240
Rattle and Role 338
Raven Bonking 251
Raven Crack 200
Raven Loonie 251
Raven's Crack 251
Raven's Foot Chimney 251
Rave On 274, 333

Reach for the Sky 138
Reasons to be Cheerful 367
Reboot 362
Recessed Corner 509
Recreational Violence 256
Recycled 369
Red Mist 78
Red Nosed Pollination 384
Red or Dead 261
Red Rum 124
Red Snapper Meets the
  Dogfish 288
Red Spider 288
Red Squirrel 253
Red X 213
Regrets Groove 384
Regulo Mark 6 459
Reloaded 71
Removal Men 102
Renascent Ability 348
Rentaghost 495
Repulse 120
Reserve Judgement 171
Reservoir Frogs 414
Resin Erection Shuffle 197
Resistance is Futile 230
Resistance, The 230
Restive Being 448
Restoree 250
Retreaty 491
Retro Rockets 490
Revelations 222
Revolva 59
Revulva 59
Reward 369
Rhubarb Rhubarb Rhubarb 321
Rhyme and Reason 171
Rhyme Crime 171
Ribcrusher Crack 183
Riding Shogun 469
Riding the Bullet 419
Right Arête 500
Right-Hand Crack 88
Right Said Fred 470
Right Slab 426
Right to Roam 230
Righty 509
Ring-Bolt Buttress 507
Ringing Chimney 184
Ringleader 183
Ringmaster 183
Ringmistress 183
Ring of Fire 234, 506
Ring Thane 119
Rinky Dinky 319

Rio Verde 144
Rippemoff 72
Rippledom 135
Ripples 164
Ripsaw 488
Rising Potential 447
Rising Sap 366
Rising Sun 469
Rite of Way 505
R'n P 316
Road Runner 470
Roaring Forties 390
Robert Blincoe 253
Roberts Roberts 382
Robin 45
Robin Hood 431
Rob's Dilemma 353
Rockbiter 206
Rock Bottom Groove 181
Rock Follies 371
Rocky Variations 477
Rolling Stone 377
Roman Candle 47
Roman Numeral X 447
Romans are Coming 447
Romeo's End 404
Roobarb 250
Roof Left 258
Roofolution 230
Roof Route 509
Roof, The 506
Roof Warrior 310
Rooster Booster pitch 1 232
Rooster Crossing 232
Roraima 27
Rosehip Wine 45
The Rotten Word 111
Rotund Roolay 105
Rouge Total 376
Rough Justice 295
Round the Bend 207
Route 1 448
Rubber-Tummy 425
Rubble Rouser 74
Rubicon 161
Rue Morgue 311
Rumble in the Jungle 177
Runaway 250
Runaway Train 275
Run For Your Wife 107
Running for Cover 470
Running on Empty 361
Running Over 85
Running Wild 250
Run Off 470

Run Ragged 397
Runts Grunt Stunt 508
Runyonectomy 382
Rupert Bear Goes Hiking 440
Russian Roulette 202
Rustie Lee 393
Ru's Traverse 262
Rusty Frog 323

S

Sack of Stones 480
Safe Haven 487
Sagittarius 206
Sag Line 55
Sago Slab 96
Sag Paneer 102
Sahara 98
Salactol 438
Salar 153
Saline Drip 237, 241
Sam and Mary 123
Sam in Your Eye 97
Sanctuarian, The 487
Sanctuary 250
Sans Identity 401
Sans Nom 496
Santiano 297
Sara Laughs 480
Sardine 234
Sarin 404
Satisfaction 84
Saturn's Ring 116
Savage Girth 423
Saweno Gancho 468
Say it With Flowers 107
S.B.S. 218
Scanner 46
Scarab 36
Scent of Spring 428
Schickster Groove 352
School's Out 105
Scientist 457
Scooby Snack 348
Scoop Route 509
Scoop Wall 64, 508
Scoopy Little Number 197
Scorpion 202
Scott's Wall 414
Scratch Race 401
Scratch Your Eyes Out 324
Screaming Target 456
Screaming Wheels 478
Screwy Driver 109
Scroll 249

Scrubber 68
Scurvey Knave 46
The Sea is a Brown Paper
    Bag 369
Sean's Roof 259
Searching for the Yeti 169
Season 420
Seated Moon 124
Seclusion, The 83
Second Day Crack 426
Second Lesson 426
Second Prize 122
Secret Agenda 431
Secret Gudgeon Society 285
Seldom Seen 383
Self Control 250
Sellar Dweller 340
Semolina Sunday 321
Senile Delinquents 485
Sensation 250
Senter Home 99
Seraphim 236
Sergeyenna 329
Sermon Wall 183
Set Fred Free 470
Setting Free the Bears 429
Setting of the Sun 84
Setting Son 468
Seven Deadly Sins 473
Seven Deadly Virtues 477
Seven Eleven 94
Seven Pounds Overweight 372
Seventh Veil 393
Sewer, The 114
Sex-Crazed Gorilla 251
Seychelles 97
Shades of Grey 226
Shaka 379
Shake 338
Shake Hands with the
    Octopus 324
Shake Rattle and Roll 85
Shaking Crack 388
Shaky Crack 37
Shame on You 420
Shanacie 419
Shang-Hai 469
Shanks 114
Shapeshifter 387
Shardlowcore 491
Sharing Best Practice 95
Sharp Practice 306
Shattered Crack 204
Shazam 312
She didn't Ken 434

Sheepish 432
Sheep Shifter 509
Sheer Indulgence 166
Sheer Power 166
Sheer Travesty 155
Sheerwater 166
She got the Bosch 277
Sheikh Rattle and Roll 218
Shelf Problem 263
Shellfish Shuffle 56
Shell Super 123
She Mail 277
Shetland Chimney 124
Shield, The 196
Shit Wall 44
Shock the Monkey 390
Short Circuit 506
Short Sharp Shock 360
Short Sport 486
Shot Yer Bolt 109
Shred Your Stick 381
Siberian Hamster 396
Sibser 369
Sickle 50
Sick With Fear 350
Sidepull Problem 239
Sidetrack 275
Sidewinder 256
Sight Beyond Sight 505
Sight, The 144
Sign My Name 44
Sign of the Times 282
Silence of the Clams 288
Silent Fear 448
Silently Sprung 461
Silent Manoeuvres 441
Silent Storm 186
Silk Coutt 251
Silver Stone 456
Silver Tongues 34
Simonstown 119
Sin 58
Sincerely Yours 473
Sin City 473
Sing for Your Dinner 467
Single Decker 420
Single Malt 421
Sinister Finish 209
Sirius 180
Sirplum 404
Sir Pryse 122
Sissy, The 160
Sisyphean 55
Sit-in Wall 89
Six Bee or Not Six Bee 414

Skid Marks 379
Skid Pan Alley 456
Skin-Flick 319
Skin Flint 94
Skylarkin 249
Skyline Pigeon 136
Slab and Arête 55
Slab and Cleft 508
Slabbering Slab 124
Slabby but Nice 123
Slab Cake 96
Slab de Lune 480
Slam the Jam 124
Slantered 195
Slapdasher 153
Slapin 153
Slap on the Pyro 438
Slay the Gray 99
Sleepers 281
Sleeping Sickness 459
Sleep On It 459
Sleepwalkers 340
Sleepy Hollow 487
SLF 491
Slim Jim 421
Slip and Slime 251
Slippery Bill 485
Slipping Blocks 442
Slip yer Foot 490
Sliver 94
Slob Team Special 470
Sloe Gin 402
Slowly Catch a Monkey 478
Slow Water Girdle 253
The Slurper 31
Small but Perfectly
    Formed 161
Small is Beautiful 145
The Small Room 114
Smartie People are Happy
    People 467
Smelting Pot 361
Smoke Gets in Your
    Eyes 123
Smutt 379
Snail Mail 352
Snail Male 89
Snails of the Riverbank 311
Snails on Strike 425
Snake Eyes 473
Snap Decision 466
Snap Dragon 341
Snap, The 319
Snatch 316
Snatchemoff 72

Sneck 206
Snerp 88
Sniffer Clarke 89
Snoozin 281
Soapsuds 37
Soapsuds Traverse 37
Socialism 389
Socket Set 419
Sock It To 'em 419
Soft Centre 417
Soft Mick 448
Soft Shoe 387
Soft Times 444
Soggy Biscuits 417
Solar Groove 448
Solar Plexus 448
Solar Wall 448
Solitaire 46, 209
Solo 448
Solo in the Jungle 174
Soloist, The 448
Somebody's Head 258
Somebody's Trademark 441
Some Coincidence 366
Somehow Super 316
Some Place 102
Something Fishy 289
Some Things Change 376
Sons of the Desert 488
So-So 200
Sound as a Carp 109
Sound as a Trout 445
Soupbones Chimney 381
Sour Grapes 141
Southerners Can't Climb 81
Southern Man 109
So Veneer 482
Sox 194
Space 138
Space Invaders 249
Spanish John 383
Spank me Senseless with a
Red Herring 279
Spare Rib 96, 100
Sparta in His Eyes 402
Spazz Energy 373
Specialist 139
Special K 63, 447
Spectrophotometry 110
Speed Freak 456
Speed Kills 32
Speedmetal Bedmoshin' 373
Speed Trials 457
Spellbound 181
Sperm Worm 160

Spider, The 402, 499
Spinball Wizard 489
Spirit of the Age 386
Spiritualist 139
Spiron 81
Spiteful Rain 122
Spizz Energy 373
Splintered Perspex 337
Splinter of the Mind's
Eye 141
Split Infinity 365
Spock 261
Spring Awakening 109
Spring is Here 281
Sprint Start 282
Squatter's Rights 190
Squawkietawkie 414
Squeak 36
Sravandrabellagola 354
Stack Wall 509
Stainsby Girls 417
Stalk, The 402
Staminaband 241
Stand-Out Arête 89
Staricase, The 252
Stark Disbelief 463
Statuesque 117
Stax a Time 384
Stealth 485
Steaming 275
Steaming Strides 379
Steam Train 391
Steel on Steel 393
Steeping the Goose 93
Steps, The 509
Steve Miller Band 240
Stevolution 230
Stig, The 441
Stille Nacht 95
Still Life 250
Still Small Voice 145
Still Wall 387
Sting in the Tail 175
Sting, The 396
Stogumber Club 365
Stolen Fruit 362
The Stomach Pump 94
Stone Leopard 249
Stone the Crows 419
Stone the Loach 285
Stonethroat 99
Stony Ground 251
Stop the Pigeon 136, 464
Stormflight 135
Storm, The 297

Stowaway 428
St Paul 47, 188
St Peter 46
Straight Leg 32
Strange Beings 195
Strange Concept 458
Strange Ways 197
Strangled at Birth 473
Strap a Doc to Me 460
Strawberry Kiss 279
Streamline 310
Strict Blueband 240
Stripper, The 323
Strip Search 145
Stuffed Badger 352
Stuff of Dreams 251
Stuff the Turkey 61
Stung 354
Sturgeon in the Cupboard 286
Sub-Atomic 491
Subterfuge 367
Subterra 355
Subversive 319
Succubus 312
Succulent Corner 396
Suckle the Honey 47
Suck on This 467
Suck yer Thumb 434
Suddenly 336
Suffocation 83
Suicide's Reprieve 388
Summat Outanowt 417
Summer Wine 352
Summons 145
Sumo 468
Sunai 444
Sun Crack 448
Sun Dance 392
Sunday Sport 102
Sunny Goodge Street 339
Sunshine Superfrog 134
Superfly 178
Super High Intensity Body
Building 237
Supernatural 481
Superocity 178
Super Orchic 374
Superstition 83
Superstring 373
Supplementary Benefit 176
Supplementary Question 122
Surface Plate 499
Surfing the Net 277
Survival Limit 249
Suryanamasker 352

Suscipiat 444
Swain's World 478
Swamp Fever 174
Swansong 85
Swan Song 441
Sweat Shop 467
Sweet F.A. 141
Sweet Surrender 182
Sweet Sweet Bulbs 427
Sweet William 141
Swine Vesicular 61
Swinging Wall 387
Swing Time 256
Switch 341
Sword and Stone 494
Sycamore 508
Sycamore Crack 496
Symmetrical Systems 352
Sympathy in Choice 226
Symphonic Crack 494
Syntax Error 50
Systems Malfunction 362

T

Tail the Dog 348
Ta Jim 478
Take Flight 484
Take Your Thyme 119
Taking Liberties 117
Tales of Pinkie Power 250
Talisman, The 481
Tame for the Trouble 323
Taming of the Shrew'd
Player 489
Tamora 126
Tank 206
Tantalus 56
Tapenard 464
Tawk the Squawk 414
Tawny Owl Pie 122
Taxing Times 448
Taylor Made 306
Taylor-Parkinson Gully 95
Tec 328
Techno Prisoners 310
Te Deum 186
Teeny Tots 468
Telescopic Demand 441
Tempting Children 467
Tendril, The 397
Tenth Heaven 480
Tequila Mockingbird 333
Tequila Tory 80
Terrace Wall 500, 508

Terrace Wall Direct 500
Terra Incognito 355
Terrorcotta 337
Terror of the Towers 488
Terry and June 414
Tetse 280
Thang Thing 480
Thank You Grooves 466
That Ball 489
Thatcher Years 176
That'll do Nicely 188
That Old DA Look 120
That Was the River 310
The B.A.R.T. Extension 53
The Love of Money is the
Root of All Evil 256
Theology 339
Theoria 297
Therapy 93
There is No Zen 164
There May be Rubble
Ahead 74, 75
There's Life in the Old
Log Yet 297
There's Method to my
Madness 260
There Will be Blood 95
Therianthropic 494
Theseus Saurus 121
The 'too small for the tall'
Wall 319
Thin Crack 509
Thinfinger 197
Thing Thang 478
Thinking 484
Thinking Outside the
Box 440
Thin Lizzy 387
Thin Thin Groove 389
Third Day Tower 426
Third Order 318
Thirsty Work 427
Thirty Nine and a Half
Steps 461
This England 473
This is the End 462
This is the Sea 310
Thomas Crapper 114
Thorn, The 45
Thor's Hammer 389
Thoth 361
Thrash Your Woodie 321
Thread Nicole 432
Three and In 428
Three Card Trick 447

Three Spheres 139
Three Tree Slab 404
The Thrill of the Chase 83
Thrills and Spills 395
Throat 428
Throwback 446
Thrutch 48
Thunder Buttress 426
Thunder Chimney 427
Thundertrapped 382
Thunder Wall 427
Thyme Out 119
Thyrsus 211
Ticket to the Underworld 68
Tiddle-de-Dum 186
Tideswell Cenotaph 250
The Tier Drop X-plodes 369
Tierfull 181
Tiery Henry 181
Tiger by the Tail 138
Tiger Crack 35
Tiger Direct 35
Tiger Groove 35
Tiger Traverse 35
Tiger Trot 64
Tigon 340
Tikka 396
Timber 494
Time Warp 193
Tin Of 232
Tip Dollar 367
Tippers 367
Tip Toe Wall 196
Tirfer Off 99
Tirfin Mandrakes 98
Tirfin USA 98
Titanic 377
Titanic Reaction 442
Titter Ye Not 362
Titus 126
To Bee a Star 414
Toby King of Wardlow
    Mires 427
Toenail Pie 161, 162
Toe Tip Crack 196
To Hell and Back 34
Toilet Gesture 234
Toilet Graffiti 115
Toilet Humour 115
Toilet, The 234
Tokyo Wall 397
Tollbar 75
Tomarwa Groove 88
Tomato Sauce 234
Tomb Raider 237

Tomorrow's Dream 358
Tom's Off Day Route 431
Too Fat to Tag 421
Too Hard for Mark Leach 226
Too Jugless for Douglas 319
Too Mellow to Bellow 427
Too Old to be Bold 155
Tooooo Long 460
Too Pumpy for Grumpy 318
Too Thin to Chin 421
Top Banana 55
Top Gear 441
Top Gobbler 93
Top MarX 213
Top Shop 261
Top Totty 468
Torchwood 116
Tors Colon 94
Tosser's Wall 391
Total Breakdown 369
Totally Awesome 161
Total Rock 376
Totonic 352
Totti for England 467
Touch and Go 431
Touch Too Much 281
Tour de France 314
Tourist Crack 505
Tourist Groove 431
Tourist Wall 505
Tout Comprendre 440
Tower Climb 200
Tower Crack 200
Towerfull 58
The Tower of Babel 58
Town Hall Clerk 427
Townships 118
Toys for the Boys 355
Toy Story 467
Tracker 116
Traffic Cops 444
Traffic Jam 48
Trainee, The 391
Trainer Tamer 172
Trampled Underfoot 311
Transit Groove 387
Transmaiacon MC 64
Trap, The 367
Traumatic 435
Treadmill, The 188
Treatment 93
Tree Surgeon 151
Trench Warfare 141
Tria 204
Trial and Error 485

Trial Run 138
Trick Cyclist 456
Trick Show 377
Tricky Dicky 393
Tricycle Man 458
Trigger 68
Trinig 250
Triple Sec 420
Triton 169
Trog 95
Troll, The 188
Trombone Practice 306
Troops of Tomorrow 206
Tropic of Cancer 342
The Trouble With Rubble 75
True Lime 200
Truffle 59
Truffles 323
Trundler, The 88
Tsetse Piece 174
Tsunami 158
TT Special 456
Tuba Mirum 61
Tumbleweed 229
Tunnel Vision 391
Turbo-Charged Monster
    Mouse 321
Turf 'em Off 72
Turf's High 98
Turkey Lurking 349
Turkey Shoot 93
Turkey Vulture Crack 80
Twang 80
Twice a Slice 259
Twilight Zone 485
Two Cave Gully 485
Two Generations 338
Two Loos 115
Two Sheep to Leicester 169
Two Step 509
Two Sunspots 328
Two-Tier Climb 509
Two Ton Ted from
    Teddington 71
Two-Way Stretch 197
Twyfords 114
Tyrannosaurus Max 295
Tyred Out 446

U

Ubiquitous, The 419
Uglier Still 404
Ugly 404
Ugly Sister 404

Ultralight 372
Um Bongo 319
Uncreased 462
Undercut to Crimp 239
Underslung 100
Under the Lifeline 463
Under Western Eyes 172
Unde-Tiered 181
Undiscovered Blacks 89
Une Crime Passionnel 312
Une Jour Parfait 190
Unfinished Business 490
Unhung 93
Uninspired 397
Union Jack 98
Unleashing the Wild
    Physique 316
Unloaded 71
Uno 258
Unpleasant 200
Unquenched 427
Unruly Behavior 92
Unstatic 263
Unzipped 220
Unzipping the Wild
    Physique 282
Up 263
Upminster Kid 420
Upstate Red 381
Up the Creek 280
Up the River Without a
    Paddle 311
Upthrutch 458, 473
Uptown Beaver 260
Up Yours 76
Uranus 116
Urban Badger 432
Urtica Dioica 250

V

Val de Mossa 171
Valentine 337
Valley of the Birds 431
Vandal 318
Vanishing Point 197
Vanishing Resources 250
Vapour Stream 188
Venom 499
Vent Your Spleen 94
Verbal Abuse 234
Verbal Abuse Start 239
Verger, The 183
Very Windy Slab 425
Viagra Falls 482

Via Vita 209
Via Vita Direct 209
Vibration 390
Vibrator 387
Vicar's Vertigo 182
Vicky 28
Victoria 402
Victoria Barcelona 28
Victoria Falls 119
Victory Roll 138
Vindicator 151
Vinegar Fly 45
Vintage Two 211
Violation of Trust 138
Violin Solo 506
Virgin King 76
Virgin on the Loose 76
Virtual Insanity 417
Visible Void 282
Vision, The 134
Viv Stanshall 425
VLC 491
Vogon 116
Voices 83
Voidless 282
Vulture's Crutch 428

W

Waddage 230
Waffle 362
Wag the Dog 348
Waldo Winchester 382
Wallaclism 466
Wall of Jericho 107
Wallop 54
Wandering Thoughts 141
War 190
Warhead 190
War Locks 356
War Memorial 312
Waste Bin 277
Watcher, The 206
Watch this Space 382
Watchtower, The 508
Water Bailiff 156
Waterloo Road 445
Water Margin 174
Water Method Man 429
Waves of Mutilation 105
Wayfarer 88
Way of the Gone Wives 320
Weakened Warrior 97
Weakling, The 177
We are not Alone 423

Weaver's Wall 196
Web, The 288
Wedgie 258
Wee Cling 177
Weedfiller 229
Wee Dimension 229
Weedkiller 232
Weedkiller Chimes 230
Weedkiller High 229
Weedkiller Traverse 229
Wee Doris 51
Wee Douglas 197
Weeper, The 381
Welcome to Hard Times 444
Welcome to My World 368
Welfare Orange 428
Wellington Route 171
Welsh Rarebit 153
Western Somoa 141
Wet yer Whistle 435
Whacky Races 456
Whasupwithi? 30
What Aches 342
What Lies Beneath 487
What's the Paint 470
What's the Thyme? 119
What the Hell 34
When Reason Sleeps 417
Where I Live 251
Whet 50
Which Depp-Artment 487
While Stocks Last 145
While the Cat's Away 121
Whine 45
Whinger, The 117
Whisper 81
Whistling Crack 386
White Bait 156
White Bait Start 156
Whitebeam 318
White Death 323
White Dove 122
White Fright 190
White Gold 324
White in the Face 251
The White Knight 46
White Life 323
White Line Fever 151
White Magic 250
White Mane 508
White Out 323
White Ridge Crawl 508
White Riot 183, 393
White Wind 461
Whiting on the Wall 286

Whoa Black Betty 263
Whore of Babylon 222
Whose is Casey? 489
Whose Line is it Anyway? 314
Who the Hell 34
Why Me? 365
Wick, The 206
Wide Crack 250
Wide Gauge 459
Wild East 239
Wilderness Years 401
Wild in Me 237
Wild in Me Start 241
Wild Man from Way Back
When 435
Wild Olives 464
Wilky's Revenge 470
William's Plays
    Shakespeare 489
Willie the Kid 112
Will it Never End 462
Willow 35
Will the Real Mill Buttress
    Please Stand Up 197
Will They 462
Will Ya be Ready? 30
Wilt 204
Wilt Alternative 204
Wimp, The 160
Windhover 63
Windows 95 277
Windy Slab 425
Winter Fingers 110
Wipe it Clean 115
Wipe Out 442
Wise Up! Sucker 388
Wish you Were Here 171
Witchcraft Wall 181
Witchettygrub 259
Witch in Stitch 387
Within Reach 373
With Juliet 489
Witness This 383
Wobbly Wheels 275
Wolfen 135
Woman in Wellingtons 435
Womb with a View 505
Women are from Venus 423
Wooden Leg 444
Workhouse, The 176
Working 9-5 259
The World According to
    Tommy Trout 285
Worm War 425
Worry Wart 204

Worse Night 135
Wot a Waste? 367
Would You Like a Sweetie? 467
Wright On 306
Wright to Left 306
Wrong Unconquerable 460
Wye Train 391

X

Xactly 212
Xageration 212
X Box 212
X-Box 440
X Calibre 27
X Certs 445
Xcursion 213
Xenophobia 444
X Files 213
X Marks the Spot 212
X Partridge 213
X.T.C. 213
Xtermination 212
Xtra Time 213
XXXX 213

Y

Yabba Dabba Doo 485
Yankee Dollar 188
Yankee Doodle 139
Yardcore 491
Y Chimney 207
Yellow Blanket 500
Yer Right Me Duck 251
Yew Cap 207
Yogi Bear 481
Yorkshire 8b 176
You Are Only Mortal 64
You Crack Me Up 93
You Dirty Duck 432
You got no Reason 171
You got Rhyme 171
You Know UFOs 435
Young Gifted and Black 263
You're Closer than you
    Think 446
You're Little 430
Your Melon 135
Your Rotten Thoughts 388
You've Addit 459
Y Should I? 213
Yuk 388
Yukio 499
Yukon Groove 196

Yus Yus 428

Z

Zander Welfare Club 288
Zanzibar 119
Z.C.T. 453
Zebedee 470
Zebedee's Got Syphilis 297
Zebedee Visits the Clinic 322
Zeitgeist 161
Zeke the Freak 160
Zero Option 196
Zippy's Roof 260
Zippy Stardust and the
    Spiders from Mars 311
Zob 150
Zorbit 508
Zowie Pop 428
Z Victor 481

42nd Street 339
90 Centimetre Diedre 86
96 Smears 440
99p Special 485

Katy Whittaker on Kudos, Font 7B, at Rubicon Wall (page 158).
Photo: Alex Messenger.